Patriotism and Other Mistakes

GEORGE KATEB

Patriotism and Other Mistakes

Yale University Press
New Haven &
London

Set in Sabon type by Keystone Typesetting, Inc.
Printed in the United States of America.

Library of Congress Cataloging-in-Publication Data

Kateb, George.
Patriotism and other mistakes / George Kateb.
p. cm.
Includes bibliographical references and index.
ISBN-13: 978-0-300-12049-3 (cloth : alk. paper)
ISBN-10: 0-300-12049-4 (cloth : alk. paper)

1. Political psychology. 2. Political science — Moral and ethical aspects. I. Title.

JA74.5.K377 2006
320.01′9 — dc22

2006047369

A catalogue record for this book is available from the British Library.

The paper in this book meets the guidelines for permanence and durability of the
Committee on Production Guidelines for Book Longevity of the Council on
Library Resources.

10 9 8 7 6 5 4 3 2 1

To John Hollander and David Bromwich

Contents

Acknowledgments

Most of the essays in this volume deal with the perplexities that inhere in the question of political motives and intentions. The field of inquiry is, to use an old-fashioned term, moral psychology. The particular emphasis is on the passions that goad innovative or extreme or excessive political conduct and other cognate human endeavors. The morally driven and creative daring of Socrates and Thoreau is discussed, and so is the radically assertive mentality that produces fanatical movements and totalitarian dictatorships. There are glances as well at the enticements of war, technological advance, political participation, and emergency action. There is even a look at the original transgression in the Garden of Eden.

It will be evident that in the course of thinking about these matters I have learned much from the work of Hannah Arendt, though I cannot resist taking issue with her on a number of points. I am indebted to many colleagues in the field of political theory; their names appear in the acknowledgments of the individual articles. I have also benefited from the intellectual company of Sharon Cameron, Arien Mack, Morton Schoolman, Tracy Strong, Dana Villa, and James P. Young.

I wish to acknowledge the encouragement and support of John Kulka, senior editor at Yale University Press, who proposed collecting the essays and helped me think about the shape and point of the book.

Last, I owe more than I can briefly say to the two scholars to whom this book is dedicated in admiration.

The previously published articles are here reprinted with some changes. Permission to reprint is gratefully acknowledged.

The following appeared in *Social Research:* "Notes on Pluralism," vol. 61, Fall 1994; "Technology and Philosophy," vol. 64, Fall 1997; "Can Cultures Be Judged? Two Defenses of Cultural Pluralism in Isaiah Berlin's Work," vol. 66, Winter 1999; "Is Patriotism a Mistake?," vol. 67, Winter 2000; "On Being Watched and Known," vol. 68, Spring 2001; "Ideology and Storytelling," vol. 69, Summer 2002; "Undermining the Constitution," vol. 70, Summer 2003; "Courage as a Virtue," vol. 71, Spring 2004; "A Life of Fear," vol. 71, Winter 2004.

The following appeared in *Political Theory* (published by Sage Publications): "Hobbes and the Irrationality of Politics," vol. 17, August 1989; "Aestheticism and Morality: Their Cooperation and Hostility," vol. 28, February 2000; "The Adequacy of the Canon," vol. 30, August 2002.

"Socratic Integrity" appeared in *NOMOS,* vol. xl, 1998 (published by New York University Press), *Integrity and Conscience,* edited by Ian Shapiro and Robert Adams.

"The Judgment of Arendt" appeared in *Revue Internationale de Philosophie,* vol. 53, June 1999, 133–154, edited by Dana Villa.

Introduction

It is easy to think that few events or conditions in politics should unsettle the seasoned observer. Leaders and followers have all the familiar passions that drive people to pursue their interests and to use force and fraud when rules and conventions get in the way. What would one expect? Human beings are what they are. As the ancient Athenians put it, "The strong do what they can and the weak suffer what they must" (Thucydides, V:81, p. 381). If the weak became strong they would do what is now being done to them; they would do what the strong always do; they, too, would ruthlessly pursue their interests as defined by their passions and, where need be, act brutally. What is there in all this that is out of the ordinary? My own disposition is to find political life unsettling more often, I suppose, than a seasoned observer would want. The essays in this collection are united by an attempt to record the idea that political life should often arouse surprise or amazement and, what is more, a good amount of bafflement.

I find, to begin with, bafflement about causes, about the passions and cravings that drive political life, and I therefore speculate about these causes. But even if I think that I have relieved some of my bafflement, the events and policies of political life often remain amazing.

"The strong do what they can." These words betray the presence of something extraordinary in Athenian action. The ruthless pursuit of interests or ends is implicitly posited in this statement, but the thrust beyond interests and ends to empire, and beyond empire to pure dynamism, is not explained. That thrust requires interpretation, despite the risk of appearing implausible or overly ingenious. Years before these words were uttered, on the eve of war with Sparta, Athenian spokesmen adduced fear, interest, and honor to account for their imperialist conduct, but then added that it is the law that the strong should rule over the weak, as if that proposition simply summarized the customary action of humanity (Thucydides, I:76, p. 44). But when the strong do all they are able to do, and then justify their deeds by reference to the immemorial nature of the gods, they are not merely invoking fear, interest, and honor, despite the allegedly irresistible pressure of these motives. The strong everywhere, not only the Athenians, are at a certain point making a leap, and rationalization makes a comparable leap. There is an unexplained surplus in the action that is sometimes registered in the stated reasons for action. There are urges behind some political deeds and policies that are not simple or clear, no matter how customary the deeds and policies might be. To be sure, the Athenian speakers wanted their audience to think that they took the presence of these urges or cravings for granted, as nothing extraordinary, nothing remarkable. We should not be so hardened; one danger is that we thereby grow more gullible, not less.

The model for political projects, for the initiation of political deeds and policies of any degree of ambition, is not a group of hungry men and women using any possible means to end their starvation, or frightened men and women trying to overcome the forces that threaten them with massacre or enslavement. Political life is ruthless or brutal, but not from desperation. Of course, people can be thrown into desperation by the effects of a political initiative. But the motive energy of politics exists beyond the realm of bodily and material necessity. And even the search for honor in the eyes of others, which certainly lies beyond the realm of necessity, still does not take us far enough in the effort to come to terms with the extraordinary qualities of much of political life.

When something shocking happens in political life, we should try to resist asking: What would we expect? Even though much of history is wrongdoing, we should do better than say: What would we expect? Yes, the human tendency to wrongdoing is indelible. Even so, analysis of any given example of it is often difficult, sometimes impossible, even when the example is not extraordinary. But if wrongdoing is characterized by excess, extremism, enormity, then analysis becomes harder. Even an inflated sense of necessity — the dominion of fear, interest, and honor, the dominion of standard power politics — does not appear very often to account adequately for the urges of activist policy.

Where the strong keep enhancing their strength and improving their means, keep extending the boundaries of their exertion, keep finding in every gain a mere foothold for a further gain and without end, should we not be at least a little perplexed? Is not empire, for example, somewhat puzzling even though it is one of the most persistent political phenomena in the human record? Fear, interest, and honor do not exhaust the possibilities of analysis when the subject is imperialism. In fact, these motives of inflated necessity — bedeviled as they are with conceptual and psychological difficulties — provide only a starting point for understanding merely standard power politics and always need filling out. The Athenian references to the inveterate behavior of the strong — divine and human, and both animal-like — touch on some passion or delusion that surpasses the conventional categories of explanation. It is as if the Athenians themselves were somewhat puzzled by their deeds, by their own dynamism, and were only able to redescribe the situation while pretending to give an account of it and presuming to justify it.

Nonetheless, political life is more than wrongdoing, whatever the sources of wrongdoing may be. It calls forth other powers than those of wrongdoing. If the organization of political life provides the will, the resources, and the opportunities for acts, policies, and methods that are often terrible, it sometimes turns on itself and achieves unexpected feats of creativity for the good, and sometimes shows restraint or even magnanimity where ruthlessness could have been expected. No view of political life is credible unless the service — if infrequently beyond the routine — of politics to moral values is kept in mind. More frequently, it renders praiseworthy service to values that are not immoral, but nonmoral and genuine. The emphasis in this book, however, is on political ruthlessness tending toward brutal excess and extremism and accompanied by intoxicated or thoughtless moral indifference and a large measure of freedom from necessity.

Political life elicits and concentrates human energies and talents and gives them large resources, scope, and scale, and the capacity to produce immense palpable effects. I hazard the thought that two qualities of political life account for much of its ability to create extraordinary manifestations. The first quality is the tendency of powerful states, elites, and strategically placed individuals to be given over to indefinite ambitions, indefinite ends, as intoxicating as they are loosely defined. The powerful are often tactically shrewd, but they are soaked in imagination or fantasy or fiction or dream, and possessed by the will (too pale a word) to rearrange or remake the world or part of it. The ambitious (for whom the words *goals* and *aims* are also too pale) are creatures of the imagination, the human faculty of making the absent or incipiently present into an idea or image that governs the attempt to rearrange or remake present reality. Imperial ambitions, for example, are in their very nature utopian, though rarely acknowledged to be such.

The second quality of political life that I highlight in these essays is the subordination or suppression of ends in favor of the ostensible means and methods. For example, political procedures are regarded as intrinsically valuable, and where their results are bad, the procedures are valued more than the results are deprecated. Or, traits of character are valued more than the good things they achieve. Or, political action becomes good in itself apart from any substantive purposes it may serve. A quick and reductive summary is that grand ambitions sponsor much of political ruthlessness or unscrupulousness or brutal, uninhibited behavior in all its amazing manifestations, and that the subordination or suppression of ends in the name of the values intrinsic to means and methods in some cases sponsors a surprising restraint, indeed magnanimity, but in other instances entails moral blindness or indifference and hence facilitates wrongdoing. I grant that the difference between means and ends is not clear, simple, or stable, but only provisionally helpful.

The essays in this collection deal with both qualities of political life and some of their manifestations and instances. A large part of the fascination of politics derives from the often wicked force of the imagination in setting the ends (often ends without a boundary), and from the moral or nonmoral or immoral attachment to means and methods apart from ends. Of course everyday politics concerns itself with limited ends attained by familiar means. But when a society has surplus strength it will undertake policies that partake of the extraordinary and will do so alongside everyday affairs. These affairs will be enclosed within or insulated from, say, expansive imperial ambitions; side by side, the mundane and the grandiose usually feed off each other. The extraordinary settles into normality, which recurrently explodes into the extraordinary. People are capable of doing anything and getting used to anything. Thus, imperialist wealth and opportunity can help to furnish life at home brilliantly, while the citizens of empire have every interest in sustaining, and ignoring or justifying, the imperial hold on the sources of their pleasure. Then too, a society of surplus strength occasionally develops institutional means that express restraint to the point of magnanimity, such as the more counterintuitive features of due process of law; or sees political action as necessary to both the cultivation and expression of virtues and desirable traits of character, again apart from the ends that make political action necessary or appear to; or promotes an attitude that sees political action as an exhilarating experience in itself, apart from the ends it attains or fails to. The means are for many people and some of the time really more urgent than the ends. The means are actual action in the present; the ends are prospective and often unrealized, despite the means, ruthlessly applied or not. Additionally, it may turn out that some remarkable features of political life defy classification as means or ends, and need a different conceptualization.

To state our summary somewhat differently: politics at its most extraordinary in its palpable effects and most surprising in its psychic sources is politics both at its morally worst and at its morally and nonmorally best.

What are the values, the commitments, the aspirations that pervade the formation of excessive or extreme ends, and that require unremitting ruthlessness or tenacity in their pursuit; that pervade the means when the means become more important than the ends they exist ostensibly to serve; or that escape confinement as means or ends? I propose three clusters of values: aesthetic, existential, and anti-instrumental. Aesthetic values drive mostly toward the pursuit of ends; existential values elude classification as either means or ends; and anti-instrumental values affirm the view that means are sometimes so special they are not just instruments, but may count more than ends.

Even when moral expectations are satisfied, what calls for attention is the regular way in which adherents to these three clusters of values sometimes do not honor the claims of morality to supremacy over all other values, or think that morality is inferior or even disregard it as beside the point. Even so, moral elements are surprisingly accorded supremacy in some cases; ruthlessness of the strong yields to restraint in the name of magnanimity. Due process of law, for example, includes counterintuitive practices that spread respect for human dignity beyond law-abiding people and spread it to even those persons accused of crime and tried for it and, if found guilty, punished for it.

Not only is it the case that the primary distinction between ends and means is either incomplete or too blunt, it is also true that the three clusters of values are not sharply separated from one another. My classification of a given phenomenon varies a bit in these essays. The reason is that the same political phenomenon as a whole or in some of its parts can appear to embody or realize the aspirations of two or more clusters. I feel the temptation to regard all the clusters as sharing to some extent in one another's nature. Indeed, it is possible to think that one or another cluster subsumes the other two as special cases of itself. Thus, the existential and the anti-instrumental clusters of values are also aesthetic in some respects. And what is the existential if not anti-instrumental? In their flight from the necessary and the useful or practical, these clusters share a common spirit that drives them toward the extraordinary and extreme.

I think that aesthetic proclivities of humanity are the most productive of shockingly immoral effects. I am not sure that this proposition or proposal is right. But at least I believe that aesthetic proclivities, for which I use the comprehensive term *aestheticism* in some of these essays, names some of the urges or cravings and some of the more subdued and self-aware motivations that lie behind many of the political phenomena that can and should arouse in us particular attention, together with horror or admiration—horror more often than admiration. Existential and anti-instrumental values play a part in the best and the worst, too, but with them admiration is more likely the proper response than is horror. Moral anxiety is almost always rightly present, even when horror is not felt but admiration is.

Aesthetic values. When I say that the first cluster of values is summed up in the term *aestheticism,* my primary but not exclusive meaning is that people look for aesthetic gratifications from phenomena that are not intended to supply them. That is, people are disposed or even feel a need to convert nonaesthetic phenomena into aesthetic ones and then demand that nonaesthetic phenomena live up to aesthetic standards. If, as they often do, phenomena fail a test that from a rationalist or a practical perspective they were not intended to endure, then a powerful psychic force can be unleashed that attempts to remedy the awful aesthetic deficiency. This conversion of phenomena takes place tacitly, even unconsciously, for the most part, but may be all the stronger for being unspoken or unconscious. Just as the working of aesthetic proclivities in a person or group is steady, so is the deliberate or indeliberate unawareness that they are experienced, that they possess the soul. These proclivities may become destructively fanatical and tireless because phenomena as given prove disappointing, and then may become entirely unscrupulous in the ensuing process of reconstruction.

Political, social, and cultural phenomena do not give what artworks give, yet much more is expected of them aesthetically than of artworks: society must as a whole or in its significant parts satisfy the cravings for such adjusted aesthetic qualities as internal coherence and order, clear patterns of activity, unambiguous meanings, an ontological purity of content, a single-minded playing of all social roles, an unmistakable distinctiveness of identity in relation to other societies, a definite shape in the mind's eye, a history that tells a story, an ongoing life that falls into a narrative, a surface that presents color to the eye or to the mind's eye.

In the *Metaphysics,* Aristotle says that the "chief forms of beauty are order and symmetry and definiteness" (XIII:3, 1078a–b, p. 1705; Cooper, pp. 270–276). I have in effect extended the range of the Aristotelian conception in Chapter 6, "Aestheticism and Morality," Chapter 14, "Ideology and Storytelling," and other essays in this collection. The most inclusive social aestheticism holds that the more a society's form, as it is, can be grasped as a single narrative or as a novel or a play or a painting, the better; when it can't, it must be transformed by political methods, as ruthless as they have to be. By an act of distorted imagination, the aesthetic proclivities move to perceive society, as it is, as conforming to these aesthetic standards; but when society fails the overly hungry imagination, the result is profound aesthetic disappointment. Then the inflamed imagination sets to work again and tries to devise strategies for imposing, by force if necessary, new institutions and purposes, a new way of life, a new overall meaningfulness on the superseded aesthetically deficient reality.

What the painter James Whistler said about nature in a lecture in 1885 applies to many political and cultural extremists who, in their unconscious social aestheticism, would never countenance being called aesthetes: "Nature is very rarely right, to such an extent even, that it might almost be said that Nature is usually wrong: that is to say, the condition of things that shall bring about the perfection of harmony worthy of a picture is rare . . . seldom does Nature succeed in producing a picture" (quoted in Craft, 2001). Where Whistler consciously and programmatically aspires to the artist's improvement of nature, many others share the craving that society — in whole or in significant parts — be like a picture, as seen or imagined by the mind's eye. This aesthetic craving can help to inspire political fanaticism; waking dreams of social beauty breed monsters. The same is true of the craving that society be a story, a sustained fiction or other kind of narrative. Let us notice that what is involved is aesthetic heartlessness of a qualitatively worse sort than that shown, for example, by those people who, with or without hesitation, watched the planes on television crash into the Twin Towers — and smoke swirling through narrow streets, and human beings (made tiny by the size of the buildings) leaping to their deaths from upper stories, and the towers collapsing — and felt the thrill of a composite experience of the sublime. The heartlessness of fanatics with plans for radical reordering of society or of those who, in contrast, invest the preservation of an established order with fanatical resolve is all the more potent because the fanatics do not call any part of their passion by the name of aestheticism, but dignify it otherwise in numerous high-sounding ideologies that appear to be as far from aestheticism as ruthlessness and brutality are usually thought to be.

In this collection I indicate my belief that all persons have unavowed aesthetic cravings, but that susceptibility to them naturally varies. I incline to the view that the most completely susceptible people tend to be intellectuals, semi-intellectuals, and pseudo-intellectuals, on the one hand, and, on the other hand, the politically ambitious and their associates. I do not mean to place all the blame on these two groups. After all, without some susceptibility among the great mass, the two groups could not successfully seduce them. But I think that the greatest need for the aesthetic gratification that comes from the imagined conversion of nonaesthetic phenomena into aesthetic ones is felt by those who are drawn to speculative ideas and to political power, and who do not recognize their aestheticism. They are the ones who manipulate the puppets that throw their shadows on the cave's wall and thereby transfix the many and lead them into a docility that may serve the fanaticism of the manipulators. The shadows are aesthetically seductive fictions that make life attractive by distorting it. Whether or not Plato thought the puppeteers cynical or fanatical, I think that even when our puppeteers think they are cynical they are owned by an idea of society as a picture or a story. The aesthetic impulse helps to propel the idealistic or ideological mission.

The aesthetic trouble with a free society is that it cannot appear coherent, shapely, and felicitously distinctive except to an initially sympathetic person, someone who detects aesthetic qualities in seemingly unpromising material and who is also disposed to move his or her aesthetic feeling and attitudes in untraditional directions. Otherwise, freedom is unlovely to contemplate or behold physically; those who live in its atmosphere can seem only licentious or ungoverned or incompetent; clumsy, unrefined, ignorantly irreverent. Democracy is a new aesthetic, as Walt Whitman tried painfully to say. It is hard for the mind's eye, and even the physical eye, however, to find a democratic society beautiful. Whitman's struggle to perceive a new beauty is emblematic of a more common hope that one need not turn away from democratic life in aesthetic revulsion. Democracy imposes a terrific strain on the schooled or self-schooled sensibility trained on models from an earlier world whose nondemocratic disciplines set the standard. The point is not so much that the deliberately aesthetic phenomena of a democratic society fail to meet priestly and aristocratic standards as that its ostensibly nonaesthetic phenomena — its way of life in countless details and its overall sense of life as an ensemble of initiatives and responses, of manners and gestures — prove difficult to convert into aesthetic ones, by acts of a possessed imagination. Then again, if democracy has cultural strength, it satisfies the conscious and unconscious aesthetic cravings appropriate to itself among the many people it serves. It satisfies the sensory cravings for color, dynamic motion, spectacle, an imagined vicarious life lived through the various media, and other cravings that also dismay many fastidious observers. There is such a thing as a distinctively democratic culture, for good and bad.

Now, it is possible to think that aesthetic standards should have no place in judging cultures and political systems. The claims of morality should be not only supreme but the sole claims heard. In his critique of political Platonism and all utopian ambitions, Karl Popper offers a sober warning against what he calls aestheticism: "I do not believe that human lives may be made the means for satisfying an artist's desire for self-expression" (1966: 165; see 164–168). Of course it is rare that anyone comes right out and says that an artist in the person of an impassioned leader should be entrusted with the power to make society the medium for his or her self-expression. Rather, Plato's position is emblematic: ascetic self-denial, not self-expression, must motivate the utopian leader. In actual cases rather than utopian schemes on paper, autocratic or collective-dictatorial power is usually claimed and accepted for ideological purposes cloaked in the rhetoric of emergency and necessity or adorned by the promise of a new social pattern that satisfies common and avowed yearnings for discipline and order. I must say, however, that despite the worth of Popper's critique, aestheticism is inevitable and in some of its forms desirable. Some of its claims must be heard and to an extent appeased.

The general point is that though equality may suit the imagination of an autocrat or an elite when the many are equal in subjection or slavery, the many themselves strive to become unequal. There is something unlovable about equality; so much so that it often feels like a condition accepted for want of a better one, and a consolation for those who cannot break out of it. If people cannot be better than those around them, they will lend themselves to the efforts of those who run their society to dominate other societies. And those who run society will always dream of plans to achieve a finer, more coherent or organic pattern of political relations elsewhere. One ingredient of imperialism is the desire of leaders to shake off the restraints imposed by democratic politics at home and treat other societies, especially nondemocratic ones, as fit for the dictatorial imposition of democracy or some other rule. Imperialism provides the aesthetic intoxication of destroying and remaking customs and relations, rules and institutions. The leaders could not get started unless the many craved some of these same aesthetic gratifications and were willing to settle for vicarious triumph over others. Athens was democratic and imperialistic; America is the same.

Do I make too much of aestheticism in the form of the determination to convert nonaesthetic phenomenon into aesthetic ones? Perhaps I do. Is there really any aestheticism at all involved in the phenomena of imperialism, reactionary autocracies and dictatorships, radical reconstruction, and, worse than all of them, totalitarianism? I actually think that the aestheticism behind these phenomena is even greater than that of democracies and semidemocracies. I do not mean that monarchies and despotisms elicit or extort greater art than democracies, though that is often the case. The point, rather, is that the ruthless adherence to the aestheticism of society as an unmistakable pattern, clear to the

mind's eye, is essentially non- and antidemocratic. Popper is right. So, to restate our examples, the craving for clear definitions, sharp internal social contrasts harmonized by the rulers, subjection to one principal purpose, consonance of numerous social roles as if they were roles in a single play or pageant,
for society as a picture that is composed to satisfy the eye and the mind's eye,
for society as one long story that is coherent to the imagination — all these
cravings are surely not democratic and not compatible with democracy.

These cravings are, I believe, a potent source of action and events in political
and social life, even in democracies. They are, so to speak, primordial, lodged
deep in the psyche. Of course they are not the only sources of what takes place.
But these aesthetic proclivities inspire, impel, instigate. They are not the whole
core but they are at the core of ideologies and religions. They can certainly
serve political and economic interests of every sort, but they are always there,
insidious, unavowed, unavowable, and not confined to any one group or class
or occupation, top, middle, or bottom. They exist everywhere, in various
degrees. And their tendency is to move in the direction of adventurism, excess,
extremism — extermination even. Aestheticism can make people ruthless without a second thought. This source of ruthlessness helps to explain the indefatigable ability of politics to surprise and amaze, not just by novel effects, but
also by the extent of the convulsion that overtakes normality.

I have no wish to deny that other drives besides aesthetic proclivities make
people ruthless with or without a second thought. A model analysis of the
heterogeneousness of motives behind a remarkable decision, if not a completely surprising one, is the account in Thucydides of the enthusiastic support that the Athenian assembly gave to Alcibiades' proposal in 416 BC to invade Sicily. He says: "All alike fell in love with the enterprise. The older men
thought that they would either subdue the places against which they were to
sail, or at all events, with so large a force, meet with no disaster; those in the
prime of life felt a longing for foreign sights and spectacles, and had no doubt
that they should come safe home again; and the idea of the common people
and the soldiery was to earn wages at the moment, and make conquests that
would supply a never-ending fund of pay for the future" (VI:24, p. 373).
Thucydides describes the motivation in such a way as to attribute one main
motive to each group. I would rather think that, as is commonly the case, each
person had more than one passion or desire. But the value of Thucydides'
analysis is not diminished: much was in play amid a common, if not unanimous, enthusiasm. Aesthetic cravings are decisive for some; economic interests for others.

Alcibiades' rhetoric before the vote, however, is what engenders the contagious enthusiasm. His aestheticism fixes on the sublime. He is the prophet of

limitlessness: "by sinking into inaction, the city, like everything else, will wear itself out, and its skill in everything decay; while each fresh struggle will give it fresh experience, and make it more used to defend itself not in word but in deed" (VI:18, 371). Alcibiades is driven more than most people by both unconscious aesthetic cravings and conscious love of beauty, but his is not the only aestheticism in evidence. There is a pervasive Athenian adventurism and a will to impose tyrannically on others and re-create their societies, even others who are sometimes democratic themselves, like Syracuse. Beyond bodily necessity, beyond practicalities, alongside inflated necessity, alongside the standard exertions of the agon of power politics, alongside even the human imitation of gods and beasts by conforming to the law of the stronger over the weaker, resides the ultimate aesthetic craving of destruction and re-creation, the craving not only for beautiful patterns but for sublimity, for the shattering of the very idea of a pattern. (I discuss the relevance to the American scene of such a desire for sublimity in Chapter 4, "A Life of Fear.")

In sum, aestheticism is the inward process by which nonaesthetic phenomena are converted into aesthetic or potentially aesthetic ones. In certain circumstances, this standing disposition is enabled to attempt the radical work of destruction and re-creation. The readiness to convulse the world because, in part, of aesthetic proclivities should be taken as a constant. The conclusion is that aestheticism in the form of unconscious and hence unavowed cravings for aesthetic ends operates with preponderantly immoral effects, those that are not only unjust or even worse, oppressive, but often evil. The association of beauty or sublimity with evil is not a new thought, but it is still worth further contemplation.

Existential values. This second cluster of values is born in the imagination and appeals to it, as aesthetic values do. But existential values are, I think, conceptually separable from aesthetic values, despite the close affinity between the two clusters. Both clusters are contemptuous toward the necessary and the useful or practical, and in some instances are prepared (or even eager) to subordinate or suppress moral considerations or to regard them as irrelevant to the greatest matters. Part of the surprise that the very occurrence of existential values in political life may occasion is precisely that the necessary and the useful are sacrificed. Wrongdoing, however, is not an aspiration that is essential to the integrity of existential values, even though many expressions of these values inflict a great deal of harm. It may be cold comfort to say that a vicious or deranged will is not involved. I must add that only in some respects are existential values related to the values espoused by the philosophical doctrines of existentialism.

Now, it is better not to speak of existential *ends* as we spoke of aesthetic ends. The means-ends duality is particularly out of place when existential values are under consideration. In my view, existential values are not ends that means can achieve. They cannot be gained as a possession; when they are realized as a way of life, no mere means-end relation holds. They are aspirations of identity. Furthermore, when they show an affinity to aesthetic values, they may manifest themselves as either sublime or beautiful: sublime in heroic episodes, beautiful in animated stability.

What then makes up the cluster of existential values? For our purposes, two ideas stand out. The first is the importance of the distinctively human status of every person equally, and the second is the importance of the human stature. (Chapter 15, "Can Cultures Be Judged?," on Isaiah Berlin, explores both ideas.) I work with the assumption that these two aspirations — that all governments should respect the status of all human beings as individuals, and that humanity should endeavor to appreciate itself in its own eyes as infinite — constitute the project of recognizing human dignity as a reality that emanates from a unique and immeasurable potentiality of human beings. The aspiration to defend and promote human stature accounts for the beautiful and sublime aspects of existential values, while the moral commitment drives the defense and promotion of human status. Respect for the human status instills inhibition; a passion for the human stature inflames assertiveness. The two components share the conviction that humanity is more than natural and is in some major respects not natural. The contrasting term to *natural* is not *superhuman* or *transcendental* or *divine*. It is simply and most accurately *human*.

Let us turn first to the respect for the human status of every person. Many of the extraordinary occurrences of insurgency, rebellion, and resolution since the European sixteenth century come from the sentiment that every person deserves to be treated by the government and other authorities in such a way as to express respect for the existential fact that human beings have more in them, actually and potentially, than other animals, and that therefore they should not be treated as animals, whether beasts of burden or prey for the stronger; they should not be treated merely as goods, things, or resources for the purposes of a few; they should not be considered merely as products of the environment, or treated as creatures to be manipulated by the administration of a schedule of pains and pleasures, or as merely lab animals (or earlier equivalents); or considered as merely material or mechanical in nature. Of course, people can be reduced by enough pain and base pleasure as to appear to be turned into any of these degraded conditions. That fact is in itself enormous: human beings can be violated radically and lose their distinctive being. Inhumanity can turn other human beings into something less than human.

(Devastations of nature can do the same.) It should be a steady source of shock that inhumanity can reach such intensity, and a steady source of dismay that we are all able to lose our nature (if only, in some instances, temporarily).

The eruptions in European and transatlantic societies and eventually in societies all over the world since the sixteenth century testify to the passion of numerous people to claim recognition for their status as individual human beings. By now, most people everywhere have learned to lay claim to the human status. The most suitable idiom for making the claim is that of fundamental individual rights or human rights. Many considerations are at work in these eruptions, but they will not be intelligible unless we see that the passion comes not only from specific grievances or even ordinary interests, but also and most deeply from righteous indignation. The feeling is keen that failure by governments and other authorities to respect the human status of all individuals by recognizing their fundamental rights is not only detrimental to the conduct of everyday life but an unforgivable insult in itself, an authoritative transgression against humanity that is not to be endured. Complications attend the theory of human rights every step of the way. The work of interpretation is endless, as is the job of practical application. But impelling the struggle for rights is a passion to be respected in one's status as human.

To be sure, the passion to be respected as a human being often seems to yield to a more intense passion to be respected in one's status as a member of this or that group or culture in particular. These latter deviations are to be expected and may ultimately crush the passion to be respected in one's status as human. The cause of individual human rights has many enemies; some of those enemies are found among the many, for whose sake their predecessors fought in the name of rights. People might think that the protection of their individual rights is too thin a gruel; much thicker are the gratifications of group and tribal identities, of one sort or another. Elites, in turn, may seek to benefit from the play of particularist sentiments.

In any event, every loss of one right or another, or serious erosion of it, is a moral loss; but it is an existential loss as well. The harm to vital interests protected by rights is a great harm, but another, immeasurable harm is lodged in it, which is existential: the profound harm that inheres in every failure by authorities and others to recognize one's status as a human being. It is not the worst thing, but it is bad enough, that sometimes people will settle for having some important vital interests satisfied — say, security and property — and not feel existentially insulted if their other fundamental rights are not recognized or, if supposedly recognized, continuously eroded. Just as particularism may numb the feeling of lost rights, so may a disproportionate valuation of some individual rights diminish other rights.

Individual status depends solely on how human beings look upon one another. The audience for the discourse of rights is human only, but it must cherish freedom and equality. There is no appeal beyond humanity, no more-than-human standard or judge; but there is no need for it. How would one reasonably defend the view that all or most people are beasts and hence fit only to be treated as beasts, or as mere animal creatures, or as things to be used or wasted?

What, however, of the aspiration to defend and promote the human stature? In whose eyes does stature matter? What audience does it have? Mustn't it have a more-than-human audience to impress, if humanity is to think well enough of itself so that it strives to elevate its stature ever more? Of what significance is humanity's judgment in its own case, its decision to praise itself?

I assume that there is no more-than-human audience; the audience can only be sufficiently enlightened humanity. Apart from humanity, there is no one or nothing on whom or which the human spectacle could register. We would need a nonhuman entity or entities that could understand human experience and think with human concepts and categories. Such beings are only mythological. In such an unbacked and unsponsored human condition, I think that we should nevertheless adhere to human stature as at least a plausible idea. The concern that motivates ideal adherence is the specialness of the human race (or self-designated special groups), not that of individuals, no matter how important a contribution is made to the human stature by individuals we call great. Indeed, if the assertion of human stature becomes a project, individuals will be sacrificed for the sake of the project, or will sacrifice themselves. The creativity and unpredictability of ordinary persons is felt to be an insufficient datum for the vindication of the idea of human stature.

Human stature is an idea meant to protect the thought that human beings are not just one more animal species. In some theories, the human stature shows itself not only in the distance between human beings and all other animals, but also in the elevation of humanity above all nature. The evidence for the idea is the fact that in a period of scarcely ten thousand years, human beings have gone from the condition of being only complex creatures to a condition ever more remote from animality and from nature. That is, humanity alone has developed astonishingly without any major change in its biological endowment, and will develop indefinitely into the future, unless it meets extinction or a universal degradation.

There is no use in pretending that an audience outside humanity exists on whom the spectacle can register. To say that the spectacle is fit for the gods is only to say that in contemplative moments and from a humanist perspective a human observer can find it astonishing. Animals do not find other animals astonishing to contemplate; they need human beings to find them astonishing in their beauty or physical powers or marvelous adaptation — not that they care. Only human beings are able to feel astonishment. Why deny them astonishment at themselves, if they feel it, given that they also feel astonishment at what is not human? A proper object of such wonder is the record of human development over the centuries and millennia that derives from humanity's unique capacity to transform the conditions of life. Is this latter astonishment felt only because of continuous changes in the surfaces of life? Is multiplicity of cultures and the proliferation of technologies only a matter of surfaces? One would have to invent a god or gods that could on the basis of a hidden wisdom take such a superficial view. As long as people are disposed to be astonished at anything, there is nothing more worthy of their astonishment — except being itself — than the history of human groupings and societies.

Some main sources of humanity's capacity for indefinite or infinite variability are inwardness, the dream-work, and imagination, all of which it alone possesses. The most simple human activity is more than animal, more than bodies in motion or machines in action. Many acts are also gestures that point beyond themselves. Double and triple meanings suffuse human facts of every sort. Almost every sensory event is also an event of the imagination or memory or will. Humanity alone among the animals is creative, not merely adaptive; it is inventive; it alone has notational systems, like language, mathematics, and music. Unlike other animals, it is essentially unpredictable; there can be no science that maps out the human future. The reason for affirming the human stature is a potentially endless profusion of novelty and of discovery and invention.

I have rehearsed platitudes. The trouble is that many people do not want to see the truth of these platitudes. They are afraid that humanity's pride in what it is as a species will inevitably turn ever more self-destructive and destructive of other species in nature. There is also a long series of reductive philosophers who attempted a cure for human pride by likening human beings to animals or machines and did so for the sake of the truth or for more peace and less savagery. But I do not think that truth is on their side. Can the platitudes I have rehearsed be demolished? Have great spirits like, say, Montaigne and Hobbes, succeeded in their humane antihumanist demolition? The idea of human stature is a component of human dignity because it seeks to save humanity from philosophical attempts to denude humanity of dignity in its own eyes and the eyes of imagined divinities. Perhaps reduced and denuded human beings are capable of even worse crimes than proud ones.

The project of human stature is memorably sustained by audacious enterprises, whether or not the project is conscious and deliberate. To the observer but also sometimes to the participants, each new enterprise shows what humanity is made of, what it is capable of, what elevates it above all nature. To be sure, the fact of cultural diversity, past and present, is by itself testimony to human indefiniteness and human unlikeness to the rest of nature and hence testimony to the human stature. But to the observer, the record of audacious enterprises is an added and endless cause of wonder. The pity is that audacious enterprises often exact an enormous cost in the lives and well-being of persons and other creatures and the rest of nature. The audacious enterprise of exerting mastery over nature without compunction and often without prudence is undeniably an assertion of the human stature; yet it is not only terrible in its effects. When not driven by necessity, the mastery is evidence of the elevation of humanity above the rest of nature. The exploration of nature is another such enterprise. Physical courage, heroism, self-sacrifice are all displayed in going to geographical limits and now in venturing into outer space. Scientific exploration has often required intellectual courage, and still does.

What of the feats of courage, heroism, and self-sacrifice that the audacious enterprises of war and conquest call forth? Animals prey on other animals, but war and conquest are human institutions. Making war when there is neither necessity nor usefulness in the endeavor can be seen or felt as an adventure, just like the exploration of earth and outer space. A game-aspect or a play-aspect is, if not distinctively human, then intensified by war and conquest beyond any animal activity. Is human stature in the form of an aspiration to sublimity perhaps displayed in all activities that recklessly endanger the security of everyday life and show fearlessness where sanity and decency would counsel peace and compromise? Or is this tendency only a deluded or stupid interpretation of the human stature?

The subject of war leads to another subject, the systemization of war in the political life and the overall culture of aristocracies. Often brutal toward one another and usually unjust or oppressive to the many in their own society, aristocracies stand for the elevation of humanity, as represented in the aristocratic class, above all of nature. Artifice is the soul of aristocracy. If war is an encounter with the sublime, an aristocratic culture seems captive to a sense of beauty. Here, too, existential values and aesthetic values are joined. From a distance, but also perhaps from within, aristocracies seem organized in conformity with the aim of encouraging a kind of beauty that not only rivals or surpasses nature, but displaces it. The passion for style in every detail of life, the constant discipline of form, the slow progression of taste, a pedantry of manners, and the disguise woven by rituals and ceremonies all indicate the constant effort to mediate activity by artifice and remove from it grossness, slovenliness, carelessness, and an animal-like immediacy. Of course the beauty of aristocracy serves many practical purposes for both itself and the rest of society; but it would be a mistake, I think, not to see that aesthetic proclivities have their own autonomy and causal power, and also work with added power when joined to existential values. Furthermore, if allied with the priestly class and the pervasive influence of religion, aristocracies have given the world a permanent depository of art and thought. These works, though hemmed in by fear of punishment or bribed by the wealth of monarchs, nobles, and clergy, are among the extraordinary works of humanity.

The cruel truth is that the dignity of the human race in its own eyes has been advanced by injustice and oppression, by the incalculable cost of injury to the human status of countless individuals. There can be a fierce struggle between components of human dignity. The institutions of war and aristocratic privilege assault the modern moral sense. From one main part of the existential perspective, however, an indelible record of wrongdoing, if acknowledged at all, cannot be permitted to pronounce the final judgment: the supremacy of morality is deposed, and existential values, whether aristocratic or heroic on some other basis, claim ascendancy. When the highest stakes are involved, morality is supposed to stand mute. Yet it is also well to remember that insistence on the human status of each person is the highest moral ideal, and it too is part of the existential cluster of values. The hope is that there is in democracy a potentiality for answering to the aesthetic proclivities morally, and without too great a cost to the human stature as existentially conceived.

Anti-instrumental values. When I speak of anti-instrumental values, I do not mean merely noninstrumental values. When those who pursue an ostensible end impede it for the sake of magnanimity or some other quality, or when those who pursue an end do not want it unless it results from the appropriate virtues or traits of character, or when an ostensibly purposive action is done more for the sake of the action than for the sake of the purpose (or at least as much), then the values in play are anti-instrumental, nothing less. Both everyday life and political life are stamped with anti-instrumentalism.

The apparent paradox is that an end is pursued by certain means, but the means seem more important than that end. This indicates that the means are more than means, even if they remain means also; and that the means contain within themselves values that are higher than the ostensible end (or are at least equal in importance). Once again human activity departs from the realm of the necessary and the useful or practical. (All three clusters of values are antipragmatic; that is what makes them interesting.) When the values embodied or expressed by the means conflict with the values contained in the ends, the ends are forced to give way, even if only partly or reluctantly. Then too, since the means are actions, they must be submitted to moral judgment, which turns out to be rather tricky at times.

I refer to just three examples that I deal with in the essays that follow: due process of law under the American Constitution; the doctrine that the virtues and traits of character employed in purposive action are, at least from one perspective, more precious than any end they may be enlisted in achieving; and the idea, most forcefully articulated by Hannah Arendt in modern times, that political action, which is thought by most people to be a means to such ends as security and prosperity, is in itself far more valuable than these conventional ends. These ends are actually only means, only instrumental, even though without some minimal security and at least an austere sufficiency, the material and institutional framework required for political action would not exist. But the designated means are the real ends, and the ends are only means.

First, due process of law. It is the most striking feature of constitutional politics, which as a whole is intended to restrain political power and make it less injurious in its effects. As defined by the Bill of Rights (and some provisions of the original seven articles of the Constitution as well as later amendments), due process is not the shortest route to a verdict in a criminal trial. Due process signifies an official resistance to temptations inherent in the exercise of power: to use it ruthlessly or brutally. A generous name for such resistance to temptation, for accepting self-imposed restrictions, for refusing to use as much strength as one has, to check oneself by various principled inhibitions on going as far as most others do in comparable situations, is magnanimity. From start to finish, from indictment to trial, then to the aftermath of the trial, and finally to punishment, restraints on state action seem to intend more than a verdict and punishment for guilt. Oddly, amazingly, these restraints seem to intend more than the truth of a correct verdict. The process must show fairness to the accused, but fairness is not the only value embodied in it; it is but one aspect of magnanimity.

The magnanimity of due process of law, then, has two principal aspects that can be distinguished, if not always sharply. Besides fairness, there is leniency, which includes impersonal hesitation or reluctance and the institutionalization of second thoughts. In all its stages, due process of law aims to respect persons in the dignity of their individual human status. Many of the people who are caught in the toils of the criminal law, whether finally judged guilty or innocent, are at the mercy of the state, and were in their lives before then often marginal or unrespectable or perhaps already found guilty of an earlier crime. Some of the finest anti-instrumental qualities, therefore, emerge amid circumstances that are least favorable to fineness, and are for that reason all the more admirable. It is possible that due process (in the American constitutional interpretation) is the most purely admirable of all political phenomena that are also moral.

Naturally, it would be the sign of a better world, a new world, if the entire apparatus of due process of law were not necessary. Aristotle's view that punishment is only a "conditional" or relative good is a symbol of the wish that no one would ever commit a crime and no one ever had to impose punishment for it. But the whole transaction is strictly necessary, and nothing better than necessary (*Politics*, VII:1332a, p. 2113). To imagine a complex civilization without any individual crime in everyday life is farfetched utopian speculation — but not nearly as farfetched, I suppose, as imagining a world without the political crimes of states, movements, and groups. (This collection is devoted to examining some of the reasons for thinking that such political speculation is farfetched). Perhaps a world without individual crime would be a world without many good things that grow from the same roots as crime does; perhaps the same holds as well for political crimes (within limits). What matters in any event is that despite the fact that due process of law lies only in the realm of necessity, some features of it can arouse not only surprise but admiration.

Here is a sampling. Fairness is exemplified by the convention or explicit constitutional provision that there be no ex post facto laws; that the judiciary is understood to be no servant of the executive power; that an accused person must know the charges against him; that an accused person must have a trial by an impartial judge, and an impartial jury from the locality where the crime is alleged to have been committed; that the method of justice is adversarial, with all the benefits to the accused person that such a method provides; and that accused persons must be allowed counsel.

Leniency is exemplified by the convention or explicit constitutional provision that the accused is innocent until proved guilty; that indictment by a grand jury is required for a criminal trial to be held; that not all pertinent evidence is admissible; that persons shall not be compelled to be witnesses against themselves; that guilt must be beyond reasonable doubt and hence verdicts of guilt must be unanimous (impersonal hesitation or reluctance); that a verdict of not guilty cannot be appealed by the prosecution (no double jeopardy); that a verdict of guilt can be appealed, often more than once (the institutionalization of second thoughts); and that no one shall be subjected to excessive bail or fines or cruel and unusual punishments (no casual endless detention and no torture or degrading treatment).

The practices of fairness and leniency do not suit a pragmatic frame of mind. Magnanimity is not a pragmatic value or virtue; its procedural manifestations give evidence of the will to respect the human status of all persons, including the guilty, those who seem not to deserve respect. Even their dignity as human beings is respected; they are not to be treated like vicious animals, no matter how vicious their crimes.

Due process of law, however, can lead to miscarriages of justice. I mention this because I wish to acknowledge that valuable procedures can produce unjust outcomes, just as elections and assembly votes can. Socrates had a more or less fair trial. I grant that if unjust outcomes were the usual occurrence, no procedure, no matter how intrinsically valuable in itself it is meant to be, could be acceptable. The means that are more than means remain means; and if they regularly fail as means, they no longer are more than means, but destructive of values more important than themselves in their self-betrayal. They become perverse, a device for odious policies, intentionally or not. This is only to say that sometimes anti-instrumental values, like aesthetic and existential ones, can issue in practices, policies, and decisions that are immoral, even when, as in the example of due process of law, the whole aspiration is toward morality.

The second example of anti-instrumentalism is commitment to the view that virtues or traits of character displayed in the pursuit of ends is of greater importance than the ends pursued. This is a doctrine that goes as far back as Aristotle's discussion of the virtues as constitutive of human happiness, and as therefore valuable to the agent's character, not only instrumentally valuable to others or the agent himself. An exemplary modern statement is in Mill's *On Liberty:* "It really is of importance, not only what men do, but also what manner of men they are that do it. Among the works of man, which human life is rightly employed in perfecting and beautifying, the first in importance is man himself. Suppose it were possible to get houses built, corn grown, battles fought, causes tried, and even churches erected and prayers said, by machinery — by automatons in human form — it would be a considerable loss to exchange for these automatons even the men and women who at present inhabit the more civilized parts of the world, and who assuredly are but starved specimens of what nature can and will produce" (vol. XVIII, ch. 3, p. 263).

I know that the doctrine compressed in this statement could easily be called existential, to use a word that of course Mill does not use. But for the purposes of the scheme of this Introduction and for no better reason, I have used the word *existential* to refer only to human dignity in its two components, individual status and human stature. The concept of individual status is indifferent to any virtue or any specific trait of character, while human stature refers in the first instance to the stature not of great individuals but of the human race vis-à-vis other animals and things in nature. The anti-instrumentalist idea at issue here is that virtues and traits of character, though useful, and though perhaps they would not have come into being and been celebrated unless they were thought useful, matter in a different way from ordinary means, and that they are irreducible to mere means, and incomparable in their value. Or, to make the point more extremely, when we say that virtues and traits matter even more than the ends of action, we propose that we should not want the ends unless they issue from them, or that the display of virtues and traits is the soul of action, whether it succeeds or fails.

A great utilitarian philosopher, Mill is nonetheless anti-instrumental in major respects. He is certainly a great champion of human dignity in both of its components, apart from utilitarian advantages. The issue here, however, is his espousal of the view that in the whole range of human activities — and the ones cited from him above do not seem to be primarily in the moral domain — benefits to humanity are benefits to *humanity* only when they issue from full human beings, not from people deformed and dehumanized by their narrow occupations. Certainly the benefits may be equitably distributed and still exact the terrible price of dehumanization. Mill knows that the benefits are not equitably distributed: owners and leaders use people. But let us leave aside the distributive question. Mill's principal anti-instrumental concern is with the "manner of men" who perform their deeds and follow their pursuits, with the "worth of the agent" (*Utilitarianism,* vol. X, ch. 2, p. 219). Character is not a means but the end. To develop freely a worthy character over a lifetime is to achieve the highest end, which, by definition, can have no justification and needs none. Occupations and vocations are not of course pretexts or incidental occasions; many kinds of work simply must get done. But to look only at the results of work is blindness, the kind of blindness that instrumentalism induces. The political relevance of this idea is, for example, that an obsessive and regimented society, especially when enchantingly prosperous, is an abomination in itself, and, being fragile, might not last long in the way of life it wants.

The question arises as to whether Mill wants us to think that when we consider moral actions, we should take a similar anti-instrumentalist view and want moral actions that come only from agents of the best moral character. The brief answer is no. But the brief answer hides the complexity of his position. Mill suggests that a person can do the right thing, but in such a manner as to repel sympathy for his act and make it "unlovable"; or fail aesthetically — that is, fail to excite admiration and the wish to contemplate admiringly the act and its agent. For Mill, the "sympathetic" and the "aesthetic" aspects are only secondary aspects of a moral act. Yet when one or both of these latter aspects are seriously faulty, the quality of morality suffers, and perhaps moral conduct becomes less likely to occur. These are serious deficiencies, but naturally they do not convert a moral act, done for bad reasons or by a bad character, into an immoral one; the moral "aspect" is for Mill always the most important. "Sentimentality consists in setting the last two of the three [aspects] above the first" ("Bentham," vol. X, p. 113). Also, he does not appear to think that every moral act must ideally be both admirable and lovable. For example, when Brutus sentenced his two sons to death, he did the right thing in upholding the law, Mill asserts; he also did the admirable thing, but not the lovable thing. (Mill even extends his position by allowing himself to say that an immoral act — say, when a brother breaks the law out of affection for a brother — can be lovable but not admirable.)

But Mill's emphasis is not on the quality of all acts, but on moral ones (though he mentions immoral ones in passing). He thinks, however, that Bentham, the head utilitarian, was culpably indifferent to the traits of character that go into the performance of a moral act. Mill does not expect or even appear to desire that the moral motive should lie behind most moral acts. But he wants moral acts to come from an undeformed character. Whenever a moral act must be performed, I infer, Mill wishes that, as often as possible, a person would be capable of manifesting moral, aesthetic, and lovable virtues or traits in the same act. Moral action must be viewed not only from the perspective of those who benefit from an agent's conduct but also from the perspective of the agent's character and the estimation made of it by both the agent and a disinterested observer. It is good for the agent to do admirable and lovable moral (and nonmoral) acts, to become an admirable and lovable person. Mill wants moral persons to be made happy by their moral actions and feel diminished by their own immorality.

What of putatively admirable traits of character shown in immoral activity? In a kind of anti-instrumental thinking, many people, not just some thinkers, wish to say that valuable traits excuse immoral deeds, or even that when valuable traits are displayed, the purpose for which they are enlisted is of no account. Courage is courage wherever it is displayed; so with practical intelligence, devotion to duty, loyalty, self-sacrifice, and so on. (I discuss this theme in Chapter 8, "Courage as a Virtue.") We must pay attention to the pervasive efficacy of anti-instrumentalist feeling. I think that the constant acceptance of wrongdoing, especially of one's own side, is made much easier by the common disposition to admire traits of character apart from their role in achieving any effect, no matter how immoral. There is a strong streak of everyday anti-instrumentalism, though obviously people must prefer winning to losing and in large part (but not exclusively) for instrumental reasons, and hence be especially sensitive to admirable traits shown by one's own side in a winning rather than a losing cause. Then again, the ability to admire the traits of those who are one's enemies or who get in one's way is not uncommon, and is a version of anti-utilitarian magnanimity. But that ability is shown for the most part fleetingly or retrospectively. Otherwise, it is displayed in the province of the best literature and is exercised sometime after the event and often by distant observers.

The third example of anti-instrumentalism is the belief that political action is an end in itself. Just as there are some philosophers and quite a few participants for whom character, and virtues and traits, are valuable in themselves, so there are a few thinkers and many participants who value action for its own sake. These latter catch the excitement and exhilaration of political involvement and convey the thought that to be in action is the best or only life, or the best part of life. (Some write of war as others write about politics.) In recent times, Hannah Arendt has been the most prominent advocate of this notion. Like many of the ideas we have surveyed, this too is counterintuitive because it is anti-instrumental. After all, what could be more practical than politics? What could be more merely instrumental? What activity could be more ruthless in pursuit of victory and therefore most attentive to the instruments that conduce to victory? Who would want politics to exist unless it were necessary? It seems to be, like punishment, only a conditional good. And like punishment, it often fails of its purpose and turns out to be, sadly for us, an instrument both dangerous and ineffective. It is at best a necessary evil.

Arendt sets herself against these views in order to impart a certain luster to political action. She is fully attentive to and appreciative of other activities and relationships that are wanted for their own sake and that few people regard as means to ends (or admit that they regard them in this instrumental way). She discusses love and friendship at their best as personal relationships that no instrumentalism can possibly fathom or even make sense of. Art is sullied when people treat it as a means to their consumption or self-realization, rather than as existing impervious to the uses made of it and demanding that it be taken in on its own terms. What is noteworthy is that Arendt puts forth the position that politics — more precisely, authentic politics — is also an anti-instrumental activity.

A crude distillation of her position is that politics is an end in itself, and that the content of politics is politics. The Greek polis provides one model of authentic politics, and revolutionary councils provide another. Authentic politics happens when the participants find in political experience their most definitive experience: an experience that is so intense and meaningful as to define them, give them their most public and most real identity. Identity does not come when sought, and it is not the possession of the person, but rather an attribute imputed to or conferred on him by those who witness his deeds and hear his words, or eventually turn them into literature. At the same time, the political actor discovers that no experience can rival political participation in creating the sense of freedom. When acting in concert, people as equal citizens or equal rebels make something new happen and they do so by finding capacities in themselves that no other kind of activity would have called forth so lustrously. These capacities—for initiative and response, for unique expression, for creative and expectant attention to the unique and hence contrasting expression of others—though present in everyday life as well, can become publicly memorable and most recognizably brilliant in political life when people engage in it noninstrumentally and for its own sake. Thus in authentic politics people are taken outside themselves, and it is there that they find out who or what they are. They are able to be free and to make a difference.

Politics is an end in itself when it is understood as an activity that should be justified not by its practical consequences but rather by the excellence of the relations it establishes among equal persons. The content that suits such a conception of politics is politics itself; that is, authentic politics looks to the introduction of a system of politics that gives a place to the very virtues and traits that brought it into being, or that strives to maintain such a system already in existence by taking whatever initiatives the system needs to remain true to itself, true to the belief that politics is an end in itself and hence that ordinary people are given the equal chance both to be extraordinary and to have exhilarating experience, if only in episodes. Necessity is banished; the practical is subordinated; the human condition of freedom is realized as something collaborative rather than in solitude.

Authentic politics is a comparative rarity, but it is not impossible that Arendt thought that many participants now and then catch a glimpse of it in any political system that is not autocratic or despotic. They love the game, just as countless observers and partisan spectators do. Loving the game may of course blind actors and partisans to the consequences of what the actors do. Arendt's anti-instrumentalist conception of political action has a hard time negotiating the moral perplexities of political life, even or especially when authentic politics exists. But it is plausible to think that some amazing or surprising creative manifestations of political life have arisen and do arise from the actions of those who love politics as the best game and see nothing outside it that matters to them nearly so much as that love.

At the end of this survey I wish only to repeat that clusters of aesthetic, existential, and anti-instrumental values infiltrate the psyches of those who lead and follow in political life. These values produce amazing effects of great wrongdoing and a few bright streams of restraint and magnanimity. They also produce audacious enterprises that excite either wholehearted or reluctant admiration. The resistance of politics to easy understanding comes from the presence of urges and cravings, drives and motivations that are in excess of basic security and material need, even inflated fear and appetites; or that willingly choose to honor human dignity in spite of fear and inflated fear. Now and then it is right to feel wonder not only at the way in which political life constantly erupts into amazing or surprising events, and even manages to stabilize shocking or occasionally felicitous political and social conditions, but also at the unpractical or hyperrational or irrational or magnanimous or heroic sources of action that hide themselves in practicality or at times even in necessity. Morality undergoes a complex fate in the ordeal of political life. Although nothing is morally worse than oppression that turns into systematic evil—and the twentieth century was not the first to witness systematic evil—perhaps all times have witnessed it—it may be that the most amazing thing about many aesthetic values and some existential and anti-instrumental values is that those who, when possessed by them, do evil, do it with more than a half-belief in their innocence and even in their honor.

References

Arendt, Hannah. "What Is Freedom?" in *Between Past and Future* (1961). 2d edition, New York: Viking, 1968.

Aristotle, *Metaphysics* in *The Complete Works of Aristotle*, ed., Jonathan Barnes, vol. 2. Trans. W. D. Ross. Princeton: Princeton University Press, 1984.

Aristotle. *Politics* in *Complete Works*, vol. 2. Trans. Benjamin Jowett.

Cooper, John M. *Reason and Emotion: Essays on Ancient Moral Psychology and Ethical Theory*. Princeton: Princeton University Press, 1999.

Craft, Robert. "Le Ten O'Clock de M. Whistler." *Times Literary Supplement*, Feb. 23, 2001, p. 15.

Mill, John Stuart. "Bentham" (1838) in *Collected Works*, vol. X. Toronto: University of Toronto Press, 1969.

Mill, John Stuart. *On Liberty* (1859) in *Collected Works*, vol. XVIII, 1977.

Mill, John Stuart. *Utilitarianism* (1861) in *Collected Works*, vol. X, 1969.

Popper, Karl. *The Open Society and Its Enemies* (1945). 5th edition, vol. 1. Princeton: Princeton University Press, 1966.

Thucydides. *The Peloponnesian War*. Trans. Crawley/Wick. New York: Modern Library, 1982.

Whitman, Walt. *Democratic Vistas* (1871) in *Walt Whitman: Complete Poetry and Collected Prose*. New York: Library of America, 1982.

PART I

Liberty and the American Constitution

Is Patriotism a Mistake?

Is patriotism a mistake? I think that it is a mistake twice over: it is typically a grave moral error and its source is typically a state of mental confusion. But the mistake of patriotism is an inevitable mistake. It cannot be avoided; almost no one can help being a patriot of some kind and to some degree. What is surprising and deplorable is that the mistake of patriotism is elaborated theoretically and promoted by people who should know better — that is, political theorists, moral philosophers, and theologians.

The defense of patriotism by some, perhaps many, thinkers is surprising. More surprisingly, however, that defense should probably not be so surprising. One of the most pronounced tendencies of contemporary intellectual life is the defense offered of what I fear I must call moral and mental obtuseness. I have in mind the general abandonment by intellectuals of a commitment to their own preconditions, which are some main values of the Enlightenment: independence of mind as an inspiration for all persons, rejection of fanaticism, and a fierce dislike of idolatry, especially group idolatry. I am not saying that

This essay began as remarks on a panel at APSA, 1996, devoted to Maurizio Viroli's *For Love of Country* (Oxford: Clarendon Press, 1995), and to the general theme of patriotism. I want to thank Roxanne Euben, Sankar Muthu, and Nadia Urbinati for their suggestions.

unless a philosopher follows the French *philosophes* in every particular, he or she betrays the Enlightenment. But there is a profound discrepancy between the values that make the thinking life possible and the values that some recent thinkers have espoused as good for others. If these others prevail, all thinkers would be threatened with persecution. Intellectual condescension would be repaid with anti-intellectual repression.

A defense of patriotism is an attack on the Enlightenment; a defense of all group phenomena related or analogous to patriotism is also an attack on the Enlightenment. Actually, the defense of patriotism is simply one part, though a major one, of a larger particularist tendency of thought, which honors membership in all groups that offer to help persons carry the burden of selfhood, of individual identity. The greatest part of the burden is the quest for meaningfulness, which is tantamount to receiving definition for the self. It is claimed that the most gratifying definition of self comes from the limits imposed and permissions granted by membership in cultural or identity groups. A large number of intellectuals have undertaken to defend the claims of group identity and affiliation as such, because the underlying idea is that only such identity and affiliation can bestow a coherent meaning on life (or establish a purpose for life). Only when life is thought to have such meaningfulness can life be endurable for people, especially for the great mass of nonintellectual people.

Therefore, I put to one side those cases where intellectuals directly or disguisedly defend their own particularism, be it based on religion, ethnicity, race, nationality, or language. That is a different kind of aberration from the one that occupies me in this paper.

Group membership and allegiance simplify life by tying the identity of each member to a structure of inclusion and exclusion, of questions and answers, of rites and ceremonies, of allowable and censurable fantasies. Supposedly, it is nonintellectual people, people who do not do their own thinking, who crave meaning the most and who must be given it by those who do their thinking for them. Thus, we find theoretical defenses of such group phenomena as religious fundamentalism, ethnic pride, and linguistic and ethnic separatism. Multiculturalism, the new name for cultural pluralism, is all the rage. And then, of course, there is patriotism, the most deadly form of group attachment, to which I will turn in short order.

One source of the defense of group attachment is postmodernism. Postmodern defenders of group-sustaining fictions don't usually tell their readers explicitly that they are defending beliefs that they could easily demolish. Rather, they are — sometimes unwittingly — faithful to the Straussian distinction between esoteric and exoteric writing, without having Strauss's courage in announcing that such a distinction exists. Strauss lets the cat out of the bag — not that he expects most people to notice. Postmodernists must think that all that the greater public will ever learn about them is, at most, their defense of group-sustaining beliefs, which are known only by the few to be fictitious, unwarranted beliefs.

Now, if one oddity is that postmodern intellectuals defend anti-intellectual social phenomena, the further oddity is that many of these intellectual defenders are convinced that there is no transcendent meaning or purpose in life and that all values are arbitrary or subjective. We find that many, though by no means all, of the defenders of tight group life (of one kind or another) are postmodernists or are sympathetic to postmodernism. That means that these thinkers combine a see-through-it-all radicalism with an accept-it-all permissiveness; they combine scepticism or atheism for themselves with a defense of orthodoxy or fundamentalism for others, with special favor naturally conferred on those groups whose beliefs give the self a shape by giving life a meaning, any meaning, preferably a system of meaning, and because of it, a coherence. I am not saying that political theorists, moral philosophers, and theologians originate these beliefs — although sometimes they do. Many of the beliefs are inherited, of course. Rather, these kinds of thinkers provide comfort and encouragement, provide rationalization, for subscribing to belief, for indulging the will to believe, for uniting a wish to have truth and a disinclination to make a serious effort to ascertain it.

The postmodernists take away with one hand what they give with another. They deconstruct the attempted meaning of intellectual systems and of some rationalist aspects of culture, but they simultaneously endorse the craving for confident meaning. They convey the message, but not in so many words, that it is better not to try to tell people the truth that there is no truth, of the sorts people want, to tell; instead, it is better for intellectuals to defend and promote fictions that these intellectuals know to be fictions and to do so because people need fictions and would languish or perish without them. The people naturally hold their fictions as truths, whereas many intellectuals see through them and still promote them. These intellectuals may not believe in the possibility of systematic truth, but they surely appear not to believe in truthfulness or honesty, either. The program of Nietzsche as Lawgiver — the pathetic and least valuable Nietzsche — is carried out, but without his compunction, and without the total candor he establishes with his readers. Notice that what is involved is not the immemorial practice of defending beliefs that thinkers know are fictions because they fear the subversive effects on morality of exploded fictions, religious or metaphysical. To the contrary, the beliefs that many contemporary thinkers want to defend conduce to immorality (by the thinkers' own standard), and these thinkers knowingly defend them anyway. And the postmodern relativism of some of these thinkers makes it all too easy to disseminate ideas that work with immoral effects. Emerson complains in "The American Scholar" that "too often, the scholar errs with mankind and forfeits his privilege" (p. 54). There is abundant reason these days to echo that complaint. Group-based meaningfulness gives solace to people, undeniably; it helps to give closure to personal identity. But if intellectuals cannot supply honest and truthful meaning, they should not supply or defend meaning they know to be unwarrantable. Perhaps, it would be best for them to remain silent, if they decided that they simply could not deprive people of solace.

I grant that theoretical support for group identity and affiliation and for the beliefs that sustain it does not come from only postmodern unbelief; it may also come from a somewhat more complicated mental condition. My point pertains especially to religious and metaphysical beliefs. I mean that some writers go through motions, hoping that the result will be their own adherence or conversion, and they recommend the process to others, especially to other thinkers. They seem to be saying to themselves: "Let us write as if we believe, and thus imitate those who, as genuine believers, maintained the tradition we now, in the face of our own unbelief, want to keep going. Let us forget or put to one side or blur what we once knew to be true, and contribute to the perpetuation of what we want to be true and what we feel we do not know enough to call false. We shall practice the traditional modes of thinking, even though they necessarily lack their old solidity. We construct simulacra that we hope will pass for, or pass into, the real thing. We will confuse ourselves and others into clarity." But this mental complication (or slow philosophical suicide) leads only to the return of once tragic constructions as farcical: farcical because flimsy. Going through these motions is not exactly covering a genuine despair with a simulated hopefulness; it is more like showing misplaced solicitude for others and the wrong kind of care for oneself. This tendency is, however, less prominent than postmodernist connivance with superstition.

There is one more oddity. I have noticed a recent tendency among some thinkers, who are non- or anti-postmodern, to defend intensity of passion or emotion. These thinkers do so because of a fear that contemporary life is shallow, that the people around us are averse to commitment and loyalty, have lost the ability to care deeply about anything outside themselves, and care about wrong, superficial things in regard to themselves. There is a growing — shall we call it — moral archaism or conservatism, fairly continuous with communitarianism, but conceptually separable from it, that values strong feelings of any sort or passionate commitment or attachment as such. Not all defenders of the passions advocate individual attachment to groups, but some do so explicitly. This way of mourning the perceived loss of depth is guided by the unexpressed surmise, I believe, that people have depth only when they have strong fathers, that depth goes only with patriarchy reinforced by patriotism and monotheism (one divinity, and pictured as father). For these conservatives, however, the newly assertive religiousness is not likely to resurrect the father and with him, depth of psyche. I call this development odd because conservatives blame the ironizing and sceptical elements in postmodernism for justifying the supposed loss of passion and commitment. Despite the overt hostility, there is thus an unrecognized alliance between some postmodernists and some of their enemies. Postmodernists offer an untruthful defense of dogma; the moral conservatives offer a sometimes insincere defense of devotion.

The difference between these two camps is this: the moral conservatives talk others and perhaps themselves into commitments, whereas the postmodernists solely defend the commitments of others. The conservatives see the corrosiveness inherent in postmodernism, but fail to observe the support lent by some postmodernists to the passionate commitments held sincerely by various groups. The conservatives also fail to see their own hollowness, even as they complain about the shallowness of the people around them. I mean that the project of urging passion, of willing passion, on oneself and others must result in an amazing self-deception. The sources of such passion in contrivance and deliberate effort is forgotten. If the postmodernists consecrate the sincere espousal by others of commitments that the postmodernists know are unjustifiable, the postmodernists are at least free, for the most part, of self-deception. That is an advantage, I suppose. But judged from the perspective of truth as well as the perspective of morality, both the particular group commitments defended by many postmodernists and the idea of group commitment as such defended by some moral conservatives are deserving of serious scrutiny and, I believe, of our reproach.

To turn specifically to patriotism as a form of group identity and affiliation: Why really do I think that patriotism in itself is a mistake? First, let us ask, What is patriotism? It is love of one's country. How is patriotism most importantly shown? Let us not mince words. The answer is that it is most importantly shown in a readiness, whether reluctant or matter-of-fact, social or zealous, to die and to kill for one's country. These two answers constitute the most common understanding of patriotism. What is one's country? Here the answer I give is not the one lodged in common understanding, which understanding would repel the answer I propose. My answer is that one's country — any country — is best understood as an abstraction, for it is a compound of a few actual and many imaginary ingredients. If the word *imaginary* is too disdainful, then substitute *imaginative* or *aesthetically induced*.[1] A country is not a discernible collection of discernible individuals like a team or a faculty or a local chapter of a voluntary association. Of course a country is a delimited territory. It is also a place, a setting, a geography; it has landscape, cityscapes, perhaps seascapes; it has old buildings as well as new ones; it has historical sites; it has a light, an air, an atmosphere; it has a special look. But it is also constructed out of transmitted memories true and false; a history usually mostly falsely sanitized or falsely heroized; a sense of kinship of a largely invented purity; and social ties that are largely invisible or impersonal, indeed abstract, yet by an act of insistent or of dream-like imagination made visible and personal.

What, then, is patriotism, really? It is a readiness to die and to kill for an abstraction: nothing you can see all of, or feel as you feel the presence of another person, or comprehend. Patriotism, then, is a readiness to die and to kill for what is largely a figment of the imagination. For this figment, one commits oneself to a militarized and continuously politicized conception of life, a conception that is entirely masculinist. Patriotism is, from its nature, a commitment to the system of premature, violent death, inflicted and accepted, in whatever spirit that suits one's temperament or that is current in one's time and place, and with victories and defeats coming as they do. The deathly passion of patriotism attained an almost parodic form not so long ago when in the country of Georgia an official (Mrs. Shevardnadze, in fact) tried to block the adoption of Georgian orphans by U.S. citizens. According to *New York Times* reporter Alessandra Stanley, Mrs. Shevardnadze said, "All the Georgian people are suffering hardship. . . . Let our children suffer, too." As Stanley said, "she casts the issue as one of national identity" (NYT, 6/29/97, pp. 1, 12). Such candor about the bond between patriotism and death is uncommon these days. In a whole book of defenses of patriotism against Martha Nussbaum's cosmopolitanism, there is scarcely any reference to the necessary connection between patriotism and militarized death.[2] Anthony Appiah appears to endorse his father's belief that Ghana is worthy dying for. And Elaine Scarry touches on international conflict occasioned by tribal national feelings. That is all.

I ask us to notice that an abstraction of the sort that I say patriotism is, is not the same thing as a principle. There is a very sharp contrast between a readiness to die and to kill for an abstraction and a readiness to do the same for a principle. A principle must be universal, but an abstraction can have any scope. To embrace a principle, which is of course abstract in some sense, is to pledge oneself to a rule to guide one's perception of the world and, if one has sufficient integrity, to guide one's conduct in it. A *moral* principle, even if a person usually lacks sufficient integrity to remain actively faithful to it in all the most tempting or desperate circumstances, governs one's conduct toward others, and the expectations one has of the conduct of others. A moral principle must be conceived as universalist, and asks for consistent application; and it aims at respect for persons or individuals, not abstract entities of the imagination. There is also a sharp contrast, on the other hand, between an abstraction like patriotism and a tangible personal interest like being protected or preserved in one's rights of life, liberty, and property, for which purpose it may also sometimes be thought necessary to risk death and to kill.

To be sure, patriotism is not only an abstraction, it is also an ideal; but it is a very peculiar one: it idealizes an entity — the country — that people feel is them or theirs. Patriotism therefore makes a certain kind of self-love into an ideal. It is a self-concern that inevitably passes into a licensed self-preference that, from the nature of things, must, in turn, attempt to be destructive toward other countries, and rarely for the sake of defending people's tangible interests. The moral disposition is to respect others for their own sake, and even to try to prefer them to oneself and one's own, though not as a matter of course to utterly self-sacrificing lengths. (There may perhaps be a moral duty to preserve oneself at a cost to others, if need be.) But patriotism is inherently disposed to disregard morality, well short of regard for others. Armed entities can never think of anything but self-promotion; their leaders never think for a moment of giving equal consideration to other peoples, much less preferring them. None of them does. The moral disposition is wholly alien to international relations, because self-preservation, no matter how defined, is permanently thought endangered. You can love particular persons without having to dislike or hate others; but you cannot love an abstract entity like a country and not dislike or hate other countries, because countries are, from their nature as organizations of and for power, in actual or latent competition. The energies of group animosity await and often receive the mobilization they desire. Those who lead the mobilization see their country as a means or base for struggle.

The highest moral principles teach restraint of self-preference, whether the self is oneself or a group-self; while, on the other hand, a person's basic rights and tangible self-interest, in a tolerable society, are supposed to be practiced or achieved without morally cognizable harm to the same rights and interests of others. In contrast, patriotism is self-idealization; it is group narcissism without any self-restraint except for a frequently unreliable prudence, and carried to death-dealing lengths. Patriotism is one of the more radical forms of group-thinking, or group identity and affiliation. Being armed is what makes it radical. I don't find much difference, at least in effects, between patriotism and nationalism.

A good patriot does not want people in other countries to be patriots. Only when a patriot is a theorist who is also an aesthete—as, say, Machiavelli was—does he want every country to contain good patriots, does his patriotism get universalized and hence converted into a principle. The aestheticized patriot wants the game of animosity to be played well by all sides. He desires to win, so he wants patriotic enemies who have enough prowess to make victory over them gratifying, even though they must not be as good as he and his side are. He sees this game that is not a game as the point of life and wants the game to go on forever; he himself may only play his patriotism like a role. But this aestheticized patriotism, if it is a principle at all, is an immoral one. Most patriots, however, are purely avaricious for victory and must prefer to contend with adversaries who are unpatriotic or much less so, and who have less prowess, despite the attractions of defeating a stronger enemy.

Patriotism is a jealous and exclusive loyalty. This fact, however, doesn't exclude cases where enemies have a common interest in maintaining the general system of patriotic loyalty. States engaged in war have cooperated in punishing mutiny in the ranks of one of them. Analogously, rulers may refuse to support rebellion in the domain of one of their fellow-rulers, despite enmity; and religions that deny validity to one another may for a time support a general religiousness against secularism. But all this cooperation across enemy lines is tactical and temporary. The logic of exclusive loyalty dictates that no state or church wants any other to succeed in gaining and keeping loyalty. For the most part, then, patriotism can't be a principle. Even if we could believe that democracies never wage war on other democracies, imperialist democracies nevertheless have subverted or preyed on other democracies, whether imperialist or not. So that there seems little plausibility to the contention that citizens of one democracy can always want citizens of other democracies to be patriots. In any event, it's odd to think that as a matter of principle patriotism can be reserved for democracies.

Now, Maurizio Viroli, in a truly fine theoretical defense of patriotism, *For Love of Country,* a work of learned originality, maintains that patriotism is not love of country as one's own country, but rather a love of country because the country is the place of free republican institutions. The patriotism he wishes to defend is, in his phrase, "the patriotism of liberty" (1995, p. 17). That is, Viroli tries to make patriotism not only a principle, but a moral principle. His patriot is committed to freedom above all, but is especially concerned with achieving, securing, or restoring the freedom of his own country. Freedom is the first principle of political morality; patriotism is the energy behind it. I take Viroli to be suggesting that a high and moral principle like freedom cannot be loved unless it is entwined with one's own country, with one's way of life and place of memory. A universal principle can be loved only through a defined particularity. I am put in mind of the Catholic view that the immaterial and spiritual God cannot be loved either without the incarnation or without such devices as Maryolatry, or statues and paintings of saints, or imposing and gorgeous houses of worship. But I think that the radical Protestant critique is right: the ultimate God gets lost in his representations; so, for patriots like the sort pictured by Viroli, moral principles risk getting lost, must eventually get lost — displaced, or forgotten, and often betrayed.

To be fair, let us look more closely at a case that supports Viroli's position, but only to some extent. And the case is a rare exception to the rule. During the time of slavery in the United States, did the high political principle of freedom elicit a dedication for its own sake, apart from its entwinement with patriotism? (One could substitute some other political principle like equal human dignity or justice or social equality and ask whether it can be respected for its own sake apart from its entwinement with patriotism or some other irrational ideal.) It seems to me that Lincoln was persuaded from the time of the Dred Scott case (1857) that slavery could be abolished only by war, but that the free states would never begin a war for the purpose of abolishing slavery; they would fight only to preserve the Union. In the South, the avowed purpose of secession could not be primarily to defend slavery: a majority of white households owned no slaves, though we know that they could not imagine themselves living with 4 million freed blacks. In any case, the main avowed purpose had to be the failure of the Union to recognize states' rights; or less legalistically, the purpose had to be to assert a separate national identity and secure it by war. Thus, in the Northern case, patriotism was enlisted for a moral end that otherwise could not be attained; in the Southern case, patriotism was enlisted to preserve the radically unjust institution of slavery. In both cases, the real moral issue — at least in the instigation of the war and for a time during the war itself — was covered over by the emotion of patriotism, which was real: in the North on behalf of the Union and in the South on behalf of the South. If it were not for slavery, Southern patriotism would not have been tried.

What lesson can be learned? Certainly, patriotism may be mobilized for a good cause. But much more easily, it may be mobilized for an unjust one. I think that Lincoln's mobilization of patriotism is one of the best instances of entwining patriotism and a high moral end. What he had to contend with was equally strong Southern patriotism. For the sake of a good cause, he felt he had to act manipulatively. The manipulation was enormous: he could not disclose the springs of his policy, though the South understood him well enough. As a candidate, he refused certain compromises on the issue of slavery. In his public positions between Dred Scott and secession, he risked the Union to contain slavery. Once president, he knew that only a minority felt as he felt about slavery, at least up to 1862, partway through the war. He would not make peace for a restored Union, if slavery were to be preserved. He was himself a patriot and revered the Union. But he hated slavery more than he loved his country. So he played the patriotism card when he had to. This is the hardest test of my contention that patriotism is a mistake. It is in itself a mistake, but it may on occasion be tactically useful for a high, moral cause. Even when tactically useful for such a cause, however, its success may exact tremendous moral costs; above all, the cost inherent in the waging of a bloody and pro- tracted war. In any event, how often in the annals of the love of country has a high moral cause been served? Perhaps more than once. But then compare these occurrences with all the occasions on which love of country has been enlisted for an unjust and often irrational or stupid purpose. How does the comparison come out? Is not the preponderant tactical use of patriotism to serve unjust causes? Wouldn't it be right — impossibly right — if no one were a patriot?

Furthermore, if political principle can be defended only when it is mixed with patriotism, so that the principle is defended only because it is ours and not because it is right or primarily because it is right, or if we call a principle right because we insist that our own commitment must be to the right, then where are we? Should we follow and imitate Lincoln and theorize manip- ulatively? No: Don't some people have to try to be honest?

I thought that was crucially the vocation of teachers. They should defend moral principles directly, and accord them the supremacy they deserve. They should not be disguised tacticians. Leave that to others. To repeat, it is better to be silent than to be a tactician. (I know that I preach.) I find it impossible to swallow Rousseau's dictum that to will the end is to will the means. I will the end and may have to use the means, but do not will to use them. I wish I did not have to use them: they stain the end to which they are putatively the indispensable means. And I should refuse to praise them or hide the truth about them. If patriotism is ever good, it is only instrumentally good, never good in itself. I also know that the thoughts and passions that called modern constitutional freedom into being and sustained it were not patriotic, but universalist, as were the ideas of the Levellers, Jefferson, and Paine, among others.

Patriotism needs external enemies. Devotion to a free constitution for its own sake is not patriotism; it has no use for enemies; it hates having them; and when patriotism must be mixed in with such devotion to give it strength, then we can be sure that the devotion is grossly imperfect. Even devotion for the sake of one's own narrow personal interest would be a less impure and much more consonant way of attaching oneself to a free constitution.

Typically enough, a moral person often has to choose between attachment to country and adherence to moral principle, especially when patriotism is most demanded; namely in those recurrent situations when patriotism is mobilized for enterprises of international tension and war. Patriotism is, if it is anything, a passion to forsake moral principle with an easy conscience. We misunderstand patriotism if we see it as given to moral doubt. The Corinthians get the point of patriotism right when they presume to remind the Spartans of what neither the Spartans nor anyone else ever forgot: "Peace stays longest with those who are not more careful to use their power justly than to show their determination not to submit to injustice" (Thucydides, 1:71, p. 41). That is, a patriot must unhesitatingly prefer inflicting injustice to suffering it, if that is the choice in any given situation. The patriot always gives his side the benefit of every moral doubt. Patriotism is on a permanent moral holiday, and once it is made dynamic, it invariably becomes criminal. The means of activist patriotism are criminal and its ends are at best semi-criminal. A person devoted to moral principle may fight for his country, but does so for the sake of universal moral principle, when its mandates happen to coincide with his country's interest—as they may, but usually only partly. I grant that a few countries show a developed patriotism that is unwarlike, at least, for the time being—say the patriotism of the Swiss. Such a condition is so rare, however, as to be unhelpful in the analysis of a general phenomenon.

The vicissitudes of patriotic feeling rarely follow what is perhaps their best pattern. We begin by helplessly acquiring love of country; we come to love its principles because they are the country's; gradually, with increased discernment, we love the principles for their own sake; then, if reluctantly, we accept the country as a grossly imperfect embodiment of the principles, while we are ever more sensitive to the grossness of the imperfection, yet appreciative, also, of the spasmodic efforts made by some fellow-citizens to reduce the imperfection or retard further imperfection; and we remain unable, perhaps unwilling, to purge ourselves completely of the original, unreasoned, instilled love or attachment. There are limits, after all, to the ability to outgrow one's early years.

I think that Alasdair MacIntyre is right (in "Is Patriotism a Virtue?") to indicate that though patriotism may be a virtue, a kind of courage, its exercise is often incompatible with universal moral principle. But I don't share MacIntyre's allowance for virtues in the service of practices that are only accidentally moral and are more naturally unjust. The practices are interwoven with vices, and the vices may even inspire or call forth the virtues. So used, or so implicated, the virtues cease doing the work of virtues, even though I would not wish to say that they thereby become vices. They become qualities or traits that one cannot help admiring, but wishes that one did not have to admire. The admiration is aesthetic, though not completely so. One is tempted to wish them out of existence in order for one's conscience to be easier. But, no, that temptation should be questioned. It should be sufficient to keep on remembering that virtues matter not only as actualizations of human potentiality and self-overcoming but also as necessary means to right conduct.

An extreme version of MacIntyre's position comes to this: it is more important to preserve certain virtues or qualities than to achieve a great outcome like peace or justice, if these outcomes do not require — cannot use — those virtues and qualities, and would spell the end of need for them. Aristotle wants to preserve private property (in part) so that the virtue of generosity can exist, and to preserve marriage (in part) so that the virtue of avoiding adultery and hence showing temperance toward women can exist (II:5, 1263b; II:6, 1265a). But these are mild cases in comparison to those where thinkers and others want war to exist so that the virtues or qualities of courage, manliness, self-sacrifice, loyalty, single-minded dedication, and extravagant expenditure and self-expenditure can continue to exist with the greatest public intensity. Patriotism is a single name for all these qualities. The motivations behind this position are aesthetic to some degree, but also have to do with an idea of human stature that is necessarily tied to heroism and adventure, to gallantry and imprudence in the face of dreaded but welcomed challenges. I do not despise these motives or the position to which they may lead, but their moral cost is often prohibitive.

Allow me to digress and say that even less acceptable, however, is the consequentialist idea that we can call a quality or trait a virtue or a vice only after a given display of it has led to a morally desirable outcome. What supposedly counts as a virtue or a vice can never be known apart from the role the quality or trait has played in a particular outcome. Every quality or trait will sometimes be called a virtue and sometimes a vice; and these alternating contradictory appraisals must be made indefinitely into the future. In response, I would say that at least when Machiavelli holds that certain virtues are often not politically appropriate, and that they produce immoral results (the greater evil), he does not stop seeing these qualities as virtues. His position is that in public life virtues have the effect of vices without turning into them. He sees private life as the appropriate arena for certain virtues. And, indeed, daily life often requires such qualities precisely for moral purposes: to show love of persons or love of principles. He thought that daily life would provide enough opportunity for these virtues, even if hidden from the public. (This is not to deny, of course, that he made comedy out of what we would call the Machiavellianism of sexual relations.)

I do not hold, of course, that any democracy — or probably any country, whether democratic or not — is merely wickedness. All democracies — to confine ourselves to those — do good things as well as quite a number of bad ones. In many sectors, a democracy is fairly decent in some of its domestic policy, and it remains faithful, despite repeated failures in hard cases, to the principles of constitutionalism. But such good tendencies go very easily with wickedness to, even despotism over, neighbors; and when a democracy is an empire, as is the case with the United States, decency at home goes very easily with quite a large amount of wickedness abroad. A democracy becomes an amputated democracy when it rules groups within its boundaries or whole peoples outside them undemocratically or despotically. I wonder whether this mixture of modes allows us to continue to call it a democracy at all.

How can one love such a mottled or hybrid entity as a country, particularly when, as in a democracy, the country's people are (always by imputation and sometimes in fact) directly and indirectly responsible for the country's wicked policies? Political institutions that embody high moral principles in their procedures and processes too often do not prevent terrible results. One does and sometimes should love persons "beyond good and evil," so to speak; but to love a country, an abstract entity capable of so much harm, especially to those outside, to those who are not fellow-patriots, but rather patriots of their own, if they are patriots at all — that is an unacceptable idea. Love of country becomes love of leviathan or behemoth, even when, and sometimes especially when, one's country is a modern republic — that is, a constitutional democracy. But I am certainly not claiming that one should stop loving one's own country in order to love other countries, or that one should love all countries equally. If love of many countries besides one's own is cosmopolitanism, then I see little value in cosmopolitanism. Worldliness is a better outlook: a nontouristic and nonanthropological appreciation of different ingredients of numerous cultures, including one's own. One should not love whole countries, at least as a patriot is supposed to. The only morally acceptable love is of persons or of moral principles, or principles compatible with morality — to leave aside love of things, human and natural. Unfortunately, sometimes love of persons conflicts with love of principles.

I also wish to maintain that even narrow self-love is vastly less egotistical than the self-inflating yet paradoxically self-sacrificing love of country. Self-love can be boundless only when one has absorbed an abstract entity like a country into oneself by identifying with it, an entity that seems to have no beginning or end, and no limits on what its leaders and members think it wants or think it must have or do. The worst degree of egotism is, of course, self-worship. But the most intense self-worship must commonly be indirect. People tend to be some-what ashamed of worshipping themselves directly and overtly. The most ef-fective indirectness is to identify with a group, and while doing so, manage to forget that one is absorbing it into oneself, so that one may more palatably worship oneself. One enlarges oneself by this process of alienation through identification because a group is not merely something external to oneself but rather something that one already imagines as one's own. One's group identity and affiliation, certainly in the form of patriotism, is thus what permits the fullest egotism.

This indirect self-worship can, however, exact a direct self-sacrifice when the group a person identifies with suddenly becomes unmistakably, literally, a force external to oneself that commands oneself to risk one's life. With the prospect of such a sacrifice, one may lose sight of one's self-worship: one nicely becomes conscientiously dutiful, almost selfless. Rather than absorbing one's country into oneself, one is — at least, initially — gratefully absorbed by, dis-solved into, a superperson, the country imagined as one person, but much greater than one person or all persons together. The I becomes a We, and the We becomes an It. By this whole process of identification, one traffics between the most unconsciously shameless egotism and the most costly self-sacrifice. One traffics between the most active fantasy life and the most passive submis-sion. Such may be the career of indirect self-worship. The upshot is that it tends to be morally safer to love yourself more than your country, if that has to be the choice.

I am not saying that indirect self-worship cannot be individually or cultur-ally resisted. The democratic individuality that may grow out of rights-based individualism can be cultivated, precisely in order to restrain or deflect self-worship. But the project of democratic individuality is very difficult to sustain, individually and culturally. The fact remains, however, that only when the meanings of rights-based individualism are taken to heart, and thereby, demo-cratic individuality strengthened, can an attempt be made, in modern condi-tions, to withstand that destructive egotism that confusedly merges one's ego and the group's ego.

Now, it is possible that for some people, the attraction of patriotism is mainly the abjection of self it imposes, rather than any indirect self-worship it may make possible. Patriotism (and some other group affiliations) signify that a person, as oneself and in oneself, is not very much. Yet by giving oneself to the group, one does one's share in keeping alive an entity that can be or become, as itself and in itself, something that matters greatly and is worthwhile. Patriotism, more than almost all other group affiliations, is a way of acquiescing in one's inferiority. What Emerson says about popular loyalty to kings and heroes can be transferred to an impersonal entity like a country. He says, in "The American Scholar":

> All the rest behold in the hero or poet their own green and crude being — ripened; yes, and are content to be less, so that may attain to its full stature.... They sun themselves in the great man's light, and feel it to be their own element. They cast the dignity of man from their downtrod selves upon the shoulders of a hero, and will perish to add one drop of blood to make that great heart beat, those giant sinews combat and conquer. He lives for us, and we live in him. (p. 66)[3]

I believe nevertheless that the more salient consideration is indirect self-worship rather than self-abjection.

I concede that my proposed analysis of patriotic group feeling as individual self-worship may be tenuous or inaccurate (and my reference to self-abjection too underdeveloped). Allow me to propose a somewhat different approach. Let us leave aside self-worship (and self-abjection) and see love of country as rather more substantially other-regarding. I still want to ask whether love of country is love at all. Perhaps love of country is an imitation of love because it is love of a false object, an object that is not an object, but one of those "dream substances, mock realities" to which Augustine refers in his *Confessions* (III: 6, p. 61). In any case, love of country is not continuous with love of persons. What is it like? It is more like cheering or rooting for a team than it is like being a member of a team and having team spirit. Patriotism is a kind of vicariousness, a living outside oneself and through something else that one partly imposes on oneself, while pretending that one has no choice but to lend or give oneself to it. To be sure, living vicariously can have direct effects on the person, to leave aside risks and sacrifices. One does not have to be a player, an actual member of the team, to be affected in various ways by the fortunes of the team for which one roots. If my team, my country, wins, I gain an inflated confidence in my own life — a confidence that frequently collapses, however, after a short while. If my team, my country, loses, I get depressed. Such habits of the mind are inevitable: we all have teams or something like teams that we root for.

But patriotism is a deadly sort of rooting. Even when persons are not mere fans or spectators, but active participants, members, say, of the armed forces, they are more like pawns than like members of a sports team. It is then that patriotism, the original passion, often gives way to concern for one's little platoon, a group of persons that one can see and care for as persons, apart from any abstract passion like patriotism. Certainly such concern for persons can bring out admirable qualities. But, to say it again, we should notice how such admirable sentiment and conduct — bravery and platoon loyalty — are enclosed within a larger pattern of activity, which can be preponderantly immoral. Also, this larger activity sometimes appears to be the game of the few who are able to make everyone else into their tools or their material. Patriotism thus tends to be voluntary self-exploitation, usually in a dubious cause.

The stakes are very high in any discussion of love of country. Indeed, I think that such a discussion must reach to the basic questions of political theory, which are, let us assume, Is government necessary? And if the answer is yes, then, What form and spirit of government best conduce to achieving the purposes that allegedly make government necessary? (There are, to be sure, other profound questions that appear in the wake of these two; above all, What, if anything, may arise that is morally admirable or that is admirable and compatible with morality, when the necessities are placated?) I believe that patriotism leads in one direction, even when patriots embrace the form of constitutional democracy, while a principled commitment to rights-based individualism leads in another direction. Patriots and defenders of patriotism may embrace the form of constitutional democracy, but they do not accept, much less embrace, its spirit.

The political outlook that derives from rights-based individualism holds that a politically organized country exists for the sake of codifying and protecting individual personal and political rights; that government, the protector of rights, is the principal entity against which rights must normally be protected; that a country's boundaries exist in order to make the exercise of rights fruitful and also to facilitate the struggle against scarcity through sensible laws and policies that can be administered properly only in territorially delimited conditions; that territorial boundaries are a way of effectively establishing but also placing some limits on an individual's positive duties of minimal samaritanism toward outsiders, while keeping in force the full range of negative duties toward them, especially duties of abstaining from violation of individual rights; and that a country is only a temporary and contingent stopping point on the way to a federated humanity. The rights-minded social contract leads not only to constitutional, democratic government but also to limited government. Indeed, the guiding utopian precept is: the less government the better, the less politics the better. Since the moral center of this outlook is equal rights, what one claims for oneself as a matter of right, one must acknowledge in or claim for others: at home in regard to one's fellow adherents to the social contract (otherwise known as a constitution) and to the fullest extent possible, abroad.

One must learn to live with the paradox that by providing security, government makes possible treating other persons morally (and for their own sake), while the existence of numerous governments, even rights-based ones, guarantees that governments will always find opportunities for immoral behavior that they will rationalize as not immoral but necessary to preserve society and government. These latter are, after all, the preconditions of individual morality. What favors such rationalization is seeing each political society as a person with all the rights of a person, especially self-preservation. Adherents of rights-based individualism confront this analogy with scepticism.

The foregoing elements help to make up a political outlook that keeps morality at the center.

Contrast this with the outlook of patriotic republicanism. According to this view, the group, the nation, not the individual, is the irreducible unit. Patriotism is dedicated to preserving and expressing or asserting the group's identity in agonistic or competitive or antagonistic political deeds that are violent or threaten to become so. We the people are one unit matched against other units. A group's identity is sustained by a distinctive way of life with a quite narrow tolerance for or patience with internal heterogeneity. The way of life nurtures activism at home and abroad. One kind of activism inspires or facilitates or provides a cover or excuse for the other. Political power created by a strong government is perceived as an opportunity for continuous initiative abroad. The republic tends to become a power base for the purposes of international rivalry. At home, republican patriots side with, when they are not promoting, continuous politicization of the people: mobilization for concerted action, a taste for inventing or exacerbating problems, a desire to multiply offices so as to encourage participation, and a corresponding desire to multiply political deeds. Democracy needs patriotism, Charles Taylor says, for "common enterprises in self-rule" (Taylor, in Nussbaum, p. 120). This is a myth because there can be no popular self-rule in a modern democracy, even with all the referendums in the world. Furthermore, patriotism needs enemies. Democracy, however, is supposed to practice enough domestic justice as not to need the distraction of foreign adventures. Statism is what republicanism comes to in modern conditions, and perhaps in some premodern circumstances as well, *mutatis mutandis*. All this energy and commitment emanating from love of country strengthens some of the worst aspects of modern political life and, in itself, this love, this patriotism, sacrifices universal moral principle in worship of a false god. Patriotism is not only disguised self-worship, not only eager self-abjection, not only voluntary self-exploitation; above all it is idolatry. As with many idols, the worship is destructive and self-destructive. The essential tie between people and society becomes sacrifice: sacrifice of oneself, of one's fellows, of one's adversaries. Would it not be better for thinkers to encourage people to learn to cultivate or tolerate a bit more the art of living with oneself rather than always moving outside oneself?

Let me end with Thoreau's words on patriotism from *Walden:* "Every man is the lord of a realm beside which the earthly empire of the Czar is but a petty state, a hummock left by the ice. Yet some can be patriotic who have no *self-respect*, and sacrifice the greater to the less. They love the soil which makes their graves, but have no sympathy with the spirit which may still animate their clay. Patriotism is a maggot in their heads" ("Conclusion," p. 578).

Notes

1. Compare Benedict Anderson (1983).
2. Martha Nussbaum and others (1996).
3. See also Emerson's "Self-Reliance," p. 268. An excellent analysis is found in Niebuhr (1960), especially chapter 4. For a brief suggestive history of states and cultures as "super-persons," see Berlin, 49–56.

References

Anderson, Benedict. *Imagined Communities: Reflections on the Origins and Spread of Nationalism.* London: Verso, 1983.

Aristotle. *Politics.* New York: Modern Library, 1943.

Augustine. *Confessions.* Trans. R. S. Pine-Coffin. New York: Penguin, 1961.

Berlin, Isaiah. *Karl Marx: His Life and Environment* (1934). 3d edition. New York: Oxford, 1963.

Emerson, Ralph Waldo. "The American Scholar" and "Self-Reliance." *Essays and Lectures.* New York: Library of America, 1983.

MacIntyre, Alasdair. "Is Patriotism a Virtue?" Lindley Lecture, University of Kansas, Philosophy Department, 1984.

Niebuhr, Reinhold. *Moral Man and Immoral Society* (1932). New York: Scribner reprint, 1960.

Nussbaum, Martha, et al. *For Love of Country.* Boston: Beacon, 1996.

Thoreau. *Walden.* New York: Library of America, 1985.

Thucydides. *The Peloponnesian War.* Trans. Crawley, revised by T. E. Wick. New York: Modern Library, 1982.

Viroli, Maurizio. *For Love of Country.* Oxford: Clarendon Press, 1995.

2

Notes on Pluralism

Constitutional democracy exists in order to give people a chance to be individuals. You look around and what do you find? People — citizens of constitutional democracies — clamoring for their groups. They demand that they be understood as group-members, as representatives of their groups, not as freestanding individuals; and that their groups be regarded as substantial entities needing and deserving not only respect but encouragement and perhaps even state subsidy. In recent years, there has been a renewed rush to join up. There has also been a renewed theorization in favor of this tendency. But, of course, devoted attachment to groups is a permanent feature of social life, whether democratic or not. My aim in this essay is to look at this phenomenon from the perspective of what I have been calling democratic individuality. I want to examine cultural pluralism in democratic societies, in particular. It must seem obvious that from any kind of individualist perspective, devoted attachment to groups, especially when widespread, looks suspicious. I do not deny that my predisposition is unfavorable. I then read a sentence by Richard Rorty and feel that such a predisposition must itself be examined. He says in regard to Nietzsche and William James that "Both would have thought the

This essay is a revised version of a lecture given at SUNY-Albany at the invitation of Morton Schoolman. I thank him and the audience for their critical and spirited response.

question 'Do groups diminish or enhance individuality?' as bad as the question 'Are parents good or bad for children?'" (Rorty, 1994, p. 191). Could it be then that a commitment to democratic individuality — to leave aside Nietzschean and other kinds of individualism — is naturally and obviously congruent with encouragement and respect for group identity and group membership? I do not think so, after all, even though I know that besides Rorty two of the most important twentieth-century theorists of the negative liberty of individuals, Isaiah Berlin and Robert Nozick, eagerly make ample room for the accommodation of intense group feelings and apparently find no liberal impediment in the way of their accommodation.[1] I hold on to my skeptical predisposition; yet I want to explore the matter.

What do I mean by cultural pluralism? I refer to the presence of diverse ethnic, racial, religious, and linguistic groups in a democratic society. This list of categories obviously does not include all possible groups. My interest is in salient cultural groups. I will pay no direct attention to political movements or socio-economic classes or to groups based on sex or sexual orientation, although one or another point I make may be applicable to these sorts of class or group. The reason I abstain from discussing them is that they grow out of something more real than the groups I consider, and they struggle against, not in behalf of, fictions. It is also the case that we never know in advance how people will categorize themselves and thus assemble themselves in group formations. I think, however, that ethnic, racial, religious, and linguistic groups are the most salient cultural groups at the present time. They are salient because they insist on their group identity assertively and often with a sense of their superiority. They think that they deserve respect and encouragement because they think they are admirable: if not superior as measured by a common standard, then incomparably or incommensurably valuable.

Cultural groups are identity groups. The key passion of group members is to *define* themselves by reference to their groups. They identify with, or lodge the most significant part of their identities in, one (or more) of these sorts of group. They think and feel that they are making a definitive or exhaustive claim or statement of fact about themselves when they say, for example, We are Irish or English, black or brown, Jew or Moslem, Anglophone or Hispanic-speaking. These attributes are not considered mere attributes; much less, as attributions. They are rather imagined as boundaries on the self's possibilities or the very elements that make it up. For people to accept their cultural groups is to accept themselves; to ignore or deny their groups is not to acknowledge who they are.

The defense, when reflexive, of group identity is a mixture of beliefs and commitments; it is tacit metaphysics reinforcing the usually unavowed preference for a code of life over ordinary morality where the two conflict, as they essentially do. When more theoretical, the defense is more subtle, but it may also evade the unpleasant features of cultural pluralism. I find the defense, whether reflexive or theoretical, vulnerable to a variety of criticisms. I have admitted my predisposition in favor of democratic individuality; and I write wedded to the doubt that democratic individuality can be reconciled with the defense of cultural group identity, despite Rorty and others. Yet, though I wish to advocate the cause of the democratic individual, I will not confine myself to individualist arguments. I do not want to content myself with trying to show the incompatibility of democratic individuality and group identity (certainly in the spirit and intensity advocated recently but also earlier). I hope to suggest as well that strong group identity, even though the cultural groups are law-abiding, is implicated in serious vices which, taken together, severely compromise the phenomenon and should disturb its defenders. The vices are intrinsic.

I mean to distinguish cultural pluralism from nationalism and patriotism. My subject is the sense of belonging to or identifying with a part of a larger (democratic) society. The part, of course, may matter more to its members than the society that surrounds it. But the part is not normally armed, whereas nationalism and patriotism conventionally refer to passions of attachment to a whole political entity, armed and sovereign. The evil done in the world by nationalism and patriotism, commonly abetted by racism or ethnocentrism, and often by religion as well, is immense. I do not, however, intend to associate cultural pluralism with evil, even though the sentiments of unarmed group identity are very much like those of armed nationalism and patriotism. It makes a tremendous practical difference whether a group is armed or not, despite the inward affinity of armed and unarmed groups. To be sure, a particular group within a society sometimes secedes successfully and becomes armed, or it manages to turn a whole society into its base and instrument. Nevertheless, my interest in this essay is with the phenomenon of cultural pluralism, specifically with the view that it is good that people in one society assemble themselves in ethnic, racial, religious, and linguistic groups. The claim is that it is good for every person to do so and good for the whole society that persons do so.

Now, the sense of group membership, the feelings of attachment, may vary in intensity. We know from everyday observation that ties may be casual, intermittent, vague, unintense. At the other extreme, they may be intense, exclusive, total, so that group members freely choose to be a "discrete and insular" minority (Justice Harlan Fiske Stone in *United States v. Carolene Products Co.*, 304 U.S. 144, 152 n. 4, 1938). There are gradations of intensity and attachment that fill up the space between the extremes. Any given group may change in the nature of its ties over time, just as any individual's feelings of group identity may undergo vicissitudes. My critical concern is with intensity and completeness of group attachment: the more intense or complete the more critical must an advocate of democratic individuality be. As I hope to indicate, the theory of democratic individuality looks with a more kindly eye on group membership not so much when it is casual or vague as when it is deliberately limited.

One last preliminary remark. At issue is not whether cultural groups should be tolerated, no matter how intense or total the group tie is. Citizens of a democracy must as a matter of right be allowed to associate, to assemble themselves in groups of practically any degree of closeness. One may wish that people could find better uses for themselves than an abridgement of their individuality. But such a wish is utopian. Individuality is episodic; its project tenuous. In any case, neither the freedom to associate nor the general freedom to live as one likes, of which free association is an indispensable part, is to be tolerated only when the quality of uses to which it is put is admirable. Rights are not properly understood as only instruments for the persons whose rights are recognized; nor only as instruments for the purposes of society. Rights are protections against governmental treatment or interference that has the effect of denying or weakening a human being's status as a person. Only where state and society are indifferent to how rights are being used, or even whether they are being used, are rights respected — provided, of course, that no valid law or due constitutional determination is violated. The proviso is crucial. What cannot be tolerated, therefore, are such cultural group practices (usually religious) as clitoridectomy, corporal punishment of children, sexual molestation of children, denial of medical treatment to children, ritualist suicidal self-sacrifice, and a group's attempts to silence or censor members or punish them formally. Denial of educational opportunities to children never should have been upheld, as it unfortunately was in *Wisconsin v. Yoder* (406 U.S. 205, 1972). The abuse and misuse of children is too often religiously consecrated. Toleration cannot extend to crimes or to injurious blockages of potentialities of experience.

The question is, Why do some theorists who are friendly to individuality (whether or not their concept is democratic individuality in the full meaning accorded it by Emerson, Thoreau, and Whitman) urge more than toleration? Why do they endorse and encourage strong group identity and group membership? Why the philosophical embrace? In trying to absorb some of the defense I find that several general arguments are put forward or hinted at.[2] Now, different arguments must be used by those not friendly to any kind of individualism. In fact, the defense of pluralism, when it is mounted by foes of individualism, is often indistinguishable from communitarianism, even though the ideals of communitarianism may sometimes be located in the ties of a whole society rather than in the ties of numerous cultural groups. Correspondingly, the critique of pluralism in the name of democratic individuality is, in many respects, a critique of communitarianism as well. But the theoretical interest is great when we find friends of individualism espousing the cause of a vigorous cultural pluralism, and espousing it as ardently as any foe of individualism.

Among the arguments for cultural pluralism is, first, the contention that cultural pluralism is inevitably present in every constitutional democracy. The inevitability is not to be lamented; it flows from the unmanipulated choices of individuals living in a free society. Further, this inevitability is not to be merely tolerated. To take such a distant attitude is inappropriate for the advocate of democratic individuality, because cultural pluralism is inextricably associated with democratic individuality. The very conditions that induce the aspiration to democratic individuality (even if they do not conspire to fortify it) also, and necessarily, facilitate cultural pluralism. Even if strong group identity and democratic individuality are opposites, they grow from the same root: a life of energetic choice. That they grow from the same root may even show that they are not opposites, after all, but have a complex if sometimes obscure kinship.

A second argument is that cultural pluralism is the indispensable basis of democratic individuality. Unless people are culturally housed in particular groups of various kinds, all of them smaller and closer than the whole society, and all of them contributing rudiments of identity, no one will ever develop the courage to try to become a democratic individual. Individuality is a difficult endeavor; it cannot be begun without the prior existence of ways of distinguishing people culturally from one another. Distinctions between whole societies do not suffice to supply differentiating characteristics. Individuality grows out of differences easy to notice but not yet personal: differences between neighbors and fellow citizens. If all were of one homogeneous cultural nature, they could not begin to imagine themselves as various individuals.

A third argument is that cultural pluralism is the consummation of democratic individuality. Identifying with a cultural group (or even more than one, perhaps) is seen as a splendid existential opportunity, an opportunity to realize one's potentialities to the fullest degree. In accepting a commitment, one finds oneself. One may more truly find oneself if one accepts a given or inherited commitment to a cultural group, rather than seeking one out. But it is better to seek one out, to undergo conversion, than to detach oneself from intense group commitment altogether. Individuality without such commitment is isolation or loneliness or even solipsism. Only in a cultural group can one live the life of democratic individuality without crippling illusions of self-sufficiency or self-creation or self-authorization.

Other arguments have been made or could be made. But I think that these three capture some of the apologetic substance. Let us look at each of them in turn.

Cultural pluralism is inevitable in a free society. I find nothing to quarrel with in the flat statement that people living in a free society will tend to assemble in cultural groups. There is no modern democracy that is homogeneous ethnically, racially, religiously, or linguistically. Through conquest, immigration, or some other historical cause, all democracies have the elements required for cultural pluralism. Of course, there are degrees of insistence on difference, as there are degrees of homogeneous integration. Over time, the proportions and intensities of difference and integration will change. The insistence on difference, however, if quiescent, will eventually manifest itself. Once manifested, it may then subside without permanently vanishing. People want to assemble themselves. Cultural encouragement to individuality, whether deliberate or not, whether authentic or not, can not — we should probably say, can never — overcome the inveterate desire or taste that people have to form distinctive groups. Freedom invigorates group formation, even if it also seduces to individuality. Some people will feel torn between the two possibilities that freedom presents; others will not find any strain between the two. Lending one's identity to an entity larger than oneself may be every bit as attractive, or more so, than trying to shape or keep one's individual identity. Indeed, the perplexities of identity seem to adhere to individual identity, not to group identity. Group identity lifts the awful burden of self-possession. The more awful the burden is felt, the more intense, maybe, the attachment to a cultural group. Paradoxical as an advocate of democratic individuality may want the situation to be, we may have to say that there is no paradox: democratic individuality and cultural pluralism are inextricably associated.

In the tenth *Federalist*, James Madison says, "where no substantial occasion presents itself, the most frivolous and fanciful distinctions have been sufficient to kindle their unfriendly passions, and excite their most violent conflicts" (Madison, 1982, p. 44). Madison thinks that the most substantial occasions involve clashes between economically unequal groups. But his basic point does not depend for its validity on the assumption that disparity of wealth is the main incitement to intense group identity. There are psychological depths beneath economic motivation. What Madison suggests is that people find not only psychological relief in group identity and group membership, but also the pleasures of animosity and feelings of superiority. His mournful conclusion is that "The latent causes of faction are thus sown in the nature of man" (p. 44). And in a free society, the latent cause is aroused and unembarrassed. I take Madison's analysis to be canonical, and, thus, the first argument in behalf of cultural pluralism is right.

But in what tone of voice should we admit the point? Madison is angry about faction largely because, in the name of justice, he is solicitous toward the better-off sectors of the population. We here are not discussing economic classes and their struggles. Still, for our own reasons, we can be angry, too, or at least feel some chagrin. An advocate of democratic individuality can lament the inevitable. There is an even less polite word than faction: herd. An advocate of democratic individuality associates weakness with wanting to be part of a herd. It means relinquishing the effort to become what or who you are (in Nietzsche's formulation) or to be what you are (in Emerson's formulation) — both notions derivative from Pindar (Pythian II). In lamenting the inevitable, an advocate of democratic individuality is saying that its friends should not welcome and celebrate cultural pluralism as a positive good, inevitable as it is. The more intense the desire for the group, the more lamentable it is. As I have said, my emphasis will be on the vices in which strong group identity and group membership are implicated. Apart from the vices, however, stands the simple idea that when herds are attractive, rightful freedom is being used to give up some of it. One is allowing a borrowed identity to substitute itself for one's own. One's thoughts and feelings become, thanks to group identity and group membership, no longer one's own, or become less so. One tends to be or become similar to others and, hence, replaceable. Let there be some regret as generation after generation, people as it were spontaneously perpetuate and often intensify cultural groups in which they have been raised or to which they convert. Let there be praise for those who resist the drive.

Cultural pluralism is the indispensable basis for democratic individuality. It is said that without committed membership in one or more cultural groups, persons could not eventually fashion a sense of themselves as individuals. On this account, individuality is an overcoming of any group attachment that effaces personal distinctiveness through unexamined immersion. But individuality must have its starting point in immersion. If group identity and group membership survive self-examination, then a freely accepted discipline can ensue. Such discipline is at least compatible with individuality or may even be its consummation. The person needs psychological security, which comes only from an early ascribed cultural identity. At the beginning, one must be less than an individual so that later one may become and stay an individual. One must wear team colors in order to discover that one is not only a team member: cultural struggles alert one to one's importance. One must be given an identity against which to rebel, an identity that, at the minimum, is found chafing. In group identity and group membership a person finds, if nothing else, the raw materials which, by being individually shaped and worked, precipitate out one's individuality. Only in a diverse society does identity become a problem. The way is prepared for persons to resolve that problem individually. In sum, if adults can loosen their group attachments, they must maintain the appearance of intense attachment for the sake of their children, who then, when grown, see through the appearance but, in turn, maintain it. Why not, then, welcome and celebrate strong attachments to cultural groups if one is an advocate of democratic individuality? If one wills an end, one must will the means. And when the means are so entwined with the end, then one must will the means wholeheartedly, not grudgingly.

My judgment is that this line of thought is plausible but not finally persuasive. I have already admitted the inevitability of strong group attachments, but I am not yet prepared to see the inevitable as positively indispensable. The reason for my skepticism is that strong initial group attachments are not overcome to a great degree often enough. Trained into close membership, into feelings of pride in the group's history, achievements, and sufferings, one tends to stay attached. One may even grow more attached the more one thinks one is coming into a fully self-conscious possession of one's inheritance. Yet one may be only tracing out the passions that have been instilled from the earliest age. One thinks that one is in possession, but one is possessed. Or, if one breaks away, and does so only in a psychologically violent way, then one may heal the injury by joining up with another cultural group. But the appetite for commitment may go forever unappeased. The will to be an individual is deflected, perhaps permanently.

The advocate of democratic individuality, then, cannot wholeheartedly accept strong attachments to cultural groups on the alleged grounds that such attachments are indispensable. The case is too speculative. An alternative speculation is that the aspiration to democratic individuality in a society slowly and imperfectly remakes the nature of group attachment. The tendency in fact has been toward less immersion, less self-loss, more ambivalence, and moments or years of secession from cultural group attachments. In becoming limited and truly voluntary, group attachments have changed, for many people, from a fate or an inheritance into something flimsier but more charming and humane. Evidences abound in American society and in other democracies of such a transformation. We can say that desirable associations are those that adults voluntarily create, and from many motives, but not out of an unappeasable appetite for surrendering their personal identity and thus gaining this or that secret or unconscious gratification. Individualists try to raise their children as potential individuals, not as members. I will return later to the theme of changing cultural groups into clearly voluntary associations.

This individualist speculation must, however, be offered warily. Although the long-term movement in democratic societies has so far been in the direction of altering group attachments in an individualist direction — as Tocqueville saw, early in the career of modern democracy — much experience goes the other way. Moods change. Group intensity is variable, but it will continue to exist at some level or other. The contemporary clamor for groups is, after all, a protest against the mottled successes of democratic individuality. Indispensable or not, strong group identity will persist. And even if not indispensable, it may play some role in its own individualist modification. Let us say, then, that an advocate of democratic individuality will not insist that strong group attachments are dispensable. Such an advocate, however, cannot welcome and celebrate them even if they are indispensable. They can be accepted only reluctantly. But what of a third argument on behalf of cultural pluralism that has been made by some who are friendly, or at least not unfriendly, to democratic individuality? Can it, unlike the arguments based on inevitability and indispensability, engender something other than reluctance? No, but let us say why.

Cultural pluralism is the consummation of democratic individuality. The heart of this argument is that unless one lives a representative life, one is not living to the fullest. One can make oneself into a project only if that project is not only one's own. One is enlarged to one's true dimensions only by giving oneself to a commitment passionately. One must take one's eye off oneself as one lives if one is to see oneself, find oneself, eventually. The best self-forgetting is devotion. Excellent devotion can be bestowed on the project of ethnicity, race, or religion, if not language. (The case of language may not be entirely relevant here; it is not usually a project in a complete existential or experiential sense. An adherence to a language is part of a larger adherence to a set of traditions or customs, whether racial, ethnic, or religious, though language can be an indissoluble part. But I will not dwell on separating language from the other bases of cultural pluralism.)

One lives representatively when one sees oneself as having a mission to be as adequate as one can be in expressing in everything one does the spirit or essence of one's race or ethnicity or religion. The aim is not to fight one's mission but to allow oneself to be taken over by it. Of course, each member of the group will make little adaptations, little interpretations, as the need arises. But the traditions and customs set a pattern to be followed. One's substance is owed to the traditions and customs: the substance is either literally biological or something close to it. Membership is fate. The long and short of it is that this line of thought posits two interlocking claims concerning the consummation of individuality. First, the person may come to realize the falseness of the aspiration to be expressively, assertively, positively oneself, just oneself, and second, then discover that one becomes an expressive individual primarily by expressing the way of life and outlook on life of the cultural group to which one has a strong attachment.

An advocate of democratic individuality can agree that there is a kind of expressiveness that is manifested when a member carries on and carries out the traditions and customs of a cultural group. Such an advocate can also think that expressiveness as such may be an overrated aspiration. But the advocate will not abandon individual expressiveness as one component of democratic individuality, and will insist that every individual has something his or her own to express that is worth expressing. This is a democratic postulate. The ordinary self is not so impoverished as to acquire substance only through intense adherence to a group pattern. On the other hand, the ideal to which democratic individuality aspires is not only individual expressiveness but its supersession — a passage to a contemplative impersonality marked by a democratically generous receptivity to all creatures and phenomena. This is the great Emersonian consummation of democratic individuality. Contemplative impersonality, however, is a radically different kind of supersession from immersion in a group. The consummation of individuality by means of strong group identity and group membership turns out to be not a consummation of *democratic* individuality. A group can consummate only a person's exclusionary individuality, if any individuality at all. Those who champion cultural pluralism and still think of themselves as friends of democratic individuality should reconsider their double espousal.

Yet, even if an advocate of democratic individuality took a more sympathetic attitude toward this third argument (and the other two), there would remain a great obstacle in the path of reconciling democratic individuality and cultural pluralism. That obstacle is the encouragement to especially grave vices — mental vices affecting the whole character — that strong group identity and group membership give. Those who welcome and celebrate an intense cultural pluralism are, therefore, the auxiliaries of vices. I think that we reach here what may be the heart of the matter.

Any strong group identity derives from, promotes, and rewards certain traits and habits that should be called by their right name — vices. These are vices from any point of view; they are bad not only because they inhibit the growth of democratic individuality. Far more importantly, these vices damage the basic moral personality. I do not see how strong group identity and group membership could ever be free of these vices. Democratic individuality is certainly not free of connection to vices, but I would like to think that the connection, though deep, is partly correctable; and it is not intrinsic. The soil or source of democratic individuality is the individualism of guaranteed rights, the disposition to be protective of one's human dignity against actual or potential state efforts to monitor or regulate or shape one's life. These efforts stem from many state motives, including the pure power interest of the state and an appalled elitist sense that the people are a plebs that needs to be managed and

improved and made reliable. Rights-based individualism can become democratic individuality only gradually, whether historically or in the experience of
any one person. If it fails to do so — and success is, in any case, only intermittent — rights-based individualism sponsors deviations from, or simulacra of,
democratic individuality. One example is what Tocqueville calls individualism: a self-absorption born of egalitarian self-doubt, individualist care of the
self, and the conviction that the greatest pleasures are found in private life
because that is where the greatest reality is found. Another example is the
materialist life: self-definition as achieved through both active mastery of the
economic environment and delighted submission to the things and goods and
sensations that money can buy. These deviations are not accidental. They are
the unsurprising, indeed probably inevitable, results of a demotic misinterpre-
tation of the point or meaning of rights. But in the Emersonian beginnings of
the theory of democratic individuality is already found a determined attempt
to weaken the tendency to deviation by appealing to the very feelings of dignity and integrity of self that misplace themselves in privatistic or economistic
individualism.

I do not believe that the defenders of a strong cultural pluralism can appeal
to their own ideal to resist its bad tendencies. One may think that there is
scarcely any difference between inevitable but partly correctable bad tendencies and those that are intrinsically bad. It may be thought that an advocate of
democratic individuality should be content to demonstrate, if possible, that
the vices associated with the soil or source of that ideal are less terrible in their
effects — much less terrible — than the vices of strong group identity and group
membership. I go on the assumption that such is the case. But I also want to
claim that intense attachment to a cultural group necessarily implicates the
member in certain major vices, and that strong cultural pluralism does not
hold within itself the resources to combat those vices. Resistance must appeal
to ordinary good sense or to a cultivated idea of democratic individuality.

What, then, are the mental vices intrinsic to an intense attachment to a
cultural group? I offer just a sampling. First, the vice of complacent confusion.
A person with a strong group commitment loses sight of the fact that one is
one, and dimly imagines that one is much larger than merely oneself. One
"introjects" the group into oneself and feels enlarged. Or, one extends oneself
so as to incorporate what is outside oneself but looks the same as oneself. Or,
one substitutes for one's little self a big entity that is allowed to occupy one's
center. The past and the fate of the group become one's own, and by this
process of absorbing and being absorbed one alienates oneself to an abstraction, or one worships oneself deviously.

Second, the vice of bad aestheticism. It consists in the desire — often unconscious or barely conscious — that the world be made up of manifestly different groups, so that life may appear as a more easily assimilable spectacle and, hence, a more enjoyable one. The individual is almost always too small and indistinct to be visible. The group is the unit preferred by the unsubtle eye. The spectacle is better when the groups are as different from one another as they can be. Part of this aestheticism is the desire that cultural groups be not only distinct but also assertive and, therefore, where possible, competitive. We exist for group rivalries; we lie under a sort of obligation to keep feuds going. I ascribe this aestheticism with its passion for unviolent enmity to a need to simplify the world and make it less resistant to categorization, to give the world a shape and a purpose that nothing else can. It is as if only sharp outlines and blunt differences could engender beauty, and only rivalry and animosity could supply the energy required to turn the world's wheel. Scarcely anyone is free of these feelings. The one good thing about them is that they introduce a form of selflessness into what otherwise would be only a collectivized egotism. The selflessness lies in one's disposability, the readiness to offer oneself to the spectacle and to its perpetual motion. But this is not the kind of selflessness that can turn into sympathy for what is different from oneself and one's group. Rather, it feeds on a lack of sympathy. It is not really like good sportsmanship. It is not even good spectatorship, so lacking in nuance is it. Some of the worst atrocities have come when bad aestheticism has been armed. The bad aestheticism of cultural groups can serve as a preparation of the sentiments for armed tribalism, for nationalism and patriotism, imperialism and colonialism, racism and crusades.

There is, third, the vice of indirect and unself-aware self-love. By means of strong attachments to cultural groups, one loves oneself. Only, one thinks that one is escaping self-love by going outside oneself. Unlike pride in one's family's past, which others often deride, the self-love at play in cultural groups seems invisible. But what is one escaping to if not to something with which one identifies? One sees oneself in the others of one's group. The narcissism is extended; it makes individual narcissism look innocent in comparison. The satisfaction sought is to be enviable but inimitable. Such a gain one can rarely procure for oneself as simply oneself. The condemnation of self-love as one of the deadliest vices is nearly universal; yet strong group attachment, which is also an expression of individual self-love, is usually praised. The disguise succeeds. The vice passes itself off as a virtue.

The fourth vice is plain dishonesty, which shows when one takes pride in one's inherited identity as a member of a cultural group, as if one had chosen it; and when one takes pride in a group's achievements even though one had nothing to do with those achievements. There is regular pressure to feel such pride. One is told incessantly to go back to one's roots and to feel the past of one's group literally as if one had experienced it. The ability to live vicariously has much to be said for it; it is one commendable use of the imagination. But taking pride in an inherited identity or in achievements not one's own is not using one's imagination. Rather one is fantasizing and doing so blatantly — that is, one is being transparently dishonest, especially to oneself. Only a moment's thought is needed to dispel the fantasy. Everything is done to block the thought.

A fifth vice is self-mystification. This vice is constitutive of the human condition. It is not confined to the mentality of intense group attachment. Nevertheless, it appears in a most developed and intractable form in group mentality. By self-mystification I mean the weakening or the loss of the composite idea that each human being is a contingency, yet an infinity; that each is unique but shares a common humanity with all other human beings. To be *contingent* means that anyone raised differently would turn out differently, and that there is no necessity to any cultural identity: no person was destined from all eternity to bear specific cultural characteristics. Mill's sentence about the intolerant English conformist has a general applicability: "It never troubles him that mere accident has decided which of these numerous worlds is the object of his reliance, and that the same causes which make him a Churchman in London, would have made him a Buddhist or a Confucian in Pekin" (Mill, 1977a, Ch. 2, p. 230). It is absurd to say that I — the person I know I am — could have been another person in the biological sense, but it is unpleasantly obvious that I could have easily acquired different traits and habits in different circumstances. I could have been *as it were* another person. To be so accidentally made up is one of many facts that point to what Emerson called the *infinitude* of each person. Because of indefinite potentiality, most of it perforce unrealized for lack of world enough and time, each of us can always choose to try to change this or that about ourselves. If, however, we conclude in fatigue or despair that character is fate, then it is one's character or temperament that imprisons the person and thwarts infinitude, it is what one incurably is and would have been, almost no matter what experiences had befallen. There is no soul awaiting incarnation that existed before one's birth and harbors one's true core of identity. Character or temperament may understandably make identity feel like eternal essence, but character or temperament is personal, not group, identity.

A person's *uniqueness* is what he or she can bring forth, the special work one can do, the unprecedented sentences one can say and write. It is unpredictability growing out of infinitude. Uniqueness is taking the next steps in one's own direction, a refusal to be distracted or diverted. The differences between groups are really less interesting and profound than the differences between individuals of the same group or different groups or no group, whenever people think and act like individuals. Group differences are visible. The diversity of individuals may be harder to notice and cherish than the diversity of cultural groups. But justice demands that the effort be made. To begin with, the prestige of cultural pluralism must be diminished. The balance to a sense of one's uniqueness is not a feeling of indebtedness and allegiance to a cultural group (or even any particular society) but an ever deepening conviction of a *common humanity* shared by all human beings. Despite all individual and group differences each is the same as all the rest: the same in unearned human dignity. A strong group feeling does much more harm to this conviction than even the most megalomaniacal individualism. Good conscience is overridden much more easily by group purposes than by individualism. The poison is in the assertion that one cultural group is by nature inferior or superior to another or to all others, or so distinctive as to be inestimably precious.

In sum, intense group attachment wars on this composite idea of the individual and, in the course of doing so, proves a potent engine of self-mystification. Even unarmed and unsovereign group feelings, when they are strong, render people unfeeling strangers to one another, rather than mysterious siblings. Strong group identity and membership enfeeble the ability to imagine oneself in the situation of another or in an analogous situation; or to imagine how it would feel to be like another. The imagination of sameness, which is fairness, and the imagination of otherness, which is empathy, are both actively discouraged.

Sixth and last, the vice of wishful thinking, the will to believe. Many cultural groups base their identity on fictions, whether religious, historical, pseudo-scientific, or ideological in one way or another. The fictions are almost deliberately not seen through, as if life itself depended on a conspiracy not only to keep going these sorts of fiction but also to keep going the universal disposition to live by fictions, to enact them. The struggles between systems of fiction can be unremitting, but all systems are united by a common interest in fixing the world's loyalty to fictions and in keeping it fixed by struggle and sacrifice. Is fiction, untruth, necessary to life? How can we know when life has never been free of it? But if life has never been free of it, does that fact not show that life cannot be free of it? Perhaps; but it would be honorable for those whose vocation it is to tell the truth to stop defending cultural pluralism in the untroubled manner that is often on display.

Of all the vices required, encouraged, and rewarded by strong cultural group identity and membership, perhaps the worst is the will to believe. It is the most regrettable because it is a gross form of self-deception (a most murky vice) and, hence, a severe blow to one's integrity. The process of drowning out one's inner reproaches and accepting one's own lies (while producing them, or later on) makes one an instrument of mendacity and, hence, an instrument of immorality. The self-deception of wishful thinking is also a severe blow to one's democratic individuality. But all the vices of strong group identity and membership are serious and together constitute a state of being neither admirable nor lovable.

I must admit, however, that none of the vices that I have surveyed is removable from the human condition. Human beings are unimaginable without them to one extent or another. Even the most resolute democratic individual will be drawn to them, if only in tame episodes. Cultural groups persist because they license vices, they license succumbing to strong unworthy temptations. What then shall we say? I find two possible strategies. The first is to determine whether there may be some usefulness in an intense cultural pluralism, apart from its questionable use as a basis for democratic individuality and in spite of its ineligibility as the consummation of democratic individuality. If there is some usefulness, the spirit in which it should be accepted is not celebratory but pragmatic (which is not exactly equivalent to cynical). The second strategy — and I here return to a point I mentioned earlier — is to suggest we should hope that, as much as possible, cultural groups become revised individualistically.

The first strategy. One use of strong group attachment is to provide relief from the demands of democratic individuality, the aspiration to which always haunts citizens of modern free societies. Relatedly and even more importantly, strong group attachment provides relief from the demands of the two deflections from democratic individuality to which I have already referred: the life of privacy and the life of materialism. Whether in its more pure form or in its deviations, the project of being or becoming something of one's own, of trying to be more than the sum of what has happened to oneself, of trying to be more than society's fool is uncertain, risky, arduous. What a relief it is to shelter in the demands, exacting as they often are, of a group code or way of life or to take from it the questions and answers that constitute an outlook on life. Strong group identity and group membership are compensatory devices that answer to the splendors and miseries of democratic individuality and to the experienced shortcomings of its deviations. And since the two deviations have serious vices of their own, the vices of egotism, coldness, insolence, moral indifference, narrow-mindedness, too much caution or too little — none of these, I say, are the vices intrinsic to democratic individuality itself — then these vices need the company, perhaps, of the vices intrinsic to intense group attachment. The two tribes of vices may now and then curb each other's excesses, although it is more likely that they confirm and strengthen each other. After all, good family people and people of business are quite ethnically or racially or religiously immersed. Either way, the vices of strong group identity and membership and the vices of the deviations from democratic individuality are compatible and form, alas, a nourishing psychological diet.

Another use of intense cultural pluralism is that in some circumstances the coexistence of, say, several ethnic or religious groups may retard a fervid and bellicose nationalism or patriotism. The group may matter more to its members than the totality of which it is territorially a part. The majority, if there is one, may not be able to count on all the citizens to endorse, say, a given foreign policy when a minority's co-religionists or fellow-ethnics in another country are threatened by the home country. A strong group attachment may help to expose the artificiality of the national or patriotic idea and make it appear as the feverish fantasy it is. To be sure, so-called hyphenated Americans (or others) are often among the most nationalist citizens, either to insist on their loyalty or possibly to enlist the power of the home country in the aims of their co-religionists or fellow-ethnics abroad. It may also turn out that political leaders may deem intense cultural pluralism as such an unstable or volatile condition that foreign adventures, meant to unite and distract, are pursued. The considerations on both sides of this issue make it hard to judge. All we can do is emphasize that in some circumstances a pronounced cultural diversity can weaken the larger and armed nationalism or patriotism in the name of a lesser and unarmed kind. The net result can be an occasional benefit to all groups and their members as well as to those who do not attach themselves; the benefit is peace to the whole society.

One last use can be indicated. The beneficiaries of intense cultural pluralism may be those who do not attach themselves and invest their individual identities in any cultural groups. Again it is Mill who supplies the guidance. His remarks in *On Liberty* on the value of conflicting partisan or zealous ideas can be used as an analogy for the value of numerous ethnic, racial, and religious groups when they are paid close attention: seen as embodying ways of life and explicitly articulating outlooks on life. It is only an approximate analogy because cultural groups, though always potentially competitive and hostile, are often complacently present side by side or at some distance, and may make their claims not at each other's expense but rather in the face of an oppressive past or an indifferent or uncomprehending present. Mill says:

> But it is not on the impassioned partisan, it is on the calmer and more disinterested bystander, that this collision of opinions works its salutary effect. . . . And since there are few mental attributes more rare than that judicial faculty which can sit in intelligent judgment between two sides of a question, of

which only one is represented by an advocate before it, truth has no chance but in proportion as every side of it, every opinion which embodies any fraction of the truth, not only finds advocates, but is so advocated as to be listened to. (Mill, 1977a, Ch. 2, p. 257)[3]

Applied to our theme, Mill's view suggests that those who struggle hard to be loyal to the aspiration of democratic individuality may learn one or another lesson useful for their individualist lives from the forcefully present cultural groups. Individualists, though they would rather not, gain from the loss of individuality of others. It is not just that the (episodically) detached individual can take pleasure in the spectacle of diverse groups; he or she can try to divorce a way of and outlook on life from its fiction and by thus secularizing or rationalizing it, by thus exposing its indeliberate symbolization, distill a useable meaning. This procedure doubtless converts devoted group members into means of edification. But the members have already converted themselves into vehicles of a discipline.

Mill also holds out the hope that in some circumstances cultural groups of an ethno-linguistic sort, which he calls nationalities, can learn from one another. He says:

> Whatever really tends to the admixture of nationalities . . . is a benefit to the human race. Not by extinguishing types, of which, in these cases, sufficient examples are sure to remain, but by softening their extreme forms, and filling up the intervals between them. . . . The united people, like a crossed breed of animals . . . protected by the admixture from being exaggerated into the neighboring vices. (Mill, 1977b, Ch. 16, pp. 549–50)

I suppose the tendency of many American religions to become mildly Protestant illustrates Mill's idea by analogy. His warning, however, must be heeded: "But to render this admixture possible, there must be peculiar conditions" (Mill, 1977b, p. 550). I would not place too much weight, any more than Mill does, on his hope. At the same time, Mill does not think that most people can ever be anything but group-animals. He is trying to draw out the best from a situation to which he is resigned. Human beings are partial and partisan to their core, and it is only group antagonism "which has kept the human mind alive" (Mill, 1985, p. 270), or will ever keep it alive. Mill is not a theorist of *democratic* individuality. Yet, an advocate of democratic individuality can doubt that cultural groups want to learn from one another and would look to individual antagonism to keep the human mind alive at some cost lower than bondage to fiction and the structural enmity of group toward group.

There are uses to intense group attachment. They are accepted without gratitude; either they are regrettable compensations or they were never intended. *The second strategy* is to discourage intense group attachment and urge that it become more and more amenable to individualist revision. Instead of welcoming and celebrating intense cultural pluralism, theorists friendly to democratic individuality should strive to elaborate the idea that the more a cultural group resembles a limited, voluntary organization, the better it is. One aim is to weaken the vices of strong group identity and membership and to make associative ties more honest, unfictional, unmystical. There is a positive aim, too. It is to build on the literature that already exists that explores the existential and experiential benefits of being an unduped participant in the maintenance of a cultural group understood to some degree as a valuable human artifice. The model would be a system of manners, or a code for a sector of life, or a purposive association that bestows the delights of association merely through the pursuit of its purposes, or a venerable institution, or some practice or activity that adds color or vigor to daily life. The participant accepts the discipline of rules or form or style or goal, but never loses sight of the notion that an individual is bigger than any artifice, bigger than any enterprise. The choice to be a participant would not be unreserved and could be temporary. It would be limited, self-limited. From such participation much good could come to oneself and others, and to the observer in each of us. Talents and gifts and virtues would be enlisted and perfected. On these terms, an advocate of democratic individuality could see that membership would be, if not the consummation of the highest democratic individuality, which is impersonal and contemplative, then at least part of the consummation of a positive and expressive individuality, a lesser manifestation of democratic individuality. If, however, I am told that this proposed individualist revision of cultural groups does not begin to understand the worth of intense group attachment, and actually denatures those groups, then an impasse would be reached, and the critique of cultural pluralism would have to end on an uncompromising note. I suspect, in any case, that there are narrow limits to an individualist revision. The vices of intense group attachment are too formidably attractive.

One last point. What I have said does not imply condemnation of strong group identity and membership when the cultural group has been or is now being victimized and is struggling to overcome its victimization or the remains of it. Solidarity is needed. But it is well for the unvictimized to say, and for those who struggle to know in some corner of themselves, that solidarity — another name for strong group identity and membership — can usually be sustained for cultural groups only by the vices that I have discussed. Consequently, cultural group solidarity is not intrinsically valuable, only provisionally and tactically and instrumentally so. The aim of liberation from discrimination and oppression should not be to stay freely immersed in categories that were once imposed. Such a choice only serves to validate the desire of people to think in categories and stereotypes. The continued validation of strong group identity and membership guarantees continued existence to discrimination and oppression elsewhere in the world and even makes it harder to condemn the past bad treatment of one's own group. Neither should the aim be to embrace as genuine the hostile ascriptions made by some groups about one's own and thus learn to be proud of what had hitherto been the source of shame. One never was what they said we all were. The aim of liberation is to become individual.[4]

Notes

1. For Isaiah Berlin, see among other writings *Vico and Herder* (1976); some mitigations appear in *The Crooked Timber of Humanity* (1991). For Robert Nozick, see *Anarchy, State, and Utopia* (1974, Ch. 10).

2. The arguments I make do not depend on any specific text. Some recent important defenses of strong cultural pluralism by those friendly or not unfriendly to an ideal roughly like democratic individuality include Charles Taylor (1992), Will Kymlicka (1992), Michael Walzer (1992), Nancy L. Rosenblum (1993), Joseph Raz (1994). A splendid critique of some of these efforts is made by David Bromwich, 1995.

3. See also Mill, 1977a, p. 254.

4. I think that Bruno Bauer is much closer to the truth about the nature of emancipation than Marx in the debate Marx stages in "On the Jewish Question" (1978). Emancipation from immersion in cultural groups is quite enough to hope for without worrying about full "human emancipation," whatever that may mean.

References

Berlin, Isaiah, *Vico and Herder* (New York: Viking, 1976).

Berlin, Isaiah, *The Crooked Timber of Humanity* (New York: Knopf, 1991).

Bromwich, David, "Culturalism, the Euthanasia of Liberalism," *Dissent* 42 (Winter 1995), 89–102.

Kymlicka, Will, "The Rights of Minority Cultures: Reply to Kukathas," *Political Theory* 20 (February 1992): 140–46.

Madison, James, *The Federalist Papers* (New York: Bantam, 1982).

Marx, Karl, "On the Jewish Question," in Robert C. Tucker, ed., *The Marx-Engels Reader 2/e* (New York: Norton, 1978), 26–52.

Mill, John Stuart, *On Liberty* (1859), in *Collected Works of John Stuart Mill*, vol. 18 (Toronto: University of Toronto Press, 1977a).

Mill, John Stuart, *Considerations on Representative Government* (1861), in *Collected Works of John Stuart Mill*, vol. 19 (Toronto: University of Toronto Press, 1977b).

Mill, John Stuart, "Guizot's Essays and Lectures on History" (1845), in *Collected Works of John Stuart Mill*, vol. 20 (Toronto: University of Toronto Press, 1985).

Nozick, Robert, *Anarchy, State, and Utopia* (New York: Basic Books, 1974).

Raz, Joseph, "Multiculturalism," *Dissent* (Winter 1994): 67–79.

Rorty, Richard, review of Richard E. Flathman, *Willful Liberalism: Voluntarism and Individuality in Political Theory and Practice,* in *Political Theory* 22 (February 1994).

Rosenblum, Nancy L., "The Moral Uses of Pluralism," The University Center for Human Values, Princeton University, *Working Papers,* No. 3, December 1993.

Taylor, Charles, in Amy Gutmann, ed., *Multiculturalism and "The Politics of Recognition"* (Princeton, NJ: Princeton University Press, 1992).

Walzer, Michael, *What It Means to Be an American* (New York: Marsilio, 1992).

3

Undermining the Constitution

This essay was conceived, titled, and partly drafted before September 11, 2001. What I am about to say does not, for the most part, deal *directly* with that awful day and the numerous consequences that have flowed from it, especially the American war in Afghanistan and the American invasion of Iraq. But as I go along, points that I make are relevant to our present situation, and some of them were actually prompted by September 11 and its continuing effects. The fact is that my main concerns are longstanding ones, but I am naturally affected by recent tremendous events and I am mindful of them in this essay. Indeed, the attack on the World Trade Center and subsequent war and warlike actions have reinforced my attention to these concerns.

My field is political theory, the study of moral principles in their application to political life. The events of September 11 and after are too recent as well as too radically unfinished to be absorbed properly into political theory. The immediate motives, the opportunistic energies, and the overarching aims of

This essay is a revised version of the Irving Howe Lecture, delivered November 15, 2001, at the City University of New York. It was a privilege to speak in the lecture series created to honor a man who remains a model of clear-eyed courage. I thank Morris Dickstein and his colleagues for the invitation. For critical remarks and valuable suggestions, I am obliged to Professor Dickstein as well as David Richards, David Bromwich, Corey Brettschneider, and Hanoch Sheinman.

those involved in the action on all sides are still imperfectly understood, and many of the consequences for numerous societies (including our own) cannot even be glimpsed. It is therefore too soon for political theorists *as political theorists* to think about these events. But the scholarly preoccupations of political theorists are tremendously caught up in terrorism and the responses to it, as well as imperialism and its impact on the domestic life of the imperialist society. How could they not be?

I want to stay with the question that I was thinking about before September 11. It is now even more topical. That question is: What do American citizens owe their Constitution? After all, the Constitution is the framework of our democracy, or, to switch the metaphor, its bedrock. Or, to switch the metaphor again, the Constitution is what holds us together. My brief answer to the question is that American citizens owe the Constitution *attention*. That is not the only obligation, of course; it is the *first* obligation, but one that is rarely urged on citizens.

We owe the Constitution attention because if we took it seriously, we would immediately see that it is a social contract or, perhaps in a better phrase, it is an agreement of the people. If any given generation does not abolish the Constitution, acceptance of it means that, by rational imputation to that generation, they have written it. Of course, if we were literally to start over again and devise a new agreement of the people, we would not likely reproduce the exact Constitution, in every detail, we now have. Furthermore, acceptance of it is much of the time tacit. I mean that citizens keep the Constitution in place out of habit, deference, a feeling for lawfulness, and some pride. These attachments are praiseworthy. But I think that the United States Constitution deserves better from its citizens. It deserves to be seen as the charter that people should re-create in approximately the same form, if it were to fall — to suffer defeat or piecemeal erosion or aggravated forgetfulness. What is more, people could perhaps renew their consent to a charter they did not write by saying to themselves that they share its commitments. It would not matter that they perhaps would change it in some ways if they had a free hand and a blank slate. I think that the Constitution merits a perpetual renewal of consent because it stands for something rare and fine. And I will try to indicate what that is as I proceed.

I say that that the first obligation is attention. Paying attention, we in our best moments could actually see that the Constitution is something rare and fine. Put more legalistically, there is always an obligation for citizens anywhere to understand the fundamental law of their land, to know its provisions, and to try to understand the purposes of the document as a whole. But in the case of the Constitution (the American fundamental law), its purposes, as far as I can make out, are something more than those general purposes specified in the preamble, which contains good words, certainly, but which may strike us now as platitudinous or undistinctive or not deep enough. Rather, we should try to understand what the Constitution in its seven articles and in the nearly contemporaneous first ten amendments (the Bill of Rights) mean by understanding what they originally meant; and then to determine whether the original meaning still holds us, as I think it should.

The originalism that I propose as a general way of interpreting the Constitution is not really the same as Justice Antonin Scalia's version as presented in his book, *A Matter of Interpretation* (1997), and elsewhere. He wants us to ascertain what any specific provision in the Constitution meant at the time of those who wrote and ratified it, and to be bound by such a meaning. Notice that he seeks to distinguish his position from that in which the interpreters of the Constitution are supposed to determine the original *intention* of the people who wrote and ratified the document. He finds the whole matter of intention murky or at least ambiguous, even though he is eventually willing to allow some reference to original intention. It is as if the Constitution wrote itself. What is especially important for us to notice, however, is Scalia's apparent assumption that words do not change meaning over time. Hence the original meaning of the words in the Constitution is the meaning they have today. The sense of the Constitution can be read off its face, so to speak.

I certainly agree that unless the Constitution remained verbally understandable by later generations, there could be no written charter to which these generations could give their tacit or renewed consent. Yet Scalia never denies that the provisions of the Constitution, with all later amendments after the Bill of Rights, require interpretation. He even endorses what he calls "expansive" rather than "narrow" interpretation. In truth, some of his opinions have given expansive interpretations that have redounded to the benefit of liberty, whether free speech or freedom from intrusive searches like using infrared imaging of individuals' houses to look for evidence of heat from marijuana plants. More often, alas, his interpretations have been narrow, so narrow as to be infernally literal-minded, with the result that he throws his considerable intellectual weight in the direction of constricting freedom or enlarging the prosecutorial and punitive powers of the state. At the end, a great degree of arbitrariness infects his method of original literalism. I grant that some measure of arbitrariness adheres to any method of interpreting a document written more than 200 years ago, and written in language that — if you will allow me to put it this way — was meant to be interpreted. The Constitution's language is general or abstract; it is most unmistakable when it specifies the structural features of the United States government and the procedures for filling federal office. But the meaning of its protections of the liberties of its citizens is always open to interpretation: conflicting interpretations that are all or most of them plausible, even if they are not equally compelling. I do not see how Scalia has provided much theoretical assistance in determining the meaning of Constitutional provisions that command those protections.

I wish to propose a rather different kind of originalism that is, I hope, in stark contrast to Justice Scalia's. It, too, is expansive, and I propose it as a guide to interpretation of the Constitution as a whole, to the spirit of the laws. Like Scalia, I urge that we go back in time to the founding to ascertain the original meaning of the United States Constitution. My suggestion is that we look at the seven articles of the Constitution together with the Bill of Rights and try to ascertain how this whole document compared to the fundamental law for any other society that existed at the time of creation and ratification. What did the Constitution and the Bill of Rights stand for in the world in which they appeared? Did any other country's law stand for the same thing, or stand for it to nearly the same degree? If we could come to some sort of agreement on the meaning of the original American fundamental law, and how that meaning compared to the meaning of any other fundamental law — express or implied — then current, we could see what we now should stand for. We could get a glimpse of how any specific provision regarding the liberties of the people should be interpreted. We could answer two questions. First, are there practices now allowed that appear to go against the original meaning and even threaten to undermine it? Second, do these practices so disfigure the original meaning that they threaten to reverse the relationship that the original United States Constitution once bore to fundamental law in the rest of the relevant world? The bulk of my attention is devoted to the first question.

But, to begin with, I will try to offer a view of what the original meaning of America's fundamental law was and a view, also, of the relationship that it bore to the rest of the world at the time. We are dealing with Western Europe in the late 1780s for relevant comparisons, the Europe of representative and thinly constitutional oligarchy in Britain, the ancien régime in France and elsewhere (with the French Revolution about to transform Europe), and with a few remains of republicanism here and there in Europe.

What, then, was the original meaning of the United States Constitution and Bill of Rights? Please remember that I am ignoring the preamble, just because its language could perhaps have been used by some other countries without too much bad faith. What country could oppose in name such aspirations as justice, tranquility, defense, the general welfare (that is, the common good), or even liberty (rightly understood, of course)?

Look again at the seven articles and the first ten amendments. We find, I believe, a document dedicated to the dignity of human beings, the equal dignity of all human beings. The original meaning of the Constitution *is* this commitment; much of the content of the document flows from it. Many specific provisions work together to contribute to the defense of equal dignity among human beings in the proposed union; and these provisions offer themselves for imitation by others in the world who would pursue the same purpose.

Furthermore, the Constitution in its time was far ahead of the rest of the world in its commitment to equal human dignity, even though we must say that some similar provisions were of course to be found in various American state constitutions, and some elsewhere. The original meaning of the Constitution is thus a commitment to human dignity. But it is also a commitment made in a world where there was no other society in which such a commitment was made, except for a brief, sudden, and partly futile period in revolutionary France. But the Constitution is morally radical even in comparison to the early French revolutionary days, from 1789 to 1791. My conclusion is that without comparison to the rest of the late-eighteenth-century world, the original meaning of the United States Constitution is badly misunderstood.

I cannot here spell out this notion of equal human dignity (a principal feature of a comprehensive view of human beings) that is contained in the fundamental law. But the core is quite familiar: government is entrusted with the task of doing its necessary work within the limits of recognizing basic individual rights. Unless these rights are recognized, the equal dignity of human beings is not recognized, and people are assaulted in their status as human beings by being reduced to the level of animals or prey or machines or things or wayward children who can never grow up. Human beings, in their strengths as well as weaknesses, must be respected in a thoroughgoing way by the rules and the officials of society.

You may find my notion of the original meaning of the Constitution and Bill of Rights no improvement over the preamble; but I suggest it nevertheless. Nowhere else in the world of the original document were human beings supposed to be treated in a thoroughgoing manner that respected their equal dignity as individuals, regardless of their social standing. Their human status as morally equal individuals was honored. We might say that the original *intention* was always to instruct the world by being ahead of it in honoring human dignity through a detailed respect for individual rights, personal and political.

A glance at just the original seven articles of the Constitution goes some part of the way in justifying Alexander Hamilton's assertion in *Federalist Paper No. 84* that "the Constitution is itself, in every rational sense, and to every useful purpose, A BILL OF RIGHTS." To be sure, Hamilton was arguing against the demands of some people for an explicit bill of rights in the Constitution. This is an argument we should all be glad he lost, brilliant as his presentation is. The Constitution is grossly incomplete and imperfect without the first ten amendments. But the fact remains, as Hamilton demonstrates, that the seven articles contain a good many guaranteed individual rights, and many of them were not known elsewhere at the time, not even in Britain. He mentions such features as the prohibition against suspending the writ of habeas corpus except "in cases of rebellion or invasion"; the prohibition of bills of attainder — that is, punitive measures taken by the legislature against particular individuals; the prohibition of ex post facto laws; the prohibition of titles of nobility (and hence the guarantee to every state of a republican — that is, nonmonarchical and nonhereditary — form of government); the requirement that all crimes shall be tried by jury; and the careful circumscription of the meaning of treason and the guarantee of due process when treason is alleged. We can add other features in the original seven articles, and these features are elsewhere defended in the *Federalist* papers: namely, denying the executive branch the power to initiate war; the prohibition of the impairment of contracts by the states; and the rule that "no religious test shall ever be required as a qualification to any office or public trust under the United States" (Art. 6). All these features are great, singly and all the more so in combination. Where else were they found? A few of them, here and there?

Then we add the Bill of Rights, with its protection, as a matter of guaranteed rights, of speech and press; of religion, including the right not to endure a federally established faith; of assembly and petition; of due process of law, with its provisions for the security of person, house, and possessions, a fair trial, and no compelled self-incrimination or double jeopardy, and no excessive bail or excessive fines or cruel and unusual punishments. When we do add the Bill of Rights to the original seven articles, we have a tremendous charter of human dignity. We tend to take it for granted. The trouble is that taking it for granted not only helps to ensure that rights will be under permanent menace, but that part of the reason that the menace exists is that it is too easy and common to be unaware or lose sight of the plain fact that at its origins, the United States Constitution was the most morally radical fundamental law in the world of nations, and by far.

If we could recapture by a simple act of historical understanding the context into which the Constitution appeared, we could see it as a world-historical event, as a revolution in moral sensibility, as one of the most remarkable occasions in the long march toward honoring human dignity in detailed and everyday practice. The United States once stood alone; with time, other societies joined it. But on the matter of human dignity, it was the teacher of the world. Is it still?

I would be a fool if I did not say that the institution of slavery stained the original document. It countenanced the distinction between "free persons" and "all other persons" (Art. 1, sect. 2); allowed for importing persons (Art. I, sect. 9); favored slave states by allowing three fifths of the slave population to count in apportioning representatives in the House of Representatives (Art. 1, sect. 2); and contained a fugitive slave provision, even though the word "slave" never appears in the original document, with the phrase "person held to service or labor" substituted for it (Art. 4, sect. 2). But it is well to notice that slaves are still called persons; abolition inheres in the word. (The word "slavery" first appears in the Constitution in the Thirteenth Amendment, which abolished it, "except as a punishment for crime" — perhaps a fatal exception.)

It is also possible to think that unless the constitutional compromise with the slave states had been accepted, there would have been no union that could have eventually had the legal footing to destroy slavery. But I realize that what I have just said is meager. Let me add that I do not believe that we can just say that out of the evil of slavery came the greater good of the Union. If I accept the view that sometimes a lesser evil may be necessary to prevent or abolish a greater evil, I do not think that such a calculation covers the rights and wrongs of the slavery compromise or gets to the bottom of the motives of those who drafted and ratified it. All I can add is that the radical moral logic of the Constitution had to wait on time and bloodshed to realize itself more perfectly. And it is still far from its practicably best realization.

I now return to the first question that I posed a little earlier. Do we currently allow practices that go against the original meaning? By my interpretation of the original meaning, do we allow practices that fail to honor human beings in their equal dignity? I think we do, and I will try to say why I think so. I will turn to the second question: Are these anti-constitutional practices so grave that they threaten to place the citizens of the Constitution in the condition of having to learn from the world about human dignity, instead of remaining ahead of the world and instructing it? My answer to this second question is not simple, and I am not sure what the answer should finally be. My gesture toward an answer will be very brief. But let us put this second question aside for the time being.

I think that the answer to the first question is obvious, or should be. There are quite a few practices at home initiated and sustained by the United States government that fail to honor human beings in their equal dignity. Of course, none of these domestic practices is an assault on human dignity as sustained and systematic and on as large a scale as slavery once was. But they are each almost as bad as legal segregation of the black race was until the 1950s and 1960s. The practices we allow as constitutional are bad enough to leave a terrible stain on our fundamental law, itself originally stained by slavery. Let me mention just three; two have to do with the right of life as an essential component of human dignity, and the third pertains to the cruelty of the American system of punishment.

In brief, I think that the then radical concept of equal human dignity that permeated the seven articles and the first ten amendments of the original Constitution is betrayed by the contemporary failure of government to work wholeheartedly toward relieving the material misery of poor children and probably also adults; by the institution of capital punishment; and by the passion for punishment that pervades the American system of criminal law.

Let me take these up one at a time. Each requires an elaborate discussion that space does not allow. I do not deny that what I am offering is a contextual interpretation of the Constitution that others will find deficient or reject out of hand. I just ask that you keep in mind the thought that guides me; namely, that the Constitution, despite its allowance of black slavery, was once the most morally radical fundamental law in the world and contained provisions that would have been shocking to most thoughtful people abroad, if they had paid much attention. Perhaps some of the provisions are still shocking — shockingly radical — even to thoughtful people who pay attention, even to some American citizens, and recurrently to many of them.

I think that the right of life, when understood as a right that should be given the same expansive interpretation that Supreme Court justices have given the right of liberty, under the due process clauses in the Fifth and Fourteenth Amendments, supplemented by the equal protection provision of the Fourteenth Amendment, would lead to the conclusion that equal human dignity is assaulted when a society allows children to perish or endure stunted lives or eventually, seriously shortened life spans, even though these children could be saved from such a fate. If the society or its agent, the government, allows children to be denied the chance to grow up and live a modestly decent life, it is guilty of causing their destruction.

When you allow something to happen that you could have prevented or now could remedy, you are guilty of causing it, especially in those cases where the ultimate responsibility is yours, and your neglect, you selfishly think, is to your interest. You save money by letting children go down the drain. It does not matter that you didn't deliberately create their terrible condition. But if the right of life of innocent human beings — which is what children are — were read as essential to human dignity, just as an expanded notion of liberty is now often read, then we would have a possible jurisprudential basis for requiring a much more adequate welfare policy. I say this as one who agrees with James Madison's general sense that if you value liberty, you must accept socioeconomic inequality. Liberty will produce unequal outcomes. It is not to be separated from good luck and bad luck, but good luck owes bad luck something.

I do not hold with those who find inequality in itself an anticonstitutional condition. I do not believe that a legitimate constitution must work, even if only gradually, to the equal material advantage of every person under it. Certainly the Constitution is not devoted to such a project. Liberty is not compatible with absolutely "fair terms of social cooperation," as it is called by John Rawls and his followers. The larger point is that a free society cannot want every person's life to consist mostly of reasonable and benign transactions with the state, of performing duties for the state (or the aggregation of one's fellows) and receiving benefits from it (or them). Such a dependent life is what the project of socioeconomic equality finally amounts to; it is not constitutional or just or compatible with human dignity.

Nor is equal protection of the laws a warrant for demanding ever less socioeconomic inequality in society. Undeniably, good sense counsels that increasingly sharp inequality in society makes it harder to call for equal sacrifices from its citizens. The social stakes are so unequal, it is as if any possibility of sincere communication between the top groups and the lower ones became impossible. After a certain far point, the rage of envy must be reckoned with. Perhaps what matters is not envy (always a censurable vice), but another sentiment — a refusal to understand why some of my fellows should have everything while I and others have nothing or next to nothing. Are we and they different species? Be that as it may, and for all the things we can say against the single-minded project of socioeconomic equality, the right of life seems to me to require saving children from stunted lives and premature deaths. I am more sure of this requirement for children than I am for their parents and other adults. Although I believe that the overall treatment of the poor in the United States is a moral scandal, I would perhaps look to other than constitutional arguments to defend adult entitlement to material adequacy (although I may be mistaken in looking elsewhere). But in the case of children, they have a right of life that not only includes protection against those who beat and kill them, but also obliges society to take adequate care of them, by one method or another.

Let me extend this point in the following way. A commitment to basic individual rights on grounds of equal human dignity is not completely confined to the rights of one's fellow citizens. *Human* rights respect no boundaries, at least in the negative sense that a country supposedly devoted to basic rights cannot abridge those same rights abroad by harmful acts of deprivation.

I do not say that those outside our boundaries have a full claim to all the advantages that we have and that it is therefore our duty to bestow them. The United States is not morally obliged to attenuate its project of cultural, scientific, and technological greatness by engaging in the perhaps futile effort to abolish poverty everywhere in the world. (Greatness, human stature, is also an aspect of human dignity.) United States aid has to be selective. But the point is negative, which means, above all, that this society, if it is to be faithful to the spirit of its fundamental law, cannot deprive innocent people of their lives for reasons of policy. Destruction of innocent life constitutes terrorism. When the United States government, year after year and for more than a decade, was largely responsible for the death through disease and malnutrition of tens of thousands of Iraqi children, we must say, to be consistent with our commitment to our own fundamental law, that the American government, with citizens' acquiescence and, in some cases, their encouragement, has been engaged in a protracted policy of denying people their human rights, and especially, their right to life, to start with. This is an indefensible policy of appalling dimensions. (It is too soon to know the cost in innocent human life of the United States war against Iraq.)

I would now turn to the second violation of the right of life. Here the life at issue is usually not that of children and it is not, in all cases, legally innocent life. I refer to capital punishment.

I think that capital punishment is, like the policies of neglecting children at home and starving children abroad, indefensible under an expanded right of life. Capital punishment is defended by a theory of punishment — violent retribution — that is abhorrent to the original meaning of American fundamental law. I say this despite the fact that capital punishment was then practiced — but so was slavery. Like slavery, capital punishment stained the original document, even though many of the provisions in the document are supremely lenient in comparison to the punitive practices of societies contemporary with it. It is precisely that remarkable and historically unprecedented leniency that made and still makes capital punishment such a disturbing anomaly.

I would say that slavery, capital punishment, and torture are continuous: they all exemplify total domination of individuals either by the state or by a state-sponsored or state-permitted institution. Such domination is total war on human dignity; it seeks to extinguish personhood itself. Nowadays only capital punishment is accepted by public opinion. But with any historical imagination, one can entertain the thought that by accepting capital punishment, one is also accepting, presumably against one's will, both slavery and torture. All three are absolute acts of the sort that finite human beings cannot assert the right to commit.

We could argue, in a tactical way, that the horror of capital punishment is that innocent people are sometimes executed, or that it is inflicted so selectively that the practice becomes arbitrary, or that the practice has always been propelled or at least fortified by racism. These are tactical arguments, although each is nonetheless true. Yet I believe that we must give some mind to the prevailing defense of capital punishment, because we find there a larger ideology of punishment that has never been compatible with the original moral radicalism of the Constitution. I will return to this ideology of punishment in a moment.

One point first. I grant that American citizens can protest capital punishment and uncorrected material misery without referring to the spirit (or original meaning) of the Constitution, and speak instead about simple justice. But I believe that to be able persuasively to designate a wrong as unconstitutional is to speak more accurately about its enormity. What may strike you as my twisting the Constitution to extract from it a result I want is instead, I believe, holding us to its original meaning, its originally radical and radically original commitment to human dignity. Putting people to death through judicial process and ignoring misery are thus each doubly wrong: these policies are not only atrocious in themselves, but represent a profound self-inconsistency, an inconsistency between the original contextual meaning of the Constitution and a number of policies and practices that betray that original meaning.

I now return to the matter of the ideology of punishment in general, not just the defense of capital punishment included in it. In what I am about to discuss I also hope to speak with a bit of relevance about the American response to the events of September 11.

American society has always shown a mean punitive streak. The wonder is that the provisions of the Bill of Rights that deal with the rights of suspects, defendants, and convicted criminals were ever proposed and ratified. For example, not forcing a person to be a witness against himself and thus to cooperate with his own hurt, no matter how much wrong he has done, is for most people morally counterintuitive and not commonly found in the criminal law systems of the majority of countries, even today. Yet alongside this tenderness toward human weakness in the Constitution, there has always been a concurrent desire in the country to punish and often to punish with a greater severity than seems called for. The late Justice Lewis Powell went so far against the original moral radicalism of the Constitution as to say that no state is required to choose the least severe punishment. He produced this malicious dictum in the course of defending capital punishment.

I think one could generalize and say that what lies behind the mean punitive streak in American culture — in sharp contrast to the enlightened leniency of the Bill of Rights — is a combination of racism and Christian Old Testament attitudes. Until racism and these religious attitudes are moderated, there is little chance for the ideology of punishment to be deflated and American practices of punishment brought into line with the original leniency of the Bill of Rights.

I stress the word "leniency" because traditionally democracy has been associated with leniency, not with the desire to punish. In fact, we could say that no democracy would have been historically possible unless leniency had been posited as a moral ideal of persuasive strength. Elites who were ill disposed toward democracy and even horrified at its prospect were made to relent for many reasons, but one reason should not be overlooked or forgotten. Some political writers managed to insert the idea that even if the great number of people, strictly speaking, did not deserve the privilege of citizenship, and that such a privilege was much more than their due, still and all, leniency toward human nature held out the hope that the large majority of people would be improved by citizenship. At the very least, they themselves would practice leniency in turn. Out of fellow feeling, they would practice leniency in the spirit of what Tocqueville unflatteringly called "guilty tolerance." They would resist oppression, but not seek to oppress the upper few or minority groups among themselves.

You can look at democracy from many angles, but from one angle democracy looks as if it were a bargain of leniency. People get more than they strictly deserve by having equal citizenship so that they can protect themselves against the powerful. But part of that bargain is surely that the beneficiaries of leniency extend it to others, especially those who are morally weak or criminally culpable. Just as the legally innocent mass of people receive citizenship, the legally guilty receive leniency in the matter of crime and punishment. You would think that a mature democracy would hold to the view that society should punish only with reluctance, and punish less frequently and less harshly than nondemocratic societies do. Theorists of democracy used to believe that democracy, especially constitutional democracy, is unthinkable without a spirit of leniency that permeates all its institutions and practices.

Racism and Christian Old Testament attitudes help to account for the mean punitive streak, for the rejection of leniency in America, the first home of leniency as a political principle. The percentage of people in prison in this country is amazing, many of them for nonviolent crimes. Prison conditions are often little short of slow torture. The facts are familiar but, alas, not as widely upsetting as they should be. I would now emphasize religious attitudes in my account of this condition.

In spurning the mission of leniency, the promoters of the ideology of punishment rely on such concepts as retaliation and retribution. Retaliation is a secular idea, but retribution seems to go very easily with Christian Old Testament attitudes. Not far from these two concepts is that of revenge. That, too, is a secular idea. But the concept with the most prestige is retribution; it seems invested with a high and mighty, indeed divine, sanction. Think of the role played in theology by blood sacrifice as expiation and by eternal punishment for temporal sins. In any case, the three concepts are scarcely distinguishable. They share the will to inflict pain deliberately in order to pay back the pain the initial crime inflicted. So, let us ask, what is the moral standing of the idea that pain should be returned with pain, preferably greater pain? (Or harm with harm?)

This is not an easy question. I have just a few sketchy points to make. I do not think that the deliberate infliction of pain (or harm) in retaliation or retribution — never mind revenge — on those who have done wrong can be considered an act of justice. What is justice? It is three things: protecting people in what is theirs, restoring to them what they have lost unrightly, and giving them what is their due, what they have earned. In addition, the motive of acting justly should be to act justly, and not merely to do a deed or enact a policy that happens to coincide with the requirements of justice, but is pursued for all sorts of other motives, some of them covertly wicked. I believe that pain can never be anyone's due, no matter what they have done, for the reason that the instruments of pain, coercion, and violence cannot properly be associated with justice. Only something positive and good can be someone's due; additionally perhaps, some accurate estimation of the quality of work that they have done. In a criminal trial, justice is done only when a not-guilty person is found not guilty (his status quo ante is restored), not when he is found guilty (nothing can restore the status quo before his crime, except in money matters). To say that a person *deserves* pain for the pain he has caused is to misuse the concept of desert. It is to cover revenge with a mask. The wrongdoer does not owe pain for the pain he has caused (or life for the life he has taken); rather he owes disclosure or acknowledgment of the truth, provided his truth is not used against him to punish him, except perhaps with his consent.

Let us recall that the first principle of morality is that we treat others as we would be treated. That is the golden rule. No matter how we are treated, we should not return the same pain for the sake of the pain. The first principle of morality is therefore against the practice of retaliation, because retaliation is dedicated to the feeling that we should treat others as they have actually treated us. Retaliation and retribution are therefore prima facie immoral; they have nothing to do with justice.

What then is ordinary punishment, to leave aside capital punishment? It is, when inflicted in the spirit of the moral radicalism of the Constitution, a lesser evil, not an act of justice. Doing justice can have nothing of evil in it; it is a pure good. The lesser evil is the *necessary* evil, and you always wish that you did not feel compelled to do evil, even when necessary. Inflicted pain, like imposed death, is always evil, and hence inflicted only when necessary, and as little as is necessary. Innocence and guilt do not affect this proposition. Thus, to be morally allowable, the lesser evil must be necessary; the only necessary evil is lesser.

The doctrine of the necessary and lesser evil comes into play when some people are compelled by authorized others to give up something of great value—say, continued existence or freedom from pain. It is so valuable that ideally it would never be given up, except for the sake of something deemed even more valuable that requires the cost. We calculate the necessary and lesser evil when we say that we inflict some pain to avoid or abolish greater pain; or we say that the right of life of the smaller number should give way to protecting the right of life of the greater number; or when we say that sometimes one right must be abridged to preserve another right that morally weighs more. Every such calculation, whether made by actors or observers, is morally ambiguous, even odious. It involves us in the very same absoluteness that I reject in the cases of torture, slavery, and capital punishment. These calculations are also liable to empirical uncertainty and harbor an innate tendency to immoral license. The very idea of political necessity is historically changeable, and always self-servingly elastic at any given time. But I do not see any other way of deciding and acting politically than calculating evils, whatever may hold in private life. Society may think that it can justly conscript persons into collective self-sacrifice, but the adherent of genuine morality must never regard conscripted self-sacrifice as just, only as dubiously allowable. Ideally, self-sacrifice would always be left to the free choice of conscientious individuals.

What justifies punishment after guilt has been ascertained through due process of law, once we deny that punishment is an act of justice, and consider it at best as a morally allowable act? So far as I can tell, only two concerns: neutralizing the wrongdoer to prevent him from repeating his crime, and deterring others from committing the same type of crime. When punishment is necessary to reduce crime—that is, to reduce the incidence of injustice through deterrence—that means the aim of justice is served by means that are not themselves just. There is no alternative. Means cannot always be continuous with the ends that they serve. The best we can do is not pretend that means are continuous or must be.

A criminal has disregarded the requirements of moral agency by misusing his free agency. But he remains a human being. Respect for his human dignity sets limits on how he should be treated. He can never forfeit human dignity because no one ever has to earn it. He cannot be treated like a noxious animal or thing.

Punishment is not justice, and retaliation is not a proper motive for punishment. The duration of neutralization must be as short as possible. Strictly speaking, neutralization is not punishment, but only a purpose served by the practice of punishment. On the other hand, the need to rely on deterrence to stop large numbers of people from committing unjust deeds shows a failure on society's part. Everyone's motive should be at least to preserve others in what is theirs and thus not take it away from them. But, I know, we are not a society of saints. So we punish to deter, but I would not exaggerate the potency of punishment as a deterrence.

Capital punishment, supposedly a sort of "massive deterrent," does not deter murder. In any case, some pain must be inflicted on the criminal if the purpose of deterrence is to be served. Such pain is not what the criminal deserves; rather, it is what he leaves himself open to. When punished, he becomes an example to others. He thus becomes useful to society. But if a person is instrumentalized so completely, however necessarily, justice is not done; only the lesser evil is.

For one cause or another, some people simply will not be deterred; but also, for one cause or another, the sizable majority of people are not kept from crime by fear of being caught and punished. Most of us are not kept from violent crime by rational calculation. If the situation were otherwise, and democracy stood in perpetual need of the deterrent effect of legal punishment, I do not see how we could say that society had met the elementary preconditions of constitutional democracy or even of a minimally decent civil society. People would be living in a state of nature, if calculation alone kept them from warring on one another. They would resemble nation-states rather than human beings. As for restoring to a person what a criminal has taken away, let us say again that only money can be restored, and where possible should be. Incarceration, like capital punishment, restores nothing to the victim; what these practices do is provide a substitute gratification to either the victim or his survivors or the enthralled spectators.

Take the case of resisting an assailant. If I defend myself, some people (I once was one of them) want to say that I am doing justice to myself by preserving myself in what is mine. Yet I am using violence to do so. There is something not right about associating justice with violence, even in the case of an innocent person who defends himself against an unjust aggressor. An act that rectifies injustice is not in itself an act of justice, if it is a violent act. More important, however, I am not doing justice to the assailant by neutralizing or overcoming or killing him. I am doing the lesser evil to him, while doing justice cannot involve doing evil. And if I manage to get him in my power, he becomes innocuous, almost innocent, and I must treat him with the least amount of pain as possible. If I make him harmless, if I am able to neutralize him, I am certainly not then entitled to kill him. So with formal capital punishment: it is too much like the original crime. We should not make a victimizer into a victim. At least the (nonpolitical) murderer does not say, I did the right thing; do as I did. The state does say, however, that capital punishment is justice: not merely what is allowed but what is mandatory; and that if capital punishment did not exist, the state would be morally faulty and do serious injustice. But this is an untenable understanding of justice. Or, if the state says it acts properly but optionally, the reply is that deliberately taking a life can never rightly be a mere available option. Justice is not optional, nor is the lesser evil when necessary.

I admit that in my argument there may be a tension between self-preservation and the golden rule. Is not the golden rule the same as the precept "resist not evil"? Is not the golden rule pure altruism and hence not for us who are not and do not even want to be saints? I do not think so. The golden rule does not say that if I have been wronged, I should let the wrongdoer go unpunished because that is how I would want to be treated if I had committed a wrong. "Trading places" is not the same as the golden rule. The question lodged in the golden rule is not, How would you like it if what you did were done to you? The scope of the golden rule is not every kind of treatment, but only the field of moral relations. If I am disposed to heed the golden rule, I want to treat and be treated *justly,* and when justice fails on one side or the other, the lesser evil of punishment may have a place.

Alternatively, if the golden rule does tend to nonresistance, then self-preservation (and that includes preservation from misery, torture, and slavery) nonetheless takes precedence over the preservation of others. Right conduct cannot be suicidal or entail martyrdom. This is my axiom. But if my self-preservation is not at stake, my steady disposition should be to practice the golden rule, to treat morally as I would be treated. The main application would be in refraining from initiating courses of conduct that I would regard as unjust if initiated against me. I thus begin with the negative meaning of the golden rule: avoiding injustice. That means that the golden rule, even though I qualify it to avoid utter self-sacrifice, still amounts to more than a rule to follow when little is at stake. All I know is this: retaliation is not part of justice, while not resisting evil is more than justice. On the other hand, never to practice the golden rule is never to practice morality, but only, in Tocqueville's phrase, "self-interest, rightly understood." If I never treat others (if only by forbearance) better than I have been treated by them, I have never been moral.

The long and short of it is this. If we start trying to produce a theory of punishment that is more consistent with constitutional democracy and, hence, with the original moral radicalism of the Constitution, we must give up our faith in retribution and retaliation. We must go so far as to see punishment, in its best administration under due process of law, not as justice but as the necessary and lesser evil, merely. We should be morally pained by the thought of deliberately inflicting pain (deprivation of life, liberty, and property) no matter how awful the deeds that we are responding to. Avoidance of as much pain as possible is not the only central moral consideration involved in the defense of individual rights — the great standard of public morality — but it is surely a central one.

As with punishment, so with war, only more decidedly. There is no such thing as a just war. That a war is necessary does not mean that it is just. First, the motive to war is never justice, not even in the sense that it is undertaken for the sake of preserving lives. Every war stems from numerous ambitions and worldly motives and interests to which war supplies a golden opportunity. Unlike a narrowly tailored criminal prosecution that has just the one goal of catching a suspected criminal and then trying and punishing him, a war is a catchall of purposes, many of them personal or partisan or factional or bureaucratically self-promoting. To say that the aim of a war is to preserve a society is usually to extend improperly the sense of the idea of self-preservation, which pertains to distinct flesh-and-blood human individuals. A personalized abstraction is fed flesh and blood. To be sure, a war can deter future attacks on a country's people, but it sacrifices so many of that country's lives that clearly other motives than preserving lives are in play.

It is unequivocally good that Nazism was defeated by violent war. Yet even when a good cause is pitted against an evil one (in the long course of history, an extremely uncommon occurrence), the very use of violent means disallows invoking the name of justice. An unequivocally good cause does not mean that the war it wages is just. The necessary means of war yoke the unequivocal good to the necessary evil. Killing the soldiers of the bad side is also evil, no matter how necessary. Correspondingly, if the clearly bad side employs scrupulously "lawful" violent means in waging its war, those means do nothing to lessen the immorality of its cause, even though the sum of expectable evil is creditably reduced. For the most part, values internal to a process have moral weight only when the process has morally allowable or morally praiseworthy aims. In any case, the moral costs of various policies that were used to prevail in World War II were stupendous.

You wage war to win it, finally, whatever motives played a part in starting your involvement in it. It becomes an adventure of us or them, and only vaguely connected, at least in the public mind, to the original motives. A purely defensive war, which is a historical rarity, waged by a guiltless party, which is also a historical rarity, is allowable, as the lesser and necessary evil, but it is not an act of justice. The evil of even the best war is a compound of necessary evil and surplus evil; the combination, in varying proportions, occurs in unspeakably huge amounts. When retaliation and retribution are woven into not only the motivation but also the prosecution of war, and divorced from the purposes of neutralization and deterrence, then the war veers toward the unjustifiable, not that I expect armed states and movements to give a moment's notice to this point. Whatever else we may think, let us try to maintain the idea that retaliation is not part of justice. A morally allowable war against the perpetrators of the terrorism of September 11 should have been a morally reluctant response. The concept of just war should be consigned to the historical museum of unenlightened, blameworthy, and essentially theological notions. And so far as I can tell, the war on Iraq is surplus evil; it has no necessity. It is a strange compound of adventurism, fanaticism, and brutal expedience.

At the start, I said my second question is whether the effect of some United States policies reverses the original relationship to the rest of the world, and puts the country altogether behind, say, Western Europe in the commitment to human dignity. No, not yet as a general proposition, is my answer, although other answers that go in divergent directions are possible. But the pity is that the United States is in the matter of poor people (especially children) and the matter of punishment (including capital punishment) behind a number of European societies. And on other issues it has something to learn from Europe. Doubtless, it is still ahead of much of the world in free speech and press and free religion. (I would have added both the right of privacy and the rights pertaining to criminal procedure — including habeas corpus — to this list if not for very recent measures and proposals mounted by the present administration in the name, supposedly, of fighting terrorism.) Above all, the United States surpasses the world in its capacity to absorb diverse people and give them their rights as individuals and the equal protection of the laws. This is a magnificent achievement. But war always threatens rights, and global or imperial ambitions always subject society to executive discretionary powers, and therefore undemocratic powers, of an indefinite scope.

A global foreign policy really does not go well with the original meaning of the Constitution, because such a policy allows political leaders to do far more evil than the necessary and lesser evil. Such a foreign policy is perforce imperialistic; and imperialism is carried on under the deluded or cynical pretense of perfect innocence or righteousness. It has been regularly true of United States foreign policy that it does or supports or encourages or permits surplus evil. Prudent good sense is often enough only a weak substitute for moral inhibition. Against the teaching of the *Federalist* papers, the United States appears to welcome having enemies. A constitutional democracy inwardly declines the more active it is abroad—even if we leave aside many particular cruel and unjust policies involved in such activism. A system of restrained power at home is badly matched with the incessant exercise of tremendous power of all kinds abroad. What is more, unlimited power used abroad cannot coexist indefinitely with the ideal of limited government at home. Power, much of it unaccountable, passes to military, police, and intelligence agencies. At the end of the road is a fused garrison state and surveillance state, much more powerful against the innocent than the guilty. That is not a free life, the life promised by the Constitution.

The Constitution's moral radicalism has radiated its influence most powerfully by hope, by promise, not by deeds. Many of our games are unworthy of our rules. To speak of trying to stay true to the Constitution's original moral radicalism is to saddle us with a tremendous burden, I know. No wonder we often run away from it. But wanting to stay true is where the greatest glory and honor would lie.

Addendum, 2005

It is wonderful to watch the Bush administration construct an imitation democracy in Iraq while steadily undoing genuine constitutionalism at home, and engage in both processes with the cooperation of the legislative and judicial branches of government. President Bush has not taken "care that the laws be faithfully executed" (Art. 2, sect. 3).

Reference

Scalia, Antonin. *A Matter of Interpretation.* Princeton: Princeton University Press, 1997.

4

A Life of Fear

We are caught up in a course of events that are nearly as opaque in motivation as they are dramatic and often tragic in their effects. The United States answered jihad by carrying the war on terror to Afghanistan, but then seemed to veer by invading and occupying Iraq. We cannot say now how the sequence will develop. The situation must change; it may change rapidly or seem to, and then change again. There will be not only new events but also new revelations about earlier events. Hunches about the future may be possible, but not predictions. Though predictions are not possible, analysis is necessary, even if it can only be strained and provisional. When motives are opaque, analysis becomes more difficult than usual, barely possible. In the present situation, motives are often opaque and become more opaque when principal actors take pains to hide them and also try to obscure the obvious (helped by the establishment press) and to distract attention (helped by the mass media). Nonetheless, we have to try to understand our situation, despite the obstacles.

Serge Schmemann says that contemporary history is the hardest to write and the easiest to criticize (2004). We are thus cautioned that those who analyze the present are prone to make serious mistakes. There will always be some opacity in human affairs; our understanding can go only so far. Principal actors themselves often cannot give a full account of their motives, even to themselves, even if they want to. Whenever several policy motives are in play, their ranking in importance will differ from one principal to another; even in the mind of one principal, the ranking may shift from time to time. It is often impossible to find a stable deepest level in many of the principals. Outside observers are reduced to piecing things together faultily. To appropriate Emerson's words about human beings in "Circles": "there is a residuum unknown, unanalyzable" (1983 [1841]: 406).

We are told that there is much to fear, but the warnings, though frequent, are often vague. Of course the destruction of the World Trade Center on September 11, 2001 by Muslim terrorists or jihadists is an event so clear and direct that it seems to need no analysis. When effects are truly dramatic, the concern on the part of the attacked party to comprehend the causes tends to evaporate or is thought frivolous or absurd, perhaps indecent. Only effects occupy the full attention, as if there were no significant prior events linked to the dramatic deeds. Officials set out to combat the effects — above all, to inflict retaliation for the sake of retaliation but also to neutralize the attackers. However, we must not let the drama and the tragedy of September 11 disable analysis.

For a start, we can entertain the thought that the destruction of the World Trade Center was intended by some of its participants and understood by many of its sympathizers as an act of revenge — a vengeful strike — against what is perceived by many Arabs and Muslims as a constellation of Western imperialism, Israeli colonialism, and Arab and Muslim subservience. All the elements preceded Bush's presidency, but he has made them a good deal worse. From the perspective of Arabs and Muslims, the Bush administration's almost total acquiescence (in spring 2001) in Israeli Prime Minister Ariel Sharon's policies was a definitive decision that served to steel the resolve to produce a dramatic act of vengeance. The constellation of elements arouses in the already inflamed religious or ethnic imagination of the Arab and Muslim world a dread of the West's tyrannical intentions and a hatred of its tyrannical deeds — dread and hatred just like those felt by Western peoples throughout their history.

The recently revealed American policy of torture of combatants captured in Afghanistan and Iraq is simply the most dreadful expression of tyranny — not in scale but in planned intensity of degradation. The pursuit of usable intelligence was not the source of the policy. How could it be? The specific deeds, if any, of those tortured were rarely known; those who were tortured were available to be tortured. The most important tactical result is that the friends and allies of the United States can henceforth treat their captives as they please in the knowledge that what they do will not be worse than what the United States has already done. But even before American torture took place, it was as if the United States had made a policy of daring Arabs and Muslims to resist and taunting them for their weakness. Then, too, the inflammation of Arab and Muslim indignation is made yet worse by an outraged sense of superior religious piety.

The political response of the weaker side in many kinds of conflict may take the form of a gesture. So obviously gestural was the attack on September 11 that it inspired the German composer Karlheinz Stockhausen to say that the destruction of the twin towers was "the greatest work of art ever," the man-ifestation of Lucifer (the demon of light) in New York. His words were shock-ing only because they disclosed the obvious. He was pointing as much to the unrestrained imagination of the planners and attackers as to the awe-struck perception of observers (Stockhausen, 2001: 76–77). His remarks after all are not far from what the 9/11 Commission says of the ambitions of an Al Qaeda principal, Khalid Sheikh Mohammed: "This is theater, a spectacle of destruc-tion with KSM as the self-cast star—the superterrorist" (9/11 *Commission Report,* 2004: 154). If KSM's desire to "make a media statement" was not bin Laden's, it was certainly congruent (2004: 154–155). The dramatic effects of September 11 dwarf those of any subsequent properly military encounter between combatants, no matter how destructive. We may therefore choose unwisely to concentrate exclusively on those effects and see the attack as an uncaused and hence inexplicable act—perhaps as pure evil. But gestures—even those that appear Luciferian—are not uncaused, not unmotivated.

The interpretation of September 11 as, in appreciable part, a gestural act of revenge is largely unthought in the United States and rarely surfaces. If it is a caricature, it is not just a lie. The American public remains incurious about the possible background causes of September 11, as if that tragedy could have no sources in grievance or the sense of being wronged and despised. In fact, the musicologist Richard Taruskin voiced a widespread sentiment when he said shortly after September 11 that the "only way" to defeat terrorism "is to focus resolutely on the acts rather than their claimed (or conjectured) motivations, and to characterize all such acts, whatever their motivation, as crimes" (2001: 36). How bizarre for a scholar, of all people, to disown an interest in causes, even the causes of crime. A refusal to try to understand the adversary sustains the brutal simplicity (should we call it Schmittian?) of Vice President Dick Cheney's more recent remark: "Such an enemy ['the terror network'] cannot be deterred, cannot be contained, cannot be appeased, or negotiated with, it can only be destroyed." Unfortunately, the 9/11 Commission report provides a variation on Cheney's theme: "It [bin Laden's program] is not a position with which Americans can bargain or negotiate. With it there is no common ground—not even respect for life—on which to begin a dialogue. It can only be destroyed or utterly isolated" (2004: 362).

We have a great deal to fear, but there is something to fear in the very war on terrorism. The government's response to fear may itself cause fear in those it is meant to protect, not only in those against whom it is waged militarily, and in those third-parties who observe and may grow alarmed by the display of American retaliatory power. For the time being, American citizens fear only the terrorists, not their own government as it fights the terrorists. What I call for (and I am hardly alone in doing so) is not to direct fear away from terrorists, but to expand the scope of fear to include the American government and its close collaborator, Israel. More accurately, I believe that we should extend suspicion or vigilance (to use a Jeffersonian word) toward the Bush and Sharon administrations. Muslim terrorism is an enemy, but it is an enemy that these two administrations have found it immensely useful to have. This realization should affect the way in which Western analysts conceive of the enemy.

Let us begin with the Bush administration. Two matters should arouse vigilant suspicion, and have done so ever more insistently. The first is the conduct of those who prosecute terrorists or alleged terrorists by means of legal or administrative procedures. The second is the war against Iraq. Prosecution is marked by what looks like a gratuitous disregard of due process of law. The war, on the other hand, was waged against a regime that had no demonstrated alliance with jihad and that in its secularism was even a bulwark against it. The common element in these two policies is that they appear to have little or no connection to an effective war against terrorism. Then, too, both policies not only are off their purported mark, but also are voluptuously excessive in the tyrannical impulses they act out. Analysis should be guided by the thought that the motives of the Bush administration are not primarily the stated ones. The motives are indeed opaque, intentionally opaque, but may acquire more clarity when many analysts put their minds to work. This essay is meant to contribute to the effort.

In his book *Bush at War*, Bob Woodward quotes President Bush on the evening of September 11: " 'This is a great opportunity,' Bush said, somewhat locating the pony in the pile of manure. It was a chance to improve relations with big powers such as Russia and China. 'We have to think of this as an opportunity' " (2002: 32). Woodward seems to think that Bush was desperate to find a small good thing amid such terrible loss; better relations with Russia and China would supply a little consolation for the tragedy of September 11. But the value of Woodward's quotation is not its quality of analysis, but Bush's twice-repeated assertion that New York's tragedy was an "opportunity." (In his subsequent book, Woodward appears to have caught up with himself.)

What is the terrorist attack of September 11 really an opportunity for? I make a suggestion with the hope of dispelling some of the opacity in the motivation. Behind all particular motives, which I will discuss shortly, there lies an overarching aim that is barely avowed and that, when avowed, is expressed in an anodyne and patriotic rhetoric. That aim is to guarantee the existence of a long-term project that will serve to justify the national security state (an ensemble of bureaucratic structures) and the economy that serves it and is served by it. Only an ideologically definable enemy can justify this system. My suggestion is not a revelation. Rather it is a statement of the obvious; it may be thought too obvious to need to be said. But it should be said because it is convenient to ignore it. The demise of the Soviet Union was the loss of the enemy that organized American life. That loss made American global hegemony possible, but the establishment demands that the national security system survive the loss. To do so, the system must have a clearly defined main enemy. A worldwide mass-cultural hegemony without a menacing enemy would not be adequate for the exercise of domination.

Without an enemy how else could the national security state and its economy thrive? The quest for political-military hegemony must be constantly challenged; what appears to impede it enhances it, even if perfect hegemony is constantly delayed or permanently deferred by impediments. The hegemonic power needs enemies, but not ones that are too seriously competitive, and it needs victories, but not a complete and final victory. The quest for political-military hegemony is, as a number of its supporters happily proclaim in their writings, imperialism, but an imperialism that is selective and interventionist rather than colonizing (except culturally). The ideal enemy is bellicose, perhaps inflamed, but manageably so. Terrorism meets that description very well, for the time being. It meets that description far better than, say, cold war with China, which would be an awfully large and unprofitable enemy to have. How would enmity with it really be managed? Bush's reference to China (and Russia) really means that the United States would not for now have to agitate the China issue in order to have a sufficiently grave antagonism to keep the national security state and economy going.

The complication is that terrorism is a metonymy for a much larger enemy, which is made up of Arabs and Muslims everywhere. By itself terrorism would seem to be a large enough enemy, but if officials thought it were, Iraq would never have been invaded. For terrorism to be adequate to the project of imperialism, for imperialism to be sustainable publicly and rhetorically, terrorism must be falsely associated with Arabs and Muslims everywhere. For this idea to take hold, ordinary people have to refuse to make distinctions among Arabs and Muslims, all of whom are assumed to be actually or potentially guilty of terrorism, just by their ascribed identity. An underlying popular racism, carefully nurtured by the establishment media and the mass media, thus helps to further the overarching aim. And with enough acts and policies of hostility toward them, Arabs and Muslims will grow more fully into the role assigned them. Intrinsic to all politics are descriptive and rhetorical simplifications that mobilize subjects and citizens, but such simplifications are coarsened further by mass politics wedded to mass media, and become more abstract, more remote from reality, whether mass politics is democratic or dictatorial, normal or insurgent.

If American imperialist ambition has existed from the start, the novelty in the Bush administration's promotion of it lies in the nature of the designated enemy, which is now solely ethnic-racial-religious. I do not say that American imperialism has been historically free of such components — far from it. Just think of the wars against the Indian nations and the war against Mexico. (Has there ever been any imperialism, any systematic career of militarily backed aggrandizement, which is free of racial or ethnocentric delusional passion? As a racial group, whites, too, have sometimes been despised by nonwhites, and whites have warred on one another with ethnocentric frenzy.) The fact remains that now these components occupy a much more salient position than they did in the period of world wars (in Europe, if not in Asia) and the cold war. In the past when racism (on which I concentrate, and by which I mainly mean aversion to the color and/or the facial features of others) has figured in American imperialism, the United States had above all in mind large economic and strategic gains that racism helped not only to define but to advance. In contrast, the present war on Arabs and Muslims holds out the prospect of no gains for American security. The national security system jeopardizes national security. What conflicts between objective American national interests and Arab and Muslim interests are there? Rather, racism allows the United States to have imperialist policies that conveniently appeal to an underlying race-based paranoia by mimicking it: a jealous fear for the country's power that grows with every victory over the enemy. The racism now seems both decisive and gratuitous — at least it seemed gratuitous until September 11. There are reasons for this development, to which we will eventually turn.

This racism shows itself not only in the invasion of Iraq, but also in the prosecution of terrorists and alleged terrorists. The abrogation of fundamental rights in the prosecution is carried so far as to seem tyrannical — that is, to employ such methods of surveillance, arrest, questioning, indictment, and confinement as to introduce a tyrannical element in American legal life. At the same time, the United States subsidizes the Israeli military despotism over Palestine, occupies the soil of Iraq, and threatens Syria, Lebanon, and Iran with violence. It is perfectly natural for Arabs and Muslims everywhere — not just in the Middle East — to fear America's tyrannical impulses. The logic of imperialism is tyranny, as both Pericles and Cleon knew and explicitly said in public.

What explains the central fact, the imperialist ambition? How far back would we have to go to hope to find a clue, if not an answer? These are not questions that we can even begin to take up here. But with an official statement like the Bush administration's *National Security Strategy* (2002), and the earlier private but influential and convergent statement of the "Project for a New American Century" (1997), we have for our time an explicit announcement — annunciation — of the high adventurous ambition that has existed almost from the start of the history of the United States. These statements have unusual candor, if only in one respect: they exult in the fact there is now only one superpower. Yet there is a persistent opacity. Neither statement goes beyond the standard invocations of national security and the will to spread democracy by using American power and influence. Why do the authors think that the United States becomes safer when it stretches itself all over the world? They take it for granted that the more active a country is the better off it will be. But that is an article of faith, and held despite the woeful experience of empires in the past.

I think that a glance at Thucydides' account of the imperialism of democratic Athens — more perhaps than a study of the imperialism of republican Rome — prepares us for apprehending the conduct of the United States. I would place the spirit of American ambition somewhere in the vicinity of three formulations in Thucydides' narrative. First, in 432 BC, the delegation of Corinth, enemy to Athens, says of the Athenians that, "they were born into the world to take no rest themselves and to give none to others" (I:70: 41). This description suits the United States as well as it suits Athens because both democracies are wild with a wildness that is akin to anarchism. Second, at the same conference at which the Corinthians speak, the Athenians reply by saying among other things, that "it has always been the law that the weaker should be subject to the stronger" (I:76, 44). The will to such power is not peculiarly democratic, of course. But from the start, the United States has possessed a strong sense of its own path-breaking legitimacy, and has combined it with unusual resourceful energy, immense practical skills, and perfectly normal moral blindness. Such a combination of traits has driven it to feats of expansion and conquest that are truly remarkable. Third, in 416 BC, there are the sentiments expressed by Alcibiades when he urges Athens to invade Sicily. He proposes a tremendously adventurous undertaking against a large, distant, politically diverse, and partly hostile island. In defending his plan, he appeals to a number of motives, but he also says that without a constantly activist foreign policy, "the city, like everything else, will wear itself out, and its skill in everything decay, while each fresh struggle will give it fresh experience, and make it more used to defend itself not in word but in deed"

(VI:18: 371). He is intoxicated by greatness and he therefore understands greatness as limitlessness. These three moments from Thucydides can guide or haunt our discussion.

In brief, American imperialism, though continuous in its history, is moody and light-blooded like that of Athens, but capable of shocking destructiveness. The United States knows and does not know its own strength, but feels it purely and deeply and therefore acts with an inextinguishable passion. However, Americans sometimes appear unable to believe that their country does what it does, and hence are unable to look at what it does in the face and recognize it. American imperialism is not (yet) imperialism with a good conscience (even to the extent that Athenian imperialism was). A few scholars and publicists have made the effort to portray imperialism as right and healthy or at least as superior to moderation, existentially if not morally; but these efforts are narrowly limited in their appeal. There must always be moral missions to hide the nature of American ambition. Exploitation comes in many styles. Despite its sympathy with the predator code, American public sentiment does not adopt the somewhat different warrior code as its own. The absence of an aristocratic tradition, even in the slave states, prevents imperialist good conscience. But it does not prevent imperialism.

The overarching imperialist aim gives shelter and encouragement to an indefinitely large number of particular motives and purposes — that is, policies, foreign and domestic, that contribute to the aim directly as well as indirectly. For those in charge, any given policy may simply be a tactic, even though what is to them merely a tactic may be an end in itself for others associated with them. In our situation, some policies may provoke the enemy to more terrorism, which also has its uses, as long as the damage is tolerable to those in charge, even if not to the victims.

Now, it may be thought that in what I have just said (and in what I am going to say) I am embarked on an attempt to produce a conspiracy theory of past and present American conduct in the world. I would never rule out a priori the existence of conspiracy in political life. What is conspiracy? It is concerted action for a publicly unavowed purpose (or briefly or barely or misleadingly avowed). The purpose is concealed, though imperfectly and not always successfully, by invoking standard values that everyone accepts. The unavowed motives must remain unavowed, but the stated motives must be stated, and accepted by the people, as the real motives. Conspiracy is luridly called "plotting"; but plotting is only planning by another name. There need be no illegality in a political conspiracy, yet there will surely be criminality of some sort (Bobbio and Viroli, 2003: 82–89). In any case, politics is often legal criminality. To call an analysis "conspiratorial" may simply mask impatience with those who reject prevailing interpretations, or unhappiness with their ideas.

A conspiracy is what the principals do not admit to. They are afraid of the word. When their plans come under critical scrutiny or adverse publicity, they may not only deliberately lie but lapse into self-deception and deny their motives, even to themselves. It is common enough that people hide from themselves when they are startled by a startled response to their motives. They may eventually not even recognize their own motives when the motives, in the beginning, are so radical as to be unavowable. They may find it as hard to believe that they conspired as their complacent or too narrowly cynical audience does. They may also come to believe their own defensive lies: their constructed world is far more respectable than the truth. They lose sight of the distinction between sincerity and insincerity. What holds for all of us in everyday life surely holds for those in power. (I do not wish to deny that some of the principals may be so proud of what they have done that they remain honest to themselves.) Although all this possible self-deception would make analysis of the Bush administration even harder, it would not erase the original clarity, the original calculations and concert of motives and plans. (Then, too, the motives could be avowed after the deeds are done and citizens not notice or care very much. What could be worse? Or is that question naïve?)

Thus, to emphasize Bush's description of the terrorist attacks of September 11 as an opportunity is not to claim that he and his administration conspired to arrange those attacks. It may never even be possible to say that he and his administration deliberately allowed them to happen, knowing or feeling close to certain that they were about to happen in the form they took. It is to indicate instead that though the administration was not happy at the start, it was relieved; and eventually it did become happy because the right kind of enemy had made it so much easier to gain popular support or tolerance for the already desired imperialist policies. If some of the principals were initially afraid that terrorism would be a distraction from other policies, they soon realized that terrorism could be made into an ample cover for those policies. The administration could persist, on the basis of a much less troubled popular conscience and with guaranteed media support and more academic support, in the overarching and longstanding (but unavowed) aim of justifying the existence of the national security state and its attendant economy. This aim preexisted the terrorist attack; the administration was therefore poised to convert any destructive event into an opportunity. And then there were particular purposes that the war on terrorism would serve and that would, in turn, help to energize and sustain it. Almost all of these subordinate purposes are also conspiracies because their motives also cannot be publicly avowed.

Yes, I offer a conspiracy theory; it would be culpably innocent to disallow it a priori. Of course, there are better analyses than the one I offer. But they, too, speculate conspiratorially, and must.

The long and short of it is that there is enough conscious awareness of the system's interest throughout the ranks of the system, abetted by tacit or habitual inclination, to permit, guide, or belatedly take advantage of many particular interests and normal moral blindness, within and outside the system, to the end of the system's preservation and expansion. A pervasive common awareness is not needed; indeed, it would make the system far more fragile: more prone to defection and guilt.

One use of an enemy is to inspire fear in the people. The Soviet Union never attacked American soil and never engaged directly with American troops in a third country, as China's did. Most people scarcely felt directly threatened by the Soviet nuclear threat, except during the Cuban missile crisis. The gift of terrorism to American imperialism, to the overarching aim of maintaining the national security state and economy, is that the terrorists killed American civilians on American soil. Hence, the fear is not so apocalyptic or remote as to feel largely unreal, as for most people the nuclear threat did and does much of the time. After all, only the United States defended the doctrine of first-use of nuclear weapons, and spoke of massive retaliation for non-nuclear military and political deeds it was not ready to tolerate. These days, there is renewed interest in the Bush administration in "small" nuclear weapons for one use or another. The upshot is that the opinion seeps down to the people that the United States is boss of nuclear weapons. (I will shortly discuss the claim that Iraq possessed a nuclear capability before it was conquered.) In contrast, terrorism creates a more palpable fear, if not entirely real except to New Yorkers. Where there is fear, there is demand for greater security. What is the national security state but a state intended to provide security against any kind of threat?

Before turning to the invasion of Iraq, I wish to discuss, as integral to the war on terrorism, the nominally legal prosecution of terrorists and alleged terrorists once they are captured or arrested. This prosecution is closely linked to the needs of imperialism, but is also partly autonomous. Just like the war on Iraq, the methods of prosecution are not conducive to defeating terrorism, but could strengthen it. Just as the war against Iraq was driven by unavowed or barely avowed motives, so, too, was and is the prosecution of terrorists. Just as the war against Iraq reaches to the redefinition of American imperialism, so the techniques and tactics of Attorney General John Ashcroft's Department of Justice reach to the redefinition of constitutional protections. Just as a steady career of imperialism provides the background for an analysis of the Bush administration's response to September 11 as a seized and exploited opportunity, so the regular occurrence of past episodes of constitutional infringement provides the expectation that any crisis, real or (partly) imagined, will provoke attempts to limit or even cancel constitutional protections. Just as racism (or ethnocentrism) has figured in the past in American feats of conquest as well as in the war against Iraq, so it now figures in the prosecution of individual terrorists and alleged terrorists.

In discussing Ashcroft's policies in the criminal law on behalf of the Bush administration, I would like to make some general points about fear of enemies, foreign or domestic, which, after all, the prosecution of terrorism is meant to allay. I posit two main and connected notions. First, until reflection and afterthoughts set in, people will have a limitless desire for security, for feeling safe. Second, in convenient disregard of constitutional limits, state bureaucracies that are entrusted with the duty to maintain security have an inherent appetite for using any methods to deter and punish crime and thus extend their control as far as they can until they are stopped. In the eyes of police and intelligence bureaucracies, constitutional protections for persons are obstacles to be removed or circumvented to the fullest allowable extent. The need for security is insatiable, and so is the inveterate bureaucratic passion for control. The two converge and for a while satisfy each other. The irony is that the fear felt by citizens can inhibit or paralyze them; but citizens' fear energizes leaders and officials and produces restless and indefatigable activity, as if the people's safety is a field on which to play spirited games or conduct interesting experiments.

The fear that is felt by citizens often has an abstract quality to it. I mean that there may not be visceral fear or keen psychological dread but rather a vague sense or (contrastingly) a fervent conviction that there is something big to be afraid of. One may not have had any recent experience of fright; one may not even think that one is likely to have such an experience in the near future. Nonetheless, one is supposed to be afraid; one complies, as if one has an obligation to be afraid; one accepts the pattern of conduct initiated by leaders and officials as perfectly proper. And if the policies are clever enough, one is afraid, though without feeling much of anything. One's imagination has been caught and one lives in its world as if it were the world. Direct experience does not circumscribe the play of imagination or the flow of media representations. Only when fear is mostly abstract can it then become limitless, unappeasable — until it is seen through, if ever. Even when under the daily threat of aerial bombardment in England in 1940, and seeing considerable evidence of it, Virginia Woolf could write with passionate honesty in her *Diary* that "I don't like any of the feelings war breeds: patriotism; communal &c, all senti-mental & emotional parodies of our real feelings" (12 July 1940; 1984: 302). Abstract feelings are parodies of feeling.

To be sure, New Yorkers were right to be afraid in the most elementary visceral sense in the immediate aftermath of September 11, and to remain anxious thereafter. Their city is the supreme target for terrorists of every kind. The supreme concentrated city is the supreme target. In its matchless physical reality, it is by far the most important American symbol, the irresistible meton-ymy. Yet the desire for controlling the people in the name of fighting the causes of their abstract (not their visceral) fear is itself limitless not so much because this desire itself is abstract (though it is) as that it is possessed by an institu-tional logic. Aren't ordinary officials also given to wanting to do their jobs as effectively as possible and to focusing on their jobs to the exclusion of every other consideration, for good or evil? The banality of evil is close to the banality of working in an organization for a good result or a neutral one because all three banalities are intrinsic to bureaucracy. Only observers can discriminate morally among the kinds of banality. Ordinarily, officials just do their work with a single mind, losing sight of the larger meaning of their activity.

I do not deny that the preservation of life and bodily integrity is the highest right—because it is the precondition of exercising all other rights and may therefore force them to yield in cases of conflict. But the circumstances in which the conflicts occur must be extreme, blatant, and also infrequent; a long-term state of emergency will wound a free state. The tendency of security to eat up all other values must be resisted because the fear can be largely abstract and therefore easily manipulable; and because whether the fear is abstract or not, people must tolerate some uncertainty about their safety if there is to be a constitutional democracy at all, if there are to be fundamen-tal rights other than the right of life. In his invaluable analysis of the fate of civil liberties in a time of terror, Ronald Dworkin says, "Rights would be worthless—and the idea of a right incomprehensible—unless respecting rights meant taking some risk" (2003: 41). Complete safety is nonexistent, in any case; to try to assure it would be an indefinite and ever-expanding process. The protection of other rights is not the same sort of process. We know much more exactly when freedom of speech, press, and religion, and the rights of criminal procedure, are protected, despite innumerable cases at the edges that require adjudication. But after a certain point, security becomes obsessive because elusive.

If the fear of terrorism is still largely an abstract fear among most American citizens, fear of their protector is so far minimal, though not nonexistent.

Their government may include individuals who fear terrorism or have empathy for citizens who feel genuine fear. But the principals of the Bush administration, though they take extraordinary safety precautions for themselves, show that they are eager to follow policies that give the appearance of fighting terrorism efficaciously but actually do little to combat it or even may intensify the will to engage in it. They are eager because their unavowed aim is to diminish constitutional protections for everyone in the long run, as the so-called USA PATRIOT Act (2001) and subsequent proposals for PATRIOT Act II (2003) demonstrate, while concentrating, in the name of fighting terrorism, on Arabs and Muslims at home and on Arab and Muslim prisoners captured abroad. (The Bush administration needs one more terrorist act on American soil for PATRIOT II and worse to become law.) The principals encourage the relevant bureaucrats who serve them to pursue the institutional logic of police and intelligence bureaucracies everywhere.

All the time, we read stories of overreaching on the part of police and intelligence agencies, apart from terrorism. But terrorism provides a marvelous cover for aggravated overreaching. We thus have a situation in which expanded control, in the first instance over Arabs and Muslims, is desired for its own sake, for the intrinsic (institutional and psychological) value of control. This desire cannot be avowed because in a democracy tyranny can never be avowed, nor can the reasons for it be avowed. On the other hand, it serves the purposes of political leaders, for whom the bureaucrats' intrinsic value of control is thus in part only an instrumental value. These political and executive purposes include the wish to be given credit for doing something dramatic in the war on terrorism; to establish precedents for treating other sectors of the population and, if need be, the whole population, in ways now reserved for Arabs and Muslims; and warning Arabs and Muslims everywhere that the United States will punish, even with tyranny, those who do not comply with American demands. These purposes cannot be publicly avowed; only the last of the three can be hinted at. And all these purposes, together with others, help to constitute the strategy that serves the overarching aim of insuring the vigor of the national security state and economy, which is an unavowable aim. The unavowable aim is served by unavowable subordinate purposes, which in turn are served by methods and tactics that are either unavowed or scarcely avowed or misrepresented.

Montesquieu says, "On the pretext of avenging the republic, one would establish the tyranny of the avengers" (XII:18, 1989: 203). I have used the word "tyranny" to describe the treatment of Arabs and Muslims. I refer to the prosecution of certain individuals in the United States, and also to such policies as: confinement in Guantánamo; the creation of a worldwide "network of detention centers with its own unique hierarchy" out of the sight of journalists, and where intimidation and perhaps torture is carried out (when it is not delegated to other countries) (Risen and Shanker, 2003: A1, 28); ethnic profiling in some contexts; new ethnically based immigration restrictions; treatment of resident aliens; easy deportations for trivial offenses; freezing assets of some organizations; the effort to choke off charitable donations to certain causes; and the use in Iraq of "tough new tactics" of occupation such as barriers, dragnets, omnipresent checkpoints, and collective punishments in the form of destroying homes and buildings, all consciously modeled on Israeli techniques (Filkins, 2003: A1, 18). In all these policies, the government has treated Arabs and Muslims at home and abroad as tyrants and despots have historically treated their subjects.

To adapt a formulation of Dworkin's, the government has acted toward Arabs and Muslims as if it estimated "those lives and freedom as worthless" (2003: 39). That is what tyranny amounts to. What else but tyranny is shown specifically in the treatment of, among others, the Guantánamo prisoners, along with John Walker Lindh, Zacarias Moussaoui, Yaser Esam Hamdi, and Jose Padilla, to mention just some of the most famous examples. The numbers of those treated tyrannically by prosecutorial methods may not be large, but constitutional violations that resemble tyranny do not have to be numerous to be symptomatic of a larger disposition. Such a disposition has already realized itself, beyond the treatment of political prisoners, in the treatment of many aliens. In any case, constitutionalism lives in the details of treatment of even a few individuals, and when the few are members of ascribed identity groups of tens of millions, then the treatment resonates.

Tyranny combines arbitrariness and repression. Both aspects are intended to spread fear among people and thus render them docile or prepare them for destruction. The methods of spreading fear that tyranny employs are punishments, threatened punishments, intimidations, and humiliations. They include executions and exterminations, torture, imprisonment for mercilessly long terms, exile, confiscation, imposed loss of earning a livelihood, unremitting surveillance, and a general isolation and dehumanization. *Arbitrariness* shows itself in the following ways: singling out one or more groups defined ascriptively and hence irrespective of any overt behavior, and condemning them to any or all of the methods just mentioned. Tyranny may also demonstrate arbitrariness by sudden changes in the rules, whether retrospectively or prospectively; or in such vagueness in the rules that people do not know what activities put them in danger; or in having the caprice of officials replace all rules. Arbitrariness reduces people to such radical amazement in being categorized ascriptively or such radical uncertainty about what is expected of them that their lives are filled with constant awareness of possible punishment or humiliation joined to a realization that others in their group have already been punished or humiliated. Thus life is dominated by sharp apprehension.

On the other hand, *repression* shows itself in too many rules, leaving little scope to free activity; in rules that prohibit the most natural or irrepressible practices and expressiveness; and in rules that suddenly introduce radical and systematic changes in the lawful and unlawful or in what people are expected and not expected to do. Repression, like arbitrariness, makes it either impossible or abnormally difficult to obey and thus shrouds all the relations and transactions of life in fear of punishment or humiliation or what is sometimes worse, continuous anxiety. Tyranny requires bravery just to engage in the very activities that require no thought for one's immunity in constitutional democracies; resistance requires heroism. As Judith Shklar has memorably written in "The Liberalism of Fear" (1989) and elsewhere, a life of fear is the antithesis of a constitutionally protected life; therefore, constitutionalism exists to prevent government from spreading fear throughout society. Citizens must work together to protect themselves from their protector, which is always prone to become a source of fear to the innocent—sometimes a source of more fear than one's fellows or outsiders. There is enough to fear in anyone's normal life without adding government to the sources of fear—much less allowing government to become its principal source.

When a government induces fear of itself in the people or in some of them while claiming to act to make them secure, we have a tyrannical or incipiently tyrannical or (oddly) a locally tyrannical situation. I repeat that I go on the assumption that the American government has expressed a tyrannical disposition toward all or many Arabs and Muslims, and acted tyrannically—arbitrarily and repressively—in the prosecution of terrorists and alleged terrorists. (Such treatment has been extended to a few sympathizers of the Taliban or Al Qaeda who may be neither Arab nor Muslim.) Other citizens and aliens should worry because precedents are being set that could, in their generality, eventually affect everyone, unless courts, especially the Supreme Court, restrain the executive agencies. At the start, judicial conduct was largely unpromising, with a few splendid exceptions. The courts gave the Bush administration most of what it claimed. Early in 2004, in the case *Center for National Security Studies v. United States Department of Justice* (No. 03-472), the Supreme Court refused to review a lower court ruling that permitted "the secrecy surrounding the arrest and detention of hundreds of people [aliens], nearly all Muslim men, in the weeks after the Sept. 11, 2001 attacks." The names of nearly a thousand people—all of them innocent of terrorism and subsequently released from detention, though many of them deported for infringing immigration rules not respected by immigrants of other nationalities and religions — will remain secret; so will the "circumstances of arrest" (Greenhouse, 2004: A1). Then at the end of its term, in its decisions of June 28, 2004, the Supreme Court undid — or at least appeared to undo — some (only some) of the constitutional damage inflicted by the government in the Guantánamo, Padilla, and Hamdi cases. The damage done to the persons of the captives remains. So far, then, the Supreme Court has avoided the most dangerous far-reaching result: the full jurisprudential validation of many of the experiments in anticonstitutionalism.

For that is what Ashcroft's (and his successor's) Department of Justice is doing: performing experiments in anticonstitutionalism. I do not agree with Dworkin that Ashcroft or his bureaucracy is driven by the strategy of "putting American safety absolutely first" (2003: 38). Rather, the strategy is to pretend that absolute safety matters most and get people to share that judgment, while actually following through on the wish to weaken constitutional protections first for a despised minority and then for everyone. The treatment of Arabs and Muslims is a sustained assault on the writ of habeas corpus, on the right to counsel, the right to confront witnesses against oneself, and to compel witnesses in one's favor to appear. The key is the assault on habeas corpus. Prisoners have been held for a long time in atrocious conditions, and without notification of specific charges and the chance to rebut them with the assistance of counsel.

In its effort to punish those associated with terrorist groups, whether or not they have committed any terrorist acts, the Bush administration has invented categories like "unlawful combatants" for foreigners and "enemy combatants" for citizens. Some guerrillas captured in Afghanistan are denied standing as prisoners of war, while American citizens suspected of terrorism are denied the protections of either the criminal law process or regular military courts. "Military tribunals" lack most of the basic features of due process of law; they are lawless legal formations. The reverse move has already been made: ordinary civilians are accused of such crimes as "theft and swindling" (Dworkin, 2003: 38) on the basis of intelligence gathered under provisions of the USA PATRIOT Act, which erodes fundamental protections against surveillance and searches and seizures. As both Ronald Dworkin (2003) and David Luban (2002: 9) have suggested, the Bush administration is using, in Luban's term, a "hybrid" model in which fighting a war is fused with detecting and punishing crime in order to deny as many protections as possible to suspects and defendants, whether they are military combatants or alleged civilian criminals. The Bush administration thus criminalizes its political and military enemies and turns domestic criminals and suspected criminals into combatants. Yet, as

Montesquieu says, "One must be just to the Caesars: they were not the first to imagine the sad laws they made" (XII:16, 1989: 201).

I think that the Bush administration, even in the absence of its war on terrorism, would have tried to weaken fundamental constitutional protections, especially in the criminal law. This administration is marked by a strong punitive streak, which is the central part of a general lack of magnanimity that is astonishing. Terrorism has supplied it with a golden opportunity to act on a prior inclination. The tyrannical treatment of Arabs and Muslims, however, serves the overarching aim of pursuing the imperial project and thus giving a mission to the national security state and economy by sharpening the identity of the enemy and deepening conflict with it. Perhaps, too, by establishing precedents for constitutional erosion now, the way is made easier for preserving imperialist policies in an ever darkening world and subduing any serious resistance to it by those segments of the American people disposed to resist.

What of the war against Iraq? In the events that followed September 11, I think that this war is the most salient policy (so far) that shows opacity in motivation. Terrorism has made it much easier to act on unavowed motives in the Middle East. Indeed, motives for the war against Iraq are either unavowed or avowed only indirectly, and are meant to remain as concealed as possible. In place of what appear to be the dominant actual motives, the stated motives are expressed in ways that try to make the war against Iraq part of the war against terrorism. On the basis of what is known the stated motives were never the real motives. The two stated strategic motives were, first, to destroy the capacity of Iraq to launch weapons of massive destruction that it already possessed in amounts sufficient to threaten or harm its neighbors, and, second, to punish Iraq for cooperating with Al Qaeda in its terrorism against the United States and its friends and allies. I go on the assumption that the principals in the Bush administration knew when they made war that Iraq had no weapons of mass destruction and had no links to Al Qaeda. It is complacent wishful thinking to assume instead that the principals were misled by faulty intelligence or judgment.

Nevertheless, just assume for the moment the sincere belief among the American principals that before the war, Iraq possessed weapons of mass destruction, and that sooner or later the American occupation force would discover them. The premise of the war would therefore have to be that the United States could not deter Saddam Hussein. Stalin and Mao could be deterred from using these weapons, but not Saddam Hussein. This is ridiculous. But it would be worse than ridiculous if the American principals sincerely believed that Saddam Hussein was as criminally insane as they said he was, and, that once attacked, he would therefore have used these weapons against a power that could annihilate his society in a retaliatory blow. The Bush administration itself would have been criminally insane to attack him and risk having such weapons used against its forces. No gain could justify such risks. We cannot impute criminal insanity to either side in this situation. To his interrogators in prison, Saddam Hussein said simply, "Do you think we are mad?" when asked why he did not use weapons of mass destruction when he had them, in the 1991 Gulf war (Johnston, 2004: A28). The proof (or near proof) that Iraq had no weapons of mass destruction (or at the least would be deterred from using them if it had them) is that the United States chose to invade it. Yet even here I cannot be certain about the extent of American recklessness. An account in the *New York Times* asserts that the United States received reports from "foreign services and other sources [it] regarded as credible that Mr. Hussein had decided to use chemical weapons against American troops in the event of war" (Jehl, 2004: A12).

The real aim is that the United States (and its friends and allies) should not have to endure to be deterred, should not have to think twice before acting as they please in the Middle East (and elsewhere). The *National Security Strategy* (2002) says that weapons of mass destruction in the hands of "rogue states" can be used to "blackmail the United States and our allies to prevent us from deterring or repelling the aggressive behavior of rogue states" (section V). The ostensible meaning is that Arab and Muslim states are enemies that cannot be deterred because they are unlike any enemies the United States has ever had to face. The true meaning, however, is that the United States will not tolerate submitting to the deterrence imposed by other states, if it can help it. The United States will act "preemptively" so as never to be deterred; to the fullest extent possible, it will secure, with its friends and allies, a monopoly of weapons of mass destruction — a hope that must one day come to grief, irrespective of American policy. In any case, we are compelled to believe that the Bush administration knew Iraq had no such weapons and that invading it could proceed undeterred and for unavowed motives.

Now assume that Iraq had substantial conspiratorial or merely cooperative links to Al Qaeda. I do not deny that that would be a different matter altogether. The policy of combating terrorism would have required that some punitive action — I do not speak of invasion — be taken against Iraq. The trouble is that there was and is no evidence of such a link; and well after the war ended, President Bush himself withdrew the accusation. But the constant and mendacious reiteration that there was a connection succeeded in persuading a majority of the American people of its truth, not only before but even after the belated presidential retraction. Racism made successful deception possible.

The long and short of it is that Iraq was invaded not because it was strong but because it was weak. Saddam Hussein was known to have no weapons of mass destruction. Defeating Iraq would provide a dramatic but easy victory. It would be a victory over Arabs and Muslims everywhere. In the short term, the lines drawn would be sharper; the enemy would be defined less ambiguously; and it would be humiliated. But in the longer term — what?

Just as the prosecution of terrorists and alleged terrorists by legal and administrative action seems like a misdirected response to the danger of terrorism, so, too, does the war against Iraq. The stated motives do not seem to be — could not be — the actual motives. There is deliberate opacity. What then are the actual motives? In our analysis, we must revert to what I have called the overarching aim of American policy: the preservation of the national security state and economy by means of an imperialist career. On this aim, the *National Security Strategy,* which purports to give an "Overview of America's International Strategy," instead presents an idealistic picture of a besieged America faced with threats greater but harder to fight than those that existed in the cold war. Almost the whole statement deals with terrorism and especially the acquisition by terrorists of weapons of mass destruction. In its fifth section, it speaks of the right of the United States "to act preemptively" in order "to forestall or prevent" hostile acts. Iraq is an enemy, supposedly because of its growing strength. I believe, however, that this statement does not give us guidance. It does show full awareness of the unique power of the United States, but hides its activist agenda under the cover of the war on terrorism, as if to say that in the absence of terrorism, the United States would be content to go about its business and let the world alone. The statement lacks candor about the overarching and longstanding aim; it will not discuss American imperialism by its right name and in its true nature.

We approach closer to the truth when we consult such interest-group documents as the statement of principles of the "Project for the New American Century" (1997) and "Rebuilding America's Defenses" (2000). Join to these two a memorandum by Richard Perle and others to Benjamin Netanyahu (then Israeli prime minister) in July 1996, called "A Clean Break: A New Strategy for Securing the Realm." Even when he is not the author, Richard Perle, a former Defense Department official and leading neoconservative ideologue, is influential in articulating a new strategy for American policy in the Middle East above all, and everywhere else that may be somehow related to the Middle East. All these documents were written before September 11, 2001. It is eerie that in "Rebuilding America's Defenses," the authors say that in the absence of "some catastrophic and catalyzing event — like a new Pearl Harbor," American military buildup would be too slow and its actions too timid (51). (Perhaps the Republican impeachment of President Bill Clinton was meant by some principals to help prepare the ground.) The high American ambition must be to discourage any attempt by one power or group of powers to surpass it in strength or even to equal it.

It's not an exaggeration to say that *for some* who took part in writing these statements or who signed them, the strategy is Israel-centered. But when the motives are Israel-centered, the strategy is not always put forth in Israel's name. Above all the strategy is offered as a guide to the United States as the only power in the world capable of world leadership and unchallenged "pre-eminence." As such, the United States is Israel's shelter. I emphasize that the strategy is Israel-centered only for some of the people involved. There are other major considerations that may converge with concern for Israel and that such concern may nicely cover. Mutual use tending toward mutual exploitation dominates the calculations.

Perle's memo of 1996 advises Israel to be skeptically cautious about the 1993 Oslo accords and hold to a steady hard-line against Palestinian aspirations; and furthermore a new strategy must aim at "weakening, containing, and even rolling back Syria." In the name of undermining Syria's "regional ambitions," a concentrated effort at "removing Saddam Hussein from power in Iraq—an important Israeli objective in its own right" must be made (3). Iraq's strength is not at issue; the country is too weak. Yet Saddam stands in the way of a new "strategic balance" in the Middle East that would enfeeble Syria and "redefine Iraq" (4). (The recent book by Richard Perle and former Bush administration speechwriter David Frum, written after the conquest of Iraq, proposes a radical and global American imperialist strategy, but familiarity with Perle's past work should help us to see what is not obvious in the book because of its length and generality—namely, that his eye is always on the success of Israeli ambitions as defined by Sharon. The book is the memo to Netanyahu in a bloated, post–September 11 form, with ambitions also bloated by the defeat of Iraq.)

If Perle is in some documents the main writer, we can find in all of them endorsement by men who came to occupy prominent positions in the United States government as a result of the tainted presidential election of 2000 and then immediately urged war against Iraq, or by men who urged the war from the sidelines. The war against Iraq was the result of a long campaign that began quite some time before September 11 (Lieven, 2002). The war was neither a preemptive war nor a preventive war: there was no danger to pre-empt or prevent, as its instigators knew. It was a deadly combination of fraternity prank and secret-society prank. Thus, from the moral point of view, it was an unnecessary war and hence an immoral one; it produced the evil of war unnecessarily—evil in itself and as a contagious example. It was yet another war thrown by the United States into the world in an unwearying succession of many American wars and military actions, as this country incessantly adds more violence to an always-violent world. The war's immorality was compounded by the impact of American (nominally UN) sanctions on Iraq since the 1991 Gulf War. The sanctions impoverished a whole society and caused tens of thousands of civilian deaths. The war against Iraq was an imperialist war, useful for the overarching and unavowable or guardedly avowed aim of preserving and fortifying the national security state and economy. But what were the more specific unavowed motives — all of them useful to the overarching aim or at least compatible with it — that in combination produced this particular war?

I begin by discounting, except for propagandist uses, the stated motive of rescuing Iraq from its suffering under Saddam Hussein's tyranny. I believe that this motive had no force among the principals involved in advocating and launching the war. They have not hitherto shown much fervor in relieving human suffering; indeed, some of them, like Secretary of Defense Donald Rumsfeld, even supported Saddam Hussein against Iran in the 1980s, while believing he had used chemical weapons against Iraqi Kurds. Furthermore, when the sanctions inflicted so much suffering, the quickest way of ending some of it was to lift the sanctions, which were kept in place for political reasons. No doubt, many Iraqis were relieved by the American conquest of Iraq and the removal of Saddam Hussein (as doubtless were leaders of Egypt, Iran, Jordan, Kuwait, and Saudi Arabia). But media attention, after the conquest, to Iraqi suffering under Saddam Hussein's oppression while he ruled is suspect; it looks like a part of the search for post facto justification of the war. When charitable attention is selective because self-interested, it is cruelty to the un-noticed. Charity itself must be selective, but the charitable attention of the media can afford not to be.

On the stated motive of promoting democracy in Iraq, I do not believe that the principals want the people of Iraq to enjoy the blessings of democracy for their own sake. However, some people in the Bush administration or close to it — examples are Cheney, Perle, and Paul Wolfowitz — have said they favor the project of spreading democracy in the Middle East. Iraq would be the beachhead. We must look on this project of Mideast "overhaul" (MacFarquhar, 2004: A9) first, as a distraction from settling the Palestinian issue in any way that Sharon and his allies reject; and second, as a method of sowing strife in the Arab and Muslim countries of the region. Cheney says that "democratic reform 'is . . . essential to a peaceful resolution of the longstanding Arab-Israeli dispute'" (quoted in Brzezinski, 2004: A19). Supposedly, when all countries are democratic they will refrain from war against one another and settle their disputes peacefully. This is a pipedream. It is hard to imagine that Arab democracies would decide through democratic processes to let Sharon's plans go uncontested. If anything, police states may act coldly and hence sometimes more prudently. Then, too, the religious and ethnic turmoil that a commitment to modern democracy would unleash in most countries in the region would prevent any of them from contemplating interference in the Israeli-Palestinian dispute. They would be too busy handling their own troubles. If a leader were to try to unite a given country by a foreign adventure, the tactic might work for a while, but not in the longer run. In any case, despite all of Wolfowitz's talk about "regime change" soon after Bush's certification as president, and despite Perle's geopolitical grandiosity, I find it hard to believe that the real motives of these two for a democratic "overhaul" had very much power in sending the Bush administration to war against Iraq. The project is too fantastical, even for hardheaded realists. Then again, I cannot be sure.

I detect five operative motives in my effort to reduce opacity. (I omit, without wanting to discredit, such speculative considerations as the wish to distract attention from corporate scandals that may touch members of the administration, and huge wartime profits for firms with close ties to these members or to the Republican Party. "Vulgar" Marxism is sometimes good analysis; better than philosophical Marxism.) None of the five considerations, when acted on, contributes to the war against terrorism and all contribute to sowing the seeds of future terrorism. Two are minor ones: first, the desire, not confined to the military bureaucracies, to have a comparatively smooth battlefield where new tactics and new weapons systems can be tried out. War, on good terms, is the best school and laboratory. Second, there is the Bush family drama. Though there may be some truth to the assertion that Bush the son wanted to avenge the attempt on his father's life by Saddam Hussein's government more completely than Clinton chose to do (while Saddam was trying to avenge attempts on his life by the American government), the larger point is that Bush the son was intent on outdoing his father. Whereas the father had left Saddam in power after defeat in the Gulf War, the son would score a tremendous media victory by deposing or killing Saddam. (Deposing is politically much better than killing: save the killing for the judges after a protracted political trial that would be a much finer media event than a sudden death.) Then, Bush's reelection would put the final nail in his father's coffin by saving dynastic honor. The two minor considerations, singly or together, did not have enough weight to send even so cynical a group as the Bush administration into war, though they helped to confirm the resolve to wage it.

As my analysis proceeds, do I take into account all possible motives? I could not possibly make such a claim. There may be relevant considerations that I have overlookeed or that I have no awareness of. There may be knowledge that I could have consulted but failed to, or secrets not yet disclosed. Let me repeat that my analysis is strained and provisional.

As I am so far able to infer, the three major and interconnected considerations are partisan politics, unreserved concern for Israel, and oil. All are either unavowable or only guardedly avowable. Each consideration penetrates deeply into the other two. In combination, these three were sufficient to send the United States to war against Iraq, but only after "a cataclysmic and catalyzing event." For Bush and some of his political advisers, partisan politics and Israel were and are closely bound together, while for other Americans, concern for Israel was and is sufficient. What of oil? I think the heart of the issue is American control of Iraq's huge oil reserves; this would rid the United States, in the future, of too much dependence on Saudi oil or oil from other unpredictable countries that may have to be treated as if they, too, had interests that deserved some consideration. (*New York Times* columnist David Brooks once said on the "Lehrer News Hour," sometime after September 11, that the real enemy in the Middle East was not Iraq but unstable and all-too-religious Saudi Arabia.) I will spend time only on the connected issues of partisan politics and Israel.

I assume the convergence of independent interests, of the separable interests of the Bush and Sharon administrations. Is that a mistake? Thomas Friedman says that "Dick Cheney . . . is ready to do whatever Mr. Sharon dictates." Indeed the Bush administration is "in his [Sharon's] pocket" (2004: A31).

Unable to decipher Friedman's words, here is what I propose. Look first at the decision to invade Iraq from the partisan perspective of Bush, Cheney, Rumsfeld, and Bush's political advisers, before turning to Sharon's perspective. From the partisan perspective, war against Iraq would be a tremendous gift to the Sharon administration and to many American supporters of Sharon and many undiscriminating supporters of Israel. Immediately after Sharon was elected Israel's prime minister in March 2001, Bush gave him permission to act in exact accordance with Perle's memo to Netanyahu. This is not to say that Sharon needed instruction; he just needed permission to do what he had always wanted. He would not suffer any American penalty. Bush's motives for giving Sharon a free hand are not of course Perle's. But Sharon wanted not only a free hand in Palestine, but also the strongest Arab regional power to be conquered, after a war as destructive to it as possible.

What are the gains to Bush himself and to the Republican Party? The first gain is independent of the Israel connection; it is obvious and historically hallowed: help in winning elections. A not-too-difficult victory over a country ethnically indistinguishable (supposedly) from the terrorists of September 11 would gratify patriotic, retaliatory, and racist sentiment in the United States. The fact that Iraq had no significant connection to Al Qaeda simply could not penetrate the public mind, and, to repeat, the myth persists despite Bush's retraction. The advantage of a short and successful war to a political party is an open secret. Everybody knows it and says it, until political argument reaches the point where the secret has to be denied — by all sides.

The second partisan gain must be unavowed. This gain is inextricably joined to Israel. It consists in the attempt gradually to detach, as much as possible, Jewish American sentiment from the Democratic Party. The stake is not so much the Jewish American vote. Republican Congressman Tom DeLay, friend of the so-called Christian Zionists, has already conceded that Jewish American voters are likely to stay mostly in the Democratic Party. (Undeniably, a shift in Jewish American votes in, say, Florida, could be expected to make a difference.) Rather, the hope is to detach, to an appreciable degree, Jewish American sentiment in the media and academy from its dislike of the Republican Party, and also to detach it as much as possible from the spirit of critique of American imperfections — specifically and for the time being, from critique of both anticonstitutional experiments and the career of imperialism. More positively, the hope is to enlist Jewish American sentiment in support of these two projects, and of course to find preponderant favor with pro-Israeli lobbies and donors of political funds.

Even before Bush's administration, a fair amount of progress had been made in these desired directions. What other meaning have such phenomena as the "Project for a New American Century" and Perle's assorted enterprises in association with *Weekly Standard* editor William Kristol, Yale professor Donald Kagan, and many others? What other meaning has the defense by legal scholars of such practices as torture (Alan Dershowitz and Sanford Levinson; the writings of both of them preceded the disclosure of American torture in Afghanistan and Iraq), ethnic profiling (Fred Schauer), show trials (Lawrence Douglas), and punishing groups, including children, for individual insurgent acts of violence (Daryl J. Levinson and Saul Levmore; for the last named, see Liptak, 2004: 5)? These scholars of the law, none of them in the government, defend measures that in their extremism are necessary only to tyranny and are historically associated mostly with it. A tyrannical cause has a tyrannical hold on their minds. For the sake of their cause, they are prepared to wound the spirit of the Constitution. On the other hand, the lawyers in the departments of Justice and Defense who prepared memorandums between 2002 and 2003 that made a case for torture were sophisticated servants of executive power rather than ideological scholars who initiated rationalizations on their own.

The government lawyers' sins show the banality of evil, not fanatical commitment to evil. The banal ones made it easier for evil to be done, while the fanatics make it easier to ratify the evil.

The additional gain for the Bush administration is to weaken the ability of the Democratic Party, tied in so many ways to Jewish Americans, to criticize the war against Iraq, a war many Democrats, including Jewish Americans, viscerally detest. (I certainly do not mean to suggest that the Democratic Party has allowed itself to be an anti-imperialist party, from Woodrow Wilson's time to the present, despite some episodic moderation on the part of Kennedy, Carter, and Clinton. Johnson was at least as bad an imperialist as Nixon, Reagan, and Bush father and son; he was probably worse than all of them.) Then, too, the core commitment of the Republican Party to the defense of privilege is enhanced by American Jewish disaffection with the Democrats because the Democrats, thanks in part to Jewish intellectuals and scholars, have worked as the party of the weaker to save capitalism from a few of its Calvinist or Social Darwinian excesses.

What is praiseworthy, but not surprising, is that Jewish Americans have been in the forefront of critique of both the war against Iraq and the several anticonstitutional experiments.

In sum, the partisan calculation was that unless blind luck — some "X factor" — interceded, the climax of Bush's partisan gains could be reelection and perhaps increases in Republican seats in both houses of Congress, and that the war against Iraq would help far more than it would hinder. The elections of 2004 have justified the Republican calculation. The capture of Saddam Hussein turned the events in Iraq into a story with at least a temporary narrative closure. That the situation after conquest has been bloody and messy has done little so far to ruin the aesthetic shape of the achievement. Indeed, in a certain quantity, American casualties incurred in overcoming resistance to the occupation of Iraq could solidify popular adhesion to Bush's policies and provide a perverse retroactive justification for invading Iraq, in the first place. But the occupation of a foreign country and the resistance it engenders produce an inherently unstable situation. The greater the effort required to defeat the resistance, the more hollow the claim that the United States invaded Iraq to clear the way for popular choice, for democracy. But so far the war against Iraq has been a net partisan gain for the Republicans. It is not a gain and may be a loss, however, for the safety of the American people.

Let us look now at the war against Iraq from Sharon's perspective. The gain of a wasted and (if Leslie Gelb gets his wish) a partitioned Iraq (2003: A27) is to remove Iraq from the list of countries that can obstruct Israel's way. The conquest of Iraq is also a stern warning to other Arab and Muslim neighbors of Israel. Israel seems now to have in Sharon's eyes something close to invulnerability. A large part of the unfinished business is with the Palestinians. Sharon's intention is to block a genuine Palestinian state and replace it with, in the words of Henry Siegman, "bantustans surrounded by Israel's armed forces and cut off from the rest of the world by a so-called security fence." The result would be to "place 15 per-cent of West bank land, home to 274,000 Palestinians, on Israel's side of the fence. It will, according to the UN, disrupt the lives of 680,000 Palestinians. If the wall follows the route approved by Sharon . . . it will effectively create at least three noncontiguous and isolated Palestinian enclaves" (2003: 16).

These purposes are aided by Palestinian terrorism, which Sharon provokes by targeted assassinations and destructive responses and a generally barbarous tyranny. The terrorism is wicked and stupid, but it is nonetheless (in Siegman's words) "not an enemy but an indispensable ally" because it supplies the pretext for Sharon to disregard Palestinian interests and advance the policy, which he had much to do with launching, of building new or augmenting old Israeli settlements in occupied Palestine (Siegman, 2003: 16). Terrorism is Sharon's golden opportunity. Only Palestinian nonviolent politics, massive civil disobedience, and other peaceful, coercive, persuasive tactics stand a chance of having an effect, as Pete Hamill (2003), David K. Shipler (2002), and some others, including a number of Palestinians, have maintained. About the recent past, Shipler said, "A hundred Palestinian children pledging peace and lying in front of bulldozers would have been more effective than a thousand Palestinian children chanting hatred and throwing lethal stones" (2002). How would Israel respond now? Perhaps not in as shame-ridden a manner as Shipler supposed in 2002, but Israel's media advantage, even in the United States, would come under stress. However, Sharon wants, like Hamas (which Israel once subsidized in order to weaken Arafat), a condition of mutual irreconcilability between Israelis and Palestinians. Palestinian moderates and secularists are neutralized and denounced to weaken their legitimacy in the eyes of the world, and to render them impotent in the eyes of their own people. The political mind of the Palestinians is killed day by day. (Of a piece with Sharon's tactic is Rumsfeld's insouciance toward the looting of Iraq's museums and libraries during the US invasion of Iraq.) Only the bearers of Palestinian rage are left to act, and with every act strengthen Sharon's oppression and American acquiescence in it.

American acquiescence increases because the administration and some of the media yoke Palestinian terrorism to the terrorism of September 11. There is no actual link, but Sharon's policies help to spread a pervasive anger among Arabs and Muslims throughout the world and hence deepen their reservoir of sympathy for any terrorism directed at either the United States or Israel. The two countries are entwined, much to the delight of the Bush and Sharon administrations. Their common interest is to characterize terrorism as (in Coleridge's phrase) motiveless malignity — that is, not a passion to inflict pain solely for the cruel pleasure of doing so, but rather a passion to inflict death and pain for no human or humanly recognizable motive. The political arts of compromise and conciliation, deriving from some empathy with adversaries (who in their weakness may not yet reciprocate it), are thereby dismissed as cowardly and immoral in the face of terrorism, the unfathomable evil. In the Israeli case, as Amos Elon has pointed out, "memory of the Holocaust has been used in Israel not only to equate Palestinians with Nazis . . . but also to provide the rationale for nuclear weapons systems" and to justify the expropriation of land and the building of settlements in occupied Palestinian territories (2004: 16). If the Palestinian resistance to occupation is seen exclusively as a historically familiar murderous anti-Semitism, what hope can there be for compromise and conciliation?

We should remember that the United States and Israel have killed many more civilians than the jihadist terrorists. When people are killed, it does not morally matter that they have been killed deliberately as a matter of policy (the military strategy of irregular forces) rather than being killed incidentally as a result of policy (the military strategy of state forces), which, it is known in advance, will inflict deaths, but is pursued anyway, because the success of the strategy is more important than the lives of those killed. The dead are dead in either case, and in neither case are they dead by accident; the larger the number of deaths, the more censurable the policy. The Scholastic idea of "double effect," parent of the phrase "collateral damage," is merely disingenuous. What is more cold-blooded: terrorist attacks or the use of advanced technology, often from a safe distance, against primitively equipped adversaries and the surrounding civilian population? (Kahn, 2002) Terrorism is not motiveless malignity; nor is it pure sadism; it is irrational politics, gestural politics at its most terrible. The attack on the World Trade Center was simply the most awful terrorist gesture so far.

Shortly after September 11, on October 4, Sharon warned the Bush administration that Israel would not be a sacrificial victim in any effort to appease the anger of Arabs and Muslims. He said, "Do not repeat the dreadful mistakes of 1938. . . . Israel will not be Czechoslovakia. Israel will fight terrorism" (Klein, 2001). These remarks were hurriedly withdrawn, but a moment of public exposure had occurred. I do not know what American idea Sharon was referring to. I can only imagine that someone in the Bush administration said aloud to colleagues that if only progress could be made toward establishing a

Palestinian state (and East Jerusalem as its capital) with full guarantees for the security of Israel within sensible boundaries, the impulse to commit terrorist acts, whether at the expense of the United States or Israel, would be weakened. The reservoir of sympathy for terrorism would be at least partly drained. We know, however, that Sharon did not have to repeat his warning. For their own personal and partisan interests, and for the interests of the national security state and economy, the Bush administration has consistently acted to sustain Sharon's interests.

If I point in the right direction when I say that the three main actual and unavowed motives of the Bush administration in waging war against Iraq are the interconnected considerations of oil, party politics, and Israel, we must conclude that at one level shabby motives lie behind the awful consequences. The war against Iraq was morally indefensible. Though a partisan himself, Senator Edward Kennedy is right when he says that the war was driven by political considerations. "There was no immediate threat. This was made up in Texas. . . . This whole thing was a fraud." Yes, a fraud, because of unavowable motives, but not merely a fraud, because not all the unavowable motives were arbitrarily partisan. The root really is the party politics of *a democratic (or popular) and radically inegalitarian imperialist state:* the usual entanglement of shabby motives with systemic ones. In other words, the root of both imperialism and party politics is the constant struggle between the parties to deepen privilege or to modify it somewhat, rein it in. Even those who aspire to modify the structure of privilege nonetheless subscribe to the principle of privilege.

The Republicans have shown since the trauma of the New Deal and FDR's four successive election victories that they will do anything to win. In a representative democracy, the party of entrenched privilege is usually more ruthless than its opposition, unless its opposition is invigorated by despair and the prospect of relief. Privilege by its very nature fears for itself with a tireless and (as it were) neurotically active fear, as if it were genuinely afraid but not entirely unhappy to be so. Apart from substantive commitments, of course, the pure agon of party politics is fierce on both sides; but the ferocity is indissociable from those commitments. The national security state and economy and the attendant imperialism are the property of both parties. The party of opposition is surely not inhospitable to the claims of privilege. But because the party of privilege must struggle hard to maintain privilege as unmoderated as possible — or thinks it must struggle hard — it will be especially ruthless in its choice of expedients. It will manipulate racism, religion, and patriotism (among other things) in order to distract attention from the system of privilege. These expedients are usually more than a match for the countercurrent of demotic resentment. That many Republican voters and some officials are sincere in their racism, religion, and patriotism helps the party greatly. But wise partisan heads know where their advantage lies. What is more, these expedients, including religion, tend to increase the hold of imperialism on the people's imagination.

The fair question is whether the United States is more secure as the result of the policies of the Bush administration. The United States had to destroy Al Qaeda bases, whatever the anger felt by Arabs and Muslims before and after the war in Afghanistan. Any American political leader would have had to retaliate. But what policies should have come after? More air-flight security features have been put in place with, I suppose, a deterrent effect. Other policies, however, have moved from the question of greater security to purposes that are not motivated by concern for American security. Though not discontinuous with the behavior of earlier administrations, the behavior of this administration seems more intent on initiating measures that are at a greater distance from their stated purposes than almost any before and, even worse, that also seem to impede those stated purposes. The word "conspiracy" is therefore more readily apt.

I have tried to indicate two things. First, the prosecution of terrorists and alleged terrorists has done nothing to increase safety while assaulting constitutional protections. Second, the war against Iraq has also done nothing to increase safety. It was launched for noncredible and discreditable reasons that cannot be avowed, and has only intensified the anger of Arabs and Muslims, while sustaining the career of an imperialism that is not only against the spirit of the Constitution but threatens it with the ruinous fate that imperialism has always tended to inflict on constitutional government. We can only dream of a saving moderation.

Addendum, June 2004 and After

I drafted this essay in December 2003, and made some revisions and a few additions thereafter. No change was made, however, in the basic argument about the motives behind the criminal prosecution of terrorists and alleged terrorists and the war against Iraq. My argument was prepared before such accounts as those given by Paul O'Neill (Susskind, 2004) and Richard Clarke (2004); the staff reports of the 9/11 Commission, chaired by Thomas Kean; and the Senate Select Intelligence Committee report. In any case, these analyses mention motives without analyzing them. A careful reading of the *New York Times* goes a long way, even though the newspaper gives a prominent place to its distortions, and when it speaks the truth, often does so in whispers — and then later atones for its candor with a spurious even-handedness.

The reelection of Bush shows how much the majority will let a president get away with. Ariel Sharon is no longer in charge, but his policies remain; they were never his alone.

This essay is a continuation of "Undermining the Constitution." I want to thank David Bromwich, Ilene Cohen, Robert G. Gilpin, Bonnie Honig, Leo Marx, Kim Townsend, Jack Turner, and James P. Young for their extensive comments.

Addendum, February 2006

I think that in many respects the activities of the Bush administration have in fact been meant not to combat jihadist terrorism, but to begin a process. I call it provisionally a process of rehearsal. The systematic mismatch between the stated purposes handed out by the Bush administration and the means and methods used supposedly to attain them means that the stated purposes are often not the real long-term motives, which are not entirely easy to understand.

Long-term motives define the idea of rehearsal. What makes it hard to think about long-term Bush administration motives and activities is that, if I may put it this way, the leading figures with their associates and advisers are already in a new world, while the great majority of the American people are in a separate world, left behind and conceptually unfamiliar with the new world that their leaders are trying to build but not explain. I don't think that the leading figures are merely old-fashioned imperialists in the American grain; rather I think that there has been within the Bush administration leadership something like a mutation, some discontinuity with the past imperialist record. Is the Bush administration then aberrant, or does it, as it hopes, initiate a permanent reorientation of U.S. policy toward the world? I am not sure. The role of accident, of the unexpected, can be sizeable. But I work with the assumption that the Bush administration is something partly new in American history.

Great power magnifies its opponents in order to justify using its strength. It not only needs enemies, it even creates them as it pleases, almost arbitrarily. It sees opportunity, where most of us are coached to see only danger. As the March 2005 document signed by Donald Rumsfeld, "The National Defense Strategy of the United States of America," makes clear, every danger is also an opportunity, and every danger is also a challenge. This document is the only main official and publicly released government statement that takes us anywhere near as close to the mentality of the Bush administration as the pre-9/11 documents of Richard Perle and his associates. Intrinsic to this mentality is an almost total disregard of the moral cost of violent means to achieve political ends. The administration acts politically as a paranoid person would, and induces paranoid responses in others.

The document from Rumsfeld's office wants "global freedom of action," an amazing aspiration, if you think about it for a minute. This is one version of pure politics, purposive without a purpose, a politics of action and augmentation for its own sake, a politics of strength, of display, of "shock and awe," of untiring expansion, of hubristic giantism. Military technologies and other sources of strength are ceaselessly promoted, refined, used, and exploited in order to show what the United States is capable of and prepare the way for further exploits. There is a fatal lack of moderation when every great danger is felt as an even greater opportunity.

The occupation of Iraq is only the beginning of what Seymour M. Hersh has called "the coming wars," whether in Syria, Iran, or elsewhere. From a long-term perspective, Iraq is a rehearsal for other wars. Bush has said more than once that there will be no foreseeable end of the war on terrorism, as if it were a war on many fronts in an indefinite series. The war on Iraq is thus the first installment of permanent war, the first stage in placing the United States on a permanent war footing. It helps begin the conversion of a constitutional republic into a "regime" — as the neoconservatives love to say — permanently disposed to find occasions for doing violent acts or making war anywhere and in any circumstances. A steady supply of dangers, even an occasional attack on U.S. soil, favors the growing sense of American global power and universal influence. Who shall be the next enemy: China or Russia? Will the struggles for resources, especially oil and natural gas, be the dominant issue? Will there be an environmental catastrophe that changes everything? Will there be a "dirty bomb" exploded on American soil? Once the structures, sentiments, and precedents are in place, uses will be found or invented for them. The whole process will be kept going.

The long-term motives behind the erosion of civil liberties and the practice of torture and degradation may now come into sight. A society in which civil liberties are abridged accustoms its people to put an inflated sense of safety or security above all other considerations, and to do so on a regular basis. The aim is to induce by repeated violation a forgetfulness of the moral reasons for guaranteeing to all persons the rights of due process and other rights like privacy. The state of emergency becomes the normal condition. In a perpetual state of emergency, traditional kinds of restraints on, and inhibitions of, the state are weakened or dissolved; this is a steady tendency of the Bush administration in many spheres of policy. The citizen's reflexes are altered: government becomes much less an object of suspicion and much more an object of deference. The citizen is transformed into a subject.

What is the long-term motive behind torture and degradation of prisoners of war? It is to coarsen the nature of U.S. armed services and by indirect influence the whole American population. Such coarsening runs in parallel to a growing acceptance by people of diminished rights. The effect of such coarsening is, with an unusual intensity, to disregard the interests of others and thus be possessed by the militant faith that the only legitimate interests are those of one's own side.

I see, then, a deliberate pattern in the activities of the Bush administration; it is an early rehearsal for making over the United States into a new kind of empire, literally global in its reach and influence, and also dominating space.

References

Bobbio, Norberto, and Maurizio Viroli. *The Idea of the Republic.* Trans. Allan Cameron. Cambridge, UK: Polity Press, 2003.

Brzezinski, Zbigniew. "The Wrong Way to Sell Democracy to the Arab World." *New York Times,* 8 March 2004: A19.

Cheney, Dick. "Remarks by the Vice President at a Luncheon for Congressional Candidate Sam Graves." April 23, 2004 (www.whitehouse.gov).

Clarke, Richard A. *Against All Enemies.* New York: Free Press, 2004.

Cole, David. "Uncle Sam Is Watching You." *New York Review of Books* 51 (November 18, 2004): 56–60.

Dworkin, Ronald. "Terror and the Attack on Civil Liberties." *New York Review of Books* 50 (6 Nov. 2003): 37–41.

Elon, Amos. "A Very Special Relationship." *New York Review of Books* 51 (15 Jan. 2004): 15–19.

Emerson, Ralph Waldo. "Circles." *Emerson: Essays and Lectures.* New York: Library of America, 1983 [1841].

Filkins, Dexter. "Tough New Tactics by U.S. Tighten Grip on Iraq Towns." *New York Times,* 7 Dec. 2003: A1, A18.

Friedman, Thomas L. "A Rude Awakening." *New York Times,* 5 Feb. 2004: A31.

Frum, David, and Richard Perle. *The End to Evil: How to Win the War on Terror.* New York: Random House, 2003.

Gelb, Leslie. "The Three State Solution." *New York Times,* 25 Nov. 2003: A27.

Greenhouse, Linda. "Justices Allow Silence on 9/11 Detainees." *New York Times,* 13 Jan. 2004: A1, A23.

Hamill, Pete. *New York Daily News,* 6 July 2003.

Jehl, Douglas. "Inspector's Report Says Hussein Expected Guerrilla War." *New York Times,* Oct. 8, 2004: A12.

Johnston, David. "Saddam Hussein Sowed Confusion about Iraq's Arsenal as a Tactic of War." *New York Times,* Oct. 7, 2004: A28.

Kahn, Paul W. "The Paradox of Riskless Warfare." *Philosophy and Public Policy Quarterly* 22 (Summer 2002): 2–8.

Kennedy, Edward, Senator. Interview. 18 Sept. 2003. Speech, 14 Jan. 2004. Reported by CNN. Available online at ⟨www.cnn.com⟩.

Klein, Morton A. "The Speech Prime Minister Ariel Sharon Should Have Made at Herzliya." 2001 ⟨www.njjewishnews.com/122503/commspeech.html⟩.

Lewis, Anthony. "Making Torture Legal." *New York Review of Books* 51 (15 July 2004): 4–8.

Lieven, Anatol. "The Push for War." *London Review of Books* (3 October 2002): 8–11.

Liptak, Adam. "Is the Group Responsible for the Individual's Crime?" Week in Review. *New York Times,* 8 Feb. 2004: 5.

Luban, David. "The War on Terrorism and the End of Human Rights." *Philosophy and Public Policy Quarterly* 22 (Summer 2002): 9–14.

MacFarquhar, Neil. "Arab Leaders Seek to Counter U.S. Plan for Mideast Overhaul." *New York Times,* 4 March 2004: A9.

Montesquieu [Charles Louis de Secondat, Baron de Montesquieu]. *The Spirit of the Laws.* Trans. A. M. Cohler, B. C. Miller, H. S. Stone. Cambridge, UK: Cambridge University Press, 1989 [1748].

National Security Strategy. 2002 ⟨www.whitehouse.gov/nsc/nss.html⟩.

The 9/11 Commission Report. New York: Norton, 2004.

Perle, Richard, et al. "A Clean Break: A New Strategy for Securing the Realm." 8 July 1996 ⟨www.israeleconomy.org/statl.html⟩.

"Project for a New American Century." 1997 ⟨www.newamericancentury.org⟩.

"Rebuilding America's Defenses." September 2000 ⟨www.newamericancentury.org⟩.

Risen, James, and Thom Shanker. "Hussein Enters Post-9/11 Web of U.S. Prisons." *New York Times,* 18 Dec. 2003: A1, A28.

Schmemann, Serge. Review. *New York Times Book Review* (25 Jan. 2004).

Shipler, David K. "Palestinians Should Switch to Soothing Israelis' Valid Fears." *International Herald Tribune,* 8 Jan. 2002 ⟨www.commondreams.org/views02/0108-03.htm⟩.

Shklar, Judith N. "The Liberalism of Fear" (1989). *Political Thought and Political Thinkers.* Ed. Stanley Hoffmann. Chicago: University of Chicago Press, 1998.

Siegman, Henry. "Sharon's Phony War." *New York Review of Books* 50 (8 Dec. 2003): 16–18.

Stockhausen, Karlheinz. Interview with Benedikt Stampa. 16 Sept. 2001. *MusikTexte* 91: 69–77 ⟨www.Stockhausen.org/the_true_story.html⟩.

Susskind, Ron. *The Price of Loyalty.* New York: Simon and Schuster, 2004.

Taruskin, Richard. "Music Dangers and the Case for Control." Arts and Leisure. *New York Times,* 9 Dec. 2001: 1, 36.

Thucydides. *The Peloponnesian War.* Trans. Crawley/Wick. New York: Modern Library, 1982.

Woodward, Bob. *Bush at War.* New York: Simon and Schuster, 2002.

Woolf, Virginia. *The Diary.* Vol. V: 1936–1941. Ed. Anne Olivier Bell. New York: Harcourt Brace Jovanovich, 1984.

5

On Being Watched and Known

The disclosure by the *New York Times* in December 2005 that the National Security Agency has been conducting warrantless wiretaps and surveillance of email in the United States since right after the destruction of the World Trade Center shows how insubstantial the protection of privacy can easily become. The further intensification of surveillance and information gathering, joined to numerous cases of video surveillance by local officials of peaceful political demonstrations, has reached the point where U.S. authorities seem as if they are rehearsing the imposition of a police state. The government's appetite for watching and knowing seems boundless. The worry about total control, which appears at the end of this paper, written in the fall of 2000, is no longer merely anticipatory and hence tactical; it answers to a change in the actual situation. The pity is that increased surveillance dovetails with the increased desire of people to expose themselves on the Internet.

Much of the time, discussion of the subject of privacy is centered in worry over easily recognizable effects on people when their privacy is violated. If a court finds that a right to privacy includes the right of married or unmarried couples to use contraception, the government's prohibition of it has been judged to be a serious harm. If a person's house is entered without a valid warrant, a court will usually find that the government has seriously violated that person's privacy.

These are just two of numerous examples where the stake is protection of privacy against state intrusion that is deemed unacceptable. A person's entitlement to be fenced in against invasion is affirmed. But when government does not honor that entitlement, and no court provides a remedy, citizens may still say that a person has been harmed in his or her vital claims. In any case, some claims are so vital that we call them constitutional rights, not only moral rights, and not merely legal rights. In the abstract, we say that by violating (or trying to violate) constitutional rights, government is treating (or is disposed to treat) people in such a way as to inflict serious disadvantage on them, thus impairing their ability to make major decisions in life freely or to remain unmolested. These are grave harms. People in a democracy need little coaching to say that they have been harmed or injured or violated, though they may need trained lawyers to formulate their claims jurisprudentially. People know that some significant interest of theirs has suffered, even if they do not always reach for the language of rights in which to express their grievance.

Now if people, by some chance, do not complain when their rights appear, in the judgment of the observer, to be violated, or if they consider the matter insignificant, or even think that they deserve to be treated as they have been treated, the spirit of the laws — if I may reify — would admonish them. It would say that when a person is treated in certain ways, even if the harm is not felt as harm or felt at all, that person has nevertheless been harmed. A person is obliged to guard his or her rights by knowing when they are violated, or suspecting that they might have been, even in the absence of a judicial declaration to that effect. Every citizen must be extremely sensitive to actual or threatened or even arguable violations. That is the heart of democratic citizenship.

By guarding one's rights, one is guarding not only one's own vital interests, but by the force of example or precedent, the vital interests of everyone else. In that sense, we are each other's keepers. Every valid assertion that my right has been infringed is simultaneously the same assertion on behalf of everyone else. Basic rights are general possessions. There is a further complication. By guarding one's rights, one is also guarding one's own personhood or human status as well as everyone else's. (Personhood and human status are rough synonyms.) I mean to say that every violation of a basic right, just by being the suppression of a vital claim or interest, is also a failure to respect the personhood of a human being. In being improperly coerced, a person is also being treated with contempt. A person is being treated, say, as if he or she were a child rather than an adult, or were a mere means to an end; or has forfeited all rights because of some offense. These forms of contempt are injuries or insults to persons and should register as an additional harm. Every basic right thus has a double meaning. The spirit of the laws — that is, the spirit of the U.S. Constitution and other comparable charters — reveres personhood, reveres the human status of every individual. Indeed, the substance of specific basic rights, such as free speech and religion, or the prohibition of self-incrimination and double jeopardy as well as, of course, the various rights clustered in the idea of the right of privacy, may be said to derive from an initial idea of personhood. Or if the practice of a given right preceded the articulation of the idea of personhood, then it is this idea that provided the rationale for the right when, for example, the codification we know as the Bill of Rights was framed, and that still provides the deepest reason for it.

But what has recently become clear (yet again) is that even if courts hold, with a putative if disputable correctness, in one or another case, that no basic constitutional right is violated, a person's human status may still be injured. The idea of human status contains more than the imperative that basic rights, as currently interpreted, be respected. It also includes the imperative that no policy, seemingly within the scope of rightful state policy, can have the effect of treating a person as if he or she were a child rather than an adult, or as a mere means to an end; or has altogether forfeited consideration as a human being because of some crime or alleged crime. If a policy has this tendency, but at least appears to violate no basic constitutional right, then it should still be condemned as injurious to human status, even though most people, for the time being, do not perceive the injury to their status, and courts do not yet recognize it. In sum, every violation of a basic constitutional right is an injury to the human status of individuals, but not every injury to human status is, at least initially and in appearance, a violation of a basic constitutional right. Indeed, injury to human status can be inflicted even if no basic constitutional right is violated: it is probable that not every such injury lends itself to formulation as a violated constitutional right. But fundamental moral rights remain even in the absence of constitutional rights.

I mean, then, to hold that the subject of protecting privacy extends to more than the violations, so far judicially acknowledged, of the constitutional rights clustered in it. To be sure, these acknowledged violations and their remedies constitute the leading part of the subject. But I would like to make theoretical room for infringements of privacy that do not apparently violate constitutional rights, or are not yet held to violate them, or that may, properly, never be held to violate them. I believe that some recent technological developments have presented us with a situation in which infringements of privacy injure our personhood, and yet courts allow these infringements to proceed. At the same time, many people do not feel that their right of privacy has been violated and that their human status has therefore been injured through nonrecognition. The technological developments that I have in mind show steady growth in capacities of watching and knowing, such as ubiquitous surveillance cameras in streets, transportation terminals, malls, stores, banks, and so on; and the computer-facilitated accumulation, storage, and retrieval of information on the body, health, habits, and tastes of everyone from infancy onward. Obviously, these are only two of many new capacities.

Intensely aggravated expressions of the capacity to watch and know are two U.S. government programs: Carnivore, which permits the FBI to record all email communications; and yet another program (shared with the U.K.), Echelon, which permits government agencies to monitor various kinds of communications worldwide. I don't pretend to name, much less technically understand, all the devices of watching and knowing that recent technology has contributed, or to be able to anticipate new ones, though I am sure there will be new ones. In this essay I will confine myself to camera surveillance and the accumulation of personal data. The agencies that try to watch and know with ever greater completeness and precision include state bureaucracies and, more commonly, private enterprises. This means that whatever may be true with regard to other rights, privacy is a right that can be infringed by private groups — private groups that war on privacy — and not just by the state. The state, however, by not prohibiting camera surveillance and data accumulation, sanctions it, and thus becomes the ultimate source of formal violations of the right to privacy — to leave aside its own, ever-increasing violations.

I am aware that the activities of watching and knowing, whether undertaken by states or other authorities or by public opinion or particular groups in society, are as old as social life itself. Yet in ubiquitous camera surveillance and in computerized data accumulation, we have a temporary logical culmination of perennial aspirations. We should not be surprised that when techniques are available they will be used; and we should not be surprised that the techniques have become available. The dynamism of modern technology has included, from the beginning, development of techniques of surveillance and knowledge about people because scientists and technicians have never discriminated among contradictory projects: relieving the human condition, controlling human populations, and performing marvels of destruction. Nevertheless, in being the logical culmination, these new devices represent the inception of a qualitatively new social system. What we are dealing with is not a tribal or village society, as once existed, made up of a few hundred or thousand inhabitants who lived their whole lives in one another's sight. Nor are we dealing with a society like the ancient city, where a fairly strict demarcation between private and public life guaranteed at least some private darkness as a refuge against the glare of publicness. Nor, yet again, are we dealing with a society in which tens or scores of millions of strangers lived in the same country and could watch and know one another only on certain terms and in certain ways. This was the situation of civilized life—to leave aside police states—until the closing decade of the twentieth century. Rather, we now find ourselves in a condition in which scores or hundreds of millions of strangers, who live in the same society, can be watched and known not only by the state but also by private enterprises and by a scattering of technical wizards. In such a society, a few strategically placed people can know most of the rest of the population in detail that is at once close and impersonal, and unprecedented in scope. American society has become a confused mixture of public and private violators of some aspects of the basic constitutional right of privacy—or if these aspects are not part of a constitutional right, then they remain part of a moral right that befits persons in a free society.

I maintain that one is being harmed when one is being observed by a surveillance camera or when detailed information about oneself is cumulatively and permanently available to state agencies, businesses, and other groups and individuals. The harm is to one's right of privacy. But the emphasis so far cannot be on actual rights violations, grave assaults on the ability of the great majority to make major decisions in their lives or to remain free of manifest molestation; instead, it must be on injuries to those elements of personhood that may not lend themselves to formulation as constitutional rights, but only as moral rights. The trouble is that in the absence of grave injuries, it is not easy to articulate one's feeling that one is being harmed, and it may not be possible to seek legal redress on constitutional grounds.

Let me initially put the issue this way: one is insulted, and insulted deeply, because one loses all possibility of innocence. Nothing I do under surveillance is innocent when I know that I am under surveillance. Is it worse to know or not to know that I am? Is it worse to be afflicted by inappropriate self-consciousness or to be duped without being aware of it? Then, too, there is no innocent detail in one's life when the anonymously curious can know it. Instead, one is crudely treated as interesting and even as presumptively or potentially guilty, no matter how law-abiding one is. Or, one is treated simply as an ambiguous or pathological specimen to be observed. The power to observe, by itself, induces in the observer the sense that the observed is ambiguous or pathological. One is placed under constant suspicion just by being placed under constant watchfulness and subjected to the implicit interrogation that exists when the accumulated information on oneself is seen as a set of integrated answers that add up to a helpless, an unauthored, autobiography. Such a loss of innocence just from these two sources is so massive that the insult involved constitutes an assault on the personhood or human status of every individual.

The difficulty of talking about the harm involved in being watched and known so continuously is, to repeat, that no palpable hurt is felt. Now, leading an observed and fully recorded life, thanks to the panoptical TV set, can be the condition of life in a tyrannical police-state, as memorably portrayed in Orwell's *1984*. There the aim is to intimidate, inhibit, spread fear and docility, mobilize masses for essentially spectatorial purposes, and, ideally, catch a few offenders and practice on them new experiments in altering the character of even those who have the greatest initial integrity. However, what I am discussing here is not yet the total and pitiless extremism of sadistic domination for its own sake, but rather the condition that has become normal life in, of all unexpected places, constitutional democracy. The very political system that stands for the principle that personhood must be respected turns out to be a system that contributes very effectively to menacing it. A free society has unleashed a set of technologies that help to undermine the condition of spirit that sustains a free society. The paradox is worse than unpleasant—if it is a paradox. May it be that democracy itself is the great instigator of technological advance of every sort just because democracy is (or has become) inescapably consumerist?

I believe that such devices as ubiquitous camera surveillance and computerized detailed information about everyone's life—and there are of course other comparable phenomena and will be more—are forms of so far painless oppression, of barely sensed degradation. This oppression and this degradation, just because they are so far painless to most people and barely sensed, are hard to complain about, even hard to talk about. One runs the risk of being thought dated, out of touch, eccentric, hyperbolic, perhaps paranoid, in merely worrying about such issues. I know that there is a burgeoning literature about these issues. But does this literature register on public opinion with a telling and lasting effect? It is all too easy to be told that if you have done nothing wrong and if you have nothing to hide, you should let being watched and known roll off you like water off a duck's back. Isn't such a sentiment still prevalent?

So let me add some other considerations to what I have already said about the insult, the so far mostly unfelt or unperceived insult, the painless oppression and barely sensed degradation. I admit that these points may not register even on those who are willing to listen. The first consideration is the sheer involuntariness of living under surveillance and having all the details of one's life on deposit and in the hands of the state and other interested groups or individuals. A person is, for the most part, powerless to avoid capture. A retreat into the woods and a life spent without most conveniences can, I suppose, reduce the quantity of being watched and being known. But some of the conveniences are not mere conveniences; the computer, for example, is a marvelous addition to the human repertory. You pay a terrible price if you give it up. Then, too, one tries to respect the privacy of others; but, in return, one's privacy is invaded. One feels a fool to care about privacy too much. If, however, one is sensitive to what is going on, one is aware that one is living on the wrong side of a one-way mirror, yet, as a democratic citizen, would not want to switch positions with the watchers and knowers.

The second consideration is that a person is not, at any given time, fully aware of the extent of the coverage. How much one has been observed and tabulated is rarely apprehended by anyone. Just before, I asked whether it is worse to know or not to know that one is watched and known. Knowing for sure is intimidating, has a "chilling effect." But an intermediate condition exists between knowing and not knowing. I suggest that uncertainty is perhaps worse than knowing for sure that in public one is scrutinized by unknown eyes and that not only the main facts but almost all the facts of one's life are recorded permanently and are forever retrievable. If, to begin with, one is sensitive to invasions of privacy, one tends to a paranoid inflation of one's predicament, but then may receive recurrent confirmation of one's dark suspicions, and then sink deeper into what is not paranoia after all. Such is the logic, when not the precise aim, of the panoptical principle.

The third consideration is the overall inequality or asymmetry that is inherent in the situation. The world is divided between those who watch and know and those who are watched and known. Even without sinister purposes, those who watch and know are able to objectify the rest. Knowing that one is being objectified, one should feel that an attempt has been made to diminish oneself. Before one tries to rise above objectification, one should see it for what it is. Each of us is treated like a lab animal, a creature that excites the curiosity and probably the desire for further techniques and projects in those immersed in the processes of watching and knowing.

This last consideration is the most comprehensive: that the new and ever more numerous techniques of watching and knowing human beings—and they are, with a mean irony, most advanced in constitutional democracies—can lead to a fundamental revision in a person's self-conception. The revision is sharply at odds with the self-conception that a democratic individual, a democratic citizen, should have, and has so far usually had. In a constitutional democracy, in which everyone is guaranteed certain basic individual rights, personal and political, a sense builds up of oneself as precious, as a whole world, as an end in oneself. I have already referred to the idea that rights aim at denying the state the power and authority to treat adults as if they were children or to reduce them to mere means, mere instruments or machines. Part of the built-up sense yields the thought and corresponding sentiment that one owns oneself, which means that one is not owned by the state or by some superior caste or by society as an abstract entity. One is enabled to treat oneself as autonomous, to an important extent and in many respects. Woven into that notion of self-ownership and in the cognate notion of autonomy is that one is inviolable. That means not only that a person should not be invaded by forces that try to use him for purposes not his own, but also that we should think of a person as having boundaries that should not be breached.

The appropriate self-conception of a rights-bearing individual is that one thinks of oneself as not being at the disposal of others. One must freely choose to work with others for common aims, which are preferably restricted and temporary. Only where there are bonds of affection or duties of love or duties to the vulnerable can one be at the disposal of others; but then we would no longer speak of being merely at the disposal of others. I am not supposed to be folded in effortlessly in some plot or plan or strategy of others. I am not supposed to be mobilizable, available either knowingly or unknowingly, for goals that I have no power to help initiate or control. The new techniques of watching and knowing cross my boundaries, and by doing that, they injure the sense of myself as inviolable. Inviolability is an important aspect of human status. I am not inviolable when I am made to blend even more than is now the case into a social mass of individualized targets of attention and scrutiny. I become just one more creature being observed, part of a continuous spectacle consumed by a few. I become an involuntary detail for technicians who live to make over the whole world into one picture.

I become merely permeable. I lose true anonymity and become either painfully known or presumptuously categorized. Invisible powers make me visible against my will. I am involuntarily disclosed (not that I want to live in a closet). I just want to be known by those who have a right to know me. In being known and watched with ever increasing facility, I no longer can say approximately or metaphorically that I own myself. My autonomy, at best precarious or even episodic, is wounded further, my boundaries further effaced. As Robert Frost (in "The Constant Symbol") said about earlier erosions of individuality: "no more invisible means of support, no more invisible motives, no more invisible anything." He was not asking for the ring of Gyges, for the power to be invisible in order to acquire impunity and thereafter commit heinous crimes. No, not at all. How can I think that my human status, part of my dignity as a human being, is respected if I am too often visible, and if some machine knows more about me than I myself know, because it does not forget, but I do? The machine is not like someone who out of fondness for me recalls some flattering detail about me that I had forgotten, or has observed some nice trait of mine that I doubted I had possessed. At the hands of the watchers and knowers I become a child again, but now an unloved foster child, even if not yet abused. I am victimized by a loss of moral rights, even if my constitutional rights are respected. But can constitutional rights really be respected when cognate moral rights are violated? Are constitutional rights safe then?

On the specific matter of being known in accumulated detail that is instantly retrievable, and transferable to who knows how many agencies and groups and for who knows what purposes, two other consequences are worth mentioning. The first is that accumulated detail about people has the effect of defining them and locking them in that definition. The identity of each is established by imputation, and the identity is equated with an exhaustive account. A person is thought to be known through and through, and without appeal, until perhaps that person has to mount a legal or political challenge to that assumption. The second consequence is that a detailed record follows a person through life, growing old with him or her, yet not losing memory as the person does. A person will not be able to start life over again, free of some of time's filthy load. A person cannot run away or hide, unless prepared to abandon everything familiar and find some alien refuge. There is no escape from a recorded identity, no escape from deeds done long ago that, if wrong, were paid for, or were not wrong but somehow technically incorrect or forgivably careless.

There is no doubt that the storage and dissemination by police agencies of lifetime records improve the capacity of these agencies to determine the identity of criminals with greater certainty. Not so long ago, the *New York Times* (March 3, 1999, p. B3) published an account of how a man who was later accused of murdering three people betrayed himself when he was arrested in an unrelated misdemeanor theft case. Detectives had the man, already suspected of murder, unknowingly provide a DNA sample just by drinking from a soda bottle or glass. He was charged with murder on the basis of DNA obtained from his saliva sample.

I am happy that a murderer was caught. But the story of his self-incrimination distresses me. Not only may the spirit of the Fifth Amendment have been violated by the police technique, but the power of other new techniques that seduce an individual into giving himself away is alarming. This is being watched and known in an extended sense. I think that the greater ease of tracking down criminals through new techniques may reach the point where the struggle against crime has tilted so far in favor of the police that the very texture of life in a supposedly free society is radically altered. I hazard to say that if criminals were always caught, especially with their own cooperation, so to speak, we would no longer be living in a free society, a society where the human status is paramount. What would become of the spirit of the Fourth and Fifth Amendments — these precious and, yes, counterintuitive amendments that mean as much to personhood as any other amendments in the Bill of Rights? Such a society is not yet a police-state, but it erects so sharp a division between the innocent and the guilty that the innocent become too grateful that they are not guilty. They become too anxious to stay that way. There must be a blurred middle ground between guilt and innocence, if innocence is not to become too proud and hence censorious, and punitive or vindictive. Democracy is antithetical to moral rigor; the concept of individual human status cannot survive it. Not that there can ever be perfect deterrence: a new thrill is added to breaking the law when policing is armed with increasingly potent devices of watching and knowing. But the perfection of the apparatus signifies the willed diminishment of human beings. We can be sure that authorities in the United States are working to achieve a world where everyone at birth is fingerprinted and made to leave a DNA deposit, not only a world in which every communication is recorded and can be retrieved. What is left of respect for the human status in all this?

Suppose I am told that this insistence of mine on personhood, on the human status, sounds adolescent. Only adolescents, some could say, care so much about their dignity and feel insults and degradations when none are intended and none would strike an adult as insulting or degrading. Adolescents worry about insubstantials because their sense of independence is so fragile and their experience of freedom so brief. Why carry on in a way, as some could say I do, that only encourages the adolescent strain that even grown-ups all too often retain? Even worse, why judge society's arrangements from an adolescent perspective, when an adult perspective should be decisive?

In answer, I would refer to Peter Weir's film *The Truman Show* (1998), a film that is sometimes discussed when new technologies of watching and knowing are the subject, and when their full potentiality to control human beings, allegedly for the sake of happiness, is projected. The horror for Truman Burbank in a hitherto pleasurable life comes when he realizes that his entire life has been shaped for a mass TV audience. He has been continuously watched and known by an audience; for that to be possible, he has been subjected to complete conditioning by a demiurgical film director who employed a cast of actors to help Truman live out his life to the point of married adulthood as if it were a spontaneous life, and in an uncannily attractive setting, or at least in a very photogenic one. When he learns the truth, despite all precautions, he rebels. He rebels against his pleasurable life because it is a lie. He goes from painless oppression and unsuspected degradation to righteous indignation. He rebels for an adolescent principle, instead of settling for a pleasurable life. He rebels not because he has been badly treated but because he has been "treated." He must overthrow authority because it is authority, benign in effect, but inhuman or superhuman in method and both mercenary and power-drunk in ambition. His relationship to the director is an extreme asymmetry.

Truman rejects manipulated adulthood and by acting like an adolescent he becomes an adult for the first time. He insists on his personhood or human status. By physical and psychological courage he escapes his enchanted confinement. The irony is that when he gets to the other side of his confinement, when he is able to leave Plato's cave, he finds himself magically deposited in a bar where an audience has been observing him on the screen, and they greet him now with screams of delight at his escape into genuine adulthood. But what shall we say about the audience? Are they manipulated by their entertainers? And are they adults? Do they have a sense of their human status? Or are they children — forever children — who are so enthralled by watching and knowing that they cannot progress to eruptive adolescence? They are safely preserved in a simulacrum of adulthood. I think that an adult version of a disposition toward adolescent sensitivity must be perpetually available if the mentality of personhood is to be safeguarded. We are not really adults otherwise; we are not even democratic citizens. As Emerson says in his essay "Politics," "Good men must not obey the laws too well."

I have so far been talking about social and cultural tendencies, and I have just isolated a few of them. All go in the direction of enhancing the ability of others to watch us from a certain angle; and to know us so that, above all, we may be known, if not to ourselves. One might say that the result is a world transparent to those who watch and know, and who themselves remain often in secrecy or obscurity. I have talked in a general way, and quite speculatively. You might think that I have talked with a metaphysical vagueness. But the sketch I have offered, if done with serious imperfection, can be done better by others, who can probably provide more than a sketch. All I am sure of is that, the risk of vagueness notwithstanding, the subject of new techniques of watching and knowing is, in part, a philosophical subject. It must be treated philosophically, but of course not only so. The stake is, to say it again, the self-conception that emerges when a society's institutions and practices try to respect personhood. If gradually, but with an apparent inexorability, the spirit of these institutions and practices is undermined by technical advances in watching and knowing — and of course there are many sources of threat to that spirit, not only techniques of watching and knowing — we would have a calamity, even if we were spared other and worse calamities like a police-state or some kind of tyranny or despotism. Insensitive now to painless oppression, however, we may become less sensitive to some future blatant oppression. Whether or not that can happen, there is such a thing as an unfelt or barely sensed calamity, odd as it may seem to speak in this way.

What are the motives in play of the watchers and knowers? Obviously, the new techniques serve a range of practical purposes, increasing efficiency in achieving some of the standing purposes of state agencies and business enterprises. Or at least that is the usual claim. But does the pursuit of efficiency serve as a cover for other motives, without replacing them? "Lust of the eyes" as the First Epistle of St. John (2:16) puts it? Some voyeurism, some prurience, some profound condescension? Or some insatiable curiosity? Or a nearly all-consuming will to knowledge, a form of rationalist aestheticism? A greed for asymmetrical relationships? Or a pursuit of proficiency for the sake of proficiency, animated by a love of overcoming obstacles in the way of attaining ever greater proficiency, with virtuoso proficiency desired because it stands as a symbol of an extraordinary superiority to ordinary humanity?

The questions are largely rhetorical. I think that we would tend to agree that all of these motives are in play. What I ask is that we not assent or stay quiet when others say that all that is involved is the motive of enhanced efficiency. We may not completely understand Heidegger when he says in "The Question Concerning Technology" that the essence of technology is nothing technological. But we must have a glimmer of what he means. Technology, technique, the proliferation of devices—all this is not only problem-solving. It is also problem-creating, challenge-creating, and more than that, it represents an attempt to rise above the level of ordinary humanity. It is semiconscious complicity in hubris, an insolence shared among a few, and distantly admired, perhaps masochistically, by most of us.

But these motives to which I just referred, aren't they motives we all have? Aren't we all prurient, curious beyond our business, in love with power and our own proficiency? Yes, certainly. Yet looked at from the outside, the new techniques take on the appearance of obsession. If there were one mind guiding the development of these new technologies, we would call that mind obsessive. Of course, there is no one mind; there is, instead, a historical cultural project in the West, the labor of many minds with the same commitment that is sustained over time. Few of the participants were or are themselves obsessive in any strict sense. But a cultural project of obsession does not need obsessive practitioners. All that is needed are devoted practitioners who supply their increments of expertise, and who also never stop to examine the nature of the project in which they are engaged. In contrast, most of us are not obsessively bent on watching and knowing countless strangers, however similar to some degree our motives are to those of the new watchers and knowers.

Suppose, however, it is said that watching and knowing are not only part of the ingrained equipment of any human being but also the specialty of philosophers and poets and novelists — to leave aside journalists. Is there a qualitative difference between the new technicians and our great and good writers? I would answer that the difference is qualitative even though not total. On the one hand, the philosopher, defined as the contemplator of the scene and spectacle of existence, is consumed by the passion to understand so as not to be taken in, and also to be the one on whom nothing is lost. The philosopher does not want to be duped, nor to miss out on what is worthy of attention; the aim is not to feel superior, whatever the philosopher may eventually come to feel, when he observes that most people are much less intensely or comprehensively observant than he is. Similarly, for the novelist who is the creator of characters in patterns of action, and the poet who is the creator of voices and perspectives: they watch and try to know human beings not to feel superior in secret, but rather to disseminate their discoveries and strengthen their readers, as if writers existed, as Keats suggests, in order to be the friends of their readers.

We should probably say that the new watchers and knowers are parodies of the philosopher and novelist and poet rolled into one. And just as the philosopher, novelist, and poet are each God-like in the disposition of intellect, so the ensemble of new techniques, and of techniques irresistibly to come, adds up to a parody of God as omniscient, the parodistic realization of God on earth. In an old theological characterization, God can watch and know everything that has happened and is happening and embrace and keep it to mind in the same instant. It is obvious that no single human mind can begin to approach this state. As Jeffrey Rosen puts it in "The Eroded Self," "Even the most sophisticated surveillance technology can't begin to absorb, analyze and understand the sheer volume of information" that is available instantly, much less, cumulatively (2000, p. 66). Our technological god knows all without knowing that it does so. But it knows enough for its purposes, alas. With regard to a given individual, the watchers and knowers can let nothing go forgotten or undetected; everyone is searched in every religious and secular sense of the word; all the particulars for the day of judgment are assembled. And the state is the god of lesser gods as well as master of us all. It aspires to become a combination of the unmoved mover and the unmoved unmover.

I have already said that if oppression is not felt as pain, and degradation is not felt at all, the human status of individuals can be seriously assaulted without protest. But suppose that somehow a persuasive public case could be made to convince people that apart from any abuse they feel as abuse, especially as abuse of a guaranteed right already declared, their personhood could still be impaired. There is at least one serious obstacle that remains. I refer to an obvious fact, which is that almost all of us, some of the time or with some part of ourselves, welcome being watched and known by people whom we do not reciprocally watch or know. There may be a loss of appetite in society for remaining private and a consequent unconcern with the new techniques, and techniques still to come. There may be an ebbing appetite for having secrets or even confidentiality, for being invisible or anonymous, for being innocent or hidden. It is as if almost everyone, if only in some moods or phases of life, has an increased desire for exposure and confession to strangers, whether casually met or heaped together in some kind of mass audience. It is as if everyone says to himself or herself, "I don't want knowledge about myself confined merely to those I know and trust. I don't exist unless I'm being watched and unless I'm known in detail by invisible or unnameable or unaccountable forces. They make me feel important; they add bulk or ballast to my ego; they give me a more intense sense of being alive or being me."

What is involved here? I suggest four elements. First, innate human sociality; second, democratic gregariousness; third, democratic exhibitionism; and last, democratic theatricality. I take up these points in order.

The aspect of innate human sociality that is relevant to our discussion is brought out when we answer the question, Who is the beneficiary of the right of privacy? The judicial answer is every individual person, and by extension, relationships that rights-bearing individuals freely form, such as couples, families, friendships, and various voluntary associations. This means that a person wants to be protected in the right of privacy, as we have been discussing it, not for the sake of one's uninvaded solitude but, instead, for the sake of being in mutually self-chosen company. But that means, in turn, that one defines one's mode of life as living in the attention of others. I believe that this is the way in which most people envisage the right of privacy—to leave aside the Fourth and Fifth Amendments of suspects and defendants. In the public mind, therefore, the case for the benefits of a protected right of privacy is less a case for the inviolability, invisibility, or anonymity of the individual than it is a case for intimacy and selectivity of company. The latter case is felt to rest not so much on the integrity or precious mystery of anyone's personality or selfhood as on the right to disclose oneself only to individuals one has chosen, and to set the terms on which one will be known and by whom. Such a right can of course be self-limited by a person's secrecy, hypocrisy, or abandonments. The upshot is that almost all of us want to be watched and known. The ideal though perhaps too flattering assumption of those who framed the right of privacy is that we want to be watched and known only appropriately. In contrast, it is only in an infrequent moment that we respond sympathetically to Rousseau's notion that our degeneration begins when we are seduced away from solitude. (Perhaps a few more such moments would be healthy for the maintenance of the right of privacy.)

The unit of privacy in practice, as it is often conceptualized, is thus not the individual but the couple, first of all, and then the family; the domain of the right of privacy is the sphere of intimacy, especially, and then the sphere of voluntary associations, which are commonly felt to matter much less. But once we acknowledge this background assumption, we then have to make another acknowledgment, namely, that most people would rather be watched and known by anonymous and invisible forces than remain unwatched and unknown altogether, if they had to choose. Because most people cannot live to themselves, their resistance to being watched and known by such forces is not likely to be strong in the absence of some specific abuse of a right or harm to some other important interest. Given our innate sociality, just barely and only occasionally held in check, the idea of personhood or human status must appear vaporous when stated abstractly and becomes real only in the face of abuse and violation. Of course, some people have a strong wish to draw the line and remain watched and known only by those they choose. But even they, if they have no taste for solitude, may find an embarrassed pleasure in being watched and known nonselectively and will surely find little trouble in putting up with unfelt or painless invasions of privacy for the sake of the immense advantages of the new techniques of communication, information, and entertainment.

The second element that facilitates acceptance of being watched and known by invisible and anonymous forces is democratic gregariousness. I say *democratic* gregariousness because I think that democratic culture encourages easy contact with strangers and not only with, say, neighbors or even fellow citizens. Exchanges of intimate details with perfect strangers, casually and even anonymously, is an everyday occurrence, and not just with travelers. Such quick, easy, and rarely remembered intimacy, which almost every democratic person engages in, has undeniable charm. Perhaps it has more than charm: it is a sign of immediate acceptance of another human being on experientially equal terms. Lines of class, ethnicity, color, and religion are crossed with such frequency and rapidity that they grow fainter and, in the long run, somewhat less important. Greater tolerance ensues. (The line or lines of gender may still be harder to cross in this respect.) Furthermore, such exposure to strangers, when they willingly receive and even return it, manifests a democratic trust in others, just as a conditioned reserve may indicate a fearful guardedness.

One complaint about gregariousness is that another line is crossed that should be respected more often. Democratic culture encourages people to act in public settings as if they were in the privacy of their homes. A certain slovenliness characterizes conduct in theaters, restaurants, and public facilities of various sorts. (I do not, of course, refer to places where crowds gather, such as amusement parks, beaches, sports stadiums, where people think they are supposed to respond to the offered activity or spectacle with a maximum of collectivized individual display.) People act as if it does not matter that they are being watched and their unaesthetic details known as they relax entirely into private personae. People in small groups — not people who are alone — behave as if others around them exist minimally or abstractly. These people either are begging for attention or are unaware that the strangers, in whose midst they find themselves, are as real as themselves. They privatize public spaces. In this privatization lies an obliviousness of the very idea of publicness and of the idea, also, that others are strangers. As strangers, they should retain some aura, some distance, some sense that they have a moral right to fences and boundaries against invasion by gross indecorum. But what if the strangers do not mind? What matters to my argument is that when so many of us behave in this fashion — when manners are deemed odious because they are experienced not only as affectation but as impediments to doing what one wants and being as one happens to want to be — then an aversion to invading and being invaded by others who have no relationship of intimacy or association to oneself is greatly weakened. The slovenly side of gregariousness makes it harder to defend the right of privacy in the absence of abuse and violation.

The third element is democratic exhibitionism, a tendency that is often remarked and talked about these days. I have nothing to add, except to say that a phenomenology of this sort of exhibitionism is needed and probably not as easy to produce as is sometimes thought. What shall we make of the delight that some people take in displaying their secrets as well as their obvious oddness on talk shows? For our purposes, one point to make is that when the worst is disclosed to an audience of millions, what room is left for privacy, what need for it? I admire the kind of courage these participants possess. But if they volunteer their secrets and ask to be watched and known, to be discussed and even envied, as they go about baring themselves, as they go about converting themselves with a quiet desperation or deliberation into freaks, the disquiet occasioned by such concerns as ubiquitous camera surveillance and the storage and retrieval of accumulated detail about everyone seem almost lightweight phenomena in comparison. What really matters is the motive for such displays.

To call the participants exhibitionists gives them a pejorative name without explaining why they act as they do. I do not mean that a single explanation covers all the participants, or even one of them. Surely, a desire for celebrity on any terms and no matter how fleeting is commonly present. Is it possible to say more about what culturally drives them? Is this kind of exhibitionism only an exaggerated form of gregariousness, or something mostly discontinuous? In either case, it seems to go well with democratic culture at its most demotic. Is there a necessary linkage between democracy — in its demotic, not yet democratically enhanced nature — and shamelessness? In *Reflections on the Revolution in France*, Edmund Burke says that a perfect democracy is the most shameless thing in the world. Let us say, instead, that an unperfected democracy is just about as shameless as we could want. By unperfected democracy I mean a democratic culture that is painfully struggling to give birth to itself in a hitherto authoritarian and hierarchical society, or an established democratic culture that always holds within itself atavisms and anomalies, or just plain forgetfulness of or indifference to its own best potentialities. Talk shows grow out of democratic culture, but where the culture is still struggling to rise, not above itself but into itself. The danger of the demotic, which is only proto- or pseudo-democratic, and which is vividly illustrated by talk shows, is that it injures the human status — not in the usual sense that the participants in talk shows are undignified, but in the root sense that if their behavior were the best that people were capable of, the idea of the equal human status of every individual could not have arisen, and with it the theory of rights, including the right of privacy. Personhood is attributed to every human being, apart from all admirable or only meritorious conduct; but if the great majority of human beings had never shown traces of some minimal merit, how could the idea of equal human status ever have emerged? If all that democracy ever was or could be was demotic, how could it have inspired and continue to inspire such devotion? If the new techniques of watching and knowing owe some part of their tremendous development to the spirit of democracy, must not the distinction between the demotic and democratic be insisted on? Must we not raise an objection when the demotic asserts itself so vigorously, and consequently throws its weight behind the assaults on the fundamental right of privacy that we are discussing? When talk shows abound, reinforced by so-called reality TV and comparable phenomena on the Internet, the difficulty of objecting to being watched and known by invisible and anonymous forces on the grounds of personhood or human status becomes greater.

A fourth element that may help to account for the ebbing of an appetite or taste for privacy is democratic theatricality. There may be continuity between theatricality and exhibitionism as there is between exhibitionism and gregariousness. Now, if democracy intensifies innate human sociability in the direction of gregariousness and exhibitionism throughout an entire society rather than confining them to particular classes, it also introduces its own kind of theatricality. Common to all elements that I have mentioned is a dislike of too much privacy, understood as either solitude or company that is chosen and selective. We might say that in all these elements is a craving for audiences of one sort or another, audiences that are larger and grander than oneself or oneself together with a few others. But I find in theatricality a disposition to which I am, consistently or not, quite sympathetic. In an authoritarian and hierarchical society, a person plays one's role as a member of a class or caste; in a democracy, one plays oneself as an individual personality, converts oneself into a style or role. This latter is the democratic sort of theatricality. (Peter Weir's Truman played himself without knowing it.)

But what does it mean to say that one plays oneself? Democracy is supposedly committed to being oneself in naturalness and spontaneity. That may be true in some parts of life, especially the intimate ones, but I would not exaggerate the presence of either spontaneity or naturalness in intimacy, either. Be that as it may, the sense I infer is that most people think that only by effort is one able to appear as one's real self because one's real self can only be one's best self. To be real to oneself one must be real to others. One can be real to others only if one puts on a performance, only if one performs oneself. This is not hypocrisy; it is not an artifice of feigning. It is too exuberant for that. One is oneself when one gives as it were a theatrical imitation of oneself. One tries to have moments when one conducts oneself as if one were presenting oneself on a special occasion. Much of everyday life is otherwise too routinized or fragmentary to call the self out of the person. This mentality is not mere narcissism, but a craving for the aestheticized reality of one's self. Even the examples of gregariousness and exhibitionism that I gave partake perhaps of the sentiment of theatricality; namely, unless one sometimes imagines oneself at the center of the attention of others, innumerable and unknown others, one would be obscure to oneself, not just to others. But if I am near a truth, then we can see that being watched and known by invisible and anonymous forces, in the absence of abuse or molestation, can be thought to be very serious with only great difficulty. The prevalent feeling in a democracy is that each of us exists as a self to be watched and known, almost as much as possible. Being watched and known is democratic discipline and the preliminary to making oneself worthy of attention.

Paul Romer, the producer who developed the *Big Brother* reality TV program, compared the European and American contestants. He is reported as saying, "In the American house, our contestants never forget they're on camera. . . . In Europe they stopped thinking of the camera very quickly." How to account for what the *Times*'s reporter Bill Carter calls the "extreme media awareness of the United States contestants"? Another producer had the answer: Americans "are all trying to produce themselves" (*New York Times*, Sept. 4, 2000, pp. E1, 9). Why make a fuss, then, about being watched and known by the practitioners of the new techniques, unless and until some substantial, not metaphysical, menace presents itself? I've tried to give the answer to that question throughout this essay.

I am left with the thought that a fallback position is needed. If you think with me that personhood or human status is damaged by the simple fact that a propitiously situated few place us under camera surveillance (not to mention other kinds of surveillance), and acquire and store countless details on each of us without our permission or even knowledge, then we must be prepared to think tactically. We must sketch an argument in whose truth we believe but that does not rely on the idea of personhood or human status in the absence of felt oppression or abuse. The postulate would be that the powers of surveillance and accumulated information, and exemplified not just by camera surveillance and databases, will inevitably be used to oppress whole populations and violate their rights, and thus deny their human status. The tactical argument would seek to present a comprehensive picture of what these new powers have so far achieved, and then project them. The underlying thought is that every power is eventually abused, and if crises do not favor power's use, pretexts will be found. I offer a version of the slippery-slope argument. The *terminus ad quem* is totalist tyranny. But there are intermediate steps between what we have now and the worst possible outcome. The trouble is that democracy, in the opinion of Tocqueville, Mill, and others, even before the technological enhancement of the powers of surveillance and information, tends to a condition that Tocqueville calls democratic despotism, which is not a cruel and grinding despotism, but rather a fairly pleasurable one. Tocqueville says,

> It would seem that if despotism were to be established among the democratic nations of our days, it might assume a different character; it would be more extensive and more mild; it would degrade men without tormenting them. . . . Above this race of men stands an immense and tutelary power, which takes upon itself alone to secure their gratifications and to watch over their fate. . . . For their happiness such a government willingly labors, but it chooses to be the sole agent and the only arbiter of that happiness. . . . The principle of equality has prepared men for these things. (1954, II, Bk. 4, ch. 6, pp. 335–337)

Aspects of the welfare state already show more than traces of such a despotism. To be sure, the subject is worried about, and not just by people whose only concern is not to be taxed as much as they are. We all have experiences of being smothered in a bureaucratic blanket. Democratic despotism is brought closer in time to us in Roderick Seidenberg's remarkably prescient book, *Post-Historic Man* (1954 [1950]). It is not, however, the worst condition. In an increasingly crowded world, we could imagine what D. H. Lawrence calls a "soft hell," a strict regimentation that hems everyone in and rations goods and feelings carefully. The soft hell is conveyed best by Eugene Zamiatin's futurist novel, *We* (1959 [1924]), or in an even softer way by Aldous Huxley's *Brave New World* (1953 [1932]). At the end of the journey, however, lies total domination, undisguisedly tyrannical, if not necessarily bent on totalitarian exterminationism.

The powers for total domination are insidiously being heaped up, not with total domination as a conscious purpose but as an expansive, incrementally adjusted, and not fully intended or admitted purpose. But a trauma can make the means of control irreversibly tyrannical. In fact, what exists potentially for an entire population is already actual for quite a number of types of people: naturalized citizens, immigrants (legal and illegal), suspects, and prisoners. Frequently, they are subjected to abuse that violates their personhood with judicial acquiescence, and we are tempted to say that they are being experimented on so that authorities may learn how to dominate a whole population in the future. We are entitled to make much of the fact that officials in a constitutional democracy can be so alienated from the spirit of the laws as to treat any person with such calculated (more calculated than impulsive) disregard of the human status. What does such disregard, even though selective, indicate about the authenticity of the political system? How can a supposedly authentic constitutional democracy contain pockets of tyranny or despotism, not to mention the atrocities it commits abroad? In any case, we cannot prophesy; we can only have our dreads. But, to repeat, the human record is clear on one thing: every power or capacity is eventually abused. The tactical truth is that present dangers are pregnant with future disasters. The tactical truth is the most important truth. We may not be heard when we say that the present situation is in itself, without further technological change, a grave assault on the human status, even though violations of an extended right of privacy have not yet been declared or even felt. But we can be heard if we make much of the potentiality that already exists for general and unmistakable oppression.

References

Huxley, Aldous. *Brave New World.* New York: Bantam, 1953 [1932].

Rosen, Jeffrey. "The Eroded Self." *New York Times Magazine,* April 30, 2000, pp. 46ff.

Seidenberg, Roderick. *Post-Historic Man.* Boston: Beacon, 1954 [1950].

Tocqueville, Alexis. *Democracy in America* (1835, 1840). Vol. 2: Bk. 4. ch. 6. Trans. Reeve/Bowen. New York: Vintage, 1954.

Zamiatin, Eugene. *We.* New York: Dutton, 1959 [1924].

PART **II**

Politics, Aesthetics, and Morality

6

Aestheticism and Morality: Their Cooperation and Hostility

It is only through the duality of the 'masculine' and the 'feminine' that the 'human' finds full realization. — *Pope John Paul II*[1]

See the power of national emblems. Some stars, lilies, leopards, a crescent, a lion, an eagle, or other figure, which came into credit, God knows how, on an old rag of bunting, blowing in the wind, on a fort, at the ends of the earth, shall make the blood tingle under the rudest or the most conventional exterior. The people fancy they hate poetry, and they are all poets and mystics! — *Ralph Waldo Emerson*[2]

This essay grows out of a thought I have recurrently had, which is that human conduct often exhibits a stronger preference for many aspirations and attainments than for morality. People have always behaved as if morality had no relevance to them when they did certain things and pursued certain aims. Naturally I do not have in mind the obvious and overwhelming truth that

Author's Note: I thank the following individuals for their help in thinking about the issues raised in this article: Jane Bennett, David Bromwich, Amy Gutmann, Casey Haskins, Alexander Nehamas, Tracy Strong, Roy Tsao, and Stephen White. An earlier version of this essay was presented at the 1995 meeting of the American Political Science Association.

people are deliberately, unthinkingly, or impulsively immoral because of self-interest, selfishness, or viciousness. I mean, rather, that we are all caught up in, and carried away by, enterprises and undertakings that involve us in immorality in an apparently idealistic way. Indeed, one is tempted to say that we are involved in an apparently innocent way. The innocence may show itself in unconsciousness of immorality or in a rationalization that denies immorality or makes it marginal or that expressly asserts that there are considerations of greater importance than morality. But whether there is unconsciousness or rationalization — and both come in several varieties — people and thinkers constantly demonstrate that they prefer, that they love, quite a number of ideal aims more than they love morality. They tacitly demonstrate an, as it were, innocent preference for, or love of, certain things despite the high, sometimes infinitely high, moral cost, or they expressly assert the subordination or irrelevance of morality. (An incidental recent reminder of this latter theoretical preference is the communitarian critique of the Kantian-Rawlsian commitment to the priority of the right to the good.)

My particular concern in this essay is the power of unaware and unrationalized aestheticism to move people to act immorally with an apparent innocence, although I also refer to a few of those theorists who rationalize the subordination or erasure of morality and do so on ostensibly *nonaesthetic* grounds. Later, I also take up specimens of what I call deliberate philosophical aestheticism, where the aesthetic relation to morality is more or less frankly contemplated and where morality does not always come out on top. The hostility of conscious and unconscious aestheticism to morality often is, in sum, great. It also is possible, however, that a more deliberate aestheticism in one form or another may cooperate with morality or may be its good friend. The picture is undeniably complex.

Let me say at the start that I do not in this essay pay attention to the great question of the direct influence of art (in its content, form, or style) on people's moral character. I presume to emphasize anxieties about beauty (and sublimity) other than those expressed by, say, Plato, Rousseau, or Tolstoy when they couple immorality and much art.

At this point, I want to mention some of the ideals that are, with a seeming innocence, pursued at high moral cost. Are these ideals perhaps also aesthetic but unknowingly so? The human record contains countless instances of these pursuits. When one has pondered that record from a simple moral point of view, the idealistic or innocent disregard of morality stands out. (I work with the assumption that people in most places and times share the same understanding of basic morality, something along the lines of simple justice practiced reciprocally.) This is not to deny the role of deadly vices. I mean only to make room for motivations that are not wicked, motivations that have their own peculiar purity, in the production of injustice, oppression, and evil. The innocence of immoral conduct depends on its being largely unconsciously immoral. To be sure, a steady stream of theorizing runs parallel to it. There is what I just called rationalization. Only theorists can consciously depart from, or make light of, morality in principle. Indeed, some theorists manage to impart the sense that the supra-moral elevation of one ideal or another is a compulsory matter or an urgent one, a matter of supreme importance that all thinking people must recognize as such.

It is well to observe that when the theoretical rationalization acknowledges that some necessary moral evil is required to achieve a nonmoral ideal, little or no regret is expressed. Doing lesser moral evil to prevent, remedy, or abolish greater moral evil, however, does normally carry regret. But when the end is nonmoral but posited as supreme, the moral cost is made to weigh little. At the same time, I am perfectly ready to grant that moral considerations often are inadmissible in a wide range of genuinely innocent practices and activities. I am not a new-style consequentialist, demanding that a moral reckoning be made of everything one does, that a moral account be given of every minute of life that one spends. All I insist on is observing moral cost and asking why theorists (but not only them) think that it should be paid, and often without regret, even when they are aware of it beforehand.

Let me offer a sampling of some of the main ideals that are ranked higher than morality and mention the theorists who contribute to the rationalization. (The theorist's rationalization may have little or no influence in the world. Ordinary people are subject to their own promptings or are driven to act by simple ideas in the air.) There is, first of all, religion, by which I mean religion in the West. Although supposedly the origin of morality, the God of the Hebrew and Christian scriptures is worshipped for his very favoritism, bloodthirstiness, and caprice, not only in spite of them. And the God made by some Christian theologians exercises sovereign predestination and constructs a place of eternal torture for many of his creatures who are guilty of uneternal crimes. By moral standards God is, in some respects, a practitioner of wickedness. But to call God wicked is considered a heinous sin, yet to hold God to a moral standard is considered impiety. Plato lamented the sanction for wickedness given by the poets' stories of the gods and rewrote the stories. Correspondingly, some Catholic theologians have tried to rewrite scripture to take the wickedness out of God. But some denominations of Protestantism have reveled in that wickedness and done so with the keenest good conscience. The Augustinian strand has been strong, and where it is not literally present, its influence — demythologized or scientized — persists. I think that the most interesting modern theological preference for God above morality is found in Kierkegaard's vindication of Abraham's decision to sacrifice his son on the command of his God. Kierkegaard elaborates what he calls the "teleological suspension of the ethical" in *Fear and Trembling* (1843).[3] On the other hand, the power of religion to inspire countless untheoretical believers to perform acts of war, persecution, and sacrifice of all sorts is abundantly manifest in the human record. The irony is not that the supposedly divine is raised above the merely human but rather that the God of morality is made to do immorality innocently and to sponsor the same in his adherents.

A second example, ubiquitous and as old as human time, is the readiness of people to preserve or advance a distinctive culture or way of life at any moral cost. The stake is as much distinctiveness or the difference from others as it is the quality of life, although distinctiveness and quality tend to get confused or conflated. Doubtless moral arguments are inserted to help defend the idea of making a culture or way of life worth any moral cost, but these arguments are so easily adopted by all sides in a struggle that one knows that the stake is not itself moral. Often it simply goes without saying that a way of life is that which must be preserved or advanced; the imitation of innocence is complete. I suppose the model theoretical text remains, after all, the funeral speech of Pericles, as presented by Thucydides, where imperialism justifies and is justified by the Athenian way of life, and the way of life is held up for a sort of mystical and supra-moral adoration. To be sure, in his speech after the second Spartan invasion of Attica during the time of plague, Pericles utters one of the few morally candid sentences ever spoken by a leader of an imperialist society: "For what you hold is, to speak somewhat plainly, a tyranny; to take it perhaps was wrong, but to let it go is unsafe."[4]

Closely related to the tendency to rank preservation and advancement of a way of life higher than morality is, third, the desire to preserve and advance the definiteness of a distinctive group identity. Although usually inextricably interwoven with a way of life, group identity can exist in the absence of a shared location. A common language, religion, or set of practices may be shared by a physically scattered group of people. But whether concentrated or scattered, a group may see its identity as a cause worth any sacrifice, with the moral cost often going unnoticed. The group is a *we*, a superperson, an incorporated self that is oneself enlarged to include everyone else or that is oneself and everyone else diminished, an imagined conversion of persons into a substance. What matters is not merely that the group lives in a certain way but that it is of one substance, precious, unique, and irreplaceable. The result is a perpetual sense that the substance is always endangered and can be easily lost or contaminated.

Theorists of race and nation specialize in this metaphorization of tribe. But whether theorized or not, whether the moral cost is present to consciousness or not, the preservation of group identity through group pride and xenophobia is a continuous source of immorality in the human record. Within one society, group identity also can be segmented and show itself in caste or class feelings or in pride of membership in one or another cultural group.

Whenever politics is made an end in itself, we find yet another (the fourth) ideal that produces immorality either unconsciously or with a good conscience. A stark theorization is given by Carl Schmitt in *The Concept of the Political* (1932). He would have us think that there is no propriety in asking the questions "Why does armed hostility exist?" and "Should it not be stopped, if possible?" Schmitt invests politics (as he defines it) with a natural ontological status; it is one of the fundamental constituent elements of the world. He says,

> The specific political distinction to which political actions and motives can be reduced is that between friend and enemy. . . . The enemy is not merely any competitor or just any partner of a conflict in general. He also is not the private adversary whom one hates. An enemy exists only when, at least potentially, one fighting collectivity of people confronts a similar collectivity.[5]

Neither difference of ways of life nor distinctiveness of group identities need be the provocation or inspiration for conflict. The mere fact that there is more than one armed group is sufficient to justify war. The existence of an armed group not only is tied to war, it exists for the sake of war. Schmitt provides a pure theorization of the abstract agon. I think that he exceeds Machiavelli, Hegel, and Clausewitz in this direction. Theoretically, there are no stakes except for winning or, second best, not losing. Does the human record give evidence of such a proclivity? Of course, the answer depends on how one reads the record. But one has the steady feeling that senseless conflict makes at least this sense: people are attracted to the pointless, the unpurposive, especially when it is extravagant, large scale, or wasteful. The more arbitrary the cause of war, the better. The less one has to defend, the better. One does not hate one's enemies; the antagonism is nothing personal. One does not even necessarily enjoy fighting. Antagonism is simply the way of the world, its pointless point, its unreason for being.

Connected to the abstract agon is, fifth, the ideal of masculinity. Included within this ideal is a passion for adventure, risk, discharge of energy, the exploration of human possibility, or a will to transgress limits or push them further. The ideal of masculinity is an ideal of heroism, virtuosity, or surprising creativity, and criminality looks like an integral part of it. I have here in mind the ideal of masculinity when it is pursued by associated men, by gangs, teams, crews, or some other kind of group. The ideal also can be understood as an expression of the desire to seize rather than to be given, to exploit rather than to conciliate, or to act only when it is difficult. The human record is filled to overflowing with such tendencies. Politics supplies an arena for them, but practically every sector of life is made to supply arenas as well. Pericles, Machiavelli, and Nietzsche are just some of the principal theorists relevant to the codification of masculinity as the project of collaborative and adventurous greatness. As theorists, they are aware of the intrinsic immorality of idealized masculinity, but probably — as with the other ideals I have mentioned so far — ordinary people (of both sexes) who commit themselves to the ideal or who admire or celebrate it do not reckon the moral cost very closely and have no interest in doing so.

Cognate with the ideal of the abstract agon and with the ideal of masculinity is, sixth, the passion to live for symbols, for what Hobbes calls "trifles" in the thirteenth chapter of Leviathan. Hobbes presents three major motives that conduce to invasive and violent conflict: gain, safety, and reputation. It is the third motive that bedevils his political theory, the motive to secure a flourishing symbolic life in which — apart from any material advantage or basic necessity — a group is accorded the prestige, honor, or deference that its members think is their due or that they want even while half-knowing that it is more than anyone's possible due. If Hobbes is the great theorist of the folly of the third motive, then it also has great theoretical advocates, from Pericles and Machiavelli to Hegel and Nietzsche. They all know the moral cost and are willing to see it paid. But when untheoretical persons live their common lives for the sake of symbols, awareness of the moral cost is only faintly present, if present at all.

I wish to add, seventh, that there are kinds of assertive or self-expressive individualism that locate the self's achieved identity in success in the abstract agon, in attaining manhood on masculinist terms, or in securing symbols. Obviously, the games are different when one person, rather than a group, tries to make his way in these endeavors. When an individual prevails, the world calls him great.

The last, as it were, innocent ideal I would mention is radical environmentalism. So far, this is mostly a theoretical movement. Those who are part of it are fully aware that they defend a cause that others find immoral or potentially so. An American poet of the recent past, Robinson Jeffers, proudly called himself an inhumanist precisely for the reason that he put the cause of nature above human ends of any sort.[6] If the present-day theorists of "green rage" are not yet prepared to say that the preservation of, say, the species of elephants or tigers is worth the destruction of human life even in great quantities, then someday they will be. Sacrifice of human ends other than life is called for now. This is no mere vegetarianism but rather a readiness to suspend (to use Kierkegaard's word about Abraham's intended sacrifice of Isaac) morality in favor of nonhuman nature.

Other ideals that are unconsciously or theoretically raised above morality can be suggested. I do not have the whole list. The reason for talking about them in this essay is really to propose that all of these ideals are, to some extent, aesthetic. None is completely aesthetic, but all are partly so. Aesthetic motives help to animate pursuit of ideals that are untheorized but enacted, or theoretically defended, at large moral cost, that are loved more than morality or are so loved that the moral cost does not break into consciousness with any force. If I am right, then the place to begin the discussion of the cooperation and hostility between aestheticism and morality is with the hostility, which is, I believe, the main part of the story. Both unconscious immorality and rationalizations of the (ostensibly nonaesthetic) supra-moral are helped along by unconscious aestheticism. A more conscious aestheticism, on the other hand, may be either more self-limiting and hence less productive of immorality or, by being given its proper name, more easy to denounce and resist. But these last speculations are uncertain.

I say, then, that despite all denials and failures of recognition, some part of the passion for religious faith, for the preservation or expansion of a way of life or a solidary group identity, for politics as an end in itself, for the project of masculinity, for acquiring the pleasures of a symbolic life, for rising in the world as a great individual, or, finally, for saving nature from the predatory verminous human race is aesthetic. All these salient (or potentially salient) features of the human record, theorized or unconsciously enacted, are to be accounted for, in part, by what I shall call aesthetic cravings. These cravings, seeking satisfaction or gratification, help to swell the amount of unconscious or rationalized immorality in the world. (To repeat, I am talking about pursuits that are immoral but not preponderantly egotistical, selfish, or personally vicious, pursuits that involve numbers of people who act idealistically. In the case of extremist and assertive individualism, the will to play one's role to the limit—an aesthetic craving—often is a good deal more important than mere egotism or lack of scruples.) When I maintain that unconscious aestheticism is responsible for a substantial amount of the world's wickedness, am I saying something surprising or something obvious? I cannot tell. But if the claim is obvious, then I still think that it needs repeating and explaining. If it is surprising, then it needs explaining all the more.

For the moment my theme is unconscious (or indeliberate or un-self-aware) aestheticism. Even when the immoral supra-moral is theorized, the ideal, whatever it might be, is not recognized as aesthetic except occasionally by a rare theorist such as Nietzsche or Hegel, and then not continuously. The immoralism of the lattter two is steady, but their characterization of its motivation as aesthetic is not steady.

Let me now leave aside the complexities and subtleties of theorizing the (ostensibly nonaesthetic) supra-moral and concentrate on human promptings that need no theorization to be potent. Later, as I have said, I discuss a few philosophers who *knowingly* give high importance to aesthetic achievement and their dubious relation to the claims of morality.

The human promptings are so intense that I call them cravings. What, then, are aesthetic cravings? A way of approaching this question is to offer this generalization: in its most extreme forms (and they also are among the great sources of immoralism), aestheticism is the effort to get from experience (let me clumsily call it non-art) what persons ordinarily seek and often find in works of art—high, low, or middling. Art should be the site where the most intense aesthetic satisfactions are found. As Frost says, "A story must always release a meaning more readily to those who read than life itself as it goes along ever releases meaning."[7] But for all of us, art (literary or other) is not enough; art is not enough art, not enough of a good thing. We all crave that the world give us and do for us what art gives and does — indeed, that the world be even more fully, more overpoweringly, what art promises to be. The much greater aesthetic urgency is directed to life, not to art. When aesthetic desires are directed not toward art but rather toward social reality, they tend to become cravings. The transaction becomes vastly more serious. If most people do not live for art, then they do live for aesthetic satisfaction and seek it mostly outside of art. But it takes unrelenting exertion in either perception or action to wring aesthetic satisfaction from life "as it goes along." My contention about the fated transfer from art to life (or the bypassing of art altogether) is supported by the symptomatic fact that aestheticians themselves routinely go beyond works of art to include nature as suitable for their philosophy, even when they cannot persuade themselves that nature is God's art or design. And, in his precritical *Observations on the Feeling of the Beautiful and Sublime* (1764), Kant goes beyond both art and nature to encompass almost all human social phenomena by means of his greatly extended aesthetic categories of beauty and sublimity. In so doing, he is simply more explicit than many others, even though he offers little defense of his procedure.

To begin with, we must ask, what is sought in works of art? Many things, of course. In trying to say what is, to begin with, peculiarly aesthetic, philosophers help us to identify essentially aesthetic inclinations. Certain objects satisfy aesthetic inclinations. On the other hand, aesthetic cravings are acute or obsessive versions of aesthetic inclinations. Works of art, in the first instance, are those objects that satisfy aesthetic inclinations or aesthetic attitudes and feelings. Burke, Kant, Hegel, Schopenhauer, Kierkegaard, Emerson, Whitman, Nietzsche, Pater, Santayana, Heidegger, Wallace Stevens, Adorno, and Marcuse, among many others, have tried to say in what the peculiarly aesthetic consists and have done so by asking, among other questions, what attitudes and feelings lead persons to like art and whatever else seems to resemble art. There is no agreement across these writings as to what is (or should be) sought in works of art, but there is a lot of powerful stimulation to further thinking. The obvious initial answer is that people look for beauty. Burke and Kant proceed to distinguish between beauty and sublimity as the two essentially aesthetic qualities in works of art, and Burke makes much of pleasure as the passion served by beauty and of astonishment as the passion served by sublimity. The oddity — perhaps it is an oddity — is that each of them poses the beautiful in opposition to the sublime, as if to say that the essentially aesthetic is made up of two main antithetical aspects. That is a complication to which we eventually will have to attend.

Start with beauty: people want beauty. I add that people not only want it but crave it, they want it not only in art and nature, and they will do wickedness to gratify the craving without quite knowing what they are doing. What is beauty? The *Oxford English Dictionary* (*OED*) nicely says that beauty is what is pleasing to the senses, especially sight, or what charms the moral or intellectual faculties. But aesthetic theory, although it deals with pleasure and pain, does not concern itself with primitive unsocialized senses. Nor does it deal solely with the pure pleasures taken up by Plato in the *Philebus* — among them, the sensory pleasures attached to shapes, odors, and sounds. Rather, aestheticians deal preponderantly with the interplay between the senses and the imagination. Clearly, because aesthetic theory considers verbal works of art, its subject is not purely sensory. Indeed literature is not sensory at all except when staged or read aloud; it is not sensory as are painting, sculpture, architecture, and music. We can aesthetically consider, say, the *Oresteia* without ever having seen it performed. But who could possibly maintain that even the more sensory arts appeal to the primitive unsocialized senses or solely to the cultivated senses? They appeal forcefully to the imagination, to which the senses minister, while the imagination is interlaced with concepts, either tacit or express. The imagination wants to be not only charmed but also thrilled or deeply gratified; it craves. What is imagination? Let us say only that it is the insistence that something beautiful is, that something beautiful exists; or, by contrast, it is the desire that something beautiful should exist, that the attractively possible should be made actual. The same goes for the sublime. (I know I am being arbitrary.)

Dr. Johnson famously says in *Rasselas* (1759, chap. 32) that the pyramids were erected "only in compliance with that hunger of imagination which preys incessantly upon life and must always be appeased by some employment." This great formulation helps us with our question of how we should identify the aesthetic and hence aesthetic cravings. These are cravings that are satisfied only when we are convinced that the world is one way rather than any other, is beautiful rather than not. And if the world is not yet what it should be, then we insist that it must be made to conform to our determination of it. What specifically do we crave when we crave beauty? I offer only a sampling of cravings, and I depend on aestheticians as well as common experience. And if they all are cravings for the pleasure that beauty gives (to use Burke's concept), then the pleasure is not simple or pure, and not easily discussed, because the imagination is deeply implicated. Here is the sampling of cravings, and they all are obvious, present at all levels of intellect and cultivation, and found everywhere:

    A.   a craving for form, shape, shapeliness, definition, or definiteness;
         a craving for coherence or unity;
         a craving for purity or consistency;
         a craving for discernible identity and ease of identification;
         a craving for pattern;
         a craving for clarification or sharp boundaries and stark contrasts;
         a craving for dualism or bipolarity;

    B.   a craving for style, for stylization;
         a craving for decorum, for *comme il faut;*
         a craving for suitability, for "fit";
         a craving for appropriate appearances;

    C.   a craving for striking surfaces, for color or colorfulness;
         a craving for novelty.

To put it summarily, cravings for beauty are cravings for the elements of beauty — for form (A), style (B), and colorfulness (C), wherever these elements are or could be found, singly or in some combination. Even more summarily, we could say that cravings for beauty are finally cravings for a certain sort of meaning or meaningfulness, and at just about any cost in morality (or, we can add, truth). Only meaning or meaningfulness can finally give pleasure to or appease the hunger of imagination, which often is unscrupulous in its quest for appeasement. These cravings are not the only aesthetic ones, and they certainly can be distinguished from all the nonaesthetic needs and passions that artworks and, by extension, nature and, by further extension, human phenomena do or should gratify. At the same time, I must admit that the craving for some of the just-mentioned qualities may be mixed with nonaesthetic desires.

Obviously, I agree with those aestheticians who extend the range of the word *beauty*. Thus the point is that people find beautiful not only the "mere" appearances of persons and creatures, things and scenes; they also find beautiful—no matter what they say—numerous phenomena whose beauty (to the socialized senses) is not only a matter of appearances, of surfaces, but also and mostly a matter of the inference or interpretation that the imagination is disposed to make. Certain cravings frequently can be satisfied only by mental work that processes reality in a manner that often is similar to the dream-work as conceptualized by Freud in *The Interpretation of Dreams* (1900). I believe that many of these cravings are aesthetic, at least in part. The hungry perceptual and mental distortions of ruthless condensation, arbitrary displacement, forced representation, and opportunistic revision figure in both kinds of work, which strain desperately to make the world come out right.

Relatedly, the extended application of the word *beauty* is equivalent to the extended application of the words naming most of the elements of beauty. I hope that when I speak later of appearance, form, or shape in the way I do— and this is a very common way—I am not, by following the example of others, merely punning on these words. That is, I hope that the extended significations show a proper similarity or continuity with the original ones (which are sensory). If, however, the meanings of these terms are only sensory, and the extensions are thought only confused inflations, then aesthetics would be a small field, much smaller than customary and much less interesting to many people. More important, I would be guilty of construing certain cravings as aesthetic that are not aesthetic at all. Following Burke and Kant, I bet, however, that, say, the appearances, forms, and shapes, the pictures and patterns, that the imagination makes up give pleasures that are not discontinuous with the pleasures given by physical appearances (and so on) in art, nature, and society. The imagination is woven into many of the latter pleasures, too. Perhaps we could say, then, that these extended applications of the word *beauty* and of the terms that name its elements are justified because the more sensory referents of this word and these terms are objects of the same kind of desire (or closely so) as the less sensory and the nonsensory—the desire that art and (social and often natural) reality provide those pleasures that come from the conviction that life has meaning, is not chaos; the desire that life be the source of these kinds of pleasure. The sensory and the imaginative satisfactions (wherever found) therefore blend into each other, while each also intensifies the need for the other. The overarching aesthetics is that of meaning. We all are practitioners of it, but too often without knowing it.

This is not to say, of course, that any aspect of social (or natural) reality can be properly discussed as if it were literally an artwork—say, a literary text or a picture, the two kinds of art that are perhaps most relevant in a discussion of the permeation of life by unconscious aestheticism. To be sure, philosophers attribute beauty or sublimity to both art and reality; both are probed for meaning, and both need and receive interpretation. However, each field toward which aestheticism turns in search of satisfaction has its own specificity and therefore requires (to a considerable extent) different technical terms and modes of inquiry. This much is granted by practically every philosophy of aesthetics, no matter how extensive its scope. Nevertheless, whatever rigorous boundary-keepers might claim, people often respond to social (and natural) reality as if it were a text or a picture but loaded with a burden that no actual text (perhaps even of scriptural status) or picture (perhaps even of iconic status) can carry or is designed to carry. The burden is imposed by aesthetic craving.

In any case, we could generalize and say that the most important satisfactions of aesthetic cravings are found in the following certainties of meaningfulness. First, they are found in the conviction that the *appearance* of persons and the appearance (in the extended sense) of social occasions and situations is suitable and is as it should be. The right style exists. Second, they are found in the conviction that one's own *experience* or the experience of one's group has form—the form of a story, pattern, or properly unfolding narrative. Each incident or component is intelligibly connectable to all others, and all of them together compose a whole. Third, they are found in the conviction that one's *identity* or the identity of one's group has a distinctive shape or form (in an extended sense) and that all the traits and qualities fit together and result in a unique or even superior style, or they are found in the conviction that one or others sustain their roles or functions or tasks with style, with virtuosity, or with surplus energy bestowed on perfecting the manner of doing. Fourth, they are found in the conviction that society's rituals and procedures, customs and practices, and institutions and arrangements all are shapely or well formed, and all help to compose *a way of life,* and hence that confusion, disorder, or rapid unpatterned change or brute immediacy has been overcome. (Recall how Socrates' Diotima in Plato's *Symposium,* 210, places well-formed activities, laws, and customs high on the ladder of love of beauty, higher than beautiful bodies and souls.)

All these (interrelated) achievements are sources of (often unacknowledged) beauty (in some sense), and therefore they are sources of satisfaction. A large part of the content of the several ostensibly nonaesthetic ideals that I discussed earlier is therefore, by my account, actually aesthetic. But these achievements do not only please; because they are craved, they provide intense gratification when they are imagined to exist, and often will be defended without mercy;

and when they are thought possible, they often will be pursued without mercy. The passion of the imagination for meaning or meaningfulness must encounter something to assuage it. How to say it? An aesthetic void must be filled or, by contrast, super-abundant energy must find discharge aesthetically.

I now wish to turn to the idea of the sublime, the companion and frequent antithesis of the idea of the beautiful. The *OED* is much less helpful with the sublime than with the beautiful. The dictionary makes reference to things that are high, lofty, or elevated, as the root of the word is thought to indicate. Burke and Kant are often revelatory on the sublime, while other theorists, such as Emerson and Santayana, scarcely bother with the distinction between beauty and sublimity, often using the words interchangeably. I do not pretend to any accuracy, but I suggest that sublimity or the sublime refers to such aspects of artworks, nature, and human social phenomena as the unbounded or boundless; the indefinite, indeterminate, or infinite; the transgressive; the overwhelming or overpowering; excess or extravagance; the massive; the massively ruinous; the oceanic; the abyssal; the overweening or overreaching; the awe-inspiring, wondrous, astonishing, or unexpectedly mysterious; and the uncanny. Not every craving that I said was for beauty and its elements is given an opposite in my sampling of the cravings for the sublime, and not every sublime craving has an obvious opposite in the list of cravings for the beautiful. But I think that there is considerable merit in the Burkean-Kantian typology (dualism). Both philosophers not only do some indispensable sorting and contrasting, they also highlight the contention that the aesthetic field is made up of contradictory cravings and gratifications.

But how could the range of aesthetic objects, conditions, and situations contain opposites? (Obviously, the relevant opposite of beauty here is not ugliness but rather sublimity.) Why see cravings for the beautiful and the sublime (and their various extensions, approximations, and attenuations) and hence their places and sources of gratification as equally essential to the aesthetic field? Burke, for one, finds the question close to unanswerable: "The ideas of the sublime and the beautiful stand on foundations so different that it is hard, I had almost said impossible, to think of reconciling them in the same subject."[8] I fail to see that he ever does succeed in "reconciling them in the same subject." It is possible, however, to suggest that, like the beautiful, the sublime, too, appeals to the imagination. Whatever appeals to the imagination is aesthetic, shall we say? The beautiful and the sublime provide initial and very broad categories to distinguish aesthetic cravings and satisfactions from each other and from other kinds. Both categories then need to be studied for their discriminations: the words *beautiful* and *sublime* do not do by themselves all the work of judgment that we require any more than the words *good* and *bad*, or *good* and *evil*, do all the work of judgment that we require in moral discourse.

If we can manage to accept the idea that aesthetic cravings are for numerous and sometimes contradictory gratifications, then we have to see what would count as nonaesthetic cravings (or motives or desires), whatever the place or source of their gratifications. In works of aesthetic theory, the aesthetic often is contrasted with the merely and directly appetitive; the reflexive and the primitively sensory; the irreducibly necessary; the purely instrumental, utilitarian, or expedient; the unreflectingly habitual; the moral; and the truth-seeking. These are nonaesthetic and often are deemed anti-aesthetic. Whenever the urge or motive is explainable by reference to any of these considerations, aestheticism has been subordinated or replaced. (We should notice, however, that an observer may, consciously or unconsciously, find some aesthetic satisfaction in contemplating the operation of any of them.) I acknowledge that there is no hard and fast way of distinguishing aesthetic considerations (and hence passions and desires) from nonaesthetic ones. But some contrast must be made.

I have tried, then, to indicate what aesthetic cravings are and how these cravings cannot find sufficient gratifications in artworks (and only rarely in nature as given) but inevitably will seek satisfaction in nearly all social phenomena — human relations, conditions, transactions, situations, and formations. The cravings are so intense and aesthetically un-self-aware that, with an apparent innocence, they regularly produce immorality in human life. In turn, the immorality is not perceived, is repressed or attributed to some other cause, or is justified but not on aesthetic grounds. The ideals unconsciously preferred to doing the right thing and avoiding wrong are, at least in part, forms of aesthetic craving, whether for the beautiful or for the sublime (in any of their elements). The ideal may be religious or be invested in the preservation of a way of life or a distinctive group identity, the ideal may locate in politics or in masculinity an end in itself or the highest end or may sanctify the aspiration of a rare individual to eminence and greatness, or the natural environment may be cherished at the expense of human life and interests. In every case, something aesthetic is at work, and passionately so, but is not recognized and hence often morally ruinous in an apparently innocent manner. Gratifications are sought beyond the repertory of artworks or the displays and effects of nature. And perhaps the most blatant case of all is group identity. How could we make sense more fully of phenomena such as xenophobia and racism and of much caste and class feeling — not just in high castes and upper classes — except by reference to aesthetic cravings?

I had better make a distinction at this point. I have two things in mind when

I speak of an unconscious or unrecognized aestheticism. First, people and theorists refuse to see that when they crave and know they crave, say, form, coherence, or dualism, or the indeterminate or the transgressive, they are actually craving something essentially aesthetic (rather than something necessary or expedient). This is my lesser point. The second and larger point is that when people and theorists crave, say, form, coherence, or dualism, or the indeterminate or the transgressive, they often represent the craving as if it were for something else (and would also tend to shun the very word *craving*). They say that they seek truth about God, are trying to follow the mandates of nature (metaphysically interpreted), or are deferring to the mandates of tradition, authority, or an immemorial code. These are the reasons they give themselves when they religiously violate morality, ruthlessly defend a way of life, carry on the project of masculinity rigidly, and so on. They do not want to see that some part of the energy of commitment to their projects comes from aesthetic cravings, cravings for form, coherence, or dualism, or for the indeterminate or the transgressive or some other aspect of beauty or sublimity. Great sincerity may lie behind pursuit of these projects as such for themselves, but the sincerity often is accompanied by aestheticism.

Yet, I do not mean to reduce human conduct or supra-moral theorization to aestheticism. I just wish to highlight one significant component, although I believe that, of all explanatory reductions, the aesthetic one is the least misleading — certainly less misleading than the reduction to economic self-interest or to an aggressive will to power. The human record is not understandable unless we take into account the force of unconscious or indeliberate aestheticism, while the theoretical promotion of supra-moral ideals also sometimes must be seen as (if only driven partly by) unrecognized aesthetic demands. The innocent assault on morality is enormous.

Does the situation improve morally when the aestheticism is self-conscious and deliberate? Or has great wrong resulted from an aestheticism that does not hide from itself and has learned its own nature? Aside from Hitler, as we watch him in newsreels and in the cinematic work of Leni Riefenstahl and also interpret some of his deeds and his final days, the human record seems to indicate that most of the wrong that has originated in aesthetic cravings for the beautiful and the sublime has resulted from indeliberate aestheticism. In its grip, people act immorally, unconsciously, and, as it were, innocently. One reason for the discrepancy in effects between indeliberate and deliberate aestheticism is that the aesthetic motive, when indeliberate, is almost impossible to own up to when the site of its gratification is not art or nature but rather human social phenomena. The motive is embarrassing. For men, it is unmanly; for women, it is insensitive. The motive also is not commonly talked about; the concept of the aesthetic is foreign to the conscious experience of most people. To be sure, there is a fair amount of everyday talk about beauty. But the range is confined to art and nature or to some specific activities — and also, of course, to sexual attraction. Many people would not recognize themselves, however, when confronted by the charge that they are relentless in their search for aesthetic gratification. It would seem impossible, furthermore, to try to disseminate, in a persuasive way, the ubiquity of aesthetic motives or cravings. The doctrine would come across as obscure, confused, or esoteric.

Another reason for surmising that indeliberate aestheticism is a much greater source of wrong than the deliberate kind is that the deliberate kind, just by being deliberate, is typically (but not in Hitler's case) a matter of cultivated attitudes and feelings far more than of cravings. Or, cravings seem to play a considerably lesser role. The properly aesthetic attitudes and feelings require a measure of self-control and might tend to strengthen self-control.

I would now like to say what I mean by aesthetic attitudes and feelings (or aesthetic inclinations), as distinct from aesthetic cravings. What are the properly aesthetic attitudes and feelings? I suppose that the way in which to answer the question is to see the attitudes and feelings that aesthetic theorists hold to be suitable for reception of and response to artworks.

As I have already mentioned, some theorists begin with things and conditions made to be beautiful (or sublime) and therefore worthy of reception. Hence these theorists exclude considerations of necessity or use and also exclude concern with the purpose of furthering morality or truth, and then they ask how a person of good judgment or taste should receive or respond to these objects and things. In short, they try to ascertain the properly aesthetic attitudes and feelings that constitute reception and response. (To repeat: most aestheticians then extend to nature the properly aesthetic attitudes and feelings that they posit as suitable to art, and a few aestheticians extend these attitudes and feelings to social phenomena.) It is worth noting, however, that other aesthetic theorists begin with aesthetic attitudes and feelings, which they define as free of concern with necessity, use, morality, or truth and then search for the objects that are worthy of those attitudes and feelings, knowing from the start, of course, what they will find — the beauty (and sublimity) of art (and nature and perhaps aspects of social life). In the same text, an unsorted mixture of both approaches can be present. Either whatever is deemed beautiful (or sublime) is held to deserve reception and response by means of aesthetic attitudes and feelings, or whatever deserves reception and response by means of aesthetic attitudes and feelings is held to be beautiful (or sublime). We should not worry about the co-presence of these contrasting approaches, whether in the same text or across texts. There might not be a determinate temporal sequence involved; rather, it might be an intuition that is then developed sequentially. Let us just take the field as it is and notice the attitudes and feelings offered, initially or eventually, as appropriately aesthetic.

I would notice some of the more frequently recurrent *attitudes*. Aesthetic attitudes are perception, observation, and contemplation; noticing and watching; staring and looking hard; studying and waiting; taking things in and letting nothing be lost; staying with the thing or condition, dwelling with or near it; caring about it while letting it be; and so on. These attitudes arouse or are aroused by essentially aesthetic *feelings* — appreciation; admiration; sometimes wonder, amazement, or astonishment. While aesthetic cravings are for the meaning that the beauty and sublimity of social phenomena (above all) provide in their form, style, or striking appearances, or in their transgression, aesthetic attitudes and feelings, although attracted to the very same elements or aspects of beauty or sublimity, seek out their most appropriate satisfaction in art and, secondarily, in nature. Ideally, there would be caution in displaying aesthetic attitudes and feelings toward social phenomena. But such caution is sometimes disregarded. And although aesthetic attitudes and feelings are bound up with pleasure, they preclude craving and hence all the moral ruin that ensues when craving does not know itself as aesthetic (or does not know itself as craving). On the other hand, by most accounts, distance and detachment go well with aesthetic attitudes and feelings. Proper aesthetic inclinations involve self-control.

One is possessed by one's cravings and suffers them to instigate one's actions. By contrast, one receives and responds to artworks with the right aesthetic attitudes and feelings when these works are allowed to be external to oneself and to affect oneself on their own terms. There is no desire to make them over. Their appeal to the imagination is not obsessive. Santayana says that the effect of art is to release us from idolatry.[9] Now, artists make art for many reasons. But when the art they make deserves our reception and response, and when we carry to it proper aesthetic attitudes and feelings, we may begin to school ourselves in the mitigation of aesthetic cravings. Art is not a substitute for life, but reception and response to it are a training for living a less crazy life. Kant's statement in *The Critique of Judgment* is very suggestive: "The beautiful prepares us to love disinterestedly something, even nature itself; the sublime prepares us to esteem something highly even in opposition to our own (sensible) interest."[10]

The moral danger is greater when people direct their aestheticism toward human social phenomena, not toward nature (ordinarily) or toward art (no matter how morally or quasi-morally objectionable the content). If possible, we must try, when we engage with social phenomena aesthetically, to bring to them aesthetic attitudes and feelings rather than aesthetic cravings. The beholding, and with it the appreciation or admiration of art, is thus the beginning of a more sane relation to social reality. Indeed, the deliberate aestheticism directed toward artworks is (subject to qualifications) the model for a deliberate aestheticism directed toward human social phenomena and, thus, the reduction of unconscious aestheticism and its offspring, innocent wickedness. Properly received, art teaches us not to expect life to give us, to a much more intense degree, what art (and nature) regularly give blamelessly (more or less), and it trains us to receive life, when we are driven to make intense aesthetic demands on it, as we receive art. Art, when properly received, can teach us that we become wicked when we confuse life with art.

On the one hand, then, art helps to validate aestheticism, and in not satisfying it in the way and to the extent desired, art, so to speak, directs it to social reality. This is art's inevitable culpability. On the other hand, receiving art as it should be received — with appropriate attitudes and feelings — is the best discipline for responding to social reality aesthetically and yet not immorally. Art can correct its own influence; it means to do so. The satisfactions of aesthetic feelings aroused by the right attitudes can encroach on the tyranny of aesthetic cravings. Yet, as I shall try to say, the effort to subdue aesthetic cravings aesthetically is not always successful, and even when it is successful, sometimes it is still morally disquieting.

How, then, does deliberate aestheticism show itself? We can distinguish between deliberate *everyday* aestheticism and deliberate *philosophical* aestheticism. Let us begin with deliberate everyday aestheticism as it is manifested in relation to activities and objects (often the products of craft) that are more or less clearly designated (or understood) as aimed especially at eliciting the aesthetic attitude of observation or contemplation and the aesthetic feeling of appreciation, admiration, or wonder. (I distinguish craft objects from works of art in the conventional sense.) These activities and objects exist to be witnessed or to be used in display and thus earn aesthetic attitudes and remain unmolested except by interpretation; they are self-contained or brought into connection with other activities and objects only on their own terms, and they are (or should be) truly innocent of implication in wrongdoing. They all satisfy the taste for form or style or colorfulness (to recur to our summary terms); they all can be judged as beautiful. Deliberate everyday aestheticism thus shows itself in such ways as appreciation of good clothes, fashion, furnishings, and ornamentation; fondness for shows, sights, diversions, entertainment, parades and processions, and circuses (as in "bread and circuses"); appreciation of ceremonies, rites, and rituals; admiration of what is designed, staged, played, plotted, or composeed; appreciation of the spectacular and theatrical; admiration of constructed objects; appreciation of popular music; admiration of athletic contests; admiration of technique and virtuosity; and so on. Deliberate everyday aestheticism easily extends its attitudes of observation and its feelings of admiration and wonder to natural scenes and effects and to many creatures and plants. (I continue to omit the aestheticism of sex. The deliberate aestheticism I have in mind is nonpossessive and is illustrated by a straight man's admiration of a good-looking man or a gay man's admiration of a good-looking woman.)

I do not wish to be inflexible. I know that aesthetic attitudes or feelings may begin in cravings, which are then restrained and transformed, and that attitudes or feelings sometimes may lapse into cravings, as in the case, say, of sports fanaticism, obsession with fashion, or addiction to entertainment. When we succumb in these ways, we know what is happening — we are held by an aesthetic craving — and we cannot help it. Furthermore, there can be no impermeable barrier between designated aesthetic activities and objects and the rest of social life. Mass politics, for example, constantly is taken in and consumed as advertisement and entertainment, with the result that the demotic erodes the democratic. The tendency to get carried away aesthetically is irrepressible. We are always restlessly seeking to find anywhere in social reality what we expect to be given (perhaps less importantly to the everyday self) by artworks, nature, and designated aesthetic activities and objects.

Is there any deliberate everyday aestheticism that knowingly extends itself to social reality, apart from artworks, nature, and aesthetically designated activities and objects? No, not usually. I have already claimed that any such conscious extension would be deemed too embarrassing or even compromising. Nevertheless, some thinkers have not been frightened out of aestheticism. They articulate a deliberate *philosophical* aestheticism and, at the same time, promise mastery of aesthetic cravings and hence a practice of aesthetic attitudes and feelings that some (but not all) writers claim is morally innocent or innocuous. As we shall see, that promise is imperfectly redeemed; cravings reassert themselves with unwelcome moral results. Or, by contrast, the philosophical aesthete can decide, after serious thought and not in the grip of cravings, that beauty and sublimity (received with the proper attitudes and feelings), even when implicated in immorality, are more important, more commensurate with the human stature, and more conducive to human vitality or happiness than is morality (or truth). We should notice that some deliberate philosophical aesthetes may concentrate on the role of artworks, but most of them take in society or self aesthetically as well. The concern for the meaningfulness that is bestowed by form, shapeliness, style, or stylization is paramount.

Yet deliberate philosophical aestheticism has a distinctive feature. It is not properly seen only or even mainly as the observer's pursuit of pleasure. Something impersonal permeates his aesthetic attitudes and feelings. The integrity of the phenomenon matters for its own sake, apart from any pleasure it may give anyone. The pleasure can be secondary, even incidental.

One group of thinkers holds that a society should be judged by the quality of artworks it produces. An especially noteworthy example is Walt Whitman, who in *Democratic Vistas* (1871) is prepared to find modern democracy a failure if it does not begin to produce its own art, especially literary art. The art must be inspired by democratic sentiment and contribute to strengthening it. Above all, the art must be the flowering of that sentiment. Whitman is noteworthy because he betrays in this work a democratic anxiety in the face of aristocracy. *Democratic Vistas* shows, in some of its parts, a Whitman overcome by distaste for his culture. But his greatest thinking, as in "Song of Myself" and other poems and in his prefaces, is a repudiation of such anxiety and such distaste. The Whitmanian repudiation grows into a new philosophical aestheticism or democratic aestheticism to which I return later. It also is true that admirers of the art of Periclean Athens and Renaissance Italy often demonstrate a deliberate philosophical aestheticism on the surface of their writings or so close to it as to make no difference.

When a moralist looks at most of those who use the profusion of splendid artworks as the highest standard by which to judge a society (but now I exempt Whitman), moral dismay is inevitable. The assumption, formulated or nearly so, is that beauty in the more usual sense — beauty as intrinsic to high art and present definitively and most impressively there — is worth any amount of injustice at home or abroad. Exploitation or imperialism is justified by the art it materially makes possible. Indeed, there is a detected affinity between the energies of art and the energies of imperialism and exploitation. Walter Benjamin's yoking of the "documents" of civilization and barbarism, in the seventh of the "Theses on the Philosophy of History," seems vindicated.[11]

But we also know, of course, that many writers have theorized a deliberate aestheticism that goes well beyond praise of artworks and nature, and beyond praise of aesthetically designated activities and objects, to reach to those aspects of social reality not customarily designated as amenable to aesthetic attitudes and feelings. More precisely, the aim of these writers is either to defend social life when in its actuality it already deserves to elicit aesthetic attitudes and feelings or to advocate that much of social life be made over so that it deserves to elicit such attitudes and feelings. A society's production of artworks is welcomed, but more beauty and sublimity are wanted than artworks (and also designated aesthetic activities and objects) supply.

What are some examples of deliberate philosophical aestheticism extended to society as such? A candid expression of such a sentiment is not often to be expected in postclassical times. When, therefore, we read Burke in some of his more radical moments in the *Reflections on the Revolution in France* (1790), we must be all the more appreciative. Earlier, in *A Philosophical Enquiry into the Origin of Our Ideas of the Sublime and the Beautiful* (1757), this great aesthetician and aesthete tries to link various passions with the two aesthetic effects and, in the course of so doing, submits many social phenomena to aesthetic consideration.[12] But in *A Philosophical Enquiry*, he does not hold any society as a whole to an aesthetic standard; he does not say that a society is to be admired and hence preferred when its institutions and practices, when its general spirit, elicit aesthetic attitudes and reward them with feelings of pleasure (as beautiful), much less with the curious (and perhaps pleasurable) pain of awful terror (as sublime).

Later, however, in *Reflections,* there are significant moments when Burke praises — one is tempted to say, unguardedly, but that would not be right — the aristocratic order of France and Europe because it meets an aesthetic test, a test that a revolutionary democracy always must fail. The most amazing moment comes when he says about the code of aristocratic honor or chivalry that under it, "Vice itself lost half its evil by losing all its grossness."[13] The implication is that aristocrats are themselves deliberately aesthetic in their conduct and that therein lies the redemption of vice — a premeditated beauty of manner, of corporate style, forgives or half-forgives vice while, perhaps, clumsiness or artlessness condemns or half-condemns right conduct (which I dare not call virtue). To be sure, Burke can turn on himself. Well after the passage on vice and grossness, he chides the French aristocracy:

> Habitual dissoluteness of manners continued beyond the pardonable period of life, was more common amongst them than it is with us; and it reigned with the less hope of remedy, though possibly with something of less mischief, by being covered with more exterior decorum.[14]

That Burke attributes conscious conformity to the mandates of aesthetic attitudes and feelings to the leaders of the old order also comes out in his assertion that the code of chivalry "obliged sovereigns to submit to the soft collar of social esteem, compelled stern authority to submit to elegance, and gave a dominating vanquisher of laws to be subdued by manners."[15] On the other hand, his judgment of the French queen, Marie Antoinette, shows a certain theoretical ambiguity. He says,

> I hear, and I rejoice to hear, that the great lady . . . has borne that day (one is interested that beings made for suffering should suffer well). . . . She feels with

the dignity of a Roman matron . . . in the last extremity she will save herself from the last disgrace and that, if she must fall, she will fall by no ignoble hand.[16]

It is not quite clear whether Burke, speaking for himself in this passage, is consciously aesthetic or imperspicuously conflating social role and theatrical role. It is also not quite clear whether he thinks that the queen is acting a role (theatrically) or playing a role (functionally). A related ambiguity character-izes the motivation attributed by Marx to great revolutionaries as well as to their farcical imitators-parodists in the opening pages of *The Eighteenth Bru-maire of Louis Bonaparte* (1852) and recurrently thereafter in the text.

In an early part of *Reflections,* Burke takes up the writing of new constitu-tions and remarks, in regard to the lower middle class lawyers, that "the evil of a moral and almost physical inaptitude of the man to the function must be the greatest we can conceive to happen in the management of human affairs."[17] What is physical inaptitude if not a failure to be personally beautiful and hence fit to grace the public stage? Burke also attributes to his opponents an indelib-erate aestheticism, indeed a craving that is not conscious of its own aestheti-cism and that would be horrified to be told its true nature. He says of the dissident clubs in England:

> A cheap, bloodless reformation, a guiltless liberty, appear flat and vapid to their taste. There must be a great change of scene; there must be a magnificent stage effect; there must be a grand spectacle to rouse the imagination, grown torpid with the lazy enjoyment of sixty years security and the still unanimat-ing repose of public prosperity.[18]

Burke knows better than anyone the strength of aestheticism's grip. He offers a deliberate aestheticism in place of an unconscious one, and he offers the device of conscious conformity to the requirements imposed by aesthetic atti-tudes and feelings to replace the aesthetic failure of uninhibited aesthetic crav-ings. That he too is, to some extent, in the grip of unconscious aestheticism is probably true as well. There is a sting in Paine's brilliant *mot* about Burke that he "pities the plumage but forgets the dying bird."[19] The *mot* is earned by the force of a paragraph two pages before:

> As to the tragic paintings by which Mr. Burke has outraged his own imagina-tion and seeks to work upon that of his readers, they are very well calculated for theatrical representation, where facts are manufactured for the sake of show and accommodated to produce, through the weakness of sympathy, a weeping effect. But Mr. Burke should recollect that he is writing history, and not plays, and that his readers will expect truth, and not the spouting rant of high-toned declamation.[20]

Burke is a complex and instructive case. He theorizes about the sublime and the beautiful but also exemplifies his theory and exceeds it. He displays aesthetic attitudes and feelings and does so across the whole field, from artworks, to nature, to social reality in all its aspects, yet sometimes he seems swept away by aesthetic cravings that he does not fully indicate he knows to be cravings or to be aesthetic. He goes almost too easily from theater to politics and back to theater, as if they were essentially the same phenomenon. His very literary style is so eloquent as to run the risk of being thought insincere or even, at times, campy or patently self-dramatizing. For all these reasons, he is, I think, one of the most important representatives of deliberate philosophical aestheticism, especially in the form of a defense of a society when, unchanged from the way it is, it supposedly deserves to elicit aesthetic attitudes and feelings. He also shows an aestheticism understood, at the same time, as a critique of any society that is, or threatens to become, unfit and unable to elicit these attitudes and feelings. Burke is not alone. Other defenders of aristocracy, whether qualified (e.g., Tocqueville) or reactive and revisionary (e.g., Nietzsche), show varying amounts of deliberate philosophical aestheticism in regard to aspects of society or to societies as wholes. But Burke, in modern times, invents the sensibility and sets the standard.

Next, there are writers who urge that much of social life be *made over* so that it deserves to elicit aesthetic attitudes and feelings. This is an activist deliberate philosophical aestheticism. Important proponents include Schiller, Nietzsche, Pater, Wilde, Marcuse, and some city planners and utopian thinkers. They occupy all places on the political spectrum, and therefore their aspirations and suggestions differ considerably from one another. In some writers, concern for the aesthetic takes and receives coloration from the concern for greater social justice. In the case of Nietzsche, the aesthetic aspiration serves and is served by what he calls life, by which he means the will to affirm life. The stakes for many of these proponents of deliberate philosophical aestheticism are thus enormous. Existence for them is made better or made more worth having when social life, not just artworks, nature, and designated aesthetic activities and objects, solicit and reward the various aesthetic attitudes and feelings. Aestheticism and morality would ideally perfect each other.

There is, however, one strand of deliberate philosophical aestheticism that is not benign, not even benign as Nietzsche's view might perhaps plausibly be considered to be. I have already mentioned Hitler. I want only to say now that fascism, to some of its initiators, adherents, and sympathizers, was a consciously aesthetic response to what they perceived as the ill-disciplined, ill-defined, swarming, incoherent, and slovenly social conditions of modern mass and surplus populations in distress. It is not only true that fascism gratified for many people cravings that did not know themselves to be aesthetic, and it is not only true that fascism was formed and enacted by a few who were willing to say or at least imply that fascism gratified their aesthetic cravings. The relevant point here is that for more detached admirers, fascism was justified as an aesthetic phenomenon, and for them there could be no higher kind of justification. They were not victimized by cravings; rather, their cultivated aesthetic attitudes and feelings gladly contemplated fascism, and they found it both beautiful and sublime. If the taste for kitsch characterized the fascist mass following, as Saul Friedlander suggestively says in *Reflections of Nazism* (1984), the taste of some intellectuals for fascism was not kitschy but rather something else — more refined and still morally lethal. Think of the admiration of especially Italian fascism felt by those such as Yeats, Pound, and Wyndham Lewis; it is aesthetic through and through, controlled and conscious. They tended to think that it was desirable for political leaders (themselves possessed by aesthetic cravings) to control and sacrifice people for the sake of a society-wide pattern or project that appealed to the writer's own aestheticism.

There is one last kind of deliberate philosophical aestheticism that has regard to matters besides artworks, nature, and designated aesthetic activities and objects. Only now the matter is not social reality as a whole or in many of its aspects. Rather, some writers have put forth the idea that the self should aspire to satisfy aesthetic criteria, should aspire to be worthy of aesthetic attitudes and feelings, and should aim to be beautiful or sublime in some sense or other. Two recent works have given influential accounts of this ideal and seem to express approval for it. I refer to Foucault, especially in the second and third volumes of *The History of Sexuality* (1984), and to Alexander Nehamas's interpretation of Nietzsche in his book, *Nietzsche: Life as Literature* (1985). A related thought is that a person's life is best lived when it is deliberately lived as a coherent narrative or story. This thought appears in Alasdair MacIntyre's *After Virtue* (1981).

In these views, the main anticipated beneficiary when the self is made into a work of art, or a life is lived as a story, is not society, nor is it the detached aesthetic observer. Although benefits to others may accrue, these writers have the individual person in view. One satisfies one's aesthetic attitudes and feelings as one contemplates oneself in process or at the end. Foucault, for example, says,

> I am referring to what might be called "the arts of existence." What I mean by the phrase are those intentional and voluntary actions by which men not only set themselves rules of conduct but also seek to transform themselves, to change themselves in their singular being, and to make their life into an *oeuvre* that carries certain aesthetic values and meets certain stylistic criteria.[21]

The arts of existence make one's existence into a work of art.

Nehamas says in rendering Nietzsche's view,

But a person worthy of admiration, a person who has (or is) a self, is one whose thoughts, desires, and actions are not haphazard but are instead connected to one another in the intimate way that indicates in all cases the presence of style. . . . But style, which is what Nietzsche requires and admires, involves controlled multiplicity and resolved conflict.[22]

Self-overcoming may lead to self-mastery, and the point of self-mastery is to acquire reality in one's own eyes. One's eyes finally see and want to see only the shaped and shapely, the beautiful.

In the course of sympathetically picturing a "premodern" ideal of a whole life for a self, MacIntyre approves of "a concept of a self whose unity resides in the unity of a narrative which links birth to life to death as narrrative beginning to middle to end."[23] Such a life will be constituted by involvement in significant social practices that are themselves shapely and regular, that require and perfect particular virtues, that are hallowed by age and not subject to individual caprice, and that reward the person with the conviction of meaningfulness. These practices, however, may be even more meaningful to the aesthetic observer than to the participants who, in MacIntyre's account, are not supposed to possess much self-consciousness. This possibility makes all the more noteworthy MacIntyre's unfriendly attitude to the aesthete as a type of character favored by modernity.

It seems to me that all three conceptions are compatible with quite a lot of immorality. Foucault, Nehamas's Nietzsche, and MacIntyre all deny the possibility of a universalist morality and use their denial as an opening to modes of individual or social life in which aesthetic attitudes and feelings are morally unencumbered. Foucault does gesture toward morality when he ponders Socrates in a late interview. He sees Socrates as proposing that care for the self (a version of "the arts of existence") might very well lead to care for others and that the best care for others comes from a person who first cares for himself.[24] But this observation appears as almost an afterthought.

I believe that if only moral *limits* were respected theoretically, then non-moral motivation (at least in some sectors of life) would not cause immorality. A person's commitment, say, to perform a role or a vocation in the most virtuosic way, or to take part in a practice wholeheartedly, but a vocation, role, or practice that was innocent in itself and also was not embedded in a larger wicked pattern or policy, could be seen as deliberate aestheticism. But the deliberate aestheticism would then be morally acceptable while also still capable of being aesthetically admirable to the person and to the observer.

The preponderant tendency, however, in those who want a self to be like a work of art or a life to be like a well-made story is not merely nonmoral and not merely intent on seeing that the idea of innocent becoming and activity retain a place in the conceptual landscape and in life itself. There is rather an eagerness to see indifference to or disregard of morality as aesthetically indispensable. Morality makes ugly through its self-examination, through scruples, inhibitions, and second thoughts. In case after case, deliberate philosophical aestheticism turns into a project for making over oneself or the world. The projects often indicate that aesthetic attitudes have transformed themselves into aesthetic cravings or that some aesthetic reason has been allowed to outweigh morality.

What are we to say after this survey of cravings not recognized as aesthetic and of consciously aesthetic attitudes and feelings allowed full rein? I began by saying that the human record, in its pervasive wickedness, gave ample evidence that people ranked many things higher than morality and that numerous thinkers rationalized that preference. I then tried to show that unconscious aestheticism is responsible for a goodly portion of such wickedness in the world and that deliberate philosophical aestheticism threatened to countenance more. My assertions are unhappy, I concede. But I have to face facts. Aestheticism, whether unconscious or deliberate, however theorized or not theorized, is inescapable. It always will be with us. No one can resist it with full success. It may, more than anything else, provide interest in life, its motion and animation. If this last sentence seems to be squarely aesthetical, then that just shows that there is no escaping aestheticism in any of the kinds I have discussed so far. Even more, aestheticism, in all its potentially immoral kinds, is a significant part of what it means to be human. Still, I wish to point in the direction of a kind of aestheticism I have so far only mentioned — democratic aestheticism — and try to say sketchily what its cultivation could contribute to the side of morality in the permanent war waged on morality by the other kinds of aestheticism.

What is democratic aestheticism? I have elsewhere tried to give a preliminary version of this idea, basing myself on Emerson, Thoreau, and Whitman and simultaneously taking some thoughts from Nietzsche and Heidegger quite against their will. I cannot here provide any new elaboration, only a few stray thoughts, and not many of them new, either.

A place to begin is Santayana's question from *The Sense of Beauty* (1896): "Are all things beautiful?"[25] It would seem at first sight that democratic aestheticism, which is a deliberate philosophical aestheticism, and available to all persons in their good moments, would want to answer the question in the affirmative. The reason would be that democratic aestheticism wants, by means of aesthetic attitudes, to receive all things in the world as equal; that it wants to bestow the various aesthetic feelings of appreciation, admiration, wonder, and so forth on everything indiscriminately; and that it wants to either abolish taste or push it well beyond its usual exercises. (What is involved, of course, is not *demotic* aestheticism, which is a celebration of popular mass artworks as the highest.) The characterization I have just given is not far from accurate. But it needs qualification.

Santayana is not disposed to say that all things are beautiful, much less that all things are equally beautiful. He does not want to abolish taste, that is, discrimination. But he does supply a thought that can be built on. He says, "Everything is beautiful because everything is capable in some degree of interesting and charming our attention."[26] He adds, "Things differ immensely in this capacity to please us in the contemplation of them, and therefore they differ immensely in beauty."[27] But it is the first formulation that can be seized on by an advocate of democratic aestheticism: in effect, everything is worthy of attention.[28] An advocate of democratic aestheticism then wishes to go on to say that the aesthetic attitude of attention often leads to the satisfaction engendered by (or inherent in) appreciation, admiration, or some other aesthetic feeling. Everything has a meaning worth pondering.

Democratic aestheticism is receptivity or responsiveness to as much of the world as possible — its persons, its events and situations, its conditions, its patterns and sequences. As a deliberate philosophical aestheticism, its primary mission is to devote attention to what lies outside artworks, nature, and designated aesthetic activities and objects, although it absorbs these phenomena in its embrace. The mission is to make the unpromising world worthy of attention; to grant standing to what seems not to merit it; and to hear the often silent or distorted appeal of everyone and everything for perception, interpretation, and contemplation, and hence for some sort of appreciation, if admiration must be withheld. Democratic aestheticism indiscriminately confers on non-art the reception that others think only art — high art — deserves. Greater than even admiration, however, is wonder or amazement, which everyone and everything can elicit just by being one more reality. Democratic aestheticism tries to make cravings for beauty and sublimity in human relations conscious of themselves as aesthetic and to curb them for the sake of morality. This cause is promoted by the cultivation of aesthetic attitudes and feelings that attain enough satisfaction if the moral sense is itself cultivated; the ideal result is that aesthetic cravings, unconscious or conscious, do not usurp the moral self, while the aesthetic self is continuously engaged and continuously appeased. Most important, democratic aestheticism shares with other deliberate philosophical aestheticisms the subordination of pleasure as its motive. Indeed, to practice democratic aestheticism, one must often disregard one's pleasure initially, and even overcome distaste.

From the start, democratic aestheticism is aware of the difficulties that the cravings for beauty and sublimity (in strict and extended senses) must and always will create for morality, and it tries to assuage those difficulties. I suppose that fact makes democratic aestheticism impurely aesthetic or compromised by morality; actually, one of its parents is morality. But that is the whole point: to assert morality's supremacy and then educate the sense of beauty and sublimity so that it serves morality rather than harming it. (Only environmentalism, in part aesthetically rooted, stands a chance of defensibly challenging the claim to supremacy of moral considerations; perhaps morality itself would, on this issue, allow its own subordination.) On the other hand, unmoralized deliberate aestheticism, an aestheticism of perfect freedom, is confined by the moral sense to artworks, nature (in many aspects), and designated activities and objects. In short, the teaching of democratic aestheticism is that we should not expect social reality to satisfy cravings that no art can satisfy and that we should direct toward social reality the aesthetic attitudes and feelings that are conventionally deemed appropriate to high art.

I have itemized the elements that fall under the rubrics of beauty and sublimity and that either are craved or yield themselves to aesthetic attitudes and feelings. As practiced by Emerson, Whitman, Thoreau, and others, democratic aestheticism tries hard to show that nearly everyone and everything is worthy of aesthetic attitudes and feelings. They try to show, first, that there is far more beauty and sublimity in the world than either conventional opinion allows or aristocratic or elitist canons of taste countenance. A revised but richer aesthetic sense reduces both craving and discrimination. Second, these writers move in the direction of saying that many things and conditions, even if they are finally not interpretable as beautiful or sublime in any plausible sense, are nevertheless worthy of attention and also worthy of the aesthetic feelings that may grow by means of attention. Although much of the world is not aesthetic in even the extended but conventional meanings of beauty and sublimity, it is still worthy of aesthetic attitudes and feelings. That is to say, the world as it is, not the world made over; the world as it is, but interpreted by the new canons of democratic aestheticism.

On the first way of looking, noticing, and interpreting, the aim is to dispel both conventional perception and the spirit of confident cultivation and to provide a morally indispensable supplement to both popular and elitist aestheticism. Some of the characteristic insights of the Emersonians (and some others) is to find beauty or sublimity where it has not been found before, to find quality either incipiently or potentially present, or to find the aspiration to beauty or sublimity amid a botched result. The supposedly anti-aesthetic elements (necessity, use, practicality, etc.) have a kind of beauty, all the more interesting for being unintended. On the second way of looking, noticing, and interpreting — the movement beyond beauty or sublimity (in any plausible sense) — the practitioners of democratic aestheticism say that the ugly or what often passes as ugly — the impure, the incomplete or inconclusive, the hybrid, the uncomposed composite, the definitively undefinable, the ill defined, the unstable, the heterogeneous, the random, the disorderly, the out of place — is worthy of attention and, from attention, appreciation. Of course, one is tempted to say that in these cases, beauty or sublimity (especially sublimity) is being redefined and reconceived, not abandoned. I suppose that there is no harm in putting it that way. The danger is that beauty and sublimity are already routinely so stretched that maybe we should draw a line somewhere. But the real point is that democratic aestheticism strains to submit the un-beautiful and the unsublime to aesthetic attitudes and feelings. No, all things are not beautiful, to revert to Santayana's formulation; nor are all beautiful things equally beautiful. But everyone and everything deserves patient attention, a look, a gaze, but not to be followed by an attempt to remedy or control or to make over.

There is some resemblance between the democratic aesthete and Plato's promiscuous and insatiable lover of boys, wine, or honor (*Republic*, V:474–75). Plato says that all those who truly love a kind of thing love every specimen, and when they find deficiencies, they redescribe them and convert them into further evidences of excellence and hence into unfailing sources of charm. In such insatiability, these lovers are like philosophers who are insatiable for truth, the only object deserving insatiability. But in opposition to Plato's philosopher, the democratic aesthete stays in this world, finds it worthy of insatiable attention, and tries to appreciate as much of it as possible. The democratic aesthete aspires to be, in Whitman's words from the Preface (1855) to *Leaves of Grass*, the world's "complete lover." But it is love at a distance; all is loved, and nothing is craved.

Santayana speaks chidingly of the mystical proclivity to "lose ourselves in the satisfying vagueness of mere being."[29] But there is a genuine nontheological mysticism that "mere being" can arouse in the receptive soul. Wittgenstein, Heidegger, and Arendt display it memorably, and it occasions one of Wallace Stevens's matchless late poems, "Of Mere Being," which renders the inconceivable fact that there is a world, much of it unreached by human meaning and untouchable by human feeling. "Mere being" means that there is something rather than nothing; it also means that any given thing, present here or there, now or then, is accidental, contingent, precarious, mutable, always amenable to different viewings and interpretations, uneternal, and perishable.

Democratic aestheticism, in the two main ways of looking, noticing, and interpeting, is driven, in part, by a sense of the amount of wickedness that comes from uncontrolled aesthetic cravings, from bad aestheticism. But if democratic aestheticism is morally driven and adheres to morality with such an intensity that it can turn into moralism — a danger that the Emersonians are keen to let you know they are painfully aware of — it is also true that the decisive effect is to enlarge the imagination of morality. By making everyone and everything worthy of attention and hence of one or another of the aesthetic feelings, it checks the tendency to condemnation and punishment. What begins in moral anxiety sometimes ends in almost total absolution. What begins in horror ends in the ascription of innocence. Because democratic aestheticism is an aestheticism, it delights in finding a field for the display of aesthetic attitudes and feelings everywhere. It takes in the whole world. It verges on practicing an aesthetic charity very much like the "Christian piety" that Santayana attributes to music as such, which serves, he claims, to express every feeling, no matter how disreputable.[30] In fact, in enlarging the moral imagination despite its initial moral dismay (or is it because of that dismay?), democratic aestheticism traces the trajectory of the teachings of Jesus, which go from a bitter call for repentance to the admonition to be like one's father in heaven, "for he makes his sun to rise on the evil and on the good and sends rain on the just and on the unjust" (Matthew 6:45).

The trouble, of course, is that the observer is in no position to absolve those who have hurt others, not him. Another trouble is that democratic aestheticism calls for personal reform, which consists in employing our democratically cultivated aesthetic attitudes and feelings in relation to all phenomena. By doing that, it dulls the urge to change the world; it leaves the world alone because the world is sufficient as it is. It could thus settle for remaining passive in the face of the very evil that helped to instigate its existence. Then, stung by such passivity and such evil, its practitioners rouse themselves to action and thus abandon their enlarged morality for the morality of condemnation and punishment. The original moral motive reclaims the practitioners of democratic aestheticism. (The wholehearted acceptance of violence against slavery by Emerson, Whitman, and Thoreau is cautionary, but what choice did they have?) The practitioners of democratic aestheticism then console themselves by saying that unless the world is made less unjust, it could not be affirmed; it could not be called innocent; it could not innocently be the site of appreciation, admiration, and wonder.

Democratic aestheticism never can escape cruel dilemmas. That some large part of the world's wickedness derives, however, from cravings that do not know their aestheticism ("Father, forgive them, for they know not what they do" [Luke 23:34]) underlies the effort to reform individuals by reforming their aestheticism. The world cannot do without the various unconscious and deliberate (undemocratic) aestheticisms, theorized or not; we are not human without them, even though they tend to make us not only human but also all too human and monstrous as well. Still, democratic aestheticism, although hardly inevitable and immensely artificial, is indispensable as both an antidote and a transcendence.

Nietzsche, early in his life as a writer, said that "for it is only as an *aesthetic* phenomenon that existence and the world are *eternally justified*"[31] and then radically qualified the remark later in the same text by adding, "Quite generally, only music, placed beside the world, can give us an idea of what is meant by the justification of the world as an aesthetic phenomenon."[32] (Does this qualification shrink the assertion by making it nearly inaccessible to nonmusical people or, by contrast, by exposing its own possible thinness?) The practitioners of democratic aestheticism do not practice the philosophical aestheticism of *The Birth of Tragedy*. They do not hold that beauty and sublimity in the common strict or extended sense forgive the unforgivable. They refuse to take the perspective of the Nietzschean god who needs all the ingredients to make his composition. That god is not unlike the Stoic god who "has need of a world like this."[33] Instead, they reconceive the aesthetic. They finally say that although aesthetic cravings are hardly the sole consideration, without them the human record is impossible to decipher, and that a newly conceived aestheticism can help us temper our aesthetic cravings. But we must also realize that it is in the very nature of democratic aestheticism to make its practitioners (and sympathizers) move uneasily, uncertainly, even as in a daze, between moral shock and a moral indulgence that is, after all, aesthetically inspired, in part.

Notes

1. Quoted in *The New York Times,* July 11, 1995, A11.

2. Ralph Waldo Emerson, *Essays and Lectures* (New York: Library of America, 1983), 454.

3. Soren Kierkegaard, *Fear and Trembling,* trans. Walter Lowrie (Princeton, NJ: Princeton University Press, 1941), esp. 79–123.

4. Thucydides, *The Peloponnesian War,* trans. Crawley/Wick (New York: Modern Library, 1982), II, 63:124. See also Cleon's characterization of the Athenian empire as a tyranny, ibid., III, 37:172.

5. Carl Schmitt, *The Concept of the Political* (1932), trans. George Schwab (New Brunswick, NJ: Rutgers University Press, 1976), 26, 28.

6. See Nicholas Everett's review of *The Collected Poetry of Robinson Jeffers* in *Times Literary Supplement,* November 25, 1994, 10–11.

7. Letter to William Braithwaite, March 22, 1915, in *Robert Frost: Collected Poems, Prose, & Plays* (New York: Library of America, 1995), 685.

8. Edmund Burke, *A Philosophical Enquiry into the Origin of Our Ideas of the Sublime and Beautiful* (1757), ed. J. T. Boulton (New York: Columbia University Press, 1958), 113–14.

9. George Santayana, *The Life of Reason,* vol. 4: *Reason in Art* (New York: Scribner, 1905), 120.

10. Immanuel Kant, *The Critique of Judgment,* trans. J. H. Bernard (New York: Hafner, 1966), 108.

11. Walter Benjamin, "Theses on the Philosophy of History," in *Illuminations,* ed. Hannah Arendt, trans. Harry Zohn (New York: Schocken, 1969), 256.

12. See the instructive discussion in Stephen K. White, *Edmund Burke: Modernity, Politics, and Aesthetics* (Thousand Oaks, CA: Sage, 1994), esp. 1–7, 22–36, 68–79. I also have benefited from David Bromwich's Gauss Lectures on the Radicalism of Edmund Burke, Princeton University, February 1995.

13. Edmund Burke, *Reflections on the Revolution in France,* ed. Conor Cruise O'Brien (London: Penguin, 1982), 170.

14. Ibid., 244.

15. Ibid., 170–71.

16. Ibid., 169.

17. Ibid., 134.

18. Ibid., 156.

19. Thomas Paine, *Rights of Man,* ed. Eric Foner (New York: Penguin, 1984), 51.

20. Ibid., 50–51.

21. Michel Foucault, *The Use of Pleasure,* trans. Robert Hurley (New York: Pantheon, 1985), 10–11. On the aesthetics of existence, the discussion in chapters 1 to 3 is especially pertinent.

22. Alexander Nehamas, *Nietzsche: Life as Literature* (Cambridge, MA: Harvard University Press, 1985), 7. For Nehamas's further explorations of aestheticism in life, see *The Art of Living: Socratic Reflections from Plato to Foucault* (Berkeley: University of California Press, 1998).

23. Alasdair MacIntyre, *After Virtue* (Notre Dame, IN: University of Notre Dame Press, 1981), 7.

24. "The Ethic of Care for the Self as a Practice of Freedom," trans. J. D. Gauthier, an interview (January 20, 1984) in *The Final Foucault,* ed. James Bernauer and David Rasmussen (Cambridge, MA: MIT Press, 1988), 7. On the shift from an aestheticized care for the self to a more universally grounded self-concern, see Foucault's *The Use of Pleasure,* 253–54, and *The Care of the Self,* trans. Robert Hurley (New York: Pantheon, 1986), 67–68. Foucault says that the shift takes place in late antiquity and the early centuries of Christianity.

25. George Santayana, *The Sense of Beauty* (1896) (New York: Dover, 1955), 79. See section 31, 79–82.

26. Ibid., 80.

27. Ibid.

28. Simone Weil made the faculty of attention central to the moral life. I find especially valuable the discussion in *Intuitions pré-chrétiennes* (Intimations of Christianity) (Paris: La Colombe, 1951), 155–59. Iris Murdoch has fruitfully explored this notion in *The*

Sovereignty of Good (New York: Schocken, 1971), esp. 34–45, 64–67, 84–90. Murdoch's whole book is relevant to the purposes of this essay, although I do not endorse the more religious passages.

29. Santayana, *The Sense of Beauty,* 80.

30. Santayana, *Reason in Art,* 59.

31. Friedrich Nietzsche, *The Birth of Tragedy* (1872), in *Basic Writings of Nietzsche,* trans. and ed. Walter Kaufmann (New York: Modern Library, 1968), sec. 5, 52. On the pervasiveness of aesthetic categories in the sense of history in Nietzsche and Hegel, see Joshua F. Dienstag, *Dancing in Chains: Narrative and Memory in Political Theory* (Stanford, CA: Stanford University Press, 1997).

32. Nietzsche, *The Birth of Tragedy,* sec. 24, 141.

33. *Arrian's Discourses of Epictetus,* trans. P. E. Matheson, in *The Stoic and Epicurean Philosophers,* ed. Whitney J. Oates (New York: Random House, 1940), I, 29:277. Nietzsche gives a rich description of the "entirely reckless and amoral artist-god" in "Attempt at a Self-Criticism" (1886) in *The Birth of Tragedy,* sec. 5, 22.

7

The Judgment of Arendt

Death deprived us of the third volume of *The Life of the Mind,* the volume on judging that was meant to complete the project that already contained a volume on thinking and a volume on willing. Of course, we cannot say what Hannah Arendt would have offered us in the third volume. We do know that *Thinking* and *Willing* contained more detailed analyses than any found in her previous work on these two themes, and also some conceptual enrichment. Arendt, however, was not a writer ever to be taken for granted; she was always capable of surprising the reader. It would therefore be best not to speculate about the contents of a volume that was never written. What we can do, instead — other scholars have in fact made the effort — is to piece together a view of judgment from works in which Arendt speaks about this subject. I propose to carry on the enterprise, with no hope of saying a definitive word.

My argument is that Arendt sets out to reconceive, to the fullest degree possible, political phenomena as aesthetic phenomena, and that her interest in judgment is an interest in aesthetic judgment, rather than in what others would consider properly political judgment. Arendt means to hold politics to the standards of aesthetic judgment, while claiming that aesthetic judgment, suitably adjusted to political phenomena, is, of all kinds of judgment, alone attentive to the most important, the most essentially political qualities of politics. She enlists Kant in her project, but the project is most un-Kantian, anti-

Kantian. Indeed, the project is her own, despite the powerful influence of Nietzsche and the ancient Greeks.

To begin, we must ask what it means to conceptualize political phenomena as aesthetic ones, and why Arendt is disposed to do so. To answer, we can initially proceed negatively. Political actions, when undertaken in the right spirit (and this proviso is of fundamental importance), are not primarily practical or moral, nor do they take their bearings from abstract and universal truth. Similarly, works of art have often been defined in contrast with what is practical (or useful), what is moral (in aim or effect), and what aspires to the truth of cognition. In understanding all aesthetic phenomena, Arendt adopts this traditional set of contrasts. To be sure, the negative approach to conceptualization is not sufficient: Arendt provides positivity, as we shall see. But let us briefly look first at the effort that Arendt makes to set political phenomena apart, to a decisive degree, from the practical, the moral, and the universally truthful. I do not mean to assert that Arendt completely excludes either the moral or the practical from the political sphere; and she actually insists on the place of a certain kind of truth in political life. Rather, she is out to *subordinate* practicality and morality to the aesthetic potentiality of politics. She also hopes to liberate politics altogether from the grip of abstract, universal truth. ✓

I believe that the most important element in Arendt's aestheticization of politics is the subordination of morality. More than either practicality or truth, morality threatens the aesthetic, when the proposed aesthetic field is political life. Commentators on Arendt have frequently found that Arendt writes about politics at its ideal best, whether in its ancient or modern forms, with scant attention to moral motives or purposes or even to moral consequences. I wish to suggest that we can account in part for such apparent disregard by attributing to Arendt the wish to aestheticize political phenomena. How does morality threaten this project? I construe Arendt to say that morality impedes aestheticization by impeding the desire to undertake politics in the right spirit. What is the right spirit? Basing ourselves mostly on "What Is Freedom?", her most extreme writing, we can say that for Arendt political actors show the right spirit when they act for the sake of exemplifying a passion (Arendt calls it a "principle"); or for the sake of displaying one's political skills (Arendt follows Machiavelli in calling this disposition "virtu"); or for the sake of the exhilaration of acting, especially when action starts something new or interrupts a seemingly necessary process or transgresses a settled practice; or for the sake of winning or excelling in political contests, quite apart from the tangible gains of victory. Aestheticized politics is pure politics, politics for the sake of politics — politics purified, to a considerable extent, from moral anxiety as well as moral goals, just as other aesthetic phenomena are held ideally to be.

Naturally, those of us who want to keep political life, even in any ideal form, under constant moral scrutiny, will not find Arendt's position morally accept-able. The scope of political effects, the scale of political consequences, may exceed the effects or consequences of any other kind of human action. If, therefore, political action is not subjected to moral standards, one wonders what kinds of action would properly be held to moral account. Arendt gives the moralist great cause for discomfort. Before we try to explain Arendt's purgative aesthetics, we must first see it for what it is. In a word, even a normal amount of moral concern, not just Socratic moral strictness, disfigures politi-cal action, by Arendt's reckoning.

Next, a concern for using political action as a means to attain concrete social goals, even nonmoral or immoral goals, disfigures or denatures it. Just as practicality is not in general compatible with aesthetic considerations, so practicality in politics, if it becomes the sole or preponderant mentality, dimin-ishes or prevents political phenomena from becoming aesthetic ones. To use politics as a means is not to engage in politics in the right spirit. Arendt insists that action undertaken in the right spirit is "neither under the guidance of the intellect nor under the dictate of the will."[1] Both the intellect and the will are appropriate for specific aims, but politics at its best has no such aims. Kant's phrase about works of art, "purposiveness without purpose," may subtly in-fluence her conception of the right spirit for politics.[2]

In regard to the place of truth in politics rightly undertaken, Arendt main-tains that opinion is the currency of such politics. "Seen from the viewpoint of politics, truth has a despotic character. . . . The trouble is that factual truth, like all other truth, peremptorily claims to be acknowledged and precludes debate, and debate constitutes the very essence of political life."[3] Where there can be no agreement, disagreement, and consent, or persuasion and dissua-sion,[4] there can be none of the give and take, none of the honest expressions of diverse outlooks, on which politics thrives. That means, above all, that the attempt to insert the allegedly highest truth — philosophical or theological truth — into political life must always turn tyrannical. When such truth is challenged, and exposed as just one more opinion, the truth-teller will try to impose it or have it imposed by a susceptible ruler. In sum, "Culture and politics, then, belong together because it is not knowledge or truth which is at stake, but rather judgment and decision, the judicious exchange of opinion about the sphere of public life and the common world, and the decision what manner of action is to be taken in it, as well as how it is to look henceforth, what kind of things are to appear in it."[5]

But to say that political action, when done in the right spirit, shares with phenomena that are customarily identified as aesthetic (that is, works of art and designed scenes and spectacles) certain negative qualities is not to say enough. Arendt tries to give positive reasons for assimilating political to aesthetic phenomena. Put bluntly, Arendt's position is that the right politics, like art, exists for its own sake: beautifully and memorably there, each is a supreme manifestation of humanity; and far from needing justification, each, in its own way, helps to justify life or, at least, helps to give life a luster that it desperately needs and that only art and politics can give it. She also adduces other specific considerations. Her most suggestive analysis is found in "The Crisis in Culture: Its Social and Its Political Significance." In that essay, she holds that both artworks and political words and deeds (when done in the right spirit) share "the quality that they are in need of some public space where they can appear and be seen; they can fulfill their own being, which is appearance, only in a world which is common to all."[6] Beauty, she says, is the distinctive characteristic of art: "beauty is the very manifestation of imperishability."[7] "The proper criterion by which to judge appearances is beauty."[8] But are political words and deeds themselves beautiful? Are they, that is, absolutely like artworks? Her answer is not entirely clear; she at least comes close to conceptualizing political action, when done in the right spirit, as being almost exactly like art. She says, "The fleeting greatness of word and deed can endure in the world to the extent that beauty is bestowed upon it. Without the beauty, that is, the radiant glory in which potential immortality is made manifest in the human world, all human life would be futile and no greatness could endure."[9] Is the beauty of political action intrinsic and does it need only to be observed by the prepared mind? Or is such beauty only incipient at best, a kind of raw material that must be worked over by the literary artist if the beauty is to be made manifest? Is the beauty only conferred? I cannot say for sure. In either case, there is no doubt that the observer is needed, whether to notice or to extract the beauty; in either case, the observer exercises aesthetic judgment. And it is also probably correct that Arendt does not mean that the political actor is driven by a passion for beauty in the strict sense. The right spirit for political action shares some of the features of making art—subordination of the moral and the practical, and the displacement of the truthful—but may have a more indirect connection to beauty as a motive. Perhaps we should take Arendt's words from the Kant lectures as definitive of her political aestheticism: "what the actor is concerned with is *doxa*, fame—that is, the opinion of others. . . . For the actor, the decisive question is thus how he appears to others."[10] Perhaps splendor of appearances is the political equivalent of artistic beauty. The splendor shines forth when political actors speak words, make gestures, and perform deeds, that seem perfect, irreplaceable, unexpectedly suitable, and able to define or redefine what will henceforth be suitable. (Let us also notice that she explicitly rejects the metaphor of a state or government as a work of art as "completely false.")[11]

Arendt adduces one other main consideration that moves political phenomena in the direction of aesthetic ones. Artworks are expressions of a distinctive human capacity: to do something new, creative, unexpected, eruptive, interruptive of routinized perception and response. Although rules and discipline enter into the making of art, art is far more than rules or discipline. Art is the freedom of humanity. Arendt conceptualizes right political action in the same way. As the Greeks practiced politics "being free and the capacity to begin something new coincided."[12] The rest of nature (supposedly) repeats itself endlessly; only human beings have the capacity to deviate and transgress, to deflect and transcend, to break free of determination and perform acts of "spontaneity."[13]

Unencumbered by very much morality or practicality, unbeholden to philosophical truth, political action, like art, signifies freedom, expresses freedom, is the medium of freedom. The human stature is therefore deeply implicated in art, and in politics when it is done rightly and understood aesthetically. Arendt's political aestheticism does not encourage self-indulgence, despite the intense pleasure (it may be) of the actor or the spectator, but rather is devoted to a restoration of human self-dignity. Those who practice politics in the right spirit do not have to worry about defending human dignity. Threats to the human stature are everywhere, but among the worst tendencies is the imprisonment of thinking and doing in a pervasive instrumentalism, whether that of producing, or fabricating, or enlisting all of politics as a means to social ends beyond itself. Of course, human life is inconceivable and unlivable without instrumental activity of every sort. Even the merest laboring is distinctively human. But beyond instrumentalism, there lies a realm of freedom; and in and because of this realm — the realm of worldliness — the human distinctiveness from the rest of nature is most fully and most splendidly realized.

Consequently, when we ask why Arendt is disposed to conceptualize political phenomena as aesthetic ones, we must finally answer that, for her, when human activity is art or is like art and is therefore properly amenable to aesthetic judgment, it most makes life worth living. It makes life worth living because it makes life most fully human. Together, beauty and freedom stamp human existence with a kind of immortality. This is not a mere end.

The stakes are therefore high. Arendt profoundly implicates the human stature in the realm of the aesthetic; specifically in artworks and in politics that is done in the right spirit. The defense of the human stature is the defense of the highest human aspirations, as well as the defense of humanity against all materialist or mechanical reduction. Artworks come forth as they can; indeed "the creative arts in our century" have experienced an "astounding recovery."[14] But politics done in the right spirit is not a frequent occurrence. Responses to artworks may be unfitting: Arendt bitterly complains about "philistinism," which either scorns art as useless or converts it into a social commodity that is prized and possessed as an indication of one's social standing or respectability.[15] Still, Arendt does not suggest that proper reception of artworks has totally vanished from the world. There has been a real "recovery of the greatness of the past" because of the decline of "genteel society."[16] Contrastingly, she finds that there is scarcely any proper appreciation of politics, scarcely any philosophical thought, past or present, that identifies the actual occurrences of the right politics and proceeds to elaborate their features. Her aim is to instruct her readers in the proper appreciation of politics—that is, to impart to the world a renovated political judgment. The usual kinds of political judgment are all marked by concern with morality or practicality or philosophical truth. They are oblivious to the possibility that politics may be assimilated to aesthetic phenomena because politics shares with artworks both beauty (or something close to beauty) and the manifestation of freedom. To be renovated, political judgment must go to school and learn from aesthetic judgment. Political judgment must become attentive to what aesthetic judges—certainly those who are instructed by Kant—concern themselves with, when they appreciate artworks. Political judgment must become very much more like aesthetic judgment in the hope that political actors will feel the pressure of aesthetic expectations and change the spirit in which they act.

In pursuit of the rehabilitation of a proper sense of politics, Arendt embarks on a theory of judgment. Her scattered remarks in several essays in *Between Past and Future*, her posthumously published Kant lectures, and a number of passages in other writings, all contribute to this theory, which was to have been formalized in the unwritten *Judging*. The truth is, however, that valuable as her remarks on judgment are in themselves, their greater value, their indispensability, comes from the light they throw on Arendt's whole body of work. Her books are exercises of political judgment. (The subtitle of *Between Past and Future* is actually *Exercises in Political Thought*.) Her remarks on judgment help us to gain a surer grasp of what she was up to all along. Her *theory* of judgment is (and perhaps would have been, even if she had completed it) much less important than the demonstration of judgment represented by her memorable books, from *The Origins of Totalitarianism* onward. We should see these books, I believe, as examples of a distinctively new kind of political judgment: a political judgment that borrows essential elements from aesthetic judgment, especially from Kant's theorization of it. Arendt's books are studiously attentive to politics when done in the right spirit—when done for its own sake, when done as display or performance, when done at the behest of a "principle," when done for the sheer exhilaration of acting, of starting something new or adventuring on something unprecedented. To that extent,

Arendt's books convey the splendor or beauty and creativity or freedom of politics done in the right spirit. In her hands, ideal politics rises to the condition of art, and the human stature is provided another prop besides art. The best politics is thus the kind that satisfies the political theorist when the theorist approaches political phenomena with the mentality of an aesthetic judge.

I grant that Arendt says that "judgment deals with particulars,"[17] rather than with common or universal phenomena, and that there is more in her books than particularist judgments. There are general and abstract analyses of the nature of political life and political action. Yet the net effect of each of her books is a heightening of the aesthetic qualities of particular political societies (Greece and Rome) or particular political episodes (the American Revolution, the early stages of the French Revolution, the revolutionary councils after the First World War, the Hungarian Revolution of 1956, the antiwar movement of civil disobedience in the late 1960s). She also says, "If judgment is our faculty for dealing with the past, the historian is the inquiring man who by relating it sits in judgment over it."[18] She may have sometimes thought of herself as a kind of historian, but her notion of being a historian, applied to herself, is scarcely distinguishable from being a political theorist.

Arendt's books are addressed to an age that she deems oblivious to the nature of politics as it has been or could be done in the right spirit. The escape from obliviousness is by way of assimilating political phenomena to aesthetic ones. The assimilation requires a perspective on politics that breaks with all the regnant ones. Only by looking at certain rare occurrences of politics can a fresh inspiration for a new political life emerge. In turn, only an aesthetic perspective can disclose the most humanly or existentially valuable potentiality of politics. Arendt employs such a perspective throughout her work. Theoretical adequacy to the best politics is what Arendt tries to provide. Only as political judgment approaches aesthetic judgment can it be adequate. The best politics is simultaneously splendid and free, and courage underlies both qualities.[19] Arendt is the modern political theorist par excellence of courage, and of the splendor and freedom that courage makes possible.

The crucial difference between conventional political judgment and aestheticized political judgment (or politicized aesthetic judgment) is that the former sees all politics as encompassable by instrumental categories. The normal political analyst proceeds to subsume political events under a few self-interested or "realistic" motives, and envisages political action as predictable. He thus fails to see that political action is sometimes driven by the very passions or principles that make action unpredictable and hence capable of being splendid and free. When action is done in the right spirit, the political analyst must be closely attentive to it and use his judgment to establish and to delineate its distinctive excellence. Arendt's work exemplifies the repudiation of subsumption. It is unusual in the attention it pays to the unusual.

At one point in her Kant lectures, Arendt distinguishes between the judgment of the Greek spectator who is a theorist and the Kantian spectator who is a judge. Although she is devoted to Kant's theory of aesthetic judgment, and makes considerable use of it, I think that the Greek notion is closer to her own continuous exercise of judgment as a political theorist. She says that the Greek spectator "looks at and judges (finds the truth of) the cosmos of the particular event in its own terms, without relating it to any larger process in which it may or may not play a part. . . . Its meaning did not depend on either causes or consequences."[20] But Kant judged political events in the light of the hope for human progress. He arranged all remarkable deeds and events into a pattern. Arendt does not pursue the significance of this distinction between Kant and the Greeks. Yet the testimony of her own work is all in favor of the Greek theorist rather than the Kantian judge (as she describes him). At the very end of the Kant lectures, she accuses Kant (as a proponent of human dignity) of contradiction: "It is against human dignity to believe in progress."[21] She does not allow *moral* hope to affect her own judgment of rare political occurrences of splendor and freedom. Human dignity, the human stature, cannot be tied to moral progress — something she had, like us, ample reason not to believe in. She sees these rare occurrences as perfectly contingent, as miracles. And if they have value beyond themselves, their value is that of examples that "teach or persuade by inspiration";[22] they are not signs — much less, guarantees — of a necessarily better future.

Now, I do not mean to suggest that all the components of politicized aesthetic judgment discussed by Arendt here and there are exemplified in her books. Of the several components, I have suggested that attention to the exceptional or novel quality of certain exemplary political occurrences and the consequent refusal to subsume these occurrences under standard categories of political analysis stand out as definitive of the political judgment shown by Arendt as a political theorist. She attends to nonmoral, noninstrumental, and nondogmatic qualities in political actors, qualities that disrupt the effort of subsumption and give reality to beauty and freedom. This kind of attention is almost unique among her contemporaries and perhaps among all but a few political theorists at any time. Arendt may hope to affect other people, whether political thinkers or actors, but she does not expect to have an easy or early influence. Much less does she expect her political theory to find agreement, as aesthetic judges ordinarily expect their judgments to converge because of a common standard of taste. She judges for herself, by herself. When political judgment is both aestheticized and philosophical (or theoretical), the work it does must be more independent, more isolated, than taste.

What then happens to other components of Arendt's (unsystematized) view of judgment, especially those that have to do with particulars, with taste, and with other related matters such as impartiality and enlarged mentality? (As we shall see, the notion of enlarged mentality is the most troublesome, yet its importance to Arendt will require us to spend what may seem like a disproportionate amount of time on it.) In these conceptualizations Arendt is trying to recapture the worldliness, the worldly code or ethic, of Greece and Rome at their political best. They provide the starting point for the political theorist or analyst who, like Arendt herself, undertakes the explicit, anxious, and risky philosophical task of assimilating political phenomena to aesthetic ones in an oblivious age, and who, by doing so, demonstrates aestheticized political judgment of a general and theoretical sort.

Particularist judgment, on the other hand, is not theoretical to any extent, but close to experience. When particularist political judgment draws nearer to aesthetic judgment — draws nearer to certain aspects of aesthetic judgment that are codified by Kant — then a true culture exists, a worldly culture in which the human stature is understood and cherished, just because political judgment attends to the distinctive features of politics done in the right spirit. The more particularist sort of aestheticized political judgment is shown in the judgment expressed by observers, spectators, and storytellers who are all members or admirers of a society in which politics is done in the right spirit, and who themselves may take their turn as political actors. Their judgment is aestheticized because, to begin with, they are disposed to look on political phenomena as aesthetic ones, or as nearly allied to aesthetic ones. Citing Pericles and Cicero as especially revelatory of ancient attitudes, Arendt finds a care for the world, a worldliness, that is motivated by fascination with the splendid appearances of both artworks and great political words and deeds and with the courage of freedom that makes such splendor possible.

Two kinds of particularist judgment stand out. The first is the judgment of the worldly storyteller; the second is the judgment of the spectator or observer who lives in a worldly society. On the first, the scholarly literature on Arendt has paid a good amount of attention to Arendt's praise of those writers who manage "the transformation of the given raw material of sheer happenings" into a shapely tale or account.[23] The political happenings, because done in the right spirit, deserve memorialization, and achieve immortality if the tale or account achieves immortality. The beautiful or admirable political act inspires beautiful, lasting utterance. Stories make culture out of politics. (Obviously not all politics lends itself to beautiful utterance; at least, Arendt does not suggest that a worthy story can be made of any political event, done in any spirit whatever. I will return to this point.)

I infer that Arendt especially likes stories when their tellers seem to show two components of politicized aesthetic judgment: first, an eye for novelty, for what is unusual, perhaps unprecedented, freely done, creative, eruptive; and second, impartiality. Historians, novelists, and poets may show politicized aesthetic judgment (or aestheticized political judgment) in their stories or accounts. Melville, Dostoyevsky, and Joseph Conrad are among the fiction writers who impress Arendt because of their political judgment: because they were profoundly attentive to the newness of major political movements and tendencies. On the other hand, she praises, above all, Homer for his impartiality. He "chose to sing the deeds of the Trojans no less than those of the Achaeans, and to praise the glory of Achilles, the hero of his kinfolk. This had happened nowhere before; no other civilization, however splendid, had been able to look with equal eyes upon friend and foe, upon success and defeat. . . . Homeric impartiality echoes through Greek history."[24] It inspired Herodotus, the father of Greek history, and is "the root of all so-called objectivity—this curious passion, unknown outside Western civilization, for intellectual integrity at any price."[25] What helped to make impartiality in the writer possible? I think that the answer is that a sense of beauty may overcome, if anything can, one's moral or practical-partisan concerns. Beauty may reside in the enemy, if only one is detached enough, has enough "disinterested delight," to override one's interests or commitments. A sense of beauty may be more objective than neutrality. Sometimes, a sense of beauty may be more moral than a sense of justice.

Then there is the spectator or observer in a worldly society. Two components of aesthetic judgment (as theorized by Kant) are here especially important. The first is taste, and the second is the enlarged mentality from which taste emerges. Arendt devotes a number of pages of the Kant lectures to Kant's idea of taste, and speaks in her own voice about taste in "The Crisis in Culture." Most succinctly, taste is (or is closely related to) what Kant calls "community sense," the sense or estimation or judgment of worldly things shared by the members of a society.[26] It is a sense of fitness or appropriateness or decorum; it registers success in measuring up to a common style. If taste aims at judging what kinds of worldly things are good or better, and what is good or better in each kind—if taste is grading—then apparently a version of subsumption is part of it. (Arendt's own judgment as a theorist of ideal politics may also exhibit something like taste.) Taste not only encourages certain political words and deeds and certain kinds of art, it also sets limits to them. It simultaneously excites and restrains because it influences creators and actors by anticipated judgment. Personal wildness or excess in artistic creation or political action is ruled out. Taste is not creative, as artistic genius and political audacity are creative, but it supplies the needed and expectant audience of observers or spectators. Spectators crave spectacle and hence the actions of those who put it on, but those who furnish the spectacle of worldly culture or politics are as nothing without an audience.

We have already seen that storytellers redeem political action from its evanescence; but their work is often belated. In contrast, the audience of spectators is immediate and exerts a direct force on artistic creators and political actors.[27] Arendt attributes to Kant the view that the "public realm is constituted by the critics and the spectators, not by the actors or makers."[28] Perhaps she is disposed to think the same herself. But there is one important difference between judges of art and judges of political action: those who are political spectators can also be political actors, in turn, whereas most of those who appreciate art cannot create it. Not only do actors internalize spectators and act, in part, with the intent of winning their favor, but the spectators often know from their own experience what it means to act. Both their action and their judgment of action are thus affected not only by the mutual dependence of actor and spectator but also by their reciprocity: in turn, each provides and appreciates the spectacle. This reciprocity is analogous to ruling and being ruled in turn, even though Arendt does not see ruling as properly political. Be that as it may, this further point could perhaps be drawn from Arendt's analysis.

Taste is not objective: there are no standards beyond those collaboratively developed by the associated spectators. But the standards are not personal or arbitrary. "Therefore taste, insofar as it, like any other judgment, appeals to common sense, is the very opposite of 'private feelings.' In aesthetic no less than in political judgments, a decision is made, and although this decision is always determined by a certain subjectivity, by the simple fact that each person occupies a place of his own from which he looks upon and judges the world, it also derives from the fact that the world itself is an objective datum, something common to all its inhabitants. . . . For judgments of taste, the world is the primary thing, not man, neither man's life nor his self."[29] Unlike moral principles, which Arendt thinks (following Kant) each individual may apprehend by himself, and without the collaboration of others, and which are the same for all, taste is in the process of continuous formation from plural sources. Judges woo (Kant's term) one another with the hope of arriving at agreement in taste; but the agreement is perhaps necessarily temporary.[30] And each one's initial judgment must be at least slightly different from everyone else's, just because individuals are differently situated from one another. (Arendt does not routinely say that judgments of taste must differ because individuals are different from one another *simpliciter,* although that thought is occasionally explicit, and the significance, for politics, if not for taste, of individual differences of character surely pervades the analysis of political action and its glory in *The Human Condition.*)

How does taste emerge? What goes into its making? Arendt follows Kant in granting "enlarged mentality" a central role. Enlarged mentality is an individual's ability to form his own judgment by first taking into account the judgments he imagines others have. In "Truth and Politics," Arendt distinguishes between enlarged mentality and impartiality,[31] even though she later conflates them.[32] Let us keep the distinction. The first thing to notice is that Arendt is not saying that each person should consult the record of what others have actually said and then try to build into one's own judgment an accommodation with their judgments, whenever possible. Rather, "I form an opinion by considering a given issue from different viewpoints, by making present to my mind the standpoints of those who are absent; that is, I represent them."[33] I must say that I find this procedure rather odd when the presumed company of judges and spectators actually get together and see and hear one another. Arendt (following Kant) is assuming, instead, a distance between judges and hence the need for a sort of impersonal and invisible communication that takes place in each person's imagination. Such distance may suit people who make uncoordinated judgments of artworks, but in politics, it suits only people who are shut out because politics is closed and unpublic. But let us leave this difficulty aside.

Furthermore, enlarged mentality is not the ability to imagine oneself as one's adversary and create arguments to support positions that one rejects (at least initially), but nevertheless tries, in the manner of Plato, Mill, and Nietzsche, to formulate as well as possible, or better than the adversary can. The point would be to test oneself by exposure to possible objections, not only actual ones. One learns from the right actual and imagined opponents. But Arendt's notion of enlarged mentality does not include this fundamental element of generous thinking.

The next thing to notice is that when Arendt speaks of taking into account the perspectives of others, she is absolute in rejecting the possibility of comprehending another person's depth of character. She says that enlarged mentality "is a question neither of empathy, as though I tried to be or to feel like somebody else, nor of counting noses and joining a majority but of being and thinking in my own identity where actually I am not."[34] Thus, to imagine the judgment of another person, I must imagine how I would judge if I were in that other person's place. *Place* seems to be a metaphor for an individual's particular social condition; or for his class or group, or perhaps for his occupation.[35]

In one text, Arendt speaks of each person's "location," which is another meta-phor for some kind of social fixedness.[36] It would not be like her, however, if she is implying that judgment is mainly a group phenomenon, and that all that enlarged mentality has to do is to imagine a handful of typical judgments that suit the main blocs — for example, classes — in society. Such an implication carries with it a social determinism that seems contrary to the strong insistence on individual unpredictability in her work. In actuality, different persons in the same place — whether class or background or occupation or region or income — make different judgments. Every person, in countless different situa-tions, has the capacity — the infinitude — to jump out of his place, avoid re-hearsed responses and speak freshly, unexpectedly. The capacity may be dor-mant, but it may suddenly appear. If Arendt shuns empathy because it seems presumptuous and destructive of human mystery, her notion of enlarged men-tality carries with it its own presumptuousness and threat to human mystery.

I must confess that I find the notion of enlarged mentality rather puzzling in itself, not just in its proposed relevance to political judgment. Why should I imagine myself in the place of another rather than trying to imagine what makes another person the distinctive person that he or she is? Well, for one thing, it may be answered, if I am to begin the effort of inferring how a person would respond to a matter ripe for judgment, I must do so on the basis of some fairly extensive prior knowledge of that person. But spectators knowing one another is not what interests Arendt. Although Arendt wants to take the judge out of his place, by an act of imagination, she does not take the judge out of himself. We can see only through our own eyes, no matter how hard we try to see through the eyes of others. Arendt does not expect miracles from imagina-tion. Perhaps she is right to suspect empathy, if it aims to understand the inwardness of another — an inwardness perhaps unknown to the person him-self in major respects, and perhaps finally inexpressible, in any case. She would certainly be right if those who praise empathy see in it a way of living by means of the lives of others, and also feel that living vicariously is the only way they can or want to live. Then, again, her skepticism toward empathy may be unsound. Let us see.

I believe that in conceptualizing enlarged mentality, Arendt is indebted not only to Kant but also to Heidegger. In the lectures, *The Fundamental Concepts of Metaphysics* (1929–1930), Heidegger raises the question as to whether "we can transpose ourselves into another human being."[37] Heidegger is impatient with the question because its premise is the Cartesian belief that each person is first given to himself as what is most certain. But each person is already with others and does not have to reach them from an initial "solipsistic isolation."[38] So far as I can tell, Heidegger is saying that we know one another because we are like one another: "the problem of the relationship of human being does not concern a question of epistemology or the question of how one human being understands another."[39] I do not know whether Arendt had access to *The Fundamental Concepts of Metaphysics,* in any form, but she must have been aware of Heidegger's tendency on the matter of empathy, a faculty that is explicitly disowned in his lectures.[40] On empathy, she certainly sounds like him. Yet we must see that her analyses of anti-Semitism, imperialism, and totalitarianism, of Greece and Rome, and of revolutionary France not only deal with what is manifest in words and deeds, but also extend to the psychology of many people remote in time, place, and culture. Arendt tries to reach their inwardness: if not their singular depths, then at least their passions and drives. She appears to attempt empathic understanding of other human beings, *especially* those who lived in periods and societies different from her own or those whose actions, more for evil than good, exceeded every norm. She tries to understand why people spoke and acted as they did. She does not imagine herself in their places; she tries to imagine them in their places. To be sure, understanding the inner sources of past events is not the same as trying to imagine how one's fellows would judge a pending matter. But there is commonality between the two mental procedures. She nevertheless rejects empathy.

Perhaps Arendt's trouble with empathy is that she understands it to mean a great body-snatching power of inhabiting others, of becoming them while remaining oneself. But the concept of empathy assumes, instead, that lodged in oneself is the whole human potentiality, and that to try to understand what animates another person, in whatever time, place, and culture, one must sooner or later look inside oneself, despite the fact that different times, places, and cultures emphasize and elicit different segments of a common human reservoir of potentiality, and have different rules, habits, codes, and practices that also must be understood; and despite the further and more important fact that individuals as individuals differ in temperament and character within and across cultures. One's inwardness is a bridge to that of others. No matter how different we are from one another, each of us can still try to understand others because inside all of us are the same tendencies, even if unexpressed and not urging themselves forward to expression. Did not Arendt look inside herself in order to fill out her understanding of often radical otherness — of Hitler or the Boers, Jefferson or Robespierre, the Greek citizen or the French resistance fighter? Indeed, her notion of enlarged mentality is based on looking inside oneself, even if one is trying to understand only one's fellow-citizens, those whose culture one shares. Just because individuals and cultures differ, looking inside oneself, however, can be only a part of the effort of understanding the inwardness of others. When she abandons understanding inwardness altogether, as with Eichmann, she claims to find no inwardness. But that must be a mistake. That he could not "think" does not mean that he did not feel; that he felt no sympathy for his victims does not mean that he had no strong feelings at all. If he was not particularly anti-Semitic, he was possessed of a belief in the racial superiority of Germans to all other peoples, and would have administered the killing of any group of non-Germans with the same bureacratic zeal he showed in exterminating Jews.

In Arendt's scorn for empathy, and for the substitution of vicarious living for courageous living that a passion for empathizing may facilitate — a scorn that is most vivid in *Rahel Varnhagen* — she threatens to make the notion of enlarged mentality politically irrelevant. On the one hand, she does not include actual knowledge of the record of one's fellows' utterances and conduct. On the other hand, she disparages the effort to understand the possible inner sources of one's fellows' anticipated views. With no knowledge of others and no attempted intuition of them, each citizen is confined to his own reading of himself, while presuming to represent others.

There are limits to empathy, of course, even in the most creatively introspective person. The inwardness of infancy and early childhood, and hence unconscious determinations, are beyond empathy. We cannot intuit one another's dream life or stream of consciousness. And just as I never understand another person fully, so I cannot understand myself fully. I cannot even, with an entire success, empathize with myself, even with my recent past and with my present. I recurrently appear strange or foreign to myself. Still, an understanding of the inwardness of others, incomplete as it must be, is a necessary part of understanding their conduct. The morality of understanding others must go beyond either the golden rule or "trading places" (that is, imagining how I would respond or feel in another's place) to understanding others in their differences from me. The morality of understanding is thus closer to the best manners in private conduct than to the best public rule-governed morality. Aesthetic judgment is indeed called for in the understanding of individuals and in conduct toward them. In truth, how could a writer create memorable characters or poetical voices that do not share his or her personal traits or ascribed social identities unless empathy is possible and the writer possessed it? What good writers do because of their talent, many others do all the time in everyday life as part of making life less unintelligible. And how can dramatic actors interpret and then put themselves into their roles, if not through empathy? Acting is not merely memorization. In sum, to the extent that enlarged mentality is not empathy under another name, empathy helps further to enlarge enlarged mentality.

To resume, the upshot of Arendt's view of enlarged mentality is that I know how another would judge when I know how I would judge if I occupied his place. We are sufficiently alike — at least as far as we participate in a common world — so that there is no mystery to be solved. Imagination must do some work. It is too easy to refuse to imagine oneself differently situated, and to think that I am only my place, that I could have no other place, and that I could therefore always be only what I am now in my present place. The imagination must unfreeze such a delusion. In a given place, any person would make the very judgment that the person actually in that place makes. The attempt to possess an enlarged mentality is really the attempt to realize how susceptible to judging differently I would be if I were literally moved from place to place, and also how comprehensively similar we are to one another, dependent for our differences on the places we occupy. In Arendt's work, people of the same society are similar enough for enlarged mentality to be possible. It is clear that, whether consistently or not, she does not posit a universality of human nature.

From recognition of this sameness-in-diversity or diversity-in-sameness, an enlarged mentality may develop, and from it, in turn, that set of society-wide standards of taste that keeps a society worldly in its art and its politics. Taste is the consummation of the particularist judgment, aestheticized and politicized, of members — citizens — of a worldly society.

I have assumed that for Arendt politics done in the right spirit is the kind of politics that needs, and repays (with pleasure and with a heightened sense of the human stature) the aestheticization of political judgment. The most obvious question to ask is whether it may be possible that politics of any kind, not just politics in the right spirit, could lend itself to aestheticized political judgment. Could not a determined judge, whether as a political theorist or as a historian or storyteller — to leave aside the spectators and actors of a properly worldly society — find in the ordinary politics of a modern society, to go back no further, the stuff that lent itself to an aesthetic emphasis on excellent appearances or on creativity, novelty, and freedom? Perhaps there are countless political occurrences that could be shaped in such a way as to contribute to the defense of the human stature? Analogously, is it not the case that aesthetic judges appreciate art that is not great or meant to be great, yet that is perceived to provide something not too distant from the gratification and inspiration that high art provides? I doubt that Arendt would have endorsed this effort, in either the political realm or the artistic one. On the one hand, ordinariness bored her; on the other hand, she truly believed in the greatness of great art and in the smallness of art that was not great. She had a mandarin sensibility. Whatever others may wish to do with the idea that aesthetic judgment offers a

206 Politics, Aesthetics, and Morality

model or an analogy or a starting point for all political judgment, and however they may wish to apply or extend Arendt's aestheticism, she, I am sure, would have resisted. She herself makes a great story of the tragic failure of a politics that began in the right spirit — the early stages of the French Revolution; and from her retelling, she reinforced her theory of political freedom as a breaking free of necessity. But her principal object in holding political phenomena to politicized aesthetic judgment is to champion the worldliness of politics done in the right spirit, not to show pity for failure.

What then of the politics that may be the most extraordinary of all, totalitarianism? I propose that Arendt tries to encompass this (in some sense) political phenomenon by employing one component of aesthetic judgment; namely, the refusal to subsume a novel phenomenon under a traditional category that misrepresents it. She is famous for rejecting the idea that Nazism and Stalinism were only somewhat exaggerated versions of immemorial tyrannies or despotisms. She insists on the unprecedented quality of both exterminationist systems. Of course, she does not aestheticize these systems; to the contrary. They are so remote from the beautiful, they are not even sublime. Instead, they are the ultimate perversion because they pervert the highest active human capacity, which is to do the unprecedented, the unexpected, the eruptive, the truly novel. The truly novel phenomenon, in these two cases, is absolutely evil. If Arendt discourages us from suffocating political splendor or ignoring political freedom because of our moral anxieties or inhibitions, she nevertheless renders with an unsurpassed power the moral horror that totalitarianism was. Yet one component of aesthetic judgment, perhaps the theoretically most important one, which is patient attention to the distinctiveness of the phenomenon that is not to be subsumed, guides her delineation of evil in *The Origins of Totalitarianism* and elsewhere.

One last point. In her lecture, "Personal Responsibility Under Dictatorship," she says that the few who refused complicity with Nazism, at great risk to themselves, "were the only ones who dared judge by themselves."[41] There is no need to insist that every time she uses the word *judgment* she means to invoke the aesthetic concept. I cannot help thinking, however, that the word is used here with the concept in mind. I mean that the resisters engaged in aestheticized political judgment to the extent that they saw the obvious — the perpetration of great evil — when the obvious was lost to sight because of the pressure of conformity and fear. Their moral judgment took on the aspect of an aestheticized judgment that perceives novelty when others see nothing special. The resisters refused to subsume evil under normality. The theorist of political evil thus joins hands with the few scattered individual resisters to it. The most theoretical sort of aestheticized political judgment meets the most desperately practical sort. Such components of aesthetic judgment as impartiality, particularist attention to worldliness, taste, and enlarged mentality all become secondary. In the face of great evil, the repressed moral sense, the plain moral sense, reasserts itself and exacts its revenge on political aestheticism. It shows (or should show) worldly political aestheticism what perverted political aestheticism is. Yet the moral sense is shored up by aestheticized judgment.[42]

Notes

1. Hannah Arendt, "What Is Freedom?" in *Between Past and Future* (1961), 2d ed. (New York: Viking, 1968), p. 152. The essay is hereafter cited as *Freedom,* and the book as *BPF.*

2. See Immanuel Kant, *Critique of Judgment,* trans. by J. H. Bernard (New York: Hafner, 1966), sect. 10, p. 55; also sect. 15, p. 62, sect. 44, p. 148.

3. Hannah Arendt, "Truth and Politics," in *BPF,* p. 241. Hereafter cited as *Truth.*

4. *Truth,* pp. 241, 247.

5. "The Crisis in Culture: Its Social and Its Political Significance," in *BPF,* p. 223. Hereafter cited as *Culture.*

6. *Culture,* p. 218.

7. Ibid.

8. Ibid., p. 210.

9. Ibid., p. 218.

10. Hannah Arendt, *Lectures on Kant's Political Philosophy,* ed. by Ronald Beiner (Chicago: University of Chicago Press, 1982), p. 55. Hereafter cited as *Lectures.*

11. *Freedom,* p. 153.

12. Ibid., p. 166.

13. Ibid.

14. *Culture,* p. 203.

15. Ibid., p. 202.

16. Ibid., p. 203.

17. Hannah Arendt, *Lectures,* p. 13.

18. Hannah Arendt, *The Life of the Mind,* vol. 1, *Thinking* (New York: Harcourt Brace Jovanovich, 1978), p. 216.

19. *Freedom,* p. 156.

20. *Lectures,* p. 56.

21. Ibid., p. 77.

22. *Truth,* p. 248.

23. Ibid., p. 262.

24. Ibid., pp. 262–63.

25. Ibid., p. 263. In an earlier essay, "The Concept of History," Arendt praises Thucydides' presentation of speeches for allowing the reader to see that "the world we have in common is usually regarded from an infinite number of standpoints, to which correspond the most diverse points of view" (*BPF,* p. 51).

26. *Lectures,* p. 71.

27. Ibid., pp. 62–65.

28. Ibid., p. 63.

29. *Culture,* p. 222.

30. Ibid.

31. *Truth,* p. 260.

32. *Lectures,* p. 42.

33. *Truth,* p. 241.

34. Ibid.

35. *Lectures,* p. 43.

36. Hannah Arendt, *The Human Condition* (Chicago: University of Chicago Press, 1958), p. 57.

37. Martin Heidegger, *The Fundamental Concepts of Metaphysics* (Bloomington: Indiana University Press, 1995), trans. by William McNeill and Nicholas Walker, p. 205.

38. Ibid., p. 206.

39. Ibid., p. 208.

40. Ibid., p. 207.

41. Hannah Arendt, "Personal Responsibility Under Dictatorship" (1964), in *Responsibility and Judgment.* Ed. Jerome Kohn (Schocken: New York, 2003), p. 44. At times Arendt seems to suggest (especially when she posits a society in which the authority of moral principles is lost) that there is only one kind of judgment at all; namely, aesthetic judgment guided by one or more elements in Kant's theory. The prior step of likening an ostensibly non-aesthetic phenomenon to an aesthetic one may not be theoretically necessary. See "Some Questions of Moral Philosophy" in *Responsibility and Judgment,* especially pp. 141–146.

42. I have benefited from the following works on Arendt's concept of judgment: Ronald Beiner, "Interpretive Essay," in *Lectures,* pp. 89–156, and "Rereading Hannah Arendt's Kant Lectures," in his *Philosophy in a Time of Lost Spirit* (Toronto: University of Toronto Press, 1997), pp. 184–94; Seyla Benhabib, *The Reluctant Modernism of Hannah Arendt* (Thousand Oaks, Calif.: Sage, 1996), especially pp. 185–98; Maurizio Passerin d'Entreves, *The Political Philosophy of Hannah Arendt* (New York: Routledge, 1994), chap. 3; Dana Villa, *Arendt and Heidegger: The Fate of the Political* (Princeton: Princeton University Press, 1996), chap. 3; Albrecht Wellmer, "Hannah Arendt on Judgment: The Unwritten Doctrine of Reason," in Larry May and Jerome Kohn, eds., *Hannah Arendt: Twenty Years Later* (Cambridge, Mass.: MIT Press, 1996), pp. 33–52.

8

Courage as a Virtue

Courage is an impossible subject. No matter what anyone says, most people (including myself) will always respect, even admire, physical courage regardless of the purpose or the cause in which it is displayed. One of the worst reproaches in the world is to be called a coward—again, almost no matter what the purpose or cause. It is merely clumsy propaganda (though clever in intention) to label as cowards the suicide hijackers who destroyed the World Trade Center on September 11, 2001. It is, I suppose, the shocking element of surprise in the attack that unconsciously helps to spare such propaganda the derision it deserves. Cowardly was the one terrible thing the suicide hijackers were not. If their religion cast an invincible spell on them, it nonetheless remains true that they needed courage to carry out their plot—a sort of courage that is closer to that shown by martyrs than by battlefield soldiers. And if we want to condemn their courage we have to say more than that they acted on behalf of a cause we abhor. In any case, bad causes do not usually stand in the way of admitting, despite President Bush's propaganda, that courage is often shown in them. To come to terms with our impulse to praise almost any show of courage really means that we should try to hold fast to the thought that the *virtue* of courage cannot be shown in a bad cause. We have to suggest furthermore that virtuous action should alone receive morally unperplexed and self-consistent admiration. Only in virtuous action can the virtue of courage be shown. In a bad cause, another kind of courage is shown, which we should learn against the odds to censure; it is an unvirtuous courage because it does not intend a moral effect and it works with the force and effect of a vice.

In "Civil Disobedience" (2001: 210), Thoreau says, "The broadest and most prevalent error requires the most disinterested virtue." He maintains that those who despite their disapproval of state policy nonetheless fall in behind it are "undoubtedly its most conscientious supporters" (210). ("Conscientious" here refers not to conscience but to dutifulness.) The issue for Thoreau is the institution of slavery and how people who know better sustain it with their patriotic allegiance. He is thus grappling with the peculiar way in which virtues (or ostensible virtues) can do the work of vices by lending their excellence to a system of wrongdoing. We should notice the false resemblance of Thoreau's view to Machiavelli's claim that when rulers practice ordinary virtues in political life (virtues like generosity, compassion, and trustworthiness), their virtues do more harm than the corresponding vices. But only a theorist who is enthralled by the project of imperialist greatness rather than devoted to limited politics would devise such an argument. He knows that ordinary virtues impede active greatness. (Luther gives a differently motivated but even more ruthless caricature than Machiavelli: acts of punishment and war are actually acts of altruistic love toward criminals and enemies.) My assertion that the virtue of courage works preponderantly with the effects of a vice does undeniably bear a formal resemblance to Machiavelli's claim, but I argue from within a moral framework, and Machiavelli does not. That makes a difference. There must be continuity between private and political morality if politics is not to be as virulent as many of its practitioners want it to be.

No, the real ancestor of Thoreau's observation is the contention of Thrasymachus in Plato's *Republic* that if the disposition of justice is to be law-abiding, then one takes part in systematic substantive injustice when one obeys the laws, which are always unjust. The virtue of justice does the work and has the effect of the vice of injustice. Underlying such law-abidingness is the will to believe what one is told and the disposition to do what people expect. Whatever the merits of Thrasymachus' claim in any particular society, the capacity of courage, specifically, to lend itself to wrongdoing is a ubiquitous fact. More than any other human trait, courage seems to be quite at home when it serves wrongdoing. It is actually the indispensable and most potent instrument of the major vices and the other psychic sources of what is most reprehensible. (This is not to say that the vice of cowardice—courage's opposite—normally functions as a virtue. Cowardice is a vice that sometimes may, for unpraiseworthy reasons, work with the effect of a virtue.) In contrast to courage, most of what are properly called virtues strain to achieve moral consequences and do so deliberately.

The unhappy truth is that courage is most praised in war. War, in its nature, is constituted by the worst wrongdoing, devoted to projects that usually have nothing to do with defending or promoting political morality, the essence of which is a commitment to human rights. Typically, all sides in a war do more harm or wrong or evil than is necessary to defend or promote human rights even when that is the purpose. The principal traditional manifestation of courage is and has been preponderantly immoral in its effects. War and its wrongdoing are unthinkable without the readiness of multitudes to show courage, or at least what people admiringly call courage, and what we should call instead unvirtuous courage. The vices and inflamed imagination of leaders are powerless without the unvirtuous courage of followers. I wish to do what Thoreau does not do: withhold the word virtue from any trait that serves wrongdoing, while not denying that these traits mimic the virtues. They show dispositions that if morally directed would be virtuous; but for a variety of reasons, can be misdirected. Much more than any other trait, courage can be misdirected and do the work of the worst vices, of vice at its worst.

What can we say to shore up the view that the prestige of courage be severed from wrongdoing, that courage is not a virtue but an unvirtuous trait when wrongdoers and the multitudes who follow and assist them manifest it? We know, to begin with, that whatever we say, our words will have no effect, perhaps even on ourselves. The idea that we could succeed in associating prestige or honor of courage only with deeds and policies that are either morally right or, at the least, compatible with morality, is naively utopian. Only a radical revision of the ideal of masculinity or manliness—a revision that is qualitatively different from that induced by radical feminism, and far more radical—could confine the honor of courage to moral deeds or those compatible with morality. Nonetheless, it is perhaps better to be naive than idle. Let us try to see how far we can get in formulating a few thoughts about courage when it is truly a virtue—that is, when courageous deeds are performed at the behest of a moral or morally irrelevant motive, when a traditionally praiseworthy trait of character serves only morality or a purpose that is compatible with morality.

Right at the start of our exploration we have to acknowledge that Plato and Aristotle, the two philosophers who provide the foundation for later thinking about courage as a virtue, find in war the natural and ideal locus of courage. Their premise is that the virtue of courage is necessary for war and that war, to begin with, is both inevitable and, at least implicitly, desirable. Against such intellectual authority it may seem futile to contend. But we should try to see what they are maintaining. Despite the tendency of their arguments, the discussion by both philosophers is valuably instructive for any student of courage and hence for any attempt to weaken the tie between courage and war. We should also remember that their discussion is framed by reflection on the best or substantially better city. Yet in many respects, the application of what they say extends into unreformed life.

In the *Republic,* Socrates defines courage as the "preservation of the belief [*doxa*] inculcated by the law through education about what things are to be feared" (IV:429c: 104). This definition works with the assumption that courage can be made into a virtue, and that only when it is cultivated and trained does it become a virtue. In sophisticated times, no virtue is spontaneous, even though its perfection requires a favorable innate endowment that only a small minority of people in a given population possesses. Courage is one of four principal virtues. (The other three are wisdom, moderation, and justice.) As a major virtue, courage helps to define the excellent person and is no mere optional trait. Courage is, above all, battlefield courage. Those who are entrusted with making war must be unafraid of death, "preferring it to defeat in battle or slavery" (III:386b: 61), "fearing slavery more than death" (III:387b: 62). In the good society, the whole society's institutions, practices, beliefs, and mores conduce to the cultivation of and training in courage in the class that must have it; namely, the warriors. The most salient point is that courage must be defined by reference to fear. Courage is therefore the overcoming of fear. It is not brainless or foolhardy. It is permeated by some — even if unusually inhibited — desire to be a coward. It also turns out that courage is itself fear, but not fear of what everyone fears naturally: death, pain, loss. The fear that is courage must be nurtured by the arrangements of the good society — or, indeed, any society. Such fear can grow only out of instilled belief or right opinion.

Courage is fear. Fear of what? Most directly in the *Laws,* Plato's answer is shame (I:647a: 27). What is the proper cause of shame? Shame at being thought a coward. That means that social arrangements must cooperate in inducing indelible horror at the thought of being a physical coward, whatever the temptations or miseries that the soldier may be subjected to. The right fear triumphs over the wrong fear. Every warrior "must be at the same time fearless and fearful" (I:647b: 28). Right belief triumphs over bodily fear. Through the Athenian stranger, Plato says, "A man becomes perfect in courage by fighting against and conquering the cowardice within him" (I:647d: 28); from childhood on, courage consists in "triumphing over the terrors and fears that come upon us" (VII:791c: 179). What does the reproach of cowardice come down to? Plato makes it clear without very much explicitness that the deepest shame should be felt when one is thought by one's peers to be a child or a sissy or a (conventional) woman (although the *Republic* allows women into the fighting and ruling class). Thus, to practice courage as a virtue is to be a man in the best sense, and the best sense is emphatically (if not exclusively) martial.

Of course, social arrangements develop a positive desire to be martial. One of the speakers in the *Laws,* Kleinias, a Cretan, says proudly that "all these practices of ours exist with a view to war . . . our lawgiver had this in view in everything he did" (I:625d–e: 4). The many, the people, in their mindlessness "do not realize that for everyone throughout the whole of life an endless war exists against all cities. . . . For what most humans call peace he [the Cretan Lawgiver] held to be only a name; in fact for everyone there always exists by nature an undeclared war among all cities" (I:625e: 4; I:626a: 4). The Athenian Stranger does rebuke Kleinias for distorting the aim of Cretan laws by making every feature conduce to prowess in foreign war (I:630c: 9) rather than "trustworthiness in the midst of dangers" in civil war; but the ideal city retains a large place for the virtue of courage in waging foreign war. Indeed, Plato builds up in both the *Republic* and the *Laws* a tightly interwoven way of life in which the self-interested ego is effaced and ties of camaraderie, loyalty, and devotion to the city are strengthened. The ultimate resource of the city is the citizen's dread of being thought a coward in war: that much of the ego is retained. Personal honor (or vanity) is narrow but intense. Why war? There are many advantages, but chief among them are these: enslaving inhabitants of defeated cities and seizing some of their wealth, while repelling the similar designs of others. In a world of cities (or nations), the city (or nation) is an absolute good to the philosophical observer as well as to the citizens of each. If the city is an absolute good, it must follow that organization for war abroad and the avoidance of civil war at home will be the principal and interconnected determinants of the whole society. Courage will be primarily battlefield courage and courage will be the most readily taxed virtue, the most difficult virtue, if one may put it that way. To revise ideas of courage in the direction I propose would mean, in part, taking issue with Plato's teaching on these points.

Aristotle adds subtlety and detail to Plato's discussion. For our purposes, what stands out is the characterization of the positive features of courage. Like Plato, Aristotle is concerned above all with battlefield courage. But though he is attentive to the part played by bodily fear as well as the fear of being thought a coward, he proposes in the *Nicomachean Ethics* a somewhat more elaborate account of what we might call the noninstrumental value of courage (and of the other virtues as well). It must first be said that Aristotle echoes the Athenian Stranger's critique of the notion that a whole society should live a life that is so much like military training that in the grim words of Plutarch (in his life of Lycurgus, the legendary founder of Sparta's famous constitution), for the Spartans "uniquely among mankind war represented a respite from their military training" (Plutarch, 1988: 35). Aristotle insists in the *Politics* that if there is war it must be for the sake of peace (VII:14, 1333a: 309). Nonetheless, courage keeps its place among the virtues in Aristotle's analysis in the *Nicomachean Ethics*, and the truest courage is steadfastness in the face of death on the battlefield (III:6, 1115a: 69). Virtue is not complete without physical courage, and physical courage is not complete without participation in war against other cities.

What specifically does Aristotle add to Plato? At least some of the time, he considers the value of courage seemingly apart from its contribution to the well-being of society. Plato had already taught in the *Republic* that the virtues, including courage, were both instrumentally valuable and, more important, valuable "for their own sake" (that is, noble in themselves) (II:357b–c, 45). For being doubly valuable, the virtues belong to the category of best things. Aristotle develops this theme interestingly. In the *Politics,* he says of the Spartans that, "Although they truly think that the goods for which men contend are to be acquired by virtue rather than by vice, they err in supposing that these goods are to be preferred to the virtue that gains them" (II:9, 1271b: 113). A supplementary idea appears in the *Nicomachean Ethics:* "Activities desirable in themselves are those from which we seek to derive nothing beyond the actual exercise of the activity" (X:6, 1176b: 286). These formulations raise the question, Does courage exist for the sake of war, or war for the sake of courage? To be sure, at the end of the *Nicomachean Ethics,* Aristotle reverts to the more mundane view that all the practical virtues manifested in military and political actions are "unleisurely, aim at an end, and are not chosen for their own sake" (X:7, 1177b: 290). In comparison to the exercise of the intellectual virtues in philosophical contemplation, the moral and practical virtues seem almost servile. To be merely useful is often close to being servile. In contrast, the individual's contemplative life is of no practical use; it can and does exist in many imperfect societies; and the moral and practical virtues are not a preparation or an outlet for the highest intellectual virtues. Contemplation is an imitation of and participation in the divine, in the more than human. Despite this apparent inconsistency on the nature of the practical virtues, courage, like the other ones, often seems prized by Aristotle as intrinsically valuable. We must grant that just as it is sometimes hard to tell whether a trait works with the effect of a virtue or vice, so it is often hard, sometimes impossible, to tell whether a trait functions as a means or end.

What, then, does it mean to suggest that war exists for the sake of courage? Aristotle's repeated view is that acting honorably or doing honorable (or fine) deeds is an end in itself. The implication is that being noble or acting nobly requires no further defense, any more than being happy in the proper sense does. In fact, being happy over a whole life is, precisely, to exercise the virtues in the appropriate activities; the moral and political activities are a central part of a whole life. To be happy is to be fulfilled as a virtuous human being. Of course, the benefits to society from the virtues are not incidental; much less are they only pretexts for the display of the virtues. Rather, the benefits cannot be severed from the virtues that have gone into their attainment. Just as the virtues would not be virtues unless they showed themselves in valuable and praiseworthy activities, so the benefits would not be worth having if they were attained without the virtues. The trouble with the Spartans is that though they wanted benefits by means of the virtues, they would not be interested in the virtues if the virtues produced no practical benefits. They were not interested in the idea of happiness as the life of virtue; they compromised the noble virtues by a single-minded practicality. (It is no accident that in the *Republic*, Plato makes love of wealth the secret passion of ambitious warriors.) In the *Politics*, Aristotle is clear that the honorable is distinct from both the necessary and the useful (I:7, 1255b: 63; VII:14, 1333a: 309). If action is to be honorable and not just necessary or useful, it must come from the virtues, not from courage only, but surely also from courage. Only action can be honorable. To be honorable is not properly understood when seen as a useful condition. He says in the *Politics*, "there must be war for the sake of peace, business for the sake of leisure, things useful and necessary for the sake of things honorable" (VII: 14, 1333a: 309). Unlike Plato in the *Republic*, Aristotle does not found the good society on a constitutive act of injustice to neighbors. He thus seems to welcome war, a little less than Plato does, as an opportunity for the display of courage. Yet perhaps more than Plato, he appreciates displays of courage for their own sake.

Is Aristotle saying that society exists for the purpose of the virtuous fulfillment of each individual? Is the good society simply a theatrical stage on which the (moral and practical) virtues can be acted out? I do not think the matter can be expressed in quite this way. In the good society, the virtue of individuals will perforce contribute to the maintenance and prosperity of society. But a properly happy society would not be happy unless its citizens were individually happy. They are happy because they are virtuous; they are virtuous because they are noble. There are, however, other advantages to the virtues. It may not be too farfetched to think that Aristotle is pointing the way to a certain outlook, which is that observers — philosophers, poets, and historians — are also great beneficiaries of the record of noble or honorable deeds. Observers, especially future ones, benefit from being allowed to be, if only in a highly mediated manner, witnesses to courage. Deeds of courage help to show what humanity is capable of. They help to show that not all of human life is submissive to the necessary and useful. There is nobility, after all. Why else is Greece so attached to Homer?

What can we take from Aristotle? Above all, the notion that the honor of courage is — at least some of the time — found in deeds that are not subject to necessity or utility. In more modern language, courage gives evidence of a hard-won freedom of action. There is something transcendent about courage as a virtue. Later, I will say more about the reconception of honor that is called for, if courage is truly to be a virtue.

But must physical courage be battlefield courage to be a virtue? The question nags because Plato and especially Aristotle do not give much attention to the moral nature of the wars that elicit courage from citizens of the good city. Plato does say in the *Republic* that ideally, when Greek cities make war on one another, if they must do so, they should look on such conflicts as civil war, not as war between peoples. The Greeks are one people. If they fight, "their attitude of mind should be that of people who'll one day be reconciled and who won't always be at war" (V: 470d–e: 145). Their mutual depredations should be limited to carrying off the harvest of the vanquished (V: 470d: 145), and no Greek city should make slaves of defeated Greeks (V: 469c: 144). Toward the barbarians, however, Plato permits the Greeks any act of severity or exploitation. Wars against barbarians make it likelier that Greeks will keep their hands off one another. Barbarians thus exist in order to be enemies. Plato reinstates toward barbarians the very mode of behavior that earlier in the *Republic* is condemned by Socrates. When one of the interlocutors, Polemarchus, defines justice as acting so as "to benefit one's friends and harm one's enemies" (I:334b: 9), Socrates rejects the definition with the simple assertion that "it is never just to harm anyone" (I:335e: 11).

Of course Socates never says that cities should follow the same morality that private individuals, who are just, follow. I suppose the implicit thought is that when citizens act politically, they are not acting personally, acting out of their own motives. Their virtues are their own; but they use their virtues to fill their roles; they act impersonally. As disciplined members of a formal group, they may therefore do anything their role calls for. In political life, they are accountable for being good citizens, not good persons. At the same time, Socrates never explains why political morality (acts of state, whether in ruling a city or acting with or against other cities) has different rules from private morality. As Plato's mouthpiece, he just takes it for granted that a city is an absolute entity whose right to endure as a city, in a world of cities and other political units, is to go unquestioned. Hence the just city cannot treat other cities as a just individual would treat other individuals.

Aristotle in the *Politics* offers an apparently novel racialist justification of slavery: wrong by nature for Greeks to be enslaved, right by nature for the Greeks to enslave everyone else. He intimates as well a racialist geopolitics in which greater Greece conquers and rules many non-Greek peoples.

We are therefore left with an indigestible fact: Plato and Aristotle produced two of the most respected analyses of courage as a virtue, yet neither of them hesitated to make courage central to morally unexamined wars. It is as if when wars are fought by a putatively virtuous citizenry, there is no room left to raise further moral questions about their organized actions. But how can courage be a virtue if its characteristic works are instrumental to the wrongdoing necessarily implicated in all wars? More strongly put, how can courage be a virtue if without it, wrongdoing on a large scale could rarely if ever take place? For what other virtue do we make such allowance? If I am accused of being anachronistic when I expect Plato and Aristotle to be more interested than they are in the moral nature of the wars they contemplate, I would direct my reproaches to those who live in our world and still think that Plato and Aristotle speak the last word, not just the first word, about courage as a virtue. A further question is whether courage, to be a virtue, has to result from cultivation and training. Can it be spontaneous?

Is it defensible to say that battlefield courage deserves admiration, even though it has worked preponderantly with the effects of vice? Does such courage — though not, even loosely speaking, a virtue most of the time — deserve nonetheless the admiration that is ordinarily bestowed on any virtue? Some may grant the point that a true virtue cannot be routinely efficacious in the production of evil or oppression or injustice, but go on to say that battlefield courage, despite all its terrible effects, is still praiseworthy as a human trait or inclination. For this thought to be defensible, the advocate must be prepared to hold that unvirtuous battlefield courage is so admirable that it is worth its undeniably enormous moral cost. Bravery is always difficult for the whole person — more difficult than anything else. Confronting difficulty is always admirable. Then, too, when the difficulty is acquitting oneself honorably in battle, there is almost no human exertion as rich in experience. The beneficiaries are thus the combatants, not just the cause they happen to serve. This defense of battlefield courage is helped along by a thought that may appease the morally anxious: such courage is usually displayed by combatants who are inwardly innocent. They do not typically intend wickedness, even though most of the time wickedness is what results from their deeds. It is not clear that most of them intend anything at all. They may be wicked to the observer, but they are sincerely not wicked to themselves. There is something about war that as it were helplessly denies to all but a few combatants (and only occasionally) a sense that what they are doing is properly subject even to moral scrutiny, much less moral condemnation. Only those who are not involved in the action can hope to judge. But then their judgment is untested; it does not rest on firsthand knowledge. In the position of combatants, their judges would do what combatants do, and think of themselves as innocent, just as combatants do. A lack of self-awareness may not be compatible with manifesting a virtue, any more than doing the work of vice is. So be it. Battlefield courage, irrespective of the moral quality of the cause for which it is shown, and despite the lack of moral consciousness inherent in its display, must still merit praise and admiration from the observer on the grounds that it conduces to an unrivaled richness of experience.

A second defense of battlefield courage as praiseworthy, closely related to the first, is that its moral cost is not simply outweighed but is actually beside the point. The courage of self-sacrifice that war manages to elicit from countless combatants consecrates their cause, even the worst one, not only those causes that are morally better. When human exertion flies in the face of the most elementary will to self-preservation, this exertion must have some kind of goodness, even if not the goodness of virtue.

Both defenses are initially or ultimately existential. Existential considerations take over the apologetic burden hitherto carried by aristocratic virtue. The underlying premise of the first defense is the belief that there are certain values — most relevantly, richness of experience — that often outweigh moral ones. The second defense has a more radical premise. It is that some potentialities — most relevantly, self-sacrifice — have an independent standing and may legitimately disallow the relevance of moral concerns altogether. When made actual, these potentialities have as great a claim on human respect as any moral virtues. Common to the two defenses is the claim that there are supreme existential values of expression that would remain latent if moral claims were allowed to veto all others. To be sure, war is action, and action is in many spheres of life subject to moral judgment. But war's action is so distinct and also so existentially significant that moral judgment may be either outweighed or not allowed any say at all.

What matters for both positions is not moral goodness, but human traits, bonds, and efforts of a special sort for which battlefield courage opens the way. The first position exonerates the inwardness of combatants in the spirit of the saying of Jesus: forgive them for they know not what they do (Luke 23:34). They are so caught up in experience they are ecstatic, they are innocent. The second position does more than exonerate; it sanctifies the inwardness of combatants by concentrating on their readiness to give up everything in a spirit of selflessness.

These themes and many besides are explored with a high intelligence by the late J. Glenn Gray in his book *The Warriors,* first published in 1959. It is one of the few books that aim at holding up battlefield courage as praiseworthy while still paying full attention to the moral issues involved. Gray does not unequivocally give the last word to moral considerations, but he certainly presents the moral case with power. Trained in German philosophy and then a combatant in World War II, he provides a subtle, often tormented phenomenological account of his experiences. In the course of his book, he accepts both of the just named defenses of unvirtuous battlefield courage as praiseworthy, but his overall achievement is not reducible to any particular position. He manages to reveal to skeptics why war attracts combatants and compels the imagination of many observers. He also reminds those who love the experience of war why they should not do so with a whole heart. Gray himself would not have done without the experience of war, but the insights he accumulates make it clear that war is ruinously expensive — to the character of those who fight as well as to the most simple moral precepts. Yet in the rapid flow of the book's contending sentiments, battlefield courage remains worthy of his admiration: he does not call it a virtue but he does find it most praiseworthy. Perhaps, on balance, the world is better for having war: on that note the book ends. In any case, only in utopian speculation — which Gray attempts in the last chapter — can war ever disappear. Its occurrence is inevitable. The situation is lamentable, but not only lamentable.

I will concentrate on the two defenses of battlefield courage as Gray presents them: praiseworthy and admirable courage, even if the word virtue must be withheld from it. It would not be uncharitable to remember as we read Gray's book that he knew as a scholar about the scale of horrors of World War I and knew as a scholar and participant about the scale of horrors of World War II.

Gray makes a case for war apart from the goals it may achieve. In that respect, his view resembles one strand of Aristotle's outlook. But if for Aristotle war exists for the display of the virtue of courage, Gray sees war as an unrivaled opportunity for experience. War, courage, and invaluably distinctive experience are indissociably joined. Each is indispensable to the existence of the other two, yet none is a mere means.

Let us begin with the first defense: by calling forth battlefield courage, war makes possible a type of experience that no other human activity affords. It is a matter of intensity: war is the highest intensifier of valuable experience. The standard is not Aristotelian happiness, but a kind of exhilaration that is perhaps not far from Dionysian intoxication; but as Gray renders it, it is available without religious feeling. Anyone — any young man, for Gray — is likely to find in war an exhilaration that surpasses any other. From within the exhilaration, battlefield courage is born. A man is swept away, carried out of himself and enabled to perform courageous deeds that he had never dreamed of or only fantasized about. Especially if one is not a professional soldier, and has had only basic training, and comes from a society that does not organize all its institutions and habits and sentiments around the practice of war, one's battlefield courage will be what I call spontaneous. Spontaneous courage will not be courage as a virtue, as Plato and Aristotle conceptualize virtue, because they tend to see virtue as that which can be attained only as the result of cultivation and training from the earliest age and in a setting that favors it. But spontaneous courage will be, in Gray's analysis, praiseworthy, as praiseworthy as the virtue of courage in Plato and Aristotle. (They both pay only a little grudging attention to the courage of ordinary democratic citizens, ignoring Pericles' pride in the spontaneous courage of the people: "courage not of art but of nature" [Thucydides, II:38: 109].)

For the first defense of battlefield courage, then, the question is, How are war's exhilaration and spontaneous courage mutually dependent? For the purpose of distilling the benefits of Gray's work for our discussion, I will add that this question can be seen from two perspectives. The exhilaration, the intensification of experience that combat arouses, as Gray describes it, is of course what the soldier feels and may or may not put into words during or right after the action. There is another perspective, that of the observer (which Gray himself sustains throughout his book). But Gray's readers are also observers and their views may not always agree with his. I distinguish between perspectives because each emphasizes different (if related) values. (I will also discuss both perspectives when we take up the second defense of battlefield courage.) All these values figure in Gray's book.

For the combatant, the experience is intense owing to what Gray calls "the enduring appeals of battle" (the title of his second chapter). It takes courage to begin to feel the exhilaration of intense experience. Such intensity contributes to the growth of the self-knowledge of the combatant by eliciting new and unsuspected courage but also in other ways. But is there a growth of selfhood? If there is, such growth would not be, I think, the same as self-realization. The experience of war may be the highest point of one's life, but it is radically discontinuous from the rest of one's life. It interrupts the arc of one's life. It need not influence the way in which one leads one's life thereafter. War may be the professional soldier's self-realization, but it is not that of the recruited soldier who, if he survives, will return to civilian life. Gray is only occasionally interested in the professional soldier. On the other hand, when Gray becomes an observer reflecting on his own experience of the intensity and exhilaration of war, he wants to get readers to share his conviction that war is indispensable because it shows what human beings are capable of: the lengths to which they will go to succeed in an enterprise, the resourcefulness they can show in the face of great risks, and, above all, the courage they can show in the face of supreme danger. The values of Gray the observer are, for much of the book, existential. The moral cost recedes or evaporates. That war is so to speak a manufactured situation, a manufactured necessity, does not signify. For the sake of his existentialism, and as part of it, Gray adopts an aesthetic perspective. His thoughts lead easily to the conclusion that life is best seen as a spectacle in which lethal conflict is the source of the greatest dramatic effect. All sides and participants are equally necessary to the spectacle. To mount the spectacle of war is a great source of the honor of the human race, of pride in human stature.

The appeals of battle arise from and call forth spontaneous courage. If you will, the pleasures of combat help to make men eager to stay in war and hence do what courage makes it possible for them to do. If the display of courage is not the end in sight, it is an exaction that many are willing to endure. War is unthinkable without it, and men may be said to want war — not only when they are bored by peace but also when they are in the thick of battle. What, then, are "the secret attractions of war" (28), as Gray recounts them? From his experience and observation, three stand out. Together they are modes of exhilaration, of experience at its most intense. The first is "the delight in seeing," the second is the "delight in comradeship," and the third is "the delight in destruction" (28–29). He attributes all three delights to combatants in general, including himself, and also hopes that readers will endorse his conclusions when he took upon himself the role of observer while still a combatant (excerpts from his wartime journals and letters are included in the book), but most profoundly when he wrote about his experience in the years afterward.

Gray hopes that readers will understand and perhaps sympathize with two of the delights (seeing and comradeship). As for the delight in destruction, it is an evil that may nevertheless foster a stronger disposition to preservative goodness than peaceful life could ever do. Of these three passions — the satisfaction of which are all delights — Gray is most eloquent (and perhaps most convincing) on comradeship. It turns out that delight in comradeship leads Gray to the theme of admirable self-sacrifice. Thus all three delights contribute to the defense of battlefield courage as a vehicle of intense experience, but delight in comradeship eventually moves Gray to what I have called the second defense of praiseworthy battlefield courage. I will take up the passions in Gray's sequence and connect them to the two defenses.

The delight in seeing is a concept Gray borrows from St. John's First Epistle, where he speaks of "the lust of the eyes" (2:16). The appeal of war is more to the imagination or mind's eye than to what we literally see. Still, the physical eyes are filled with pleasure by the sight of foreign lands; by the armaments of war, the explosion of bombs; by groups marching in order; by "the captured enemy in a cage" (29). Witnessing these tableaux, the mind also feeds on the spectacle of war. Ugliness itself has an aesthetic appeal (30), and scenes of battle have a "fearful beauty" — Gray alludes to Yeats's phrase "terrible beauty" about the Easter uprising in Ireland in 1916 (32). In moments of abstraction from the human cost of war's havoc, "the scene was beyond all question magnificent" (33). Gray candidly pictures the way in which the aesthetic faculties may suspend the moral ones. Most important, the major aesthetic gratification of war is not the impression of beauty that these phenomena leave with the susceptible participant-observer, but rather the feeling of the sublime (33).

Gray says, "Astonishment and wonder and awe appear to be part of our deepest being, and war offers them an exercise field par excellence" (34). He takes issue with those who think that a feeling of the sublime must arise from a feeling of superiority to the "blind forces and lifeless powers of nature" (35). No, the sublimity of war is not triumph over forces, human or natural, but instead "a recognition of power and grandeur to which we are subject" (35). The experience of sublimity is an extraordinary intensification of experience. But the crucial point is that under the spell of wonder at apparently superhuman forces, soldiers are detached from a sense of self and hence subordinate themselves to the effort of war. "We are able to disregard personal danger at such moments by transcending the self, by forgetting our separateness" (35). (Is the sense of self really lost when the self is witness to its own transcendence, I wonder?) Perhaps not every soldier can lose himself in rapt contemplation in the midst of danger, but it is "a common-enough phenomenon" (36). One sees a duty to make the sublime occurrence materialize or continue. Indeed, Gray thinks that if the world ends because of some tremendous explosions, "there will be those who will watch the spectacle to the last minute, without fear, disinterestedly and with detachment" (36).

Aesthetic considerations have a sizable part in the play of courage. Courage is needed for the creation of sublimity, but the impression of sublimity in turn also increases courage. Yet, as Gray says, the delight in seeing with the mind's eye, which appears "to be a noble quality in men," has a moral cost. Does Gray think that sublimity of this sort outweighs the moral cost? He equivocates, but he is certain that "aesthetic ecstasy . . . is always pressing us beyond the border of the morally permissible" (39). He does not take the way out that consists in saying that the aesthetic and the moral are both valuable, but incommensurably so, and that one's choice between them is therefore a mere preference without a reasoned basis; one simply chooses. Gray leaves the matter hanging at this point in the text, but subsequently allows morality to catch up with the aesthetic and eventually subordinate it. Yet the memory of the sublimity of war remains together with its intimate tie to spontaneous battlefield courage. It haunts morality with a sense of the existential costs of morality.

The second and most salient appeal of war is the tie of comradeship. Like the feeling of sublimity, comradeship also involves a loss of sense of self, or at least an attenuation of it. But unlike the essentially aesthetic quality of the delight in seeing or imagining, the delight in comradeship is, in Gray's view, a moral passion. Comradeship is devotion to one's fellows. The trouble is that the devotion is so exclusive that the cost to others does not register on oneself. Only one's comrades retain reality as human beings. Comradeship is therefore, in my judgment, not a moral passion but a quasi-moral one; it is really existential. Its other-regarding demands on the self can be even more strenuous than those of impersonal morality, but it effaces the moral claims of all people but one's "little platoon." Comradeship mimics morality while betraying it. Many combatants experience this devotion and the intoxication that goes with it. Gray expects disinterested readers to sympathize fully. But the quasi-moral is likely to work with the force of immorality. Moral commitments may consequently preclude sharing Gray's love of comradeship wholeheartedly. In any event, by being the greatest reward of battlefield courage, comradeship is its greatest instigator.

It is at this point that the advantages to selfhood of intensity of experience give way to the willingness to sacrifice oneself. Delight in comradeship is so great that it transforms itself into dying for one's comrades. It rises above itself. The underside, of course, is that if one is willing to sacrifice everything, one is also willing to force adversaries to do the same. What I have labeled the first defense of battlefield courage merges with the second.

What makes delight in comradeship the great source of battlefield courage and drives it to the extreme point of self-sacrifice? I suppose that someone at the point of dying can rarely put into words the causes of his heroism. There are, of course, famous last words, but they cover more than they reveal, and though they signify, they explain little. Gray makes a strong effort to disclose the mentality of combatants, while reserving for himself as a philosophical observer the capacity to articulate ideal reasons. To be sure, ideal reasons capture a good part of what combatants feel, but there remain considerations that only a philosophical observer can be sensitive to. Let us begin with these ideal reasons.

Gray says that many veterans who are honest with themselves will admit that "participation with others in the chances of battle had its unforgettable side." Though hard to express and to make intelligible to those without the experience, "Probably the feeling of liberation is basic" (44). Gray then goes on to distill the highest value of the experience of war in the company of comrades. "Many of us can experience freedom as a thrilling reality . . . only when we are acting with others for a concrete goal that costs something absolute for its attainment" (44). But this thought with its affinities to German Idealism is underlain by a remarkable effort to speak an unpleasant truth (if truth it is). He says, "Individual freedom to do what we will with our lives and our talents, the freedom of self-determination, appears to us most of the time as frivolous or burdensome. Such freedom leaves us empty and alone, feeling undirected and insignificant. Only comparatively few of us know how to make this individual freedom productive and joyous. But communal freedom can pervade nearly everyone and carry everything before it" (45–46). He knows that he has voiced an antidemocratic sentiment. After all, the Athenian democrats had defined freedom as doing what you want and living as you like. But communalism is a tremendous delight; it is freedom from freedom. The individual self is not large enough. "With the boundaries of the self expanded, they [the combatants] sense a kinship never known before. Their 'I' passes insensibly into a 'we,' 'my becomes our,' and individual fate loses its central importance" (45). The echoes of Plato's characterization of the fate of the individual self in the ideal ruling and fighting class must be deliberate. The bond among warriors is tighter than any other in the world.

Now, the "communal ecstasy" (46) of this comradeship, Gray says, is unlike the aesthetic ecstasy of the sublime fed by the appeal of battle to the mind's eye. The whole person is caught up in comradeship, not merely his contemplative fascination. A common mortal danger and a common effort to repel that danger help to account for loyalty to the group. It is loyalty unto death. There must be a "superpersonal will" in charge (41); the military command must be in place; there must be organization; any fighting unit "must have a limited and specific objective" (42). With these preconditions met, the fighting unit will develop a passionate comradeship once in the thick of battle. All this intense experience, however, has its telos beyond itself. Under the severest pressure, comradeship becomes self-sacrificial courage. Is it love of comrades that makes each soldier selfless? Not quite. Gray speaks of "the assurance of immortality that makes self-sacrifice at these moments so relatively easy" (46). Perhaps there is a religious basis for this assurance. But Gray prefers to make it this-worldly. The closest he comes to a flat explanation is his remark that "death becomes in a measure unreal and unbelievable to one who is sharing his life with his companions. Immortality . . . becomes a present and self-evident fact" (46). In other words, "the self that dies is little in comparison with that which survives and triumphs" (47).

In a later chapter, "The Soldier's Relation to Death," Gray speaks in a different tone about self-sacrifice. The writing is at times actually morbid. Here he is more interested in those who have a relation to death and hence to self-sacrifice that is "not so common" (121). Even though it is not so common, it is "closer to representing the essence of the fighting man" (121–22). Some who fight "can learn to regard death as an anticipated experience among other experiences" (122). Indeed, death is "a supreme kind of experience" because "They look out upon the world as adventure" (123). These combatants are dashing, lighthearted, careless of their own lives and those of others. They verge on the inhuman (124). Yet they are admirable. Their action unto death is in itself a philosophical commentary on life. The most thoughtful of them "regard death as that absolute in human existence which gives life its poignancy and intensity" (122). They are at the furthest remove from those whose exhaustion makes them welcome death on the battlefield (104) or those who find in dying atonement for the killing they have done (120). The adventurous are uninterested in morality but very much interested in the proper existential relation to death and hence to life. Gray's own existentialism is most keen when his writing becomes impassioned about courageous adventurers. But when he says that for the poetical or philosophical nature, "death is an adventure in knowledge," it is hard to see how any but a more or less religious attitude is at work, not an existential one.

When Gray writes about the soldier's relation to death, he leaves the average experience of combatants behind. He is thinking aloud philosophically. He is appealing as an observer to other observers; and they can say that the words are impressive, but have no necessary force. The words do not fascinate, much less persuade those for whom the moral question of the rightness of the cause in which self-sacrifice figures is paramount. The argument is at its most serious when Gray tries to render the mentality of the great mass of combatants. When they are immersed in comradeship, but not inclined to philosophize, battlefield courage comes over them and they perform feats of selflessness that they could not have planned to perform, being unprofessional soldiers temporarily removed from civilian life. Their feats are antithetical to the tenor of their civilian lives. Their courage is not virtuous in the ancient sense; it is spontaneous, an unpremeditated response to common peril. But it is a response that is unthinkable without the favoring circumstances of the battlefield.

Before finally expressing admiration for such self-sacrifice, Gray stages an argument. He attributes to unequivocal defenders of war the view that the capacity for self-sacrifice brings men to "a recognition of their true nature and their essential relationships" (48). There is a "mystical element" in war" (47). Opponents press the point that "As often as not, it [self-sacrifice in war] puts itself at the service of an evil cause" (49). Gray's exasperated judgment is that "What our moral self tells us is abhorrent, our religious self and aesthetic self yearn for as the ultimate good" (49–50). Can he break out of the dilemma? He introduces a number of suggestions. Among them are these: his favorable reference to Christian theologians who taught that "without the supramoral act, we human beings are not able to lead even a normally moral existence" (50); and his contention that self-sacrifice, like attraction to the sublime, "makes possible the higher reaches of the spirit into the realms of poetry, philosophy, and genuine religion" (50). Extremism makes moderation dependable; the best and the worst are joined at the root. He concludes, "Are we not right in honoring the fighter's impulse to sacrifice himself for a comrade, even though it be done, as it so frequently is, in an evil cause? I think so" (50). Why exactly? There is no exactness; there probably cannot be any. There is only, at the last, a proud existential or perhaps a quasi-religious sentiment: "our species has a different destiny than is granted to other animals" (51). By the time Gray is finished, he has buried moral considerations, though with a troubled conscience.

I have no doubt that Gray has made as good an existential case as anyone for the idea that battlefield courage as such is praiseworthy, admirable. As we have seen, that case is built on two main facts: battlefield courage goes with unusual intensity of experience and it expresses itself with striking frequency in the form of self-sacrifice. The upshot is that it is praiseworthy whatever the cause that prompts it. War, the manufacturer of necessity, has more to do with human greatness of stature than almost any other activity and is inseparable from all other great activities. Against such an outlook, the moral voice insists that there must be expressions of physical courage that are in fact separable from war and battlefield courage, that show forth human greatness, and that also are moral or compatible with morality. In the next section, we will turn to these alternatives.

Gray's third enduring appeal of battle is delight in destruction. Intensity of experience is once again the key matter. What combatants are capable of is here shown not in self-sacrifice but in the urge to level, waste, and kill. Both combatants and observers (including Gray himself) can take pleasure in witnessing or imagining destruction. For combatants, this pleasure is a compound of two pleasures: fighting for the sake of the pleasure of fighting unto death, and fighting for the sake of the pleasure of prevailing by means of inflicting death; the pleasures of mortal contest and of victory in mortal contest. (The destruction of structures and artifacts and perhaps the desolation of nature also provide pleasure.) Both pleasures ultimately stem from a love of violence: the sheer pleasure of violence. But he says that this delight is "a radical evil" because soldiers turn into"berserkers and destroyers" (51). He is ashamed of feeling this delight, this "ecstasy without a union" (56). Nevertheless, he cannot resist trying to draw something praiseworthy from this abomination. His theme is how promixity to destruction may call up a tender preservative love. "The object of one's care is less essential than the presence of the need to take care and preserve" (85). Once again, the existential value of a human trait is prized above the benefits that may accrue from its display. I am afraid, however, that the passages on preservative love do nothing to lessen the terribleness of the urge to destroy that precedes it. It is not clear how many soldiers have this feeling. In any case, battlefield courage in itself is not at issue, although the wish to praise and admire it is harshly assaulted by its connection to baseness in human beings and to what is lower than baseness — inflamed criminality. Gray simply could not find the delight in destruction void of some compensatory grace. But the cruel destruction far outweighs the preservation, which is called forth only to palliate the destruction. In such a context, the preservative love has no moral importance; it comes close to self-indulgence; at the least it is self-serving.

Gray makes the enduring appeals of battle, the secret attractions of war, not only vivid but philosophically noteworthy. He shows conceptual delicacy in linking battlefield courage with both intensity of experience and the willingness for self-sacrifice. He provides a complex existential account of battlefield courage. This leads him to inhabit Aristotle's intermittent view that though fighting does not exist for the sake of the pleasures of fighting, war may exist for the sake of courage as much as courage exists for the sake of war. Gray is suggesting that the "delights" of war absolutely depend on battlefield courage to keep war as a practice intact, and that courage enhances existence — enhances even the life of the combatants who die. The enhancement of life is yoked to the necessities of war. The rejoinder to Gray (which is also an endorsement of his moral side) is that the moral costs, the costs to the lives and decent well-being of countless people, are well beyond exorbitant. Gray would not part with his experience of war, but he would, though with some ambivalence, see the world free of war.

Let us begin where he (almost) ends. Let us suggest that for all the existential benefits of battlefield courage, for all the temptation to admire it irrespective of the cause in which it is shown, we would be glad to see it disappear from the world, along with war. In its place, we would begin with an admiration of other kinds of physical courage, and then see where that response led. It would be too easy, though not necessarily false, to say that intellectual courage and moral courage are intrinsically superior to physical courage. Let us therefore stay with physical courage. When could we admire it without running into a wall of moral objections? Is it not in fact sometimes needed for the sake of acting morally or compatibly with morality?

Gray's richness of mind facilitates a much less existential defense of physical courage. He also greatly helps to rebut the tendency of Plato's and Aristotle's teaching that virtuous courage requires cultivation and lifelong training. Rather, courage can be spontaneous and is perhaps all the more remarkable for being uncultivated and only minimally trained. Not indoctrinated right belief but common, if unreflective, sentiments provide the spur. Gray is also free of the difficulties that come from calling battlefield courage a virtue even when — perhaps especially when — courage is shown in the habitual commission of immoral deeds that contribute to a larger scheme of wrongdoing. The result of Gray's meditations is that he gives life to the thought that the courage of the world — whether on the battlefield or elsewhere — is spontaneous courage. It comes and goes, even when under military discipline. In war it occurs amid conditions of manufactured necessity — not artificial, as in sports; not urgent, as in some dangerous peaceful occupations — but manufactured by the inexhaustible irrationality of reason of state. If battlefield courage is so morally dubious, we must think again as to when spontaneous courage is properly admirable and praiseworthy, when in fact we can call it a virtue, though not as Plato and Aristotle define virtue.

There is one more lesson that emerges from Gray's book, and it is the most important one. He makes the idea plausible that strictly speaking there can be no "moral equivalent" to battlefield courage. The reason is that there is no activity that is moral or morally compatible that provides equivalent existential advantages to those of war. We can find a number of activities that come close, but if we think comradeship unto death an existential advantage, we are not likely to discover any activity existentially equal to it. The existential significance of the self-sacrifice of comrades unto death is only rarely encountered in peaceful activities that are moral or morally compatible — though of course, miners, fire workers, and police, among others, can lead dangerous lives. To be sure, some experience off the battlefield can be as intense as war, to use the other existential criterion. (Are we sure that action where the risk of death is ever present is intense, rather than unreal?) It does not suffice, however, for the moral minded to say that war is not needed for the "delight in seeing," whether the reward is beauty or sublimity; or even that there can be comradeship, or something like it, in many spheres of life, even if not typically unto death. We must concede to Gray's existential outlook what we have to: we must admit that serious losses are inflicted on certain existential values by moral claims. But then we can go on to think about peacetime physical courage within a moral framework. Within a moral framework, let it be said, existential values will find a large place, but not the dominant one, not the primacy desired by a number of thinkers, including Gray some of the time. But because we want to admire and praise physical courage in the right way, we must have examples of it as a virtue — when its traditional entanglement with wrongdoing is left behind. And the more spontaneous, the more uncultivated or untrained, that virtuous courage is, the better.

I would like to offer some utopian speculation about courage as a virtue. Whatever the existential losses sustained in breaking the link between courage and the battlefield, the moral gains are considerable. We must look for activities in which physical courage of a high order can be displayed and individuals can reasonably expect to earn honor for that display in their own eyes as well as the observer's. We already bestow honor on most of them, but to burnish it we should try to stop bestowing honor on battlefield courage and see it as the organized criminality that it is. Thus, there are activities that have existential affinities with battlefield experience in their intensity; some of these activities may contain the element of personal risk (even unto death, though rarely), whether for the sake of comrades or only in their company. Probably the intensity and the risk are not typically as great as they are in battlefield experience. Absolute self-sacrifice does not define these activities. Once again, so be it. These moral or morally compatible activities benefit the souls of the participants and produce immense advantages for others. Another advantage is the help they give philosophical observers in shoring up human stature and establishing the honor of the human race, though not through killing.

In thinking about courage as a virtue, as I have defined it, one would think that the sensible next step would be to enlist the help of William James's celebrated essay "The Moral Equivalent of War" (1910). The essay is undeniably rich; it is written by a fierce opponent of American imperialism and by a self-described pacifist. Yet so intent is James on seeing war as perhaps the most important revealer "of what men and women are able to bear" ("The Energies of Men" [1907]: 1228) that he gives much more to unqualified defenders of war ("the war-party") than they deserve (James, 1910: 1290). James is captivated by the possibility that it is good for young people especially to be "owned" by their country (1292), disposed in their conscripted service to pay "the blood-tax" they owe it (1291), and ready to submit themselves to a collective discipline in the name of "a stable system of morals of civic honour" (1290). James fears the softening effects of peace; he is anxious for the retention of "manliness" (1290); he is afraid of relaxation in competition; he is an apostle of strenuousness. He is victimized a bit by both the Social Darwinian and the Teutonic rubbish of his period, sensitive and generous soul that he was. Furthermore, he defines the moral equivalent of war as the enlistment of all young men in the war "against *Nature,*" the "immemorial human warfare against nature" (1291). He does not appear to confine the war against nature to the eradication of disease and the remedial anticipation of catastrophe. In a more environmentally sensitive age than his, identifying the worst enemy as nature as such, rather than humanity's irresponsibility toward nature, would hardly register as moral. The irresponsibility is as bad as war, or worse.

So we must turn to other writers for assistance, especially Tocqueville. Once again, he does better for democracy than almost all democrats. In the second volume of *Democracy in America* (1840), he writes splendidly about the changes in the exercise of courage and the bestowal of honor effected by the replacement of aristocratic culture by democracy. His description of the aristocratic (essentially medieval) ethos is a succinct characterization of a world that by his time was seriously attenuated but had lingered, and that had not ever sunk deep roots in the American colonies (at least in the northern ones). To follow Tocqueville's account is to receive the best instruction on the moral equivalent (or near equivalent) of war, to the extent that moral or morally compatible activity may have important existential qualities.

In Tocqueville's telling, feudal aristocracy preferred "great crimes to small earnings" precisely on grounds of the human stature, the human greatness, of the elite (3.18: 244). That is just one indication of how bold and brilliant vices would readily be set above "quiet, unpretending virtues" (244). Among the virtues, as the aristocracy understood them, especially honorable were those virtues "which are conspicuous for their dignity and splendor and which may be easily combined with pride and the love of power" (244). The feudal nobility went so far as to place military courage "foremost among virtues and in lieu of many of them" (245). Tocqueville does not hesitate to call the aristocratic notion of the highest virtues an inversion of "the natural order of conscience" (244). Indeed, running throughout Tocqueville's chapter is a systematic contrast between "notions of right and wrong diffused all over the world" (242) and the "special rules" that make up the aristocratic "code of honor" (251). As elsewhere in the book, he says that the clash between aristocracy and democracy is not only a clash of worlds, but also a clash between the peculiar but partial aristocratic abandonment of ordinary morality and democracy's full acceptance of ordinary morality as its organizing principle.

What we have been seeing as a conflict between existential values and moral ones, Tocqueville renders as a conflict between upper-class warrior values and moral ones. Reading him is an ideal preparation for thinking about the revision of courage as a virtue. He familiarizes us with the idea that democracy changes all values in a democratic direction, even courage and honor. He is most instructive on the sources of honor in a democracy. They include practice of the "quiet virtues that tend to give a regular movement to the community and to encourage business" (248). Honor is to some extent displaced away from physical courage and on to success in business. Love of wealth, which is censured in other cultures (even if hypocritically), is praised when associated with boldness of enterprise (248). But democracy shares some of the sources of honor with aristocracy. Indeed, both cultures look upon physical courage as the highest virtue.

Then Tocqueville unexpectedly says that in America "martial valor is little prized" (249). Whether or not democracy can love war and still be consistent with its commitment to human rights, American democracy has always loved warriors and even war itself: so much of its history involves initiated armed conflict. Be that as it may, the fact remains that American democracy has made a specialty of according honor to risky physical activities that have nothing to do with war, and Tocqueville notices that fact. He says that "the most esteemed courage is what emboldens men to brave the dangers of the ocean; privations of the wilderness" (249). The motive may be money, but the virtue involved in getting it seems to exceed the gain; the gain could not possibly be the sufficient psychological explanation (or the main source of our admiration).

Our theme is physical courage. We therefore cannot appropriately say that any activity that requires some kind of boldness or strenuousness, or some kind of competitive zest, or that manages to attain fame and with it honor, but that does not hold great physical risk, can be seen as analogous to physical courage on the battlefield. Battlefield courage undoubtedly shares attributes and advantages with other activities that carry no physical risk. But let us stay with physical courage in the face of supreme risk to life and limb. If we do, we easily see that Tocqueville's examples of braving the dangers of the ocean and enduring the privations of the wilderness are often morally compatible exercises of physical courage; they provide intensity of experience and bring the prospect of death more near. To be sure, there may be no selflessness in such exercises and usually no certainty that some comrades will die and that those who survive will nevertheless have been willing to die for comrades and comradeship. We can then add such activities as dangerous sports and other athletic activities, and the exploration of space. With or without expensive technology, these and other activities can be individual or collaborative undertakings, but they all surely give physical courage ample scope for its display. They provide tests of character under trying circumstances and allow a person to measure himself or herself without harming others. They help to make courage a virtue and they emphasize that if courage in some of its expressions may require basic training, it cannot emanate from cultivation or indoctrination. If it did, it would most likely be criminal. If not purely spontaneous, physical courage as a virtue is comparatively spontaneous.

And then what of the unspeakable courage of women who bear children when they live in a place where, as they know, more than a few die giving birth? Not to mention the pain of childbirth in the best of circumstances. In a political vein we can add the practices of nonviolent politics when dissenting or rebellious participants confront those willing to use violence against them or threaten them with the awful prospect of a prison term. A more dangerous nonviolent political act is to rescue or give refuge to the persecuted at grave risk to oneself. Nonviolent politics is politics at its moral best, sometimes collaborative but always individualistic because conscientious; and it becomes admirable and honorable when, but of course not only when, it requires the physical courage that peaceful resistance without retaliation often depends on.

In sum, humanity will always need physical courage. William James, for one, has a marvelous description of people's pluck during and after the San Francisco earthquake of 1906, which he lived through (James, 1906). The struggle to preserve oneself and others or the passion to sacrifice oneself for others can continue without war. Courage is not only a practical necessity, it is also an enlargement of humanity. The task is to confine it morally.

The unfortunate general judgment is that democracy has not yet adequately revised physical courage and the honor that is accorded to it. Democracy still regularly implicates courage in terrible wrongdoing by its appeals to both gullible patriotism and gullible masculinity. Unvirtuous courage thrives on the mindlessness of "right belief." But at least democracy gives impetus to private, often individualistic, physical deeds of enormous risk and lavishes honor on them. Courage can be and is shown without stain. Comradeship unto death should cease being the paradigm of courage and the apex of honor. How great, really, are the existential losses we countenance when we try hard to deny praise and admiration to comradeship unto death?

Addendum

There is a large area of inquiry that we cannot address in this essay: how individual suicide can be an act of virtuous physical courage when the person takes his or her own life to avoid the possibility of degradation in one's status as a human being, or acts before the degradation is complete and the thought of suicide vanishes along with all other thoughts. Suicide is often seen as cowardly on the questionable but plausible assumption that fear of death is a smaller fear than that of pains. Whatever one's opinion of suicide as such, it seems to me that to take one's life because one knows that one is or soon will be degraded by one's suffering — the degradation caused by suffering but conceptually distinct from it — is an admirable act of virtuous physical courage. It is certainly at least compatible with morality; as a self-regarding act, it may not be a moral or immoral act in itself. The act is a defense of one's personal honor, and it adds to human stature by defending the honor of the human race in one's own person.

In private life, a degenerative disease like Alzheimer's in its earliest stages can rightly be judged by the patient as an inevitable degradation to be avoided by a timely suicide. But apart from disease, there is the fate of inmates in concentration camps and death camps. Bruno Bettelheim in his remarkably perceptive book *The Informed Heart* (1971), and Primo Levi in four magnificant and endlessly instructive nonfiction books (three on the camps and one on the journey home), contemplate this awful subject memorably (1989, 1995a, 1995b, 1996). (I do not say these writers are the only ones.) I take from them a twofold meaning of degradation. First, becoming completely the plaything of others, utterly incapable of free agency or even a passive personhood; and second, becoming unable to think of anyone but oneself, of anything but one's literal survival, and becoming as a consequence unable to be moral, even in a minimal, negative sense. The effect of systematically, unrelentingly, and minutely inflicted suffering is degradation; but degradation may not be felt as its own kind of suffering. The accumulation of pains is likely to monopolize one's consciousness. The feeling of degradation requires, however, some awareness, as from a distance, of one's situation. One must still be able to ask oneself, What have they made (or do they mean to make) of me?

I believe, after reading Bettelheim and Levi (both of them suicides but years after their camp experience), and less equivocally than they, that suicide to avoid degradation in camps is an honorable act of physical courage. It is all the more honorable because degradation is not one's fault; the experiences that cause it are far more than human nature should ever be asked to bear. The act of suicide would be in no sense punishing oneself for failure or dishonor, much less wickedness. On the way to degradation, the captors absolutely refuse recognition of one's human status as a rights-bearing person. The injury to it is mortal. But it is possible, by a leap into a last freedom, to die rather than to persist for a while, and thus bravely to sacrifice oneself for one's honor as a human being and, by that, exemplify the stature of the human race. Is there a better existential affirmation?

Those who avoided or freely ended their degradation in the camps were, according to the testimony of these two writers, very few. In praising suicide in the camps, I am not deterred either by the fact that sometimes suicide by one prisoner would cause others to be punished or by the contention of Bettelheim that most prisoners eventually became suicidal, so that "Psychologically speaking, most prisoners in the extermination camps committed suicide by submitting to death without resistance" (245). A passive longing for death is not the same as a virtuous act of physical courage. To be sure, both writers chose to survive. Bettelheim converted his imprisonment into an occasion for objective inquiry, by splitting himself into two: sufferer and observer; and thus escaped some of the degradation. Levi, on the other hand, did not take his own life because he wanted to survive in order to give witness. Perhaps their intellectual mission spared both of them some of the worst ravages, but Levi especially is merciless about his own awful adaptation. How could I possibly take issue with either of them? But about others, I can only say that in their place, though I do not know what I would have actually done, I hope that I would have had enough courage to take my life for the right reason. Yes, there were some who survived and then went on to lead normal lives; a few, perhaps, as if nothing had happened. Neither my fortunate lack of experience nor the example of survivors, however, stops me from admiring those who took their own lives out of a sense of personal honor and maybe a sense of the honor of the human race. Not that I wish to say that those who went on living for as long as they could were dishonored by a degradation they did not bring on themselves. Can I have it both ways?

Plato says, as we have seen, that death in combat is better than the literal slavery that awaits those who surrender. But imprisonment in camps, at its worst, is worse degradation than at least some institutionalized slavery, and it is honorable to avoid or end degradation, especially where the motivation is not so much to end suffering as it is to abort the degradation that various physical pains and psychological humiliations can cause. Degradation consists in becoming incapable of acting either freely or morally. It is worse than death, and physical courage, and doubtless other kinds, too, are needed to choose to die by one's own hand before one's time, totally innocent.

References

Aristotle. *Politics.* Trans. Benjamin Jowett. New York: Modern Library, 1943.
——. *Nicomachean Ethics.* Trans. Martin Ostwald. Indianapolis: Bobbs-Merrill, 1962.
Bettelheim, Bruno. *The Informed Heart.* New York: Avon, 1971 (1960).
Gray, J. Glenn. *The Warriors.* 2d ed. New York: Harper Torchbooks, 1970 (1959).
James, William. "On Some Mental Effects of the Earthquake" (1906). In James (1987): 1215–22.
——. "The Energies of Men" (1907). In James (1987): 1223–41.
——. "The Moral Equivalent of War" (1910). In James (1987): 1281–93.
——. *Writings, 1902–1910.* New York: The Library of America, 1987.

Levi, Primo. *The Drowned and the Saved.* Trans. Raymond Rosenthal. New York: Vintage, 1989 (1986).

———. *The Reawakening.* Trans. Stuart Woolf. New York: Touchstone, 1995a (1963).

———. *Moments of Reprieve.* Trans. Ruth Feldman. New York: Penguin, 1995b (1981).

———. *Survival in Auschwitz.* Trans. Stuart Woolf. New York: Touchstone, 1996 (1947).

Plato. *Laws.* Trans. Thomas L. Pangle. New York: Basic Books, 1980.

Plato. *Republic.* Trans. G. M. A. Grube. Rev. C. D. C. Reeve. Indianapolis: Hackett, 1992.

Plutarch. "Lycurgus." *Plutarch on Sparta.* Ed. and trans. Richard J. A. Talbert. New York: Penguin, 1988.

Thoreau, Henry David. "Civil Disobedience" (1848). *Collected Essays and Poems.* Henry David Thoreau. New York: The Library of America, 2001.

Thucydides. *The Peloponnesian War.* Trans. Crawley. Rev. Wick. New York: Modern Library, 1982.

Tocqueville, Alexis de. *Democracy in America.* Vol. II. Trans. Reeve, Bowen, Bradley. New York: Vintage, 1954 (1840).

9

Technology and Philosophy

Let us begin with a general definition of the word *technology*. In its current meaning, it names the means or methods used to help people move from place to place, communicate, produce, construct, create, fabricate, but also destroy; to observe, to calculate, and to think. (This list is obviously not exhaustive.) Technology is thus made up of all kinds of equipment—tools, machines, and devices—that assist the work of human muscles, senses, and brains, and thus the realization of human purposes and ends. Our question is: Is *modern* technology a subject of philosophical interest? Philosophers can make any subject interesting, and not just to themselves. At its best, their work has a tendency to arrest our habit of taking things for granted, of seeing phenomena as normal or as a matter of course. Philosophy, from Socrates on, is often a challenge to common sense. Philosophy is amazed at the way in which common sense is unamazed; and then in another sense of amazement, philosophy is disposed to be amazed at the phenomena themselves. Philosophers have sometimes characterized our steady condition as sleep; their hope is to awaken those who hear or read them. Thoreau said that "Moral reform is the effort to throw off sleep" (Thoreau, 1985, p. 394); so too is the reform of one's perception. To be awake is to experience amazement repeatedly; it is to marvel. I submit that modern technology is worthy of amazement, and that some philosophers have tried to awaken us to amazement.

I refer, however, not to the prowess, the marvels of technology: we are fully awake to them, whether as active users or passive consumers. Instead, I have in mind the marvelous fact, the amazing fact, of modern technology as a human relation to nature and human beings. There is nothing ordinary, universal, or inevitable about that relation. Naturally, I do not mean to belittle anyone who looks with amazement at any given example of modern technology or at a set of connected examples. The feats of modern technology are staggering; the capacity for ever more feats in the future seems intact. Yet, this prowess, this capacity, grows out of some passions or drives or motives that repay attention; they are culturally and historically special. Philosophers, especially German and American ones, have tried to uncover them, and have done so, marveling not only at the feats and triumphs of modern technology but also at the mentality and condition of spirit that launched modern technology, and have helped to keep it in its tremendous course of continuous inventiveness and permanent revolution.

The whole meaning of modern technology cannot of course be contained in any single philosophical system or tradition. Nor is philosophy needed on one level of explanation. There are, after all, countless consumerist pleasures, active powers, and special interests served by the development of modern technology; there are also countless accidents and strokes of fortune that went into its making. No particular story about modern technology could be adequate, no interpretation sufficient. But some thinkers have a powerful contribution to make to our understanding of modern technology; they add depth.

But, first, what is the *unamazed* commonsense attitude toward modern technology? I hope that I am not too reductionist when I attribute to common sense the view that modern technology is just extraordinarily successful problem-solving, a terrific display of resourceful ingenuity, a splendid and constant show of adaptability to circumstances. Of course, problem-solving, ingenuity, and adaptability are traits essential to the story of modern technology. But what originally energized these traits? What has helped to call them forth repeatedly, once modern technology is launched? Why have they appeared more in the West than any place else? Why have they appeared in such profusion only in the period that begins with the Italian Renaissance and the German Reformation—the period that many scholars call modernity? Both modern science and modern technology begin in that period—not from scratch, of course, but in any case substantially. Whatever drove the beginnings of science and whatever drives it still, the career of modern technology is not wholly subsumable under that of modern science. As Heidegger says, modern technology is not simply applied science, although it is that, too (Heidegger, 1977, p. 116). The will to work technologically on nature and human beings is conceptually independent of the will to know for its own sake, which is characteristic of science.

I suggest beginning with Karl Marx's views. He is surely one of the first to think philosophically about modern technology, especially machine technology housed in factories. The question that I think should be put to his work is whether he philosophically challenges our common sense or, instead, expends his genius in keeping us asleep. Who could doubt that his work aroused many people from the 1880s on, and then aroused a large part of the world after his death? His vision seemed to have awakened people to their place in the world, to their true identity and interest. He powerfully insisted, what is more, on the distinctiveness of modernity. Yet I believe that this great philosopher actually helped to strengthen common sense in its mental sleep, rather than awakening it to amazement. What I mean is that the tendency of the Marxist system is to see modern technology as an intense concentration of human practicality, not as an achievement stemming from passions, drives, and motives that enlist the desire for success in solving problems in a much larger and rather mysterious project.

Marxism does deserve tribute for insisting on the way that technological capitalism, especially in the period from the middle of the eighteenth century onward, had transformed Europe and affected the rest of the world. In "The Communist Manifesto," Marx and Engels say of the European bourgeoisie:

> It has been the first to show what man's activity can bring about. It has accomplished wonders far surpassing Egyptian pyramids, Roman aqueducts, and Gothic cathedrals; it has conducted expeditions that put in the shade all former Exoduses of nations and crusades. (Marx and Engels, 1978 [1848], p. 476)

Marxism thus points to the marvels (and depredations) of modern productive technology, and does so comparatively early and certainly with compelling rhetoric. Just by that effort, carried out in much of their writing, and culminating in *Capital* (1867), Marx, and Engels, too, perform one of the duties of philosophy in the face of common sense.

But something large is missing. I mean that Marxism offers only a little help and poses an enormous obstacle in the attempt to give an account of why it was the West that launched modern humanity on the career of technology. Marxism's insistence on the role played by individual and class economic self-interest explains something about the persistent use made of technology by modern capitalism, but next to nothing about the mentality of its emergence. When we turn to the most ambitious foray into the philosophy of history and historical change made by Marx (with help from Engels), we are given a much too narrow base for our speculation. I refer to a passage in *The German Ideology*, a work written in 1845–46 (and then withheld from publication). Marx says there that unlike other German philosophers who habitually explain historical change by reference to philosophical innovations, to changes in ideas and conceptions, a true realist must begin with certain physical or biological premises. These premises must organize the writing of history; they must provide the basic cause of the epochal transformations in the human condition that have taken place from time to time, and with greater speed and perhaps greater self-consciousness in the past few centuries. Nothing psychological or spiritual or philosophical is needed to make sense of history.

What are these premises that provide the key to understanding historical change? Marx gives three (Marx and Engels, 1978, pp. 155–57). The first is that in order to live and go on living, human beings must engage in some kind of labor. The second is that "the satisfaction of the first need . . . leads to new needs" (p. 156). That is, wants expand, even if their satisfaction is not required to keep bare life going; and these expanded wants are felt as imperiously as needs for food, dress, and shelter. The artificial becomes as necessary as the natural. The third premise is that male and female must engage in sexual intercourse if the race is to go on. Thus, production and reproduction constitute the foundation of human existence. What gives this truism its intended force is the Marxist contention that much of the time people carry on their various activities unaware that the real, but largely hidden point or aim of all their activities, is to keep life going. Noneconomic and nonsexual activities have the same ultimate point or aim as economic and sexual ones, or are ultimately at the service of economic and sexual ones. Humanity is driven by the mission of life, even though it often believes that it is inspired by other and more flattering purposes. All its ideas, conceptions, and philosophical systems have only one source, if mostly hidden: the imperatives of the mission to keep life going. No aspect of human life has freedom from these imperatives, even though people characteristically deceive themselves into thinking that their creations, their culture, their various activities are not only severally autonomous, but also the unconstrained and unpredictable source of their particular and variable definitions of how to respond to nature, how to respond to the mission's undeniable imperatives. Marx is saying that even inequality and class domination have simply been the best instruments of these imperatives.

Marxism wants us to marvel at the wonders of capitalist productivity, but not at their psychological or spiritual or philosophical causes. These wonders have occurred, Marxism suggests, because humanity is always trying to increase productivity, always serving economic rationality, even when it thinks it is doing something else. The dialectical change from one economic structure to another is, for all its violence and drama, a steady story: growth in productivity. Thanks to an accumulation of technical knowledge, which is inevitably sought, human productive capacities have gradually increased, despite setbacks, through time; but thanks also to some fortunate circumstances, these capacities have grown with a relentless acceleration from the time of the European discovery of the New World. Marx is not exactly saying that modern technology was *fated* to happen. He is saying, however, that modern technology, propelled by the self-interested profit-seeking of the entrepreneurial class, has served the imperatives of the mission of keeping life going, and until recently has done so better, more fully and efficiently, than any conceivable alternative. In short, the relation to nature and human beings that modern technology manifests is nothing to wonder at. Human beings have always had the same relation: they must produce in order to keep life going, where life requires that strict necessities of food, dress, and shelter, but also the acquired necessities that developed productivity creates, be satisfied. Marxism elaborates both the old adage that necessity is the mother of invention and, to some extent, the reverse, which is that, as Thorstein Veblen puts it, invention is the mother of necessity.

Other philosophers challenge the contention that humanity has always had the same relation to nature and human beings. They see in modern technology something in addition to improved productivity, and hence something in addition to the old story in which humanity does battle with natural scarcity in the most effective way possible (even if that way, to be effective, had to be ruthless and unfair). They also see something besides the reign of what neo-Marxists have called "instrumental rationality," the pursuit of means to means, with ends forgotten. Neo-Marxists hold that there is a zeal that lets nothing stand in the way of ever-greater efficiency in the production of more and more goods, and all this for the sake of ever-greater profits, and in total disregard of the costs to workers or to nature, while all higher purposes recede, dwarfed by the technological process. Despite the suggestiveness of this critique of instrumental rationality, however, there is another kind of amazement at this process. A number of philosophers express it. What do they see?

I will refer to three thinkers who, explicitly or not, take issue with Marxism and with the commonsense attitude to modern technology that Marxist philosophy has helped to fortify, or even to create. These three are Max Weber, Martin Heidegger, and Hannah Arendt—all German, or German in origin.

Now, I do not say that trying to awaken us to amazement should be the only office of philosophy. There is intellectual advantage when some philosophers, and Marx is one example, side with common sense and embolden it. But other philosophers go in the other direction and produce the ideas that help to change people's relation to nature and social reality, and thus re-create common sense altogether. Marx gives an example, also, of this interpretative power. In this war among the offices of philosophy, a given philosopher can move from one side to another, from time to time. Let us say that the archetypes are Socrates, the gadfly; the Sophists, who defend and abet common sense; and Plato, the lawgiver (even if a devious one). For the purposes of this essay, Weber, Heidegger, and Arendt are gadflies: they try to sting us into wonder about modern technology; while Heidegger also emerges as a kind of lawgiver or prophet, but more negative than positive.

I will be very selective in discussing the philosophical challenge to common sense and to Marxist and neo-Marxist philosophy on the matter of modern technology. What holds Weber, Heidegger, and Arendt together is their inclination to regard modern technology as stemming from the passions and drives and motives of excess or extremism, not from resourceful practicality. In the background is a great page from the Third Essay of *On the Genealogy of Morals*, where Nietzsche says, "measured even by the standards of the ancient Greeks, our entire modern way of life, insofar as it is not weakness but power and consciousness of power, has the appearance of sheer *hubris* and godlessness." We violate nature and "we cheerfully vivisect our souls" (Nietzsche, 1969, sec. 9, p. 113). Not only are the displays of technological prowess, in their profusion, a cause for wonder, the passions and so on underlying them are the amazing heart of the story and must be attended to, if the displays themselves are to be properly appreciated and properly marveled at.

I find in Weber, Heidegger, and Arendt the following themes, all of which are first stated or suggested by Weber in *The Protestant Ethic and the Spirit of Capitalism* (1904–5). All the themes go against both philosophical Marxism and common sense. First, it is a fact worthy of meditation that, in its origin, modern technology is not a human-species-wide phenomenon, but a distinctively Western one. Although the West was and is indebted to the scientific and technical achievements of other regions and cultures, it is responsible for modern technology. In the three thinkers, and others as well, the Western distinctiveness is rendered ambivalently: celebration and profound disquiet are mixed together in the analysis of both the feats of prowess and the underlying passions that provoked those feats. I would add that such ambivalence is one of the most prominent features in a lot of writing about technology.

A second theme is that, just as modern technology was not a universal phenomenon, so there was nothing inevitable about it in the West. All three philosophers have a keen feeling for accident and contingency, for roads not taken, for opportunities either not accepted or forced into being. A third theme is that the passions, drives, and motives that helped to promote technology are, to a significant extent, instigated or inspired by ideas, religious or philosophical, that manage to be absorbed into the self-conception that many individuals in a cross-national cultural setting hold of themselves. Modern technology is not only applied science; even more profoundly, it is philosophy or theology enacted. Philosophers and theologians are the originators. Other people go along or are carried along, because of the original reasons, or because of their own varied reasons, half-reasons, and nonreasons.

The long and short of it is that only in the West, but contingently so, modern technology emerged, and did so because of the birth and spread of hard, abstract ideas that are not explainable in the Marxist manner as inevitable reflexive responses to material circumstances. And it has emerged and continues to flourish as a special and particular project; what is more, a project of excess and extremism. The modern West, best seen as the creator of modern technology, is not only distinctive, it is anomalous in comparison to the rest of the world; and the anomaly is stupendous and perhaps monstrous. The marvel lies not only in the results of the project but, to begin with, in the fact that the project of modern technology was ever undertaken and then sustained. Humanity in the West has had a certain kind of relation to nature and human beings not to be found elsewhere, or found in a much diluted form.

Now, Weber's aim, to start with him, is not to account for modern technology, but to explain the rise of capitalism. It turns out, however, that for Weber capitalism is only one, though a major, expression of Western distinctiveness. Common to all features by which the West has distinguished itself from the time of the Greeks onward is rationalism, rational method, a continuous displacement of superstition and wishful thinking in regard to nature and human beings. Every aspect of Western culture — its architecture and art, its political systems, its science, its scholarship, even its religions — has been characterized by rationalism. Now, rationalism is a rather elastic term in Weber, no doubt. But his accumulation of examples adds up to one of the best brief overviews of Western distinctiveness ever attempted.

Capitalism is the example that occupies most of Weber's attention in *The Protestant Ethic and the Spirit of Capitalism*. The role of capitalism in developing technology, and also the role of technology in developing capitalism, do not figure with much explicitness in Weber's book. He discusses modern technology, including its noneconomic motives, in *Economy and Society,* and says that economic calculation is "the main emphasis at all times" (1978, Talcott Parsons, trans., I: 67). His primary interest is in the preindustrial origins of the spirit of capitalism, the period of the sixteenth to the eighteenth centuries. What matters, however, is the *affinity* between capitalism and technology, not their causal connection. They partake of a similar attitude to reality. Both are manifestations of what Weber conceptualizes as rationalism, rational method in any given sphere of life. Hence what Weber says about the rise of capitalism, we may plausibly apply to modern technology.

But what is the connection between rationalism and that excess and extremism to which I have referred? Rationalism would seem to be the very opposite of excess or extremism, and if culturally anomalous, then certainly not monstrous. Yet this is where Weber's analysis, and the analyses of Heidegger and Arendt as well, take on a heightened interest. The contention is not simply that too much rationalism — rational method after a rather distant point — turns against itself and becomes inhuman, though that thought appears in Weber. Rather, the contention is that the passions or drives or motives that push rationalism everywhere and to an apparently limitless extent are themselves not rational, but irrational. Reason in the form of rational method is at the service not so much of everyday basic interests as of a philosophical or religious outlook on life or reality, or the world, or nature and human beings. Weber's thought is more vividly expressed earlier by Herman Melville's Captain Ahab in *Moby-Dick:* "all my means are sane, my motive and my object mad."[1]

What I wish to propose is that in distinct contrast with or in explicit and sharp opposition to Marxism, a number of German thinkers as well as a number of earlier American writers have thought they glimpsed rational method in the service of something not always distinguishable from madness. Method in madness, for the sake of madness, but also the rational method itself, by its unrelenting quality, often veering into madness, and thereby partaking of the nature of the end. Ahab's formulation does not cover the whole subject; it may not even cover his own experience. All that the narrator of *Moby-Dick* credits Ahab with is "some glimpse" of the truth about himself. A littler later (ch. 46, "Surmises"), the narrator speaks of Ahab's "subtle insanity" and "strange imaginative impiousness." The excellence of Melville's analysis is that he takes pains to distance Ahab from his crew. Ahab is aware that love of the chase is an "evanescent" feeling among the crew. "The permanent constitutional condition of the manufactured man, thought Ahab, is sordidness." By sordidness is meant only plain self-interest, which can be enlisted, however, in a leader's enterprise, an enterprise that is so self-absorbed that the usual motive of self-interest or even love of the chase does not originate or drive it. Of course, Ahab is not an inventor, nor a symbol of modern technololgy; but his injured and outraged stance toward life strongly resembles the composite of drives and passions and motives, of obsessions and mental leaps, attributed to modern technology by some philosophers.

Indeed, rational method, when sufficiently uninhibited, looks as if it were the end itself, so intensely gratifying is its use, while the ostensible end (whether rational or irrational) appears to be a pretext. Edmund Burke supplies the political analogy when he describes political revolution: "criminal means once tolerated are soon preferred. . . . Justifying perfidy and murder for public benefit, public benefit would soon become the pretext, and perfidy and murder the end" (Burke, 1970, pp. 176–77). Yet what he says about revolutionaries can be said about many other political actors, for whom political office is an attractive invitation to use criminal means in conscienceless good conscience. So, to a certain extent, with modern technology. The very distinction between extreme means and extreme ends in modern technology is volatile, so regular is the transformation of each into the other.

From one perspective, at least, modern technology often looks like madness, or like nonhuman giantism, to use Heidegger's concept (Heidegger, 1977, p. 135). There must be madness when modern technology shows itself at least as dramatically in destruction as in productivity. One is tempted to say that modern technological weapons of war are not, to those who invent or design, command, or use them, qualitatively different from the means of economic production for civilian uses. The psychology is the same in both cases. How could we fail to have our sense of wonder quickened when we observe that the technological spirit passes so easily and quickly from peace to war, as if there were no humanly real difference between them? To find in that move mere practicality, ordinary problem-solving, is to be lost in a dream, just as those who set the "problems" to be solved are in the grip of hubristic ambitions. The more important point, however, is that something like madness — call it irrationality — sets modern technology in motion and helps to keep it in motion.

In Weber's analysis there would have been no modern capitalism, but also no modern science or (we may add) modern technology, without something irrational. This is not to say that for Weber Western rationalism has been implicated in irrationality from the start. But he does wonder at the thought that the West has applied rational methods to areas of life left comparatively untouched by such methods elsewhere. These methods appear irrational to those outside the West, and they also appear irrational to some Western philosophers.

Weber locates the source of modern rational irrationality in the Protestant idea of work as a calling, the practice of work as worldly asceticism. The tremendous energies of modernity were unleashed not by worldly self-interest, by prudence, calculation, or the concerted effort to deal with needs that are either primary or added to primary ones, or even by the high aim of relieving the human estate, but rather by systematic self-denial. If the world were run by a more conventional self-interest, or even by a decent commitment to human betterment, it would be an easier and less productive place, with less wealth but less poverty, less misery. Greed exists everywhere, Weber says, but the rational and methodical pursuit of profit is the essence of capitalism, and distinctive to it. And apart from the causal connection between capitalism and modern technology, each phenomenon, considered separately, is driven by the application of rational method to limitless purposes, whether limitless profit or limitless technical achievement. Both purposes signify the presence of the inexhaustible, the insatiable, the unappeasable.

But why the limitless? In regard to capitalism, as we have said, Weber makes much of the Protestant notion of one's work as one's calling. Thus, Protestantism, especially Calvinism, shifts the notion of vocation or calling from religious practice to the everyday work done by all persons in the world. Why the shift? Weber says

> the religious valuation of restless, continuous, systematic work in a worldly calling, as the highest means to asceticism, and at the same time the surest and most evident proof of rebirth and genuine faith, must have been the most powerful conceivable lever for the expansion of that attitude toward life which we have here called the spirit of capitalism. (Weber, 1958 [1904–5], p. 172)

By a curious alchemy, which Weber suggestively but sketchily describes (pp. 114–15), and persuasively emphasizes, anxiety over salvation or damnation led persons to find both distraction from anxiety and palliation of it in unremitting work. Success in work gave some possible clue to one's fate in the afterlife; success in creation was a pious imitation of God. Worldly blessings were an arbitrary sign of God's favor, not a loving expression of it. Success in work, at the same time, went to those who applied the most rational method to their work, while they disciplined themselves to labor much harder than most people, including their fellow Christians. They were driven most powerfully not by economic interest but by a religious conception that was not rationalist and not even rational, but an affront even to many Christians. In short, religious anxiety lies at the root of capitalism understood as a special case of the method of rationalism. The tremendous tower of economic achievement rests on a base that is not worldly, but religious. Only a passion not worldly, not itself rational, apparently, could inspire such stupendous worldly results, and could achieve them only by a wholehearted use of rational methods.

We can say that if religious anxiety helps to account for the emergence of capitalism in the West, something like it may help to account for the emergence of modern technology in the West; and, furthermore, something like it may help to account for the distinctive rationalism of the West from the Greeks onward. Weber's analysis of the sources of a compulsion to use rational method cannot be confined to Protestantism and capitalism, as he indicates by his prefatory consideration of Western distinctiveness, even if he withholds the theme of the irrational basis of rational method until he discusses capitalism.

I suggest that Protestant anxiety, now present with us in the form of a secular work ethic, is just one manifestation of a general anger at the world that seems to exist in the West much more than elsewhere, and from the Greeks onward. I do not say that anger at the world is the only passion or drive or motive that underlies modern technology — the technology of production and destruction. But it is one of the few main elements. (I will briefly mention some others at the end.) And when I speak of anger at the world I include anger at oneself and the tendency to project or imagine divinities that are given to anger at us. There is a recurrent disposition in the West to feel radical dissatisfaction with nature or reality or the world; to wish it otherwise; to find fault with the given to the point of undying regret that things are as they are; and, along with all this, to look with perpetual discontent at oneself and strive to improve oneself by making oneself an object of perpetual surveillance and solicitude.

Of course I highlight only one part of the moral temper of the West. It is the part that Weber and later German philosophers highlight. I believe that they have caught something noteworthy that should figure in the effort to explain Western distinctiveness and with it, modern technology. Early in the second chapter of *Walden* (1854), "Where I Lived, and What I Lived For," Thoreau says

> Why should we live with such hurry and waste of life? We are determined to be starved before we are hungry. Men say that a stitch in time saves nine, and so they take a thousand stitches today to save nine tomorrow. (p. 396)

In the sentence "We are determined to be starved before we are hungry," I find a formulation that exceeds in significance the particular economic point that Thoreau is making. He is mindful of the "desperation," as he elsewhere puts it, that characterizes modern life. We make ourselves sick so that we "may lay up something against a sick day" (p. 328). (To be sure, he is prepared to admit that he has sometimes been a "half-starved hound" ranging the woods, "not that I was hungry then" [p. 490].) He laments the general situation. Whether we lament it or not, the insight remains: we cannot seem to make sense of the Western anomaly unless we perceive modern technology as flowing not from need or lack but from fullness of energy. And as Thoreau suggests in a spirit not remote from Weber and post-Weberian philosophers, fullness of energy breeds anxiety, anger, dissatisfaction, and self-dissatisfaction, and they reciprocally increase energy. Modern technology comes not from hunger: we are determined to be starved before we even feel hunger. Satisfied need does not appease the psyche. We cannot believe our own fullness, or, we refuse to accept fullness as fullness. In that fullness we are determined to act not merely as if we are hungry but as if we are starved. We are starved no matter how much we eat. We are also eager for the opportunity of emergency, or necessity. We pretend to a bare need when what we suffer from is an excess of determination—a determination to use up energy in anger, anxiety, dissatisfaction, and self-dissatisfaction. And what we find is that energy accumulates with its expenditure. Success provokes dissatisfaction. What I am submitting to doubt is the contention that the modern technological project has been instigated by a memory or anticipation of starvation—a determination never (or never again) to be starved. Rather, indefinite hoarding ("standing reserve" in Heidegger's phrase) is a preparation for some future breakthrough, some magical moment of use, some deed that leaves the world unrecognizable (Heidegger, 1977, pp. 3–35, 36–49).

All this is not solely Protestant; and if modern technology is *modern* technology, there is nevertheless a perfect consonance between modern technology and salient features of the Western spirit from the Greeks onward. It is impossible to say whether religion and philosophy originate these features of the Western spirit. But at the least, religion and philosophy in the West have codified and sanctified and thereby emboldened anger, anxiety, and so on. The ultimate cause may be buried too deep in obscure and accidental psychic processes, past and present, for us to unearth.

Heidegger and Arendt amplify the story told by Weber, and also told, well before him, by Thoreau and Melville and others in the United States. In such essays as "The Age of the World Picture" (1938), "The Question Concerning Technology" (1949–50), and "Science and Reflection" (1954) (all three in Heidegger, 1977), Heidegger finds the origin of modern technology in Western metaphysics. He emphasizes the outlook of thinkers as lawgivers, and sees in them the true bearers of the passions and drives and motives that are the foundation of modern technology, rather than assigning the inspiration to common Western humanity as a whole. When philosophers are not content to awaken wonder at the world, but instead strive to remake the world, they sometimes succeed. Their greatest success is modern technology. Modern technology is, to repeat our phrase, a certain relation to nature or reality or the world; it is therefore not merely the inevitable application of that immense scientific knowledge that grows once humanity is rid of communal or religious superstition and repression. Certainly that is part of the story, but for Heidegger it is not the principal part. Rather, modern technology is the materialization of Western metaphysics, which is the parent of both modern technology and modern science. Indeed, the technological aim drives the development of modern science. Western metaphysics is just one interpretation of reality, just as its offspring — modern science and modern technology — are particular relations to reality, to what is given.

Heidegger means to show that Western metaphysics — and metaphysics includes theology — is a continuously if sometimes covertly reiterated Platonism. By his method of exegesis, Heidegger tries to persuade us that Platonic metaphysics converts the world into a picture for the mind's eye, and by doing that, prepares Western humanity to lose sight of the mere fact of existence, the unsummoned thereness of reality, of the given. Metaphysics inveterately reduces the world. The purpose of the reduction is to make the world intelligible and hence manageable, fit to be worked on, and made ready to have practical order imposed on it. The world, as given, is disliked; it is disliked in large part just because it is given; the dislike engenders anger, and from anger comes rebellion. Western humanity is and has always been at war with given reality, to a much greater degree than the rest of humanity, and in a remarkably distinct manner. Technology is the most spectacular campaign in the great war waged by Western humanity against nature or reality as given. To repeat: the deepest cause of that war is not scarcity, not the failure of nature to make better provision for a necessitous humanity, but, instead, a Western willfulness, a will to power, to mastery, an overflow of energy that wants to shake the world to pieces and make it over. The craving is either to put the human stamp on reality or at least to rescue nature from the absence of any honestly detectable stamp, any detectable natural purpose or intention. As Nietzsche says: humanity, in its *asceticism,* "wants to become master not over something in life but over life itself, over its most profound, powerful, and basic conditions" (Nietzsche, 1969, sec. 11, pp. 117–18). Western humanity cannot let things be on their own terms or coax gently from them their own best potentiality; it is so far unable to practice what Heidegger calls *Gelassenheit.* Western metaphysics is the sponsor of anger and hence of repeated violence toward nature.

Hannah Arendt, in *The Human Condition* (1958) and other writings, continues the philosophical effort to restore a sense of wonder at the very fact of modern technology, at the relation to reality that modern technology stands for. She speaks of world alienation in the modern age, a process that she dates from the discoveries of Copernicus and Galileo and their impact on the thinking of philosophers. In her writings, I find two sequences. In one, world alienation begins in those discoveries that discredit the senses and force the skeptical mind back on itself to find its warrant for certainty there rather than in the testimony of inadequate senses concerning the deceptive world. There are other events. The Renaissance and Reformation combined with the European invasion of the New World to produce a profound disorientation, a loss of worldly assurance, a loss of the feeling that it is possible to be at home in the world. The world and its possibilities are made too vast. From such alienation, resentment grows, and with resentment the project of making the world over, and then persisting in undoing and remaking it forever. Resentment is the key concept for Arendt; it is much broader than Nietzsche's *ressentiment,* but has some of the latter's qualities.

Again, it is resentment not at nature's scarcity, but as its sheer otherness that drives the project of modern technology, which is the project of mastery and domination. There is in fact an alternative and superior theoretical sequence in Arendt's writings. Arendt leaves the impression that Western humanity perhaps never wanted the world to be a home, and that if it were more congenial to human expectations, Western humanity would have been even more alienated, more resentful at the given, more disposed to inflict a technological simulacrum on it. In this account, resentment is prior, certainly among thinkers. Western thinkers have always resolved to be alienated from the world. Resentment spurs the developments that culminate in pervasive modern world alienation, which then further intensifies and spreads and, as it were, popularizes resentment. She shares with Heidegger a disposition to see the ancient Greeks as already living for the sake of imposition on otherness: their metaphysics and their science, even their politics, seem animated by the same, or roughly the same, mentality as modern science and technology (Arendt, 1958a, p. 301).

This is not to say, however, that Arendt loves nature and the natural. She has her own snobbery. She is repelled by all those human beings whose labor (especially agricultural) makes them, in her eyes, indistinguishable from natural creatures who are totally absorbed into nature's "metabolic" processes. She loves existence as such, she loves the world, but she does not seem to love the natural. (Compare this to Thoreau, who loves the natural, the primitive, but is disgusted by the sensual and the sexual.) The climax of Arendt's story is in her essay "The Conquest of Space and the Stature of Man" (1968[1963]), in which she claims that the upshot of space exploration will be the flight from the earth and the colonization of space (pp. 265–80). World alienation could thus lead to a radical earth alienation. From space, human beings will look down on their earthly habitation from a distance both physical and metaphysical and thus consummate their restless resentment at earthly and worldly limitation. "Modern rationalism is unreal," she concludes, "and modern realism is irrational" (Arendt, 1958b, p. 300).

Common to Heidegger and Arendt is the wish to promote a feeling of astonishment that a world is just there, given without there necessarily being a giver; and beyond astonishment at givenness, grateful adherence, or attachment. Gratitude would show itself in, among other ways, an acceptance of limits on the will to rebel against nature. To try to subdue it to the satisfaction of human needs is inevitable; the process must go on, if human life, and not only life but civilization, are to go on. It is the Western rebellion at all limits, the anger or resentment that givenness provokes, the imperious rage to remake the world so that humanity becomes the only maker, even in destruction — all this is not compatible with gratitude for existence and perpetually substitutes wonder at human achievement for wonder at the fact of existence itself.

"We murder to dissect," says Wordsworth in his poem "The Tables Turned" (1798). We pretend to understand the living thing when we study it dead, after we have killed it. The word *murder* indicates Wordsworth's judgment that only the murderous would dissect, and that dissection is but a continuation of the act of murder. Hatred or dislike of the creature or natural thing is behind the dissection — a burning desire to master it by knowing it when it is no longer itself.

But the question arises as to where a genuine principle of limitation on technological endeavor would come from. It is scarcely conceivable that Western humanity — and by now most of humanity, because of their pleasures and interests and their own passions and desires and motives — would halt the technological project. Even if, by some change of heart, Western humanity could adopt an altered relation to reality and human beings, how could it be enforced and allowed to yield its effects? The technological project can be stopped only by some global catastrophe that it had helped to cause or was powerless to avoid. Heidegger's teasing invocation of the idea that a saving remedy grows with the worst danger is useless. In any case, no one would want the technological project halted, if the only way was a global catastrophe. Perhaps even the survivors would not want to block its reemergence.

As for our generation and the indefinite future, many of us are prepared to say that there are many things we wish that modern science did not know or is likely to find out and many things we wish that modern technology did not know how to do. When referring in 1955 to the new sciences of life, Heidegger says

> We do not stop to consider that an attack with technological means is being prepared upon the life and nature of man compared with which the explosion of the hydrogen bomb means little. For precisely if the hydrogen bombs do *not* explode and human life on earth is preserved, an uncanny change in the world moves upon us. (1966, p. 52)

The implication is that it is less bad for the human stature and for the human relation to reality that there be nuclear destruction than that (what we today call) genetic engineering should go from success to success. To such lengths can a mind push itself when it marvels first at the passions, drives, and motives that are implicated in modern technology, and then marvels at the displays of technological prowess. The sense of wonder is entangled with a feeling of horror. We are past even the sublime, as conceptualized under the influence of Milton's imagination of Satan and Hell.

It is plain that so much of the spirit of the West is invested in modern technology. We have referred to anger, alienation, resentment. But that cannot be the whole story. Other considerations we can mention include the following: a taste for virtuosity, skill for its own sake, an enlarged fascination with technique in itself, and, along with these, an aesthetic craving to make matter or nature beautiful or more beautiful; and then, too, sheer exhilaration, a questing, adventurous spirit that is reckless, heedless of danger, finding in obstacles opportunities for self-overcoming, for daring, for the very sort of daring that Heidegger praises so eloquently when in 1935 he discusses the Greek world in *An Introduction to Metaphysics* (1961, esp. pp. 123–39). All these considerations move away from anger, anxiety, resentment, and so on. The truth of the matter, I think, is that the project of modern technology, just like that of modern science, must attract a turbulence of response. The very passions and drives and motives that look almost villainous or hypermasculine simultaneously look like marks of the highest human aspiration, or, at the least, are not to be cut loose from the highest human aspiration.

Note

1. Melville, 1851, ch. 41, *Moby-Dick*. Leo Marx instructively discusses this passage in *The Machine in the Garden* (1964), pp. 298–302.

References

Arendt, Hannah, *The Origins of Totalitarianism,* 2d edition. (New York: Meridian, 1958a).

Arendt, Hannah, *The Human Condition* (Chicago: University of Chicago Press, 1958b).

Arendt, Hannah, "The Conquest of Space and the Stature of Man," in *Between Past and Future,* 2d ed. (New York: Viking, 1968 [1963]).

Burke, Edmund, *Reflections on the Revolution in France* (New York: Penguin, 1970).

Heidegger, Martin, *Discourse on Thinking,* John M. Anderson and E. Hans Freund, trans. (New York: Harper, 1966).

Heidegger, Martin, *An Introduction to Metaphysics,* Ralph Manheim, trans. (New York: Doubleday Anchor, 1961).

Heidegger, Martin, "The Age of the World Picture," in *The Question Concerning Technology and Other Essays,* William Lovitt, trans. (New York: Harper, 1977).

Marx, Karl, *Capital,* Ben Fowkes, trans. (New York: Vintage, 1977 [1867]).

Marx, Karl, and Engels, Friedrich, "Manifesto of the Communist Party," *The Marx-Engels Reader,* 2d ed., Robert C. Tucker, ed. (New York: Norton, 1978).

Marx, Leo, *The Machine in the Garden* (New York: Oxford University Press, 1964).

Nietzsche, Friedrich, *On the Genealogy of Morals,* Walter Kaufmann, trans. (New York: Vintage, 1969 [1887]).

Thoreau, Henry David, *Walden* (New York: Library of America, 1985 [1854]).

Weber, Max, *The Protestant Ethic and the Spirit of Capitalism,* Talcott Parsons, trans. (New York: Scribner's, 1958 [1904–5]).

Weber, Max, *Economy and Society.* 2 vols. Guenther Roth and Claus Wittich, eds. (Berkeley: University of California Press, 1978).

PART III

The Adequacy of the Canon

IO

Socratic Integrity

The word *integrity* is derived from the Latin word *integer,* which means whole or wholeness and hence entirety or completeness and, by implication or extension, being unimpaired, uncompromised, and uncorrupted, and being blameless. Things and conditions as well as persons can have or lack integrity. We can say that a person has integrity, then, when he or she has a certain concentration or purity or consistency. We can spell out these meanings a bit by saying that one has or shows integrity when one is entirely present (episodically or over a whole life) in what one does; one is all there; and one has all one's force of character and resources of action at one's disposal and under one's control. Relatedly, one has or shows integrity when one acts as oneself only, rather than unconsciously or thoughtlessly mixing in with oneself the attitudes or habits of others, imitating others without a sense of self-loss. Yet another description of integrity emphasizes a person's ability to remain steadfast to a commitment through thick and thin, overcoming internal and external obstacles, and devoting his or her whole life to that commitment or defining one's identity by reference to it. Integrity may also include standing alone for the sake of some commitment or other and refusing to go along with others or be incorporated in their plans or deeds. Thus, one remains whole by refusing to be included in an objectionable larger whole.

These brief accounts of integrity are derived from common usage, and they also seem to suit Socrates quite well. That we apply to Socrates descriptions of integrity that probably were derived in part from his words and acts in the first place is a harmless circularity. He has helped mold later ideas of integrity. And if returning to his words and deeds may revivify a sense of his integrity and his right, even, to help define integrity, the fact remains that integrity as Socrates practiced it shows some strange features. My purpose in this essay is to explore some of these features. For the most part, I concentrate on Socrates as Plato presented him in the *Apology of Socrates,* with some attention to the *Crito.* Whether or not the Socrates of the *Apology,* especially, was the real Socrates in every main feature cannot be established. Let it suffice to say that if it were not for the *Apology* but also the *Crito,* Socrates would not have been as influential in helping define integrity as he has proved to be. The hold of Socrates on the imagination altogether, but certainly on the understanding of the meaning of integrity, would be much less without these two works.

The strangeness of Socrates is owing to his negativity. It is no revelation to say that Socrates wrote nothing and maintained that he knew nothing. These are among his most famous manifestations of negativity. But his negativity is comprehensive and calls for an accounting that makes it constitutive of his integrity. That is, he may be a model of integrity because he is so extensively negative.

I use the word *negativity* to include more than the two manifestations just mentioned. Socrates practices negativity also in the sense that he says no to the doctrines of others without producing one of his own; his inner voice never says yes, but only no; he works on the hypothesis that the content of his wisdom is nothing, is ignorance; he knows what injustice is, not what virtuous excellence is; he knows how to act by abstention, avoidance, self-denial, and noncompliance; and he is prepared to contemplate eternal nothingness after death. There are other manifestations of negativity as well. Socrates' unforgettable presence is thus put together from elements that seem to lack any fullness, any positive definition. His integrity is nevertheless perfectly full; as a personage, he is most positively defined. But his fullness and definition arise from negativity. (At the end of this essay, I will qualify this assertion.)

Thinking about Socrates may lead us to decide that any kind of integrity that takes him as a model must follow him in accentuating the negative (to negate an old song). To put it more strongly: there may not likely be a *secular* integrity unless negativity is, so to speak, affirmed. This is not to say that every feature of Socrates' integrity must be incorporated into all versions of secular integrity. Thoreau, for example, is powerfully inspired by Socrates and is equally negative. Yet he may be even more secular than Socrates, and he certainly introduces creative changes in the theory and practice of secular integrity.

On a theoretical level, perhaps the starkest contrast to Socratic integrity is found in the Aristotelian ideal system: a picture of full virtuous excellence authenticated by reference to a confident understanding of human nature and the human condition. Aristotelian integrity is integrity of a radically different kind, and to one who prizes the Socratic model, the Aristotelian kind can look both spurious and dangerous.

It may be useful to see in Socrates a model of two kinds of integrity, one intellectual and the other moral. He shows *intellectual* integrity by a single-minded intensity or concentration in pursuit of truth or of wisdom, but this pursuit issues in only a perpetual dissatisfaction. It is as if intellectual integrity must lead not so much to a strict skepticism as to a residual tentativeness or uncertainty about what one accepts as true. Some conclusions that others offer are clearly mistaken or confused. Socrates is prepared to say no to them, but to say no (even many times) does not automatically produce a yes (even after a long time), that is, a definite conclusion amenable to sustained elaboration. What his intensity or concentration earns him is the right to maintain that he has avoided common or prevalent errors. His truth or wisdom is negative: freedom from avoidable error on the most important matters.

Socrates shows *moral* integrity in his strict avoidance of injustice. He tries to demonstrate purity in his conduct toward others. He thinks he may be doing good to people by being continuously available for conversation and thus getting them to think. But when he engages in worldly action, in acts of citizenship, his whole concern is to avoid injustice. Depriving others of what is theirs, in accordance with their own understanding of what is properly theirs, is injustice; he will not ever act so to deprive them. His justice is abstention from the dispossession of others. In contrast, actively giving them or distributing to them some worldly good they lack but may deserve is not his moral aim as an actor in the world. He does not claim to know what anyone is positively owed. As for himself, after the Athenian jury finds him guilty, he can say that what he really deserves at the hands of Athens is "free meals at the prytaneum."[1] But it is only at the end that he estimates his own worth, and he does so only to throw irony on the requirement that he propose a counterpenalty to the death penalty proposed by his prosecutor, Meletus. Socrates does not have to know what anyone is worth because he does know what doing injustice amounts to. The avoidance of injustice lies within his power and places no exceptional demand on his knowledge.

The two kinds of integrity, which I have separated, exist, of course, in the same person. How are they connected? Do they have the same root in one commitment? Do they have equal worth, or is one kind an instrument of the other? Or are they only accidentally copresent? I am tempted to say that Socrates' intellectual integrity is at the service of his moral integrity and therefore does not exist for its own sake, for the sake of exact understanding. The fury that drives him to destroy the argumentative positions of others (as shown in some of Plato's inconclusive dialogues like the *Euthyphro*) is the conviction that assurance about one's rightness of opinion is rarely justified but that out of unearned assurance grows the strengthened proclivity to act unjustly. To purge himself and other people of substantive ideas is to induce greater hesitation in action.

Socrates' intellectual integrity is thus a weapon in his war on opinions that engender or nurture injustice. He would not be so relentless in examining others if he did not think that he could slow them down. He is not, however, offering a positive vision, for he has none to offer. His intellectual integrity does not prepare the way for correct substantive ideas about virtue or matters of any other kind. No clever intellection is needed to ascertain the nature of injustice. That is why I am tempted to think that for Socrates, intellectual integrity is a means to reducing the amount of injustice in the world — a purpose for which his life itself is a means. In regard to his own opinions, his intellectual integrity steadies his soul in his own determination to avoid doing injustice. At the same time, to promote the intellectual integrity of others by his relentless questioning — even though most people will not likely attain a high level — is to serve a moral cause. What I say here is only a rough first statement about Socrates' intellectual integrity.

If we proceed with the assumption that the center of Socrates' integrity is moral integrity, we can look at some of its prominent features in their negativity. Then we will have reason to return to his intellectual integrity.

In the *Apology,* Socrates says that he is convinced that he has never wronged anyone deliberately.[2] This is a tremendous claim for a person to make about himself; the presumptuousness is considerable of entering a judgment about oneself and one's whole life heretofore. The majority of the jury finally does not agree with Socrates about himself. They thought that he has wronged the whole city, and quite deliberately. Now that he has been formally accused, they are ready to see as injurious the whole tendency of Socrates' life as a questioner, even though he thinks that his questioning is the greatest service that can be rendered to the city. The dispute cannot be settled amicably; the city has the last word. There is, however, nothing or very little that is speculative about doing wrong in the specific sense of acting unjustly toward another person. On this matter, Socrates makes a case that seems right, and none of the accusers tries to rebut it.

Socrates recounts in the *Apology* two political episodes in which he was involved. These episodes offer powerful support for the moral judgment that he makes of himself. In the first episode, he acts by being the only one to vote no; in the second, he acts by refusing to obey an order. Dissent and non-compliance constitute the salience of his active or direct citizenship, which is therefore negative. Moreover, in both cases, he is hardly a volunteer. When he dissents, he has to vote because it is the turn of his tribe to serve on the panel that prepares the agenda for the Assembly. When he refuses to obey, he is picked by the Thirty to carry out a mission. For the rest of the time, he refuses involvement; he does not give speeches in the Assembly;[3] and he explicitly refers to the fact that the public speech he gives to the jury, which is, as it were, wrung from him, is unique: the dire accusation against him occasions his first appearance (of any kind) in a law court.[4]

In the background is Socrates' general abstention, which derives from his wish not to implicate himself in the wrongdoing that the Assembly regularly sponsors. He says:

> There is no man who will preserve his life for long, either in Athens or else-where, if he firmly opposes the multitude, and tries to prevent the commission of much injustice and illegality in the state. He who would really fight for justice must do so as a private citizen, not as a political figure, if he is to preserve his life, even for a short time.[5]

The public voice of the leadership tends to corrupt any group of people. To answer that public voice with one's own voice in public would lead to nothing but the ruin or death of the person who made the effort and hence to the waste of an opportunity to do what one could do in one's everyday way to fight injustice. Socrates would wish to be the same person in public life as he is in private,[6] to speak in the same private voice about public matters, especially when injustice is urged. Although private interest regularly succeeds in cloaking itself in public purpose, a sincere private voice in a political place is not heard, or it is ridiculed or denounced as harmful. Socrates concerns himself with his own purity, but he conceives his purity as inseparable from avoiding injustice — that is, from not being an instrument of wronging others.

A principal negative element of Socrates' integrity is to abstain from hope-lessly unjust active citizenship. Nevertheless, he does not absent himself from his duty on the panel of the Council of the Assembly when it is his tribe's turn. Thus, in the first episode, 406 B.C., ten victorious military leaders in a battle off the Arginusae Islands were severely criticized for neglecting to pick up the dead and rescue survivors. Pressure built to try the leaders as a group, rather than separately, and the panel succumbed; Socrates was the sole dissenter on the panel. The issue was, to use a modern term, due process of law: fairness dictated separate and unrushed trials and in a proper court. Seeming niceties of legal procedure provided Socrates the unwanted but accepted opportunity to stand up for principle. What is the principle? Avoiding injustice. Eventually six were tried together, condemned, and executed. The result was a foregone conclusion; injustice had to happen.[7]

Notice that in opposing public pressure in 406 B.C., and then seven years later at his own trial retrospectively explaining his dissent, Socrates does not appeal to any special, much less subjective, notion of injustice. Instead, he tries to hold Athens to its own principle of right conduct, which here involves not positive reward but deprivation: punishment in the form of death. The principle is that we should not harm — in the sense of wronging — the innocent; stated more narrowly, we should not harm — punish — those who have not been found guilty by means of a proper legal procedure.

The same conception of injustice covers the second episode. Socrates refuses the order by the Thirty in 404 B.C. to apprehend Leon of Salamis and take him to Athens and certain death.[8] He does not say that the Thirty had no legitimacy and hence could not validly order anyone to do anything; he does imply, however, that Leon was an innocent man who was the victim of official persecution. He includes the treatment of Leon as among the crimes of the Thirty, who sought cynically and self-protectively to implicate as many people as possible in them.

If the principle that Socrates stands up for is part of Athenian life and not of his invention, he adheres to that principle even to the point of self-sacrifice. He is willing to sacrifice himself, his life, rather than abandon the principle. He will adhere to his negative morality, cost what it may (to use Thoreau's phrase from "Civil Disobedience"). This is where the moral novelty of Socrates in the *Apology* is found.

As he is well aware, many men risk death in battle.[9] Whatever any particular soldier's motivation may be — whether fear or interest or honor, or only conformity or habit — premature death or, perhaps just as bad, the threat of enslavement is a constant accompaniment. War is the central institution of citizenship. Socrates likens himself, in his dissent and noncompliance, not only to a soldier who does his duty but also to Achilles.[10] But these comparisons obscure the main thing, which is that Socrates risks life and freedom in situations in which no one else does. He stands alone, as one person, as his naked moral self. He has only himself to fall back on. His courage is for the sake of refusing to be an instrument of injustice. The enemy he fights alone is his own city, when the city fails to be faithful to its own best principle, which is also his own: not to wrong or penalize the innocent (actual or putative). The city does not risk itself by avoiding injustice in the matter of the military leaders or of Leon. Morality on these occasions is free of cost to any licit interest. Socrates is not asking the city or anyone else for the kind of sacrifice he asks of himself.

Where is the precedent for Socrates' action, for his distinctive moral heroism? In the ordinary sense of self-sacrifice, Socrates is self-sacrificingly moral; his moral integrity is extreme. Moral integrity must cost something, but one can have some measure of it without practicing it, "cost what it may." We need not build extreme self-sacrifice into the very definition of moral integrity. To be sure, he is not hounded or put to death because of either of the two episodes; there is no indication that they played any role in the accusations against him or in the judgment of his guilt and the sentence of death. But when he acted, he did not know whether he would lose his life or anything else valuable as a result. He took enormous chances, chances that no one else would have taken. That he was over sixty when he did so does not mean he would not have done so if the occasions had arisen when he was younger, even if it is true that for at least a few people — whatever may hold for Socrates — to contemplate death is easier when older than when younger.

Let us also notice that just as there is nothing religious in Socrates' understanding of injustice, so does neither the answer of the priestess at Delphi nor the existence of Socrates' inner voice have anything to do with his moral heroism. There is probably a connection between Socrates' courage in the cause of avoiding injustice and a surmise he entertains about what it means to be dead. (I shall return to this point.) But that surmise is purely Socrates' own; it comes from no divine instruction; it promises no reward in the afterlife for moral heroism; it is purely secular.

That Socrates is also a hero of another kind as well — a hero in the cause of truth in the negative sense of dispelling errors — is undeniable. Here, there may be something religious in the inspiration of his courage. The inner voice does not deter Socrates from appearing at his trial and speaking as he does.[11] The answer given by the priestess — no one is wiser than Socrates[12] — is construed by Socrates as a mandate to pursue wisdom, cost what it may. He says that if the city were to offer to release him from the charges against him on the condition that he henceforth abstain from his inquiries, he would reject the proposal. "I should reply: 'Athenians, I hold you in the highest regard and affection, but I will be persuaded by the god rather than you.' "[13] Something religious may fortify him here to be self-sacrificing, but it is not anything conventionally religious. In any case, the motivation of his dissent and noncompliance for the sake of avoiding injustice has different grounds from his persistence in philosophical questioning, even though this persistence is finally also for moral purposes, for the sake of enabling others to promote or lend themselves to injustice less.

The question arises as to the importance of Socrates' dissent and noncompliance. They were not followed by a subsequent deed or gesture of protest, much less by resistance alone or with others (if others could be found). Furthermore, Socrates fought in three battles just before or during the Peloponnesian War and thus did in fact lend himself to the systemic promotion or defense of imperialism — that is, injustice on a great scale. Although Diogenes Laertius records that Socrates turned down Charmides' gift of slaves,[14] there is no indication that Socrates criticized the institution of slavery — the capture of slaves in war and the codification of their bondage in law. Isn't it the case, then, that in risking his life in the two episodes, Socrates is courageous but for reasons that show a lack of proportion: too much courage in small affairs and none at all in large ones? And by doing nothing to try to change the system, doesn't he strain at a gnat in each episode and swallow a camel?

Certainly, by reformist and pragmatic standards, Socrates' negative citizenship had no political effect in his time, however one may judge his later influence by example in the annals of conscientious and nonviolent politics. Perhaps, after all, he is interested only in the future — in his subtle and long-term effects on the moral imagination. He has no illusions about his immediate efficacy: he says that he would have perished long before if he had been politically outspoken.[15] To the charge that he takes a heroic stand only in comparatively minor public situations, one can offer a reason that Socrates does not give. (Indeed, he does not indicate any awareness of the possibility of misplaced or disproportionate heroism.) The reason, however, is not foreign to Socrates' world. It is implicit, for example, in the successful effort of Diodotus, as recorded by Thucydides, to reverse the Athenian decision (428 B.C.) to kill the population of Mytilene, a rebellious confederate.[16] Certainly Socrates would not have given a speech like Diodotus's. Deliberately, even if transparently, Diodotus employs arguments that do not fully represent his own views. He clothes moral reasons in tough-minded calculations. He thinks he would not have been heard otherwise. He speaks to win. Morality needs him no less than it needs Socrates, even if Socrates' integrity is greater.

In any event, common to Socrates and Diodotus seems to be a hopeless resignation to the occurrence of large-scale tendencies of wrongdoing, especially toward other cities. The wrongdoing is systemic; it is almost unconscious, so ingrained and inveterate are the cultural causes of it. To be aggressive, predatory; to act to the limit of one's capacity and to attempt to act beyond it; to desire to possess more than one's share, as if true satisfaction exists beyond mere satisfaction; to see in one's power not so much a stake to defend as a precondition for transgressive adventure; and to thrive on risk, especially to one's continued existence — all this is the project of individual and group masculinity, the project of hubris and pleonexia, of rejecting the very idea of limits. This project is so driven that it cannot be withstood. But there is no excuse for base, small-minded horrors; people know better, or ought to; no imagination is required to see the wrong. People should not be carried away and in a real or manufactured passion initiate or sanction an atrocity or a profound evil of detail. That they do know better is proved by their occasional second thoughts.

The Athenian Assembly rescinded the decree condemning the Mytelinians. But the Athenian ship carrying the decree made no haste to reach the city, so reluctant was the mission.[17] Likewise, Socrates says that the Athenians eventually realized that the decision to try the military leaders as a group was illegal.[18] (Later in the *Crito,* he says that the many who casually put men to death would as casually bring them back to life if they could.[19] Socrates' words do not imply that the people do villainy and then repent but, rather, that they are generally incontinent and their incontinence sometimes causes them to feel a vague disquiet. Their bad deeds are halfhearted, partly unmeant.)

The view that I have just sketched is only one possible way of making plausible the pattern of Socrates' political episodes against the background of his general abstention. There is no doubt that my rationalization has an affinity with the perverse notion that, say, a country can do anything it likes in the field of foreign affairs as long as it treats its prisoners of war correctly and follows other rules of war or that a system of slavery is tolerable as long as the slaves are not constantly brutalized. But the sense of things that I would like to attribute to Socrates contains no excuse for the large-scale tendency or system of wrongdoing in the midst of which a morally heroic episode suddenly appears, with the overall wrongdoing left untouched. Socrates excuses nothing: his general abstention is a general condemnation. When the Socrates of the *Gorgias* says that Pericles left the Athenians much wilder than they were when he took over,[20] the assertion is in keeping with the sentiments of the Socrates of the *Apology.*

I do not mean to suggest that the negative and episodic politics in which Socrates engages is the only politics compatible with some measure of integrity, whatever Socrates may have thought. One can imagine a tolerably good officeholder devoting himself or herself to doing only the lesser and necessary evil while also doing as much good as possible. But we have to strain hard to imagine someone like that. Those who are attracted to office are not attracted to a strict economy of wrongdoing. They are eager to do, to act, even if they are not devotees of the project of masculinity, cost what it may to morality, or even if they are not eager to pursue it precisely because it is immoral. The world cannot do without officeholders, but it has something to learn from pondering the nature of Socrates' citizenship. His episodes teach a lesson beyond themselves: the baseness of particular political decisions may direct attention to the larger tendency or system in its regular and cumulative wrongdoing. To the extraordinary excesses of politics-as-masculinity, ordinary moral resistance may be futile, whereas extraordinary gestures of independent and solitary self-sacrificial morality may alone have a countervailing grandeur. These gestures have the masculine antimasculinity that answers to political hubris and pleonexia.

There is one more noteworthy episode in Socrates' political life — his refusal to escape from prison and from capital punishment. This refusal, too, may be seen as self-sacrificial morality: sacrificing oneself rather than doing injustice. The question is what principle covers Socrates' decision. In the *Apology*, the principle that covers his dissent and noncompliance is to avoid wronging the innocent (actual or putative), which he carries to a self-sacrificial length. He does not expect from any other person or any collectivity self-sacrifice for the sake of avoiding injustice. Nevertheless, Socrates' own integrity is partly defined by a willingness to risk death or some great loss in order to uphold a commonly accepted principle.

This principle is not only regularly breached in self-interested disregard of justice, but it also seems to allow people to suspend it if their own life or freedom is somehow endangered through no fault of their own — as when, for example, their choice is the one faced by Socrates: to be an instrument of injustice or to risk suffering a loss of life or other great right. He insists on preferring others to himself, preferring death to serving injustice. But what is involved in his staying in prison to face death, rather than escaping? It does not do to say that Socrates disobeys the state only when it acts with procedural irregularity and always obeys it when it acts with procedural regularity. It is clear that he would never obey, in any circumstances, a validly issued order to cease philosophizing with others. He is not a pure proceduralist. Procedural irregularity matters decisively to him when it is a device of substantive injustice. That it makes sense for us to speak of the inherent morality of procedural regularity is not relevant to the Socrates of the *Apology*.

He claims to know that he is innocent of the charges. He is innocent in his own eyes. He does not corrupt the youth by teaching new divinities, much less by teaching atheism. By not escaping he therefore becomes an instrument of political injustice, this time to himself. If before, especially in regard to the Thirty, he had risked death by his intransigent refusal to obey, he is now obedient unto death, his own unjust death. Why is he obedient? In the *Crito*, Socrates gives a number of reasons for his decision. Among them are two basic principles, as well as several considerations not neatly connected to either of the two principles. Socrates may stay to die, however, not because of any principle or consideration but because in his integrity he does not want to associate the practice of relentless questioning (in the name of dispelling errors) with anything less than heroism, physical heroism like that of Achilles in the face of certain death soon to come. Comparing himself with Achilles better suits the Socrates of the *Crito* than the Socrates of the two episodes in the *Apology*.

The given reasons do not satisfy. They are thrown out in a rush as if to overpower the auditor and leave him little time to answer. Likening himself to the frenzied worshipers of Cybele, an earth goddess, Socrates says that his arguments sound in his ears like the music of flutes: "The sound of these arguments rings so loudly in my ears, that I cannot hear any other arguments."[21] This sound is not the sound of intellectual integrity. More important, the reasons do not satisfy because in moral complexion, the *Crito* is perhaps closer to the *Gorgias* than to the *Apology*. The *Crito*, like the *Gorgias*, gives too much to an almost masochistic severity to the self, to the practice of authoritative punishment, and to servile deference to properly constituted authority. Socrates opens up a vast gulf between what he allows political authority to do and what he allows individuals to do. This is not the same gulf as separates the morally allowable suspension of morality in cases of terrible risk for individuals and the insistence, for oneself, that one face terrible risk instead of subordinating the vital claims of others to one's own.

When we try to find the principle, two emerge. The first is the same one invoked in the *Apology*: a self-sacrificing avoidance of doing injustice or being its instrument. The second one is altogether novel: when treated unjustly by the state or others, an individual should never retaliate. The difficulty is to ascertain which of the two really covers Socrates' refusal to escape. I do not think that we can unambiguously determine the matter. The cause of the ambiguity lies in ascertaining the agent that is the recipient or beneficiary of Socrates' enactment of — submission to — moral principle. Is it the city and its laws? Or is it those men who, acting by means of a valid and intrinsically fair legal procedure, arrived at a substantively mistaken, perhaps maliciously motivated, and seriously unjust decision? (It was only by a comparatively small majority: if only thirty votes, out of five hundred or so, had changed sides, the outcome would have been different.)[22] In his discussion with his old friend Crito, Socrates appears to shift the identity of the object of his self-sacrifice. He also seems to shift the identity of the source of the injustice done to him.

The upshot is as follows: if it is men, not the laws,[23] who visited injustice on him, then to seek to escape their judgment is to retaliate against them in the sense that he would treat them unjustly, as they had treated him. The whole avowedly novel and peculiar doctrine of nonretaliation is first enunciated in the *Crito,* with the implication that to escape would be to treat unjustly the jurors who had condemned him to death unjustly; to treat them as they had treated him. The retaliation is not in kind; rather, it repays an unjust effect with an unjust intention (vengeance). Retaliation is made to look worse than the initial act of injustice.

But it is not clear to me that the doctrine of nonretaliation as Socrates initially formulates it pertains to the mistaken and perhaps malicious jurors. Perhaps a more suitable referent awaits these unprecedented words:

> For there is no difference, is there, between doing evil to a man and acting unjustly? . . . Then we ought not repay injustice with injustice or to do harm to any man, no matter what we may have suffered from him. . . . Are we to start in our inquiry from the premise that it is never right either to act unjustly, or to repay injustice with injustice, or to avenge ourselves on any man who harms us, by harming him in return. . . . I myself have believed in it for a long time, and I believe in it still.[24]

As an individual who is also an uncommon citizen but one who is not necessarily — or necssarily not — setting himself up as a model for collectivities and their leadership, Socrates says that it is right to abstain from punishing the *guilty.* To punish them is to harm or injure them in some sense, and to harm or injure them is to treat them wrongly or unjustly. (The distinctions between these notions tend to disappear.) To give those who have wronged oneself what the world thinks they deserve is to render them injustice. Socrates avoids injustice when he accepts it for himself. The idea is amazing, but it does not really refer unawkwardly to the jurors.

To what or whom can it refer less awkwardly, even if still not with a perfect fit? After the words just quoted, Socrates begins to speak of the city, not of the particular men who condemned him. If he escapes, he would harm the city; at least part of that harm consists of doing injustice to it. Is the city (condensed into its laws, which are then impersonated by Socrates to speak to him, but of course in words that he has composed and that may, in some respects, be unusual if not novel and unprecedented) — is the city, despite his express denial, guilty of injustice, or wrongdoing, to him? To try to escape would then be to retaliate, to return harm for harm, wrong for wrong. If the city, however, is not guilty, then the doctrine of nonretaliation, as I have said, would not be clearly illustrated by his refusal to escape. But Socrates never says flatly that the city is guilty; to the contrary, as we have seen.[25]

Perhaps the city is both guilty and innocent. That would mean that both the principle of nonretaliation and the principle of never wronging the innocent (cost what it may) would be needed to cover Socrates' refusal. If the city, is, from one perspective, innocent and only the jurors are guilty of injustice, a case could be made for saying that to escape is to harm the innocent. In accordance with Socrates' insistence that he will not harm the innocent, cost him what it may, he will accept the verdict and wait to die in prison. But if the city is, from another perspective, guilty, Socrates will accept the verdict and not retaliate, not return harm to the city for the harm it inflicted on him. He will not harm the innocent. Also, he will not harm — that is, punish or wrong — the guilty, no matter how much conventional opinion may think that the guilty should always be punished or harmed or wronged by the aggrieved party.

The city is innocent if men, not the laws, effected the miscarriage of justice. The city is guilty if its laws, despite their overall acceptability, could ever lead, through their failure to ensure against drastic human imperfection, to serious injustice. The city is perhaps guilty or perhaps innocent if it sincerely but mistakenly thought that it did the right thing.[26]

Whether the city is innocent or guilty or both or not quite either, the harm done by escaping from its judgment is the encouragement given others to disobey a law whenever they thought they could safely do so and for any self-serving purpose whatsoever. Socrates has the laws say: "Do you think that a state can exist and not be overthrown, in which the decisions of law are of no force, and are disregarded and undermined by private individuals?"[27]

Socrates then supplements this generalized conception of harm with three considerations: if he were to escape, he would be guilty of three vices. First is the vice of ingratitude toward the laws that provided the framework within which Socrates was born and reared and educated. The laws deserve greater honor and obedience than one's parents do; the laws are more truly parents than biological parents are.[28] Second is the vice of faithlessness to an implied agreement to obey all laws and decisions. Socrates was free to emigrate without penalty, but he stayed, as if to say that he had freely chosen an allegiance into which he was born but did not have to retain.[29] Third is the vice of unfairness because Socrates was given a chance to persuade the city that it was wrong but he failed to take the chance.[30] (Apparently, Socrates did not regard his speech at the trial as an effort at persuasion, and he did not want others to see it as such, either.)

These vices are condemnable apart from any direct harm they may inflict. (But their example could prove contagious and thus eventually become a direct source of harm to the city and its laws.) Socrates' escape would display these vices. They would be imputed to him after the fact by a candid observer, himself or another, but they would not motivate the escape. Fear would motivate it, and perhaps also hatred and a spirit of revenge. Moral integrity precludes acting from such motives or passions, just as it precludes acting in such a way as to display major vices like ingratitude, faithlessness, and unfairness in the course of acting from fear or hatred or vengeance. Detestation of the vices should be enough to overcome the strength of powerful self-concerned emotions. Socrates wants to avoid moral taint for his own sake and also for the sake of the city and for the sake of other individuals.

I have said that I do not think that Socrates' reasons (whether general principles or particular considerations) satisfy. They do not seem to cover suitably his decision not to escape from prison and death. Neither of the two principles is really appropriate to govern the relationship between an individual citizen and the city or its laws or even between an individual citizen and a group of citizens formally entrusted with an official responsibility (as the jurors were). In the *Apology*, after all, Socrates' concern is to avoid wronging innocent persons when they are the targets of official lawless action. He seeks to protect individuals against the state. But he sides with official injustice in the *Crito*. He treats the city as if it were a hounded and vulnerable individual and thus transforms political duty into a relationship of such personal intensity that it threatens to become malignant.

The principle of nonretaliation, however, shows a moral refinement that is even more extraordinary than the principle of never harming the innocent, cost what it may. But the view that nonretaliation is exemplified when a prisoner cooperates with an unjust punishment is a terrible stain on the very idea of moral integrity; it is a disfigured moral heroism. Such obedience, especially when it is defended by a refined principle, sets a worse precedent than does any kind of disobedience, however motivated, and it also outweighs the value of the example set when an independent thinker faces death alone in a triumph of physical courage. Martyrdom to principle is, of course, poignant. Without it, Socrates' hold on the imagination would be less. If Socrates had escaped into exile, what would Plato have written about him?

Does the Socrates of the *Apology* inevitably lead to the Socrates of the *Crito*? I have already indicated that the *Crito* seems closer to the *Gorgias* than to the *Apology*. I mean that Socrates' arguments in the *Apology* show a freedom of spirit that they do not show in the two other works. Only in the *Apology* does he defend dissent and noncompliance as justified. He seems to have invented these modes of individual citizenship and then compounded his moral originality by practicing these modes to the point of risking loss and destruction. Yet it may be possible, I do not deny, that there is some consonance of character between the Socrates of the *Apology* and the Socrates of the *Crito*. In both works, he is careless of death. In the *Apology,* he risks death to avoid being an instrument of injustice. In the *Crito,* let us say he goes to his death to avoid displaying the vices of ingratitude, faithlessness, and unfairness. Perhaps the avoidance of these vices matters more to the Socrates of the *Crito* than any abstract moral principle, even though adherence to one or the other principle is what provides the pretext for Socrates' moral gallantry. Perhaps he fears being thought a coward more than he fears anything else. Or perhaps the matter is simply that as Socrates says, a man who subverts the law by escaping from prison may well be supposed a corrupter of youth, and thus Socrates for the first time will have been proved guilty of the crime that originally he was falsely accused of.

The long and short of it is that Socrates shows moral integrity when he acts for others, not for an (as it were patriotic) abstraction like the laws or the city. I say *abstraction* because Socrates barely indicates that the institutions of the Athenian polity embody moral principles worth defending for their own sake; rather, the institutions happen to be those of Socrates' own city. Devotion to one's city as such is devotion to an abstraction. In contrast, he acts for others, for other specific individuals, or for his fellow citizens as individuals when he dissents and refuses to carry out a murderous command and when he imagines himself choosing death or other punishment rather than acceding to an offer to remain free and safe provided that he stops questioning others. He consummates his moral integrity when he self-sacrificingly practices the principle of not wronging the innocent, cost what it may. This principle is made vivid in the *Apology,* not the *Crito*.

I have said that his intellectual integrity is for Socrates a means to the end of his moral integrity and that he also tries to induce some intellectual integrity in others to reduce their proclivity to urge or support injustice at home or abroad. Yet to say that his own intellectual integrity is a means to this double moral end is not a formulation that I am certain of. Accordingly, I would like to point out some considerations that do not all go in the same direction.

Socrates' moral integrity is most fully demonstrated when he risks himself rather than lending himself to injustice. Does his intellectual integrity show itself so riskily? Throughout his life "as a sort of a gadfly,"[31] he knows he incurred animosity. The old charges against him were that he studied and speculated about things in the heavens and beneath the earth, that he made the worse argument appear the stronger, and that he taught these practices to others.[32] These charges did not win him favor, only fear and ridicule. Socrates denies the old charges but thinks they provide a propitious background for the accusers and their new charges, namely, that he corrupts the young and believes not in the same divinities that the state believes in, but in new ones.[33] He denies the new charges, too, but he also knows that animosity lies behind them, just as it lay behind the old charges.

Socrates, however, does not seem to say that he had ever thought, until the formal accusation against him, that he was risking death by his practice of persistent questioning and perpetual dissatisfaction with the answers. To be sure, he antagonized specific sectors of the Athenian population by showing the hollowness of their answers to the basic question of what human excellence is, or what it means to excel in what human creatures are naturally capable of,[34] or how it is possible to educate people to attain human excellence. Still, if he tended to brand as ignorant and presumptuous the answers offered by political leaders, poets, and craftsmen, if he could say that those with the highest reputation for wisdom were the most unwise "while others who were looked down on as common people were much more intelligent,"[35] he did not think, it seems, that he was endangering his life or his continued ability to reside in Athens, despite some apprehensions.

Socrates' intellectual integrity becomes truly risky when he senses that the outcome of the trial could be his death, and yet he refuses to ingratiate himself with the jury or to plead for forgiveness or leniency. He also insists that if offered a dismissal of the charges on condition that he desist from his public philosophizing, he would refuse the offer. He would go on asking questions and finding the answers ignorant and presumptuous, even if told beforehand that his persistence would lead to his execution.[36] Indeed, "whether you acquit me or not, I shall not change my way of life; no, not if I have to die for it many times."[37]

It is at the end that intellectual integrity shows itself as self-sacrificing; Athenian tolerance lasted a long time, and it was not inevitable that Socrates would ever have had to face death for the sake of persisting in a life of questioning and not answering. Athens respected and even encouraged *parrhesia,* frankness. This is not to deny that Socrates would have persisted until the end, cost what it may, even if the end had come much earlier. So if intellectual integrity is the means to a moral end, it is nevertheless true that Socrates would have died for the sake of the means. The means are irreplaceable. Still, to be prepared to risk much or everything for the means is not to make the means the end in itself.

Socrates risked death also for the sake of his end, which is negatively moral and consists in the will to avoid treating any individual unjustly. As we have seen, however, Socrates' moral integrity countenances his general political abstention: he would not die young in the wasted effort to change a tendency of policy and a masculinist system of culture that had to produce injustice on a large scale. His moral integrity is self-sacrificing only narrowly and episodically. He has never sought opportunities for moral self-sacrifice. But he has always sought opportunities to practice his intellectual integrity and to try to encourage it in others. He has tried to sow dissatisfaction with received opinion on what is good in life and what human excellence is. What is more, he has inhumanly neglected his own interests and remained poor so that he could engage others philosophically.[38] And then he dies, it appears, not because of original and independent moral integrity but because his intellectual integrity somehow catches up with him unawares, and fatally. He regrets nothing and would now deliberately face death rather than ceasing to philosophize with others. Isn't his moral integrity therefore only incidental and his intellectual integrity central? Isn't it more likely the case that neither is a means to the other? Isn't it certainly the case that intellectual integrity is not a means to moral integrity? Aren't the categories too rigid?

In spite of all, I believe that everything in Socrates' intellectual life is devoted to the moral end of reducing injustice in the world. He grants that he has stayed alive rather than participating actively in politics with its risk of death or exile or some unsustainable loss. We grant also that he does not try to be a systemic reformer. Rather, he stays alive to force people, one by one, or a few at a time, to face themselves. His every word, the whole method of ruthless examination (*exetasis*), is devoted to the questions of how to act, what to want, how to conduct a life, what to live for. He is trying to induce, by his perpetual dissatisfaction with answers, not skepticism but moderation. He is trying to erode the sources of pleonexia and hubris, which derive their force in part from unchallenged opinion about the goods and ends of life. If he has been generous, though parsimonious, in risking his life for the avoidance of injustice, still he has not wanted to die before he was old, so that he could continue to moderate Athens, at least to attempt to do so, with only a mild expectation of some small success. Perhaps the future Athens will vindicate him.[39]

In any event, nothing is finally important to Socrates but the struggle against injustice. His labor is animated by the conviction that a disabused mind favors a less raging heart. What is more, intellectual integrity is not required to know what injustice is. I do not see in Socrates a pure will to truth: error irritates him because it is usually an instigation to injustice or a rationalization of it. The most public and powerful errors of opinion concern the goods and ends of life:

they all pertain to excellence or happiness. But they are productive mostly of injustice and eventual ruin. High idealism, always mistaken, is corrupting when publicly enacted. It is as if Socrates desires that the questions that social life incessantly raises, if only implicitly, should never be answered; as if he wants the whole subject of positive excellence and composed happiness to remain suspended so that people would concentrate their energies on living more moderately and therefore more modestly. The result would be some reduction of injustice at home and abroad. Socrates' method of intellect, like his whole self, is a sustained refusal to be an instrument of injustice.

Socrates examines others because they do not examine themselves. At best, under Socrates' pressure, they may ultimately learn to examine themselves a little, make their improvident conclusions into questions that are not readily answered. Although the phrase "the unexamined life is not worth living"[40] need not refer to self-examination, the context gives it such a connotation. People crave this or that worldly good. Socrates asks them and wants them to ask themselves, If they possess that good, is it really good? Does it really give happiness? Does it permanently allay the craving that led to its pursuit or, rather — in T. S. Eliot's words from "Gerontion" — does the giving famish the craving? If people do not have some wordly good or prize, Socrates wants to delay them in their pursuit so that they may ask themselves, Do I really want this? Couldn't I be happier or less unhappy without it or with less of it? Am I in a competition for no good end? Am I playing somebody's else's game?

Socrates' conception of self-knowledge is, therefore, inseparable from moderation or temperance. Critias, of all people, says in the *Charmides,* a dialogue about temperance, that the phrases "be temperate" and "know yourself" are equivalent.[41] The self-examining person can learn to say, "How many things I can do without!"[42] Self-examination therefore helps make life somewhat more worth living. But the practice of self-examination is uncommon. If it is odd, perhaps blasphemous, for Socrates to claim that he is guided by an inner and divine sign or voice,[43] it is at least as odd to practice self-examination, as he says he does,[44] and to encourage it in others. For a moral purpose, Socrates is inventing the practice of self-examination, and clearly, his practice of it is far in advance of that of his interlocutors.

From the perspective of this essay, it is worth noticing that Socratic integrity, moral and intellectual, is dependent on division within the self, not on being at one with oneself, not on having a conventional psychological integrity or wholeness. Self-examination is self-division, and from self-division comes self-knowledge. Self-knowledge turns out to be mostly negative: Socrates discovers that he does not really want the worldly goods and prizes that he is supposed to want; his desires are for other things, which are not positively described. And he also learns to resist certain descriptions made of him; specifically, those of his accusers. He knows himself sufficiently so that they cannot overpower him into forgetting who he is,[45] even though he may not have a full understanding of who he is or think that he can define himself or be defined by others. The results of self-examination are what they are.

Self-examination is an uncompletable process. It should last until death, and perhaps beyond. Socrates never claims perfect self-knowledge. It would be incompatible with having a self. The Socrates of the *Phaedrus* says that he does not know whether he is as proud as Typhon (a usurpatory monster with a hundred serpents' heads) or a more gentle creature: he is a question to himself.[46] He can imagine himself capable of the worst. This searching self-exploration, marked by some trepidation, that is formulated in the *Phaedrus* goes well with the Socrates of the *Apology*.

What is pertinent here is that by practicing self-examination, Socrates shatters his oneness. He breaks himself up into a watcher and a watched. The watcher is not always morally suspicious; it is not the Christian conscience. Although it is distinct from the inner voice, the watcher does reinforce the work of the inner voice, but this voice prohibits Socrates from doing anything that may be *personally* bad — injurious — for himself to do. Neither the inside watcher nor the inner voice is *directly* moral. What, then, is self-examination? The self examining itself may show something like "the ability to hold converse with myself" that Antisthenes, a friend of Socrates, says is the advantage of philosophy.[47] But a conversation needs more than one speaker. Is the self-examining self two selves?

In the *Apology*, Socrates does not say enough about self-examination for us to decide conclusively that it is a dialogue between me and myself (in Hannah Arendt's formulation).[48] If it is, however, does the watched self talk back to the watcher? Does Socrates internalize his public method of examination? If so, then the watcher or examiner is the superior, but not exactly as reason, in the *Republic*, is superior in dignity to the passions and appetites, which, when the soul is not trained, reason constantly battles and often loses to. Socrates refers not to any special training or higher education, but only to self-examination and the kind of examination by others that may encourage self-examination.

Perhaps in its persistent retrospection, self-examination is similar to interpreting a dream one has: one's wakeful experience is like a flow of dreams, and only a kind of internal secession from the experiencing self permits one to understand what one was up to or what one has been pursuing without quite knowing why. Implicit is the hope, however, that the inside watcher or examiner is not altogether too much like the amorphous I in the dream that is dreamed along with the rest of the dream. The hope is that the inside examiner is not so entangled with the examined that there is no possibility of genuine distance and difference between these two aspects of the self, no possibility of genuine self-examination. The hope is that self-examination is not a trick of language, an incorrigibly contaminated process, from the start.

Socratic self-examination is not merely self-consciousness; it is not merely reflexive consciousness, the ability to speak sentences about oneself. It is not, at least to begin with, the ability to imagine oneself in the place of another or to imagine what it is like to be another. It is also not quite Thoreau's "doubleness," in which "I can stand as remote from myself as another" thanks to "a part of me, which, as it were, is not a part of me, but a spectator, sharing no experience, but taking note of it, and that is no more I than it is you."[49] Socratic self-examination may be one of the seeds, but Thoreau's doubleness is closer, I think, to late Stoicism (though still far from it in important respects).

Whatever Socratic self-examination is, whatever it is most like, and whether or not it is genuinely possible, it is a principal negative component of Socratic integrity and shows, once again, how such integrity is made from negatives. Self-examination can be difficult or painful or disorienting; it is almost unnatural. It surely is not nicely compatible with being splendidly virtuous, which contains nothing tentative or perplexed or self-doubting. It is not useful for self-realization or the display of aristocratic virtues. To become less disposed either to serve as an instrument of injustice or to lend one's strength to the initiation or maintenance of injustice is its ultimate end. The way to greater moderation or sanity is self-examination, joined to examining and being examined by others; the way is not Aristotelian habituation from an early age.

It is obvious that the moral origins of Socratic self-examination do not determine the later history of the practice. Socrates inaugurates thinking about the potentialities of inwardness, but its story in the West contains much diversity. Not all those who have strenuously practiced self-examination or who have theorized its practice are morally motivated, as Socrates is. Inwardness as the site of freedom or self-renewal or positive inspiration is an essential part of the Western fabric, but I do not think that the original conception of inwardness, which is Socratic, contains all these later developments. To say as much is neither to praise nor to reproach Socrates. His conception is what it tremendously is.

Why does Socrates care about injustice to the extent that he does? Why is he so passionate to see less injustice in the world and disposed to risk death rather than being an instrument of injustice? Why are his moral integrity and, derivatively, his intellectual integrity so intense? There is no conclusive way of answering these questions. I am not even sure that such questions should be asked; indeed, there is a sort of crass impertinence in raising them. Still, the temptation to speculate is hard to put down. The speculation I offer mixes references to Socrates' statements and to his psyche.

One can say simply that for Socrates, human beings, unlike other creatures, are capable of justice and injustice. That is their distinctiveness. Socrates does not know what full distributive justice is; he does not know humanity or any particular human being, even himself, well enough to know how to confer such justice. He does know what injustice is; he knows what undeserved and deliberately inflicted pain or suffering or dispossession is. He knows what people tend to shun or shy away from. He also knows that those who resent injustice when it is done to them are quite prepared to do it to others, whether initially or in retaliation.

From all this, a possible conclusion is that the truly significant aspect of human distinctiveness is the capacity to do injustice. Socrates' aim is to curb it: everyone agrees that certain kinds of pain or suffering or harm are bad. The badness is enough reason to curb it. Then add: to persuade people to be less unjust is not to take them closer to human excellence (one component of which would be the ability to confer full distributive justice), but it is to take in hand a distinctive human capacity — the ability to do injustice — and to transform it into a better expression of human distinctiveness, the ability to refrain from injustice. Such a line of reasoning is suggested by what Socrates says in the *Apology* in regard to the elusive nature of human excellence and the limits on human knowledge concerning it.[50]

One possible reason that Socrates cares (and that we should care) so much about injustice, then, is that the honor of being distinctively human in the most feasible way is at stake. But I do not believe that in thinking about Socrates, we should put too much weight on the idea of human distinctiveness. We may incorporate too much Plato or Aristotle into the Socrates of the *Apology*, even if we highlight the negativity of the manner in which he may conceive of human distinctiveness.

A related reason, present in the *Crito*, is taken up with an eye on eventually introducing the doctrine of nonretaliation. Socrates says that doing injustice is bad for the agent, not only for the victim. The agent harms himself in harming another. This would mean that Socrates has tried to abstain from injustice for his own sake, not that of others, and that he urges the same attitude on others: "For if we do not follow him [the wise man], we shall corrupt and maim that part of us which, we used to say, is improved by justice and disabled by injustice."[51]

The *Gorgias* intensifies the idea: it is better for oneself to be the victim of injustice than its perpetrator. But when Socrates in the two episodes must choose between being an instrument (never the initiator) of injustice and risking death, he does not say that he would rather be dead than impaired. Such an interpretation is possible. After all, when Socrates claims in the *Apology*—and it is a shocking statement—that an unexamined life is not worth living, he says something similar. But the choice of an examined over an unexamined (in a sense impaired) life is a choice that can usually be made without risk of death or of any other great loss. Only sluggish people refuse to choose an examined over an unexamined life; their lives are therefore diminished radically and needlessly. Their cowardice is moral, not physical. They choose their impairment amid ease and safety.

I think, however, that the point made by Socrates' conduct in the two episodes is that he will never assist injustice to save himself; he would rather die. Only when the issue is escaping unjust punishment and the city is likened to a parent greater than a biological parent does Socrates say by means of a rhetorical question that it is better to be dead than impaired: "Then is life worth living when that part of us which is maimed by injustice [i.e., by doing injustice] and benefited by justice [i.e., by doing justice] is corrupt?"[52] The *Crito*, however, as I have said, could be thought closer to the *Gorgias* than to the *Apology*, in which the perspective of the victim's suffering, not the advantage of the agent's soul, is paramount.

To be sure, Socrates does say in the *Apology* that if the Athenians (because of Meletus) put him to death unjustly, Meletus and they would do more harm to themselves than to him (or at least as much harm).[53] This probably means, however, that Socrates is more valuable to Meletus and Athens than life is to Socrates. On the one hand, Socrates is valuable because he is unique in his power to get people to think about why and how their pursuits and policies are making themselves unhappy and harming others; on the other hand, life matters less to him than it does to others. I do not think we can import into this sentence the comparative advantage or disadvantage to the soul of the agent, whether Socrates or the city, of doing and receiving injustice. By his assumption that he is not guilty, Socrates is saying that Athens does not have to choose between doing and receiving injustice, but between doing and not doing injustice.

If we stay with the *Apology* in pursuit of why Socrates is so passionate about injustice and why he prefers dying to being its instrument, we can say that Socrates has an opinion about death that leads him to make lighter of it than most people do. That he was over sixty at the time of the episodes of dissent and noncompliance and that he is seventy when he explains himself under accusation may have some bearing on his readiness to refuse to abet or do injustice to others, cost him what it may. But I doubt it. Xenophon does go so far as to have Socrates say that to die now at the hands of the state would spare him the hardest part of life (old age) and give him the easiest death (quick and painless poisoning).⁵⁴ Perhaps Socrates did put the matter in this way, if only to himself, but the prudence manifested in these words does not suit the Socrates of Plato's *Apology*. There is something tonally different from prudence when toward the end of Plato's *Apology*, he says, "I am persuaded that it was better for me to die now, and to be released from trouble."⁵⁵

Socrates' old age does not really affect his heroism; most elderly people cling to life as ferociously as young ones do. Nevertheless, Socrates thinks about death in such a manner as to leave the impression that he has never cared too much about staying alive for its own sake. He does not love life with a blind attachment; he seems to need reasons to go on living. Perhaps the cause is temperament or some obscure distaste or revulsion. A more worthy reason would be the prevalence of injustice. We shall turn in a moment to a kind of explanation that Socrates himself provides. Whatever the reason, Socrates is continually unintimidated by death and not only when he is risking it in the name of avoiding injustice. Not dreading death absolutely, however, makes it easier for him to risk his life and then to face certain death with equanimity. This is not to say — Socrates does not say — that it was easy, routine, a smooth matter of course, for him to risk death. He sometimes speaks as if he felt danger, felt fear for himself, when he stood alone.

The *Apology* contains two main and interrelated points concerning death. The first is Socrates' contention that the good person cannot be harmed; the second is Socrates' assertion that either there is no afterlife or if there is one, it can be an opportunity for unending conversation among the dead. Either hypothesis would help make it easier for Socrates to risk or face death. We leave aside the powerful but metaphysically laden utterances about the philosopher's affinity to death in the *Phaedo*, great as they are. The Socrates of the *Apology* has no positive soul-metaphysics of the sort found in the *Phaedo*.

Concerning harm to the good man, Socrates says: "Meletus and Anytus can do me no harm: that is impossible, for I am sure it is not allowed that a good man be injured by a worse."⁵⁶ He also says, even more unconditionally, that "no evil can happen to a good man, either in life or after death."⁵⁷ The first contention refers to the harms of (judicially imposed) death, exile, and loss of political status.⁵⁸ The second formulation refers to harm to the good person's affairs in general, but the central harm is (judicially imposed) death.

Although in his speech after conviction and before the penalty, Socrates calls imprisonment an evil and surely considers exile a terrible fate, especially for himself,⁵⁹ he concentrates in these two statements the claim that for himself, death and other judicial penalties — but especially death — are not harms, certainly when inflicted unjustly. Although not harms, they are still not things that Socrates actively seeks or unequivocally wants. He is, after all, a human being and only a human being. He takes pride in having risked his life by dissent and noncompliance, as if he felt the risk as a risk and the possible cost as a cost. Reconciliation to death, even though perhaps present throughout his adult life, is not fully consummated until the eve of his death.

We can distill his claim in this way: in devoting himself as an episodically active citizen, as a general nonparticipant in politics, and as "a sort of gadfly" to the cause of diminishing injustice and not lending himself as an instrument to its perpetration, he has labored to prevent people, at home and abroad, from being deprived of what is theirs. He has also risked much that is rightfully his in doing so, even though being deprived of what is rightfully his — especially life — does not matter too much to him. That kind of deprivation matters a great deal more to others. A really good person does not attach himself very tightly to even the rudiments of his existence or to his existence itself; a really good person also knows that often those he wants to protect are (or have been or will be) themselves initiators or instruments of evil.

In short, Socrates devotes himself to preserving people, who are not exactly worthy, in possession of those things that are not exactly important, except to their unimproved selves. (The preservation amounts to abstention from unjust taking.) For Socrates to be deprived of life or something else is not really to be harmed, but because people are as they are and because they will more or less likely remain so, despite Socrates' unstinting efforts, they will feel themselves harmed by such deprivations. Despite their incredible readiness for military self-sacrifice, people ordinarily want to go on living as long as they can and as prosperously as possible. They are within their right to do so. What people rightfully want, Socrates will try not to deny them, even if he himself must lose those things that people rightfully want.

Self-examination has made Socrates more moderate, less intensely attached not only to the prizes of the world but even to the level of day-to-day life that moderate people satisfy themselves with. Perhaps an initial disposition also has moved him in a self-denying direction. Then, too, the divine sign or voice never seems to deter him from risk or self-sacrifice, as if to give its negative blessing to Socrates' independent resolve to struggle in his own way against injustice. These elements all help detach Socrates from ordinary self-concern, including concern with his death from any cause but particularly his death from the injustice of others.

The question persists, however: Why is Socrates, now and before, so calm about death? Why does he mind dying less than most people do, certainly than most people taken as natural individuals not disciplined into martial collective self-forgetful self-sacrifice? Socrates goes very far when he says, "For no one knows whether death may not be the greatest good that can happen to man" rather than the greatest evil, as most people think.[60] Why would anyone think, instead, that death may be the greatest good? The rate of suicide is low even among the desperate.

Socrates eventually answers this question when he addresses the jurors who voted to acquit him. The answer, however, seems to violate the heart of the claim that Socrates knows nothing that is worth knowing. His unashamed claim to ignorance has up to this moment rested on the view that the most important power — being able positively to live well — must depend on wisdom, and wisdom is knowledge of what being dead amounts to. He says:

> For to fear death, my friends, is only to think ourselves wise without really being wise, for it is to think that we know what we do not know. . . . And if I were to claim to be at all wiser than others, it would be because, not knowing very much about the other world, I do not think I know.[61]

His very last words at the trial express total ignorance: "But now the time has come, and we must go away — I to die, and you to live. Which is better is known to the god alone."[62] One is tempted to say that his search for wisdom all along has been to learn what others think death amounts to and how they adjust their way of life to their thoughts about being dead. Everywhere he turned he found not wisdom in the form of acknowledged ignorance, but ignorance presented as wisdom, with horrible consequences for self and others. Love of life is feverish because the thought of Hades is so appalling. We cannot be wise unless we know what being dead amounts to, and no one living knows that. Hence no one is wise, least of all Socrates, who at least is knowingly ignorant.

The trouble is that Socrates thinks he knows something about death. It is clear that he takes issue with a common view that in Hades souls survive in a condition of longing for life. At least, Socrates in Hades would not long for life. It is also clear that what he tells the jurors who voted for his acquittal comes from no divine source, no oracular priestess, no divine sign or voice and that what he says could not have come from self-examination or the method of examination used with others. At the end, Socrates, careful to deny that he has speculated about conditions beneath the earth, does just that. Perhaps this speculation has sustained him for a long time in his struggle against injustice. Perhaps his city thought that his aberrance — what we call his integrity — was underlain all along by an unorthodox idea of what being dead amounts to. To that extent, perhaps his old and new accusers were right.

When Socrates says that death is one or another of two states, he does not allow for the possibility of a third. Death is either nothingness or it is a "migration of the soul to another place" where the opportunity presents itself for endless conversation with and examination of the other dead.[63] Socrates would want to talk especially with the very types of human being that he, when alive, found especially wanting, poets and men of worldly affairs. The latter possibility is charming because it implies that a lifetime of experience — anyone's experience — could be the source of an endless duration of interpretation, though it would help if Socrates were on hand as midwife of interpretation. But this latter possibility, an unorthodox version of an orthodox view, does not suit Socrates as one whose intellectual integrity prohibits wishful thinking. However, the notion does suit him as one who, while alive, seems to aspire to be an undistracted, disembodied intellect.

Of course, we can never know for sure what Socrates thought. The first possibility, however, does perfectly suit Socrates' intellectual integrity. Death is nothingness; it is like not having been born yet; it is not a condition of any sort (personal or otherwise). Gregory Vlastos says: "So far from allowing Socrates a belief in the prenatal existence of the soul, Xenophon does not even credit him with the usual, old-fashioned, belief in the soul's survival in Hades."[64] Xenophon's omission is not proof of anything, but it is interesting that writings that Xenophon dedicates to the attempt to make Socrates as unthreatening as possible do not declare Socrates' acceptance of the soul's immortality.

A supposition that death is nothingness need not sponsor moral integrity; it can as easily go with libertinism or apathy. Socrates' case is different. He finds the prospect of nothingness appealing, not disgusting or disturbing. He does not repeat the saying of Silenus that it is best never to have been born, but he comes close. He says:

> if death is the absence of all consciousness, and like the sleep of one whose slumbers are unbroken by any dreams, it will be a wonderful gain. For if a man had to select that night in which he slept so soundly that he did not even dream, and had to compare with it all the other nights and days of his life, and then had to say how many days and nights in his life he had spent better and more pleasantly than this night, I think that a private person, nay, even the Great King of Persia himself, would find them easy to count, compared with the others. If that is the nature of death, I for one count it a gain. For then it appears that all time is nothing more than a single night.[65]

Only a few days and nights in one's life are sweeter than dreamless sleep or the nothingness of death, and they do not weigh as much as the other days and nights.[66] Being dead forever is nothing more for the dead person than a single night's dreamless sleep is for a living one. To risk or face death may be a little easier for a person who not only thinks that death is nothingness but also believes that life is a burden.

Surmising about death as Socrates does, why has he gone on living in the absolutely arduous way he has? Why didn't he lead a more ordinary life or a moderately pleasurable one? The answer can be, finally, that he could not help living as he did. I mean that he was driven irresistibly and from the beginning, from before the time the priestess gave her answer, which in any case Socrates did not have to construe in the activist way he did. Driven by what? By the one positivity that perhaps can be attributed to him: that he was driven by affection and compassion for others. Indeed, all Socrates' negativity stems from that one positivity and is dictated by it. It is his energy, his eros. He is more than just the friend of the Athenian jurors that he says he is.[67] The whole image of Socrates as a model of intellectual and moral integrity, as a supreme hero of self-denial and self-sacrifice, as a master of negativity, needs one, if only one, positivity, and that must be a positive commitment to others. He cared for them more than he cared for himself. He lived and died for them. He made them his superiors by deeming them worthy of his self-sacrifice. But he did not think that they were his equals, and this is precisely why he had to care for them and in the way that he did.

Notes

1. Page 37a. All page number references are the standard margin pages of Plato's works and refer to the dialogue being discussed. I used the translation of the *Apology* and the *Crito* by F. J. Church, revised by Robert D. Cummings (Indianapolis: Bobbs-Merrill, 1956). I also regularly consulted the translation by G. M. A. Grube, *The Trial and Death of Socrates*, 2d ed. (Indianapolis: Hackett, 1981); and read the translations by Benjamin Jowett, *The Dialogues of Plato* (New York: Random House, 1937), vol. 1, 401–38; Hugh Tredennick, *The Last Days of Socrates* (Baltimore: Penguin, 1959); and R. E. Allen, *The Dialogues of Plato* (New Haven, Conn.: Yale University Press, 1984), vol. 1.

In thinking about the *Apology* and the *Crito*, I found instructive and helpful the following works: Hannah Arendt, "Thinking and Moral Considerations," *Social Research* 38 (1971): 417–46; Hannah Arendt, *Thinking*, vol. 1 of her *The Life of the Mind*, 2 vols. (New York: Harcourt Brace, 1978); Hannah Arendt, "Philosophy and Politics," *Social Research* 57 (1990): 73–103; Thomas C. Brickhouse and Nicholas D. Smith, *Socrates on Trial* (Princeton, N.J.: Princeton University Press, 1989); W. K. C. Guthrie, *Socrates* (Cambridge: Cambridge University Press, 1971); Richard Kraut, *Socrates and the State* (Princeton, N.J.: Princeton University Press, 1984); Alexander Nehamas, "What Did Socrates Teach and to Whom Did He Teach It?" *Review of Metaphysics* 46 (1992): 279–306; Josiah Ober, "Gadfly Ethics in Context: The 'Socrates and Athens' Problem in

Apology and *Crito*," unpublished manuscript; Christopher Reeve, *Socrates in the Apology* (Indianapolis: Hackett, 1989); Gerasimos Xenophon Santas, *Socrates: Philosophy in Plato's Early Dialogues* (Boston: Routledge & Kegan Paul, 1979); Gregory Vlastos, *Socrates: Ironist and Moral Philosopher* (Ithaca, N.Y.: Cornell University Press, 1991); and A. D. Woozley, *Law and Obedience: The Arguments of Plato's Crito* (Chapel Hill: University of North Carolina Press, 1979). I have also learned greatly from my students at Amherst and Princeton, where I have been privileged to teach the *Apology* and the *Crito* over a period of forty years. My special thanks to Neera Badhwar, J. Peter Euben, Donald R. Morrison, and Alexander Nehamas for their criticisms and suggestions, and to John Cooper for many enlivening discussions of Socrates.

2. 37a.

3. 31c.

4. 17d.

5. 31d–32a.

6. 32e–33a.

7. 32a–c. For Europtolemus' initially successful but then failed speech in the Assembly to block the group trial, see Xenophon, *Hellenica* I: 7: 14–33, trans. by Rex Warner as *History of My Times* (Baltimore: Penguin, 1966, pp. 47–51).

8. 32c–e.

9. 28e.

10. 28b–29a.

11. 40a–b.

12. 21a.

13. 29d.

14. Diogenes Laertius, "Socrates," in R. D. Hicks, trans., *Lives of Eminent Philosophers*, 2 vols. (Cambridge, Mass.: Harvard University Press, 1950), vol. I, II: 31, 161.

15. 32e.

16. Thucydides, *The Peloponnesian War*, III: 41–48.

17. Ibid., III: 49–50.

18. 32b.

19. 49c.

20. 28516b–c.

21. 54d.

22. 36a.

23. 54b–c.

24. 49c–e.

25. 54b–c.

26. 51a.

27. 50b.

28. 51a–b.

29. 51d–e.

30. 51e–52a.

31. 30e.

32. 19b.

33. 24b.

34. 20a–b.
35. 22a.
36. 29c–d.
37. 30b–c.
38. 31a–b.
39. 39c–d.
40. 38a.
41. 164–65.
42. Diogenes Laertius, "Socrates," vol. 1, II: 25, 155.
43. 31c.
44. 29a.
45. 17a.
46. 230a.
47. Diogenes Laertius, "Antisthenes," in Hicks, trans., *Lives of Eminent Philosophers,* vol. 2, VI: 6, 9.
48. See note 1 for citations of Arendt. Arendt makes much of a passage in the *Gorgias,* in which Socrates says: "It would be better for me that my lyre or a chorus I directed should be out of tune and loud with discord, and that multitudes of men should disagree with me rather than that my single self should be out of harmony with myself and contradict me" (482b–c). See *Plato's Gorgias,* trans. W. C. Helmbold (New York: Liberal Arts Press, 1952), 50.

According to Arendt, Socrates' regular practice of self-examination is entwined with his dread of the self-reproach that wrongdoing would cause him: he stays blameless so that he can be internally harmonious. But I doubt the Socrates of the *Apology* believes that he can ever attain steady internal harmony, perfect freedom from self-reproach. Furthermore, Arendt assimilates self-examination too closely to conscience; she makes it too directly moral.

See also Bonnie Honig's thoughtful essay on integrity and self-division, "Difference, Dilemmas, and the Politics of Home," *Social Research* 61 (1994): 563–97.

49. Henry David Thoreau, "Solitude," in *Walden* (New York: Modern Library, 1937), 122.
50. 20a–b.
51. 47d.
52. 47e.
53. 30c, d.
54. Xenophon, *Recollections of Socrates and Socrates' Defense before the Jury,* trans. Anna S. Benjamin (Indianapolis: Bobbs-Merrill, 1965), 6–9, 146.
55. 41d.
56. 30c–d.
57. 41c–d.
58. 30d.
59. 37b–e.
60. 29a.
61. 29a–b.
62. 42a.

63. 40c–41c.

64. Vlastos, *Socrates,* 103.

65. 40c–e.

66. Why are most dreams bad dreams, and why are bad dreams continuous with most of wakeful life? The Socrates of the *Republic* suggests that the reason is that dreams, like daily life, are the scene of temptation to wrongdoing. He says: "Our dreams make it clear that there is a dangerous, wild, and lawless form of desire in everyone, even in those of us who seem to be entirely moderate or measured" (572b). See Plato, *Republic,* trans. G. M. A. Grube, rev. C. D. C. Reeve (Indianapolis: Hackett, 1992), 242. Temptation makes life as well as dreams a burden to one whose sense of injustice is keen. There may be a connection to the Socrates of the *Apology.*

67. 29d.

I I

Wildness and Conscience:
Thoreau and Emerson

In the United States, political theorists, whether housed in political science or philosophy departments, pay almost no attention to Emerson and only a little to Thoreau. Outside the United States, political theorists pay no attention at all to either. There are good understandable reasons for this neglect. The changes that have come over the United States and the world since the middle of the nineteenth century appear to make irrelevant all that Emerson and Thoreau say about political life. Then, too, what they do say is rather small in quantity and is not at all systematic.

The changes in the American scene include such phenomena as the ravages and blessings of corporate capitalism, unending technological innovation, global imperialism, world wars, mass immigration, mass society, the growth of state and private bureaucracies, and the dizzying shifts in the surface of life and in the scale and speed of social change. How can Thoreau and Emerson continue to be relevant to political theorists, even to political theorists of

This is a revised version of an essay read as a Spencer lecture at Oxford in 1999. I thank the Spencer Committee for their invitation. I benefited from the criticisms of Sharon Cameron, Leo Marx, Alan Ryan, Nancy Rosenblum, Richard Fallon, Ruth Grant, George Shulman, and Jack Turner. I have also learned much about Thoreau's arts of perception from Sharon Cameron's book *Writing Nature: Henry Thoreau's Journal* (1985).

democracy, when the world has altered so drastically since they wrote about politics? Indeed, even in their own world, they were remote from, and very disdainful toward, the raw expressions of political life such as party politics, interest politics, clamor over public policy, mass movements, the urge for structural reforms, and so on. Some people even at the time considered them archaist, obsolete, quixotic, deservedly marginal. Why, then, not ratify the judgment of many of Emerson's and Thoreau's contemporaries and the preponderant judgment of succeeding generations?

My answer is that their seeming remoteness from the steady politics of their own time is what enabled them to perceive truths about the deeper causes of the situations and events they distanced themselves from; and that in regard to the greatest issue of their time — slavery — they were as alert and responsive as almost anyone else and far more so than most others. They chose their causes with a caution that was both scrupulous and self-conserving. Their seeming remoteness should therefore have commended them to succeeding generations. Those deeper causes are not easily named; much less can they be adequately explained. But they make up an underlying condition, a condition of the spirit or of the will that drove and still drives particular political events while helping to account for the more permanent conditions or recurrent situations. I invoke here the theme of American wildness. Thoreau and Emerson are among the most trustworthy guides to American wildness; among American writers, only Melville is in their class; and among European writers, only D. H. Lawrence (in *Studies in Classic American Literature,* 1922) — and thanks in part to his reading of Emerson — deciphers the American wildness in a compelling manner.

I don't claim that wildness of the sort I am about to describe is either peculiarly American or purely democratic or, of course, that it is the only sort of cultural wildness that the historical record shows. But the wildness of America and perhaps any country that is comparatively free of pre- and nondemocratic ingredients is noteworthy and not observed often enough by political theorists and other commentators who attend to the gross effects of political life. Where the influence of social science is strong, it may be that the depths of social reality remain undiscussed or even their existence unsuspected. The history of the twentieth century makes a shambles of social science; but, then, no nineteenth-century philosopher, not even Nietzsche, seems to prepare the way for understanding the wars and exterminations of the twentieth century. In general, closeness to events and situations may hinder curiosity as to their psychic sources, as if there were no psychic sources of any complexity, as if there were only self-interest unimaginatively pursued, with or without ideological rationalization. Thoreau and Emerson try to look hard at the American wildness, and though they see self-interest everywhere, they are not content to see only self-interest or even to see self-interest itself as a simple passion in need of no philosophical examination. They see fanaticism in the narrowest of pursuits as well as in the largest and most amorphous ambition. They know how fantasy or the urge of fiction rules our lives, and often cancels prudent self-interest.

By definition, wildness is excess and extremism, especially in the forms of insatiability and transgressiveness. Some phrases capture aspects of wildness: going the distance, breaking through, "scoring," going one knows not where, moving just to be in motion. History is full of wildness, but it should always give the inquirer pause and reason to marvel, despite its ubiquity. We must add immediately that American democratic wildness grows in the same soil as democratic ordinariness, which has been said by many theorists, led by Tocqueville, to be characterized by restraint or modesty or mediocrity or mildness or by an unexorbitant and easily placated range of appetites and wishes. Furthermore, American democracy has never had — except in the pseudoaristocracy of Southern slave society — a division along class or caste lines where those at the top may be said to be wild in their exploits, adventures, overreaching, and predation, but wild, so to speak, in accordance with their standing in life and code of life, while the many, in accordance with their stations in life, lead circumscribed lives. In contrast, American wildness emerges unpredictably from all quarters. The wildness of assertive individualism in a democratic culture lives right next door to the modesty, and sometimes in the same breast.

It is precisely the absence of aristocracy — of what Emerson calls the "feudal mischief" ("Fortune of the Republic," 528) — that helps to account for both the peculiar wildness and the pervasive modesty and ordinariness. The absence of aristocracy means, above all, equality, equal individual rights; but it also means that there is no domination and direction of the cultural and spiritual life, of taste and public display, by the few, the hereditary few, the best born and most privileged. Democratic people are more on their own. They do not live under an army of occupation that an aristocracy in effect is, and remains even when some of its substantive power is stripped from it. The people are therefore unoppressed in any obvious and constantly reiterated way. When they are not oppressed in the main, not mere subjects, and when they are aware of their constitutional entitlements, people develop a mentality that permits a mildness or modesty or mediocrity that is undeferential. They become free in a manner that does not exist when a society provides them only with presumptive security in privileges, but not the chartered or contractual security of equal individual rights. Democracy lacks a top that presses on the psyches of the great number underneath. The democratic wildness is intensified in America by the fact that, from the start, America was a place to escape to and there try to make a new start — America as the scene of the canceled past.

At their best, unoppressed ordinary people, guaranteed certain rights as persons, may grow to think that in a new secular way there is something equally precious about themselves. They need not, though some will, transform that feeling into the wildness of arrogant self-assertion. To be sure, ordinary people will resent self-assertion when it threatens to become anything resembling the old aristocratic easy dominion or aspires to the imposition or reimposition of fixed hierarchy; they resist it with bitter anger. Yet central to the disposition of ordinary people in most times is a lack of continuously fascinated interest in exercising political power or translating popular will into a continuous stream of public enactments. The greatest passion is not to have political power exercised too energetically over them and to resist encroachments thought needless.

The democratic culture of equal individual rights ideally induces equal restraint in each person; restraint does not come from a hereditary upper stratum that owns a country, and runs it like a conquered province. Such democratic restraint is meant to be and is always operative as an inhibition on any wildness that is directly predatory against fellow citizens. Yet there is a democratic wildness nevertheless: the very condition of not being oppressed, not being pressed down, not being formally graded and ranked, releases energies that seem to burst all restraint. The tragedy is that when democratic people fail to recognize others as full equals, their wildness works tremendous wickedness. Nonwhites have been the principal victims of such failures of recognition, which have been a compound of sincere and cynical racism, of pride in whiteness (especially northern European), and of distaste for the nonwhite or the not quite white enough. Racism was for Emerson and Thoreau the supreme manifestation of American democratic wildness; in certain respects, it continues to be so. Racism has existed and exists everywhere, not just in democratic societies; the fact is that it is anomalous only in democracies; it is a direct political betrayal only of democratic principles.

Of course, race-pride and racism are not the only sources of inflamed self-assertiveness. Despite the hold of traditional religions on many Americans, an innovative and often extemporaneous religiousness frequently erupts. There has been, from the start, a religious wildness, an extremism of the spirit that undergoes transformations into mentalities that are highly heterodox and frequently verge on the secular or become godless while still permeated by religiousness. One especially important expression is the strange, un-Catholic fusion of religion and the pursuit of wealth. The pursuit is an act of worship more religious than any formal worship would be that propitiated God so that he would grant success to the pursuit. And then Social Darwinism came along to give a belated and speciously scientific rationalization for economic rapacity and for the democratically acceptable dualism of winners and losers. Perpetually in the background, of course, is the original Calvinist dualism of winners and losers, with all the wildness of endeavor that Calvinist anxiety helped to inspire, even as it also helped to inspire modern democracy.

Emerson asks in his first book, *Nature* (1836), "Why should not we also enjoy an original relation to the universe?" (7). American democratic wildness often stems from that very impulse, anarchic, desocialized, religious, or quasi-religious in essence. Many people are disposed, if only fitfully, but some people obsessively so, to pit themselves against the world; to test themselves against it; to do battle against it; either to tame it and settle down in it or to prevail in successive encounters with it; to leave a mark on the world or set a record in battling against it. The world is not fixed; its shapes and structures are fluid; it is a standing temptation to wild exertion and self-assertion. Only the will is sacred. Let it be said that this is not the Byronic insolence of deviance or aristocratic eccentricity.

Even when the wildness is organized, the organization is not feudal or despotic, but rather more like wild bands or groups in which individual members never lose sight of themselves as egos that exist prior to the organization that enhances wildness and makes it effectively predatory and aggressive. Tocqueville can speak of entrepreneurial Americans as "a company of adventurers" (*Democracy in America*, I:17, 308). The institution of slavery itself, though a legal system and a kind of culture, also bore these adventurist marks. Interested control of the government was and is often the aim, so that it can be made the mere instrument of aggression, while the struggles of political parties, though coinciding in large part in the time of Emerson and Thoreau with the struggle of slaveholders, and later of buccaneer capitalists, against the rest of society, against ordinary persons, is in itself, some of the time, a partly separate contest and exists for the sake of the partisan agon.

There is no understanding American democracy, therefore, without understanding two things: the anger of ordinary persons at the attempted imposition, no matter how slight or subtle, of old regime hierarchies and standards; and the wildness of those who express their wildness in self-originated adventures and enterprises. Theorists usually ignore both, their attention fixed on the play of masses and forces, but not on the sources. In contrast, Emerson and Thoreau — of course, not only them — show throughout their work acuteness in observing both the anger of modesty violated and the wildness of existential self-assertion. (By the way, people don't usually feel violated by the unaristocratic self-assertion of others; they expect it, especially in moneymaking and spirituality.) These writers teach that excess is inveterate and inevitable in American life; it is normal, but it comes principally from the wildness, rather than from the defensive anger. Thoreau's formulation in *Walden* that too many people in America are determined to be starved before they are hungry is as good a one-sentence description of American wildness as there is, I think (*Walden,* "Where I Lived," 396). Unleashed, democratic wildness is not divine, but demonic: it makes almost something out of almost nothing.

Emerson, far more than Thoreau, admires the human wildness. That is a fact we must take in as fully as possible. There is no doubt that in many writings such as *Nature,* the "Address" at the Divinity School at Harvard (1838), much of *Essays* First and Second Series (1841 and 1844), and *The Conduct of Life* (1860), Emerson encourages individual audacity in both active and spiritual life. His influence went, for a time, preponderantly in that direction. He hates the inherited Christian view of life as a place of submission, sacrifice, punishment, and defeat, and urges rebellion against it in the name of a brave self-trust, but not for the sake of "luxe, calme, et volupté." Thoreau certainly led a much more nonconformist life than Emerson did, but was only slightly impressed by individual wildness when it did battle with nature or when it raced to win worldly prizes. At the same time, he can say, "I love the wild not less than the good" (*Walden,* "Higher Laws," 490); for him wildness is, or is like, natural innocence; human exertion, however, often strikes him as socialized savagery. The larger point is that in the writing of both, we find a daring that seeks to break with the old world and find new forms and a new voice. Emerson and Thoreau are wild writers, but disciplined by a mastery of the English language that is breathtaking.

The largest point, however, is that both Emerson and Thoreau try to reconceive democratic wildness and find better channels for it. That means that in regard to political life, both of them tend in an anarchist direction, but do so for new moral purposes. Thoreau, especially, develops a view of individual conscience as a force in politics; that is to say, confronted with politically organized and systemic wildness, which itself verges on the anarchic, he answers with a moralized wildness, but one that is meant for almost unorganizable individuals. Thoreau and Emerson exemplify and advocate a moral sensitivity and therefore a political irritability that are exceptionally keen; and Thoreau, in particular, works with the notion of individual conscience and tries to make it a weapon of wildness against the criminal wildness of social groups, no better than bands and gangs, who enslave blacks, dispossess Native Americans, and manipulate the government into making war against Mexico in order to rob it of half its territory. Emerson and Thoreau help us to see that the worst and the best in American democratic life are offspring of wildness, and tend to one or another kind of anarchy. (A writer like Whitman can suggest in *Democratic Vistas* [1871] that, spiritually or existentially, the democratic worst is worse and the democratic best is better than what the old order shows.) To understand democracy in America, then, is to reckon with anarchic or near-anarchic wildness in many forms as well as with the social modesty of democratic ordinariness.

I wish eventually in this essay to take up Thoreau's idea of conscience as it figures in his most important piece of political writing, "Civil Disobedience" (first presented in 1848, and first published in 1849). But let me turn preliminarily to the general sense of politics and political morality that is found in Thoreau, and also in Emerson, who influenced Thoreau's sensibility profoundly. I have already said that both writers tend to anarchy. One thing that I mean is that anarchy is their highest hope. They see in the felt need for government only a sign of human deficiency. Thoreau's first words in "Civil Disobedience" are:

> I heartily accept the motto, — "That government is best which governs least;" and I should like to see it acted up to more rapidly and systematically. Carried out, it finally amounts to this, which I also believe, — "that government is best which governs not at all;" and when men are prepared for it, that will be the kind of government which they will have. (203)

Emerson had already said in his essay "Politics" (1844) that "The appearance of character makes the State unnecessary" (568). Neither writer thought that humanity in fact would ever be so grown up as to dispense with government; but government had to be constantly eyed with both suspicion and regret. At best, government is a lenient regulation of civilized anarchy, not a powerful instrument of grand projects.

To be sure, both of them indicate that constitutional democracy is the preferred form, but Emerson insists that democracy should be seen only as suitable to "modern times" and as happening to coincide with the "habit of thought" and the "religious sentiment of the present time." He goes so far as to say that democratic political institutions "are not better, but only fitter for us" ("Politics," 563). Other times and places and sentiments have judged and will judge differently. Emerson sees undoubted advantages in the way in which democratic government has advanced the protection of persons and of property, the object for which government is now supposed to exist (560). But he does not find in the national government or even the closer state governments moral phenomena of any dignity, or an opportunity, in their processes, for new moral relations or experiences.

Thoreau is somewhat more concessive, at least overtly so. He says, "The progress from an absolute to a limited monarchy, from a limited monarchy to a democracy, is a progress toward a true respect for the individual." But then he asks, "Is it not possible to take a step further towards recognizing and organizing the rights of man?" ("Civil Disobedience," 224). He does not seem hopeful that it is possible. But two formulations capture his ideal. First, he says that "government is an expedient by which men would fain succeed in letting one another alone" (204). Second, he invokes the moral necessity that the people be governed only by their consent, but immediately renders that idea as individual consent, and not only to membership in political society. Even one's enfranchisement in the system of elections isn't enough for the reality of individual continuous consent. He says that government "can have no pure right over my person and property but what I concede to it" (224). He means, freely and thoughtfully concede to it. When the disagreement between government and me concerns a truly weighty issue, the gross imperfection of political authority becomes blatant, hard to ignore. Government then forces the issue of its authority. But at the extreme, when its policies or specific acts are wicked, it becomes an alien imposition, authority in forfeiture, as we shall see when we discuss Thoreau's act of civil disobedience.

Given that neither Thoreau nor Emerson rarely says or suggests anything positive about government in general or anything enthusiastic about democratic government in particular, each could conceivably propose that democratic government, at least, had a title to the full obedience of the body of citizens; that democratic government, for all its inevitable association with human deficiency (in citizens and officials alike), possessed *legitimacy*. Although they don't use this term, they worry about the problem. The original title of Thoreau's paper that is posthumously called "Civil Disobedience" was "The Relation of the Individual to the State" — that is, the nature of the allegiance owed by the citizen. The word *allegiance* figures importantly in his paper. Thoreau refers to William Paley's political writing on the duty of submission to government (1785), and would have found the phrase "civil obedience" in it. Do Thoreau and Emerson, then, endorse the legitimacy of democratic government, and thereby counsel full obedience to it; perhaps even counsel conscientious obedience to it, as Paley for one does on behalf of his own government? The brief answer is no, for both writers. In the case of Thoreau especially, there will be a turn to conscientious disobedience, as if to say that the normal relation between the individual and the government is at most a hesitant, reluctant, unentire, provisional allegiance, an allegiance and hence an obedience that the government must earn every day, and often enough fails to earn. Thoreau explicitly calls the authority of the U.S. government inherently "impure" ("Civil Disobedience," 224); an impurity that cannot be removed, no matter how well government behaves; it can't be removed from any democracy and certainly not from any other kind of political system. Coercive powers, though authorized by the people, define the impurity of government. And when government initiates or sustains grave wrongdoing, inherent impurity becomes active illegitimacy.

Both Emerson and Thoreau initially incline, then, to near-anarchism for as it were existential reasons rather than moral ones. Their wildness shows itself not as the wildness of predators who systematize anarchy by aiming to use government as an unholy engine, but as an ingrained irreverence toward government as a contemptible and intrusive servant. This nonmoral, innocent, and anarchic disposition then grows into moral horror when government does the bidding of wickedness embodied in wild predators. If we wish to speak sequentially, we could say that existentially loose allegiance transforms itself, especially in Thoreau's mind, into a disaffection that is impersonally, theoretically, defended on moral grounds. But perhaps, in Thoreau's case, it is not possible ever to disentangle the existential from the moral, or either of them from the aesthetic.

I would like to introduce some systematization into the reflections of Thoreau and Emerson on government in order to indicate the reasons for their overall political scepticism, even aversion. (These two writers differ in some substantive respects, but Emerson is the root and Thoreau the most interesting foliage.) Neither one makes light of politics. In "Intellect," Emerson holds up the question of "the basis of civil government" as paradigmatic of the struggle to think, which he, following Pascal, calls "the hardest task in the world" (420). But both he and Thoreau approach the specific task of thinking about politics, of doing political theory, with the sense that it is a distraction from other matters they would much rather think about. Yet their moral sensitivity and the derived political irritability compel their reflections on government. Even if government were not the instigator or instrument of wickedness, it still would be somewhat odious. What is at issue here is not simply the point to which I referred earlier, namely, that the existence of government is testimony to human deficiency: the moral weakness of all of us and the ambition of some of us. Beyond that *donnée* there are many things that government undertakes that are deplorable and yet not wicked, yet so deplorable as to weaken allegiance to it. Government often insults citizens by the content of its regulations, not only by the very fact that it regulates.

If only all politics could be like the town meeting: that sentiment seems to be often at work in the political reflections of Emerson and Thoreau. In the town meeting all the citizens are neighbors; politics has little connection to coercion and violence; affairs are close enough to perceived experience as to lose almost all the unreality and abstractness of remote effects and undecipherable motives and fantastic purposes; consent is personal and continuous; and above all, affairs are simple enough to be democratically processed. Only here is modern democracy true popular self-governance. Explicitly in Emerson's "Historical Discourse" (1835), on the two hundredth anniversary of the incorporation of the town of Concord, and all but explicitly in Thoreau's work, the sense is that when political life is a more formalized neighborliness where little common action is needed, but when needed, intelligible to all and forgivable by those who opposed any particular decision, the questions of political theory lose both their urgency and their comparative intractability.

But a town is only a town; it is incorporated into a state; and the states compose a union. Both the particular state and the whole union, each established as a remedy for the situation in which numerous strangers live together, and for problems of scale and threat, and for the sake of securing the opportunity for private or political augmentation of power and wealth, engenders problems, in turn. This complex situation creates the initial looseness of allegiance to government and the eventual emergence of conscience as a counterweight. I am not suggesting that Emerson and Thoreau sentimentalize small town life or the actual activity of town meetings, and see in its displacement by larger political systems a tragic fall. They would not reverse the flow of history, much as they find fault with a good deal of its net result. The culture of democratic spirit in the modern age, after all, has grown with the attenuation of political democracy. They were not themselves especially eager participants even in local affairs. Their anarchic tendencies flourished because of absorption in their vocations as writers and in the failure of any kind of politics to appeal to their imagination as writers, to their sense of human adventure.

In any case, Emerson says that "Every actual state is corrupt" ("Politics," 563). Intrinsic corruption does not account all by itself for what I have been calling wickedness; nor does it account for something lesser, which I will call obnoxiousness. What is the corruption? Its root is in partisan organization. "A party," says Emerson, "is perpetually corrupted by personality" (564). Leaders, attracted to position and influence, turn party organizations into personal vehicles. The organizations may be necessary to the system, and may even be admirable when they stand for one or another basic principle. But it is the leaders who are the main beneficiaries: they "reap the rewards of the docility and zeal of the masses which they direct" (564). The corruption lies in the regular reversal, effected through parties, by which the people's agents become the main beneficiaries of political action. Gaining official power becomes the end and serving the constituencies becomes incidental. It is well to notice that

Emerson yokes docility to zeal in the masses, as if to say that ordinary persons, forgetting their self-respect, instrumentalize themselves and are essentially passive, whether they are docile or zealous. Or, as Thoreau puts it: "the people must have some complicated machinery or other, and hear its din, to satisfy that idea of government which they have. Governments show thus how successfully men can be imposed on, even impose on themselves" ("Civil Disobedience," 203).

Thoreau, however, is not an immediate perfectionist; he allows that, as he puts it, "All machines have their friction; and probably this does enough good to counterbalance the evil" ("Civil Disobedience," 206). He allows that some injustice may be "part of the necessary friction of the machine of government," and calmly adds, "let it go, let it go." Why let it go? His answer is finally rather sinister: "perchance it [the friction] will wear smooth, — certainly the machine will wear out" (211). The real trouble comes when "the friction comes to have its machine, and oppression and robbery are organized" (206). But aside from this latter, aggravated condition, Thoreau is content, and Emerson with him, to let political life, in its necessarily mottled way, proceed without them, and without any inclination, on their part, to commit themselves to it with a full allegiance. It is the realm of what Thoreau, following Paley in word, though unlike him in spirit, calls "expedience." Let us in fairness to Paley notice that he defines expedience not as opportunism that takes moral shortcuts but rather as that which conduces overall to human happiness, generously understood. Indeed, " 'It is the will of God that the happiness of human life be promoted' " (Paley, 298). To act expediently is therefore obedience to God's will and for that reason a moral obligation. But to reduce (or elevate) political morality to the promotion of happiness does not suit Thoreau's disposition at all. Happiness often goes well with a cynical (utilitarian) rationalization of its cost. In any case, he regularly uses the word *expedience,* for the most part, to mean a morally untroubled, even complacent, practicality.

In the normal scene of political life, then, Emerson and Thoreau leave their readers with three choices: to try to play a part in the political game by seeking and holding office; to let oneself be enlisted in the game, but without really affecting the play or even understanding, much of the time, what is going on and why decisions are made as they are made; and, last, withdrawing to the sidelines and hoping that one will be left alone. But sooner or later, politics impinges on those who would gladly be left alone. Politics moves out of the realm of expedience; intrinsic corruption is accompanied by policies that are actively insulting and obnoxious. Those who are personally or morally sensitive and hence made irritable by what goes on must pay attention to politics. Some response, some gesture or deed, may be called for. Regular involvement

in a party or movement is out of the question because steady politics necessarily shapes, misshapes, the participant in its own image. In my schematiza-
tion of the reflections of Emerson and Thoreau, I have not yet reached wickedness, only what is actively obnoxious.

When I speak of what is obnoxious without being wicked, I have in mind a
general point that preoccupies both Emerson and Thoreau and a specific issue
that mattered greatly to Thoreau. The general point is formulated by Emerson
as the incessant movement by government out of its proper dual role of enforc-
ing basic justice (protecting persons and property) and attending to the arrangements of basic expediency and into what Emerson calls "the blunder" of
"undertaking for another" ("Politics," 567). Emerson means the blunder of
governmental activism that seeks to channel the energies and direct the activities of the people. Even in the first half of the nineteenth century in the
United States, Emerson observes an enormous surplus of legislative enactments and executive decisions. He says:

> when a quarter of the human race assume to tell me what I must do, I may be
> too much disturbed by the circumstances to see so clearly the absurdity of
> their command. Therefore, all public ends look vague and quixotic beside
> private ones. . . . This is the history of governments, — one man does some-
> thing which is to bind another. A man who cannot be acquainted with me,
> taxes me; looking from afar at me, ordains that a part of my labor shall go to
> this or that whimsical end, not as I, but as he happens to fancy. ("Politics,"
> 567)

Emerson is intent on making limited government — that is, the limited scope of
governmental activity even safely within constitutional boundaries — essential
to rightful (or legitimate) government. Government is not wise to do everything it is constitutionally permitted to do. Beyond narrow limits, government
must turn into a system beyond any but the slightest control of the people who
are governed. They become subjects; and if they are not subjects through and
through, as under other political systems, they are nevertheless subjects to
some extent. The promise of democracy to end subjecthood, not only subjection, is unredeemed. Government acts as if it does not exist and act solely
through the permission of the people and their sensible delegation of limited
power. It is no wonder that Emerson says that "Good men must not obey the
laws too well" ("Politics," 567). Too many laws (and directive regulations)
have nothing to do with either basic morality or basic expediency.

The specific obnoxious issue that mattered to Thoreau, apart from actual
wickedness, was the religious tax. In 1833, the Congregational Church was

disestablished in Massachusetts, but the town still collected a parish tax. At the age of twenty-one, in 1838, Thoreau refused to pay the tax. As he says, in "Civil Disobedience," "unfortunately, another man saw fit to pay it" (215). He adds that he risked jail for his tax-refusal; but the town authorities allowed him henceforth to stop paying the tax. As part of the arrangement, he made a statement explaining that his grounds for refusal were that he should not be compelled to support an organization that he had never joined. Thoreau's deeper implication is that it is a grave insult to be made to support an institution that professes a faith and attempts to answer for its adherents the most important questions about life. This is a denaturing of philosophy, an obtuse coercion of intellect. It is an attempt to impair one's intellectual integrity; even to affront one's intellectual (as distinct from moral) conscience. The affront consists in being treated as if one were in need of perpetual tutelage. Each mind must attempt to answer — or at least come to terms with — the most important questions by itself and for itself, whether large metaphysical questions or particular moral ones. For government to serve as the agent of a church is for government to wound people in the center of their being, despite any good governmental intention. Even if a person happens to agree with the teachings of the church that is sustained by governmental compulsion, he or she is still insulted by the very compulsion itself. Once again, the state strays outside the realm of unquestioned justice and the realm of mere expedience and tries to settle disputable matters that must be left to individual judgment. Contrastingly, Thoreau lets us know that he has not declined paying the highway tax ("Civil Disobedience," 219).

So far, the determined suspicion of government shown by Emerson and Thoreau may seem unradical and not to partake of the wildness that I tried to identify earlier. Their anarchism or libertarianism is surely serious and at war with any easygoing acceptance of governmental activity. But where is the wildness? If not already found in the elements I have isolated so far, it is seen in the most distinctive aspect of their teaching, especially that of Thoreau, in the doctrine of moral conscience as resistance to government. I believe, however, that there is wildness even in the anarchic tendencies that I have up to this point mentioned. In accumulation, they sever any link between conscience and obedience to the law, except when the law codifies basic morality and hence serves as a "memorandum," in Emerson's term ("Politics," 559). Still, when conscientious refusal becomes actual on an incendiary issue like slavery, and is not merely principled refusal over a safely confinable issue like a church tax, then the wildness of conscience faces the wildness of aggression and unlimited exploitation. The loosened existential tie of hesitant and incomplete allegiance turns into a morally driven disaffiliation. The theory of allegiance changes its coloration.

Allegiance turns into disaffiliation because of the wickedness of slavery above all, a wickedness compounded by an aggressive war of dispossession against Mexico, waged mostly at the behest of the slave interest. The American national government protected and expanded slavery; the laws of many southern and border states institutionalized slavery. Slavery was a system of organized gangsterism that was all the more abhorrent because it existed in the only democracy in the world. Emerson saw slavery as made possible only by racism—a racism that permitted some people to half-think that black people were not fully human. I say half-think or half-believe because there is ample evidence that even white racists intermittently recognized the full humanity of blacks, but then reached opportunistically for any argument that came along that could rationalize the holding of slaves, either by them or by others.

Both Emerson and Thoreau were abolitionists, but neither they nor anyone else could readily imagine how slavery would be abolished. The fact is that the possibility of compromise was reduced constantly by the militancy of the slave power and by the corresponding militancy of anti-slavery forces, whether those of abolition or containment. Eventually, only war could end it, and did end it. But before the irrepressible conflict, Thoreau decided on an action that was a gesture. For six straight years, from 1843 to 1848, he refused to pay the head tax (the poll tax) of nine shillings ($1.50) in Massachusetts. He was arrested once, in July 1846, and spent one night in jail, and was then released when someone paid the tax for him—an intervention he bitterly protests in his essay (220), just as he had bitterly protested the same kind of intervention in the earlier matter of the church tax. Conscience must cost the person something. It acts only for the benefit of others, not oneself; it is resistance on behalf of others. By not paying the tax, "I felt," he says, "as if I alone of all my townsmen had paid my tax" (216). (He alone had paid the regrettable but imperative moral tax levied on all those granted the unspeakable benefit of existence.) He resumed paying the tax in 1849, however.

The gesture seems curious. Even Emerson thought poorly of it at the time. Massachusetts was a free state: why break the law in a free state, when your cause is to end slavery in southern and border states? Why signify your disaffiliation from the government of Massachusetts in refusing to pay the state's most general tax, when the state allows no slavery within its borders? Surely Thoreau's gesture is misdirected? To these questions I have no answer that would not be glib. Thoreau does not elaborate schematically. We can perhaps attribute to him the view that Massachusetts must sever its connection to the

Union, whose Constitution and laws allow and protect slavery, and whose policies expand slavery. Slavery has some economic benefit even to free states. Massachusetts knows better than to do what it does. Thoreau's disaffiliation enacts in miniature what Massachusetts should enact in magnitude. And until Massachusetts follows Thoreau's example, he will remain disaffiliated from Massachusetts; he will have seceded from it. He must break the law to show that his reluctant and provisional allegiance has given way to a so-far peaceful rebellion. To be in jail as a result of a conscientious act is simultaneously to withdraw decisively and to be withdrawn forcibly from political society. Thoreau didn't know how long he would have to stay in jail after his arrest; the law didn't specify a term. As it is, he says that if numbers of people had done or would do what he did, and filled the jails by their refusals, the effect would have been great and instantaneous. They would have shamed authority and clogged its system. But not many, if any, followed suit.

Breaking the law for moral reasons, in the manner of Thoreau, is conscientious wildness, pitting oneself against the massive forces of organized and legal wildness. Thoreau is helping to invent a practice of conscientious politics. The law must be broken: there must be anger and it must be ritualized. His intention is to show that he refuses allegiance to Massachusetts. Of course, history gives numerous examples of patient martyrdom and passive resistance. But Thoreau is not sustained by any faith or religious hope; he is not in service to an otherworldly mission. His notion of conscience has nothing to do with remaining loyal to a persecuted religious denomination. Socrates is his model, but Socrates broke no law deliberately. On the other hand, Thoreau is not taking part in a violent and insurrectionary movement, which also may call for self-sacrifice, but where no self matters much as a self, except for the selves of leaders. It is difficult, in any case, to see how conscience could ever be reconciled with the use of violence. There may be morally allowable uses of organized violence, but probably not conscientious ones.

An army of initially conscientious soldiers may just be possible, but the logic of military engagement precludes a conscientious army. Thoreau says, rather unexpectedly, that "a corporation has no conscience, but a corporation of conscientious men is a corporation *with* a conscience" ("Civil Disobedience," 204). But I think that conscience and a sustained policy of almost any kind are not compatible. When it is political and not for a course of action that one pursues in one's own life, conscience is for serious gestures. It is the insistence on an individualist perspective in political life. However, the later embrace of John Brown's violence and then war with the South, by both Emerson and Thoreau, placed them in the realm of the (merely) morally justifiable or allowable, in the realm of the necessary and lesser evil. This realm is no longer that of conscience. Movement into it shows how conscience may induce a sense of moral urgency, which may then overwhelm conscience and replace it with either inflamed fanaticism or a more familiar sense of duty. Even in "Civil Disobedience," Thoreau endorses the right of violent revolution when government's "tyranny or its inefficiency are great and unendurable" (206). Conscience cannot make up the totality of moral politics, but it is an irreplaceable ingredient. Morally tolerable politics also requires a nonindividualist or collaborative perspective, which entails organization and all its personally damaging compromises.

What is Thoreau's position? As an American citizen, he feels a personal responsibility for the existence of slavery. It doesn't matter that he owns no slaves and lives in a state that doesn't permit slavery; it doesn't matter that slavery long preceded his own existence and, he fears, may outlast him. I suppose that implicit in his position is something roughly like Kant's first statement of the categorical imperative. If a lot of people, each thinking for and acting as himself or herself, were determined to oppose slavery — many more than now do — slavery would be mortally injured. And just because many people refuse to oppose it, they perpetuate and even strengthen it. It doesn't matter that any person, as one, can do only a very little to end slavery (unless, naturally, he has great official power; but those in power have no interest in ending slavery). One must imagine oneself multiplied indefinitely, rather than associated with many others in a common course of action. One says to oneself, imagine that a lot of people acted as I do. Whether or not they do, I must act in the right way, even though it costs me something and even if it turns out that I am alone, or nearly so, in acting as I do, and have next to no effect. Thoreau says, "For it matters not how small the beginning may seem to be: what is once well done is done forever" ("Civil Disobedience," 212).

A thought like the one I just described seems suggested in Thoreau's essay. But I wouldn't press the point. Yet the fact remains that he does feel somehow *personally* responsible for perpetuating slavery unless he takes some action. Going into politics doesn't fit his character: he would have to make too many compromises and then, at the end, probably have little to show for it. He will act nevertheless. Unless he acts he will consider himself, no matter how indirectly, an "agent of injustice to another" ("Civil Disobedience," 211). We may think that he unduly stretches the notion of personal responsibility. We may even think that he does so out of an exaggerated sense of his own importance. But to think this way is, I believe, to refuse to enter into a world where people of moral sensitivity, because of slavery, lived traumatically even though untouched in their own immediate lives by what traumatized them.

It is therefore especially important to notice that Thoreau takes pains to

present himself as characteristically averse to doing good, to acting philan-
thropically. He says, "I came into this world, not chiefly to make this a good
place to live in, but to live in it, be it good or bad" ("Civil Disobedience," 211).
Even more emphatically, he says:

> It is not a man's duty, as a matter of course, to devote himself to the eradica-
> tion of any, even the most enormous wrong; he may still properly have other
> concerns to engage him; but it is his duty, at least, to wash his hands of it, and
> if he gives it no thought longer, not to give it practically his support. If I devote
> myself to other pursuits and contemplations, I must first see, at least, that I do
> not pursue them sitting upon another man's shoulders. I must get off him first,
> that he may pursue his contemplations too. (209)

And in other writing Thoreau laments the very onerousness of insistent conscience (*A Week*, "Sunday," 60–62). He would hate being thought philan-
thropic. If a person seeks distant wrongs to remedy, the chances are good that
he is overlooking wrongs that he is inflicting closer to home. An abolitionist
can exploit his own servants. Thoreau says in *Walden*, "What *good* I do, in the
common sense of that word, must be aside from my main path, and for the
most part wholly unintended" ("Economy," 380). He goes so far as to claim
that "Philanthropy is almost the only virtue which is sufficiently appreciated
by mankind. Nay, it is greatly overrated and it is our selfishness which over-
rates it" (382). Our pity is incurably infected by self-pity and by our passion to
condemn in others our own unpurged faults. Thus, it is not philanthropy that
inspires his abolitionism and his abolitionist gesture. At least, Thoreau would
have us believe that it is not philanthropy, that it is not positive benevolence.
Rather, he does not wish to lend his support to the exploitation of others; even
though he is not himself a direct exploiter, he benefits to some extent by
leaving the exploitation undisturbed.

His abolitionism is not philanthropy to slaves; it is only restoring to them
what has been wrongfully and wickedly taken from them, their freedom and
the fruits of their labor. It is repairing an evil, not improving an already tolerable condition. There can be no obligation in conscience to increase any good
for adults (unless they are friends or lovers, perhaps). But where Socrates
refused to cooperate in the initiation of evil, as in the case of apprehending
Leon of Salamis, and turning him over to the Thirty and to an unjust death,
Thoreau is seeking to end established and systematic wrong. Unless he felt
implicated in such wrong, however, he would not feel obliged to act to end it.
In that respect, he is like Socrates. He insists that he is implicated in injustice;
he rejects the thought that if he took no interest in slavery, all that he would be
guilty of is merely allowing an evil to proceed for which he bore no respon-

sibility. He also insists that he almost tries to avoid occasions for moral action. Thus, Thoreau wouldn't necessarily care to relieve suffering that was no one's fault, and that resulted in no exploitative benefit to himself. Rather, he, like Socrates, will not be an agent of injustice. To act against injustice, he must be able to take injustice personally.

I have to grant that some of the time, Thoreau seems to build into the avoidance of injustice a demand that entails not merely some cost to the agent, but complete self-sacrifice where necessary. A people as well as an individual must avoid injustice, "cost what it may." "If I have unjustly wrested a plank from a drowning man, I must restore it to him though I drown myself" ("Civil Disobedience," 207). The example of the drowning man is taken from Paley's book (218). Arguing by what he thinks is an analogy, Thoreau is willing to contemplate the end of "their [Americans'] existence as a people" — that is, as a union of free and slave states — if breakup is needed to end a system in which free states strengthen the establishment of slavery and sustain the predatory warfare instigated by the slave states ("Civil Disobedience," 207). (The slave-holders who loved slavery more than the Union were of course willing to sacrifice the existence of the Union.) But I see no analogy between preserving one's life and preserving the Union. Even if there were, Thoreau's political argument as a whole does not require — it may even be injured by — such extreme supererogation, such a demand to go beyond what most philosophers (not only Paley) consider as strictly morally due — certainly in the case of one desperate individual pitted against another desperate individual, where each is morally allowed to be self-preferring. Acting from conscience from its nature doesn't entail martyrdom. To be sure, Thoreau doesn't say that a drowning man is obliged to allow the other to have the plank without trying to secure it for himself first; he only says that one must not wrest the plank from the other. Correspondingly, Paley's example is not one person wresting a plank from another, but only "where two seize upon a plank, which will support only one" (218). Yet Paley allows each to prefer himself at the expense of the other. "When our life is assaulted," even if involuntarily, Paley says, "all extremities are justifiable" (218). I assume that Thoreau at the least envisages some situations where each is obliged to prefer the other's life to one's own. But even this latter demand is more self-sacrificing than most philosophers consider morally imperative.

Can an expectation of unconscripted altruistic self-sacrifice unto death be routinely included in basic morality, and even seen as its distinctive act? Those who are sympathetic to the claims of conscience still hold that there are morally acceptable limits to preferring others to oneself. In fact, Thoreau does not say that one person is morally obliged to die to set another one free. Eventually, however, he will praise John Brown for freely risking his life for emancipation. However, if Brown did morally supererogatory acts, he nonetheless did acts of violence, acts of war, which are not acts of conscience, even if conscience played a role in turning Brown away from indifference to or acceptance of slavery. (To be sure, conscientious civil disobedience was meant as an explosive gesture, though nonviolent, just as Brown's violent raid was also meant as an explosive gesture. There is some gestural affinity between Thoreau's act and Brown's.) Nonetheless, the fact remains that slavery could be abolished only through many deaths, volunteered or conscripted, and sanctioned for the most part by the cause of the Union; that is for a dramatically political (patriotic) cause, not an overtly moral one. Sacrifice had to be collectivized, organized, and commanded. Leaving aside the matter of the drowning man, we can still say that Thoreau's moral negativity is quite wild in its combination of parsimony and extravagance, of reluctance and risk.

Thoreau's conscience drives him to enlarge his sense of responsibility and then to act on it without any assurance that his action will have an effect. His conscience obliges him to break the law, never, except incidentally, to obey it. He says, "The only obligation which I have a right assume is to do at any time what I think right" ("Civil Disobedience," 204). His conscience tells him what is right. Is he being subjective in his invocation of conscience? Is he appealing to some idiosyncratic interpretation of common principles? Or is he relying on some special religious or metaphysical doctrine to influence his position? Is he elevating his mental powers above the level of his fellow citizens? I think that the answer to all these questions is no. (The drowning man example is extreme, though not idiosyncratic. It is after all in line with some of the teachings of Socrates and Jesus.) Actually, Thoreau is doing nothing but intensifying an idea of obligation that many Americans should find congenial: its essence is rejection of an orthodox definition of obligation (reiterated by Paley) as obedience *in conscience* to the command of a superior, whether God or human master, just because it is a command (Paley, 34–35).

To be sure, Thoreau says that his obligation is to do what he *thinks* right, as if setting himself up as a uniquely unaccountable judge. But I read this phrase as conveying the idea that it is only thinking, thoughtfulness, anyone's not only his, that can establish the very nature of obligation and the existence of a particular obligation. The rest of "Civil Disobedience" as well as some other political essays of his, including "Slavery in Massachusetts" (1854) and "Life Without Principle" (published posthumously in 1863), make it clear that he uses the term *conscience* to name nothing subjective or idiosyncratic or special or personally superior. Everybody has a conscience; conscience tells each of us right from wrong; but it does not merely speak to us, it urges us to abstain from wrong. Conscience is taking with the utmost seriousness what everyone professes, and many fail to take seriously. This is the core of moral conscience as Thoreau conceives it. It is conscience because one must think about the obvious when it is overgrown by indifference, comfort, and self-serving rationalization, or more commonly and worse, when it is bruised and shoved aside by either sensual complicity or the momentum of companionship in mischief. One often has to fight hard against one's conscience, and almost as often defeats it. It has to be touched to live. One must think strenuously in the silence of moral solitude, and permit, in that silence, the obvious to emerge. One must be alone with oneself, even if not physically isolated, to let conscience — our common possession — speak. Here is where Thoreau's most important departure from Paley — an undeniably subtle and enlightening comprehensive political philosopher — occurs.

It cannot be emphasized enough that Thoreau's notion of conscience contains nothing merely personal, not even so much as a personal interpretation of the inner working of conscience or the judgment it had to make of slavery. Many kinds of action could follow from this judgment, but the judgment itself all people had to reach, provided they didn't deceive themselves. Thoreau never says that those who uphold slavery do so because they think that slavery is morally right. But if slavery is the worst wrong, not to resist it when one is implicated in it is to turn oneself into its agent. And when, a few years after Thoreau's tax refusal, citizens in free states were compelled by new laws in 1850 and 1854 to assist in the capture of runaway slaves, the conscientious citizen's implication in slavery became more palpable and more unpardonable. Thoreau assumes agreement on the immorality of slavery; otherwise he couldn't work on his readers as he does; he doesn't think that the wrongness of slavery has to be demonstrated; he assumes that everyone believes that if the comprehensive wrong, slavery, is not wrong, nothing is wrong; and he couches the appeal to his audience as an appeal, at the last, from them to themselves ("Civil Disobedience," 220); as an appeal from oneself morally asleep to oneself when one has made the effort to "throw off sleep" (*Walden*, "Where I Lived," 394). He assumes that white people can know that slavery is as wrong as anything can be and still not think that blacks are equal to whites, even though they should. He is trying to awaken whites from racism, so that they feel, on behalf of black slaves, the defensive anger that ordinary democratic persons feel toward caste arrogance. Thoreau does not define the world like Huck Finn, in Mark Twain's novel of 1884, who yokes conscience with obedience to the laws of property in slavery, religiously reinforced, and experiences his goodness in not informing on the runaway slave as a temptation that risks damnation. It is too early for the considerable amusements of Twain's irony.

Thoreau's attitude to the people varies in tenor in "Civil Disobedience" and other writings. He is sometimes harsh about their moral inattention while at other times he praises the people of the free states as morally better than their governments. But there must be hopeful expectations behind his act and the words he uses to explain his act. There must be respect for, not only disappointment in, democratic ordinariness. Yet the truth remains that injustice isn't excused when done or allowed democratically; it is made worse. Inherently valuable procedures betray themselves when they give means or cover to great substantive wrongs. There must be affinity between the morality of means and the morality of ends. Paley himself allows that "if the ends be bad, the means cannot be innocent" (Paley, 164).

Thoreau says that we have a right to assume only certain obligations. One cannot assume any obligation that carries with it the possibility of becoming an agent of injustice; one's rights do not include that one. One must be sparing in assuming obligations; one can't be a machine for doing as many right things as possible. A morally overburdened life is not a joyous life, but a morally insensitive life and a life without a corresponding political irritability would be an inhuman life. To discharge one's moral responsibilities needn't be part of one's self-fulfillment; it is just conscientiously inescapable.

Thoreau's idea is that every obligation must be consciously and voluntarily assumed; and the only aim of a sense of obligation is to do the difficult right thing, the act that is determined or ratified by conscience. That is to say, one is obliged only to do the substantively right thing in each case of moral decision or when faced with some continuous situation that demands a moral response. Nothing commendable in the structured habitual or institutional background has any moral weight. I find in Thoreau no concession either to the idea that an enfranchised person's obligation can ever extend to the readiness to abide by all laws and policies, whatever their content, that have been made by a valid procedure, or to the idea that every protected, unenslaved, or otherwise undispossessed person accumulates an indebtedness to society that obliges him or her to abide by all laws and policies that have been made by valid procedure. Neither one's tacit consent to membership in political society nor one's secure and unhampered course of life is a source of obligation because neither can enlist conscience. It sometimes seems as if Thoreau sees no moral field between conscience and expedience. Only when a peculiar difficulty intrudes itself must conscience, as Thoreau knows it, come into being: the difficulty of seeing that one's own good fortune is wrapped up with harm to others. Conscientious obligation may override even the most praiseworthy procedure and the most lucid gratitude for great benefits received. Allegiance is to the right, to just treatment of individuals, not to government or to society; and the greatest service that one can offer one's fellows is to encourage them in the avoidance of injustice. They know what injustice is, after all.

When a conscientious person obeys the government, one obeys only the right that government happens to do, not the government itself. What is right is not right because government commands or does it. To make the point again, Thoreau does not acknowledge the legitimacy of any government. Government can't be legitimate: in itself, even properly constituted political authority can never be worthy of obedience for what it is. No human institution is above individual conscience. That doesn't mean that a democracy without slavery would be illegitimate, though the U.S. government is made illegitimate by slavery. Rather, the question of a government's rightful claim to authority is superseded in the conscientious citizen's mind by particular judgments, as the need arises. At moments of necessary decision, there is either expedient obedience or conscientious disobedience. "A very few," Thoreau says, "as heroes, patriots, martyrs, reformers in the great sense, and *men,* serve the state with their consciences also, and so necessarily resist it for the most part" ("Civil Disobedience," 205). Typically, politicized conscience is resistance. Thus, conscience has much to do with politics. Thoreau's orientation to life is intensely ethical: he must recurrently see political affiliation as a major moral issue on which every conscientious person must take a personal stand. The actions of government are sometimes so serious in their consequences that they can't be merely expedient or inexpedient. To think that they are exhaustively covered by these latter categories is to adopt an impermissible attitude of moral complacency or indifference. Therefore, since Thoreau can't attach conscience to allegiance, he must attach it to resistance.

Let us admit that Thoreau is untroubled by the thought that he is, to a great degree, the bearer of an outlook that only democracy nurtures; and that he is like a child instructing his parents in the lessons they somewhat absent-mindedly taught him. Thoreau doesn't turn on himself as Socrates does in the *Crito* when he impersonates the Laws of Athens in order to have them say how much he owes them. But Thoreau's fault is slight: the evil of slavery in democracy has made him forgivably forgetful of the dependence of his anger on the spirit of democracy, and of his imagination of wildness on the life of democracy.

In effect, the conscientious individual has no state. He or she will remain unpledged, will withhold express consent to membership in political society, with all the moral abdication inherent in such consent and its derivative allegiance. If there is consent to political membership at all, it is barely tacit. We should notice that while in Thoreau's view, political allegiance is always morally problematic, allegiance to morality, in contrast, is imperative as a matter of course. Indeed, just because allegiance to morality is imperative, political allegiance is morally dubious. Consent is necessary for a person's political membership, but morality is binding apart from anyone's consent. Consent has nothing to do with the authority of moral principles: I am not free to decide whether or not I will do right.

Anything more than begrudged political consent would also endanger Thoreau's larger existential imperative (given as a friend to another friend): "Consent only to be what you are" (*A Week,* "Wednesday," 220). One's citizenship or political membership can't define one's identity. In "Walking" (1862), Thoreau sums up his own status. He says, "I live a sort of border life, on the confines of a world into which I make occasional and transient forays only, and my patriotism and allegiance to the state into whose territories I seem to retreat are those of a moss-trooper" (251). (A moss-trooper is a shadowy brigand or plunderer.)

It may be asked, How can there be conscientious disaffiliation if there is only tacit membership to begin with? In her own essay "Civil Disobedience," Hannah Arendt goes so far as to claim that the dissent contained in civil disobedience is the first genuine act of consent that a citizen can make (88). But I don't think that we have to answer as Arendt does. It's perhaps enough to say that people knew that Thoreau was American and lived in the United States and they didn't usually think about express or tacit consent to membership, anyway. The only question is whether his disobedience registered on them, on his fellows and neighbors, as he wanted it to do. And does it still register on us?

It is clear that unless Thoreau had written his essay on civil disobedience, the act itself would have counted for little, except perhaps to make it easier for Thoreau to live with himself. But living easily with himself was never his motive. (He was as hard on himself as he was tender, sometimes, to others.) To be sure, he needed an act so that his words against slavery could have something behind them other than the passion for eloquence in a just cause; but it is also the case that without words, the eruptive wildness of conscientiously breaking the law could appear trivial or self-indulgent. The words and the act need each other, and they form together one memorable deed. The act of disobedience inspired many other political actors later, while the words, inspired and aided by Emerson, still carry many a lesson in political theory. I would conclude by pointing to some of these lessons.

The setting that I have in mind, then as now, is an imperial democracy, the United States; but the lessons can apply, I think, to other democracies when some allowances are made. Let me recall that for Emerson and Thoreau, genuine democracy is found only in town meetings, where politics is face to face, and is, above all, simple enough for unexpert but attentive democratic understanding and where the stakes of politics aren't very large. Here if anywhere, allegiance (for political as well as existential reasons) can be full, or, in my language, the question of political legitimacy is solved. But enlarge the polity, and a set of consequences follow that must loosen allegiance and locate conscientious citizenship in opposition, resistance, and disobedience, rather than in loyalty and devotion to the state and its projects.

Let me mention some of the judgments passed on an enlarged and complex polity that figure explicitly or by suggestion in the reflections of Emerson and Thoreau. Deceit of candidates aside, elections are almost like a blank check for the future, and serve only clumsily and confusedly, if at all, as a judgment on the recent past. Elections aren't like a constituency's delegation of power for some specific and narrow purpose. In an enlarged representative system, politics becomes abstract, too complex for common understanding, too divorced from popular control. Politics becomes the self-serving enterprise of professional politicians; governmental ambition seeks out occasions to regulate life and thus encroaches unnecessarily on freedom; guaranteed rights often lose out in hard cases; both moral conscience and intellectual integrity are affronted by governmental efforts to settle moral or philosophical disputes best left to an individual's considered judgment; and great wickedness recurrently is done, at home and abroad, whether at the behest of the indefatigable power interest of government or the ruthless economic or other interests of various groups. Every type of human transaction or sentiment is coarsened or made brutal in its political mode; perhaps conscience, too.

Since the time of Emerson and Thoreau, every political imperfection has grown. There is greater wildness and also greater system: each pretends to compensate for the other, while the tendency is for each to thrive with the other. The United States still has all the impulses of wildness. Even some of the new technologies of controlling the people and their supposed wildness show the insatiable wildness of managerialism. This last fact points to a larger one; namely, what is crucially different from the time of Emerson and Thoreau is the tremendous increase in the discretionary power of executive and administrative officials. All citizens and noncitizens are dependent on the decisions of officials acting with legally (but often improvidently) delegated power. The rule of general laws is displaced by personal rule over citizens, in many sectors, whether in everyday life or in the pursuit of imperial foreign policy. Sometimes the policies administered are benign, sometimes innocuous, too frequently sinister or potentially so. The properly democratic complaint can't be, except occasionally, that popular will isn't translated into laws and policies; there can't be literal popular self-government; on numerous issues, popular will is either divided or scattered or unformed. The complaint should be, instead, that there are too many laws and policies, with the result that people are often subjected to the will or discretion of officials. The unfelt pain of being known through and through, being watched much of the time, being affected by as it were invisible power—all this grows and grows. Foreign policy is full of wicked effects: the waste and criminality of imperialist wars and other military interventions, and of cruel economic measures. Modern democratic government is unlimited even when it respects many fundamental individual rights, though the erosion of some rights, especially in privacy and criminal law, is pretty steady. Government is usually not better than the average level of public opinion but it has the liberty, often, to be very much worse.

Confronted with such a part-friendly, part-alien, part-monstrous hegemony, the idea of legitimacy undergoes serious attenuation. How can genuine consent be given or implied when government has such liberty to be so active, energetic, discretionary, when it has so much surplus power, when it is so full of the ability to mobilize people in undertakings not their own, to initiate change and shape the common fate? How can there be legitimacy when government is unlimited and, what is more, recurrently wicked, when the aims and capacities of government exceed the grasp of any rational theory of the necessity for government, or its expedience? On the one hand, increased governmental activism exacerbates what I have called the existential scepticism toward government as such and toward government as interference. On the other hand, such activism continues to distress conscience over a fairly broad range of issues. I don't say that it becomes illegitimate again, as it was when slavery existed, or that violent overthrow would now be justified. After a certain point, however, the question of legitimacy is shelved, or at least appears misguided. Room is left for a measure of allegiance: democratic procedures are still better than not and still better than others; and the advantages of a decent life pursued by tens of millions in the safety of constitutional rights that are protected by normal democracy constitute a staggering achievement that does not wholly rest on the exploitation of some by others. But the cost of democratic politics to morality, as well as the harm done by the quantity of discretionary power to the status of citizens as free beings, is very large. It gets awfully hard to remember that democratic politics itself is intrinsically a more moral system than any other. Yet what alternative is there?

If room is left for a measure of allegiance—more than Thoreau, for one, would have wished to grant—and especially an allegiance based on the government's constitutional respect for fundamental individual rights for all, room is also left for the work of conscience, basically as Thoreau sketches it, in creative acts of no-saying and disaffiliation, especially to protest failures by a government, which is supposedly dedicated to fundamental individual rights, to respect them at home or abroad. This work can be done and has been done in Thoreau's spirit. The principal purpose must be to protest wickedness and, if one has the courage, to refuse being its agent. The point is not to let the sentiment of democratic legitimacy inhibit action by stifling conscience, as long as protest is nonviolent.

I grant that there are not many issues as clear-cut as slavery, unless capital punishment is such a one, as I think it is; whereas the issue of abortion in our time, for example, is disputable. Abortion is one of those uncommon moral questions that are fundamental and also are defended by equally or nearly equally compelling arguments on opposite sides. In its radical indeterminacy, this is not the sort of question that originally called forth Thoreau's conception of conscience, where all the right was on one side. Nonetheless, on either side in the matter of abortion, one can act in Thoreau's spirit. Conscientious passion can properly find itself on either side, and so can conscientious and nonviolent lawbreaking, so great are the moral stakes for each side. (Or is it rather the case perhaps that a pro-abortion person should concede that conscience could be only *against* abortion, while the pro-abortion position has rights on its side, but not conscience? Personal rights, in this rare instance, outweigh the claims of conscience, even if it speaks with one voice?) In any event, a good person should not obey many laws too well. Possible service in the military should always make a young person wary. Good democratic wildness must face up to bad democratic wildness, one anarchism against another, despite the awful unevenness of the struggle. That is the lesson of Emerson and Thoreau.

Works Discussed

Arendt, Hannah. "Civil Disobedience" (1970) in *Crises of the Republic*. New York: Harcourt Brace Jovanovich, 1972.

Emerson, Ralph Waldo. "Historical Discourse" (1835) and "The Fortune of the Republic" (1863, 1878) in *Miscellanies*. Ed. Edward Waldo Emerson, *The Complete Works of Ralph Waldo Emerson*. 12 vols. Boston: Houghton Mifflin, 1903–4, Vol. 11. All other references are to Ralph Waldo Emerson, *Essays and Lectures*. New York: Library of America, 1983.

Paley, William. *Principles of Moral and Political Philosophy* (1785). Indianapolis: Liberty Fund, 2002.

Thoreau, Henry David. *A Week on the Concord and Merrimack Rivers (1849)* and *Walden* (1854) in *Henry David Thoreau*. New York: Library of America, 1985.

Thoreau, Henry David. "Civil Disobedience" (1849) and "Walking" (1862) in *Henry David Thoreau: Collected Essays and Poems*. New York: Library of America, 2001.

Tocqueville, Alexis de. *Democracy in America*. 2 vols. Translated by Reeve/Bowen/Bradley. New York: Vintage, 1954. Vol. 1 (1835).

Valuable Commentary on Thoreau's Politics

Bennett, Jane. *Thoreau's Nature: Ethics, Politics, and the Wild.* Thousand Oaks, Calif.: Sage, 1994.

Cavell, Stanley. *The Senses of Walden* (1972). 2d ed. San Francisco: North Point Press, 1981.

Richardson, Robert D. *Henry Thoreau: A Life of the Mind.* Berkeley: University of California Press, 1986.

Rosenblum, Nancy. Introduction, *Thoreau: Political Writings.* Ed. Nancy Rosenblum. Cambridge: Cambridge University Press, 1996, pp. vii–xxxi.

Shulman, George. "Thoreau, Prophecy, and Slavery." Unpublished manuscript.

Turner, Jack. "Performing Conscience: Thoreau, Political Action, and the Plea for John Brown." *Political Theory* 33 (August 2005).

12

Prohibition and Transgression

In his "A Letter to Augustine," William Connolly says that "you peer more deeply into this abyss than anyone before and most after." The abyss is "the depths of the human condition" (*Identity/Difference: Democratic Negotiations of Political Paradox,* p. 126; hereafter *ID*). Connolly's tremendous praise for Augustine's power as a moral psychologist is all the more telling because Connolly himself is a subtle and resourceful practitioner of this mode of inquiry. (Assume with me that a principal part of reflection on the human condition is reflection on human nature.) I have no doubt that he was drawn to Augustine because of an affinity between their interests, but also because he thinks that Augustine, though god-intoxicated, will always have much to teach even the most nontheistic student of moral psychology. Even if Connolly's own tendency, which is neither religious nor secular, "subverts Augustinianism and neo-Augustinianisms," it "remains close to Augustine in certain ways" (*The Augustinian Imperative: A Reflection on the Politics of Morality,* p. xxxi; hereafter *AI*.)

In this essay, I wish to explore aspects of Augustinian moral psychology that

This essay was written for William Connolly's Festschrift, *The New Pluralism,* edited by Morton Schoolman and David Campbell (forthcoming). I wish to thank Sharon Cameron for her criticisms.

Connolly himself explores. My perspective is friendly to Nietzsche and indebted to him, as Connolly's is. I hope to make some distinctions that are not foreign to Connolly's undertaking, but that may strike a somewhat different note. I think that Augustine's fervent Christianity may reduce some of his power to instruct nontheistic and antitheistic readers in moral psychology. I will be guided throughout by the conviction that Augustine both enlarges our conception of human nature and misrepresents human nature. He enlarges our conception of human nature by enlarging our awareness of human capacities, for good and bad, especially when these capacities in society at large are unexpressed, unadmitted, or unnoticed; and he simultaneously misrepresents human nature in his pursuit of composing a theological picture of existence — a picture that is more inclusive than Connolly's "Augustinian imperative," which is "the insistence that there is an intrinsic moral order" (*AI*, p. xxvii). There is more than morality in the Augustinian world-picture.

Augustine contributes profoundly to the truth about human nature, and some of the truth he introspects, intuits, or discovers is a hard-earned pessimism. But not all of Augustine's pessimism is true; some of it is necessitated by the effort to fill out his theological system. I mean that Augustine works with such theological fervor that some of the time he imposes on a generally valid and generally available pessimism a theological interpretation of existence that provides a false depth to his pessimism. To be sure, Augustine (like others) can express truth about human nature theologically; but then we must "demythologize" the writing and translate it into secular terms. If there is some rhetorical or imaginative loss, there is gain in truth. However, when vice is transformed into sin, and when sin is traced to the original sin in the garden, the needs of a theological interpretation of existence may displace the search for truth. Even more, when offense to God, not intentional harm to others, is seen as the highest sin, Augustine's pessimism loses a fair amount of its secular relevance. I do not say that his religiousness invariably leads him astray; it may rather sharpen his initial insight or even prompt it. In any case, I will try to point out some of what I think remains of permanent validity, unhurt by theological commitment, and sometimes reliant on it.

Now, it is not only a matter of damage done to moral psychology by the distortions effected by theological commitment. The mere fact of decisive difference between the Christian worldview and all others, but especially the pre-Christian outlooks of Greece and Rome, makes it difficult to assess the comparative merits or depth of their moral psychologies. It is likely that Augustine is the deepest of all Christian moral psychologists, but is Connolly right to see him as peering into the abyss more deeply than "anyone before and most after"? (*ID*, p. 126). The possibly superior claims of Plato to universal validity—not to mention the Greek dramatists and historians—are not the whole issue. The fact is that every moral psychology pays attention, whether consciously or not, to the numerous ways in which human beings are and must be affected by the particularities of their culture. If, for example, a culture is polytheistic or does not assert that god or the gods made the world from nothing, much of the mental atmosphere of that culture will be significantly affected and take on features absent in a culture devoted to an idea of god as one and omnipotent.

Human beings are capable of conforming to an indefinitely large number of world-outlooks, with the result that their psyches are in some main respects, though not all, different from place to place and time to time. To some extent, therefore, it is not possible for us to adjudicate the rival claims of Plato and Augustine to have the greater depth. Perhaps Plato in the common judgment of posterity probes most deeply of all into the psychic recesses of classical humanity while Augustine does the same for devoutly Christian humanity. But is Plato a more adequate moral psychologist for the classical world than Augustine is for the Christian world (say, through the middle ages)? Do we know enough to say? And is there a moral psychologist yet more adequate for his or her different world than Plato or Augustine is for his?

Yet there is after all a common humanity—common instincts, capacities, and traits—across cultures and through time. In certain aspects, moral psychologists through the ages can be measured by the same standard, as if they constituted one species. Plato's impact survives the loss of the classical world, and Augustine's survives the heterogeneity or attenuation of the Christian world. With a common humanity, the claims of Plato and Augustine become commensurable, though their ranking will always remain open to dispute. At the same time, analysis of what is particular to a culture may some of the time be more instructive to the student than analysis of commonality. On many occasions, we may learn more about the common human condition by a deep analysis of particularity than by a deep analysis of commonality. The simple fact of indefinite plurality instructs us in the vastness of human nature, a truth that helps to protect us against the flattening effects of any theoretical reduction. Even more important, deep analyses of particular cultures make life altogether more interesting, more gratifying to contemplate in the extended range of its diversity.

Who am I to be lecturing Connolly about cultural difference?

A distinctive contribution that Christian theology has made to moral psychology is inquiry into the ways in which norms of various sorts are violated, or appear to be violated, on account of drives that do *not* come only or primarily from the appetites, desires, or fantasies of the body or the senses; or from worldly motives such as wealth, prestige, glory, office, influence, and domination; or from ideological motives that impel people to any degree of excess or wickedness with little or no sense of transgression. (In my discussion, I will exclude ideological motives.) There are transgressions that are, or seem to be, impelled to a great extent by drives that signify resistance to a given prohibition for the sake of resistance or that find in a given prohibition an incitement or invitation to resist it. (My formulations are tentative.) In the considerations that I examine, bodily or worldly gains, when they exist, are not the philosophically most interesting point of transgression. Relatedly, moral transgression may be of secondary importance or nonexistent. Prohibition is experienced as an impediment, but not merely to familiar desires, even the grandest or cruelest. On the other hand, transgression may be experienced not simply as transgression but also as necessary for one's dignity or for pursuit of a purpose that raises no moral questions. The stakes involved are those of self-conception, and how one's self-conception depends on the nature of the relationship one has to supernatural (or other superior) authority. How one appears in one's own eyes matters at least as much as how one appears to others — a sentiment more Christian perhaps than classical. Through a certain self-consciousness, the Christian self doubles itself and haunts itself. Yet how one appears in one's own eyes is closely bound up with a more than human authority that one posits or accepts on faith. The transgression, however, has relevance for secular readers.

I wish to look at two all-too-famous analyses made by Augustine where transgression is the theme and where the role of prohibition is not felt solely as a barrier to familiar private or public desires. What is the general validity of the analyses made by Augustine? Outside his theology what value do these analyses have for the nonbeliever? Augustine intimates that he touches bottom, that he has seen the sources of the greatest evils in human life. Has he?

Before I turn to Augustine's analyses of two acts of transgression — stealing pears, and eating forbidden fruit in Eden — allow me to offer an assortment of kinds of transgression in order to place Augustine's two cases in a larger scheme. I want to emphasize that transgression of moral rules plays a variable role in this scheme; transgression may sometimes be only an offense to the majesty of the lawgiver and inflict no intentional harm on others, and therefore have no immoral content. I distinguish as follows.

Ordinary transgression. It occurs when a norm or rule gets in the way of a specific appetite or desire or passion. Often there is an act of will or determination or resolve that strengthens and concentrates the appetite or desire or passion, often to the point of ruthlessness, just as there is likely to be a flash of the imagination that inflames any of these three. Bodily reflexes are not paradigmatic. Ordinariness is Kant's radical evil: self-preferment overriding the rules that protect everyone. Typically, the transgression harms others through injustice or offense, directly or indirectly, but occasionally it does not.

Measured transgression. It occurs when a person or a group adheres imperfectly or selectively to a prohibition or set of prohibitions. It may think that authority makes or issues some excessively difficult or even unnecessary demands or commands, but there is no basic questioning of authority. The transgression is not likely to harm others.

Spiritually vainglorious transgression. It occurs when a person or group feels resentment over not being recognized as an equal or as a superior to the authority that prohibits, even though a skeptical or hostile observer may plausibly doubt the merits of the claim to such recognition. What is involved is not vainglorious worldly ambition, which I categorize as ordinary transgression. A friendly observer would regard spiritually vainglorious transgression as a legitimate claim to dignity in one's own eyes. When such dignity is involved, the transgression is not likely to harm others, unlike worldly ambition, which is sometimes meant to and often does.

Deliberately guilty transgression. It occurs when a person violates a prohibition for the sake of violating it and thus acts perversely. A person turns away from the prohibition for no reason or for a twisted reason or for a reason that is not at all transparent. Here the arbitrariness or seeming arbitrariness inheres in the transgression rather than in the prohibition. The transgression may or may not harm others.

"Innocent" transgression. It occurs when a person or group feels righteous indignation or some kindred emotion. The prohibition is thought arbitrary or not quite comprehensible or even pointless, and hence insulting or manipulative or sadistic. The transgression is not the same as civil disobedience or conscientious noncompliance, both of which protest (directly or by proxy) the substantive injustice of a command to do something or cooperate with it, though there is kinship between the two sorts of lawbreaking. By definition, the transgression does not harm others.

This list is by no means complete. Furthermore, it is not always obvious or indisputable in what category to place a given act of transgression; the act may perhaps fit in more than one; the categories may even blend into or tinge or anticipate one another. We may even feel that ultimately one or more of these categories have no real existence. Interpretation of the transgressive act is indispensable but is sometimes afflicted by the elusiveness of the phenomenon. But at the risk of oversimplification, I suggest these distinctions. To repeat, my main interest is in two particular acts: the theft of pears by the sixteen-year-old Augustine and his friends; and the first couple eating forbidden fruit in Eden. A secular observer may come to interpret the first act as an instance of deliberately guilty (or perverse) transgression, the second as an instance of "innocent" transgression. Augustine agrees with such an interpretation of the first act. But since he can never see any act of transgression as innocent, even if the word is put in quotation marks, he ultimately interprets the fall of Adam and Eve as spiritually vainglorious transgression. We must add, however, that as his analysis of stolen (forbidden) pears and the eating of forbidden fruit proceeds — both are strange fruit — he supplies qualifications that are important enough to make us wonder whether he thinks that what is involved in both cases is only ordinary transgression after all, and indeed transgression arising from the passions of companionship, which wring from him a measure of sympathy. Yet despite his sympathy, Augustine's rhetoric is powerfully enlisted in the cause of condemning transgression when he preponderantly interprets it as either deliberately guilty or as spiritually vainglorious — not to mention his constant eagerness to condemn every kind of transgression and find for it a suitable punishment, which is always harsh and sometimes infinitely merciless.

Let us begin with the theft of pears in the year 370. The account appears in the second chapter of the *Confessions* (written in 397–98) and takes up six pages or so (sections 4–10). Augustine's writing is always dense and questing, but these pages are also restless, and perhaps inconclusive. Born in 354, he had experienced conversion to Christianity in 386. Thus when he wrote the *Confessions,* he was a mature man looking back at his youth, and he was looking back at his non-Christian years from the vantage point of one who was reborn or profoundly converted. He has every interest in making the before-and-after dramatic. This is not to say that he invents episodes; it is only to say that conversion guarantees that the mentality of the person before his conversion will be significantly discontinuous with his mentality now. The memory of the deed may be accurate, but the later construal of it need not be the construal that Augustine would have given at the time of the deed or at any time before the conversion. The person's past will be a source of distasteful amazement, not of accepted continuity with the present. It will be described in a spirit of condemnation; one wonders how one could have been as bad or stupid as that. Still, if the conversion is to count as profound, the person must have been either bad or stupid before he underwent conversion.

Augustine does not spare even his pre-adolescent childhood (recounted in Book I) from condemnation. He refuses to see it as in any sense innocent. He refers to lying and to cheating at games as a boy. He says, "I even stole from my parents' larder and from their table, either from greed or to get something to give to other boys in exchange for their favorite toys" (*Confessions,* I:19,

p. 39; hereafter *C*). He not only denies that children are innocent, he also likens the activities of adults — "grown-up games known as 'business'" — to the games children play; he subsumes all human action, when not transfigured by grace, under the same condemnation. That the adult games are "less creditable" than those of children barely matters (*C*, I:9, p. 30). Children are as inwardly guilty as adults; guilty adults are only stronger children. To think of adults as children is not to extenuate adult crimes, but only to incriminate children as fathers to these crimes. To grow up truly can only mean conversion — a leap, a rupture with all that one has been, and certainly not a recovery of innocence, which one never had. It is not clear, however, whether Augustine holds that children sin because of their will, as adults and presumably adolescents do. In any case, Augustine does not say that children should not be punished, even though he often says in *On Free Choice of the Will* (begun c. 387, finished c. 395) that the presence of the faculty of will in human beings alone makes their punishment justifiable. Will is the "power to accept or reject" one's inclinations toward what one sees or touches (*On Free Choice of the Will*, III:25, p. 146; hereafter *F*).

Augustine's childhood is a preparation for a sinful adolescence in which some of the sins are those of lust, where transgression is what I have called ordinary. But the famous sin that he analyzes is the theft of pears that he as a "boy of sixteen" carried out with a gang of friends. For the most part, Augustine presents the theft as deliberately guilty transgression, to use the phrase from our scheme. This is anything but ordinary transgression, though it is surely common enough in various forms of mischief and purposeless adventure; human beings of any age engage in this kind every day. To highlight the nature of the deed Augustine compares it to the crimes (or alleged crimes) of Catiline (c. 108–62 BC) and presents it in a worse light than all of Catiline's reputed deeds. The theft of pears was, we could say following Augustine's lead, perverse (*C*, II:6, p. 50), while Catiline was (in Sallust's probably tendentious phrase) "a man of insane ferocity" (*C*, II:5, p. 48). Augustine finds it much easier to understand this man, whom he takes to be a ferocious political and personal criminal and who he believes committed numerous serious crimes, than to understand himself as a petty but unneedy thief.

Is it odd or not to find systematic ruthlessness easier to understand than one minor act of perversity? I cannot say. Augustine insists, however, that at least "Catiline did not love crime for crime's sake" (*C*, II:5, p. 49). To be sure, Augustine quotes Sallust as saying that Catiline "chose to be cruel and vicious without apparent reason," but Augustine disagrees. He finds unperverse reasons for Catiline's actions and therefore saves Catiline from the imputation of transgressing for the sake of transgressing. Catiline wanted "honor, power, and wealth" and for the sake of these ends, Catiline "committed his crimes" (ibid., p. 49). The greatest crimes, the crimes of political policy, arise not from perversity but from the ruthless attempt to secure certain worldly ends that everyone dreams of. Augustine says that the motives of crimes are typically "either the desire of gaining, or the fear of losing" some worldly object or other (p. 48). These motives impel to what I have called ordinary transgression.

Does Augustine explain ruthlessness? In the *City of God* (begun 413, finished 426), he does distinguish the ruthlessness that comes from a love of country interwoven with a sense of honor or glory from the ruthlessness that pursues domination for the sake of domination irrespective of glory. There are varieties of worldly vainglory. At least, concern for glory "makes a man fear the disapprobation of sound judges," and thus supposedly excludes "barefaced crimes" (*City of God*, V:19, p. 212; hereafter *CG*). But ruthlessness of method and means, whatever the ends in view, is to be expected. It is not as if Augustine ranks in the scale of crimes the perverse but petty theft of pears above the great crimes of political policy or personal ambition and hence as deserving greater secular punishment. Rather it seems as if perversity reveals a darker truth about humanity than murderous or unscrupulous ruthlessness does, especially when ruthlessness occurs as a matter of policy. Policy is often either impersonal or not merely self-regarding. In contrast, perversity is more than merely playing "grown-up games," whereas war and conquest are only that. Perversity is precisely doing, indeed loving, transgression for the sake of transgression and therefore holding the prohibition in a special sort of contempt. In this light, the offenses against God's will that perversity produces are much more serious than the vast injustices that ruthless human beings inflict on other human beings in (as it were incidental) defiance of God's law.

What does it mean to love being perverse, to love transgression for the sake of transgression? Augustine spends several pages trying to get to the bottom of the matter. He tries to recall his feelings at the time (*C*, II:8, p. 51); he is thus straining not to let his converted self totally misrepresent the person he was before the conversion, despite the inescapable influence of that conversion on his memory. For one thing, he is certain that he did not join others because they were all "compelled by any lack" (*C*, II:4, p. 47). He had plenty of his own pears and they were much better to eat than the ones he stole, which he did not eat. Then, too, Augustine allows that he might have committed the crime by himself if he really desired someone else's more excellent pears (*C*, II:8, p. 52). Nevertheless, there is a puzzle; a refrain of the *Confessions* is that Augustine is a puzzle or problem to himself. Stealing inferior pears with a gang of friends is, however, an emblematic puzzle. "Can anyone unravel this twisted tangle of knots?" (*C*, II:10, p. 52). Of course, God can, he says. But God has not spoken directly. Augustine's explanation will go as deeply as it can, but perhaps never really can get to the bottom of the matter.

Augustine asks "what pleasure I had in the theft" (C, II:6, p. 49). He thus works with the assumption that pleasure (or happiness) or the avoidance of pain is the constant human aim. (This hedonism extends to concern for salvation itself.) When an act is deliberate and done with full awareness that it is a transgression, its aim must be pleasure or the avoidance of pain. The deliberately guilty transgressor is seeking pleasure or trying to avoid pain. What is the pleasure, what is the pain avoided, in such transgression? Clearly it is not a question of the appetites, as Augustine makes clear. Indeed, in the *City of God*, Augustine insists that "we must not attribute to the flesh all the faults of a wicked life"; the Devil has no flesh (CG, XIV:3, p. 551). It is not even a question of sensory or aesthetic gratification. Augustine found then and finds now no beauty in the theft, "not even . . . the shadowy, deceptive beauty which makes vice attractive." The theft also lacked the elevation of great ambition and the great vices that accompany great ambition (pp. 49–50). If not the appetites or worldly ambitions or sense of beauty, what then?

In much of his analysis, Augustine can only repeat the assertion that he simply loved to do the wrong thing; that "he had a greedy love of doing wrong" (C, II:4, p. 47); that he enjoyed the theft; that he loved mischief; that "I loved my own perdition and my own faults, not the things for which I committed wrong, but the wrong itself" (ibid.). These formulations, however, redescribe the problem; they do not solve it. The problem is to explain, if possible, why the adolescent Augustine (or anyone at any time) loved or loves doing the wrong thing, when the appetites are not the driving force, and neither is the attraction of sensory beauty. What is in Augustine's nature, what in ours? What is the pleasure in view, or the pain avoided? Is there a decipherable motive to perversity, to transgress for the sake of transgression? Or does perversity precisely lack motivation, and is thereby arbitrary or gratuitous? Augustine says he did wrong "for no purpose" (C, II:4, p. 47); "I loved evil even if it served no purpose" (C, II:7, p. 51). If so, then the theft of pears threatens to become inexplicable. Yet, transgressing for the sake of transgression means transgressing for the sake of the pleasure one gets from transgressing. "I loved nothing in it except the thieving" (C, II:8, p. 51). Pleasure is the motive. But isn't pleasure (or the avoidance of pain) always the motive for any act, when one accepts the hedonist psychology as truthful? To invoke pleasure takes us a step closer to a solution, perhaps. But what is the pleasure, if not an appetitive or aesthetic one? What is the pleasure in thieving for no purpose?

I think that Augustine comes closest to solving the problem — at least for a devout monotheistic culture — when he takes back his earlier rejection of the idea that the theft of pears lacked any resemblance to the dignity of great ambition and the (worldly) vainglory or pride that lies behind it, and in the next page, posits such dignity. Of course the dignity is spurious to religious eyes. Without mentioning the word *pride,* he nevertheless attributes to the adolescent Augustine the ambition of imitating "in a perverse and wicked way" the powers of God (*C,* II:6, p. 50). Is the attribution fair, or simply the only way out of the philosophical puzzle, at whatever cost in accuracy to rendering the mentality of the adolescent boy? He will eventually elaborate the project of the deluded imitation of God in the *City of God.* But the hidden will to the imitation of God is here sketched.

To transgress for the sake of transgression turns out to mean to transgress for the sake of the particular pleasure of thinking that one is acting like God, the god of power. This would be spiritual vainglory. Augustine compares himself, however, to a powerless prisoner "who creates for himself the illusion of liberty by doing something wrong, when he has no fear of [secular] punishment, under a feeble hallucination of power" (*C,* II:6, 50). In Augustine's interpretation, deliberately guilty transgression therefore is not so much a source of pleasure as an attempt to mitigate the pain of humiliated inferiority. Surely, such a consideration has an application not confined to devout monotheistic cultures. At any time or place, people can see life as dominated by symbols of prohibition; revenge against authority takes the form of a symbolic rejoinder; an act of theft is actually an act of defacement or vandalism. The imitation of God (or some more-than-human power) cannot be creation, only decreation. Perhaps, then, we can say that at least some acts that appear to belong only to the category of deliberately guilty transgression belong also to the category of spiritually vainglorious transgression, which is often rebellious in nature. Or, the act appears at first to fit in one category and then it slides into another.

Augustine's analysis of the theft of pears contains a second motivation besides the one we have been discussing, however the first one is to be categorized. He says that he is quite sure that he would not have committed the theft "on my own" (*C,* II:8, p. 51). As the analysis unfolds, Augustine makes repeated reference to the influence that comradeship had on his decision to join the gang that stole a neighbor's pears. On the one hand, he would have been ashamed to be less dissolute than his companions; he did not wish them to despise him (*C,* II:3, p. 46). He says, "I used to pretend that I had done things I had not done at all, because I was afraid that innocence would be taken for cowardice and chastity for weakness" (ibid.). Augustine adds, "we are ashamed to hold back when others say 'Come on! Let's do it!'" (*C,* II:9, p. 52). On the other hand, he loved the company of his friends; he stroked his glowing desire "by rubbing shoulders with a gang of accomplices" (C, II:8, p. 52). He loved the applause of his friends for his bad deeds. His grim conclusion is that "this was friendship of a most unfriendly sort," but he cannot resist restoring mystery when he adds that he was bewitched by it "in an inexplicable way" (C, II:9, p. 52). But it does not seem inexplicable, certainly not as hard to explain as loving to transgress against a prohibition just because it is a prohibition.

The question persists. Why should companionship, and not only in adolescence, often define itself as transgressive? What is "the thrill of having partners in sin" (C, II:8, p. 52)? Is there a mystery here, too? If companionship makes all the companions feel stronger than any of them would feel alone, is the typical tendency of enhanced strength an increased proclivity to act transgressively? Does power exist to be misused; is the mind of power disposed to believe that prohibitions exist to be transgressed? In a renowned formulation in the *City of God*, Augustine asks rhetorically, "Remove justice, and what are kingdoms but gangs of criminals on a large scale? What are criminal gangs but petty kingdoms?" (CG, IV:4, p. 139). If Augustine's gang of adolescents is not a habitually criminal association, there is nonetheless some continuity between criminal adolescence and criminal adulthood, while the predatory character of all adult associations, official or irregular, is highlighted. Yet enhanced strength is not the only matter that Augustine mentions. There is also loyalty to comrades; it is enclosed within transgression but is not in itself transgressive. Some part of comradely loyalty exists supposedly untouched by the mischief and the vandalism; it is not exclusively a wish to impress comrades or avoid earning their ridicule. Not only may there be honor among thieves; there may also be love, if not the best love. If so, the deliberately guilty act of transgression may also appear to be only ordinary transgression, where the felt superiority of human ties obscures the criminality of the act and hence facilitates transgression, even if it does not necessitate it.

Augustine gives central place to the interpretation of the theft of pears as a perverse act, as a deliberately or willfully guilty act of transgression. But the richness of his restlessness pushes his analysis into two other directions. First, he opens up the incriminating possibility that pride or spiritual vainglory, arising from a certain sort of humiliation, may actually supply the energy for the act of transgression; and, second, he opens up the extenuating possibility that loyalty to one's fellows may have the side effect of enlisting one's energy in criminal exploits, even though no one by himself may have a particular liking for transgression. Comradeship is impersonally corrupting. Of course, loyalty to one's fellows can, even unintentionally or indifferently, help to sustain the worst policies of atrocity. That leaders can count on it in advance also emboldens the initiation of such policies. The extenuation therefore can never be other than small; it is always cruelty to victims. Who can unravel this twisted tangle of knots?

My sense is that when we deduct what a secular outlook might have to deduct from Augustine's analysis, his complex and unself-confident analysis of the theft of pears contains powerful instruction in the nature of transgression. Much of the analysis is independent of theology; its worth is even independent of the redescription of vice as sin, if sin means not any offense to any authority but only offense to God's authority. Even if a pure example of deliberately guilty transgression may be found mostly in literature or theology, and even if actual examples tend to resist being placed in only one category of transgression, the phenomenon of perversity mixed with or resulting from other psychological elements commonly exists. Perhaps perversity must always be explained as the result of other psychological elements, even if it is something in itself. In any case, the effort to explain perversity as a human, not satanic, phenomenon, and to resist seeing it as nonhuman "motiveless malignity" or gratuitous bad will, is exemplary. It is exemplary because Augustine moves uneasily back and forth between claimed knowledge and admitted uncertainty. On the theme of perversity and apparent perversity, we should feel greatly indebted to Augustine.

The second act that Augustine discusses memorably, and that I want to take up, is the disobedience of Adam and Eve in Eden: their fall, their sin. Augustine also takes up the rebellion of some of the angels and tries, oddly, to impute human motives to bodiless creatures who are supposed to be nonhuman. Indeed the psychology of Adam and Eve — minus the rancor of defeat and with it, the perverse will to vandalize God's felicitous creation — turns out to be almost indistinguishable from that of rebellious angels. (I am fascinated by the thought that one who believes in angels sees in them, when they are rebellious, only human passions. There are no limits to a gullible believer's epistemological presumptuousness.)

The story of man's fall has been endlessly written about, especially by Christians. It is a sketchy story yet so suggestive that it gives itself over to indefinite interpretation. It is as it were shallow in its psychology, its imputed motivations, but correspondingly it has a bottomless depth, once one's literary imagination has been captured. It certainly provides Augustine with the opportunity to interpret the human condition. Like Connolly, who sustains a continuously incisive reading, I am absorbed by Augustine's analysis (*AI*, pp. 94–127). Perhaps everybody should be allowed, at least once in a lifetime, to interpret the original sin. My interpretation is mostly a study and critique of

Augustine's and not freestanding. I mean to proceed by using the scheme, already introduced, of kinds of transgression.

The story of the fall — what tradition calls the original sin — has helped to organize Christian civilization. It is no mere story, but a world-opening and world-sustaining myth. Its brevity is part of its greatness: it is only one chapter long (Genesis, 3:1–24). It has engendered much of Christian theology, especially that of Augustine and the Protestant reformers. It has, in demythologized forms, influenced secular pessimism in various degrees of pessimism. It proposes to answer such questions as to why there is death, why there is a preponderance of pain in human life, and why human beings hasten death and inflict more pain on themselves than would naturally exist. The short form of the explanation is that human beings refuse to do what God tells them to do; for whatever reasons they disobey even God, not only parents, superiors, and political authorities, all of whom are assumed to be worthy of full obedience. But of course the psychology of disobedience turns out to be in Augustine's analysis another twisted tangle of knots. If in the story of the pears, however, Augustine is intermittently candid about his uncertainty and leaves the reader not quite decided as to what Augustine's emphasis is and how therefore one should explain the theft, he is less willing to admit uncertainty in his construal of the fall. The more abstract and less personal the story, the greater is Augustine's confidence in his analysis. Yet it is not possible to say where Augustine places his largest emphasis. If he professes no uncertainty, a well-intentioned reader will still find it in him.

One secular difficulty with the story is that Adam and Eve were created by human imagination. They are characters, not people. Furthermore, they were born or came into being as adults without a past, without parents and relatives, and especially without infancy and childhood. Their psyches have no layers. They also have no fellows. They can speak and understand without having slowly acquired language over the years. When they do the forbidden deed, they have no history of prior activity; the only prior deed is verbal: before the fall, Adam names the living creatures at God's request (Genesis, 2:19–20). Thus at the time of the fall, Adam and Eve are inexperienced to the point of blankness — call it innocence. Yet adult readers of Genesis are supposed to see themselves in Adam and Eve; indeed, they are supposed to see in the couple the original parents of all humanity. Above all, they are supposed to see in the original sin their own innate — that is, inherited — proclivity to violate prohibitions; to be creatures disposed to disobedience and transgression. Nevertheless, we must let all these mythical difficulties evaporate if we want to see how Augustine interprets the story and, as secular readers, learn from him what we can about the subject of prohibition and transgression.

Genesis is spare in its description of the disobedience of Eve and then of Adam. God tells Adam (before the account of the creation of Eve from Adam's rib, the second account of the creation of the female), "You may eat from every tree in the garden, but not from the tree of the knowledge of good and evil; for on the day that you eat from it, you will certainly die" (2:16–17). There is, however, no indication that Adam could possibly have had the experience to know the meaning of the terms *good* and *evil*, even though readers of the book will know and may just assume that what they know, Adam and Eve must have known. But at the minimum we have to allow that Adam and Eve must know the difference between obedience and disobedience.

The tempter promises that eating the forbidden fruit will open Eve's eyes and give her the god-like capacity to know good and evil. Again, it is hard to see that Eve knows the meaning of the promise. Why does she succumb to temptation? In the translations I follow, her motives do not include the desire to grow wise (by knowing the difference between good and evil); rather, she eats because she "saw that the fruit of the tree was good to eat, and that it was pleasing to the eye and tempting to contemplate" (3:6). Not only the appetite but also the aesthetic sense is attracted.

However, the King James Bible and two modern revisions of it say that Eve saw that the fruit was "to be desired to make one wise"; so do some other translations. But I rely on the unrevised *New English Bible* throughout. Of course, my analysis would have to change somewhat if this translation is incomplete. But I see no reason to abandon the unrevised *New English Bible,* which is superior in style to the revised edition, and no reason to accept instead the revised reading that Eve found the fruit desirable "for the knowledge it could give." The Latin Vulgate, known to Augustine, does not attribute to Eve the thought that eating the fruit could make the eater wise; neither does the Douay Rheims translation of the Vulgate or Robert Alter's recent translation, *The Five Books of Moses* (pp. 24–25). *The Interpreter's Bible,* in its original edition, reports the suggestion that the words that attribute to Eve a desire to become wise are the interpretative addition of a glossator (vol. 1, pp. 505–506). Perhaps the most important consideration is that Augustine only says that man was "delighted" with the serpent's statement that if the fruit were eaten, "you will be like gods," as if amoral powers of authority and command, rather than "knowing both good and evil," were the essence of being like gods (CG, XIV:13, p. 573).

Why did Adam eat? Nothing is said except that "She also gave her husband some and he ate it" (Genesis, 3:6). How do they try to exonerate themselves when they are accused by God of transgression? Eve simply says, "The serpent tricked me, and I ate" (3:13). Adam with apparent simplicity says, "The woman you gave me for a companion, she gave me fruit from the tree and I ate it" (3:12).

From the couple's awareness of their nakedness, God recognizes that they have eaten the forbidden fruit (3:11). Although God created humanity "in our [God's] image and likeness" (1:26–27), he now says that eating the forbidden fruit, not being created in God's image, has made "the man become like one of us, knowing good and evil" (3:22). In order to prevent Adam from gaining immortality by eating the unforbidden fruit of the tree of life, God expels Adam and Eve from Eden. The story in Genesis, until interpreted (as it should and will be) tells of ordinary transgression, nothing more complex. The transgression is the more fascinating because it is not an act of immorality: there is no injustice in it; the fruit does not belong to another human being. The (only) offense is to the majesty of the prohibiter. The words of the tempter direct the attention of Eve to the forbidden fruit, but once he has her attention, her act is on its face only an instance of ordinary transgression: the pleasure of the senses and a sense of beauty together cause the transgression of eating what she is not supposed to eat. There is no uncontestable textual indication of impious curiosity or a thirst for knowledge for the pleasure of knowledge. Adam chooses to disobey God for no reason other than to do what his wife does. From these simple elements, theology and philosophy have constructed an enormous structure of imputed meaning. There is nothing inherently wrong with that; the trouble is that, for skewed theological reasons, the imputed meaning soaks life in imputed human sinfulness. I certainly do not question the urge to interpret the bare story of Adam and Eve and take it beyond the category of ordinary transgression; but I do question the necessity of always interpreting disobedience as incriminating and hence as the principal basis for pessimism concerning human nature.

In Augustine's analysis in the *City of God,* which is spread out in parts of Books XII to XV (and mentioned elsewhere), I find four of the five kinds of transgression that I have schematically isolated. I find ordinary transgression, spiritually vainglorious transgression, deliberately guilty transgression (perversity), and even innocent transgression (so to speak). The last of these is barely present, but it is present, if only so that Augustine may discredit it. He makes the most of the three other kinds. In attributing a psyche to Adam and Eve, he presents one explanation after another for the original transgression; but if a reader is asked whether Augustine ranks these three, I do not know what the sure answer should be. Perhaps a plausible answer is that he appears to give more or less equal weight to spiritually vainglorious transgression and deliberately guilty transgression; and, as in the story of the pears, ordinary transgression enters as an extenuation. Innocent transgression is mentioned only to be turned into further incrimination.

I will begin with the kind of transgression that Augustine begins with, and end my reading with the kind that Augustine ends with. The first is deliberately guilty transgression and the last is ordinary transgression. But I will take up second his third kind, and take up third his second. Thus I will move from deliberately guilty transgression to spiritually vainglorious transgression and then to "innocent" transgression before ending with ordinary transgression.

The first, then, is deliberately guilty transgression or perversity. Augustine's account of perversity seems to be a bit different from the one he gave in the *Confessions* but close to *On Free Choice of Will*. He proposes the idea that among creatures, only angels and human beings possess will. Let us recall that Augustine defines will as the "power to accept or reject" one's inclinations (*F*, III:25, p. 146). Having a will makes possessors of it responsible for their actions; all other creatures, lacking will, cannot be held accountable for their behavior. As creatures of will, human beings are created capable of freedom. Perhaps, for Augustine, having a will and being capable of freedom are exactly synonymous. Original sin came out of a condition of undamaged will, out of the first or lesser freedom, which contained the ability to sin or abstain from sin. The freedom of the saved in heaven is the greater freedom, which lacks the ability to sin (*CG*, XXII:30, p. 1089). It is not clear in Augustine's analysis how in the absence of the ability to choose to sin, it would be appropriate to speak of freedom, even greater freedom; but he does so anyway. (Even if it does not belong, freedom is too good to leave out of heaven.) What is more, Augustine eventually says that the condition of will after the fall is different from both the original condition and the condition to come: the damaged will of fallen humanity is marked by ignorance of truth and the weakness of will incurred by bondage to the flesh (*F*, III:18, p. 128). He makes this apparent concession to radical frailty very late in the book on will; if he had made it sooner, I do not see how he could have consistently gone on to say what he says about everyone's responsibility for being a sinner and making sinful choices.

It is not univocally clear therefore to what extent Augustine attributes to humanity after the fall free choice of will — that is, the freedom to abstain from sin, if they have a will to do so, if they are determined to do so. In fact, he affirms against the Pelagians that only by the grace of God are people capable of abstaining from sin in this life. How can people born with damaged will still be responsible for sinning as Adam and Eve, born with undamaged wills, originally were? Yet he also insists that only where there is free choice of will can punishment (not merely pain or penalty) be rightfully inflicted. Certainly Augustine is always justifying punishment, including eternal punishment for temporal sins. Throughout his writings he speaks as if people always get what they deserve, which is usually punishment. His position seems, however, to come to this: able to abstain from sin or not, people deserve punishment. Such a position is untenable; it seems a lapse from Augustine's intellectual integrity. The problem of sin and responsibility cannot be solved on Augustine's own conflicting terms. So let us disregard his remark about the altered condition of will owing to the original sin, and proceed on the assumption that after the fall, people have strength of will sufficient to abstain from sin, if they choose to do so. I do not see how his argument could get started otherwise.

As if there were not enough trouble already, Augustine is not of one mind on the question of what the will to sin means. At times, he speaks as if the will to sin is driven by the pressures of familiar desires, by the wish to find pleasure and avoid pain by their satisfaction. When he speaks in this way, the story he tells is unremarkable: people disobey because they are tempted by unobscure desires. Their whole story is ordinary transgression. But he is not at all consistent on this score. We have already seen that in the *Confessions,* he renders transgression for the sake of transgression as transgression for the perverse (obscure) pleasure of transgression, and then tries to say in what the pleasure consists. In the *On Free Choice of Will* and the *City of God,* he alternates between the pleasure of transgression (apart from its anticipated benefits) and what Connolly nicely calls the idea of "pure will" (*AI,* pp. 44, 115 and passim). I incline to the view that perverse pleasure (the satisfaction of obscure desires) rather than pure will is what is involved preponderantly, even though Augustine produces sentences that appear to enunciate a doctrine of pure will.

Let us look for a moment at the notion of pure will as a contrast to perversity. As it is presented in the *City of God* (which recapitulates many of the teachings of *On Free Choice of Will*) it would seem to mean a will unaffected by any consideration or end or purpose and unconditioned by innate temperament or prior experience. Pure will is thus a gratuitous will, a will that its bearer probably cannot explain to himself. It partakes of the random, even of the uncaused. A pure will is an uncaused will—uncaused by either conscious pressures (internal or external) or a course of rational deliberation; an uncaused will is not moved by the pursuit of pleasure or the avoidance of pain. Augustine struggles with the idea of uncaused will, but not as a god-like attribute. Perhaps he is drawn to pure will because, as we have said, Adam and Eve have no past and have no experience before they fall. But Augustine also seems to attribute pure will to human beings after the fall.

Augustine says that "nothing causes an evil will," even though "it is the evil will which causes the evil act" (*CG,* XII:6, p. 477). When Augustine says that nothing causes an evil will, he really means *nothing.* That is, "one should not try to find an efficient cause for a wrong choice. It is not a matter of efficiency, but of deficiency; the evil will itself is not effective but defective." To be defective is to defect from God to something of "less reality" (*CG*, XII:7, p. 479). Trying "to discover the causes of such defection — deficient, not efficient causes — is like trying to see darkness or to hear silence" (*CG*, XII:9, p. 480). Deficiency or defection occurs because creatures of will, like all other creatures, are created out of nothing (*CG*, XII:1, p. 472; XII:6, p. 479). What does that mean? Its meaning is not, I think, that desire stems from lack, as in Plato. Rather, Augustine intends to repudiate the belief that nature, which is God's creation, suffers from inherent deficiency. He wishes to attribute all deficiency, including that which derives from will, to nothing, from which God created everything. Only the uncreated — God alone — is fully real and hence incapable of defection. The greater the deficiency in the degree of reality, the greater will be the departure from the goodness of created nature. Human beings transgress from pure willfulness in pursuit of unreality. Their freedom, wrongly used, makes them the least real of all creatures. I am afraid, however, that this is an explanation that does not explain. We are left with a view of uncaused will that dissolves into nothingness before our eyes.

The conclusion is that Augustine employs an idea of perversity (or deliberately guilty transgressive will), rather than an idea of pure will. He is intelligible only if we take him to say that pleasure, or avoidance of pain, of some special kind is moving the human being, as it moved Adam and Eve, to transgress for the sake of transgression. The pleasure that Augustine detects in Adam and Eve is not quite the same as that which he attributes to the gang of adolescents: the compensatory pleasure of spiritual vainglory or pride that covers an attempt to mitigate the pain of humiliated inferiority. I do not think that Augustine attributes an aboriginal dejection to Adam and Eve. For him, their wish for exaltation appears to come not from impotence but from an initial sense of unused strength that knows no way of expressing itself except in transgressive action. This orientation seems less like perversity and more like a spiritually vainglorious self-conception, though I grant that it is not always possible to rule out dejection altogether when self-assertion is present. Pride blends easily with the dejected emotions of envy and jealousy. In any case, the category of deliberately guilty transgression is made to yield, if not completely, to the category of spiritually vainglorious transgression.

At the heart of vainglory or pride is the will. (The will is intrinsic to both spiritual and worldly vainglory, but the subject here is spiritual vainglory.) There is no pride without will and hence no evil without will. The evil will causes the evil act (*CG*, XII:6, p. 477; XIV:11, p. 568). But at the heart of the will is pride. This statement and its reverse are both true. Pride is the essential manifestation of the will. Pure will is actually will that is inflamed by spiritually vainglorious passion. Augustine asks rhetorically, "could anything but pride have been the start of the evil will?" (*CG*, XIV:13, p. 571). If that is so, there is never such a thing as a pure will, an uncaused will without purposive content that is capable of authoring deeds that do have content. What holds for Adam and Eve holds for all human beings, even if Adam and Eve were not abject and the rest of us are. Transgression for the sake of transgression is not pure willfulness, but an act that satisfies the desire for a certain kind of pleasure (of self-conception) that is independent of ordinary or worldly appetites and passions (no matter how vain and ambitious) or of an attraction to sensory beauty.

Augustine tries to indicate the beginnings of the fall. What helps to prepare the way for the pleasure that is perhaps most agreeable to a sense of spiritual pride, or even definitive of it, is an unnoticed inner movement in the mind and heart of both Adam and Eve that inclines them to defiance or disobedience. "It was in secret that the first human beings began to be evil; and the result was that they slipped into open disobedience" (*CG*, XIV:13, p. 571). In modern language, we could say perhaps that the cause of the supposedly uncaused will is found in unconscious promptings, undetectable stirrings of creativity and initiative, for good and evil. Should we add that they come from we know not where? They are not repressed longings — Adam and Eve had no childhood; but in human beings after Adam and Eve, these longings take their time to mature, and might never become conscious, or quite conscious. Augustine says, "The fall that happens in secret inevitably precedes the fall that occurs in broad daylight, though the former is not recognized as a fall" (p. 573). There is a fall before the fall. Spiritual pride is its source. Is it injured pride?

As I have said, the pride of Augustine's Adam and Eve does not seem to begin in a certain sort of dejection, like that of the transgressive adolescents in the *Confessions*. Perhaps he thinks that the pride of Adam and Eve is closer to that of the rebellious angels than to that of human beings after Adam and Eve: some envy or jealousy rooted in an ache of unused strength, not humiliation. He defines pride as "a longing for a perverse kind of exaltation" (*CG*, XIV:13, p. 571). "The exaltation itself is in fact already an overthrow" (p. 573). Involved here is a self-conception that Augustine associates with all acts of transgression that resent subordination and the obedience enjoined on the subordinate. Submission is not only to the commands of a superior but also to the status of being subordinate. The tempter could not have succeeded "had not man already started to please himself." Indeed, man became "too pleased with himself" (p. 571). Man was delighted with the tempter's well-founded assertion, made to Eve, and repeated by God after the fall, "you will be like gods, knowing both good and evil" (Genesis, 3:5, 22). By speaking of man, Augustine is attributing these dispositions of Adam and Eve to all humanity.

Since Adam and Eve fell before the fall, they were never innocent: such is Augustine's radical suggestion.

Was unfallen man proud of his incipient powers because they were so remarkable? And did this pride grow out of an initial secret chagrin that stemmed from being blocked in rightfully exercising powers awaiting expression? From chagrin, did he begin to feel that the command to abstain from self-expression was insulting, and that obedience was dishonorable? Why accept everything passively as a gift from God and not strive instead to seize or realize possibilities? Augustine says that Adam and Eve wished "to abandon the basis on which the mind should be firmly fixed, and to become, as it were, based on oneself and so remain"; the "original evil" is that "man regards himself as his own light" (CG, XIV:13, p. 571). Adam and Eve wished to make themselves "their own ground" (p. 573). The forbidden fruit is not a special substance that magically transforms them into self-exalting creatures. Their very transgression shows that they wish to depose God and take his place, not only to imitate him. Augustine demands subjection, which is a perfect obedience to the will of God. Such subjection is the highest human condition. Perfect (pure) obedience to God's will is a complete guide to conduct and it makes the difficult and often futile work of knowing the difference between good and evil unnecessary. (Augustine's political theory and ecclesiastical theory show a similar advocacy of nearly unqualified obedience.)

Abraham, a model of subjection, was willing to kill his own son in obedience to God's extraordinarily difficult command, but Adam and Eve could not obey the one easy command they were given. To be fair, Augustine does not go as far as Kierkegaard in *Fear and Trembling* in vindicating to an only nominally Christian society Abraham's decision by redescribing it as a "teleological suspension of the ethical" (p. 100); Kierkegaard is admiring of Abraham, though also appalled by him (p. 90). But Augustine is ruthless in another direction. He says that eternal death will appear as an excessive punishment only to those who do not know "how to measure the immensity of the wickedness in sinning when it was so immensely easy to avoid the sin" (CG, XIV:15, p. 575). In *Totem and Taboo*, Freud says that there is "no need to prohibit something that no one desires to do, and a thing that is forbidden with the greatest emphasis must be a thing that is desired" (p. 69). By making so much of how easy it was for Adam and Eve to obey the supercharged taboo, Augustine is turning Freud inside out. (Alas, Freud does not reckon with the possibility that a prohibition itself may be perverse.) Of course, the command is easy to obey only if one is disposed to humility. Yet without experience of defeat where would humility come from? God never asks Adam and Eve to love him or be grateful. Are they supposed to have these feelings without instruction?

Augustine wants to pull down human spiritual pride in the face of God. Secular thinkers, however, can find benefit in his wariness concerning the hubris of rebellious angels and disobedient human beings. Although Adam and Eve are scarcely hubristic to those who do not accept Augustine's reading, his indictment of them can be redirected toward the pervasive desire of civilized humanity to be its own base or ground, to resent what is merely given, to endeavor to remake and reshape, to alter or abolish nature, to depose nature as it is and replace it as much as possible with nature as humanly remade. Secular people can learn from Augustine's indictment of vainglorious self-conception as destructive, not merely creative. Humanity destroys as it creates. How is the balance to be struck?

Deliberately guilty or perverse transgression, then, gives way in large part to spiritually vainglorious transgression in Augustine's analysis of the original sin. There is, however, a moment in the *City of God* when he entertains the thought that the transgression of Adam and Eve was innocent, so to speak. Augustine quotes Paul (1 Corinthians, 15:56): "sin gains its power from the law" (*CG*, XIII:5, p. 514). But then Augustine goes on to trample over the subtleties of Paul's teaching and render the law's strange effect on the sinner as simply a further indication of the sinner's evil proclivities. The law encourages transgression, does the work of entrapment, but bears no blame for doing so. By itself, the fact that the prohibition increases the desire to transgress it should be not only an extenuation of the transgressor but an incrimination of the prohibition. The transgression becomes innocent in a manner of speaking. Instead, in Augustine's analysis, the fact of increased desire to transgress is only further incrimination of the transgressor. Augustine says that "the prohibition increases the desire to commit the unlawful act," but the next words are "when the love of righteousness is not strong enough to overcome the sinful desire by the delight it affords" (ibid.).

It is interesting that Augustine acknowledges that prohibition may encourage transgression. I suppose that he did not have to insert this point into his analysis. But because he is, despite his theological need, a true philosopher after all, he will often make trouble for himself by speculating beyond the boundaries of safety. Nevertheless the only response he can offer to a troubling thought is to invoke a rare emotion: a love of righteousness so strong as to overcome the strengthened temptation that God, as author of the prohibition, places in the way of a creature that is already weak just by being human. There is finally no innocent transgression in Augustine's system, not even in a manner of speaking, unless we cite a passing remark in which Augustine allows that Adam "was unacquainted with the strictness of God," and perhaps mistakenly thought that his offense was "pardonable" (*CG*, XIV:12, p. 570). But to be uncomprehending of punishment and of death as the supreme punishment, not to mention eternal death after earthly death, is, for Augustine, not sufficient to establish innocence or even to mitigate the punishment of guilt. "Need I say more?" he asks with satisfaction (ibid.).

More than one kind of transgression is present in Augustine's analysis of the original sin. The last kind that he considers is what I have called ordinary transgression. It has a sympathetic quality, but may lack the gravitas of the other kinds. Adam transgressed, Augustine says, not because he was seduced into thinking the serpent spoke the truth, as Eve was; rather, Adam fell in with Eve because they were "so closely bound in partnership"; Adam "refused to be separated from his only companion, even if it involved sharing her sin" (*CG*, XIV:11, p. 570). Adam's fault was loyalty, a trait that led him to commit an unforgivable sin deliberately. Perhaps such loyalty was not romantic love (as in Milton's *Paradise Lost*, where Adam and Eve had sex before the fall; in Augustine they could have had nonconcupiscent sex, but did not, perhaps because the fall took place too soon for them to find their parts), but closer to that comradeship in stealing pears that so engrossed Augustine in the *Confessions*.

From a democratic perspective, the stakes are greatest when the possibility of innocent transgression (as right in itself, not as the lesser evil) is theoretically allowable. Two religious thinkers, Paul before Augustine and Kierkegaard after him, open up that possibility for both religious and secular adherents, rather than striving to close it off. A brief comparison between Augustine and them could be instructive, especially because Paul and Augustine are often joined together in one tradition, while Kierkegaard, a Lutheran heretic, centuries after them, belongs by temperament in their company.

In a delicate passage in his letter to the Romans, Paul approaches the idea that some transgressions are, so to speak, innocent. Paul makes the claim of innocence, though the claim is hesitant or ambiguous. When he retracts it, the retraction is rather willed. He asks, "Is the law identical with sin?" (Romans, 7:7). The meaning of "the law" is not stable in Paul's discourse. Most obviously, it refers to the prohibitions against covetousness in the great commandments of Moses. At his most antinomian, Paul is therefore quarreling with some of the great commandments and in the name of innocent transgression. But sometimes the law is not described explicitly: it can refer to the numerous prescriptions of the Mosaic law. Paul is championing faith above laws and works, love above the conformity that comes from ritualism or fear of God's punishment. He verges on separating goodness from obedience. He answers, "of course not": law is not identical with sin. But then he says, "But except through law I should not have become acquainted with sin. For example, I should never have known what it was to covet, if the law had not said, 'Thou shalt not covet.' Through that commandment sin found its opportunity and produced in me all kinds of wrong desires" (Romans, 7:7–8). At most, there is a slight or tentative inclination to do a deed; but prohibition intensifies such an inclination by defining the deed as a transgression and therefore invests the inclination with a force and hence an importance it would otherwise lack.

Whatever his retractions or his efforts to climb above his initial assertions, Paul asserts that prohibition induces or excites the will to transgress: the commandment "produces in me all kinds of wrong desires." It is only when a human being is uncommanded and is filled with a sense of liberation that he may do the right thing in the right spirit. But under the regime of command, where every prohibition is charged with the surplus significance of sin, which is offense to the majesty of the divine lawgiver, transgression is inevitable. Transgression is a response to what is felt as a taunt: I dare you to disobey. The law "seduced me" (7:11). Paul continues: "There was a time when, in the absence of the law, I was fully alive; but when the commandment came, sin sprang to life and I died" (7:9). The spirit of Paul's words is hostile to the all-too-human craving for the mystery that adheres to nonmoral prohibitions when they are charged with dread. Of course, all that Paul says about the law assumes the redemption offered by faith in Christ. Yet it seems to me that with some adaptation, his words about the demoralizing effects of prohibition, and not only when there are numerous laws, might be applicable to Adam and Eve (and all their children). The aim need not be complete exoneration, but only extenuation within a Christian framework, and a democratic leniency outside it. There is something innocent in their transgression and recurrently in ours.

To bring the point home, we must psychologize with the help of Paul. Let us attribute the following anachronistic thoughts to Adam or Eve.

It had not occurred to me to break the law until I was told not to do so. I did not even know that it was possible to disobey until there was a prohibition. Once there was a prohibition my whole mentality changed. The prohibition was invested with an inscrutable importance and was supported by equally inscrutable warnings of the dangers of transgression. I sought the reason for the prohibition and was told none and could find none. The prohibition struck me as an act of pure will by the prohibiter, arbitrary or gratuitous. It is less comprehensible than a reverse equivalent of perverse transgression would be. A needless prohibition is like a false accusation. Why was the tree of knowledge planted in the first place? If as a permanent test or temptation, then its mere existence enslaves. Why should eating be so charged with importance? Why should there be a taboo when there is no strong desire to do the tabooed thing? Why should Eden contain any prohibition? The prohibition's meaning was like a secret kept from me. Who can resist trying to find out what the secret is? (There turned out to be no secret, only punishment for wanting to know.) The prohibition opened up an otherwise unimagined and undesired opportunity. But if I refused the challenge and unquestioningly obeyed an inscrutable command, my whole self-conception would have been radically changed. I would have remained forever in perpetual uncertainty and impure docility. I was never a child. I would have been less than human if I had complied, even though it turns out that I am not more than human for having disobeyed.

The line of psychology suggested by Paul has application beyond monotheism or any religious outlook. A noteworthy and partly contrasting picture is offered by Kierkegaard in *The Concept of Anxiety*. It is still religious, but he is willing to propose what he calls a psychological analysis that is secular for as long as it can be, and only after that point does he become religious in his interpretation. The psychological analysis portends Heidegger's ontology and Sartre's existentialism. Kierkegaard holds that every man is like Adam, but not because he has inherited sinfulness from Adam, but because like Adam every man must lose his innocence in a certain kind of transgression, which Kierkegaard recurrently calls a leap (p. 31). A leap has the "suddenness of the enigmatic" (p. 30). A temptation, but not the sensual kind, is a spiritual test or trial, which is not to be wanted yet also not to be shunned (p. 174). Prohibition (of some spiritual endeavor) induces anxiety in a person hitherto innocent of a determinate endeavor. Anxiety is the "qualification of the dreaming spirit" (p. 41). In children, anxiety is intimated as a seeking for the adventurous, monstrous, and enigmatic (ibid.). In adults, there is undeniably a desire for the forbidden (p. 40); but Kierkegaard's interest is in the spiritually forbidden, symbolized physically by forbidden fruit. The prohibition of spiritual endeavor necessitates a leap, not a series of easy steps. Once awakened by the prohibition into anxiety, one is also awakened to "freedom's possibility" (p. 44). Adam did not need the Devil: "one need merely assume that Adam talked to himself" (p. 45). To be sure, we cannot expect that Adam was able to understand all that was involved in the prohibition or in the guile of the Devil. But once anxiety is awake, the condition is comparable to "the dizziness of freedom, which emerges when . . . freedom looks down into its own possibility" (p. 61).

I take Kierkegaard to be saying that freedom is shown in the leap across the boundary-line, the transgression that is a spiritual leap into guilt, the spiritual guilt incurred in committing the absolutely indispensable sin of rejecting complete and unquestioning obedience. No science can understand the spiritual leap that is inherent in moving in a moment from the anxiety of innocence to the ambiguous anxiety of spiritual guilt (p. 61). Adam became an adult and we become adults when we dare to awaken to anxiety and then transgress; that is, to put it in secular terms, we try to possess our life by entering unafraid into a direct relation with the highest principles of freedom. I think that Kierkegaard sees Adam and Eve as the inventors of freedom through disobedience, a disobedience that is not sensual, but spiritual. This may not be a reassuring innocence; it is an innocence of transgression. Paul also hints at it, but Augustine cannot bear to countenance it. (He feared his own wildness.)

One last word. "Innocent" transgression is a serious questioning of prohibitions and of their source. I think that there are several versions of such transgression; the attitudes and feelings that animate them are congenial to the democratic spirit. To finish our treatment of the theme of prohibition and transgression, I would like to suggest that the versions in Paul and Kierkegaard have relevance to democracy, which in itself is a system of questioning prohibitions and their source. I think that these two thinkers do more unintentional good to democracy than Augustine does. What then is Augustine's value to modern democracy? I have already said that he enlarges our conception of human nature. I mean above all that he did the inestimable favor of enlarging awareness of the self's inward and introspective capacities and exploring its richness, and thereby encouraging people to revere one another's human dignity, the founding sentiment of modern democracy. At the same time, his explorations of the complex and unsettled nature of the passions contributes to a realistic pessimism that is not intrinsically inimical to democracy and that can contribute to a greater sobriety of democratic expectations. (For the secular reader in general, some of his pessimism is surely applicable to cultures that are not devoutly or only culturally Christian, whether democratic or not.) Yet when it comes to prohibition and transgression, Augustine the driven theologian, for all his exceptional acuteness, for all his wisdom, harms the sentiments of democracy.

In his novella, *The Tables of the Law,* which is a meditation on Moses, Thomas Mann tries to probe the mentality of the prohibiter. Mann reconstructs the reasons for the absoluteness and severity of the commandments and for the multiplication of prohibitions that not only regulate life but prescribe practically every aspect and detail of it. He says of Moses, "His birth was irregular, hence it was he passionately loved order, the absolute, the shalt and shalt not. In his youth, in a blazing fit of rage, he had killed a man; so he knew better than the innocent, that to kill is very fine but to have killed is most horrible, and that it is forbidden to kill. His senses were hot, so he craved the spiritual, the pure, the holy; he craved the unseen, because he felt that the unseen was spiritual, holy and pure" (p. 1). With some changes, Mann's portrait of Moses becomes a portrait of Augustine.

Mann's story reminds us that prohibitions come from only human beings, whatever the claim for more-than-human authority, and warns us that to worship the unaccountable and surround it with ferocity and unapproachability is but to worship the extremist psychology of one man or perhaps a few men. Majestic prohibitions are projections on to others of the lawgiver's own unusually strong transgressive impulses; his remorse for these impulses may have the odd result of intensifying his need to cajole others into facing restraints so majestic that they may eventually strengthen people's desire to transgress for the sake of transgression or, more likely, to transgress out of an outraged innocence. A network of mystification and humiliation is established. By its pervasive cultural influence, a civilly rebellious democratic politics exists in part to dismantle this continuously re-created network. When the law does not codify basic morality, but nevertheless pretends to an importance higher than morality, it enslaves the spirit. Democracy is a refusal to leave authority majestic, absolute, unaccountable, and pleased to multiply prohibitions obnoxiously; authority must be transparent and reasonable. When authority is otherwise, transgression is a gesture by which to express both shock and righteous indignation, and then it is perhaps innocent.

Works Cited

Alter, Robert. *The Five Books of Moses.* New York: Norton, 2004.

Augustine. *Concerning the City of God against the Pagans.* Edited by David Knowles. Translated by Henry Bettenson. Baltimore: Penguin, 1972.

Augustine. *Confessions.* Translated by R. S. Pine-Coffin. New York: Penguin, 1961.

Augustine. *On the Free Choice of the Will.* Translated by Anna S. Benjamin and L. H. Hackstaff. Indianapolis: Bobbs-Merrill, 1964.

Connolly, William E. *Identity/Difference: Democratic Negotiations of Political Paradox.* Ithaca: Cornell University Press, 1991.

Connolly, William E. *The Augustinian Imperative: A Reflection on the Politics of Morality* (1993). New edition. New York: Rowman and Littlefield, 2002.

Freud, Sigmund. *Totem and Taboo* (1913). Translated by James Strachey. New York: Norton, 1962.

Genesis in *The New English Bible.* New York: Oxford University Press and Cambridge University Press, 1970.

Genesis in *The New Interpreter's Bible.* 12 volumes. Nashville: Abingdon Press, 1952.

Kierkegaard, Soren. *Fear and Trembling: A Dialectical Lyric* (1843). Translated by Walter Lowrie. Princeton: Princeton University Press, 1941.

Kierkegaard, Soren. *The Concept of Anxiety* (1844). Edited and translated by Reidar Thomte and Albert B. Anderson. Princeton: Princeton University Press, 1980.

Mann, Thomas. *The Tables of the Law (Das Gesetz)* (1943). Translated by H. T. Lowe-Porter. New York: Knopf, 1945.

Paul, *The First Letter of Paul to the Corinthians* in *The New English Bible.*

Paul, *The Letter of Paul to the Romans* in *The New English Bible.*

Hobbes and the Irrationality of Politics

It is commonly understood that concern with civil war dominates Hobbes's political theory. A few years before the Restoration, he said: "all such calamities as may be avoided by human industry, arise from war, but chiefly from civil war."[1] His work is held together by the effort to understand the causes of civil war and to offer proposals for its long-term prevention. In *Leviathan,* his one political work written in the midst of civil war, Hobbes also hints at the most expeditious way of ending it; namely, to accept the conqueror as the new ruler and to do so without scrupulous legitimist worries over the dispossessed (and executed) ruler or his heir. Naturally, no political theorist is indifferent to civil war (or to the intense turbulence that may precede and augur it). Indeed, no rational person can be indifferent to it. But Hobbes is surely unsurpassed, perhaps unequaled, in his concern with it. Even people in Hobbes's situation, or in comparable ones, seem less agitated by it as a brute fact, less affronted by its mere occurrence. For Hobbes, civil war is always senseless. If he thinks that much of political, as distinct from administrative, activity is irrational, he finds in civil war the perfection of such irrationality: political passions, themselves intrinsically verging toward madness, going

This is a revised version of a paper given at the APSA Convention in September 1988. I wish to thank William Connolly, David Johnston, Nannerl Keohane, and Sidney Maskit. I am also indebted to the late Judith Shklar.

over the line and into wasteful darkness. The question is why his concern with civil war is as all-absorbing as it is.

We must immediately add, however, that he confronts the prospect of perpetual tension and war among nations with an almost perfect equanimity.[2] I think that the emphasis in the above quotation is not on the greater chance of avoiding civil war in comparison to international war, but simply on the greater horror of civil war. If his immediate experience teaches him that it is "chiefly" civil war rather than international war that causes avoidable calamities, the historical record he has at his disposal would not necessarily sustain his judgment — not to mention what later generations have endured and witnessed. (What greater calamity befell Athens than the failure in Sicily?) Even if civil wars are worse than international ones, the latter are still bad enough to pose a grave theoretical problem. There seems to be a discrepancy that requires our attention, and it is a matter of some significance in the overall attempt to understand Hobbes's political theory.

I think that in his obsession with civil war, Hobbes may be read as providing three distinct arguments to show the unwisdom of deliberately carrying social disagreement to the point of violence. I would call them the extreme argument, the moderate argument, and the unexpected argument. Each argument can be seen as a sufficient case. All three arguments try to show that nothing justifies past or present social groups in using violence against established political authority, and nothing could do so in some more remote future. Relatedly, nothing justifies or could ever justify embarking on a course of dissent and agitation, because it can lead a society to slide into a civil war that no one originally wanted. The instigators of disturbance rarely live long enough, he says, to see the ruinous consequences of their acts.[3]

I would like to take up each argument: there are complexities that may repay exploration. Confronted with these complexities, one may finally decide that Hobbes is not only an advocate of subjection, but also a profound emancipator. His ability to emancipate all individuals, even citizens of constitutional democracies, is part of my theme. He emancipates, to some degree, in spite of himself, when his honesty gets in his way. To some (perhaps greater) degree, he emancipates because he means to do so. He emancipates even as he pursues his own purposes, but also when he is used by later readers for their purposes, not his. Insofar as he develops a radical, special individualism, he is an emancipator.

I am engaged in placing into three separate arguments ideas that Hobbes makes flow together as if they constituted just one argument. But I do not think that these ideas are all of a piece, and the differences among them are not explainable only by reference to changes over time in Hobbes's thinking.

My thesis is that the extreme and moderate arguments assemble considerations that should, but do not, foreclose another argument, which for that reason I call the unexpected argument. It is especially for the sake of presenting the unexpected argument that I take up the other two that contrast so vividly with it. To anticipate: Hobbes unexpectedly seeks to discourage tendencies that cause civil war so as to strengthen the capacity of the nation-state — above all, England, of course — to conduct a foreign policy that actively, not to say aggressively, seeks to preserve the life of the body politic as if it were a real entity, even at the expense of lives of individuals. But, perhaps, Hobbes may himself finally supply the resources to undercut this unexpected argument.

Throughout this article my emphasis will be Hobbes's own: civil war as the result of an attack on more or less absolute authority, rather than as the result of an initial rivalry between socioeconomic groups. Hobbes's arguments can and do sometimes apply, however, to the latter case, *mutatis mutandis*.

The Extreme Argument

To put it schematically, Hobbes thought that the *aims* for which civil wars are fought (or threaten to be fought) and the *motives* that invest such objectives with their lethal power are both discreditable. Hobbes is thus engaged in a deflationary project with the intent of exposing both foolishness and cynicism. The result of it, he hopes, would be to strengthen society's will to have social peace and to endure absolute government, which is claimed to be the best guarantor of social peace, by far.

In regard to the *aims* of those who rebelled against Charles I, Hobbes says in the dedication to *Behemoth* (finished in 1668) that the "seed" of the civil war was "certain opinions in divinity and politics." These were the effective causes.[4] In all his political writing — created amid turbulence, civil war, or restored peace — Hobbes devotes great energy to persuade his readers that to fight over religious and political opinions (and hence over desired religious and political practices) is foolish. He is trying to eliminate the causes of civil war at their doctrinal root. We may distinguish and say that Hobbes thinks that for social groups to use or threaten violence in the name of their *religious* opinions and practices is to make or risk war over a matter where knowledge is impossible. Knowledge is claimed, but the claim is always false. It is therefore the height of folly to make or risk war when no sect possesses truth or can possibly do so. On the other hand, Hobbes thinks that the *political* struggle for such aims as guaranteed constitutionalism or mixed government or popular self-rule is foolish because all these practices, if attained, would turn out to be incompatible with the maintenance of a settled society. Their aspirants, therefore, all show culpable political ignorance: they would "lay the foundation of their houses on sand."[5]

Let us take up *religious aims* first. Now, Hobbes's own theological beliefs are notoriously a matter of controversy. I cannot discuss them with the care and fullness they deserve. David Johnston's *The Rhetoric of Leviathan* has made a highly intelligent and well-executed contribution to this subject.[6] All I wish to do here is make a few rough generalizations.

The foundational assertion that Hobbes makes and repeats is that

> the nature of God is incomprehensible; that is to say, we understand nothing of *what he is,* but only *that he is;* and therefore the Attributes we give him, are not to tell one another, *what he is,* nor to signify our opinion of his Nature, but our desire to honor him with such names as we conceive most honorable amongst ourselves.[7]

I do not believe that Hobbes is an atheist, despite the contentions of Polin and Strauss[8] and the apparent tendency of Johnston's analysis. Though the natural "seed" of religion is four human proclivities that Hobbes disdains, "Opinion of Ghosts, Ignorance of second causes, Devotion towards what men fear, and Taking of things casuall for Prognostiques"[9] he also insists that any dispassionate and profound inquiry into the nature of things will yield belief in "one God eternall," "a First, and an Eternal cause of all things."[10] Natural reason teaches that the world is not eternal, but was created; that is, caused to come into being by a first cause totally other in nature from its creation, its creations.[11] Undeniably, Hobbes's view is somewhat different in a later and purely scientific work, where he says that the words *infinite* and *eternal* lead only to confusion: the human mind cannot comprehend them. He will purposely "pass over" these questions and "content myself" with scriptures, custom, and "reverence due to the laws."[12] For all that, there is no compelling reason to doubt Hobbes's profession.

I fail to see how anyone who reads the following passage can think Hobbes an atheist:

> For as a man that is born blind, hearing men talk of warming themselves by the fire, and being brought to warm himself by the same, may easily conceive, and assure himselfe, there is somewhat there, which men call *Fire,* and is the cause of the heat he feeles; but cannot imagine what it is like; nor have an Idea of it in his mind, such as they have that see it: so also, by the visible things of this world, and their admirable order, a man may conceive there is a cause of them, which men call God; and yet not have an Idea, or Image of him in his mind.[13]

This is one parable deriving from Plato's story of the cave, and trying to rival it, that does not pale utterly in comparison. A fierce repudiation of atheism is implicit in it. But equally fierce is the repudiation of any elaborated theology that claims to have arrived at the truth about the nature of God. For Hobbes, theological disputes cease being harmless and turn lethal when they incite human beings to a self-intoxicated zeal, bigotry, and persecution. Wars (civil or foreign) over religion are not wars over the nonexistent, but wars over the unknowable. Not even revelation alleviates the mysteriousness of God's nature. But apart from revelation, and relying solely on natural reason, Hobbes is adamant that the principles of natural science are "so farre from teaching us any thing of Gods nature, as they cannot teach us our own nature, nor the nature of the smallest creature living. And therefore, when men out of the Principles of naturall Reason, dispute of the Attributes of God, they but dishonour him."[14]

Rational worship would be amazed contemplation of the nature of things, but Hobbes knows that such an attitude is beyond most people. It is uncommon to feel the passion of disinterested "admiration" at the emergence of novelty in the world, at "the course of heaven," and at "the strange effects of the elements and other bodies."[15] The unphilosophical "voluptuous men" do not know how "great a pleasure it is to the mind of man to be ravished in the vigorous and perpetual embraces of the most beauteous world."[16] Unable to revere the world, most people need desperately to make sense of their suffering. In a proto-Nietzschean mood, Hobbes suggests that all religions are devices invented and accepted for the purpose of appeasing the common pain and "each mans private misery," and deflecting responsibility for these sufferings away from rulers and back on to the sufferers themselves. Hobbes applauds the founders and lawgivers of ancient commonwealths for inculcating the belief that misfortune came from "neglect [of worship], or errour in their Ceremonies, or . . . their own disobedience to the lawes." Such a belief made people "the lesse apt to mutiny against their Governors."[17] If people are disposed to crave elaborated theologies — actually, theodicies, which, for Hobbes, are the heart and soul of theologies — wise statesmen will cultivate that disposition by producing theologies that account for suffering by reference to the fault of those who suffer.

However, Hobbes turns on himself. His critique of free will, developed ferociously in his extended dispute with Bishop Bramhall, helps to defeat the strategem. Even though he knows that most people will not attend to his difficult rebuttal, Hobbes confesses that there is danger to piety in publishing all speculations on free will, including his.[18] Still, one does not have to be a metaphysician to be impressed by the sense of human creatureliness that permeates his work: the sense that appetites and passions dominate the helpless creature and absolve him or her from any ultimate responsibility. "The De-

sires, and other Passions of man, are in themselves no Sin."[19] Hobbes pities
even criminals. We cannot help being what we are. As readers of Hobbes, we
should also take in fully that Job answers to Hobbes's idea of what it means to
be a philosophical human being. The reason is that Job maintains his innocence against his false comforters and accepts his suffering although he has
done nothing wrong to deserve it. Job is overcome not by contrition but by an
impression of power that is scarcely distinguishable from a sense of beauty.
Hobbes makes it clear that the God of scriptures is, more than he is anything
else, the God of power: his right to rule mankind "is to be derived, not from his
Creating them, as if he required obedience, as of Gratitude for his benefits; but
from his *Irresistible Power.*" God is pure power: "God has no Ends."[20] The
possession of irresistible power carries with it the right to afflict, which "is not
always derived from mans sinne, but from Gods Power." As he says in his
exchange with Bishop Bramhall, God's afflictions are not always punishments.[21] The God of scriptures had the right to make innocent Job suffer and
to have made Adam suffer even if he had not sinned. The God of scriptures
even "afflicts other living creatures, that cannot sinne."[22] Irresistible power is
"above all law, so that nothing he doth can be unjust."[23]

If, then, Hobbes sees the social utility of the belief that people suffer because they deserve to, he also insists on their creaturely innocence in the face
of unfathomable and afflictive power. I think that Hobbes believes in a demythologized or secular version of the teaching of the book of Job. Suffering is
everywhere, and no one and no creature deserves it. Nature is what it is, and its
maker's mind is beyond our knowing.

The trouble that Hobbes sees as a plague is that for a long time Christian
sects and denominations have elaborated theologies that are not only intrinsically preposterous, but set people against each other and against the state.
The modern state must inculcate a uniform religion. Hobbes's general position
is that any religion must be free of ideas that lead people to challenge authority, as, say, Catholicism does on grounds of papal supremacy or Protestantism
on grounds of conscience or church reform. A uniform religion, publicly established and taught, however, need not be intolerant. Hobbes praises the
Roman policy of "tollerating any Religion whatsoever in the City of Rome it
selfe; unless it had something in it, that could not consist with their Civill
Government." The Jews alone were not tolerated because they refused subjection to any "mortall King or State whatsoever."[24] Above all, no religious
doctrine can be taught that incites strife by pretending to know God in a
different way from that of the established religion. Hobbes is resigned to the
realization that the seeds of religion "can never be so abolished out of humane
nature, but that new Religions may againe be made to spring out of them."[25]

But he will not resign himself to bloody religious dispute, in which (in Matthew Arnold's phrase) ignorant armies clash by night.

Concerning *political aims* as a source of turbulence and civil war, Hobbes can be as unrelenting as he is toward religious ones. Hobbes's antagonism to those who instigate civil disturbance in the name of constitutional limits on state power, or the establishment of mixed government and shared power, or the revival of the spirit of ancient popular self-rule is famous and widely discussed. The extremism of his case consists in asserting that to want such things is, in effect, to want what contradicts the very nature of a settled society. On this subject, Hobbes's mind sometimes shows a curious reversion to scholasticism. It is as if he is saying that he (alone) has the correct definitions and that from these definitions an entire substantive doctrine inexorably follows. By definition, sovereign power is not subject to or held accountable to the laws it alone has the right to make. By definition, the sovereign power is unitary. By definition, the sovereign power can, of course, be a democratic assembly, but only in an oxymoronic sense is democracy a government. To be sure, Hobbes does not content himself with such an unpersuasive definitional strategy. His passion for order is fed by what he thinks he observes, and it issues in the attempt, for example, to demonstrate that limitations on power may interfere with requisite action in time of need or emergency; that mixed government exaggerates social tension by granting it institutional embodiment; that sovereign assemblies (whether aristocratic, oligarchic, or democratic) are prone to confusion and indecision; and that a monarch's self-interest is more likely to coincide with the common good than is an assembly's. But Hobbes presents even his empirical evidence dogmatically.

Thus, if an unreligious reader of Hobbes can find Hobbes's sincere theism unrepellent and his political theology sensible for his time, a constitutional-democratic one must rebel (so to speak). In regard to political aims, the Hobbesian strategy of extreme deflation simply does not work and did not work in his own time. Above all, historical experience teaches many more lessons concerning constitutionalism, mixed government, and popular self-rule than Hobbes is willing to learn or teach. If there have been long-lived absolutisms, there have also been long-lived constitutional aristocracies, oligarchies, and democracies. When Hobbes is in his all-or-nothing mood, history refutes him. Undeniably, the will to constitutional mixed government for England did produce turbulence and civil war in Hobbes's lifetime. The effort may be thought, from his and other perspectives, too costly. But the resistance to it may be judged needlessly unyielding. The aim in itself is not incoherent or self-defeating. He could have learned from Machiavelli, if he did not want to learn from history, that the institutionalization of tension, dispersed power, enjoined collaboration, and popular participation could conduce to the avoidance of civil war rather than to its promotion. Hobbes's emancipatory potentiality is not found in the extreme form of his critique of political (as distinct from religious) aims and aspirations.

We turn now to Hobbes's effort to show up the *motives* behind the profession of seditious religious and political doctrines. He is not content to challenge these doctrines and attempt to show their substantive foolishness. His analysis contains a supplementary theme, which is that those, and they are always only a few, who originate and disseminate seditious doctrines do so for discreditable motives. Naturally, this critique of motives can only be supplementary: doctrines can be killed only by substantive rebuttal, but they can be wounded if their articulators and advocates are personally sullied.

It seems to me that in considering what Hobbes says about the motives of the fomenters and conductors of sedition, we come to the heart of his teaching on human nature. Despite his express avowal that human reason can never penetrate to the true nature of anything, including human nature,[26] Hobbes manifestly thinks we can go a long way toward achieving a serviceable comprehension. Practically every page of his political, historical, and theological writing is about human nature. There is a Protestant quality to his fascination with it because he is interested in himself. It turns out that in writing about the leaders of sedition he is writing about himself; more precisely, he is writing about what he could have become had he not succumbed to reason and turned into a theorist of civil peace. His impulses are those of the seditious, but they, unlike him, act on them.

At the beginning of *Leviathan*, Hobbes gives his method for understanding human nature. Its essence is self-knowledge. To know oneself is to read oneself. To read oneself is to have the courage, it may be the positive appetite, to look deeply. To look deeply is to look for the worst, expecting to find what is bad. To read oneself, one must "take the pains." If one takes pains in reading oneself, one may read mankind.[27] Despite the generality of Hobbes's teaching, despite its apparent application to all humanity, Hobbes's real object of inquiry is not all humanity, but the instigators of sedition. And they can always only be a few.

The most inclusive word to describe these few is *ambition*. Ambition is "the other sort of discontent, which troubleth the mind of them who otherwise live at ease, without fear of want, or danger of violence, [it] ariseth only from a sense of their want of that Power, and that honor and testimony thereof, which they think is due them."[28]

These words come from Hobbes's first political treatise, *De Corpore Politico*, completed (in 1640) before the actual outbreak of the English Civil War in 1642. This characterization appears toward the end of the work, and its chapter is titled "Of the Causes of Rebellion." One may generalize about all his writing: Hobbes's crucial teaching on human nature will generally be found in those places that deal with the causes of turbulence, sedition, and civil war, rather than in those more abundant pages where human nature is discussed scientifically or in a determinedly technical vocabulary or where it is imagined in the absence of coercive authority. For Hobbes, human nature is social nature, no matter how "unnatural" our sociality may be. As he finally says in *De Homine* (1657): "they who consider men by themselves and as though they existed outside of civil society, can have no moral science because they lack any certain standard against which virtue and vice can be judged and defined."[29] (I may stretch his meaning a bit.)

People are actually what they are before your eyes, provided you have trained your eyes to perceive what you see (or been guided by someone, like Hobbes, who through self-examination has trained his eyes).

What is Hobbes's finding? What does he find in himself and hence in others who are not common men? Hobbes suggests or explicitly indicates that the possession of some natural or acquired superiority inflames the self and induces pride, and therefore an itch for public power, or a too sensitive sense of honor, or a too assertive love of honor. But it is built into the very nature of the social condition that only a few persons could have any sort of natural or acquired superiority in relation to their fellows. Indeed, it is only in society that there can be usable superiorities: only where there is social peace can *individual* superiorities signify. Even in international wars, individual superiorities are regulated by a social purpose. But in the anarchy of individuals there is only individual natural equality, the equality of cunning and physical prowess. It is not the case that there are two sorts of human nature, so to speak, but rather that though anyone would be changed by the possession of some distinct comparative advantage, only a few could ever find themselves in that position. Intrinsic to human endowment and material nature, scarcity constitutes the human condition.

More precisely, only a few are able to initiate the disturbance of a whole society. All individuals experience a need to act out of pride or honor or love of power, but most of them (because of their meager resources or abilities) must ordinarily confine those passions to their families or immediate circles. Their passions do not jeopardize civil peace. A few, however, the lucky or favored ones, are able to ignite turbulence, sedition, and civil war, even though they are too few to carry it on by themselves. Hobbes frequently speaks in *Leviathan* and elsewhere of how they must "seduce" or "corrupt" or "bewitch" the rest, the many, in order to recruit the needed manpower. "Ambition can do little without hands."[30] A few have sometimes succeeded in arousing, organizing, and commanding the many and thus introduced civil war.

Common people take no notice of subversive ideas unless "set on" by preachers and others to whom they defer. For their own ends, a few instill "needless fear" (or some other passion) into common men in order "to make use of their Hands."[31] Religious and political ideas that challenge the established religious and political order are therefore mere vehicles of ambition. To gain influence, power, reputation, honor, or glory, a few make up and spread ideas that manage to fill the many with foolishness, with false fear or false hope, concerning this life or the next. Hobbes often suggests that those responsible for the introduction of seditious ideas do not believe them: they only want the gullible to believe them.

Both *Leviathan* and *Behemoth* analyze specific religious doctrines, for instance, by reference to the way they facilitate the power of priests and presbyters over governments and subjects.[32] At other times, Hobbes writes as if preachers and university teachers did sincerely believe the ideas they produce and disseminate. On the other hand, now and then, Hobbes suggests that the many are not taken in, but rather go along when they think that new doctrines are vehicles for some increase in their material well-being: in the civil war, very few of the common people "cared much for either of the causes, but would have taken any side for pay or plunder."[33] Nevertheless, his preponderant teaching on seditious motives is that subversive doctrines are confected to advance the intense desires of a few for such psychic gratifications as the pleasure of domination, the pleasure of prestige, or the pleasure of making a difference and making things happen. These are the pleasures of ambition. Strong monarchic government seems especially to arouse such undesirable emotions as envy or spite or malice.[34] "Seditious blockheads . . . were more fond of change than either of their peace or profit." At the same time, his preponderant teaching is that the many come to believe new doctrines and are incited by them.[35]

Hobbes allows that "many times well-natured men are subject to" ambition. He is obviously referring to himself. What saves him from subversion (he claims to think that he is not subversive: almost no one has ever agreed with him) is his philosophy: all true philosophy "can never appear propitious to ambition."[36] Hobbes repeatedly says that all human beings are averse to society and can scarcely be made to endure each other's company. Yet as one takes in his whole analysis, it emerges that only the gifted and privileged few are inveterately anti-social.

Hobbes locates in three groups the presence of those motives that are by far the most threatening to the peace of society. In *Leviathan*, he identifies them as the rich, the potent, and the learned.[37] In *De Homine* he says "dispositions are frequently made more proud by riches and civil power; for those who can do more demand that they be allowed more, that is, they are more inclined to cause injuries, and they are more unsuited for entering into a society of equitable laws with those who can do less."[38]

He elsewhere adds that those who to themselves seem wise or learned "are most frequently censorious and anti-social in disposition."[39]

In almost all his political writings these three groups figure as decisive. In aggregation, they amount only to a small minority. Yet their natural or acquired advantages equip them for winning over many others. The most sustained account comes when Hobbes distinguishes people (that is really to say, advantaged people) from social insects.[40] He charges all humanity with the same tendencies to restlessness, vanity, emulation, and arrogance. His whole work, however, is preoccupied with those whose position in life exaggerates these tendencies and enables them to act on them publicly. Riches, high status, and learning all engender the vice of megalomania. Though common sense tells us, and Hobbes is not needed to make the point, that material desperation may dispose to sedition,[41] Hobbes is confident that any halfway intelligent ruler will know enough to avoid or alleviate it. Especially in the form of want is desperation administratively preventable. (He brands as unfit for society those who will not share their superfluity with the needy.) Even desperate fear in the form of apprehended punishment can be reduced.[42]

When we consider the three basic human motives that Hobbes attributes to all human beings,[43] we should realize that it is only the third that is a continuous source of potential or actual turbulence, sedition, and civil war. Regarded as individual motives not in the hypothetical war of every man against every man, but in the social condition (as theoretically they must be), the desire for gain and safety can be accommodated nondisputatiously, nonviolently, and more or less certainly. For ordinary persons, security has a moderating effect on the desire for goods; even a moderate desire for fame and power is acceptable.[44] The real political problem, for Hobbes, is how to handle the third motive, the desire for reputation (or glory, honor, prestige, and concomitantly for position, influence, or power), when it exceeds moderation, as it naturally tends to do in those situated to feel it keenly. "But those men are of most trouble to the republic, who have most leisure to be idle."[45] "Man is then most troublesome, when he is most at ease."[46]

Hobbes's aim is not to destroy all those who have natural or acquired advantages. (After the war, he does say it would have been better for the state to have killed 1,000 seditious Presbyterian ministers than to have sustained the eventual 100,000 deaths of war.)[47] He says that the universities are the "core of rebellion"; nevertheless, "they are not to be cast away, but to be better disciplined."[48] In this remark, we may find Hobbes's general strategy. He wants the ruler to induce the rich, the potent, and the learned to support him, instead of disturbing him, or each other, and to do so by making himself the sole fount of honor and rewards. The talents and energies of the potentially seditious are indispensable, but they must be properly channeled. Where benefits do not bind, severity must be used.

However, Hobbes does not believe that the will to defy authority or disturb order, just for the sake of not being docile, if for no other reason, can be totally eradicated in privileged or talented people. "Ambition and greediness of honours cannot be rooted out of the minds of men."[49] For this reason, Hobbes's ruler will rely on the cooperation of at least some in the intellectual minority to do his bidding and use them to immunize the great majority against any new subversive doctrines that may somehow leak out. If censorship and general control over university instruction and intellectual publication (religious and secular) fail utterly to extinguish such doctrines, the people can still be made indifferent to them. Loyal intellectuals will instruct them in their duties unremittingly. "It is therefore manifest, that the Instruction of the people, dependeth wholly, on the right teaching of Youth in the Universities."[50] The greatest part of mankind are instructable: needy or covetous or inclined to sensual pleasures, they are too busy or too lazy to think for themselves; and they take their ideas where they find them.[51] Unless first misled, "the minds of the common people are like clean paper, fit to receive whatsoever by Publique Authority shall be imprinted in them."[52]

Given, then, the extreme argument that subversive ideas are wholly foolish in substance and are put forth insincerely (for the most part) and out of untransparent and discreditable motives, we are able to see why Hobbes develops the need for Leviathan, a government that is not merely strong enough to deter or prosecute crime against individuals and to alleviate poverty and encourage industrious pursuits. A strong but not an absolute government can keep people safe from each other and free from hunger. But what creates the need for an absolute Leviathan, which is an all-watchful government, is the tendency of a few to use a whole society as a medium for their irrational antisocial motives, and to refuse to accept a condition in which they are loyal and obedient to the ruler and the law equally with the common people. In Christian times, religious and political doctrines are the causes of turbulence, sedition, and civil war and only an absolutist government (as distinct from a merely strong, effective, and efficient one) can restrain subversive doctrines and inculcate disciplinarian ones. In an incautious moment, but not an aberrant one, Hobbes says that his deflationary analyses can save his society: "For were the nature of human actions as distinctly known as the nature of quantity in geometrical figures, the strength of *avarice* and *ambition,* which is sustained by the erroneous opinions of the vulgar as touching the nature of *right* and *wrong,* would presently faint and languish."[53] Hobbes then adds what he nowhere else suggests, namely, that his teaching could even lead to "immortal peace" for all mankind, "unless it were for habitation, on supposition that the earth should grow too narrow for her inhabitants, there would hardly be left any pretence for war." This unique bit of global utopianism aside, Hobbes's hopeful rationalism is unmistakable. It permeates his work. The radical truth about the emptiness of doctrines and the motives of those behind them can supposedly bring social peace.

The Moderate Argument

This argument also works with the assumption that religious and political doctrines are, in Hobbes's age, the source of the energy behind agitation, sedition, and civil war. In various places in his writings, however, he suggests that he is willing to take some opinions as ineradicable. English mental reality may never be completely reformable, even by Leviathan. What he demands is that certain opinions be revised. He also insists that the aspiration to make any doctrine prevail by force must be weighed against the moral duty of preserving life from the occurrence of humanly inflicted premature and violent death. Never far away is his radical mockery toward the content of subversive religious and political doctrines and the motives of those who originate and disseminate them. Nevertheless, Hobbes mixes in with his radicalism a more conciliatory attitude. Despite its conciliation, however, his readers can see even this attitude as meant to be sufficient to discourage and discredit the will to turbulence, sedition, and civil war. Perhaps those made hostile by Hobbes's radicalism can suspend their feelings and consider a more relenting kind of argument that occasionally surfaces, one that was especially relevant to his contemporary English audience (and, by extension, to us).

Concerning *religious doctrines,* Hobbes shows his moderation by bowing to the inescapable fact that the people of Britain (and, of course, almost all of Europe) will profess and practice the Christian faith. Even though he gives abundant testimony to his conviction that about God humanity can only know that he exists, and cannot know anything about his nature, Hobbes is willing to go along with the claim that God has revealed himself and that the Bible contains the revelation. Hobbes is no more a Christian than he is an atheist. However, his world is Christian. We know that he does not think that most people can live with his bare contemplative theism. There will always be elaborated religions because human psychological frailty requires them.

It is a matter not of inducing belief for the sake of civil peace, but of regulating belief so that it not become a pretext for civil war. To be sure, Hobbes thinks that a politic ruler can perhaps nudge the established religion in a direction positively favorable to this or that aim or ambition of the ruler or his state or even in a direction favorable to some broader social purpose, like, say, resignation to one's lot. But I do not think that a narrowly elitist conception of religion is central to Hobbes's thinking. One indication of that is his rejection of the idea of eternal punishment for sinners. Though he denies the existence of the incorporeal soul, he claims to believe in an afterlife for the resurrected body after the last judgment. What is striking is that the fate of the damned is not everlasting torment, but a second death (eternal nothingness). Hobbes promises the saved a blissful *earthly* immortality, a condition like that forfeited by Adam; there is no kingdom of heaven except on earth.[54] People have always thought that fear of hell is a greater inducement to good behavior than hope of heaven. Hobbes simply abandons such fear and with it an immemorial device of social discipline (Locke, but not Rousseau, goes that far). To be damned is not so awful when all it may be is nothing, perhaps preceded by punishment. Who would be terrorized by such a prospect? Hobbes does say that false beliefs about the afterlife redound to the worldly advantage of the clergy and may lead people to prefer submission to them rather than to the ruler when salvation seems to require political disobedience.[55] Surely, however, he could have found a way of squaring civil peace with the usual Christian beliefs about hell and even found advantage in them. That he does not try is part of his emancipatory power. He is repelled by the cruelty of eternal punishment and finds it unbelievable and unworthy of belief.[56]

Among other writings, *De Cive* and *Leviathan* explore ways by which Christianity may be made safe for society. The discussion is most detailed and resourceful in Part 3 of *Leviathan*. What matters for our purposes is that Hobbes reduces Christian duty to two things. All that is necessary for salvation, for gaining entrance into the kingdom of God, is, first, faith that Jesus is the savior and second, the readiness to obey the laws of one's society.[57] The upshot is that the ruler must set down the articles of Christian faith and the regulations concerning Christian worship. Hobbes proceeds to instruct the ruler in those articles and regulations. He admits that in speaking of religious doctrine ("paradox"), he is introducing some novelty. He excuses himself by saying that he is propounding (that is, proposing for consideration) rather than maintaining (that is, legislating) doctrine.[58] In the midst of civil war, he waits for the reestablishment of unchallenged political rule and with it the final authoritative determination of doctrine. Obviously Hobbes hopes that the new ruler will be guided theologically by him. He provides what he supposes is a politically acceptable version of Christianity. It repudiates Catholicism root and branch, chastises Presbyterianism, and places the Church of England securely under the ruler's control. (Surprisingly, he says that the principles of belief and church organization of the Independents are "perhaps the best," especially on the grounds that they most respect individual conscience and they most resemble original Christianity.)[59]

To an orthodox Christian of one or another kind of orthodoxy, such Hobbesian moderation is not really distinguishable from Hobbesian extremism. Hobbes is aware that the tendency of his revision may founder on the elementary possibility that some people may sincerely believe that a command of God may conflict with the command of a ruler and sensibly prefer to risk either civil turbulence or civil penalty, or fight a civil war, rather than lose eternal salvation. Hobbes calls this conflict "the most frequent pretext of Sedition, and Civill Warre, in Christian Commonwealths." He acknowledges "it were madnesse to obey" man rather than God.[60] He tries to sum up all that is necessary to salvation, as we have seen: first, faith that Jesus is the savior and, second, readiness to obey the laws of one's society. But it is manifest that some do not find this enough, and the second precept assumes as a matter of course precisely what is being disputed.

Hobbes's final stratagem is to try to provide reassurance to those who are torn. He uses the story of Naaman the Syrian emblematically (2 Kings, ch. 5). Cured of his leprosy by Elisha, a Jewish prophet, Naaman accepts the God of Israel as the only God. Because of his office he asks the prophet for permission to worship in his old way whenever he has to accompany his master. Without replying directly, Elisha bids him farewell. Hobbes converts this story of conversion into a general lesson to the effect that if one professes or worships falsely, but is inwardly faithful, one is as faithful as one has to be. The outward denial is not the individual's responsibility if commanded by the ruler; it is, instead, the ruler's responsibility. In fact, the false words and acts are not the individual's own, but those of the ruler. Analogously, and terribly, Hobbes says, "For if I wage war at the commandment of my prince, conceiving the war to be unjustly undertaken, I do not therefore do unjustly; but rather if I refuse to do it."[61] Hobbes also narrowly circumscribes the range of permissible martyrdom. Christians should ordinarily go along outwardly with the religious prescriptions of even infidel (i.e., non-Christian) rulers: what matters is what is in their hearts, which is untouchable by the ruler and is God's only concern. If, therefore, Christians can be exonerated if they obey infidel rulers, so can they be exonerated if they obey a ruler they think is heretical or sacrilegious. Naaman set the allowable precedent.[62] There must be no agitation or rebellion for the sake of religion, no matter how reasonable it may seem. God forgives unholy performance when there is inward piety.

The use of Naaman is as far as Hobbes can go in quieting Christian anxiety over the possible conflict between the word of God and the command of the ruler. Naturally, everything that Hobbes says about Christianity is underlain by his own disbelief in it. A true believer is not likely to find an allowable precedent in Naaman's conduct. Only time is able to resolve the dilemma, bringing with it indifference, unlimited tolerance, or pervasive disbelief (if not disestablishment in England). Time did the work his moderate argument could not.

Concerning *political doctrines,* Hobbes shows in his post-Restoration writings a certain acceptance of, perhaps it is mere acquiescence in, a regular share of political power by Parliament. Especially in *A Dialogue Between a Philosopher and a Student of the Common Laws of England,* he seems to take it for granted that England will never endure any form of government but a mixed one. When Hobbes writes the *Dialogue,* this does not yet mean that there will be a guaranteed constitutional set of limits on political power, much less that there will be anything like popular self-rule. Rather, the houses of Parliament will collaborate with the King in making laws and setting policy. In the *Dialogue,* the Lawyer says that in Saxon times, the kings made laws by the advice of the "wisest and discreetest Men of the Realm." The Philosopher agrees, and adds: "there is no King in the World, being of ripe years and sound mind, that made any Law otherwise; for it concerns them in their own interest to make such Laws as the people can endure, and may keep them without impatience, and live in strength and courage to defend their King and Countrey, against their potent neighbours."[63]

The English Parliament since the Norman Conquest is of the "same nature" as the Saxon one. Peers and representatives are by imputation "the wisest and discreetest Men of the Realm." Especially sensible are laws that "restrain the Levying of Money, without consent of Parliament."[64]

Hobbes had already made some provision for consultative government in *Leviathan.*[65] But he is so out of the way in his mention of the idea, so insistent on his repudiation of mixed government, and so emphatic in granting the king the absolute right to call or not to call for deputies to be sent him, to heed them or not heed them, and to dismiss them at pleasure, that regular consultation with the people cannot be considered a feature of Hobbes's desired monarchic sovereignty. (He jealously reserves the word "representative" for the king.) To be sure, he continues to affirm the supremacy of the king in the Dialogue, and to invest sovereignty in him alone. The king makes the laws. Nonetheless, Hobbes has moved to a muted acceptance of regularly consultative government.[66]

He cannot be said, however, to have moved far enough. Any defender of what we call representative institutions wants a great deal more than Hobbes gives. At the least there would have to be a redefinition of sovereignty so that not the king, but the king in Parliament, would be sovereign. That would mean the mixed government that Hobbes could never bring himself to accept because, as I have said, he was scholastically locked into a definition of sovereignty supplemented by a stubborn conviction that mixed government is a standing invitation to turbulence, sedition, and civil war.

Most important, Hobbes disallows any claim by right to what we call representative institutions, much less to universal suffrage. What he cannot bring himself to do is respond sympathetically to the moral sentiments that pervaded much of the opposition to the Stuart monarchy before and during the civil war and that survived its restoration. Even at his most concessive he does not choose to say in so many words that some part of the passion behind English resistance to the Stuarts came from a motive that could not simply be discredited. That motive was a sense of human dignity — as voiced, for example, by the Levellers — that consisted in the desire of people not to be dependent on the unconsensual will of one man (or a few men). The wish of a people not to be entirely passive, not to be entirely decided for, not to have to live in anxious anticipation of a unilateral will (even if often benevolent) is not at all the same thing as the positive will to dominate others, to assert oneself at the expense of others, or to stand out in eminence distinctly from others. Hobbes does not equate one wish to the other. He just says nothing about the sentiments of dignity, except perhaps in the casual sentence, "every man, where he can be present by Nature, desires to participate of government."[67] His silence is an avoidance of extremism on this point, but is still an inadequate gesture.

Hobbes is certainly aware of such sentiments. This awareness shows itself in his insistence on the idea that only consent to be governed creates legitimacy in government. If a person is protected, he has consented to obey; if he has consented, he is obliged. Hobbes is never satisfied to say simply that if a person is protected, he is obliged to obey the protector. Hobbes is acknowledging that people in his world have the sentiments of (to use a modern term) self-determination (as distinguished from aggressive self-assertion), sentiments that are the core of a sense of human dignity. He insists on saying that "no man is obliged by a Covenant, whereof he is not Author."[68] The mere fact that he makes as much of consent as he does is his tribute to the sentiments of dignity. But it is a terribly tactical tribute. Hobbes has no procedure in a settled society for giving individual consent to membership in society and no electoral procedure by which a whole people gives its continued consent to the existence of political authority. On the other hand, he assumes that the only way government comes into existence in the first place is through conquest, not by voluntary "institution." The sequence of chapters in *Leviathan* does not parallel a historical sequence: although Hobbes's discourse moves from the state of nature to a discussion of covenants and then to a discussion of the nature and institution of sovereignty, he does not think that a government will be created by warring individuals who magically agree to stop warring. Governments typically emerge from conquest by a foreign or domestic group. Here, too, he finds consent where hardly anyone else would: he finds it under life-threatening duress. His theory of consent, whether in the conquered generation or in succeeding generations, appears hollow.

What makes it actually not hollow, but narrow, is Hobbes's affirmation of the priority of the value of staying alive (unenslaved) over any other value in life. Hobbes would have us think that if one's life is safe, and kept safe, because of a protector, one has consented to obey the protector, even if one has not actually done so. One has consented in one's capacity as a rational agent. A rational agent is one who prefers an unenslaved life to anything else in life. One must not merely grudgingly obey the protector while waiting for a chance to unseat him and replace him with another (or with a system) one likes better. One must full-heartedly and unreservedly accept him. One must act as if one has actually consented to his power. This goes for the immediately conquered as well as their descendants. Hobbes's theory of consent is a theory of rational consent only, and so little are people inclined to be rational (until better instructed) that the theory of rational consent is a theory of implied consent. Its full formulation is: if what oneself and others, as rational agents (or reasonable creatures), would try to create, already exists in fact — namely, a government under which lives are safe — we may be said to have created it by mutual agreement, and to be obliged to obey it as if we had actually created it, whatever its source or structure. Sovereignty by institution applies especially to the generations after conquest.

All of this means that, for Hobbes, the sentiments of dignity can never justify civil war or even agitation. If constitutional procedures and limitations and representative institutions already exist, Hobbes (after the Restoration) is willing to see them go on, provided no absolute moral claim is made for them, and the king is accorded supremacy. On the other hand, if they do not exist, nothing can excuse agitation or violence in behalf of their introduction. In regard to political principles, the moderation of Hobbes's second argument to discourage civil war lies in allowing some of the political practices of human dignity (e.g., regular consultative representation), and even accepting them (when properly understood) as compatible with the king's sovereignty. But he will not theoretically bless the sentiments that create and sustain them; he is afraid that these sentiments will always seek guarantees for the appropriate practices. Even worse, where these practices do not exist, or exist only in an attenuated manner, or are endangered by an assertive king, the sentiments of dignity may upset peace and threaten the preservation of life.

In sum, Hobbes does not always say that the sentiments of human dignity drive people to pursue inherently foolish political aims or that the sentiments are in themselves discreditable. Rather, the sentiments, and the practices that satisfy those sentiments, are of qualitatively lesser significance than living a normal span of (unenslaved) life. They are never of sufficient weight to justify serious endeavor in their behalf. Though not utterly foolish, such endeavor would still be irrational.

The question then arises as to why Hobbes values staying alive as much as he does — as much as, or more than, any political theorist ever has. Obviously, premature violent death is not the only event of civil war. Those who manage to stay alive live poorly, uncertainly, and amid devastation. But Hobbes's theory, though it makes reference to such disasters, is most itself when it concentrates on staying alive rather than risking death and hence on staying alive rather than being dead. Yet in its concentration, the theory says next to nothing as to why staying alive is the highest good. It is, of course, very easy to draw the conclusion for oneself that lives should not be thrown away in pursuit of aims that the theorist has tried to show are worthless and are propagated by a few who do not believe them, but see in them only the vehicle of ambition. Hobbes's job is more difficult, however, when he concedes, if only reluctantly, indirectly, or late, that some of the religious and political aims and motives that arouse discontent and may issue in civil war have some merit. How does a theorist persuade his readers that meritorious though some of the aims and motives may be, there is a value more meritorious yet, in fact, absolutely meritorious?

My inference is that Hobbes thought that not much could be said or should be said. Worldly men, he says, love the earth. I think Hobbes includes himself among them.[69] Being alive should be pleasure enough, as long as one is not enslaved, to which he sometimes adds, as long as one is not so materially miserable as to become weary of life. Indeed, in a successfully ruled society, there will be more than "a bare Preservation"; there will be "Contentments." At one point, Hobbes goes so far as to include within the unrenounceable right to life the right to things "without which a man cannot . . . live well."[70] He never adds, however, that life is unworthy of being lived in the absence of political freedom, excellent virtue, magnificent culture, or anything else that has ever been deemed part or all of a good life or the good life. Living one's own life quietly is miracle enough, and the longer one's life, the better. (Hobbes is perplexed by suicide and doubts it should be considered a felony: he who takes his life is not *compos mentis.*) I think that Hobbes believed in no afterlife. This is the only life. In comparison with being dead, being alive is everything, and it is infinitely better than being nothing. Everybody would be better off if they thought so, if they were rational enough to think so. To be told (or reminded of) just a few words about life's sweetness, despite all its pain, should be enough. Hobbes, let us say, simply wants people to "love the earth," no matter how they live. He also knows that most cannot and do not, any more than most can adopt his bare contemplative theism.

I interpret his contention that "the first, and Fundamentall Law of Nature . . . is, to seeke Peace and follow it"[71] as a stratagem for morally compelling people to prefer life to anything in it. He makes it a duty to stay alive rather than risking death in behalf of any purpose but trying to preserve it. If he cannot persuade people to prefer life — indeed, if he must, to begin with, endeavor to persuade them — he knows that he must have recourse to some religious consideration. He certainly cannot rely on a constantly overriding biological instinct of self-preservation. Human history is the record of people throwing their lives away. Of course, in a well-governed society people will go about their business and not threaten the peace. But suppose they have been "seduced" or "corrupted" or "bewitched?" Only a religious appeal can be useful (and even it may not be successful). Teach therefore that the laws of nature are also the commands of God. To risk one's life needlessly is to disobey God. To disobey God is to risk forfeiting salvation.

Notice, however, the complexities in Hobbes's position. Like Locke, he needs a moral God, but, unlike Locke, he gives many indications that he does not believe in the existence of one. He needs a threat of punishment in an afterlife, yet explicitly says that the loss of salvation is equivalent only to eternal nothingness.

Notice, also, that Hobbes needs a moral God, the God of morality, not only for the sake of supporting one's duties to others, but also, and crucially, for the sake of supporting one's duties to oneself. Everybody can see that most of the time unless one treated others as one wants to be treated oneself, one will suffer. No individual can ever count on impunity, no matter how powerful.[72] Only rulers may feel impunity. Doubtless appeal to a moral God may help rein them in, but Hobbes counts on prudence, not on religion, to keep rulers from abusing their office. The hard problem that a moral God can "solve" is to dissuade people from pursuing plausible (that is, not utterly foolish) ends out of plausible (that is, not really discreditable) motives, when the pursuit endangers social peace and hence the preservation of life. However, Hobbes leaves the attentive reader no warrant for believing in a moral God; he must rely on Christianity, which his bare contemplative theism erodes.

If the duty to stay alive is ungrounded, the idea of implied rational consent is jeopardized, and along with it, both the moderate argument meant to discourage civil war and, perhaps, Hobbes's political theory as a whole. Only in utopian circumstances would people be rational enough to prefer staying alive to achieving anything that risks life. Leviathan himself would have to coexist with Christianity for the foreseeable future. As long as Christianity holds, Hobbes knows that there will always be a chance that people, no matter how well instructed, can find a reason to challenge the sovereign in the name of God. Furthermore, Christianity cannot always be counted on — far from it — to pacify longings for such secular political objects as constitutionalism, mixed government, and even popular self-rule.

Perhaps not even in utopian circumstances would people find the moderate argument believable, much less the extreme one. Or, if they found it believable, they still would not find it livable: the price of peace may seem to many ordinary and uncorrupted persons, not only to the advantaged few, the nearly complete sacrifice of the distinctively or eminently human. He needs and we find another argument meant to show the unwisdom and irrationality of turbulence, sedition, and civil war, and hence to discourage them. Is it less vulnerable?

The Unexpected Argument

Hobbes does not so much argue as recurrently suggest that disturbing or shattering social peace is irrational because it weakens or even eliminates (if only temporarily) a society's ability to conduct international relations and to fight wars against foreigners. It is as if the only rational conflict is war between states (or populations). The more obedient a people, the more effectively can the sovereign conduct foreign policy. Hobbes's position seems sensible. But it may not be sensible, in part for reasons that Hobbes himself may help us take seriously. Indeed, it is hard to see how Hobbes can hold it and still be consistent with his most particular teaching.

I find Hobbes's position odd because he accords supreme value to preserving life from the possibility of humanly inflicted premature violent death, yet wars are a great, even perhaps the greatest, cause of such death. How can Hobbes not only look with equanimity on the perpetual occurrence of international war (there is no hope of constant peace between any two nations),[73] but also suggest that societies exist for the sake of making war? In *De Cive*, he says:

> But it is a manifest sign that the most absolute *monarchy* is the best state of government, that not only kings, but even those cities which are subject to the

people or to *nobles*, give the whole command of war to one only; and that so absolute, as nothing can be more. . . . *Monarchy* therefore is the best of all governments in the camps. But what else are many commonwealths, than so many camps strengthened with arms and men against each other.[74]

The tone of this book seems more militarist than Hobbes's others; in it he is more prone to describe society as an organization for making war. But the book is not untypical. In *Leviathan* he distinguishes between a family and a commonwealth on the grounds that the latter cannot "be subdued without the hazard of war."[75] Hobbes's defense of absolutism is constant, and is explainable sufficiently by his feeling that it is the best system of government for conducting foreign policy. He thinks that absolutism best pacifies a people and thus best mobilizes them, and then it most efficiently commands them.

Further, how can Hobbes try to show that ambition and vainglory motivate individuals to pursue ruinous aims in society, yet appear to urge rulers and their nations to pursue those very aims at each other's expense? Or, more moderately, how can he try to show that plausible aims, plausibly motivated, can never outweigh the value of staying alive, yet urge an overriding seriousness to the pursuit of international war?

Hobbes often says that a principal aim of a ruler is to defend his subjects against foreign enemies.[76] That idea seems harmless enough when the typical case would be interceding with foreign governments on behalf of a particular individual when he has somehow got himself into trouble abroad. But that is not what Hobbes means. He has in mind protecting a whole people against foreign invasion and conquest. To one who affirms the priority of unenslaved life over other considerations, foreign occupation should not seem a terrible thing. Only if the invader's intent is to enslave or massacre a people would resistance to him be the right policy. Hobbes nowhere indicates that the regular aim of nations is to enslave or massacre populations, at least not in the dealings of European nations with each other. There was a time when "in the war of nation against nation, a certain mean was wont to be observed."[77] Perhaps that lenient time has passed. But whether or not Hobbes thinks it has, he does not say that European wars are now wars of enslavement or massacre.

Does he think that rulers, in order to provide for the material subsistence of their people, must make war on each other? That each society is a band of desperate people who would perish unless they risked the little they had in a struggle to acquire an adequate long-term supply? Hobbes does in fact say that "in old time" some groups lived by "rapine,"[78] but he does not suggest that this is now the norm. To be sure, he does worry about overpopulation, but advises that able-bodied poor people be sent to "Countries not sufficiently inhabited:

where neverthelesse, they are not to exterminate those they find there; but constrain them to inhabit closer together, and not range a great deal of ground, to snatch what they find; but to court each little Plot with art and labour, to give them their sustenance in due season."[79] He does not advise European countries to colonize each other. One day, perhaps, all the world will be "overcharged with Inhabitants," and then "the last remedy of all is Warre; which provideth for every man, by Victory, or Death."[80] This bit of ingenious futurism has no place in his general view of international relations.

Thus, neither personal survival nor strict material necessity figures in Hobbes's endorsement of perpetual war between nations. It appears, instead, that Hobbes has patriotic or national sentiments, and they are fed from two sources. First, he thinks that a people — certainly, the people of England — are a family or are like a family. In *De Cive,* he says that "a great family is a kingdom, and a little kingdom a family." He repeats the thought in *Leviathan;* and in *A Dialogue,* he traces the emergence of some actual governments from the wars or agreements of families in ancient times.[81] (If there is anywhere in Hobbes literal sovereignty by actual institution, it is in this brief historical account. Sometimes "Lords of Families" peacefully created an aristocracy, sometimes rebellion against kings produced democracy from anarchy; but all the great kingdoms, England included, were created by war and conquest out of small families.)[82] All these statements leave one with the impression that Hobbes feels the patriotism of kinship or ethnic solidarity and feels it so strongly as to imagine his society as bound together by blood, and his ruler as the parent.

Patriotic sentiments show themselves in a second way in the following passage from *A Dialogue:*

> LAWYER: But you have heard how, in, and before the late Troubles the People were of another mind. Shall the King, said they, take from us what he please, upon pretence of a necessity whereof he makes himself the Judge? What worse Condition can we be in from an Enemy! What can they take from us more than what they list?
>
> PHILOSOPHER: The People Reason ill; they do not know in what Condition we were in the time of the Conqueror, when it was shame to be an English-Man, who if he grumbled at the base Offices he was put to by his Norman Masters, received no other Answer but this, Thou art but an English-Man.[83]

These feelings of national shame are hardly appropriate to a radical individualist who prizes life more than anything in life. I do not think that Hobbes means here to equate the feudal service introduced by the Normans with slavery (which of course he never obliges or counsels anyone to accept).[84] Hobbes is not even above speaking of a "we" that refers to precedessors who lived six hundred years ago. It may be that he is appealing to patriotic feelings in order to strengthen his case for unquestioning obedience, which he desires for the sake of avoiding the greater evil of civil war. He does, after all, say that there does not follow from international war "that misery, which accompanies the Liberty of particular men."[85] But I find it hard to discount his own national feelings altogether. Throughout *Leviathan*, he is free in the use of the word (foreign) "enemies." My impression is reinforced by the reference he makes in his autobiography to his personal hatred of his country's enemies: the coming of the Spanish Armada during his mother's pregnancy meant that he was born with fear as a "twin," fear that accompanied him throughout his life as a second self (perhaps).[86]

Maybe one should say that for Hobbes civil peace is both a means to international effectiveness and an end in itself; and that there is no way of knowing what finally matters more to him, civil peace for the sake of life or civil peace for the sake of effectiveness in war. In any case, we cannot fail to see that a sufficient reason Hobbes has for deprecating civil war and defending absolute Leviathan is a great anxiety regarding foreign affairs. He is entirely too comfortable with the paradox that was to bother Rousseau: the state exists to make war (between individuals) impossible, but makes it (between states) inevitable.[87] The cure is the disease metastasized. It will not do to suggest that the nation-state is, on balance, the best protection of individuals, and then say no more, offer no further indication of a wish to transcend the nation-state. "On balance" is not theoretically adequate to the task of protecting every individual, the task of the social contract. In one strand of his political theory, then, we find that a readiness to have (international) war for the sake of the group's freedom from foreign domination coexists with a hatred of (civil) war or even agitation in behalf of political freedom whether in the form of constitutionalism or mixed government or popular self-rule.

There is another bit of evidence for thinking that foreign affairs crucially mattered to Hobbes, even though patriotic sentiments do not appear on its surface. I refer to the most famous passage in Hobbes, the rendering of the natural human condition, in the thirteenth chapter of *Leviathan*. I believe that as an account, this rendering is incoherent except when it refers to international relations; and that as a piece of implied advocacy, it is not consistent with some principal elements in Hobbes's political theory even when it is taken as a guide to the conduct of international relations. However, when read as an account of and guide to international relations, it lends strength to my claim that for Hobbes, a sufficient case for avoiding civil war and therefore for having and obeying absolute government is that only on these terms can the ruler be internationally efficacious. Only thus does one's own country have a chance in international competition.

It is obvious that the three motives and three aims that are supposed to dominate individuals in a state of nature are the ones the Athenians invoke to cover their city's imperialist conduct, at the first congress at Sparta in 432 B.C. The model for and the inspiration of the thirteenth chapter of *Leviathan* is a passage in Thucydides that deals with the motives and aims of states, not of individuals, whatever it may mean to say that a state has motives or aims. In Hobbes's (loving and lovely) translation, the Athenians say they acted "chiefly for fear, next for honour, and lastly for profit."[88] In *Leviathan,* we find the same thought, altered somewhat in the phrasing: "So that in the nature of man, we find three principal causes of quarrel. First, Competition; Secondly, Diffidence; Thirdly, Glory. The first, maketh men invade for Gain; the second, for Safety; and the third, for Reputation."[89]

Hobbes's assumption seems to be that the true nature of individuals shows itself in the absence of coercive political authority (or some other kind of deterrent). But the notion is perplexing. Hobbes is conflating desperation and impunity. He throws into his picture every conceivable horror; he wants to overpower our imagination. A closer look exposes a theoretically indiscriminate assortment of horrors, as far as the natural condition of individuals is concerned.

My point is that in the natural condition, the Thucydidean mentality can coherently, if problematically, refer only to armed groups. Of the five examples of an actual state of nature (as distinct from the hypothetical case of the war of every individual against every other), only two refer to individual conduct (armed robbers and household thieves); both cases deal with "profit" only (and only in a haphazard sense); and both are instances of some people spasmodically preying on others, not of the constant war of every man against every man. The state of nature of the American savages exists between families, not individuals, and "the brutish manner" of their life excludes considerations of honor. The other two illustrations refer to the clash of armed groups: civil war and international relations.

What really matters is the reference to international relations. Unlike civil war, this is a permanent condition, and it is the real referent of the thirteenth chapter. A formulation pertaining to individuals actually suits nations only, especially great ones: war is "perpetual in its own nature; because in regard of the equality of those that strive, it cannot be ended by victory."[90] No nation can ever achieve a final victory over all possible enemies. Here "feelings" of desperation or of necessity are, as a matter of course, entangled with "feelings" of strength or impunity or invulnerability. Only here is the spectrum of human motives and aims on display, concurrently and fully, and on the part of all the actors, at least the unweak ones. Hobbes's true meaning is that in the dealings of armed groups with each other, a sense of necessity can drive each to the same course of behavior that a sense of invulnerability can; that strength never feels strong enough to be contented and never weak enough to be constrained to forbear from activist endeavor. Each strong power always feels both threatened and tempted. Most of the time there is no sequence from security to material aggrandizement and then to a concern with honor or power for its own sake.[91]

The supreme irony is that Hobbes encourages nations to be what he warns individuals not to be: activist, uncontented, and ambitious. Even an unremitting concern for reputation (that is, for honor or prestige) is encouraged because reputation is power. Power is everything: "present means, to obtain some future apparent Good," become the end, the good itself, so rife and so seemingly indistinguishable are the occasions of peril and opportunity.[92] Worst of all, Hobbes exceeds almost all others in claiming that moral motives or limits have no place in international relations. Harming even innocent foreigners does not breach natural law because those who are not subjects or bound by treaty must be considered enemies as such.[93] The explanation of the supreme irony is that only docile individuals provide the matter out of which an audacious nation can be fabricated.

Whenever, therefore, in the same passage or chapter (say, chapters 8, 10, and 13 of *Leviathan*, when they deal with power or honor) Hobbes seems to be simultaneously ridiculing and justifying the same thing (for example, the pursuit of power or honor), the explanation may sometimes be that he is ridiculing the pursuit when an individual engages in it, but justifying it when an armed group engages in it.

The trouble is that Hobbes's analysis personifies a nation and makes it into a collective individual.[94] One main result of his claim that a multitude is made one person when it has a sovereign and that the sovereign "beareth the Person"[95] is to facilitate thinking of a nation as an individual and thus ensuring that international war will be thought normal and inevitable — that is, natural. He reasons as if a nation's being or life were just like that of an individual, and thereby accords a nation an absolute natural right to existence worth any sacrifice of individuals and never itself to be given up for the sake of a larger union, if such a union can offer a greater hope of peace. He unhesitatingly transfers to collectivities the vocabulary that is unconfusing only when used about individuals in their attributes, motives, aims, and experiences as well as rights. This transference is the most ingrained kind of political irrationality.

What is more, the transferred words insensibly take on an inflated meaning as if to adjust to the transference, but nevertheless simultaneously retain their personal connotations in a kind of hysterical doublethink. One would have expected and hoped that an individualist theorist as radical as Hobbes would be the last person to think herd thoughts. This metaphorization can only lead to theoretical results that are seriously discrepant from the affirmative individualism of the physical individual that permeates Hobbes's work.

There is no rational analogy between individuals and nations. It is not merely the case that the analogy is imperfect. Nations are fiction: their bonds tend to degenerate into kitsch, which favors crime and aggression. I do not refer to crazy mob or crowd behavior, but to a steady if not always overt feeling of group identity that sustains the armed group in patterns of national policy. The necessities of the collective individual are only imaginary necessities, as imaginary as the collective individual itself, and they get their undeserved legitimacy from the thoughtless conceptual assimilation of the group to the individual. For an individual to be in distress, to suffer want or fear or to die, is one thing, but to say that a nation does so is to engage in the very sort of sentimentalist irrationality that Hobbes is otherwise eager to warn us against. Similarly with the group's ambitious excesses: if all individual excesses stem from fantasies, those of the armed group stem from the fantasies of a spurious identity: group identity. The armed group may feel itself as a distinct and homogeneous substance, different in nature from other armed groups, and susceptible to any voice that inspires either a dislike of otherness or a virile taste for abstract antagonism.

It is only by projection and introjection that anyone identifies with a collectively in that weird combination of selflessness and selfishness. One must lose one's self to a larger self from which one regains oneself magnified. To some degree these psychological mechanisms are inevitable, but Hobbes should fight them, not smooth their way. They go against his clement rationalism. Yet I do not see how we can make sense of key elements in Hobbes's political theory unless we ascribe to him an unpurged patriotism or ethnocentrism. Something obdurately conventional remains inside him. He tries to see through everything except national feeling. He cannot shake free of the sickest of all sick political thoughts, the abstract we. To want nationhood, whether the numbers are few or in the millions, is to *want* war and death.

Ironically, his national attachment causes him to produce an account of international relations that may vindicate his country's enemies just as much as his own in policies that are ruthless, unyielding, and altogether untempered by moral considerations. (Does he perhaps think that only the English are innocent and have to be instructed in international realism?) The morally allowable suspension of morality in cases of individual desperation or necessity is converted into a theory that encourages the metaphorization of necessity and the superstitious inability to know the difference between a necessity and opportunity. Moral permission for the individual's need becomes moral license for the group's atavism. Obedience to laws of nature obliges only individuals in Society, while states may continuously invoke the right of nature. Hobbes consecrates the idea of a nation-state whose aims are indissociable from perpetual war and are not merely circumstantially served by war. Armed groups are like teams put together in order to play games; they are not like individuals struggling to survive. And like teams, they are usually basically similar in aims (whatever their constitution), yet sustained in their enmity by an inflamed partisanship that fantasizes a complete mutual otherness. Armed groups are teams that cannot bear to think that they are playing. If they shed blood, they must believe that it is for something real. On the other hand, the rare candid political aesthete sees the play, but ignores the blood. Instead of satirizing this folly, Hobbes in effect promotes it.

As always with Hobbes, there are mitigations. He can be ironic about those kings who, secure in their power not only at home, but also abroad, become adventurist and seek "Fame from new Conquest."[96] This point has the merit of suggesting that a nation may not be a collective person, but rather the instrument of the ruler as one all-powerful natural individual. Even more severely, he includes among "those things that Weaken, or tend to the Dissolution of a Commonwealth" an expansionist foreign policy: "the insatiable appetite, or Bulimia, of enlarging Dominion; with the incurable Wounds thereby many times received from the enemy; And the Wens, of ununited conquests, which are many times a burthen, and with lesse danger lost, than kept."[97] One may add that Hobbes is free of any taste for a missionary or ideologically driven foreign policy. Also, despite the unifying effects of a common enemy, he does not urge rulers to exacerbate international tensions and engage in wars abroad in order to rally the people at home and avoid their civil strife. In fact he goes so far as to advise kings against aiding rebels against other kings. "They should rather, first, make a league against rebellion and afterwards, (if there be no remedy) fight one against another."[98] These passages are only mitigations, slight ones at that.

As is commonly the case, however, Hobbes undercuts himself, and in doing that evinces his emancipatory power. He introduces a concept that is not a mere mitigation of his commitment to the war-state, but actually opens up a radical critique of it. Thanks to Howard Warrender,[99] that concept can be seen in its ramified significance. I refer to Hobbes's contention, present in both *De Cive* and *Leviathan*, that each individual has an unrenounceable right to life.

One can never be thought obliged to risk or sacrifice one's life for any purpose, though of course one may have to risk or will even lose it in the effort to save it. If, as we have seen, the idea of the duty of self-preservation is a device to dissuade people from embarking on civil war or activities that threaten it, the idea of an unrenounceable right to life is crucially a device that works with the effect of psychologically strengthening each individual against the claims of any government, including, or perhaps especially, *Leviathan*. Moreover, the duty to preserve oneself can reinforce the psychological effect of the right to do so, and thus become another device against the claims of government.

Hobbes says:

> And therefore there be some Rights, which no man can be understood by any words, or other signes, to have abandoned or transferred. As first a man cannot lay down the right of resisting them, that assault him by force, to take away his life; because he cannot be understood to ayme thereby, at any Good to himselfe. The same may be said of Wounds, and Chains, and Imprisonment.[100]

The right by nature to do anything whatever to preserve oneself is a right each of us has equally with all others. It exists not only where there is no government (or other protector) or where its protection has temporarily lapsed, but also where there is a government and one is threatened by it. No matter what one does, no matter what obligation one owes, no matter what wrong one has done, no matter what the cost to innocent others, one can never owe or forfeit one's life. We must notice, however, that the unrenounceable right establishes no corresponding duty in others to respect it. When government is impotent or in abeyance, I have a right to do what I must to save my life, inside or outside society, and so does everyone else, even at my expense. Similarly, a functioning government may have lawful designs on my life (or bodily integrity or freedom); but I have the right to elude or resist those designs. One may always "without Injustice, refuse" to cooperate with one's own hurt or ruin at the hands of Leviathan itself.[101]

Hobbes's theory teaches that in the most important respect, therefore, every human being under every government always lives in a state of nature. If nations exist in a state of nature because there is no government above them all, the most important illustration of the state of nature between individuals is a settled society. The reason is not so much because the passions are (by their very nature) irritable and transgressive, but much more because every society always has some life-threatening purposes or projects, which every individual has the right to avoid or resist for himself. The other side of the coin is that the ruler, no matter his origins, is always a conqueror, and the state his personal property. He is always in a kind of state of nature with his subjects, as they are with him. The idea of society as a state of nature is a brutal but demystifying and hence emancipatory notion.

Now, Hobbes takes no steps to guarantee his radical idea institutionally, although a conception of society that was even less naturalistic than Hobbes's own would require guarantees. In Hobbes's theory, the ruler will use and treat individuals as he sees fit by right or by strength. He will overpower them and their unrenounceable right to life. I do not think, however, the idea is thereby eviscerated. It is possible to think, rather, that even in the absence of institutionalized guarantees, a climate more favorable to individual integrity would develop if a ruler and the people alike accepted Hobbes's teaching on this matter. Clearly, however, institutionalized guarantees best suit (some manifestations of) the unrenounceable right to life.

It may be asked, what is the source of this unrenounceable right? The answer is not clear. There is no answer in Hobbes's answer: "Nature gave a right to every man to secure himselfe by his own strength, and to invade a suspected neighbour, by way of prevention."[102] Hobbes leaves no natural teleology standing: "the universe, as one aggregate of things natural, hath no intention."[103] In addition, Hobbes has theoretically disabled himself from appealing to an overriding instinct in human beings to self-preservation and thus from somehow deriving a right from an instinct. Spinoza's apparently similar teaching on the right of nature in his two tractatuses is even more obscure to me than Hobbes's. In Hobbes the true ground is, I think, a feeling: Hobbes's passionate tenderness toward all human beings, especially vulnerable ones. With what right, with what possible authority, could anyone require a fellow creature not to try to preserve itself?

In any case, the unrenounceable right to life is made by Hobbes to yield a number of important consequences. A seemingly narrow idea has immense explosive power. It shakes Hobbes's own theory; it should shake any theory, and any practice. Hobbes himself draws the following consequences. The general failure of authority revokes one's allegiance. Prisoners of war may change allegiance. Those engaged in the very activity that Hobbes dreads most—namely, civil war—may rightfully resist their capture. One may lie under torture. The ruler is wrong to compel a person to bear witness against himself in a criminal proceeding. One may try to elude or resist one's legal punishment. Indeed, at one point Hobbes even says that the ruler's right to punish is his personal natural right to overcome hostility; it cannot be a right understood as inhering in sovereignty precisely because no subject has the right to authorize his own hurt or ruin.[104] (There is kinship between the right to life and the rule of law, and Hobbes brilliantly expounds and extols the rule of law in chapters 26 through 28 of *Leviathan*.)

All these ideas tend to erode the mystique of political authority. Insofar as they do so, they give evidence of Hobbes's emancipatory power. We must now bring the matter home to the issue of Hobbes's commitment to the personified nation and thus to the inevitability of war. Hobbes tries to deal with the fact that wars can sometimes be fought only if the ruler conscripts able-bodied men. He does his best to establish the ruler's *covenantally based* right to conscript, not merely his natural *power-based* right to overcome impediments to his will. Thus, he is unwilling to conceptualize conscription in the way that he (sometimes) does punishment. His unpurged national feeling blocks the move. Yet his readers may make the move for him.

How can one be obliged to conscription and yet have an unrenounceable right to life? Assume that a given war is not a war directed at the enslavement or massacre of the population. Also take into account all that Hobbes says or suggests concerning the inferiority of the value of all things in life in comparison to (unenslaved) life itself. One should conclude that though Hobbes may prefer able-bodied men to forget both their duty and their right to stay alive, and to lend themselves to the patriotic endeavor to defend the life of the personified nation at the expense of their literal lives, Hobbes's most distinctive concept teaches that they should not. They should be ready to accept surrender, provided they do not anticipate enslavement or massacre.

Hobbes is, to be sure, equivocal. This shows itself in the fact that he formulates the social covenant in two different ways. Initially and at least twice thereafter, he wants us to conceive that we are held together in society solely by the pledge not to harm each other. Yet elsewhere he includes the provision that we pledge our "mutuall ayd against . . . enemies abroad"; that we oblige ourselves to "join together against a common Enemy"; and that we oblige ourselves "to assist him that hath the Sovereignty, in the Punishing of another."[105] He thus gives both a minimal and an expanded version of the social contract. The minimal contract is a drastic departure from traditional thought because it conceives of a population as contingently thrown into life in the same place and time and held together by rational good sense (abetted by fear of punishment). The expanded one re-establishes traditional thought on a new basis by continuing to see a population as a people that have ties that are more profound and more ancient than the ties of rational good sense and that antedate the very idea of a social contract and may very well outlive it. Further, the expanded contract in itself creates an artificial reason to die and kill; the minimal version truly seeks peace.

I do not see how the expanded contractual understanding is compatible with the idea of an unrenounceable right to life. I therefore do not see how Hobbes can succeed in the perhaps frightened effort he makes at the very end of *Leviathan*[106] to stabilize the rather erratic discourse on conscription that appears in chapter 21. He awkwardly adds a law of nature to those he had already listed in chapter 15. The addition comes as a belated discovery. The awkwardness is disarming, but it is also a sign of his own doubts. He says that "every man is bound by Nature, as much as in him lieth, to protect in Warre, the Authority, by which he is himself protected in time of Peace."[107] That seems to seal able-bodied men into a system of conscription. The matter is not so simple, however. The phrase "as much as in him lieth" may be the key. In chapter 21, Hobbes says that some men have "naturall timorousnesse" or "feminine courage."[108] Allowance should be made for them: they should be let off or permitted to buy their way out. Even though the sovereign may punish with death their refusal to fight, they are guilty not of injustice (that is, a breach of covenant), but of cowardice, of acting dishonorably. But Hobbes has already taught us how cheap a thing honor is. He is even prepared to say that it is good if most subjects lack fortitude, which is necessary for soldiers, "yet, for other men, the less they dare, the better it is both for the commonwealth and for themselves."[109] The implication is that the ruler can always put together an adequate volunteer army—provided people do not resist paying their taxes. Finally, the best that Hobbes can do is to give conscription a shaky theoretical defense. Maybe that is all that he wants to do.

Hobbes cannot bring himself to reject conscription outright. He does not follow through on his sentence, "for it can never be that Warre shall preserve life, and Peace destroy it."[110] His national sentiments obstruct the logical unfolding of his theory, which is properly completed by Kant in *Perpetual Peace*. The essence of any self-consistent contract theory is the preservation of all human lives, or as many as possible, and on minimally decent terms. Yet his theory emanates from his deepest philosophical self, not from his national feelings. Though he seems to try to construct a sufficient argument to discourage civil war, and anything that may help bring it on, by invoking the dangers of the international state of nature, the most distinctive element in his political theory defeats his strategy. His real passion, we may then say, is probably on the side of the fragile individual, on the side of the ordinary person, not on the side of all those (in power or aspiring to it) who gain from the mystifications that crush him. For that reason, even when on behalf of civil peace for the sake of life rather than for the sake of waging wars, he crudely discredits or insufficiently esteems some of the aims and motives that instigate civil war, he is still an emancipator. The notion of the fragile individual can also be used in spite of Hobbes's intentions, but in line with his real passion, to defend the necessity for constitutional democracy, as well as to defend resistance to it when its heightened sense of legitimacy encourages its adventurism abroad. His most general power, however, consists in getting us to wonder whether any value can ever justify losing and taking life, even if we choose some other way of valuing life than by reference to an unrenounceable right. At the same time, on our own but perhaps fortified by him, we can reject the common contention that only those willing to die and kill for political and civil freedom deserve to have it. If I am told that what I cherish and benefit from depends on the willingness of others to risk death and to die, all I can say is that I must admit to living exploitatively.

In sum, one can say that Hobbes is radical in the intensity of his wish to subdue people to obedience and that he therefore gives too little to political freedom and too much to the alleged necessity of war. But he is even more radical in his ability to set them free because his analysis exposes the vanity of elites and imparts a reverence for mere being. Free of absolutism, people can still be freed some more by Hobbes. The individualism that is centered in the sense of individual fragility is always able to engender radical results. Though one must heed him selectively, he is, in truth, an emancipator.

Citations of Hobbes's Writings

Autobiog: *The Life of Thomas Hobbes of Malmesbury.* Trans., Parsons and Blair. In *Interpretation,* 10 (1982), pp. 1–7.

Beh: *Behemoth or the Long Parliament.* Ed., Ferdinand Tonnies. 2d ed., New York: Barnes and Noble, 1969.

De Cive: *The Citizen: Philosophical Rudiments Concerning Government and Society.* Trans., Thomas Hobbes. In *Man and Citizen.* Ed., Bernard Gert. Garden City: Anchor, 1972. I have consulted the translation by Richard Tuck and Michael Silverthorne, *On the Citizen.* Cambridge: Cambridge University Press, 1998.

De Corp: *De Corpore Politico. The Elements of Law Natural and Politic,* chs. 20–29. Ed., J. C. A. Gaskin. New York: Oxford, 1994.

De Homine: *De Homine.* Trans., Wood, Scott-Craig, and Gert. In *Man and Citizen.*

Dialogue: *A Dialogue between a Philosopher and a Student of the Common Laws of England.* Ed., Joseph Cropsey. Chicago: University of Chicago Press, 1971.

Elements: *Elements of Philosophy.* In *The English Works of Thomas Hobbes,* Vol. 1. Ed., Sir William Molesworth. London: Bohn, 1839.

Human Nature: *Human Nature.* In *The Elements of Law,* chs. 1–19.

Lev: *Leviathan.* Ed., C.B. Macpherson. Baltimore: Penguin, 1968.

Questions: *The Questions Concerning Liberty, Necessity, and Chance.* In *The English Works of Thomas Hobbes,* vol. V.

Thucydides: *The History of the Grecian War Written by Thucydides.* Trans., Thomas Hobbes. In *The English Works of Thomas Hobbes,* vols. VIII, IX.

Notes

1. Thomas Hobbes, *Elements of Philosophy, The English Works of Thomas Hobbes*, vol. 1, ed. by Sir William Molesworth (London: Bohn, 1839), 8.

2. Thomas Hobbes, *A Dialogue Between a Philosopher and a Student of the Common Laws of England*, ed. by Joseph Cropsey (Chicago: University of Chicago Press, 1971), 57.

3. Thomas Hobbes, *Leviathan*, ed. by C. B. Macpherson (Baltimore: Penguin, 1968), ch. 27, 342.

4. Thomas Hobbes, *Behemoth or the Long Parliament*, ed. by Ferdinand Tonnies, 2nd ed. (New York: Barnes & Noble, 1969), v.

5. Hobbes, *Leviathan*, ch. 20, 261.

6. David Johnston, *The Rhetoric of Leviathan* (Princeton, NJ: Princeton University Press, 1986). See also the instructive discussion by William E. Connolly, *Political Theory and Modernity* (New York: Basic Blackwell, 1988), ch. 2.

7. Hobbes, *Leviathan*, ch. 34, 430.

8. Leo Strauss, "On the Basis of Hobbes's Political Philosophy," *What Is Political Philosophy?* (Glencoe, IL: Free Press, 1959, ch. 7), a discussion of Raymond Polin's *Politique et philosophie chez Thomas Hobbes*.

9. Hobbes, *Leviathan*, ch. 12, 172.

10. Hobbes, *Leviathan*, ch. 11, 167; ch. 12, 170.

11. Hobbes, *Leviathan*, ch. 31, 401.

12. Hobbes, *Elements*, 410–414, at 414.

13. Hobbes, *Leviathan*, ch. 11, 167.

14. Hobbes, *Leviathan*, ch. 31, 404.

15. Thomas Hobbes, *Human Nature*, ch. 9, 59.

16. Hobbes, *Elements*, xiv.

17. Hobbes, *Leviathan*, ch. 12, 17–18.

18. Thomas Hobbes, *The Questions Concerning Liberty, Necessity, and Chance*. In *English Works*, vol. 5, 199.

19. Hobbes, *Leviathan*, ch. 13, 187.

20. Hobbes, *Leviathan*, ch. 31, 401.

21. Hobbes, *Questions*, 229, 237.

22. Hobbes, *Leviathan*, ch. 31, 397–399.

23. Hobbes, *Questions*, 146.

24. Hobbes, *Leviathan*, ch. 12, 178.

25. Hobbes, *Leviathan*, ch. 12, 179.

26. Hobbes, *Leviathan*, ch. 31, 404.

27. Hobbes, *Leviathan*, intro., 82–83.

28. Thomas Hobbes, *De Corpore Politico*, ch. 27, 163.

29. Thomas Hobbes, *De Homine*, trans. by Charles T. Wood, T. S. K. Scott-Craig, and Bernard Gert. In *Man and Citizen*, ed. by Bernard Gert (Garden City, NY: Anchor, 1972), 68–69.

30. Hobbes, *Behemoth*, 70.

31. Hobbes, *Dialogue*, 65, 76.

32. Hobbes, *Leviathan*, ch. 47, 706–708; Hobbes, *Behemoth*, 13–26.

33. Hobbes, *Behemoth*, 2; Hobbes, *Dialogue*, 65.

34. Hobbes, *Behemoth*, 23, 27, 110, 114.

35. Hobbes, *Behemoth*, 113.

36. Hobbes, *Behemoth*, 107, 96.

37. Hobbes, *Leviathan*, ch. 27, 341–342; ch. 30, 379.

38. Hobbes, *De Homine*, 66.

39. Hobbes, *De Homine*, 66.

40. Hobbes, *Leviathan*, ch. 17, 225–227; also Thomas Hobbes, *The Citizen: Philosophical Rudiments Concerning Government and Society [De Cive]*. In Gert, *Man and Citizen*, ch. 5, 168–169.

41. Hobbes, *De Corpore Politico*, ch. 27, 163.

42. Hobbes, *Leviathan*, ch. 30, 387; ch. 15, 210; ch. 30, 389–390.

43. Hobbes, *Leviathan*, ch. 13, 185.

44. Hobbes, *De Homine*, 60–61.

45. Hobbes, *De Cive*, ch. 5, 169.

46. Hobbes, *Leviathan*, ch. 17, 226.

47. Hobbes, *Behemoth*, 95.

48. Hobbes, *Behemoth*, 58.

49. Hobbes, *De Cive*, ch. 13, 265.

50. Hobbes, *Leviathan*, ch. 30, 384.

51. Hobbes, *Leviathan*, ch. 30, 384.

52. Hobbes, *Leviathan*, ch. 30, 379.

53. Hobbes, *De Cive*, dedic., 91.

54. Hobbes, *Leviathan*, ch. 38, 478–491.

55. Hobbes, *Leviathan*, ch. 38, 478.

56. Hobbes, *Questions*, 214, 216.

57. Hobbes, *Leviathan*, ch. 43, 610.

58. Hobbes, *Leviathan*, ch. 38, 484.

59. Hobbes, *Leviathan*, ch. 47, 711.

60. Hobbes, *Leviathan*, ch. 43, 609–610.

61. Hobbes, *De Cive*, ch. 11, 245. In Tuck and Silverthorne, ch. 12, 133.

62. Hobbes, *Leviathan*, ch. 42, 527–531; ch. 43, 625.

63. Hobbes, *Dialogue*, 165–166.

64. Hobbes, *Dialogue*, 63.

65. Hobbes, *Leviathan*, ch. 19, 240–241; ch. 22, 284.

66. Hobbes, *Leviathan*, ch. 19, 241.

67. Hobbes, *Leviathan*, ch. 22, 280.

68. Hobbes, *Leviathan*, ch. 16, 218; also ch. 21, 268.

69. Hobbes, *Leviathan*, ch. 46, 689.

70. Hobbes, *Leviathan*, ch. 14, 142; ch. 30, 376; ch. 15, 212.

71. Hobbes, *Leviathan*, ch. 14, 190.

72. Hobbes, *Leviathan*, ch. 15, 205.

73. Hobbes, *Dialogue*, 57.

74. Hobbes, *De Cive*, ch. 10, 234.

75. Hobbes, *Leviathan*, ch. 20, 257; also, ch. 17, 224.

76. E.g., Hobbes, *De Cive*, ch. 13, 260.

77. Hobbes, *De Cive*, ch. 5, 166.

78. Hobbes, *De Cive*, ch. 5, 166.

79. Hobbes, *Leviathan*, ch. 30, 387.

80. Hobbes, *Leviathan*, ch. 30, 387.

81. Hobbes, *De Cive*, ch. 8, 205; *Leviathan*, ch. 17, 224; *Dialogue*, 158–161.

82. Hobbes, *Dialogue*, 161.

83. Hobbes, *Dialogue*, 59.

84. See Hobbes, *De Cive*, ch. 8; also *Leviathan*, ch. 20, 255.

85. Hobbes, *Leviathan*, ch. 13, 188.

86. Thomas Hobbes, *The Life of Thomas Hobbes of Malmesbury*, trans. by J. E. Parsons, Jr., and Whitney Blair. In *Interpretation*, 10 (1982), 1–7.

87. Jean-Jacques Rousseau, *Extrait du projet de paix perpetuelle de M. L'Abbé de Saint-Pierre*. In *The Political Writings*, vol. 1, ed. by C. E. Vaughn (New York: Wiley, 1962, reprint), 365. See the discussion in Stanley Hoffmann, *The State of War* (New York: Praeger, 1965), ch. 3.

88. Thucydides, *The History of the Grecian War Written by Thucydides*, trans. by Thomas Hobbes. In *English Works*, vol. 8, 81; vol. 9.

89. Hobbes, *Leviathan*, ch. 13, 185.

90. Hobbes, *De Cive*, ch. 1, 118.

91. But see the citation (note 96) from *Leviathan*, ch. 11, 161.

92. Hobbes, *Leviathan*, ch. 10, 150.

93. Hobbes, *Leviathan*, ch. 28, 360.

94. On the perils of personifying a nation, see the excellent analysis in Charles Beitz, *Political Theory and International Relations* (Princeton, NJ: Princeton University Press, 1979), 52–53 and *passim*.

95. Hobbes, *Leviathan*, ch. 16, 220.

96. Hobbes, *Leviathan*, ch. 11, 161.

97. Hobbes, *Leviathan*, ch. 29, 375.

98. Hobbes, *Behemoth*, 144.

99. Howard Warrender, *The Political Philosophy of Hobbes* (Oxford: Clarendon Press, 1957), 18–21 and *passim*.

100. Hobbes, *Leviathan*, ch. 14, 192; also ch. 14, 199; ch. 15, 212; ch. 21, 268.

101. Hobbes, *Leviathan*, ch. 21, 268.

102. Hobbes, *Leviathan*, ch. 26, 335.

103. Hobbes, *Questions*, 237.

104. Hobbes, *Leviathan*, ch. 21, 273; ch. 21, 270; ch. 14, 199–200; ch. 21, 269; ch. 14, 199; ch. 21, 268–269; ch. 28, 353.

105. Hobbes, *Leviathan*, ch. 14, 190; ch. 15, 201; ch. 18, 228–229; ch. 17, 227–228; ch. 26, 315; also ch. 21, 268; ch. 28, 353.

106. Hobbes, *Leviathan*, in "A Review, and Conclusion," 718–719.

107. See also Hobbes, *Leviathan*, ch. 29, 375.

108. Hobbes, *Leviathan*, ch. 21, 270.

109. Hobbes, *Behemoth*, 45.

110. Hobbes, *Leviathan*, ch. 15, 215.

$I4$

Ideology and Storytelling

One of the most striking features of Hannah Arendt's analysis of totalitarianism is the prominent role she gives ideology. Even before she added the chapter "Ideology and Terror: A Novel Form of Government" (first published in English in 1953) to the second edition of *The Origins of Totalitarianism* (1958), she had extensively discussed (in the first edition, 1951) the work that ideology did in making totalitarian movements and dictatorships successful, if only temporarily. In this book (in both main editions), her teaching is that we cannot make sense of the totalitarian phenomenon if we do not emphasize the hold, the power, of ideas. The tacit lesson is that people who initiate or cooperate in protracted policies that have murderous effects on a large scale must be driven by ideas. However vicious people can be in their overtly unideological face-to-face relations in everyday life, they cannot be involved in murderous policies unless possessed, at least to some extent, or only spasmodically, by ideas — more accurately, by a system of ideas. To design and carry out an atrocious policy requires more than the nameable vices: pride, envy, vanity, anger, vengeance, greed, cruelty, and others. The system of ideas not only sanctions but impels these policies, and shapes their realization. There is no straight line between the nameable vices and murderous public policies; ideol-

I wish to thank Judith Barish, Jerome Kohn, and Roy Tsao for their suggestions.

ogy must enter the picture and transform human beings into actively ideological creatures. Ideology may employ the practiced vices or it may, contrastingly, induce people to overcome their inhibitions, their reluctance to give in to their vices. Ideology is, in any case, indispensable to murderous party dictatorships (as it is to any murderous policy enacted by nontotalitarian governments). Such is the thought that appears to govern Arendt's presentation.

What persuades Arendt to make so much of ideology in her analysis? I think that Arendt's view is that unless people are beside themselves or are carried out of themselves — unless people are not quite themselves — they would not plan and execute murderous policies on a large scale. Such policies are not the direct enactment of, say, the vices of anger or vengeance or cruelty. Nor are the policies merely the clever strategies employed by one or more of the vices to realize an aim, as, for example, Iago's envy or gratuitous spite or some violent ambivalence in him devises a clever scheme to ruin Othello's felicity. No, where there are exterminationist public policies, the quintessence of totalitarianism under Hitler and Stalin, ideology plays the pivotal role. An analysis that derived their exterminationism from their personal pathology would not be satisfactory.

In her notes on Dostoyevsky's *The Possessed,* Arendt attributes to Dostoyevsky the argument that when atheism spreads, man "is no longer owned by God," but is "possessed by ideas which act like demons" (1967:2). She also says that the strength of the novel is in the concrete presentation of characters who are embodied ideas, who live for their extreme and conflicting ideas (3). In a very suggestive but compressed and inconclusive set of notes, only four pages in length, Arendt asserts that ideas chase "ordinary thoughtfulness" out of the head of the character Stefan Trofimovitch Verhovensky; he thus "borders on criminality," and produces (perhaps must produce?) a criminal son. The father is under "the domination of phantoms because there is no reality behind them" (2). (Notice that it is being dominated by ideas, not, as with Eichmann in Arendt's picture of him, being without ideas or vaguely attached to misrepresentations of them, that constitutes thoughtlessness. This is a more satisfactory account of Eichmann than the one we usually take away from her book on him.) The worst villain, Peter, son of Stefan Trofimovitch, however, is not the servant of an idea, she says, just because he is a nihilist; he is modeled on Nachaev. But I think Arendt may make a misstep here: nihilism, nihilistic indifference, is after all an idea. Peter's seeming ideological indifference stems not from an inactive mind but from the conclusion he has reached that all things are pointless or meaningless and that therefore anything goes. Destruction is sustained by a philosophically grounded frivolity that stems from an overpowering philosophical disappointment. In any case, Dostoyevsky's sense is that ideas motivate extreme ambitions of policy — destructive and utopian. Whatever differences Arendt had with him, she, too, holds to this view. Of course, her notes on *The Possessed* were prepared some years after the second edition of *Origins* and even after *Eichmann in Jerusalem* (1963). But I think that her analysis of totalitarianism inhabits the same mental universe as Dostoyevsky's novel (even though the only references to him in *Origins* are citations owed to Hans Kohn).

I say that Dostoyevsky and Arendt inhabit the same mental universe because they share the attitude that people crave meaning (or meaningfulness), which only ideas can give. Immersion in the everyday life of the senses, activities, and affections simply does not suffice. When old ideas, old systems of ideas, fail, new ones are imperative and will be sought and then adapted. Somewhat like Dostoyevsky, Arendt believes that life is unendurable for people without the meaning that a system of ideas can alone provide. Again, somewhat like Dostoyevsky, Arendt herself needs meaning. The paraphrase that she provides of some leading notions of existentialist thinkers in France and Germany, but especially Camus and Sartre, in notes for a lecture called "The Spiritual Quest of Modern Man" (1952), indicates a sympathy for the way in which these thinkers are driven by the effort to delineate — if not remedy — the crisis of meaninglessness brought on by the enfeeblement or refutation of belief in the theological or religious God.

The phenomenon of totalitarianism is of course not fully explainable by the death of God, but for Arendt the effort to explain it must seriously attend to the impact of the crisis of meaninglessness. She is a philosopher who is capable of extraordinary feats of comprehending human phenomena that are alien or repugnant to her; but I think that we must add that on the significance of the question of meaninglessness she reads herself first in order to read the world. That does not imply that if totalitarianism came into being and stayed for a while because it provided a solution to the crisis of meaninglessness, then Arendt must have therefore felt a measure of sympathy for those who were taken in by it or even for those whose rage for meaning may have initiated and sustained it. Arendt shows no sympathy for either category of people. The trouble is that she is a great friend and advocate of intellectual modes — among them, religious belief, stories, narratives, myths, legends, and what she calls philosophical or metaphysical or theological "fallacies" — that are not nearly as unlike — *formally speaking,* and apart from content — ideology in general and totalitarian ideology in particular, as she tries to make us believe. Her own passion for meaningfulness is everywhere in evidence. She says that from the perspective of the "thinking ego" "a life without meaning *is* a kind of living death" (1978:87). If Arendt has any sentimentality, it is on this issue. Her

writings show almost no trace of a cultivated ability to endure meaninglessness, and she certainly does not seek to cultivate that ability in her readers.

I think that Arendt is absolutely right to make ideology central to totalitarianism and hence to see the crisis of meaninglessness as implicated in the rise
and strength of totalitarianism. I differ from her on the identification of those
people who crave meaning the most, who crave it so much that they will go to
any lengths to detect or impute it or intellectually impose it on reality; and then
having found it, try to remake the world in its image with a total devotion, a
total lack of restraint. My sense is that ideology matters the most, and by far,
to totalitarian leaders, upper cadres, middle bureaucrats, and intellectual sympathizers. It matters somewhat but only intermittently to the large majority of
people. By perhaps exaggerating the need of masses for the meaning that
ideology confers on reality, she may consequently underestimate the part
played in the rise of totalitarian leaders by the various bodily and mental
shocks sustained by populations in times of war, defeat, and material misery,
eloquent as she is about these traumas. A strong leadership was wanted in a
sea of troubles. The mass crisis to which totalitarian movements responded
was, in the first instance, much more a crisis of demoralization and dispossession than a crisis of overall meaninglessness.

To be sure, defeat in war was a terrible blow to the patriotic psyches of the
losing populations, and patriotism is itself either an explicit ideology or an
inculcated myth. In either case it is a giver of meaning. But patriotism was not
an element in the stated totalitarian ideology of either Hitler or Stalin, despite
the uses they both made of it when it suited their tactical convenience. Patriotism is an ever-present ideological background element, an element, by the way,
that Arendt praises. She asks rhetorically, in an unfortunate passage in "Truth
and Politics," "why shouldn't a liar stick to his lies with great courage, especially in politics, where he might be motivated by patriotism or some other
kind of legitimate group partiality?" (1968a: 249).

I wish to say, then, that the appeal of ideology was strongest to those actively involved in the design and command of totalitarianism, and this minority found in the shocks of defeat and widespread misery an opportunity for a
new beginning, for the sustained attempt to realize their ideology and, by
doing that, to make the world freshly meaningful. In trying to enter this suggestion for revision in Arendt's analysis, I am guided by a remark Nietzsche
makes in *Beyond Good and Evil*. He says, "Anyone who has looked deeply
into the world may guess how much wisdom lies in the superficiality of men.
The instinct that preserves them teaches them to be flighty, light, and false.
Here and there one encounters an impassioned and exaggerated worship of
'pure forms,' among both philosophers and artists: let nobody doubt that

whoever stands that much in *need* of the cult of surfaces must at some time have reached beneath them with disastrous results" (1968a, sect. 59: 261). Intellectuals, when they do not despise the masses as incurious and anti-intellectual, attribute to them far too much concern for some large meaning in life. The caution in analysis that Nietzsche here recommends is all the more striking because of his deep anxiety that the death of God at the hands of modern science would lead to the absence of all meaningful content for the human will: "man would rather will *nothingness* [*das Nichts*] than *not* will" (1968b, third essay, sect. 28: 599). Perhaps he had already corrected his own anxiety in the earlier passage from *Beyond Good and Evil*. His caution is superior to his anxiety. Nonetheless I am far from denying that all people desire and even crave meaning, but not necessarily the comprehensive sort that ideologies or other systems supply.

Arendt's work is permeated by concern with meaningfulness, by anxiety over meaninglessness. Yet the connection between her concern and anxiety and her analysis of the nature of totalitarianism turns out to be a complex matter. My view is that one cannot intensely want meaningfulness and still be in a position to be surprised by the eruption of totalitarianism, which is to be explained (but certainly not exclusively) as a fanatical response to the crisis of meaningless-ness. Arendt assembles all the insights to enable us to see totalitarianism in this way, but something prevents her from saying outright that the quest for mean-ing can turn inhuman, and that therefore the quest for meaning must be held under continuous suspicion.

At this point I would like to take up the concept of meaning as it figures in Arendt's work and then return to her treatment of totalitarian ideology and its relation to the question of meaning in life. Although Arendt provides little analysis of the concept of meaning, she does offer some hints. I will try to fill out her understanding of meaning. What she calls "the quest for meaning" or "the appetite for meaning" occupies her in many of her texts. She often *defines* thinking as the quest for meaning; the quest for meaning is "reason's need" (1978: 78). Roughly put, the quest for meaning is not the desire for an ordi-nary explanation that remedies one's ignorance, that adds one more bit of knowledge to one's store of knowledge, while leaving that store cumulatively richer but basically unaltered. In general, Arendt distinguishes the quest for meaning from the quest for experiential and scientific knowledge. Thinking is not the same as knowing. She says "the faculty of thought . . . does not ask what something is or whether it exists at all — its existence is always taken for granted — but what it means for it to be" (57).

Obviously if we could manage to arrive at an understanding of what it means for any given thing or all things to be, we would have acquired knowledge in some sense; we would have learned a new fact of major proportions. We would have learned the not obvious point or purpose for which any given thing or all things exist. We would have discerned a telos not our own. Arendt says that such meaning may not be easy or even possible to pin down. She follows Auden in holding that each [person] "was meant to be." It is not clear, however, who or what meant any person to be. But being meant is enough to have meaning; having meaning is to be intended. Then she immediately adds, "But this being 'meant to be' is not a truth; it is a highly meaningful proposition" (57). There is a contrast, then, between truth and meaning, a matter that will occupy us.

Arendt seems to endorse Bergson's view that meaning is "ineffable" and that it is "slippery," that it refuses to be grasped and always "slips away" (122). On storytelling, in particular, Arendt says that it "reveals meaning without committing the error of defining it" (1968c: 105). It is important to see therefore that although Arendt insists on severing the love of meaning from the desire for certainty, I do not think that we should make too much of ineffability and indefinability as crucial features of Arendt's understanding of meaning. Elusiveness or inconclusiveness, yes; inadequacy of articulation, yes; but perhaps nothing beyond that. I really do not see how the concept of meaning can bear so much weight in Arendt's work if ineffability and indefinability are crucial. The quest for meaning would be meaningless if it never came to some conclusions, if only provisional or incomplete. The Socratic thinker may be content to be perpetually dissatisfied with any attempted articulation, but most people and most thinkers are not. If people want meaning as much as Arendt suggests they do and should, they will not rest until they have persuaded themselves that they have it or some part or glimpse of it.

Arendt's interest in severing the quest for meaning from the quest for knowledge is nothing less than an attempt to sever meaning from the claims of almost all kinds of truth, not just scientific truth. At one point she says that people are able to think, "that is, speculate meaningfully, about the unknown and the unknowable" (1978: 71). If we accept her framework, and emphasize that the unknowable is what is unknown, we are told from the start that metaphysical thinkers deal with matters about which nothing can be honestly or truthfully said. She calls these systems "fallacies." What matters is that metaphysical systems confer meaningfulness on life, whatever the purposes of the metaphysicians. To put it bluntly, it seems as though she knows that results of the quest for meaning are false, empirically false, but she wants us to respect them, even though she and we know that they are false. We must hide from the truth while pretending that it is irrelevant to our enterprise. At one point in her writings, she does say, however, that a particular "fallacy" has some "truth inherent in it." But this fallacy is not a whole system, but only one idea in it, namely, that the realm of action should be understood from the spectator's viewpoint, not the actor's. The truth in the fallacy is conceptual; it is, precisely, that not the agent but the spectator "can hope to understand what actually happened in any given chain of deeds and events" (1977: 52).

Even if false, the results of the metaphysical quest, we could say, were meant to be true, though I am not sure that Arendt believes that philosophers typically try to be honest. Let us agree that other motives besides the quest for truth impel philosophers, and that the quest for meaning in the face of the claims of truth may be one of those motives that deflect a philosopher from truthfulness. Still, if we thought from the start that the best we could say about a thinker is that all that he or she wanted to do is impose a pattern of meaning on the world, I wonder what respect for the thinker we would retain.

We could of course say that although the philosophers' results, doctrinal metaphysical systems, are not literally true, they are still true in some other sense. Adapting Feuerbach, we could say that their esoteric meaning is poetical, a truth about human nature and the human condition, not about the possibly unknowable nature of nonhuman things. (Arendt herself offers the thought that metaphysical systems are only projections of the experience of the thinking ego as it tries to think, of its experiences with itself.) But Arendt does not seem to want esoteric poetical truth. She appears to urge us to separate truth from meaning altogether, and for the sake of declaring that truth has no relevance to the quest for meaning and hence to our wish to esteem that quest. She arranges Kant so that his critique of pure reason makes room not for *Glaube* but for thinking (1978: 63), the "purposeless quest for meaning" (213, 78). It seems to be the case that meaning is never truthful and, worse, that truth is always meaningless. The quest for meaning is a self-enclosed language game, just as the quest for knowledge is.

Does this mean that by these moves, Arendt shows that she really wants untruths, lies, to decorate the world with unwarrantable beliefs that confer meaning? She tries to fend off the attempted destruction of metaphysics by the logical positivists, her contemporaries. She does not want us to say that the quest for meaning issues in meaningless propositions. But the propositions are not truths. By calling metaphysical and theological systems "fallacies," she admits that she has "joined the ranks of those who for some time now have been attempting to dismantle metaphysics." Alluding to Shakespeare's *The Tempest,* she nevertheless warns those who join the dismantling effort to be "careful not to destroy the 'rich and strange,' the 'coral' and the 'pearls,' which can probably be saved only as fragments" (1978: 212). But if truth, even in a nonliteral but nevertheless genuine poetical sense, is ruled out of court when doctrines are assessed, retribution is never far away. Mustn't we use empirical truth to discredit meaning-conferring modes when we think that any of them can turn or has turned into an instrument of evil?

The truth is meaningless; let there be meaning. At one point, Arendt says that "All the metaphysical questions that philosophy took as its special topics arise out of ordinary common-sense experiences; 'reason's need'—the quest for meaning that prompts men to ask them—is in no way different from men's need to tell the story of some happening they witnessed, or to write poems about it" (1978: 78). I think that for Arendt only stories or other intellectual modes that can be construed as stories are meaningful. She actually tends to see every intellectual mode that imparts meaning as a kind of story. Meaning is in the telling, not in the ineffable, not in the untold and untellable. The richest meaning, however, comes from what we ordinarily call stories—fictional compositions such as novels, short stories, plays; but Arendt also straightforwardly treats biographies, autobiographies, and historical accounts as stories. (I will refer to the latter genres as stories in the expanded sense.) In her essay on Lessing, "On Humanity in Dark Times," she says, "No philosophy, no analysis, no aphorism, be it ever so profound, can compare in intensity and richness of meaning with a properly narrated story" (1968d: 22). (As she adds, in the remark quoted earlier, a poem can reach the same meaningful richness.) To be sure, she refers to the way in which "thoughtful remembrance" of a course of events like the French Revolution can lead to a "condensation of happenings into concepts" (1977: 59). She herself is a master of such condensation. Yet her overall teaching is that we should judge philosophical, theological, and other abstract systems on the basis of the standard set by storytellers and poets in their successful quest for meaning.

Now, I have indicated that we could treat metaphysical systems as poetically true, truth in disguise, not literally true. As for stories (in the fictional sense) and poems, we of course do not judge them by their literal truth, but employ several sorts of standard. One such standard is being true to life, or being "poetically" true in the sense of teaching a lesson in moral psychology that rings true or opens the eyes. Another standard, which is substantially different from such kinds of truth, is meeting the needs of the imagination. I think that Arendt is most devotedly committed to the last-named standard for judging not only stories (in the fictional sense) and poems, but all intellectual modes that can be construed as searching for meaning, not for knowledge; quite surprisingly, these modes appear to include biographies, autobiographies, and historical accounts, where the normal expectation is knowledge and only such meaning as is compatible with it. But the imagination needs reality to be aesthetically compelling. The need can be a craving. All of Arendt's work shows that craving. I understand her as sharing the passion that she attributes to Socrates: "What I called the 'quest' for meaning appears in Socrates as love, that is, love in its Greek significance of *Eros,* not the Christian *Agape.* Love as Eros is primarily a need" (1978: 178). To be sure, she distinguishes between the thinking ego and the real self (87). So, let us say that whatever may have been true of Arendt as a person, the inference that we can plausibly draw from her work is that Arendt's thinking ego craves meaning for essentially aesthetic reasons, and that she attributes to people in general (whether or not their thinking egos are persistently active) the same craving or at least a strong need, even though it is apparently not erotic in the Socratic sense.

For Arendt, the purpose of thinking, which is the source of stories (in both the fictional and expanded senses) and poems, as well as many other intellectual modes that (she thinks) cannot and should not be expected to stand up to the claims of any kind of truth, is to generate meaning, or meanings, or meaningfulness. "Seen from the perspective of thinking, life in its sheer thereness is meaningless" (87). It is true that the volume *Thinking* contains a qualified impeachment of thinking for deserting thereness, the radiance of appearances, "the immediacy of life and the world given to the senses" (87). But Arendt makes it clear that thinking as deserting the senses, as abstraction from the immediately given, is intrinsic to human beings and their stature. There is no humanity without thinking. If, then, Arendt befriends the unprocessed world of sensory appearances, she befriends even more the processes by which this world is converted into meaningfulness. She thus praises not only stories (in the fictional sense), but also any intellectual mode that can be likened to stories or studied as stories are, and from which all the advantages of stories in the usual fictional sense can be gained. Mustn't we say that Arendt tells stories about various intellectual modes so that she can assimilate all these modes to fictional stories? (She of course hates ideologies, but I wonder if she can consistently do so. We will return to this matter later.)

Can we further characterize the meaning that stories (works of fiction as well as stories in the expanded sense: biographies, autobiographies, and histories) offer? Leave aside metaphysical systems for the moment. Any given story makes sense of personal experiences, actual or vicarious. The sense it makes must be — and here, a range of verbs is needed to catch Arendt's view — detected or inferred or pieced together or imputed or allowed slowly to emerge. Meaning is not obvious; experiences do not bear their sense on their surface. An intellectual effort must be made to apprehend meaning, which is invisible. But something more than patience is necessary. For one thing, distance from the experience is required. In several works, Arendt discusses the role of the observer or spectator, the one who abstains from involvement so that he or she may distill the sense from the action that the actors themselves — too busy in their exertions and passion to compete, excel, or prevail — cannot distill. Actors and spectators exist for the sake of each other. Only when Odysseus hears a bard sing Odysseus' own story of his quarrel with Achilles does Odysseus start to cry. "Only when he hears the story does he become fully aware of its meaning" (1978: 132). What is true of Odysseus is true of all people in their experiences. Most people cannot tell their own stories, literally or allegorically. But everyone can have moments of reflection, of retrospection, in which the effort is made to catch up with oneself and what one has been through, or consider imaginatively what others have been through. In any event, stories (in the fictional and expanded senses) redeem experience, save it from flowing away into the void. The key to telling stories (in these two senses) is to permit the passage of time to withdraw oneself from the experience or achieve "alienation" from it; then one repeats it in imagination and thereby allows the meaning to emerge for the first time (1968c: 104; also 1978: 77, 85–87; Dempf, Arendt, and Engel-Janosi, 1962: 2–5). To repeat in one's imagination, however, is to do much more than strain toward an accurate remembrance. It is to give form or shape to whatever has happened. Memory and information are the malleable servants of the memorable.

Of course, Arendt doesn't insist that the meaning or sense that is elicited or distilled should be or even can be neatly formulated. We have already referred to her belief that "storytelling reveals meaning without committing the error of defining it" (1968c: 105). She mentions a thought from Heraclitus that perhaps can be extended to cover her expectations for stories: "Apollo . . . 'does not speak out nor does he conceal but indicates' . . . that is, hints at something ambiguously" (1978: 143). This formulation can then be applied to all meaning-conferring modes, especially metaphysical (including theological) systems.

Then again, there are times when Arendt seems to expect and admire more than ambiguous hints — something more definite and achieved. This is especially the case when the experience to be rendered meaningful points beyond itself to an invisible realm or to an invisible and harmonious order. The world as a whole can be the unit of meaningfulness, can be one grand story, when it is construed metaphysically. Arendt contemplates some of the great metaphysical systems from the perspective of the meaningfulness that they elicit from or confer on the whole world. (To repeat: Arendt holds that these systems are "fallacies," but are not properly called falsehoods, even though both words are ultimately traceable to the same Latin root.) When she deals with the meaningfulness that metaphysicians impute to the world as a whole, it is clear that she is asking us to regard metaphysical systems as stories or as analogous to or sufficiently like them. One trouble for her conception is that when metaphysics is discussed, the claims of truth become irrepressible. The metaphysicians themselves (we have to assume, whether or not Arendt does) wanted to be taken as telling the truth when they spoke doctrinally. They wanted to be believed. They are often believed, even if not completely on their own terms. But whatever their motives, we must, to begin with, study them as engaged in doing more than trying to make the world more interesting or aesthetically compelling. When they inspire action by direct appeal or by a slower and more indirect influence, they do so because at least some of their adherents think that a given system is the truth.

What, finally, is meaning for Arendt? An event, or an experience, or a condition, or a whole individual life, or the world as a whole, can be made to be meaningful if the thinking imagination takes hold of mere thereness or "sheer happenings" and manages to persuade the reader or auditor that sheer happenings point to or actually fall into a pattern or design, or betray the presence of an intention or purpose that is more than that of the actors or that of human beings altogether. The difference between meaning and meaninglessness is *not* like the difference between speech and noise, or like the difference between the intelligible and the unintelligible, or even between the interpreted and the uninterpreted. Rather, it is the difference between the aesthetically compelling and the aesthetically disappointing. Or, it is the difference between what has been aesthetically enhanced beyond its own powers of self-enhancement and what is simply accepted as given. All meaning takes the form of a story, whether or not the intellectual mode is a story in the ordinary fictional sense. Perhaps it is only meaning that makes reality felt as reality rather than as a nightmare or hallucination. Indeed, by making no attempt, in her essay on Dinesen, to distinguish between historical accounts and fictional accounts, Arendt is implying that what matters is not fidelity to fact but the plenitude of meaning. (She anomalously discourages the creation of "fiction" in the telling of stories [1968c: 97]. By "fiction" I think that she means here some self-serving evasion or cover-up.)

In *The Human Condition* (1958), she does say that the "distinction between a real and a fictional story is precisely that the latter was 'made up' and the former not made at all" (186). The stakes are nonetheless raised in Arendt's discussion of every person's life as an enacted story. "The real story in which we are engaged as long as we live has no visible or invisible maker because it is not made. The only 'somebody' it reveals is its hero. . . . *Who* somebody is or was we can know only by knowing the story of which he is himself the hero—

his biography, in other words; everything else we know of him, including the work he may have produced and left behind, tells us only *what* he is or was" (186). One's life turns out to be in the hands not of ourselves, but of those who either play our stories on the stage or write them up after we are gone. Arendt is always insistent that one cannot know who one is, which means that one cannot know one's own story while living it and cannot survive its completion to know how it all came out: therefore, he who lives the story can never tell it.

I am afraid that this is aestheticism run rampant; it deviates too grossly from the common understanding that we know *who* we are in a way that no one can know us. Her own stony rejection of the possibility of empathy is surely applicable here. If any story is untellable it is the story of any person's life. Actually, a life overflows every aesthetic form and boundary. As a whole, it is not a story at all. One's life is not a trajectory of character; everybody dies unconfessed. I can give myself away and still not be known.

Notice that Arendt sometimes writes as if what matters is finding or rescuing what has been overlooked; but much more is involved. Indeed, in her essay on Isak Dinesen, Arendt appears to endorse the view she attributes to Dinesen. By being made into a story, "an unbearable sequence of sheer happenings" in one's life "become what she [Dinesen] would call a 'destiny'" (1968c: 104). When events are patterned into a destiny, they form a sequence that inevitably discloses that a point or purpose existed from the start. Randomness is subordinated or effaced. When contingency is perceived as necessity, it only then becomes meaningful. Arendt does not abandon Stoicism, after all, certainly not when dealing with life stories. (In fairness, we should point out that on one occasion, she yokes together two ideas she usually keeps apart. Following Marx, she calls bodily processes "the fateful automatism of sheer happening that underlies all human history" [1977: 59].)

A life has meaning when, perhaps only when, it has a destiny that the storyteller can ultimately discern afterward and then disclose. Thus, Arendt, a leading theorist of freedom as rejection of destiny, and of contingency as the guarantor of the reality of the will, has moments when even these high commitments yield to the imperatives of meaning for the life story of a person. In apparent contrast, she regularly deplores the hubristic tendency to resent what is given, just because it is given, and seeks instead to transform it into something made over. But to grant such desperate benefit and such prestige to storytelling is to admit that the given is never good enough. Its basic deficiency is that it does not have meaning until transformed. Meaning is craved so keenly that aesthetically untransformed reality is disowned as lifeless or inhuman. Thus, there are important moments in Arendt's work where the quest for meaning overrides every other consideration. This fanaticism, so to speak, is barely mitigated by Arendt's resistance to easily found or easily stated meaning.

The context also seems to indicate that Arendt accepts Dinesen's judgment that "All sorrows can be borne if you put them into a story or tell a story about them" (1968c: 104). Stories facilitate reconciliation with one's suffering, one's whole life. In other places, Arendt says that the net result of stories (in the most inclusive sense: fictional, expanded, and metaphysical), and hence of a conviction of meaningfulness, is that one achieves reconciliation with life beyond oneself; one feels at home in the world. A great device of reconciliation is precisely to see necessity, if only aesthetic necessity, in sequences of apparently random occurrences, and come to feel that things had to be this way. A person had not been a victim of mere chance. One kind of story, what Arendt calls myths, can offer us "that comprehensive whole in which we feel spiritually at home" (*OT* 1: 435; see 434–35; see also for her related espousal of legends as "belated corrections of facts and real events" (*OT* 2: 207–11). Without myths and legends, without aesthetically compelling departures from literal truth, we are lost in darkness, or what is almost the same, pointlessness. In "Truth and Politics," she speaks for herself when she says straight out that the political function of the storyteller (historian or novelist, as if there were little difference between them) is to bring about a Hegelian " 'reconciliation with reality,' " "to teach acceptance of things as they are." This acceptance "can also be called truthfulness" (1968a: 262). To leave aside the odd equation of acceptance and truthfulness, stories, according to Arendt, do not render things as they are; what we accept from them is the rightness or beauty of a wholly constructed and patterned world, a world elsewhere. (This is not the same as poetical truth in moral psychology.)

In Arendt's account, stories (in the most inclusive sense), begin in resentment toward life as given, but they transform what is otherwise meaningless or only incipiently meaningful into something impressively meaningful, something aesthetically compelling, and thus effect a reconciliation with life. But the reconciliation may be not with life so much as with a meaningful simulacrum of life—not paradise or utopia, but life replaced by a constructed representation of life, thanks to the power of imagination. Resentment is deflected or distracted; it is enchanted.

Arendt stages a struggle between meaning and truth. We cannot properly end the struggle by saying that they have no relation to each other and hence are not in competition with each other. (Arendt herself occasionally speaks of "the truth of a story," as in "Action and the 'Pursuit of Happiness' " (Dempf, Arendt, and Engel-Janosi, 1962: 5). Now, if Arendt does not believe in the possibility of truth, then the issue is dissolved. But things are not so easy. On the matter of truth, Arendt's teaching is of course subtle and complex, as always, but elusive. What makes it elusive is her distinction between rational truth and factual truth (1968a: 231 et seq.). She is eloquent in affirming human dependence on the integrity of factual truth against the efforts of massive liars, propagandists, and image-makers in either totalitarian or democratic societies. Factual truth is the truth of details. (Yet she can also speak of a genuine and "undeniable affinity," though limited, between lying and acting in the world, because the liar, like the actor, wants things to be different, wants to change the world" [250].) Rational truth, at the other end of the spectrum, is not clearly defined, but seems to mean the alleged absolute truth of one metaphysical system or another. What is not highlighted in Arendt's reflections on truth is the sizable middle realm of empirical truth, warrantable beliefs about historical and natural sequences and conditions, the very subject of some of her greatest writing.

Arendt is confident that Kant himself "would certainly have been prepared to sacrifice truth to the possibility of human freedom; for if we possessed truth we could not be free" (1968d: 26–27). I suppose that she is saying that if enough people knew that determinism is true, they would give up the aspiration to freedom. But the model is not Kant but Lessing, who, she says, would have sacrificed truth unhesitatingly "to humanity, to the possibility of friendship and of discourse among men" (27). I believe that the case against truth is truthfully made when we say not that we must be prepared to sacrifice truth to some other end, but rather that metaphysical or theological or religious absolutes that are put forth as truthful are not truthful, are never warrantable. Moral truth, however, does not need any of these absolutes. It is odd, by the way, that Arendt can simultaneously admire the meaningfulness that metaphysical and other systems confer on reality, even though they are "fallacies," while disparaging them in other texts not because they are false but because they are true.

What matters finally is not the inadequacies of Arendt's conceptualization of truth but her seeming willingness to sacrifice it, as she understands it, to other values. Whatever the tension she shows in adjudicating between the claims of truth and the claims of political freedom, she is clear that the claims of meaningfulness must prevail over the claims of truth. Nonetheless, I would quote a formulation that appears in "Religion and Politics" (1994 [1953]). She says that "freedom of thought and action is possible only under conditions of insecure and limited knowledge, as Kant demonstrated philosophically" (370). The wisdom in this view surpasses that of her other formulations.

There is a complication that I must mention because it may be relevant both to Arendt's views of truth and to her analysis of the role of ideology in totalitarianism. The complication is as follows. Without systematically incorporating her own religious belief into her published writings, she gives an unmistakable indication that biblical religion is the truth. I know of no other way of reading her essay "Religion and Politics," to which I just referred, than to take it as saying that biblical religion is the revelation of God's existence and of his words, and that therefore biblical religion is not to be seen as a meaning-conferring intellectual mode and nothing more, but rather as the truth, and the truth that of course makes the world meaningful. But, Arendt implies, the bestowal of meaning is not the point at which to start when considering the Bible. And even though the loss of belief does have the effect of emptying the world of meaning, the effect is incidental to the brute fact that the divine truth of revelation has been abandoned. To insist that biblical religion is just one more meaning-conferring system, and, even worse, to liken totalitarian ideologies to religion by calling these ideologies "secular religion" is to commit "blasphemy" (1994: 379).

In a letter to Karl Jaspers (March 4, 1951), she says that she holds to "a kind of (childish? because unquestioned) trust in God (as distinguished from faith)." But she insists that all "traditional religion as such, whether Jewish or Christian, holds nothing whatsoever for me anymore" (Arendt and Jaspers, 1992, letter 109: 165–66). Not faith, but trust — but religion nevertheless. Her religiousness, however it is to be understood, thus allows her to see all metaphysics as fallacies undeniably open to "dismantling" (even if generously), while exempting religion from the functionalist analysis of ideology.

Arendt is religious in some traditional sense in at least certain of her utterances. She recurrently expresses an unargued skepticism toward Darwin's theories, and also seems to disparage Deism as an ideology, which is here defined as a "mere pseudo science and pseudo philosophy" (*OT* 2: 468). She goes on to say that a theology based not on revelation as "a given reality" but rather on an *idea* of God would be "as mad" as a zoology that was no longer certain of the physical existence of animals (468–69). Her religiousness is one reason why she does not confine herself to pointing to the shock of wonder that there is a world at all — a sentiment that recurs in her work. She must add gratitude to wonder. Her trust makes her "happy" (Arendt and Jaspers, 1992: 166). To be grateful seems to suggest that there is an entity toward whom or toward which gratitude is properly directed. Wonder by itself cannot carry the burden of deriving from unbelief a feeling of attachment to the world.

In the first edition of *The Origins of Totalitarianism*, Arendt says that the real choice is that "between resentment and gratitude as basic possible modern attitudes" (*OT* 1: 438). The impossibility of gratitude when the biblical God is no longer believed in will engender nihilism. The essence of nihilism is the essence of totalitarianism. Only a nihilist can eventually become a totalitarian leader: "In his resentment of all laws merely given to him, he proclaims openly that everything is permitted and believes secretly that everything is possible" (438; see also *OT* 2: 387). Anything that is possible is permitted — or rather, must be permitted by us because there is nothing above us to give or withhold permission. A believer may resent God, may "resent the very fact that he is not the creator of the universe and himself" (*OT* 1: 438). But the *unbeliever* may also resent that same fact, and then proceed to become a re-maker of the world and of human nature itself (*OT* 2: 464–65). I think that Arendt is saying that nihilism did not kill God, but when belief in the biblical God died, nihilism had to follow. Still, to lament the loss of belief on the grounds that without it a culture could not hold together or that the old order could not endure or that people would perish from unbelief is only to offer pragmatic or what Arendt calls "atheistic" reasons for sponsoring belief ("Notes," 1967: 3).

Yet it must be mentioned that, at least on one occasion, she herself engages in a bit of functionalist analysis when she claims that modern ideologies are "far better fitted to immunize man's soul against the shocking impact of reality than any traditional religion we know." She rejects Marx's characterization of religion as opiate, and says that compared with "the various superstitions of the twentieth century ["political or psychological or social" ideologies], the pious resignation to God's will seems like a child's pocket-knife in competition with atomic weapons" (1968b: 135).

I say that Arendt is religious; but I do not mean that her work is a political theology. To the contrary. It is nevertheless a matter for serious regret that Arendt, precisely as a secular political theorist, encourages her audience to want meaning, to want it more than almost anything else (certainly more than what they may consider empirical truth), even though unrevealed. If Arendt herself has a truth that fills the void, the void for many people can be filled not by biblical revelation of truth but only by some kind of story, one or another meaning-conferring mode. Isn't that Arendt's reason for suggesting that, to the fullest extent possible, most of these modes should remain undisturbed by the claims of truth? If people cannot be attached to life unresentfully by biblical truth, then they must be attached to life by stories (in the most inclusive sense) that introduce meaningfulness into the world and thus perhaps appease resentment. I think that this is Arendt's position. I do not think that I am taking interpretative liberties.

Yet if we disregard the religious complication, which has only a slender overt textual basis, we as unbelievers are left with the strong impression that Arendt befriends all but one of the intellectual modes that give meaning to life, that introduce meaningfulness into it. She is unremitting in her denunciation of ideologies, even when they remain politically inert. My point is that whatever she may say, ideology is not much different from these other modes, including religion, in the functions they fulfill. She bitterly denounces functionalist analysis. She insists on trying to isolate ideology, but it cannot be isolated. In fact, she herself gives indications that it cannot be. It, too, gives meaning to life and is powerful just because of that. That is actually Arendt's point, but a point that she does not allow to interfere with her celebration of the quest for meaning. Why not then draw the lesson that we should be sparing in endorsing the quest for meaning? And sparing on the grounds that whole systems that confer meaningfulness tend to sacrifice the claims of truth — that is, warrantable empirical beliefs — whatever they may profess? Worst of all, these systems drive the perpetration of atrocities and do so at least partly in the *unavowed* name of meaningfulness, in the *unavowed* name of particular aesthetically compelling distortions of reality.

Those who devise the systems and those who try to realize them in the world probably would not recognize themselves as questers for meaning, as aesthetically driven. They typically hold that they are in touch with reality, or in touch with deeper strata of reality. Ideologists and ideologically motivated leaders and their associates boast of their adherence to truth, the truth of their cause or mission, no matter how many lies, big and small, they promote in pursuit of their end. They do not, of course, love truth for the sake of truth; they do not inquire into truth, but borrow from existing doctrines that they proceed to cheapen even further; they love their preconceived truth because it has a particular content. In fact, they may even call the truth whatever they feel that they must believe. In an elaborate sense, the wish is unconsciously father to the thought. The particular content serves all sorts of psychic and material interests. Nor do they abstractly love meaning for the sake of meaning, apart from its particular content. Even if they could be engaged in an abstract discussion of meaning, they would be uncomprehending or soon lose interest. Although they are aesthetically driven, their aesthetic cravings can be satisfied only by a particular pattern, not by any pattern whatever. They are not pure aesthetes of meaningfulness, desirous of finding meaning wherever it could be found — as, say, Arendt is, within very broad limits.

We all need stories of some kind. But different people need different kinds of story, whether anecdotes or novels, myths and legends, or metaphysical systems. Many people prefer no story to one with an uncongenial content. That means naturally that aesthetic cravings are entwined with urgent nonaesthetic considerations. A person wants certain main matters in life to be made aesthetic, their unattractive rawness transmuted into a gratifying form. Only a few want stories as stories, and the more the better, and the more kinds the better. Only a few have a *craving* for a formed or shaped reality, especially the whole social or natural reality outside their personal lives. These few are, let us say, full or parody intellectuals. But most of them do not always recognize the nature of their passion.

Thus, it is manifestly clear that Hitler, for example, believed in the *truth* of racism: he believed that Aryans were inherently and unalterably superior to non-Aryans, especially Jews, Slavs, and Gypsies. Stalin believed that capitalism was evil because it renounced equality on behalf of individual inequality. He believed in the *truth* of the "science" of class struggle. Once launched in power, however, both Hitler and Stalin grew ever more intoxicated by the beauty of a pattern, an imagined picture of the world in which either the Aryans ruled or the nameless masses ruled. It is the beauty of a pattern or picture that helps greatly to permit falsehood to be taken for truth and that makes falsehood so deadly. To the intellectually vulgar, to those who devise, consume, and work to realize ideologies, only distortion and untruth can be a source of beauty, and the beauty is correspondingly disfigured. (Compare what Arendt says on the aversion of erotic Socratic thinking to "ugliness and evil" [1978: 179].) It is hard to think that either Hitler or Stalin (or anyone) could have been so ruthless, so fanatical, unless they had become obsessively seized by their design on reality. They were zealots of meaning and haters of obstructive empirical truth. As Arendt in her strange, remarkable essay on Hermann Broch sympathetically formulates his idea about extremists: "They are aesthetes insofar as they are enchanted by the consonance of their own system, and they become murderers because they are prepared to sacrifice everything to this consonance, this 'beautiful' consistency" (1968e: 122–123).

I would now turn to Arendt's treatment of ideology, especially totalitarian ideology, with the intention of indicating that Arendt herself sometimes draws totalitarian ideology quite closely to other meaning-conferring modes of thought, even though she is insistent on setting ideology apart.

At some distance from *The Origins of Totalitarianism,* and familiar with Arendt's subsequent writings, we can say that this book is devoted to a question that Arendt takes from Daniel Ellsberg. In her essay "Lying in Politics," (1972), which deals with *The Pentagon Papers* and the causes of the Vietnam War, she sets herself to answer his question: "How could they?" (1972: 33). By the time she is finished, Arendt offers a parallel text to *Origins*. In "Lying in Politics," she explores the mentality of those who could pursue a war that defied common sense and common humanity: the image-makers, the problem-solvers, the ones who loved pure theory at the expense of reality. They were not vicious, but deluded. If they lacked the passions of abstract vengeance and hatred — passions that dominated totalitarian leaders — they nevertheless shared much else. "How could they?" The answer is that the makers of the Vietnam War were captured by a passion to impose a pattern on reality, at whatever cost. Arendt does not call them ideologues (or aesthetes), but many of the traits that figure in her concept of ideology appear in her discussion of the mentality of the Vietnam War-makers. We can generalize her point: the waging of a large war is the best model for and schooling in the protracted ruthlessness that marks the practice of totalitarianism. Permanent revolution is permanent war, while massive war is totalitarianism carried on for different purposes. Aesthetic infatuation with abstract patterns dominates the mentality of war leaders and totalitarian leaders alike.

"How could they?" How could the totalitarian leaders and their associates, followers, accomplices, and subordinates have done what they did? How could policies of such large-scale atrocity have been conceived and executed? How could totalitarianism exist? Arendt's answer revolves around the concept of ideology. We can piece together Arendt's definition of the phenomenon. Totalitarianism is a political system of terror imposed on a population in order to maintain total domination, the purpose of which is to actualize an ideological interpretation of reality at any cost. The given reality must be replaced by a new one through relentless destruction and equally relentless reconstruction. The destruction is envisaged as purification, and the process of reconstruction aims to achieve an ever greater purity. Arendt makes a signal contribution to our understanding of the methods and workings of terror as well as to our understanding of the nature and appeals of ideology. She is unequaled in this effort. In this essay, I concentrate on ideology.

What is ideology? At one point, Arendt calls it (in the particular form of anti-Semitism after 1914) "a weird mixture of half-truths and wild superstitions" (*OT* 2: 53). (Notice how, at least here, she invokes truth to discredit ideology.) More fully, she repeatedly refers to ideology as fiction or a fiction. Ideology is, in her analysis, an all-embracing fiction that aims to instigate and guide the work of destruction and reconstruction. Why does she call it fiction? She must think every ideology empirically false — not only post-1914 anti-Semitism — even though she does not commonly use the word "false" in writing about it. Suddenly starting to talk about the relevance of truth in political life would seem incongruent. Yet ideology is fiction, a system of fiction. What other contrast to fiction could there be, in this context, besides truth? Her analysis does suggest that any comprehensive theory of nature or history must be largely fictional. (How far apart are these comprehensive theories from admirable metaphysical fallacies?) For Nazism (with earlier race thinking, anti-Semitism, and racism in the background), nature is the struggle of races;

for Stalinism (with Marxism and Leninism in the background), history is the struggle of classes. These two struggles turn into world-organizing fictions when they are seized by totalitarian ideologists.

Notice that Arendt does not accept the usual, Marx-inspired view that ideology is either deliberate or unconscious rationalization in the sense of offering a justification that is meant to hide the reality of economic and political class-interests. Rather, ideology is fairly transparent and fairly predictive of future conduct. Although she makes something of the cynical manipulation of ideological belief by elites, she does not always exempt them from it. Nor should she do so, if she is to be consistent. Ideology seduces and then possesses those who adhere to it, and they find themselves and their interests remade by it. It is the promise of a new world.

When the word "fiction" is used, but not to mean a lie about a particular fact, we are obviously in the realm of stories. Is an ideology in Arendt's concept, then, a kind of story? I do not think that she ever says so. It is as if the word "story" is too hallowed to be extended to cover ideology. We have seen that Arendt herself appears to assimilate every meaning-conferring intellectual mode to a story or a kind of story. She appears, however, to exempt religion, biblical religion, most definitely, from the category of story, on the grounds that revelation is trusted to be *true*. (I do not know what other word to use.) But she also seems to refuse to allow ideologies to be included as stories. It turns out, however, that as she accumulates characterizations of totalitarian ideologies in *Origins*, they are often described in the same terms, or nearly the same, as those she uses for stories in every sense: ordinary, expanded, or metaphysical; and also included are two genres she takes up briefly in *Origins*, namely, myths and legends. But both religion and ideologies (whether totalitarian or not) are excluded.

There is brilliance in extending the notion of story to include many meaning-conferring modes; but there is something arbitrary in excluding ideologies. As for excluding religion, all I can say is that to an unbeliever, religion is just another meaning-conferring mode, with no more claim to deference than any other such mode. Whatever is worshipped becomes a religious object, whether it is divinity, a leader, the group, or wealth. But our concern here is primarily with Arendt's exclusion of ideology from the category of respectable meaning-conferring modes. My main contention is that there is no difference, in nature, between ideology and other meaning-conferring modes. There are of course differences in content; also, we may like some modes better than others, and some particular specimen within a mode better than another specimen, and even think that some specimens or even modes have a better influence on people than others. But then our judgment relies on considerations independent of the power of a specimen or of a whole mode to confer meaning on reality. We must appeal to truth or morality or both much more regularly than Arendt does. As we have seen, she typically does not want the claims of truth, in particular, to get in the way of meaning.

The differences among meaning-conferring modes that I would emphasize concern how they are taken by those attracted to them. The question is whether or not any of them incites fanaticism; that is, fanatical adherence of such intensity as to encourage utter ruthlessness. I think, however, that nearly any meaning-conferring mode can incite fanaticism, even fictional stories in the narrow sense. Certainly metaphysical (including theological) systems and religious faith and cultural myths and legends — all of them meaning-conferring — have done so and can be counted on to do so again. I grant that fanaticism can attach itself to metaphysics (especially) only when it is cheapened and then taken with a complete literalism. Arendt refers to the fate of Darwinism at the hands of murderous racism and to the fate of Marxism at the hands of murderous revolutionaries. The fact remains that any meaning-conferring mode can be a cause of fanaticism. Arendt says that ideologies remain "harmless . . . as long as they are not believed in seriously" (*OT* 2: 457). Of course, any idea would be harmless in that condition. But any idea can, in certain circumstances, appeal with such force as to gain serious, literal-minded adherents who then become fanatical in their enactment of that idea.

I wish to add that although Arendt occasionally uses the word "fanaticism," its sense is not prominent; the passionate belief that is invested in ideology does not figure very much. Absolute literal-mindedness does figure, but in dealing with Hitler and Stalin and their respective associates, we are confronted not only with literal adherence to doctrine. The literal-mindedness derives from an extraordinary intensity of commitment. Relatedly, I think that the higher the rank in the totalitarian party hierarchy, the more intense the ideological passion, the greater the fanaticism. Where there is fanaticism there is obsession with the meaning conferred by the ideology on all of reality, with the story that the ideology tells about reality. Fanaticism is, in part, a condition of being overpowered aesthetically, as I have said. The nameable vices are dwarfed by the scale of atrocities and could not on their own lead to totalitarian practices. Only the passion for a particular meaningfulness could do so.

The appeal is precisely that the idea confers meaning on all of reality, a new, attractive meaning that, if pursued ruthlessly, promises a new world. What accounts for the transition to fanaticism? Arendt speaks of favoring circumstances such as the feeling that there are superfluous and lonely masses of people. A few leaders see in them the raw material of a new opportunity; the people themselves find meaning in being captured and caught up in new projects. Instructed by Arendt, however, I doubt that there can be any general theory to account for the initial appearance of a particular fanaticism. In a revelatory footnote to her essay of 1954, "Understanding and Politics: (The Difficulties of Understanding)," she says, "An event belongs to the past, marks an end, insofar as elements with their origins in the past are gathered together in its sudden crystallization; but an event belongs to the future, marks a beginning, insofar as this crystallization itself can never be deduced from its own elements, but is caused invariably by some factor which lies in the realm of human freedom" (1994: 326). Fanaticism is a free (hence unpredictable) leap into mental bondage, and it can never be fully understood, just as a *system* of fanaticism like totalitarian dictatorship is a transcendence of its elements and therefore can never be fully understood.

It is noteworthy—it has been noticed and discussed many times—that Arendt's work on totalitarianism after *Origins* downplays the importance of ideology in totalitarianism, especially in its maintenance as a system. The concept of thoughtless conformity to the administration and execution of a policy of legalized or authoritatively sanctioned murder on a vast scale that *Eichmann in Jerusalem* explores and that is famously distilled in the phrase "banality of evil" takes the place of ideological fanaticism. In a letter to Mary McCarthy, written in the wake of the controversy aroused by the book on Eichmann, Arendt goes so far as to say: "If one reads the book carefully, one sees that Eichmann was much less influenced by ideology than I assumed in the book on totalitarianism. The impact of ideology upon the individual may have been overrated by me" (Arendt and McCarthy, 1995: 147). (She also says that she will postpone speaking about the "contrast" between radical evil and the banality of evil [148].)

That people can play their part in a policy of atrocities unthinkingly and mechanically is undeniable. But I think that it would be misleading to see Eichmann as devoid of a passionate commitment to something other than his career. If not personally an anti-Semite, he was surely a devoted patriot and believer in Germany's racial destiny as defined by Hitler. He would have worked to kill any category of the population, if ordered to do so, but simply would not have understood a command to round up and kill loyal non-Jewish German patriots. Such rigorous devotion cannot be understood without some reference to an initial fanatical zeal, a zeal instigated by Nazi ideology. Only a prisoner of a fiction, only someone aesthetically intoxicated by a design for a new reality, could possibly be so immune to moral considerations. If the inability to think, as Arendt defines that inability—here, as the inability to put oneself in the place of others—is made into a *sufficient* explanation of Nazism, from the top to the bottom of the party hierarchy, and masses beneath it, the resulting analysis is too reductive. Indeed, it is ideology that helps to sustain

the inability to think, just as the inability to think initially draws the susceptible to an ideology. Ideology is indissociably linked to the inability to think, but
they are two distinct phenomena.

Whatever Arendt's second thoughts, I believe that her original analysis of
totalitarianism in which ideology holds central place is essentially correct. At
the same time, I think that the hold of ideology on the great mass of people
may be exaggerated in *Origins*. Numerous people have numerous motives and
susceptibilities. If they like stories that make reality more meaningful, they
tend to like even more some immediate answers to the daily problems of
staying afloat. Active participants in the party and state are the most ideologically driven. The parallel text, "Lying in Politics," makes this clear.

Ideology is of capital importance. The main reason is that an ideology tells a
life-encompassing story. An ideology confers meaning on life by first explaining the sources of calamity and then inflaming the will to change over reality so
that a plenitude of desirable meaning may be realized. The story changes the
hearts of those who succumb to it. Falling under the spell of an ideology is just
like undergoing a religious conversion and remaining devout. As with religion,
so with ideology: under the spell, leaders, their associates, and their followers
may in some conditions be merciless in defending or spreading a doctrine. So,
too, patriots or loyalists use arms in defending a way of life that is based on
myths and legends that make them feel that their way of life is superior and
irreplaceable. In all cases, the claims of truth and the claims of morality are
spurned when critics say that these claims conflict with and override any
ideological or religious or cultural or political commitment. Alternatively, the
defenders maintain, not always cynically, that a higher truth or higher morality is incorporated in the commitment. Arendt strenuously resists, however,
the likening of ideology to religion or metaphysics or cultural outlook. She
hates any analysis that effaces substantive differences in the name of a func-
tionalism that shows how ideology plays the same role in the affective and
intellectual lives of its adherents as religion or metaphysical systems or myths
and legends. Her waspish rejoinder to Jules Monnerot's excellent criticism of
"Religion and Politics" is a case in point (1994: 384–86; for Monnerot's letter
on her article, see Monnerot, 1954: 131–34).

For all her irritation, there are uncanny resemblances or affinities between
ideology and meaning-conferring modes that Arendt herself draws to her
readers' attention. In addition, a determined reader can find yet other resemblances that beg to be pointed out. All this means that there are significant
affinities between what Arendt admires and what she deplores. She admires
some of the very same characteristics in stories (in all senses: fictional, ex-

panded, and metaphysical) that she deplores in ideologies. The best and the worst — or, at least, the good and the bad — often emerge in her work as kindred. This is the case not only with stories in all senses and ideologies, but also with such pairs of concepts as action and lying; genuine political actors and totalitarian elites; warrior heroes and sinister secret agents; those who bind themselves by promises for authentic political action and conspirators; the homelessness of philosophical thinking and that of the masses in modern life; the abstraction from reality and the senses that is shared by genuine thinking and ideology; contingency and meaninglessness; meaning and untruth. None of these exemplify the dialectical unity of opposites, or the Platonist teaching that the worst can only be the deformation of the best, but something tragic that I find hard to grasp, as if Arendt were repelled not only by what she deplored but also by what she admired (and were largely indifferent to everything in between). In any case, our attention here is directed toward the affinities between stories (in all Arendtian senses) and ideologies, especially totalitarian ideologies. (Metaphysical doctrines are frozen thinking, ideology is cheapened metaphysics, totalitarian ideology is a perversion of ideology because it is, deliberately, "a political weapon, not a theoretical doctrine" [OT, 2: 159].)

I mention first those moments in *Origins* when she is at least fairly explicit about the affinities between stories and ideologies. The major declared affinity lies in the ability of ideologies, just like stories, to satisfy in the masses (we should say, in adherents, especially) what she calls a "longing for fiction." The human mind as such is drawn to believe that "structural consistency is superior to mere occurrence." Furthermore, all human beings, Arendt says, "need the constant transformation of chaotic and accidental conditions into a man-made pattern of relative consistency" (*OT* 2: 352). Consistency is close to meaningfulness because it is practically the same as regularity, the absence of chaos and accident. Mitigating again her emphasis on the needs of the masses rather than on those of elites and their followers, we find Arendt saying that totalitarian movements "conjure up a lying world of consistency which is more adequate to the needs of the human mind than reality itself; in which through sheer imagination, uprooted masses can feel at home and are spared the never-ending shocks which real life and real experiences deal to human beings and their expectations" (353). The needs of the human mind that ideology serves are the needs that stories (in all Arendtian senses) also serve. She also says the generalizations of propagandized ideology establish "a world fit to compete with the real one, whose main handicap is that it is not logical, consistent, or organized" (362).

At these moments in *Origins,* Arendt herself appears to subsume ideology under the comprehensive category of story. But there are also moments when her descriptions betray unremarked affinities between totalitarian ideology and the meaning-conferring modes she admires. Here are some examples. Arendt says that an ideology, unlike "a simple opinion," claims "to possess the key to history, or the solution for all the 'riddles of the universe,' or the intimate knowledge of the hidden universal laws which are supposed to rule nature and man" (159). On this account, how do ideologies, whether total-itarian or not, differ from some metaphysical systems and most theology, both of which modes Arendt asks us to admire and cherish? Further, when she discusses the way in which totalitarian ideologies deduce everything from a single premise and then try to force reality into conforming to the logical tracing out of the implications of that single premise, she says that such log-icality has a coercive and murderous force. She then traces the hold of such logicality, even when murderous, to our "fear of contradicting ourselves" (473)—the very fear that she elsewhere calls the common root of Socratic conscience and the categorical imperative. But the more relevant point is that an intricate deduction from a single premise is a trait of many metaphysical systems, including theological ones. She also says that ideologies "are never interested in the miracle of being" (469). Yet her consideration of metaphys-ical systems in *Thinking* demonstrates that a number of these systems also fail to show that interest, fail to register the shock of wonder (fused with admira-tion) at the fact that there is a world at all.

All stories, in whatever intellectual mode, coerce the mind. Anything with a plot coerces reality and, correspondingly, forces the mind to keep going until it discovers the denouement. There is a craving for resolution. Also, Arendt says in summary that all ideologies contain totalitarian elements and only total-itarian ideologies develop them fully: total explanation of the nature of things, abstraction from experience and the senses, and deduction from a single prem-ise (470–71). But all three "totalitarian" elements can easily be found in meta-physical systems, and sometimes developed as fully as they are in ideologies.

In sum, ideologies, whether totalitarian or not, whether murderous or not, are not different in their appeal from fictional stories, historical stories, per-sonal stories, myths, legends, religion, and metaphysical systems (including theology), if that appeal stems from the ability of any of these intellectual modes to confer meaning on reality. To the extent that the success of totalitari-anism depends on its ideological power to organize reality into meaningful-ness, ideology performs the same function as these modes. The only difference is in content at any given time. But almost any content that is apparently innocuous can turn lethal. Then the claims of truth and morality press them-selves urgently. The most harmless mode is fictional stories that do not hide their fictional quality; but even they are not completely harmless. Practically any specimen of any of the other modes has induced and can induce fanaticism, the ruthless will to realize the ambition to make the world over in accordance with the aesthetic imperatives of a fiction or story about the world or picture of it.

How odd, how right. The best aspect of Arendt's analysis of totalitarianism is the patiently and brilliantly elaborated view of the place of ideology in it. Her continuous sensitivity to the human need for converting reality (non-aesthetic, unaesthetic) into something aesthetically compelling enables her profundity in regard to the nature of totalitarianism. Yet, I think that her steady encouragement of that need, which she felt keenly and which she (somewhat misleadingly) attributed above all to the masses rather than to intellectuals, semi-intellectuals, and pseudo-intellectuals, is one of the less good features of her work. The less than good element (I dare not call it bad) in her work facilitates the best. This is another kind of affinity.

Is there a lesson? Our greatest teachers, and Arendt is one of them, should encourage us to endure meaninglessness. Not that anyone can live without moments in which things appear to cohere or add up or fall into place or resemble a pattern with an intention or purpose. We all need, in Robert Frost's words, "a momentary stay against confusion." But the quest for *overall* meaningfulness (contra Arendt and perhaps Frost) should be disowned, and local meanings allowed to suffice. It is curious to watch Arendt in *Thinking* try to read Heidegger as a philosopher straining to answer Leibniz's question, "Why is there anything at all and not, rather, nothing?" In his *Introduction to Metaphysics*, Heidegger is actually working to wean us from that metaphysical question, so that we may rest in an attitude of wonder at the fact that there is a world at all. In contrast, the question of why sends us in search of what is now untenable — what Leibniz called a sufficient reason — and hence in search of some transcendent point or purpose that is supposed to confer and guarantee an overall meaningfulness (for Arendt's discussion, see 1978: 145 ff.).

If atheism is deemed an ugly truth, then we should learn to say with Keats (the worshiper of beauty) that "an eagle is not so fine a thing as truth" (Letter to George and Georgianna Keats, 14 February–3 May, 1819, in Keats, 1970: 230). Aestheticism should not interfere with our effort to come as close to the truth as possible. Indeed, the constraint of truth need not be a constraint at all. It can be a release into an uncommon beauty. In other words, atheism's overall meaninglessness may make particular meanings all the more precious and, what is more, may intensify wonder at the fact that there is a world at all. But if Arendt holds that atheism is an ugly falsehood, a falsehood that must sponsor meaninglessness, disagreement with her must remain unresolved.

References

Arendt, Hannah. *The Origins of Totalitarianism.* 1st ed. New York: Harcourt, Brace, 1951. Cited as *OT 1*. 2d ed. New York: World (Meridian), 1958. Cited as *OT 2*.

——. "The Spiritual Quest of Modern Man." (1952). The Hannah Arendt Papers at the Library of Congress. Available online at ⟨http://memory.loc.gov/ammem/arendthtml/mharendtFolderP05.html⟩.

——. "Religion and Politics." *Essays in Understanding 1930–1954.* Ed. Jerome Kohn. New York: Harcourt Brace, 1994 (1953).

——. *The Human Condition.* Chicago: University of Chicago Press, 1958.

——. *Eichmann in Jerusalem.* 2d ed. New York: Viking, 1965 (1963).

——. "Notes on Dostoyevsky's *The Possessed*" (1967). The Hannah Arendt Papers at the Library of Congress. Available online at ⟨http://memory.loc.gov/ammem/arendthtml/mharendtFolderP05.html⟩.

——. "Truth and Politics." *Between Past and Future.* 2d ed. New York: Viking, 1968a.

——. "What Is Authority?" *Between Past and Future.* 2d ed. New York: Viking, 1968b.

——. "Isak Dinesen: 1885–1963." *Men in Dark Times.* New York: Harcourt, Brace and World, 1968c.

——. "On Humanity in Dark Times." *Men in Dark Times.* New York: Harcourt, Brace and World, 1968d.

——. "Hermann Broch: 1886–1951." *Men in Dark Times.* New York: Harcourt, Brace and World, 1968e.

——. "Lying in Politics." *Crises of the Republic.* New York: Harcourt Brace Jovanovich, 1972.

——. *On Revolution.* New York: Penguin, 1977 (1963, 1965).

——. *Thinking. Life of the Mind.* Vol. 1. New York: Harcourt Brace Jovanovich, 1978.

Arendt, Hannah, and Karl Jaspers. *Correspondence 1926–1969.* Eds. Lotte Kohler and Hans Saner. Trans. Robert and Rita Kimber. New York: Harcourt Brace Jovanovich, 1992.

Arendt, Hannah, and Mary McCarthy. *Between Friends: The Correspondence of Hannah Arendt and Mary McCarthy, 1944–1975.* Ed. Carol Brightman. New York: Harcourt Brace, 1995.

Dempf, A., H. Arendt, and F. Engel-Janosi, eds. *Politische Ordnung und Menschliche Existenz.* Munich: Beck, 1962.

Keats, John. *Letters of John Keats.* Ed. Robert Gittings. Oxford: Oxford University Press, 1970.

Monnerot, Jules. Letter to the Editor (Henry Kissinger). *Confluence* 2:4 (1954): 131–34.

Nietzsche, Friedrich. *Beyond Good and Evil. Basic Writings of Nietzsche.* Ed. and trans. Walter Kaufmann. New York: Modern Library, 1968a.

——. *Genealogy of Morals. Basic Writings of Nietzsche.* Ed. and trans. Walter Kaufmann. New York: Modern Library, 1968b.

15

Can Cultures Be Judged?: Two Defenses of
Cultural Pluralism in Isaiah Berlin's Work

My contention is that in Isaiah Berlin's work there are abundant elements for two defenses of radical cultural pluralism, even though he does not distinguish them. One is the aesthetic defense; the other is the anti-universalist defense. I begin with the aesthetic defense, which is not often discussed. I grant that I have assembled the aesthetic elements from various portions of Berlin's work, and do not deny that Berlin himself might have dismissed my attribution and thought that I had taken improper interpretative liberties with his work.

I should say at the beginning that my view is that the best case for cultural pluralism sees it as the inevitable, if often not very admirable, outcome of

A version of this essay was given as the second annual Judith N. Shklar memorial lecture at Harvard University, April 1999. I thank Stanley Hoffmann for his kind invitation and the members of the audience for their spirited scepticism. I also wish to thank Jeremy Waldron and Amy Gutmann for their encouragement, and Jonathan Riley for his detailed response (2002).

It is worth noting that Shklar admired Berlin's work, and thought that they shared an intellectual affinity. Yet her writings are free of aestheticism, and she sometimes reproached it, while I believe that Berlin's work is immersed in it. She was also much further away from anything resembling relativism than Berlin was. If both she and Berlin are to be classified as liberals, I would say that they are as different as two liberals can be.

personal freedom, which is the highest value. But Berlin occasionally derives the worth of freedom from its role in securing pluralism, and thus reverses this liberal evaluation (1998a: 58). I will not discuss the tie between liberalism and pluralism in this essay.

The Aesthetic Defense

In reading and rereading some of Berlin's work, whether to teach him through the years, or to think about him after his death in 1997 had elicited an abundance of commentary, I have been struck by his aestheticism. If you are bothered by his work, as I am, though deeply respectful of it, you may try to locate the source of that concern. And if, at the same time, you may suffer, to some extent, but not to the same extent as Berlin, from aestheticism, as I do, then you may grow sensitive, perhaps hypersensitive, to it when it appears in the work of any major political theorist.

Let me now enter at least a provisional definition of aestheticism as I use the term in reference to Berlin's work. By aestheticism, I mean first, the disposition to look or hunt for beauty (and sublimity), in matters present to the senses or the mind; and second, the disposition to regard some inherently nonaesthetic phenomena as more or less aesthetic phenomena, and therefore to justify these nonaesthetic phenomena as we justify manifestly aesthetic phenomena — namely, by their imputed beauty (or sublimity). Therefore one considers other values, like morality or truth or usefulness, as irrelevant to the appreciation we bestow. Artworks are for us manifestly aesthetic phenomena, whatever else they may also be or have been. And an aesthete prizes them above all else for their beauty. A radical aesthetic move is made when an aesthete chooses to see or conceptualize what appears to be an inherently nonaesthetic phenomenon as a thing of beauty and prize it for its beauty. My suggestion is that Berlin's own political thought (as it comes out in conceptual essays as well as in essays on texts in political and moral theory) is fundamentally aesthetic in its orientation. Berlin is an aesthete in a quite comprehensive sense.

I don't mean to take advantage of any bad connotations the word *aesthete* has. I'm not wholly ashamed of my own aestheticism. What worries me, however, is the disposition, shown by Berlin, to use the perceived or imagined beauty of an inherently nonaesthetic phenomenon as a way of exempting it from moral or epistemological scrutiny. To state my interpretation briefly, I claim first — and this is almost incidental — that Berlin celebrates any culture that produces artworks of great beauty, even if that culture seems morally deficient and organizes its life around pervasive untruth. But that claim fades into insignificance in comparison to another one, which is that he tends to look upon practically any culture or way of life as if it itself were a work of art, and as such, except in egregious cases, which are rare, deserving of aesthetic contemplation and of aesthetic praise, almost no matter how severe a judgment of it by the standard of morality or of truth would be.

I don't attribute to Berlin the extreme and narrow view that a culture exists only to produce art and is justified only by great art. Nor do I mean that Berlin is sympathetic to the effort "to impose an aesthetic model upon reality, to say that everything should obey the rules of art." Such an activist and romantic aestheticism is repugnant to Berlin because it presumes to treat human beings as "stuff" (1999: 146–47). A way of life does not have to be made over aesthetically for it to deserve to be regarded aesthetically. Furthermore, Berlin does not usually establish the comparative worth of cultures by the quality of their art. Berlin's aestheticism is more subtle and perhaps more insidious than any easy, untroubled, and perhaps slightly vulgar or hysterical aestheticism. The whole point, in any case, is that Berlin is, in principle, averse to comparing the worth of either works of art or whole cultures. For him, the realm of the aesthetic and of the putatively aesthetic is made up of phenomena that demand and deserve not to be compared, one to another, but to be admired, each one, in itself, for itself—to be admired as both excellent and sufficient. Ranking artworks or cultures is out of order philosophically, no matter what one's personal aesthetic preferences may be.

I speak very broadly; numerous details are needed if Berlin's aestheticism is to be delineated accurately and fairly. I hope to mention some of these details as I go along. But my sense has grown that Berlin's work is animated by aestheticism, and the net effect can be quite disturbing. If Berlin is a liberal, he is a liberal with only part of his soul.

His aestheticism shows itself even in his intellectual method, which is a method of generosity. He shows an extraordinary ability to restate philosophical positions that he does not fully accept or accept at all. In restating them, he enhances them. It may be that he even sympathizes with some positions toward which we think he ought to feel dislike or abhorrence. (In fact, in a given essay, he sometimes attributes a position to a thinker and then in another essay presents that position as his own.) Feeling sympathy or not, he gives the impression of an intimate impersonation of ideas, of making them not so much believable as capable of being believed in by others, though not by ourselves. This is a rare gift that we should treasure. But enhancing philosophical outlooks and systems through inspired exegesis and thereby presenting them to the reader as worthy of serious but not necessarily credulous attention—to aestheticize them—is not the same as, is discontinuous with, promoting the view that almost all cultures deserve aesthetic apprehension. A culture is activity, often based on, to use Berlin's own description, a "set of illusions and fantasies" (1999: 119); it is not a system of thought offered as a deliberate and impersonal contribution to speculation.

My aim, then, is to explore Berlin's aestheticism — in regard to artworks and cultures — and also to try to say why he espouses it. Of course, more than his temperament is involved, more than his reflexive or cultivated tastes or his habits of mind. He has commitments of a very serious sort and among these commitments, one, above all, drives him to emphasize the realm of the aesthetic and the possibly aesthetic. He is not self-importantly self-pleasing, but philosophical, in his aestheticism.

What, then, is Berlin's ultimate commitment? I find that he is desirous, and urgently so, to defend the human stature. Let me add that this is my phrase, not Berlin's. I adapt Hannah Arendt's phrase, "the stature of man," as it appears in the title and body of her essay "The Conquest of Space and the Stature of Man" (1968).

Berlin wants to defend humanity against the effort, sustained if not concerted, made by some human beings, especially but not only some philosophers and some scientists, to reduce humanity in its own eyes, and to do so not for the sake of making it more modest and less cruel, as Montaigne and Hobbes did, but to reduce it out of a devotion to telling what is held to be the truth. Such devotion to truth, of course, may mask other urges like a rage for order or a will to power. In any case, Berlin wants to refute, if possible, philosophical arguments that make human beings into something mechanical or only animal, into material, or bodies in motion, or, on the other hand, predetermined by nonhuman or more than human forces. He is against all forms of determinism, as his famous essay "Historical Inevitability" (1954) richly demonstrates. He believes that these determinisms are not proven; and he hopes that they will never be proven. Even more, he does not want them believed, even if one day they seem to be proven, as he indicates in " 'From Hope and Fear Set Free' " (1964).

Much of Berlin's work is given to challenging one kind of determinism or another. His philosophical project is to uphold the human stature. He invests himself in the passion that has mastered German philosophy since Kant and even before. For that reason, he is much closer to Hannah Arendt and Leo Strauss than he is to practically any liberal, even Mill. Aestheticism is Berlin's gorgeous weapon against reduction, against determinism in all its forms.

Berlin aspires to defend human dignity, to use the term of Pico della Mirandola in the Renaissance. Dignity is at least a more familiar notion than human stature. But where Pico tries to establish human dignity by placing humanity in a hierarchy with god above it, the angels perhaps not quite as good as it (such is Pico's radicalism), and other creatures below it, Berlin has no hierarchy. He has only humanity and other creatures; and he has no interest in the other creatures. He is nevertheless quite close to Pico, who locates human dignity in humanity's protean, self-creating character. Berlin's constant question is, in effect, How shall the human race think of itself, and therefore treat itself? How shall we think of ourselves, though unaided by any supernatural revelation, and in the face of some philosophy and some science? To think of ourselves too lowly is to guarantee that we will treat one another basely, inhumanly; or block human unfolding. In the words of Kant from *Perpetual Peace*, human beings need only "to realise consciously that they are not free beings for them to become in their own eyes the most wretched of all earthly creatures" (1991: 123).

In truth, there is ample evidence that can be used to repel determinism of every kind. In his excellent book on Isaiah Berlin, John Gray says that for Berlin the defining characteristic of human beings and the source of their excellence is the faculty of choice. Writing in "John Stuart Mill and the Ends of Life" (1959), and elsewhere, Berlin emphasizes the necessity and difficulty of choice, and links it to much that is remarkable and praiseworthy about human beings. Yet I find the term a bit anemic, a bit too academic, and would rather underline Berlin's emphasis on creativity, human creativity. Berlin is also aware that it is not impossible that individual choice may itself be deterministically explained. Furthermore, he is not constantly preoccupied with the fact that ordinary individuals go about their everyday lives making choices and then trying to live with or evade the consequences of these choices. His work does not glow with the novelist's fascination with everyday particularity. When I say that Berlin is, instead, philosophically interested in human creativity, I mean that the rebuttal or refutation of every determinism depends especially on the mysterious creativity shown, on the one hand, by artists in every medium, whether verbal, musical, painterly, or some other, and shown, on the other hand, by those mysterious contingencies that go into the creative formation and continuous elaboration of a culture or whole way of life. Neither kind of creativity is ordinary; neither is merely personal, though eminent individuals create art and may stand out in the creation of cultures. (To be fair, Berlin does not, in the manner of Nietzsche or Leo Strauss, tie the human stature to the existence of the sort of high excellence that only a few can reach, and only on the backs of others. In that respect, he is closer to Arendt, for whom the stature of the whole human race is not dependent on the highest type of man.) Of course, Berlin never denies that creativity exists in other forms and expressions besides art and ways of life. He refers to "the unpredictability of all human activities" (1999: 147).

But my interpretation of his work inclines or even induces me to hold the view that he is drawn to those sorts of creativity that either must be regarded aesthetically or can, he suggests, lend themselves to being regarded aesthetically. It may also be plausible that creativity in aesthetic modes or in modes that may perhaps lend themselves to aesthetic attitudes are the clearest cases of creativity, free and eruptive creativity, whereas other forms and expressions of human creativity may be so tied to the necessities or practicalities of the human condition or to ubiquitous human aims and goals that creativity may seem too much like adaptability or Rousseau's "perfectibility" or even an expectable response. Or the creativity of, say, scientific inquiry, may seem too closely guided by the logic of the next step (in Arthur Koestler's phrase), too closely locked in a developing pattern, to be felt as genuinely and eruptively creative, even though it regularly is. But artworks and whole ways of life keep their mystery. Their essence is mystery. Why they are as they are cannot really be explained; surely, not fully explained. They are simply there, and if not totally gratuitous or unpurposive, their aesthetic qualities lift them above all possibility of being encompassable by the usual kinds of explanation. They are subject to limits but not strict determinants. The effects of creativity are not exhaustively traceable to antecedent causes, much less could they have been predicted. Unpredictability is another way of referring to creativity. But the unpredictability at issue is essentially benign because of its link with beauty or sublimity. Horrible human unpredictability is another matter, an inverted creativity.

Thus, the very sign of human stature, the very source of human dignity, the very core of human distinctiveness, is valuable, unpredictable creativity, especially that creativity that is either manifestly aesthetic or (supposedly) lends itself to aestheticized apprehension. When human beings create beauty or sublimity, when they allow the observer to experience the attitudes and feelings appropriate to beauty and sublimity, then if that observer is also a philosopher, he or she may engage in the great effort to defend the human stature against all determinism, all reductions, all stupendously inaccurate simplifications.

In his radical aestheticism, then, Berlin is suggesting that it is legitimate for the philosophical observer to regard cultures, whole ways of life, aesthetically; to consider them as if they were, from one valid perspective, like works of art. If they are like works of art, then we can contemplate them, appreciate them, praise them. We can carry to their study that set of attitudes and sentiments we normally think appropriate for artworks, but only for artworks. Berlin's radicalism consists in the effort, precisely, to break with normality by extending to cultures the kind of receptivity that most people think is suitable mainly for artworks, and if otherwise suitable, then only for nature and for a few human activities.

Now, the stakes are great for Berlin when practically any culture or way of life is introduced as significant evidence for unpredictable creativity and hence for an affirmation of the human stature. He has to convince us that human beings are sufficiently free of one necessity or another when they form and keep their ways of life. Not only Marxist economic determinism, but Montesquieu's partway geographical determinism, Spencer's imperatives of adaptation, a political determinism of friends and enemies, and any theory of inevitable progress or inevitable decline or endless recurrence are not finally to be trusted to explain why a culture is as it is, much less why the art it produces is as it is.

But if the stakes are great for Berlin, they are also great for all those who worry, as I do, that the conversion of cultures as wholes into aesthetic or near-aesthetic objects suitable for our contemplation, appreciation, and praise may imply an immoral aestheticism or one indifferent to the claims of truth. If every way of life rests, at least to some extent, on untruths and on this basis or some other, institutionalizes or inveterately practices wickedness, then the cost of Berlin's aestheticism is high; for some of us, too high. If we cannot regard cultures except aesthetically, which turns out to mean that we can only appreciate them and do so in an aesthetic frame of mind, then we theoretically countenance injustice and untruth. At the same time, the contrast on this score between artworks and cultures is stark: we need not countenance injustice and untruth in our appreciation of artworks, even if we agree that aesthetic judgment excludes moral and epistemological judgment. Could there not be, then, some other way, than aesthetically, of resisting determinism and hence defending and affirming the human stature? Or, if there is none, is there another way, perhaps, of defending and affirming human dignity, apart from the concept of human stature and even apart from the question of determinism? Let me suspend the question of alternatives for a while.

There is one complication that I must mention here, which seems to go against what I have been saying about Berlin's aestheticism. Berlin only occasionally speaks of aesthetic judgment, but when he does, he means by it the sort of judgment we would have to use if human beings were determined in their conduct. He says that if people lack free will, we could not attribute responsibility to them. All we could do is regard them as if they were objects and then observe them aesthetically. Of course, Berlin wants to be able to believe in free will and continue to attribute moral and other kinds of responsibility to people. When he speaks in this manner, about aesthetic judgment, as in " 'From Hope and Fear Set Free' " and "My Intellectual Path" (1998) he is defending the possibility of moral judgment and seeming to relegate aesthetic judgment to a hypothetical and lamentable status. This usage is, however, incidental and uncharacteristic. So that when he comes to cultures and whole

ways of life, although he does not usually refer explicitly to aesthetic judgment, he is clearly suggesting that they are to be regarded like artworks; and
like artworks, they are free, unpredictable and finally mysterious creations.
The aesthetic and the undetermined go together, and the claims of morality
and truth declared out of bounds, a conceptually improper encroachment of
practical or epistemological judgment on aesthetic appreciation.

Even in regard to one's aesthetic response to human beings, Berlin reports
with sympathy, even if without overt endorsement, the view of J. G. Hamann
in the eighteenth century that understanding a person is like understanding a
work of art because the spiritual essence of a person is the same as that
person's style, and that, in turn, a person's style is continuous with the spiritual
essence or style of a culture (1973: 8). At the extreme, this position holds that
what is most interesting in life is art or like art or aspires to be like art or can be
taken as art. Berlin's explicit references to aesthetic judgment as the only
proper judgment of human beings when philosophy has discredited free-will
are only by the way. His typical view is that the realm of the aesthetic, the
realm of beauty and sublimity, is the repository of human stature, not the
symbol of the degradation of a determined world.

In passing, I wish to point out that Berlin does not square his emphasis on a
whole culture's distinctive style with his defense of group pluralism within one
society, when that pluralism grows out of several different and adjacent "con-
stellations." Does not a society's own internal pluralism interfere with its
distinctive style, with its imputed claim to make a pure, unhybrid contribution
to global pluralism? (In regard to the sacrifice of individuality to pluralism on
any scale, Berlin is mostly silent.)

The Heart of the Aesthetic Defense

I would now like to take up notions used by Berlin to establish the idea
that cultures or whole ways of life are not to be regarded except aesthetically,
which turns out to mean, not be judged at all, but only appreciated. The first
thing to notice is that an aestheticized attitude toward a culture is an outsider's
perspective, that of one who contemplates a culture as a whole. An aesthetic
perspective must be an external one. This attitude cannot be held by the people
in that culture; it cannot be their self-understanding, except maybe for a
few writers or painters or aesthetes. Most people do not live—at least deliberately—in order to contribute to the creation of a collaborative work of
beauty and hence to provide aesthetic pleasure to themselves, much less to
observers. Indeed, Berlin never denies that it is proper for members to criticize
their own cultures on moral and epistemological grounds. He produces a code

meant only for observers. Berlin is thus speaking to his audience above the heads of those who live their various ways of life. Undaunted by this unbridgeable gap between a culture's self-understanding and an aestheticized perspective, Berlin proceeds on the assumption he attributes to Vico as well as to J. G. Hamann and Justus Möser (in the eighteenth century) that a single style pervades all activities and manifestations in a culture, or with a slightly different emphasis, that every age has its own style (1973: 8–13). With the concept of style as central, we are in the realm of aesthetics. I fail to see how we can take the measure of Berlin's achievement unless we at least work with the hypothesis that Berlin is encouraging us to hold an aesthetic perspective on cultures and doing so ultimately for the sake of defending the human stature.

To adopt an aesthetic perspective not only means to find mysterious cultural creativity everywhere, it also means, as I have said, to consider the claims of morality and truth as irrelevant or out of place. An overriding concern with morality and truth — or to put it negatively, with the avoidance of wickedness and of untruth — does not get the point. And, tactically, it clouds or compromises the perception of beauty. Such a concern also gets in the way of defending the human stature by placing the clearest and most vivid examples of human creativity, which are aesthetic or amenable to aesthetic apprehension and praise, under suspicion. Truth and goodness get in the way of paying tribute to human glory. (Revealingly, Berlin says that "some wish to call" pagan [as distinct from Christian] morality "aesthetic," 1972: p. 64.) And if most people do not consciously live to contribute to making their culture into something like a work of art, they, too, certainly, should not be encouraged to allow truth and goodness to get in the way of their devotion to their culture. Their devotion to it, from whatever reasons or causes, is precisely what permits observers to defend the human stature. People are thus turned into the usually unwitting but indispensable servants of styles and hence of the (at least partly) undetermined creation of beauty that is contemplated by aestheticist observers.

The philosophical heart of the aesthetic attitude toward cultures is found in Berlin's idea of the incommensurable value of cultures, first articulated by Vico, and made truly influential by Herder later. Berlin calls his own view *pluralism*. But he is no ordinary pluralist; he is a radical pluralist because he affirms the idea of the incommensurable value of each culture as a whole, of "a plurality of incommensurable cultures" (1973: 12). In Berlin's writings, the aesthetic perspective requires the idea of incommensurability, though the converse does not seem to hold, as we shall see later. This idea means that there can be no common aesthetic measure that allows us to compare and rank all those things and entities that we perceive and admire because we take an aesthetic perspective on them. If cultures (like individuals) must engage in exclusion, as any stylization must; if in their acts and practices, they must sometimes choose among possibilities that are incompatible and of incommensurable value, the aesthetic observer has only to admire them as one admires art: inclusively.

First consider art. Grading and ranking artworks, or styles or schools or periods of art, within one culture, or grading and ranking art that emanates from various cultures, is usually a misconceived enterprise. There should be no common standard for beauty: to think there should be is not to understand what beauty is. To be sure, aestheticism as such is not linked by necessity to incommensurability. Some theorists would say that it is precisely the function of taste to compare and rank works of art by means of a set of standards that have been carefully worked out. Differences between high and low art, between popular and mass art, should be noticed and accommodated. In contrast, Berlin's aestheticism rejects comparison and grading, most tellingly in respect to cultures and ways of life — that is, in respect to what is only dubiously amenable to aesthetic judgment, to begin with. His aestheticism leads him conceptually to need and hence to invoke the idea of incommensurability. And he chides Montesquieu for thinking "that art has absolutely rigid criteria . . . and there is no question of the relativity of taste" (1998b: 88).

Let us acknowledge that Berlin is not idiosyncratic. In spite of the urgings of the doctrinaires of taste, many people are quite content to greet each work of art in itself and find it sufficient, without caring to assign it a grade. That is Berlin's aesthetic attitude. He actually renounces aesthetic *judgment* because it is potentially censorious. Rather, his aesthetic counsel to us is to look for the coherence of a culture, which is its style, and also to isolate particulars for praise and admiration. To say that cultures are incommensurably valuable is not to say that they are equally valuable. That still would be to retain the mentality of grading and ranking. We should rather see cultures as equally needed, not for a teleological purpose, but to show how extensive human creativity is. Each culture is a whole world. Why compare worlds? Analogously, we do not say that apples are better than oranges, or even that they are equally good. They are incommensurably valuable, and are equally needed to develop our sense of nature's bounty, even if we prefer one to the other, as a matter of personal taste, or like them equally, or dislike both. Each is likeable and liked by many people. That is enough to establish their value. Aestheticism thus works as a kind of objectivity: "values are absolute quite independently of what you may think or want" (1998b: 100). The more significant consideration is that the aesthetic observer must turn his back on the claims of morality and truth or resist their temptations; they are aesthetically irrelevant.

Notice that I say that for Berlin the claims of morality and truth are irrelevant, not that these claims are secondary and fit to be subordinated for the sake of aesthetic appreciation of a way of life. Berlin could not consistently uphold the overall idea of incommensurability and still assert that the claims of beauty are greater than the claims of morality and truth. There is therefore a double incommensurability. Beauty, morality, and truth are incommensurably valuable, just as, within the realm of beauty, not only art but whole ways of life are incommensurably valuable. The entire aesthetic realm is separate from other realms and has responses and receptivity to it that are its own; within that realm, grading and ranking mistakenly hinder our generous and sympathetic appreciation. Aesthetic incommensurability in this double sense is thus crucial for the defense of cultural pluralism and, with it, for the defense of the human stature.

I notice that in one case, Berlin cautions against the idea of breaking up experience into "autonomous realms." He says that pluralism does not mean, for example, that politics is an autonomous realm of means and that morality is an autonomous realm of ends. Rather they are together in one realm of ends. But different cultures pursue incommensurable ends, and do so because they have radically different "moralities" (here Christian or pagan) (1972: 64); that is, they have different organizing principles. I think, however, that this is just another way of saying that cultures rather than realms of endeavor are autonomous. All the activities of any culture are of a piece; they compose a stylization that is incommensurably valuable. To a disposed observer, like Berlin, aesthetic apprehension, by denying the relevance of moral and epistemological claims, establishes its own autonomy, the autonomy of the observer who renounces all practical judgment. The aesthetic realm is the observer's only home, and is fit only for him. Such is Berlin's characteristic presupposition.

I grant that there are many sorts of entity that Berlin thinks are valuably plural, not only artworks (on the one hand) and cultures, societies, and epochs (on the other). Sometimes, he also speaks of a plurality of ideals or temperaments or values: these terms are bunched together with cultures in the last piece he wrote, "My Intellectual Path." Elsewhere he speaks of incommensurably plural moralities or virtues (1972, passim; 1988: 7–14). Now, the whole issue of incommensurable value is large and enormously complex, and it may arise outside the aesthetic realm, and need not always be linked to, much less confined to, aesthetic judgment. And it need not always be associated with relativism. We could say, for example, that there is no way of ranking the virtues of courage and moderation; or ranking the value of being male or female, young or old, straight or gay; or ranking the sanguine and melancholic temperaments; or ranking the values of a long life and a glorious life. Ideals like fashionableness and voluntary poverty cannot be graded or ranked:

they simply exploit different sectors of human possibility, and the observer can see the fineness of both. In all these cases, genuine incommensurability is present. (These are not cases, however, that illustrate a separate problem: the *difficulty* of determination by the measure of one standard.) Is it possible, after all, that wherever incommensurability is believed to obtain, the *observer* should make room for aestheticism? I leave aside the predicament of the *actor*, the person who must act yet is faced with a choice between incommensurably valuable experiences or attainments or courses of action.

The philosophical situation becomes altogether different when Berlin speaks of incommensurably valuable moralities, as he does in his celebrated essay, "The Originality of Machiavelli" (1972) and elsewhere, and of incommensurably valuable societies, cultures, ways of life, as he does throughout his work, but concentrated in *Vico and Herder* (1976) and *The Crooked Timber of Humanity* (1991).

Let me persist: what is really happening when Berlin says that cultures and ways of life are incommensurably valuable? I have already mentioned that Berlin characterizes the essence of a culture as a distinctive style. Berlin proceeds with the assumption that the style of every culture results from the working out of basic principles or commitments or more broadly, the working out of a religion or metaphysics or code of life. He follows Vico in thinking that every culture is the embodiment of a set of answers its people give to "different questions of the universe" (1973: 6). Structures, institutions, practices, customs, and tendency of policy all stem from these usually systematized answers. The values of a society, even if not perfectly consonant theoretically or actually consistent, are not individually isolated, but form a "constellation" that provides the heart and soul of a way of life (1998b: 100–101). The constellation yields a net achievement, which is a style that shows itself in a society's principal activities. In brief, unnecessitated beliefs organize and stamp a culture, and these beliefs are as various as the creative genius of grouped humanity can make them. One can point to the discussion of organizing principles or beliefs in Montesquieu and Rousseau as relevant precedents for Berlin's view.

Berlin insists that these organizing beliefs, these fundamental principles or commitments, are beyond the reach of epistemological criticism, just as their enacted consequences are beyond moral judgment. Of course, to be asked to suspend epistemological and moral criticism — criticism informed by a wish to point out untruth and wickedness — is not automatically to embrace aestheticism. One may have other designs. But in Berlin's case, the tendency of his work is to get us to think that epistemological and moral criticism is out of place when we apprehend cultures. If we see them as like aesthetic objects, unitary and individuated, we must be led by the perception of their beauty and sublimity, when we contemplate them, to the celebration of human creativity and then to the defense of the human stature. For this sequence to be possible, Berlin must mean that even if there is universalist or cross-cultural truth or morality, it is irrelevant. His further implication must be that the human stature cannot depend on our ability to ascertain truth or achieve justice.

In opposition I wish to assert — that is all I can do — that the defense of the human stature, even if that defense actually requires reliance on human creativity as shown in the formation of numerous unfated ways of life, which the observer wishes to regard like works of art, does not outweigh the claims of truth and especially of morality. I insist on the supremacy of moral considerations; to think otherwise is to invite or endorse barbarism. And by moral considerations, I certainly do not mean either hedonism or human flourishing. I also wish to assert that human dignity is a larger idea than human stature, and contains another component that is indissociable from morality. I call that component the human *status* of every person, which like human stature is also a non- and anti-utilitarian idea. To honor that status, gross forms of oppression must be avoided; more positively, fundamental rights must be respected. Human beings, as such, must be given their due. What unites human stature and individual status is the same refusal to see human beings, collectively or individually, as animals or machines or material or bodies in motion, and the same hope for a world in which that refusal permeates social actuality. Let me add that the discovery of truth, whether in science or experience or philosophy, should be sufficient to defend the human stature. (In any case, no animal that has language can be wholly determined or wholly predictable.) Truth is enough for the human stature, while justice is required to recognize the status of individuals. The realization, necessarily imperfect and impure, of truth and morality registers awareness of and pays tribute to human dignity, in its twofold quality, human stature and individual status, the double reason that humanity should not hold itself in low estimation as wholly determined creatures or entities, and not treat one another wickedly.

What after all would the defense of the human stature come to, if injustice and other kinds of grave immorality were not only prevalent but also theoretically countenanced? The whole notion of human dignity would be hollow. Human dignity must not only be celebrated, as when human stature is theoretically affirmed. Human dignity must also be honored in practice, as when the human status of every person is recognized, and ideal recognition occurs when government recognizes and protects every person's fundamental rights, and everyday life is permeated by the spirit of such recognition. But somewhat less than the ideal counts: some portion of justice. It is good to think about the human stature more than Anglo-American philosophy typically does. But if the human stature, from a perspective like that of Nietzsche, Heidegger, and Strauss, but also Berlin, conflicts with the human status of every person—if, that is, the claims of the two components of human dignity may sometimes be incompatible—the claims are nevertheless commensurable. Individual status must prevail over human stature, because the claims of morality are supreme. The Nietzschean perspective on the human stature is hardly the only one. Then, too, when the human stature is made to rest on the energies released by untruth, it is compromised.

In my assertions, I must finally rely on a methodological point. I believe that it is a profound mistake to carry the analogy between a work of art and a culture (or way of life) as far as to place a culture entirely in the aesthetic realm. It is an undeniable fact that a culture often emits a detectable style that unites and vivifies the main aspects of that culture's life. In regard to dead cultures, why not aestheticize, within broad limits? Why hasten to moralize? But the undeniable fact of cultural style is not enough to compel the conclusion that a whole way of life is very much like a work of art. A way of life is made up of repeated acts, activities, and enactments that implicate everyone who takes part in them in consequences, great and small. These consequences must be submitted to moral judgment. The field of moral judgment is not confined to individual choices. A way of life is made up not of harmless rituals and routines, but of relations of power that beg to be assessed. Aesthetic appreciation should not replace practical reason.

But there is no talking an aesthete out of his position. Then, too, Berlin's deepest commitment, which is to the human stature, is not only deep but also honorable. But his defensive aesthetic strategy, if I have described it accurately, is quite dubious; and it is not likely to appeal to many people, even radical pluralists, who would prefer other strategies, even though some of these pluralists are unconscious aesthetes or aesthetes too embarrassed to acknowledge their aestheticism. I think that it is only fair to Berlin to say that the elements for an alternative nonaesthetic strategy are found in his work. Abandoning the aesthetic strategy, however, means that the high value of beauty (or sublimity) cannot be enlisted to fend off the claims of morality and truth as irrelevant or inappropriate.

The Anti-universalist Defense

There are important elements shared by the nonaesthetic and aesthetic strategies. These elements include Berlin's commitment to defend the human stature against all determinisms and reductions, and to do so by emphasis on human creativity as it shows itself in the unpredictable and irreducibly unexplainable formation of cultures. And the notion of the incommensurable value of cultures is once again the key to Berlin's strategy. If his aestheticism initially moves him to invoke the idea of incommensurability, this idea can also, and does sometimes, stand apart from his aestheticism.

This alternative nonaesthetic strategy proceeds by way of denying universal standards of truth and morality. Incommensurability becomes the point of theoretical departure, not a necessary device along the way (so to speak). When incommensurability of cultures is maintained, practical moral judgment is supposed to be rendered helpless. In the absence of universal standards, each culture stands in itself, valuable in itself, free of criticism on the basis of universal standards, and really not to be judged at all by an outsider. Berlin rejects Hegel's view that any particular culture is only "a link in the chain of the world spirit's development" (1975: 53). In sum, incommensurably valuable cultural diversity as such, rather than the cumulative sublimity of such diversity, becomes the royal road to the attempt to resist all kinds of determinism and reduction.

I would now like to take up this alternative nonaesthetic strategy. To Vico, Berlin attributes the view that a proper sense of human creativity rejects the very possibility of one universal and timeless "standard of truth or beauty or goodness" (1973: 5). This is Berlin's view, too. I also think he endorses the Herderian idea that different ideals in different ages were "each in its way valid for its time and place and can be admired and appreciated by us now" (1999: 63). To be sure, he does say that a minimum of common values gives sense to the idea of natural law and distinguishes morality from "such other notions as custom, or tradition, or law, or manners, or fashion, or etiquette" (1969: xxxi). He even speaks of "the central values" that are "common to human beings as such, that is . . . to the great majority of men in most places and times" (1969: xxxii). But when pluralism is his subject, this near-universalism, predicated on a "nucleus of needs and goals, a nucleus common to all men" (1969: xxxii), is practically invisible. He does not allow near-universalism to shape his pluralism. I assume that he rejects universal standards. This rejection, however, leads us back to the question of incommensurability. Let us in this context look again and more closely at what Berlin means by this notion.

Most generally put, in Berlin's view, valued things are valuable; and they are not only valuable, they are often incompatibly valuable; and whether compatible or not, they are incommensurably valuable. Incompatibility and incommensurability are two distinct notions, even though Berlin sometimes conflates them. One notion may apply in a given case, while the other does not. Typically, Berlin is interested in cases where both apply. I think, however, that

Berlin could not (or should not) be content to show that valued things, or even good things that deserve to be valued, may be incompatible: there is no revelation in saying, for example, that the organizing constellation of values of a warrior society exclude or are incompatible with those of a commercial society. (A given society's actual practices are nevertheless quite likely to be internally driven by incompatible values, apart from any group pluralism within it.) There *would* be a revelation if Berlin could sustain the thesis of incommensurability, in regard to cultures, the thesis that it is philosophically invalid to judge and rank cultures, *while avoiding becoming a relativist*. He insists recurrently that he is not a relativist, that he believes only in the incommensurability of values, especially the incommensurable value of a given whole way of life in relation to any other (1998a: p. 57; 1998b: 100–101). Does he sustain the thesis of incommensurability, in regard to whole ways of life when not regarded aesthetically, but rather in the light of the denial of universal standards? I do not see that he does.

I should have thought that if you reject universal standards of morality and truthfulness, you must be a relativist, even if you deny it and call yourself by some other name. Nothing is gained when Berlin defines away the problem by saying that a relativist is one who believes that any principle is either a subjective preference or a helplessly determined judgment and nothing else or more. Allow that the organizing principles of a society together with its associated values are not the mere preferences or choices of any one person or group, and are not irresistibly dictated by conditions. Still, cultures can certainly be judged and ranked when some cultures, more than others, are organized by untruth and consequently systematize wickedness. Untruth by itself is bad enough. My point is that if there were no untruth or wickedness, the thesis of incommensurability would be greatly instructive on some matters, but would lack much of its power to disturb.

I think that Berlin is misguided in his denial of universal standards. Almost all cultures know the difference between a lie and a truth, even if they organize their ways of life by beliefs that turn out to be false. Almost all cultures work with the same rough idea of what is elementarily just or unjust, even though it is often quite difficult or even impossible to decide particular cases rationally; even though it is humanly impossible to adhere fully and perfectly to justice; and even though it is close to humanly impossible to accord supremacy to justice over all other purposes and aspirations. Whatever he says, Berlin is a relativist. His extension of the incommensurability thesis to whole ways of life, when done nonaesthetically, is relativism. (I say this, despite Steven Lukes's illuminating effort to leave the question open [Lukes 1998: 8–10].) Relativism is a seductive error; plausible points can be made in its defense.

Finally, however, you can believe in the incommensurable value of each culture, nonaesthetically, only if you are a relativist.

There's nothing at stake if someone, in an idle mood, tries to rank societies, when each of them is committed to basic organizing principles that do not significantly incorporate untruth and do not lead to conduct that is systematically immoral. Then too, to say that "value systems," in Berlin's phrase, are objective because it is possible for us, though often difficult, to understand why societies subscribe to them, possible also "with sufficient imagination" to "enter into a value system which is not my own, but which is nevertheless something I can conceive of men pursuing while remaining human, while remaining creatures with whom I can communicate" is not to use the word *objective* correctly (1998a: 57). People have in fact believed and do now believe in all sorts of wickedness-sustaining untruths, but the values they adhere to are not objective simply by being humanly understandable. I cannot think of any value or constellation of values that totally resists comprehension. That cannot mean, in turn, that almost all values ever held and acted on are objective in the proper sense of the word. If they are not subjective, they are not objective, either.

I know that I must enter several qualifications (or apparent ones) of what I have just asserted about the moral and epistemological faults of the incommensurability thesis when applied in the spirit of relativism to ways of life. Here are just five qualifications. First, as conformists, which is what everybody is much or most of the time, people have everywhere and at all times maintained roughly the same average kind and degree of compliance with what is expected of them. From the perspective of human inwardness, people, past and present, are basically the same in the wish to go along with prevailing standards, even though their outward practices differ greatly and the kind and amount of systematic wickedness sustained by their conformity also differ greatly. The human race steadfastly retains a fairly constant inward culpability and innocence at all times and places. Some people are just morally luckier in their conformity than others, but all are equally susceptible to being conformist. Second, there is often more than unexamined conformity; there is a sincere conviction that the practices and beliefs of one's society are right and good, and deserve to be followed. Again, from the perspective of inwardness, people are, everywhere and at all times, roughly equally sincere in their wish to be good and speak honestly, no matter how substantial the variations in the conduct expected of them.

Third, I grant that in many cultures, especially tribal ones and other kinds in the past, the idea of universal morality and the idea of the unqualified search for truth and right understanding did not exist. These concepts were unavailable to people in such societies. I agree that they cannot be blamed for what they could not know or understand, but that should not prevent us from holding that such societies, though not guilty, were still deficient, and that we should not place them on the same level as cultures that possess universal standards, even though cultures acquainted with universal standards have done inconceivably more evil than cultures without them. Universalist societies have also done a greater amount of good, which of course does not excuse or balance the evil but only palliates it. Fourth, many cultures, past and present, are scarcely knowable, if at all, to outsiders or to people who live after them. (This is not to say that a society is unopaque to insiders.) What we do not know well enough we should not judge and rank, except when confronted with massive wrongdoing; but then add that we should be careful how, in our unknowing, we praise or otherwise validate them. Fifth, it is certainly true that an overall assessment of any culture's success in attaining a measure of systematic justice and avoiding reliance on untruth can be excruciatingly hard and liable to change. In making this reckoning about one culture, and then about another culture for the sake of comparison, we encounter good reasons for moral doubt or confusion and surely for moral disagreement and even indeterminacy or undecidability. All in all, which society was morally better, Athens or Sparta? Which society harmed other ones more and benefited them more? It is a good deal harder to say than I would like. But some comparative assessment, some commensurability, is possible, and we start with the presence of gross evils sustained at least in part by gross untruths. Berlin himself, on rare occasions, admits that we should be "free to criticize and condemn," even as he also insists that no matter what commitments we are studying, "we cannot pretend not to understand" them (1988: 11).

These qualifications, which I partly withdrew as I stated them, do not really lend any assistance to the thesis of incommensurability. Some of them, however, may play a role in Berlin's advocacy of this thesis. He does not overtly make much of any of them or anything like them in his work. But in combination, these qualifications may enjoin us, as sceptics toward cultural incommensurability, to be cautious and restrained in our judgments of other societies, past and present, even as we, on anti-relativist grounds, reject the idea of incommensurability in regard to whole ways of life. Berlin's notion of the incommensurable value of cultures, in general, tends to grant *immeasurable* value to every culture. But only human individuals are each of them immeasurably, even infinitely valuable. A human being is above price. But no culture or way of life, or distinctive element in a culture or way of life, is immeasurably valuable; nor is it unmeasurably so, to leave aside its art or artefacts. But it is certainly right to say that the universal principles of any society are immeasurably more valuable than any of its others. The deep trouble is that Berlin sometimes conceives of each culture as an individual, an existential unit, with all the immeasurable value that only persons possess. He not only appreciates but works with such an assumption, which he attributes to Herder and also to German historical jurisprudence (1999: 125).

I think, furthermore, that almost every culture in its pride wants to be measured by common standards, and evaluates itself comparatively. Where is the gratification when a society judges itself valuable by reference only to its own peculiar standards? A society is usually not content to say simply that its ways are its ways, and let it go at that. Most people understand that to claim, for example, that a particular practice is moral just because they say it is means that there is no such thing as morality (or justice or propriety). The self-enclosed declaration is only a declaration, a mere expression of approval. It is not a judgment at all. Societies typically claim that they are better than other societies, or the best of all of them. The standards used may not be universalist, but must be more than local; it is understood that societies must endure trial by contrast; and the comparisons often make reference to morality (or justice or propriety) and to truth. Otherwise self-praise is pointless, while self-criticism, if it exists at all, is reduced to mere anxiety over internal consistency. Only philosophers with some high theoretical ambition invoke the idea of incommensurability when they speak of whole societies or cultures or ways of life, and claim that it is only fair to judge them by their own standards. And only societies thought deplorable or even worthless by everybody else could possibly find solace in this idea.

Contrastingly, if an Emersonian or Millean or Nietzschean individual tries to live by his own law and measure up to standards he sets only for himself, the same difficulties are not involved. Such an individual is trying to escape trial by contrast: that is how he defines his autonomy. He hopes that others will develop along their own lines; the more, the better. But societies are continuously comparing themselves with others by common standards and competing with them for many of the same things. And as with individuals, so with societies: whatever they may do or say, two common standards remain applicable to all of them: morality and truth.

A climax is reached when, in "My Intellectual Path," Berlin takes up the question of the Nazis. (Earlier, he had accused Hitler, rather lamely, of flouting "values which are of an extremely universal kind" (1999: 141). He calls Nazi values "detestable," and Nazi deeds "wickedly wrong." Can an advocate of incommensurability condemn any society, including Nazi Germany? Berlin's reasoning is curious. He refuses to see the Nazis as "literally pathological or insane"; rather, they are "totally misguided in believing that some beings are subhuman." He says, "I see how, with enough false education, enough wide-spread illusion and error, men can, while remaining men, believe this and commit the most unspeakable crimes" (1998a: 57–58). Berlin here falls back on universal standards of morality and truthfulness. But in his work he has only rarely appealed to a common or universal morality, even in its negative form of avoiding "extremes of suffering" (1988: 17). And I am not aware that before his last writing he ever employed the universal standard of truthfulness in assessing a society. The Nazis, but years after their defeat, compel him explicitly to reintroduce universal standards belatedly and in an improvised, almost sheepish manner. Even so, his remarks indicate as clearly as any lengthy exposition that the thesis of the incommensurable value of ways of life is untenable, certainly for anyone straining to refuse the available temptation of relativism. Much earlier, in his essay on Montesquieu, bad conscience had already driven Berlin to employ a general, cross-cultural standard for judging societies. He says that Montesquieu pleads convincingly for vastly different ways of life that satisfy human needs "no less satisfactorily and fully than other cultures" (1955: 158). Yet this is a serious misrepresentation of Montesquieu (later corrected, 1998b: 88). Montesquieu detested the prevalence of despotism in the world. But Berlin wants us to think that most cultures have been or are happy. The general standard is no sooner introduced than it is turned, alas, into a general exoneration.

The Two Defenses Compared

There are two strategies, then, that a purposive reader can find in Isaiah Berlin's work to defend cultural pluralism and to defend it (ultimately, but not solely) for the sake of the human stature: the aesthetic strategy and the anti-universalist strategy. I cannot help feeling, however, that what moves Berlin most profoundly is the aesthetic strategy. I do not deny the sincerity of his troubled rejection of universal standards of truth and morality on the grounds that there is no conceivable authentication, no more-than-human umpire who could set down unquestionably valid standards. History is a game of change and it has no umpire. But for all the weight of Berlin's historicism, I am left with the impression that the aesthetic strategy is stronger than the anti-universalist strategy, and that it is closer to Berlin's heart. It is the eros of his pluralism.

I think that Berlin's aesthetic strategy is stronger in some respects than the second, anti-universalist strategy, not only because, as I have tried to indicate, the anti-universalist strategy is based on the mistake of relativism. The advantage of the aesthetic strategy is that it is purely external and does not pretend to know any particular way of life from the inside. Furthermore, an external perspective, though all-forgiving in its effect, does not have to pretend to call untruth by the name of relative truth or wickedness by the name of relative morality. Is it possible that aesthetic indifference to the claims of morality and truth does less harm to either than relativism does?

Close to Berlin's heart is the advice that the mind's eye should contemplate the beauty of each way of life. Such beauty impresses on the mind the power of human creativity, which is the best argument against every reduction and determinism. We should not let anxiety over injustice and untruth desensitize us to beauty, the beauty of the stylization of any way of life. We should train ourselves to ignore content, so to speak, and look to form and shape, to manner and style. We must replace the claims of morality and truth with an endorsement of the aesthetic. And the indefinitely large accumulation of cultures, past, present, and to come, should provoke awe, a feeling of sublimity: human creativity is unpredictable, indefatigable, and endless. No culture (or period) could ever contain all that is valuable in life. Utopia is an amputated reality that pretends to be all-inclusive. Of course, Berlin cannot say that the creation of numerous distinctive cultures is more important than the reduction of injustice and untruth. Such an assertion would reinstate the very commensurability among high values that in his aesthetic strategy he is trying to discredit. Yet, if the stakes are as great as the defense of the human stature, perhaps Berlin is entitled, by his own rules, to say that the endless human creation of beauty to the point of sublimity is, after all, more important to the philosopher than the reduction of injustice and untruth, precisely because nothing is more important than defending the human stature against its many enemies. It is, at the last, an existential perspective that provides the philosopher with a measure, and by that measure, the avoidance of the degradation inherent in every reduction and determinism guards the human race, and nothing matters more than that. Nothing matters, perhaps, except that.

There is, then, a sort of very fierce religion of humanity in Berlin's thought. I use the word *religion* deliberately. Berlin prefers that his powers of argument and articulation build up an outlook on life that is not rationalist in the inclusive moral and epistemological sense. Rationalism cannot be trusted with guarding the human race by preserving the necessary aesthetic attitudes and feelings that lead to upholding the human stature. If Berlin's outlook is not fundamentally irrationalist, it is quasi-religious. I do not refer to his very intense loyalty to the Jewish tradition, despite his personal unbelief. I mean, instead, that he comes to associate creativity with religious — not merely theological or metaphysical — inspiration. For him, religion is the greatest source of energy in human affairs, the greatest source of that creativity that issues in an endless profusion of ways of life, not only in the creativity of great poetry, music, and painting. Religion is the greatest source of the aesthetic realm. Berlin is only grudgingly reconciled to the realization that the spread of knowledge will certainly kill some realms of the imagination founded upon nonrational religious beliefs and hence shrink some sorts of human freedom (1964: 194–97). He implies, with chagrin, that only a rationalist wants to know the worst and thus be set beyond hope and fear. Berlin wants to preserve not only hope but a fear that is like awe.

I take from Michael Ignatieff's *Isaiah Berlin: A Life* (1998) this extract from a letter Berlin wrote in 1981 after hearing an apparently rationalist sermon preached on the Jewish New Year. Berlin says that "the validity of a religion [should] not, in my view, depend on its moral implications: it is transcendent, absolute, orders things which, in human terms, may be horrifying (as so often in the more bloodshedding exploits in the [Old Testament]) but *are* the essence of a truly religious attitude" (294). Am I wrong to say that when words like these come from an unbeliever, he must be an aesthete? Human life is made interesting for him, and worth guarding, only when its creative energies are stimulated to extremism by untruth and issue in what paltry moralists condemn as wildness and wickedness. But, to say it again, such aestheticism in Berlin's case is finally not personal. He loves beauty, but he loves human dignity more. Interested in much more than his own aesthetic gratification, Berlin wants to defend the human stature, and he is sincerely convinced that one key to its defense must lie in aesthetic attitudes and feelings, whatever the cost to morality and truth. Judging and ranking cultures by the extent to which they avoid or reduce injustice and untruth entangles us, Berlin seems to think, in indifference to creativity and hence to perils to the human stature. Human dignity is at stake. But, truly, Berlin appears to me to be, despite his liberalism, unaware that human dignity involves not only the stature of humanity, but also—and I would say more importantly—the status of each individual person, a status that only the recognition of individual rights can fully protect. This should be the moral aim of every culture and it needs no untruth, no religion, and no elaborate metaphysics for its defense.

Note

In a revealing letter to Marion (Mrs. Felix) Frankfurter, written in the United States as a young worldly man of thirty-one in 1940, Berlin says about the culture of the United States as compared to that of England that it is "Aesthetically inferior but morally superior." At this stage he is willing to rank two cultures and by two different measures. Even though he gives no philosophical importance to his personal preference, he chooses, despite a little ambivalence, the aesthetic over the moral, English culture over American. The doctrine of incommensurability has yet to make its appearance. In a nice gesture, he adds: "Perhaps England was like that vis a vis France or Austria in 1840" (2004, 327–328).

References

Arendt, Hannah. "The Conquest of Space and the Stature of Man." *Between Past and Future,* 2nd ed. New York: Viking, 1968.

Berlin, Isaiah. "The Counter-Enlightenment." 1973. *Against the Current.* Ed. Henry Hardy. New York: Viking, 1980.

——."'From Hope and Fear Set Free.'" 1964. *Concepts and Categories.* Ed. Henry Hardy. New York: Viking, 1980.

—— "Historical Inevitability." 1954. *Four Essays on Liberty.* New York: Oxford, 1969.

—— "In Conversation with Steven Lukes." 1998b. *Salmagundi* no. 120 (Fall 1998): 52–134.

——Introduction. 1969. *Four Essays on Liberty.*

—— "John Stuart Mill and the Ends of Life." 1959. *Four Essays on Liberty.*

——*Letters 1928–1946.* Ed. Henry Hardy. Cambridge: Cambridge University Press, 2004.

—— "Montesquieu." 1955. *Against the Current.*

—— "My Intellectual Path." 1998a. *The New York Review of Books* 45:8 (May 14, 1998): 53–60.

—— "The Originality of Machiavelli." 1972. *Against the Current.*

—— "The Pursuit of the Ideal." 1988. *The Crooked Timber of Humanity.* Ed. Henry Hardy. New York: Knopf, 1991.

——*The Roots of Romanticism.* Ed. Henry Hardy. Princeton: Princeton University Press, 1999. [Lectures delivered in 1965.]

—— *Vico and Herder.* New York: Viking, 1976.

Gray, John. *Isaiah Berlin.* Princeton: Princeton University Press, 1996.

Ignatieff, Michael. *Isaiah Berlin: A Life.* New York: Holt, 1998.

Hegel, G. W. F. *Lectures on the Philosophy of World History: Introduction.* Trans. H. B. Nisbet. Cambridge: Cambridge University Press, [1830] 1975.

Kant, Immanuel. "Perpetual Peace." *Kant's Political Writings.* Ed. Hans Reiss. 2nd ed. Cambridge: Cambridge University Press, [1795] 1991.

Lukes, Steven. "Berlin's Dilemma." *Times Literary Supplement* March 27, 1998: 8–10.

Pico della Mirandola, Giovanni. *On the Dignity of Man.* Trans. Charles Glenn Wallis. Indianapolis: Hackett, 1965.

Riley, Jonathan. "Defending Cultural Pluralism." *Political Theory* 30 (2002): 68–96.

The Adequacy of the Canon

The impetus of this essay is the question, Is the canon of political theory adequate to the task of enabling readers in our time to take in and comprehend the awful events of the twentieth century? This question can be broken down into two questions. First, Does the canon up to the end of the nineteenth century make, or help significantly to make, these events intelligible, if not expectable or predictable? Second, Are there any political thinkers in the twentieth century, plausibly eligible for canonization, who offer this kind of help? I incline to the view that the canon up to the nineteenth century does something to help, but probably not enough. The awful events of the twentieth century seem, if only in their scale, to break out of the conceptual net found in the sequence of canonical texts written up to 1900 or so. On the second question, I believe that two prominent Nietzscheans did what Nietzsche himself did not quite do: they made a substantial contribution to our ability to encompass the awful events of the twentieth century. I refer to Heidegger and Arendt. And I refer to Arendt not as one influenced by Heidegger but as a thinker in her own right, inspired by Nietzsche as Heidegger was, but doing her own political thinking to our inestimable benefit. These two thinkers are not alone in offering assistance, but they stand out.

Naturally, I do not say that the only value of the canon up to the nineteenth century or of the plausibly canonical writers of the twentieth century is found in helping readers in our time to make sense of the awful events of the twentieth century. Nor do I want to suggest that the only aspect of the twentieth century that is of interest to the student of political theory is the series of atrocious events. For example, the continuing phenomenon of unlimited government parasitically or culpably sheltered by constitutional democracy is of compelling interest. I confine my interest to awful events — actually, deliberate policies, some of them carried out quickly and some over a longer period of time — because facing the worst is surely one of the purposes of reading the canon, just as it is, of course, of reading anything worthwhile in the whole field of the humanities. It may be a matter of temperament only, but I think that facing the worst is actually the most important purpose that could be served by the canon and by a good deal of the politically relevant humanities as well. But it is not the only purpose.

I should say right away that facing the worst, trying to comprehend awful events, whether or not those of the twentieth century, consists to a great extent, even though not exclusively, of making some sense of the motivation of leaders who initiate these events and of the motivation of followers who sustain the leaders. In other words, I look to the canon for enlightenment in *moral psychology* — to use an old but not worn-out term — and I also look to the canon for some assistance in the supplementary endeavor of *moral phenomenology*. Moral psychology is the nonscience that looks externally at initiators and their followers; moral phenomenology is more detailed and often consists in self-characterization by agents, real or fictional, and for this latter enterprise, nothing comes close to equaling imaginative literature. But moral psychology is my basic concern in this essay. I should add that an interest in moral psychology is not exhausted by the wish to explain the motivations behind initiating and sustaining terrible deeds. The effort to know the springs of human conduct as broadly as possible — and from the useful vantage point of political life, its necessities and opportunities, disciplines and psychic enlargements and distortions — is intrinsically bound up with studying the canon.

Now, by awful or atrocious events in the twentieth century, I mean, primarily, but not only, World War I, World War II, the use twice of atomic weapons, their repeated threatened use by the United States, the theories of nuclear deterrence, the gulags, the Holocaust, induced famines, such American wars as the Korean War and the Vietnam War, and numerous massive massacres. My stress is not only on initiation but also on maintenance, and much less so on neglect and indifference. The theme is the scale of humanly inflicted suffering on human beings and the mentalities that permit the initiation and implementation of such deeds. I grant that the distinction in responsibility between causing something awful and letting it happen or continue is often slight or nonexistent and also that the amount of suffering that is neglected when it could be mitigated or ended can be enormous or even unprecedented. Indeed, neglect can be deliberate, a pragmatic substitute for infliction. Blameworthy indifference and malevolent abstention are phenomena in their own right. Some of what I say in this essay will, I hope, be relevant to these phenomena. But my main emphasis is on deliberate infliction.

Let me just mention that besides instruction in moral psychology, three other uses of the canon are, in my judgment, especially important. They may be put in the form of questions that the canon strives to answer: Why, if at all, is government necessary? What are the claims of morality when governments and citizens act? What, for good and ill, is distinctively political? But the compound question before us is, Does the canon before the twentieth century prepare us for the awful events of the twentieth century and make them at least partly intelligible? And if, in the twentieth century, Heidegger and Arendt — especially Arendt — help, how do they help?

My principal interest has been for as long as I can remember the wish to find instruction in moral psychology from the canon. Then, trying to see what light it throws on the awful events of the twentieth century, I find myself somewhat disappointed, though I am willing to grant that I may be anachronistic and therefore expect the wrong kind of instruction from the canon that runs from Plato through the nineteenth century. Alternatively, I may fail to see that this canon actually does offer adequate instruction for my purpose; I may not read carefully enough. My halting conclusion is that whether or not the canon up to 1900 could have been adequate, it is not completely so, and should not be thought to be so, despite the fact that it remains invaluable for instruction in moral psychology.

In the twentieth century, there is no break in human nature. Unchanged human nature, however, produces discontinuity in the scale of atrocious effects of deliberate state or movement policy, and could produce yet greater atrocities in the future, and even culminate in the extinction of humanity and much of nature. These are the new facts that have to be pondered. Yet writers in the canon did not contemplate such a scale because they gave scant attention to certain human capacities that have always existed and always been in play. Nor were the atrocities with which they were familiar usually traced to these capacities. But when the scale of destructive wrongdoing is as immense as it was in the twentieth century and could possibly encompass massive human and natural retrogression or decay, or inconceivable ruin, then we must pay attention to overlooked or barely noticed causes, if only we can get hold of them.

Yet if the twentieth century is discontinuous in scale of atrocities, is it not anachronistic to expect the canon up to 1900 to enable readers to face the worst in the century that followed? With few exceptions, political theory, even at its canonical best, does not aspire to predict the course of the future. But it is not prediction that is wanted. What, then, is? We can reasonably want the moral psychology that is so variously, intricately, and subtly on display in the canon to prepare readers for anything awful, whatever the scale. Are we not entitled to expect that the major politically relevant elements of human nature will be assembled in the great and good texts that are available for our instruction? The texts usually presume to speak timelessly: the human psyche is laid bare. The common root of all diverse cultures is allegedly exposed. This is the overt or tacit premise in the canon.

What is more, I think that the preponderant tendency in the canon is pessimism concerning human nature. Such pessimism is not monochromatic; it is not always deep dyed; it may be softened by a guarded hopefulness; it is certainly put forth in substantially different hues. But Plato, Aristotle, Augustine, Aquinas, Machiavelli, Hobbes, Locke, Rousseau (in spite of himself), Kant, probably Hegel, Mill in his stoical moods, Nietzsche in his way—all of them and others, too—paint a composite, even heterogeneous, but unmistakably sad or dark or tragic picture of humanity, a humanity corrupted more by privilege than by adversity, though sometimes more by humiliation or weakness than by privilege. They all say the worst they know about humanity. They think that only in exceptional or almost miraculously contrived circumstances can the worst passions of humanity be restrained or diminished and some of the best capacities brought out. The unreformed normality is, however, very grim. In such grimness, the canon retains a power to instruct that I wish to affirm. I only want that power enhanced, especially for the task of facing the awful events of the twentieth century, but also for casting a long backward look at the experience of the centuries before that. We could say that the canon up to 1900 either is not pessimistic enough or that the very nature of its pessimism concerning human nature needs some alteration or amplification or redirection.

The twentieth century is discontinuous with previous history in the scale of its atrocious effects, yet I would have wanted the canon up to 1900 to be more nearly adequate to these awful events. My view is that the discontinuity of the twentieth century is caused by capacities or tendencies in human beings that of course long predate the twentieth century. Is it possible that these tendencies could not have been noticed sufficiently? Or, perhaps there seemed to be no need to notice them when awful events through time were thought to derive wholly from yet other tendencies that make up the composite pessimism in the canon? But I think that there has always been need to notice them. They help to account for many of the awful events all through time. Only, in the twentieth century, these immemorial tendencies in all human beings cannot any longer be overlooked; without them, that century is not intelligible.

I find that three factors work to make these tendencies to pursue atrocious policies metastatic in their effects. First, the numbers of people alive, from the late nineteenth century onward, has drastically altered the scale of effects of concerted human action, whether aggressive or defensive; whether masses are mobilized or passive; whether they are instruments or victims, or both (as they usually are). One way into the story of atrocities in the twentieth century is to highlight the not-innocent availability of those who have suffered as much as or more than their victims: masses who become politically usable when they are populist, usually resentful, and often undemocratic in spirit if not in their nominal citizenship. An egalitarian passion serves to make them yet more usable. Second, technological advances have armed immemorial tendencies in human nature with gigantic powers. Third, religion no longer satisfies religious craving to the same extent or on the same terms, at least not where technological prowess is most advanced. In sum, the same old human nature, but radically potent and swimming or drowning in enormous numbers of people, many of whom are spiritually greedy or can be persuaded to become so, produces effects that are unprecedented in scale. I return to these aggravating factors below.

Not all three factors are always present; in the case of some massacres, for example, technology can be rudimentary, or the population not shockingly larger than it had been, or religious beliefs not very different from what they had been. In these cases, however, the adequacy of the canon is still impeachable because of its comparative neglect, above all, of the part played by one tendency in human beings, the proclivity to be prey to imagination and the intertwined proclivity to fail to exercise imagination. The vicissitudes of imagination are, I think, a key element. To be sure, from the eighteenth century on, benign imagination has been discussed as one key to right conduct. But that discussion does not range as far as we need, despite its continued usefulness. In this essay, I do not presume to offer anything like a full account of imagination, or an inventory of its uses (especially its good uses), or of the consequences of its failure to be used. I submit only preliminary considerations. What I say is tentative, with many loose ends. But the scale of horror makes it urgent to try again to understand the causes of horror.

Human beings have always been creatures who live in their imagination and who also refuse, when it suits them, to exercise their imagination. We have the inborn mental capacity to make the absent present (on one hand) and (on the other) the present absent. Memory, too, makes the absent present, but what is absent and then recalled — if only imperfectly — actually happened; in contrast, imagination makes the absent event or condition that has never existed present to the mind. In general, creative imagination is much more than new images (in the literal sense). It is primarily a partly unconscious process that comes to conscious fruition verbally, and produces unpredictably new ideas and concepts. It is projective or innovative thinking that signifies at least a partial break with old ways of thinking. But the story does not stop there. I am especially interested in what I will call "hyperactive imagination"; the contrasting term is "inactive imagination" (or moral blindness). The canon does not do justice to this theme of imagination in its vicissitudes. But when hyperactive imagination and inactive imagination are seen in combination as causally efficacious in the production of awful events on an unprecedented scale, then we may have to say that the canon up through the nineteenth century must be challenged in its very pessimism. I do not mean especially that the canon at its most pessimistic is not pessimistic enough, but rather that we must put forth against the canon, where necessary, a pessimism that is ever mindful of the imagination both in its aggressive exercise and in the human disinclination to exercise it benignly. In a vague way, one can hold that this revision adds up to a greater pessimism, from one point of view, but to a lesser pessimism, from another.

Say that the pessimism of the canon stands on the prevalence of numerous vices and that the especially salient political ones are pride (or arrogance), mere vanity (emptiness never to be filled), envy, jealousy, anger, resentment, vengeance, greed, indecent curiosity, and a perverse and an apparently unmotivated malice. They have always yielded appalling effects in everyday life and in political life. Nonetheless, in thinking about adequacy of the political canon, I wish to highlight the relationship between these vices and the vicissitudes of the imagination.

It is possible to hold that without imagination there would be no vices, that there would be only appetites or instincts or reflexes or comparatively unmediated impulses (a condition somewhat like Socrates' city of pigs); that vices are emotions and hence are always woven with or even out of active or purposively inactive imagination, out of a passionate sense of possibility or a false sense of impossibility, or a will to redesign or obscure reality. That may be so, but now the subject becomes intractably difficult for me.

So let me summarize the relationship in this unsatisfactory, schematic, and temporary way: the vices are the irritants that set the imagination in motion and concurrently keep it selectively inactive; reciprocally, both hyperactive and inactive imagination sustain and increase the hold and ferocity of the vices and give direction and method to them. The horror is that hyperactive and inactive imagination (or moral blindness) in combination make it easy, or easier, to commit atrocities on a large scale and not feel regret or remorse, whether after victory or defeat. On every level, the participants have little or no conviction of vice. Indeed, as I indicate later on, hyperactive imagination, when it initiates effects on the scale of twentieth-century atrocities, seems to be distant from or even to lose connection with any of the vices and does its worst work unprompted by any of the vices, including indecent curiosity and gratuitous malice. The sense of possibility develops its own momentum; if it is abstract or fanatical enough, it can eventually supply its own motivation. The momentum is experienced as destiny or mission, that is, as a necessary pattern that must be taken to completion. Aestheticism becomes dominant. Either a solitary gesture or a protracted atrocious policy can be felt as a single leap into or out of the void. An alternative (also aesthetic) formulation is that the initiators and leaders tend to conceive of themselves as the most visible actors in a drama of which nothing merely human is the author. They must be submissive to their prominent roles. Ordinary pessimism, ordinary realism, do not appear to me to go far enough in making sense of what possesses those who initiate atrocious effects on an unprecedented scale. On the other hand, when imagination remains inactive, one can feel innocent because one feels insulated, even liberated, from one's own motives. In this context, who but the blind can feel innocent?

The assistance provided by Heidegger and Arendt and some others should be seen as making a contribution to moral psychology that helps illuminate the awful events of the twentieth century and that also casts light back on the course of human history. I propose to see Heidegger and Arendt — perhaps Arendt a good deal more than Heidegger — as theorists of the imagination, especially in its political relevance. I do not say that these two great philosophers do all the work that has been done or that should be done. Nor does it matter that neither thinker offers a lengthy exposition of the very nature of imagination. They offer instead an indispensable stimulus.

When confronted by such humanly inflicted and humanly endured catastrophes as the two world wars, the use and threatened use of atomic weapons, and the exterminationist policies of Nazism and Stalinism and other so-called Marxist-Leninist dictatorships, we have to try to understand how such policies could have been initiated and carried out in a burst or over some years. Hannah Arendt insisted that we could not make sense of Nazism or Stalinism if we relied only on the inherited theories of tyranny or cruelty or on the standard pessimism that attributes to human beings a limitless zeal for power or wealth or self-aggrandizement. Even the Greek concepts of hubris and pleonexia — intoxicated or unconscious insolence and intoxicated or compulsive overreaching — do not take us far enough or even, perhaps, always in the right direction, though their power to incite reflection is great. Even Augustine's self-lacerating and self-perplexed analysis of stealing pears as a sixteen-year-old (in the second book of the *Confessions*) or his profound speculation on the mentality that led to the fall of Adam and Eve (in Books 13–15 of *The City of God*) still do not, I think, in their inexhaustible suggestiveness take us all the way.

These theories and concepts together with the standard pessimism must retain a place in any analysis of the twentieth century, but they must make much more room for both the aggressive exercise and the self-protective refusal of imagination. I would add that the canon's grimness is not adequate for just the two world wars, not even the first one, which was the source, inspiration, and model of most of the humanly inflicted catastrophes of the twentieth century. So, I would now like to offer a view that presumes to interpret the humanly inflicted catastrophes of the twentieth century in a manner that I believe the canon up to 1900 does not fully engender. Naturally I make no claim for any originality on my part. In what I am about to say, I rely to a very great extent on Arendt and Heidegger and also of course to some lesser extent on other thinkers during the twentieth century. Undeniably, the canon up to 1900 aids us, but maybe not always on its own terms.

I begin, to say it again, with the scale of humanly inflicted suffering in the twentieth century. Some human beings are responsible for the deliberate murder, torture, mutilation, derangement, and dispossession of millions and millions of other human beings, and over comparatively short periods of time. The absolute numbers of victims in the twentieth century is unprecedented, despite large-scale slaughters and traumas in the past. If I am told that although the absolute numbers were larger than ever, the percentage of human beings evilly treated, out of the total human population, was not larger and may even be smaller than in the past, my answer is that such a concern for percentages rather than for absolute numbers is, in fact, part of the mentality that makes large-scale atrocities possible. The failure to take seriously nothing but percentages shows a callousness that is part, though a familiar part, of the story of humanly inflicted suffering all through time. Every person counts immeasurably: that is one point. The other point is that an immense accumulation of murdered or savagely treated persons still matters, despite the immeasurability of each person; the scale of atrocious effects still matters, even when we say such things as the following. First, each person dies only one death; a group of persons does not literally endure a group-death in addition to the death of every person in the group. One person does not die the death of one other or many others. Furthermore, the most intense sensations or experience of pain and suffering can register directly only on that person. No sympathizer can feel directly the accumulated pain and sufferings of a group of people. Yet the suffering of multitudinous others can register on the imaginative observer (or fellow sufferer). Although the losses sustained by great numbers of people cannot be summed and experienced by any single person, the observer should try to come to terms with the scale of suffering. The observer can strain to imagine the victims, one by one, as a succession of universes passing into extinction. Benign imagination, recognizing present reality in spite of everything that obstructs such recognition — all the passions or the hard shell of indifference or inadvertence — is crucial.

Now, the scale of atrocities was immense that was perpetrated by, say, imperial Rome, imperial Spain, European and American expansion in North America, and societies holding African slaves. In each example, inflicted or occasioned deaths numbered in the millions. All the examples preceded the twentieth century. Do not these atrocious policies discredit the contention that the twentieth century was discontinuous in the scale of awful effects? I still think not, because the numbers of dead or degraded in earlier atrocities accumulated over many decades or centuries and, in each case, under successive leaderships. But the awful events of the twentieth century that I have singled out all occurred in roughly sixty years (1915 to 1975) and occurred in many places. (Stalinism and Maoism had the longest run.) The combination of concentration in time and dispersal over the world seems to me unprecedented. Even in regard to earlier violent and atrocious policies, notice how rarely any canonical (or other political) text tallies the numbers or even gestures toward the scale of suffering. Does Machiavelli — even worse, do his commentators — ever mention the hundreds of thousands or even millions slaughtered by imperial Rome? In rare canonical moments, Hobbes estimates that "near 100,000 persons" died in the English civil war,[1] and Hegel says that in the New World, "nearly seven million people have been wiped out" by Europeans.[2]

If an unprecedented scale of deliberately inflicted pain and suffering in the twentieth century is granted, at least provisionally and even skeptically, I now return to the three factors — obvious except to the unimaginative — that facilitated (and helped to encourage) the commission of awful events and will facilitate it in the twenty-first century and beyond. Begin with the recent large growth of total human population in the societies that inflicted or endured the suffering. The sheer fact of numerousness inflames the imagination of power that initiates atrocious policies. Here, imagination, making the absent present, turns hyperactive and wants to alter reality on the basis of a new design for it.

In the hyperactive imagination of power, human beings are conceived as instruments or impediments, as raw material or dirt or disease. With so much human raw material at one's own disposal to use in realizing the new design, and from another perspective, with so much humanity piled up and imagined as imperfections in or obstacles to that design, why not use or degrade and destroy human beings? There are, after all, so many of them. New instruments and impediments can always be found. When masses of people are lost, they are figured as either necessary sacrifices or disposable waste. In either case, they exist to be processed for the sake of the design. The designers scarcely if at all feel the cost of the design as a cost; it is imagined as part of the fabrication of the design, when the cost is not itself the design.

The scale of atrocious effects in the twentieth century is, furthermore, unthinkable without the magical technological prowess that culminates in, but is hardly confined to, the development of atomic weapons. Indeed, atomic weapons were actually used only in World War II (although especially the United States expressly threatened their use on quite a few occasions afterward) and not in the other atrocities of the twentieth century. But the other atrocities did rely on — perhaps we should say, were intrinsic to, or not readily conceivable without, or entailed by, or were the preponderant motive behind — enhanced technological prowess. The growth in human capacities is first of all, even if not always chronologically first, a growth in the power to dominate and destroy. The growth in the capacity to monitor, detect, organize, mobilize, enchant, debase, coerce, and kill is an integral feature of the development of modern technology, just as previous technology served, *mutatis mutandis,* the same purposes all through time. Technology is power, and power will always be abused; it exists to be abused, to perfect intimidation, coercion, humiliation, mobilization, and violence.

Abundant populations and technological prowess are two of the necessary conditions for large-scale atrocious effects in the twentieth century; they help to account for the enormously greater destructiveness of hyperactive imagination joined to moral blindness. It is tempting to say that given these two conditions, the past human record, by itself, would indicate — strongly suggest — that large-scale atrocious effects would inevitably appear. The pessimism of the canon up to 1900 should have flowed smoothly into the twentieth century. But does it do so? It might be safer to say that the canon could have taught this lesson quite without intending to do so. I mean that the succession of political theories — or, at least, most of the texts in the succession — exemplify or are symptomatic of the imagination of power, the *will* to redesign reality, if circumstances are favorable. Few of these texts are a call to arms; few hold that it is desirable that political actors strive, by violence if need be, to realize the theorists' design or some other design that the actors themselves have drawn up. But the canonical writers should have known from their own inner workings how attractive the prospect of shaping reality is, how attractive it is to imagine that what is lamentably absent is gloriously present. (Not that the reality that any particular theorist ever wanted to replace was really good or met even a judiciously minimal level of justice.) But the explicit theme of political imagination is not prominently on display in the canon, though Plato, Hobbes, Burke, and Nietzsche and a few others are self-consciously and indubitably instructive on it. Without consideration of this theme, the human record becomes even harder to decipher.

If the canonical writers up to 1900 could not have been expected to deal with the numerousness and technological prowess that we have known for the past century and a half, they could have been a good deal more explicit and revelatory about hyperactive imagination, the passion to design or redesign reality. Numerousness and technological prowess greatly favor this sort of political aestheticism and magnify, many times over, its atrocious effects. But the strength of the inveterate aesthetic political passion has always been great and too often unnoticed. It invisibly accompanies high-minded projects of reform, renovation, restoration, or redemption.

I now take up again the death of god, the third factor that favors the imagination and helps make it hyperactive in the twentieth century and even earlier. The exacerbated will to redesign reality we ordinarily call "fanaticism." I believe that none of the atrocious policies with their stupendous scale of effects could have occurred without fanaticism. No doubt, Hobbes and Burke are canonical critics of modern revolutionary fanaticism, and both theorists throw a harsh and only a partly distorting light on its nature. But they both rashly exemplify their own fanaticism, which is an obsessive adherence to order. Many in the canon certainly address the ruthless pursuit of ends by those in control and those who try to struggle free of that control. Some in the canon are painfully aware of the effects of religious fanaticism. But what of the fanaticism shown by both sides in the two world wars, Nazism and Stalinism, and in other protracted atrocious policies in the twentieth century? They are all cases of secular fanaticism. Their irrationality is not nominally religious in the usual sense. Perhaps it is a paradox, but it may be the case that secular fanaticism will tend to be worse, more limitless, than religious fanaticism. Even before god died, were not slavery, imperialism, torture, and massacre mostly unreligious activities? At the same time, it may also be the case that in a more secular age, it is easier to call religious fanaticism by its right name. Putting these last points together, one could say that the death of god makes room for a more limitless fanaticism, while making it easier to brand as fanatical the ruthless religious politics and its atrocious effects, in the past. (Who can ignore the way in which religious fanaticism laid Europe waste in the sixteenth and seventeenth centuries?) And should religious fanaticism inspire societies or movements in the twenty-first century to commit atrocities on the scale of those in the twentieth century that impelled the analysis in this essay, then it will be time to reexamine the political centrality of the death of god as a factor. There is in any case never any reason for much shock or surprise if some expressions of murderous fanaticism are religious.

Let me take up the second point first, namely, that we now can speak easily of politicized religious fervor as fanaticism. The canon up to 1900, for the most part, is pious toward religious piety. The canonical theorists are all themselves heterodox in belief or unbelievers, but few until the Enlightenment admitted as much. Give Leo Strauss his due: political philosophy is characteristically politic, all too politic. Out of fear of authority or mistrust of the people, canonical writers do not think that they can call the (steady if sometimes suspended) devotion shared by all classes to one or another politically and socially active orthodoxy by its right name, that is, fanaticism — what the Enlightenment at last loudly calls enthusiasm. Only recalcitrant devotion to heterodoxy is branded as fanaticism. But the canonical theorists knew better.

I want to say that belief, orthodox or heterodox, is built out of aesthetically compelling falsehoods and unwarranted beliefs. The process by which believers sustain their belief is not cynical, but it is surely not driven by a quest for truth. It is driven by something typically opposed to truth, namely, a quest for meaning, for an overall meaningfulness in the world. The quest for meaning is satisfied by comprehensive and aesthetically compelling fictions or stories. Armed and aroused, belief can be merciless because the meaningfulness of the world is at stake. Unconscious aestheticism becomes licentious. The canonical theorists more or less know that common opinions about the nature of the world are false, but most of them guard their scepticism — until the Enlightenment. In that caution, the canon for us must show some inadequacy. The death of god is, in part, the growth in the ability of observers to call religious beliefs false and condemn them as fanatical, when they are ruthless. Of course, I introduce the word "aesthetic" in full awareness that not all the canonical theorists would have appreciated the word or even quite made sense of it. But the idea that human beings are driven by cravings that demand that social and natural reality have coherence, purpose, and meaning is hardly foreign to many in the canon up to 1900. What are such cravings, if not aesthetic?

Fanaticism, secular and religious, and by whatever name, has always existed. I now return to the first of the two points: secular fanaticism can be worse than religious fanaticism. That is part of what modernity signifies. I mean that the death of god achieves two cultural results—certainly in the West. First, inherited religion becomes less and less able to confer meaningfulness on the world. Second, and more important, the very ability to devise comprehensive and aesthetically compelling fictions and stories about a transcendental or supersensible realm and get people to believe them with sufficient strength to build a whole culture around them nearly evaporates. Let it be allowed that there is a strong possibility that thinkers—but also half-thinkers, would-be thinkers, and pseudo-thinkers—need comprehensive meaningfulness more than ordinary people do, even if great and good thinkers struggle to discipline their need more than ordinary people do. The fact remains that ordinary people are susceptible to a kind of enchantment that lies over the bedrock of their intellectual indifference. They can be aroused for a while and enlisted in causes. Their imagination can be gratified and captured. They can have, if only briefly, satisfactions they did not dream they could have. A few can acquire an addiction to comprehensive meaningfulness. On the whole, however, new doctrines eventually fade; their hold over ordinary minds fades. In any case, meaningfulness is now mainly secular: its vehicles are nation, class, race, ethnicity, or civilization (way of life). (Some parts of the Islamic world are currently an exception to the secular rule but not guilty, or not yet guilty, by their independent force, of atrocities comparable to those of the twentieth century in scale. Perhaps when technological prowess, or ingenuity that compensates for the lack of prowess, comes to fanatical Islam, it will enroll itself in the annals of colossal evils in modern times.) But whatever the case with Islam, all secular doctrines that insist, without appeal, on categorizing people along group-identity lines can be made or forced to yield a comprehensive or overriding meaningfulness. All are seductions of the susceptible.

Devout leaders, not cynical ones, inspired fanaticism in the twentieth century, in which almost every fanaticism was secular. They were more susceptible than their followers. There were no protracted policies with enormous atrocious effects without an initiating secular fanaticism that devoured the leaders, who then managed to spread their contagion among their indispensable following. None of the secular fanaticisms had any built-in limits. Although religion can inspire an utterly merciless fanaticism, it usually holds within itself some respect for moral limits to which appeal can be made. And religion's fanatically atrocious policies stem in significant part from the worldly motives of those who act in its name. What I say is naturally not meant to exculpate religion. It is only to suggest that when we try to face the worst in the twentieth century—understand that "worst" as worse than almost anything else in previous centuries, because of the scale—we cannot begin to understand the various atrocious phenomena without the category of fanaticism. In turn, we cannot understand fanaticism without the category of aestheticism. Leaders want to make the world meaningful by design. They are prepared to act without moral limits. Their aestheticism overrides every other consideration and does so, at least for a time, guiltlessly. The scale of results of such fanaticism, such secular aestheticism, given numerousness of population and technological prowess, must be and has been enormous. Indeed, so great is the scale of effects that it is impossible to assign to any of the vices — the four deadly sins (that are not weaknesses of the flesh) and their variants — sufficient power even to will it. Even the worst psychopathology cannot lead directly to such a scale. Given the scale of effects, every leader is a midget in comparison to the powers unleashed; there is some horrible discontinuity between even the most obsessive purpose and the scale of ensuing atrocities. The policy makers amaze themselves with their own power. There is no proportion between potency and mere vice or between potency and mere goal. At the end of its journey, the initial hyperactive imagination arrives at the unimagined, which is, to the victims and the observers, unimaginable.

The leaders of atrocities are merely human beings at their worst; what makes them the worst is that they are the most deluded by their own imagination. They live in another world. They are detached from reality, except strategically and tactically. They are realistic in everything but their aims. Of course, the pessimistic moral psychology of the canon — to the extent that it does not reckon with the imagination — must be inadequate. Only an imagination grown hyperactive by aesthetic cravings that are not recognized as what they are, can, in the work of persisting in policy despite the unprecedented scale of awful effects, function as a fatal substitute for vices or personal pathology. In scanting the theme of the active imagination, the canon's adequacy to the twentieth century is abridged and so also, perhaps, its adequacy throughout time. Its pessimism can mislead us.

I have suggested that the theme of imagination's vicissitudes is not confined to the fanatical and ruthlessly hyperactive force of imagination. There is another side to the story. If aggressive imagination is the rabid capacity to make the absent present, to imagine a different reality, to have designs on reality, the complementary phenomenon is to fail to see the reality that is present and thus to treat it as if it were absent, and instead to define all reality as one's own little piece of it. The theme of imagination's vicissitudes and their role in political life must include the failure of benign imagination, in the particular sense of moral blindness. Such failure is humanly congenital and incurable, but it must be understood, if policies with atrocious effects of unprecedented scale are to be faced. Hyperactive imagination cannot do its work without the accompaniment of moral blindness.

The initiators introduce the aesthetically compelling fictions and stories, redefinitions of the world through new or rearranged categories, that seduce the susceptible, including themselves. But the fanatical drive to realize what has been hyperactively imagined, to make actually present what has hitherto been absent, could not proceed unless the initiators and leaders used their capacity, all the while, to make absent what is present. The present is not allowed to be present. The people they lead and the people they destroy must cease being people in their eyes, must lose their humanity and become unreal or less real or caricatures of reality. On the other hand, it helps that the followers, to be suitable instruments, must have an added incentive to stay, in their own way, blind to what they do. This blindness, which is always at one's disposal, is guaranteed to turn lethal when the fanatically aesthetic contagion has been spread by the initiators. As far as politics is concerned, hyperactive imagination, within souls who possess it, is indissociable from inactive imagination in leaders and followers alike. Those who design a new reality must be selectively blind to existing reality. Then when they are able to pursue their imaginative design without limitations on their conduct, they must absolutely refuse to see what is present before them because they want to see only what they imagine. When followers are seduced, they are fortified in the disposition not to see what they are doing. Failure of imagination is also in part a phenomenon of aestheticism because the, as it were, unseeing violence done to reality is done for the sake of realizing or defending the design, its shape and meaning. My emphasis will be on the moral blindness of followers.

Perhaps an alternative formulation is that blindness is not inactive imagination or a failure to use imagination, but rather another kind of active use of the imagination. It replaces what is there by what is not, as if by a process of illusion or hallucination, or by what Orwell called "doublethink." In any case, what goes on is more than ordinary self-deception. I will not explore this conceptual issue here.

William James titled one of his most trenchant essays "On a Certain Blindness in Human Beings" (1899). His subject is expansive, but one of his meanings is that almost no one grants equal reality to others. It is necessarily the case that each person must be more real to himself than anyone else can be: he is conscious to himself in a way that no one else can be conscious to him. But with the exercise of imagination, another person can at least be understood as real to herself as he is to himself. One cannot inhabit another while remaining oneself; one cannot inhabit another at all. The inwardness of another is absent, that is, invisible, but it can be made present with a little bit of benign imagination. One can take thought and say to oneself, I am not the only reality. Whether other people are like me or different, with me or against me, more foolish or less, I cannot deny their reality as fellow human beings. They matter to themselves as I matter to myself. They are almost certainly as well intentioned or sincere or as conformist as I am. To entertain such sentiments is not necessarily to feel compassion or even empathy. It is not to imagine yourself in the place of another and thus show sympathy, or to imagine another person inside yourself and thus show restraint. These familiar moral operations of the imagination, conceptualized by Rousseau and Adam Smith, do indeed show that a large part of the cure for the pathologies of hyperactive and inactive imagination is the cultivation of the moral imagination. These operations certainly work against blindness. But the feeling for the human reality of others is a distinct use of the benign imagination, and lack of such a feeling is a distinct and awful deficiency. When one is morally blind, one refuses to allow the present to be present; one loses sight of it, even though it is there.

And when, by yet another semipathological process of both using the imagination and refusing to use it, the I incorporates itself into a We, one can still make the very difficult effort to say to oneself, in a momentary suspension of group feeling, that these outsiders are as real to themselves as we are to ourselves. This moral use of the imagination, in which blindness lifts for a moment, does not automatically lead to the affirmation that they are as good or as morally right as we are; just that they are as inwardly innocent as we are, as devoted to themselves as we are to ourselves. (Of course, the moral claims of content must reassert themselves. The final judge of the merits of the case, however, must be a third party, except of course when there are atrocious effects. In such a case, anyone at all should be able to judge the obvious, but most people will not choose to; they will substitute partisanship for judgment.) Every side is likely to contain only a few persons who are capable of at least this momentary or episodic use of the moral imagination and thereby redeem not their side but the honor of humanity, if you allow me to put it that way.

I call the self-incorporation of oneself into a We a double process of using the imagination and refusing to use it. My reason is that by identifying with a group to the point of merger and self-loss, one sees oneself as everywhere present in others and everywhere absent as oneself. One therefore claims to be what one is not (dissolved helplessly in solidarity or camaraderie with others) and also claims not to be what one is (an individual). In miniature, strong group adherents show the symbiosis of hyperactive and inactive imagination.

The negative power of the inactive imagination to produce enormous atrocious effects manifests itself in another way, in another kind of blindness than the denial that others are as real to themselves as I am to myself, but a kind that does not preoccupy William James. The phenomenon is familiar enough, but perhaps has not been considered sufficiently by the canon up to 1900. I refer to blindness to the overall policy that enfolds one's own small contribution to it. One wills not to see with the mind's eye what one cannot see with the body's eyes. The literally invisible is made to remain altogether invisible and regarded as absent or nonexistent. Here too, the present is not allowed to be present. Such blindness is the normality of followers on every level. Being seduced by a fanatical (fantastic) doctrine makes it even easier to remain in blindness, which is the normal condition of the heart. One loses sight of — if one ever had in sight — the policy or system in which one plays one's small part. One does one's job, one goes through the motions, and comes to the end of the day. Some may even find fulfillment in their work. People are routinely able to compartmentalize their lives in another way: nice at home, they are beasts at work. Or, followers can shield themselves or be abstracted from the preconditions of what they do and the effects they help to produce. This latter tendency is especially pronounced in bureaucratic management of atrocities. But the former tendency, compartmentalization, shows itself in war and in direct superintendence or direct commission of other atrocities. From a political perspective, the most important meaning of the examined life — certainly, if Socrates is the model — is inquiry into the larger system or policy in which one is asked or told to play one's part. Even where the effects of fanatical doctrine have worn off, such inquiry is so difficult as to seem unnatural or suicidal.

The phenomenon of inactive imagination is the core of atrocities on an unprecedented scale in the twentieth century. I mean that though we may want to single out the initiators (and perhaps also their sadistic underlings) for special censure and call persons of these two sorts monsters, the indigestible truth is found elsewhere. It is found in blindness, the blindness of those who, though seducible by doctrine, lack hyperactive imagination but also characteristically lack the ability to grant that others are as real as they are, that everyone is as real to himself and herself as one is to oneself, and who also lack the ability to examine themselves sufficiently to notice the larger pattern that enfolds their everyday contribution to that pattern. The inertial force of blindness, in its two aspects, is the key to atrocious policies. Without followers, hyperactive imagination is powerless. To be sure, without initiators, ordinary people would content themselves with vices and pathologies and their confined effects, which are appalling enough. But they (we) are susceptible — seducible to some extent and for a while by what is aesthetically compelling, by the narratives, stories, myths, and pseudo-explanations, by the ideologies, that misrepresent reality to reshape it and make it more gratifying. There is a universal if shallow yearning to be taken in.

Seduction is more the fault of the seduced than of the seducer. To be seduced is to be given a mostly aesthetic inducement to stay blind, to forget altogether that one is blind. But even untouched by fanatical doctrine, one has too many reasons to stay blind. Then, too, we must not leave out the pleasures of collegiality and the pleasures that inhere in the web of organizational relations. These kinds of pleasures can be so absorbing that one's job, at whatever level, becomes utterly detached from its content; it becomes part of a whole self-enclosed world. Thus, followers lend their numbers to victimize people like themselves, they cooperate in their own victimization, and after a while, their leaders victimize them as if they were the enemy.

I have no rigorous way of accounting for any particular design created by a hyperactive imagination. I also cannot find plausible any account that presumes to explain why at any given time seducers are successful or why their designs are lethal. But I believe that the pessimism of the canon does not treat sufficiently the ferocious power of the creative, hyperactive imagination. On the other hand, the pessimism of vices, present in the canon and of course present in the politically relevant humanities, does, however, make a substantial contribution to understanding some part of the energy behind blindness. But blindness is not a comprehensive term for the vices; blindness is a motivated failure to see reality, a readiness to treat the present as absent, a refusal to allow the present to be present. Does the canon up to 1900 address this matter sufficiently?

Now, contingency has a lot to do with the successful initiation of protracted policies that pile up an immense human cost, whether the purpose precisely is to pile up that cost or whether the purpose is pursued regardless of any cost. There is no necessity of occurrence in any given time or place, but we should expect atrocious policies to appear — we do not know where or when. To repeat my suggestion: the pessimism of the canon up to 1900 does not adequately prepare us to expect the atrocious scale of the two world wars, the use or threatened use of atomic weapons, the Holocaust, the gulags, the induced famines, the wars waged by the United States in Korea and Vietnam, the massacres all over the world. A lot of the canon teaches that we should always expect the worst from people in actual, unideal societies. Nevertheless, the scale of wrongdoing in the twentieth century is discontinuous with that which the pessimism of the canon presumes. Augustine's idea of original sin and Kant's idea of radical evil are profound contributions to moral psychology but were not framed with this scale of wrongdoing in mind. (Only some of the biblical god's acts are on this scale, but what is his moral psychology?) Nietzsche really did not envisage the scale. Perhaps not even Dostoyevsky in *The Possessed* envisaged it, though I think he came pretty close.

What I would have expected is that the canon should prepare us to see that the scale of effects does not increase because of increased vice. To be sure, new developments in a combination that favored the unbridled play of imagination's vicissitudes — unreligious and boundless fanaticism, numerousness, and magical technological prowess — could not be foreseen. To expect that they could have been is foolish. But the real issue is not the favoring conditions that change with time but the steadiness of human nature, the unchangeable hold of imagination's vicissitudes, the transformative power wielded by those vicissitudes over the vices. Ideally, the canon would have taught that at any given time human beings will be destructive up to the limit of their technological capacity. To the imagination in its vicissitudes, the size of the moral costs — the scale of atrocities — does not matter. A large part of the reason is that the aesthetic significance of the policy (its logic, pattern, or design) will overpower the sense of costs. Indeed, the aesthetic significance may well increase as the costs increase. Reality is kept at bay by aggressive or passive aestheticism. Such steadiness, not merely in the nameable vices but in hyperactive imagination and moral blindness, and perhaps to the point of infinite destruction and self-destruction, is missed by the canon up to 1900.

The atrocious politics in the twentieth century that I have singled out cannot be poured into one mold. It is possible, however, to adapt Aristotle's view of the dynamism of superiority and inferiority as found in Book 5 of the *Politics*. Speaking very abstractly, we could say that putative equals, like the great powers in World War I, may become fanatical in struggling to claim superiority or resist inferiority. Next, as a result of defeat, a prior arrogant superiority turns into a humiliation that seeks vengeance. Nazism answers, in part, to that description. Or, exalted by victory, a prior humiliated inferiority seeks to revenge itself on the past. This last point may help to account in part for Stalin, Mao, Pol Pot, and their kindred.

The twentieth century is the century of mass slaughter, mass murder. The conduct of both world wars demonstrates the readiness, sustained by blindness, to pay the cost of mass murder in the fanatical pursuit of aesthetically compelling ends, especially an aesthetically gratifying picture of the world in which one side or the other is master. I am not saying that all sides are morally on a level. No, only that the pursuit of victory was so ferocious, by even the better side, that the moral cost of its victory subtracts an appreciable quantity from its moral advantage. In both wars, the good side perpetrated atrocious policies in the name of not surrendering or winning. On the other hand, the Holocaust and gulags, the massacres, the induced famines and cultural revolutions, and the use and threatened use of atomic weapons demonstrate that mass slaughter may as well be the purpose itself of policy. The number of deaths (actual or threatened) in these latter policies is so large that one cannot simply say that the infliction of death is a reluctantly employed tactic on behalf of some further end. When means are terrible on a large scale, they are not only means but are signs and displays of superhuman power. And if following Aristotle, we say that an element of vengeance figures in the use of such so-called means, as is likely, the vengeance is abstract, personalized (the target group of countless persons is figured as one monstrous person), yet impersonal (one's own group is imagined as a superperson through which one has being and identity). I say "abstract" vengeance because face-to-face bloodthirstiness or bloodlust—a staple of the canon's pessimism—is not nearly as important an ingredient as the aesthetically compelling thought of boundless vengeance. And only as abstractly aesthetic, as sublime, can vengeance be boundless. Mass slaughter is needed for the story or narrative of the destiny of abstract personages to come out right, to have the right shape. The motivation is therefore not sadism, even though the personal sadism of a minority (in aggregation) can be accommodated by the protracted policy.

The long and short of it is that the canon up to 1900 has scanted the interconnected themes of hyperactive imagination and inactive imagination: on the one hand, fanatical and aesthetically compelling designs on reality, and on the other hand, blindness in the double sense of refusing to accord full reality to everyone but oneself or one's group and refusing to examine oneself in relation to the enfolding policy in which one finds oneself doing one's particular and often little but necessary job as well as one can. The complex interplay of making the absent present and the present absent is scanted. In facing large-scale policies of destruction, we should therefore hesitate before rushing directly to human wickedness as the undiscriminating explanation, as canonical writers often do. I gladly admit, however, that the canon can improve moral sensitivity and thus assist us—despite its politic reticence (before the Enlightenment) about fanatical commitments that groups make to unwarranted beliefs—in the often shunned task of calling a spade a spade.

I also realize that the canon's pessimism can profitably disabuse its readers of optimism concerning human beings. Where would moral indictment be without Socrates, or moral disappointment without Jesus? The canon revolves around these two characters. Their nearly unlivable ideals are haunting, impossible to exorcise completely. (We should pay special attention to the way in which canonical writers fearing for the safety of the political realm, even when some of these writers despise it, make strained and often overly ingenious efforts to neutralize the radicalism of both of them.) Then, too, there are many particular passages in the canon that insidiously insert themselves in one's sensibility, the manner by which one characteristically looks at the political and cultural realms, and affect one's perception to an extent that one is scarcely aware of. Even for the task of being adequate to the unprecedented scale of atrocities in the twentieth century, the canon up to 1900 cannot be dispensed with. I myself have sought assistance from Aristotle, among others. Still and all, the canon up to 1900 is not sufficient in its net sense. It may not take us close enough to the plausible belief that when hyperactive imagination and inactive imagination work jointly, the scale of awful effects, no matter how vast, has no moral significance but is likely to have an overriding aesthetic significance. In this respect, human nature has been and will remain pretty constant. That means that we can expect future atrocities on as large a scale as those of the twentieth century, or even larger, or at least we need not be surprised if they occur. Who knows but that human extinction and extinction of many other species lie at the end of the journey of technologically conditioned imagination in its vicissitudes.

In closing, I want to mention, without exploring, the several contributions that Heidegger and Arendt made in the twentieth century to our understanding of the scale of atrocities. I do not mean that these two are the only political or politically relevant thinkers who help us understand the atrocious twentieth century. Simone Weil on group self-love as the cause of much oppression, Sartre on the imagination and on the pathos and terror of unsponsored freedom, and Foucault on the mentality of technicians and on the biopolitics of the twentieth century are invaluable. I have relied on them all in my composite analysis of these atrocities. But I have obviously relied most on Heidegger and Arendt. I have tried to bring together the following elements from their writing.

In the case of Heidegger, the essays intelligently collected in *The Question Concerning Technology* by William Lovitt give instruction on the nature and effects of Nietzsche's teaching that god is dead and on the human effort to replace god that was mounted for centuries before Nietzsche's teaching. To replace god is to receive the world, as it presents itself, with infuriated alienation and resentment and consequently to respond to it with a fanatical spiral of self-aroused will to treat the world as material to be known comprehensively as material and thus as ready to be remade, reshaped, and stamped with the human image, at any cost to human beings or to the human essence. The task is rationalistic and technological; technology drives the rationalism, drives the science; a fundamental irrationality underlies the rationalism and the fanatical and unbounded quest for ever more potent technology. In the process, human beings themselves become material in the hands of leaders and directors and technicians, the raw material or "standing reserve" for unprecedented projects made possible by technological prowess. There seems little resistance, on anyone's part, to using or being used. All this is lodged in Heidegger's remark that "the essence of technology is nothing technological."[3]

In an undeservedly notorious but actually profound remark, Heidegger says in his Bremen lectures of 1949, "Agriculture is now a motorized food-industry — in essence the same as the manufacturing of corpses in gas chambers and extermination camps, the same as the starving of nations, the same as the manufacture of hydrogen bombs."[4] The repetition of "the same as" makes the point that content does not matter to technicians because they can convert any purposive activity into an activity that has no purpose but the activity itself. The difference between production and destruction is insignificant because either activity to them is above all a glimpsed and taken (if not always forced) opportunity to show their skills in displays of virtuosity. Any society intent on ruthless production will find a seamless continuity in turning to mass destruction. Human beings, like human wants, are merely problems to be solved. Brilliantly inventive technicians and scientists consummate what I have been calling moral blindness. And from a sufficient physical distance, the hyperactive imagination of the leaders and initiators converts their purpose into something as if it were seen from a height: a pattern to be imposed and completed, as if human beings and everything human were only material that awaited its aesthetically (dramatically or categorially) compelling shape and representation.

The canon of political theory can never be wholly adequate, even when supplemented by the politically relevant literary humanities. Humanly inflicted suffering is a bottomless subject, while the larger subject of moral psychology is an unending, undying subject: it is what Socrates is eager to think about in Hades indefinitely, if there be a Hades. Nonetheless, the canon can be made more adequate to the subject of human suffering on an unprecedented scale in the twentieth century. The most important political theorist in this endeavor is Hannah Arendt. On the matter of hyperactive imagination, her analysis (in *The Origins of Totalitarianism*, 1951, and subsequent editions) of the craving that reality conform to the expectant aesthetic sense and of the zeal with which initiators and leaders strive to reshape the world in accordance with their imperious fictions is indispensable. (All I do is emphasize the word "aesthetic.") The highest totalitarian aims are not practical or pursued by a utilitarian calculus. Utility concerns only the efficiency of methods. Although she does not extend this idea theoretically back to World War I — she does refer to the "insane nationalism" responsible for "the catastrophic decline of Europe"[5] — it deserves a larger place. We can see the fanaticism of nationhood working to produce an unprecedented scale of atrocious death and suffering. This is not quite the same as "the catastrophic decline of Europe." As it is, her discussion of both anti-Semitism (racism, more generally) and of imperialism in *The Origins of Totalitarianism* introduces the theme of the rage to remake social life as an embodied and enacted fiction, the rage to bring to perfection the lethal drama of charged categories (that is, of ascribed identities hardened to stone).

Her posthumously published *Thinking* (1978) is marvelously suggestive of the way in which the quest for meaning dominates philosophical thinking and is independent of the quest for the truth of cognition. Totalitarian ideologies, but really all ideologies, are merely parodies of philosophical thinking. The main difference — and it is enormous — is that totalitarian and other fanatical ideologies are murderous. She shows how human numerousness — what she calls, perhaps following Nietzsche in *Thus Spoke Zarathustra* (First Part, "On the New Idol"), superfluous populations — favors the large scale of murderous activity, whether the targets and victims are the initiators' own populations or their declared enemies. Then, too, both aspects of blindness (denying full reality as human beings to other human beings and having no interest in the protracted policy that enfolds one's everyday contribution to it) are memorably captured in her concept of the banality of evil in *Eichmann in Jerusalem* (1963) and in adjacent ideas in other writings.

Altogether, Arendt breaks new ground, even though her ideas of course need revision. In the background is her interest in what she sees as the radical break with the past in the nineteenth century, the dissolution of the trinity of religion, authority, and tradition. She says, "Kierkegaard, Marx, and Nietzsche are for us like guideposts to a past which has lost its authority. They were the first who dared to think without the guidance of any authority whatsoever."[6] That break is Arendt's version of the death of god, and we can connect it to the atmosphere in which fanaticism becomes mostly secular and achieves its boundlessness. There are symptomatic affinities and causal relations between the dissolution of the trinity of inherited social bonds and the unprecedented scale of atrocious effects in the twentieth century. But the three philosophers whom she singles out do not prepare us for the simple thought that the same human traits and passions can effortlessly remain themselves in the face of an unprecedented scale of atrocious effects. Undeniably, Kierkegaard and Nietzsche offer insights on hyperactive imagination and Marx on blindness (especially in his fertile and extendable notion of commodity fetishism). (By the way, does Freud help? Most of all, perhaps, in his theory of the dream work in *The Interpretation of Dreams*, 1900. Lacan's reworked Freudian view of the psyche as thrown incurably off-center at an early age and as therefore ever afterward falsely appeased also helps.) Yet Arendt's notion of living by and for fiction casts a tragic light on the whole human record, and she, more than anyone else, in the range of her interconnected ideas on the human condition, takes the canon into the twentieth century and, I am sure, beyond.

Notes

1. Thomas Hobbes, *Behemoth* (Chicago: University of Chicago Press, 1990), 95.

2. G. W. F. Hegel, *Lectures on the Philosophy of World History. Introduction: Reason in History,* trans. H. B. Nisbet (Cambridge, UK: Cambridge University Press, 1975), 163.

3. Martin Heidegger, *The Question Concerning Technology,* trans. William Lovitt (New York: Harper, 1977), 35.

4. Berel Lang, "Heidegger's Silence and the Jewish Question," in *Martin Heidegger and the Holocaust,* ed. Alan Milchman and Alan Rosenberg (Atlantic Highlands, NJ: Humanities Press, 1996), 7–11, 17.

5. "Rosa Luxemburg," in Hannah Arendt, *Men in Dark Times* (New York: Harcourt, Brace & World, 1968), 43.

6. "Tradition and the Modern Age," in Hannah Arendt, *Between Past and Future,* 2d ed. (New York: Viking, 1968), 28.

Index

Abolitionists, 258–264

Abortion, 270

Abraham, 291

Abstraction, patriotism as, 7–9

Adam and Eve, 277, 283–293, 391

Adorno, Theodor, 125

Aesthetic cravings, 131, 395, 397; for art, 124–130, 132; attitudes and feelings vs., 132–134, 135, 139–142, 144; for meaningfulness, 128–129; use of term, 123, 124, 126; wickedness in, 145–146

Aestheticism: of Berlin, 362–374; definition of, 362; deliberate and self-conscious, xix, 131–142; democratic, 142–147; demotic, 143; destruction and re-creation in, xxi; everyday vs. philosophical, 134–140, 143; in free society, xviii; in group rivalries, 32, 120–121, 123; in ideologies, xx, 142; inevitability of, xix, 142; inward process of conversion, xxi; of meaning,

127–129, 345; and morality, xxi, 117–149, 151; in patriotism, 8, 10, 142; in religions, xx, 119–120, 123, 131, 359; romantic, 363; ruthless adherence to, xix–xx, 123, 390; social, xv–xvi, 124, 131–134; subordination of pleasure in, 143; unconscious, 123–124, 128, 131; use of term, xvi

Aesthetic judgment: Arendt on, 150, 157–158, 159–160, 165–167; Berlin on, 370

Aesthetic theory, 125–130

Aesthetic values: in aristocracies, xxvi; existential values in, xv–xvi; in political life, xv–xvi, xviii–xix, xx, 156–157

Afghanistan, war in, 41, 60, 75, 88

Alcibiades, xx–xxi, 66–67

Al Qaeda, 76, 83, 88

Ambition, 305–307, 309, 310, 319

Anarchy, in wildness, 250–251, 253, 254, 257

Angels, belief in, 283